Environmental and Nature Writing

Environmental and Nature Writing

A writer's guide and anthology

**Sean Prentiss
and Joe Wilkins**

BLOOMSBURY ACADEMIC
LONDON • NEW YORK • OXFORD • NEW DELHI • SYDNEY

BLOOMSBURY ACADEMIC
Bloomsbury Publishing Plc
50 Bedford Square, London, WC1B 3DP, UK
1385 Broadway, New York, NY 10018, USA

BLOOMSBURY, BLOOMSBURY ACADEMIC and the Diana logo are
trademarks of Bloomsbury Publishing Plc

First published 2017
Reprinted 2017 (three times), 2018

Cover design: Eleanor Rose
Cover image © Getty Images

A catalogue record for this book is available from the British Library.

ISBN: HB: 978-1-4725-9252-1
PB: 978-1-4725-9253-8
ePDF: 978-1-4725-9255-2
ePub: 978-1-4725-9254-5

Names: Prentiss, Sean, author. | Wilkins, Joe, author.
Title: Environmental and nature writing : a writer's guide and anthology /
Sean Prentiss and Joe Wilkins.
Description: London ; New York : Bloomsbury Academic, 2016. |
Includes bibliographical references and index.
Identifiers: LCCN 2016012261 (print) | LCCN 2016026775 (ebook) |
ISBN 9781472592538 (paperback) | ISBN 9781472592521 (hardback) |
ISBN 9781472592545 (epub) | ISBN 9781472592552 (epdf)
Subjects: LCSH: Natural history–Authorship. | Natural history literature. |
Environmental literature. | Ecology–Authorship. | Authorship. | BISAC:
LANGUAGE ARTS & DISCIPLINES / Composition & Creative Writing. |
LANGUAGE ARTS & DISCIPLINES / Journalism.
Classification: LCC QH14 .P74 2016 (print) | LCC QH14 (ebook) | DDC 508–dc23
LC record available at https://lccn.loc.gov/2016012261

Series: Bloomsbury Writers' Guides and Anthologies

Typeset by Newgen Knowledge Works (P) Ltd., Chennai, India
Printed and bound in Great Britain

To find out more about our authors and books visit
www.bloomsbury.com and sign up for our newsletters.

For each home ground we need new maps, living maps, stories and poems, photographs and paintings, essays and songs. We need to know where we are, so that we may dwell in our place with a full heart.

Scott Russell Sanders

Contents

Part II The Craft of Nature and Environmental Writing   37

3 Seeing the World, Believing the World   39

4 Living Maps   51

5 The Writer in Place   67

Part III Nature and Environmental Writing Anthology   169

Creative Nonfiction   169

Fiction   265

Poetry

Part I

An Introduction to Nature and Environmental Writing

1

The Trailhead

Chapter Outline

Relevant readings

Creative Nonfiction: Chelsea Biondolillo, "Geology: An Investigation"; David Gessner, "Nature Writing by Numbers."

Fiction: Lydia Peelle, "Mule Killers."

Poetry: Joe Wilkins, "Seven Devils."

Free write

Think about the last time you saw some new, grand place—a stretch of rocky coastline, a desert canyon, an old courthouse with ornate stonework, a decaying factory. What was your first reaction? Take ten minutes to describe the physical place, as well as your emotional reaction to it. What did you see? What did seeing this place make you feel? What did you think of as you gazed at it?

Now, trade your free write with a partner. What are the similarities and differences between your and your partner's physical descriptions and internal reactions? Share and compare with another group of two. What conclusions can you draw about the ways we as human beings approach and make sense of the world around us?

Vignette

We park at Windy Saddle, double-check our packs, and then start down the trail, which moves through dense forest for a time before switchbacking down a steep scree field. To the north, the first of the seven peaks, Devil's Tooth, grows starker, rockier as we drop into the valley. We take our first break along a creek, drop our packs and munch on peanuts, rinse our necks and faces. While my friend studies the map, I pull out my journal and the book of poems I happen to be carrying, James Welch's Riding the Earthboy 40. *I read a few poems, jot down notes: images of the world around me, the names of trails and creeks and peaks. We move on. Up a forested ridge and out into the rocks, and down again, crossing the west fork of the creek, then up once more, past the shallow Bernard Lakes and on, in the fading light, to the abandoned fire lookout at Dry Diggins.*

From the raised porch of the lookout, the vista is astonishing, is more than one could ever hope for: the rough slope of Hell's Canyon directly below us, that deep, vast absence of rock and shadow—yes, we look down on wisps of clouds—and beyond to the high shoulders of the Wallowa and Blue Mountains of Oregon. We sit on the porch until the sun sinks. Half drunk on mountain wind and the rhythms of Welch's poems, I scribble lines that I think might lead to a poem: You say: I will teach you mountains, The music in your bones, *and* A wind that shifts the skulking cedars.

But we've stayed too long. The lookout, full of mouse droppings, which might mean snakes or hantavirus, is no place to camp. In the mountain dark we shoulder our packs once more and hike back to the lakes to pitch our tent. A light rain falls. We heat dehydrated spaghetti on a cook stove and eat in silence. The rain slackens. Picks up again. Beats against the side of the tent.

We wake to sunlight, our tent steaming dry. We hike up and up, ever up, the alpine meadows full of beargrass, fireweed, burnt snags, bright flowers. The buzzard profile of He Devil Peak looms before us, the trees at this elevation gnarled and stunted. We hike on. Finally, we make camp on a small headland jutting into Sheep Lake.

The next day we scramble up a talus slope and slowly edge our way toward She Devil Peak. I get halfway up and find a rock shelf, tell my friend I'll wait here. I feel like I simply must get out my journal and write. I'm working on a poem; I know it now. Something about the rocky starkness of this mountain land, something infused as well with the sharp, evocative, surreal sounds of Welch's poems. And now I begin to hear my father's voice, my father, who died when I was only nine, who as a young man worked as a backcountry ranger, who must have spent many days and nights tromping just like this from lake to lake, mountain to mountain. Something about this landscape, about these two peaks flanking the rocky shelf I sit upon, He Devil and She Devil: I'm both here and not here. I don't know that my father ever hiked the Seven Devils, but these mountains are somehow beyond time for me. The land itself lets me be the boy I was and never was, the man I am and might be. Lets me hear my father's rocky, long-gone voice.

We climb down. The next day we hike out, drive home. I keep working on that poem. A few days on, I have a draft called "Seven Devils." I call my friend, and we make plans to meet later that night so I can show him, but I don't make it. Physically and emotionally worn out, I fall asleep early. I sleep all night. I wake knowing I have made two journeys, both far and necessary.

—Joe

Motivations: The physical world, the internal world

Perhaps you, too, have taken a journey deep into one backcountry or another and been thunderstruck by the beauty of the landscape, as Joe was in the Seven Devil Wilderness. Or perhaps your most vivid memories of place have to do with visiting a striking city-scape: San Francisco, Hong Kong, Istanbul, Grand Rapids, Vancouver. Or maybe you're thinking now of something smaller, simpler, more intimate—sitting in the grass in your neighborhood park, noticing the sounds of the frogs and the knotted shadows of the oak, that doe stepping from the cover of the blackberries as the sun goes down, even the way trash tangles on the banks of your slow, urban river.

Whether deep in mountains or on a city street, we've all experienced those moments of great, troubling beauty, moments where the natural and built worlds command our attention—and strike something deep within us. And when that internal bell is rung, those emotions reverberating, we often feel compelled to share the experience. There are many ways we might do this. We might elbow our hiking partner and point. We might pull out our phone and snap a picture. Maybe we carry a sketchpad or paints. Or we open our journal, like Joe did, and use language, our species' primary tool of communication, to try to describe that place and explain the emotional power it holds for us.

This is the reaction we will talk about in this textbook—the urge to write about the landscapes and places of our lives (both the beautiful, like Joe's Seven Devils, and the battered, like a polluted river)—and this is just what Joe attempts in his poem "Seven Devils" (included in the anthology). Using figurative language and a sharp, searching voice, Joe describes his intense physical journey through the Seven Devils, as well as his own emotionally charged internal wanderings.

The Seven Devils' landscape itself sent Joe deep into memory, story, and imagination. And this is where it all begins for nature and environmental writers: we confront (and are confronted by) the fraught and sometimes terrible beauty of a dynamic landscape, and in fits and starts we slowly see the complex ways the natural world and human experience (whether personal or sociocultural) are wound together. After these experiences, we turn, then, to the page and, with as much grace, intelligence, and imagination as we can muster, attempt to describe, recreate, and interrogate these journeys in language.

But why? Why write? What do we hope to get or give with this writing?

These are good questions, and the answers are manifold and mysterious. For his own part, Joe felt a kind of emotional cleansing as he reread the final draft of "Seven Devils"; with the poem, he'd narrated a number of journeys that were important to him—his and his friend's hike, his father's death, his own fatherless journey into manhood, and his mother's strong example—and he felt the kind of catharsis many artists feel as they complete a work that they think might speak to some audience. Which brings us to what we might hope to give with our writing: Joe wanted the poem to speak to an audience not just about his own physical journey, but about our many journeys through time and place; about the ways place refracts and intensifies our experiences; about the extreme, mysterious power of landscape itself. And he hoped, though you can be the judge of this, that the poem might inspire others to sit with and observe landscape as well, to consider how a place might shape their own lives and stories. Joe hoped his poem might do what the poems of James Welch did for him on that hike in the Seven Devils: allow him to look up from the page and see the physical world around him more clearly, treat it more carefully.

We call this kind of writing—writing that is as concerned with the physical world as it is with character or plot, writing that speaks to the ways human journeys are bound up in landscape and place, writing that allows us to see the natural world and our place in it more clearly, writing that inspires and challenges us to enter and know the natural world, writing that helps us move through that world with more care and wonder—nature and environmental writing.

Nature and environmental writing

This textbook has many different audiences. Some of you may come from a background in environmental science or environmental studies and long to apply your knowledge of nature to the making of stories; others might be writers who have stories but long to learn more about how to set them in place; still others might be environmental activists or journalists hoping to bring about change. Despite our differences, we all share profound experiences of place and the impulse to write about those experiences; we are all interested in writing that honors and investigates the natural and built worlds.

With our varied backgrounds in mind, as a way to make sure we all get started on the same trail, this textbook initially endeavors to introduce you to the complex, dynamic genre that is nature and environmental writing. We do this by spending time in Part I defining, classifying, and tracing the history of nature and environmental writing (see Part III, which contains an anthology of contemporary nature and environmental writing, as a valuable resource for coming to know and appreciate the genre).

However, this textbook is primarily designed to teach readers how to use the techniques of creative writing to turn our interactions with nature and environment into powerful stories. As such, this book focuses more fully on our shared desire to write essays, stories, and poems in the nature and environmental writing tradition. Part II, then, which is the heart of the book, offers ways to think about and practice the techniques of craft that will help you become a stronger, more effective nature and environmental writer.

Part III, as mentioned above, is an introductory anthology of contemporary nature and environmental writing. While we could have added hundreds of other amazing pieces, our hope is that these selections offer you immediate access to some of the best nature and environmental writing being done today. In addition to this anthology, we highly encourage you to read widely. Get hold of books by authors in the anthology, ask teachers and peers for recommendations—read, read, read!

With all this in mind, perhaps our first order of business is to more fully define nature and environmental writing. For a humorous and wise guide to nature and environmental writing, make sure to examine David Gessner's "Nature Writing by Numbers," which offers a step-by-step comic narrative on how to write in these two genres. Or else we can go back to Joe's vignette about his journey in the Seven Devils and his impulse, even as he hiked, to write about that journey. Can we say, perhaps, that the natural world and our internal experiences are mutually informing, are in fact inextricable from one another? Sure! Though we live in a society and culture that often attempts—via various technologies—to obliterate place, we must remember that the physical world, the world of rocks and trees and rivers, is, in fact, the wellspring of human reckoning itself. We're built of the same stuff as grass, as apples and elk, and when we get right down to it, we depend on the natural world for nearly every kind of sustenance, from physical to spiritual.

Let's have this stand, then, as our first criterion: nature and environmental writing is writing that honors the connection between the natural world and human experience, that understands them as parts of a whole, that reckons with the complex forces of place and landscape in human lives.

What else? If we take a look at Lydia Peele's powerful short story "Mule Killers," we see a deep connection between the protagonist's family and their ancestral farm in rural Georgia, but we also see that human history—tractors and other advances in technology—begin to bring a force to bear on the natural history of the land, as the mules are led to slaughter and more and more acres are plowed under. So, we might say that in nature and environmental writing the natural world must be understood as dynamic and, further, that the relationship between the natural world and the human world is also in constant flux.

"Mule Killers," like much nature and environmental writing, makes an ethical claim on us as well. The story asks us to consider whether technological advances are true "advances"; it asks us to consider whether tractors and gasoline engines did more harm than good to the landscape and to the characters of the story:

These days, my father remembers little from the time before the tractors. The growl of their engines in his mind has long since drowned out the quieter noises: the constant stamping and shifting of mule weight in the barn, the smooth sound of oats being poured into a steel bucket. He remembers the steam that rose from the animals after work.

And we're not done yet! Consider Chelsea Biondolillo's slanting, song-like essay, "Geology: An Investigation." "In geology, an unconformity is a missing layer of the Earth's history," Biondolillo writes, as she adroitly illuminates for us a few tenets of planetary, as well as personal, geology:

> It's a lack of proof, a century's worth of centuries blown away, settled under the sea or still floating in a slant of sunlight just this morning, when you woke up late. We know it's gone, because the layers below are jagged, like a mouth propped open. Sometimes, it's difficult to tell the chronological order of the sedimentary deposition: there are many ways for the weather to throw rocks around. There are always parts of the story left out.

Listen to that voice: so wry and wise and alive, so precise and musical. This, too, is a marker of nature and environmental writing: writing that is vivid, rich, and graceful—an experience unto itself.

And, finally, all of the pieces mentioned above intimately know their worlds both on a sensory level (what it looks, smells, feels, sounds, and maybe tastes like) and on a natural history level. These authors know what the landscape looks like, where the rivers flow, the intricacies of an Alaskan watershed or a mountain slope or a mule. They are experts in language and in landscape.

If we are to take stock now, **nature and environmental writing** is writing that:

- Speaks to the shifting, essential relationship between the natural world and human experience;
- Understands the natural world as in flux, and honors the dynamic relationship between the natural world and the human world, as each brings forces to bear on the other across time;
- Makes ethical claims about the ways we live with the natural world;
- Seeks to make reading itself a sensory experience by employing evocative language and vivid descriptions;
- Possesses a strong understanding of the natural history of the place or places in question.

So if these are the traits nature and environmental writing share, how, then, do we differentiate between nature writing and environmental writing? Though there are dissenting voices, most understand the differentiation as a matter of emphasis. **Nature writing** is writing that highlights the intricacy, beauty, danger, fear, and/or current conditions of the natural world, especially as it is perceived by a particular consciousness and spoken about in a particular voice. Joe's poem "Seven Devils" would be classified, then, as nature writing, as would Chelsea Biondolillo's essay "Geology: An Investigation."

While doing many of the same things as nature writing, **environmental writing** also speaks—and does so directly and purposefully—to the ways humans influence (and often misuse) the natural world. As such, in environmental writing, the ethical implications become far more pointed, far more political. Lydia Peelle's short story "Mule Killers" serves as a strong example of environmental writing: as Peelle's characters mourn their poor decisions and struggle to accept their fates, she asks us to mourn our poor decisions and question our mechanized, industrial fate as well. In fact, Peelle might even be challenging us to do something about this, both in our own lives and in the wider world. And this is absolutely what environmental writing endeavors to do: it seeks to challenge the reader to make changes in their daily lives and to advocate for environmental justice and sustainability in the wider world.

The trailhead

The book you hold in your hands is a nature and environmental writing textbook; as such, it is something of a hybrid: it is a text that attempts to define, classify, and otherwise speak about nature and environmental writing, yet it is also a text that endeavors to offer instruction in how to write graceful, powerful essays, stories, and poems in the nature and environmental writing tradition. With this first chapter, we have begun our discussion of the definitions and classifications of nature and environmental writing. We continue this discussion in Chapter 2, where we follow the historical trails of nature and environmental writing. Starting with Chapter 3 (and Part II), we turn our attention toward the craft of writing in the nature and environmental writing tradition.

Despite the hybridity of this text, we begin this long, daunting journey— we shoulder our packs and take those first steps, begin to match our strides with the landscape about us—with a single hope: that through our study we might write our own nature and environmental essays, stories, and poems, and we might open the eyes and hearts of our readers and introduce them to new areas that must be seen, experienced, or protected.

Exercises

The following exercises will help you practice the techniques learned in this chapter.

A. Choose a book from your shelf—one you've read before—and take a walk or go on a hike. At some point, take a break and read. How does the hike or walk change your experience of the book? How does the book change your experience of the hike or walk?
B. While looking at the same book from Exercise A, examine how the book uses place/setting/landscape. How does the book describe location?
C. Consider the list of traits for nature and environmental writing included in this chapter. Does each of the readings for this chapter meet the criteria for either nature or environmental writing? Or both? Why or why not? What about the book you chose from Exercise A?

Prompts

The following prompts will help you practice the techniques learned in this chapter.

A. Write a poem that occurs both in a particular place and in memory. Move back and forth between those two realms as you see fit.
B. If you were to be reincarnated as an animal, what animal would you want to be? Why? Write an essay that considers these questions.
C. Think of a place in your life that you would least like to lose. Do you have a house you'd hate to have sold? Is there a park you'd hate to see developed? Is there a mountaintop you'd hate to have logged? Write a story in which you imagine the loss of this place.

2

A Short History of Nature and Environmental Writing

Relevant readings

While all other chapters begin with a list of creative nonfiction, fiction, and poetry selections to read from our anthology, we have chosen to not do that in this chapter's "Relevant readings." We removed the selections here since each piece in our anthology fits into one or more of the below listed subgenres of nature and environmental writing.

Rather, what you will find throughout this chapter is that we briefly mention many anthology pieces in the various sub-genres. And we offer you the opportunity to explore the anthology on your own and to see where the pieces you chose might fit among our categories.

Free write

Let's pretend for a moment that we have a time machine, you and I, and we'd like to travel back to the moment when people first began writing about the natural world. When and where would that be, do you think? And why do you think so? Jot a few ideas down.

Now, what about the moment people began writing about what we now call the environment (where people interact with and affect nature)? Which time and place would we aim our time machine at now? Why? Again, write some of these ideas down.

Now, look back over what you've written. Are the times and places the same or different? Why? Share your ideas with a partner.

Vignette

On September 26, 1752, the first of my European relatives, forty-seven-year-old Johannes Georg Beck and his fifteen-year-old son, John Jacob George Beck, left their home along the Enz River in Germany, bound for Pennsylvania. They boarded a ship, the Richard and Mary, and soon landed in Philadelphia. Once in this new world, they migrated to northeastern Pennsylvania, to what was then the frontier, the home of a number of native peoples, the wild frontier. They settled on the edge of the Slate Belt, a geological region that has been mined for slate, then tilled for corn, and now developed for power plants and hosieries.

*There, just miles from where I grew up, Johannes and John Jacob home-
steaded. Within the year, Johannes's wife, Anna Maria, arrived with the rest
of their nine children. By 1775, Johannes had died and was buried in a grave
in the Old Beck Family Cemetery (just upriver from my childhood home). His
marker is the oldest in the cemetery.*

*Now when I, a tenth generation Pennsylvanian, return to the Slate Belt
from my new home in Vermont, I return to a landscape that feels deeply famil-
ial. My stories have been birthed in these old, exploited hills. This landscape
fathered and mothered my family of Becks, Millers, Halls, and, now, Prentisses.
We are a people of slate, rich soil, cornfields, ice storms, and hot, humid summer days that chase us into our Delaware River.*

*When I visit my mother and father, I go for hikes. Just a mile from my child-
hood home, I explore one of the earlier homesteads of my ancestral family. As
I walk through the crumbled cellar walls, I say,* Right here, they hauled water
from the river. Right here, they built a stone row. Right here, they planted
fields of corn. Right here, they lived and died.

Pennsylvania is my historical landscape.

*But I am more than just a son of Pennsylvania. I am also a person who lives
not just in place but in words. When I think about my writings, I think about
their genealogical past, their lineage. Not via blood and birth but via idea,
metaphor, and image. I think about the history of my ideas and narratives. Just
as with my family's past, I can trace my literary roots back many generations.
And I need to be able to do this, to know who my literary grandparents and
great grandparents are. My literary aunts and uncles too. Every writer should
know where they come from and which trails they traveled to get where they
are now.*

*For me, my authorial lineage begins with the words of Desert Southwest
writers like Edward Abbey, Charles Bowden, and Terry Tempest Williams. It
comes from Pennsylvania where Abbey's great novel,* The Fool's Progress, *takes
place. Bits of my lineage come from Oregon and the great outdoorsman, Ken
Kesey. One poetic part of my literary tree was born out of Ohio's James Wright.
Another part was birthed a world away, the ancient Chinese poet, T'ao Ch'ien.
Each literary ancestor brings something new to my voice, my ideas, the genres I write in. And what's best is that I don't yet know my full history. I have
not yet discovered all the writers who will teach me. This literary genealogy is
expansive.*

*We all have history. With our families and with our writing. And our his-
tories are what shape, create, and motivate us to find our muses, to write our
words, to live our lives in the best ways we know how. The places we are from*

grow our language and evolve our ideas and tones. And the writers we love shape how we see our homes, how we see the arc of our lives as well. Our histories in place and on the page affect who we are, what we have to say about place, and how we will say it. Will we whisper it like a Pennsylvania autumn breeze, cry it like a Pennsylvania spring rain, or scream it like a Pennsylvania summer thunderstorm?

—Sean

A short history of nature and environmental writing

This textbook devotes itself to helping you learn to write nature and environmental essays, stories, and poems. As such, it may seem strange that before we talk about writing—about craft and technique and form—we devote an entire chapter to history. Yet, contemplating where we come from—as Sean outlined above—is necessary for understanding why and how we might write in the first place. And just as each nature writer needs to contemplate their history or lack of history in a place, their love for a landscape or their bitter hatred, their deep knowledge of a land and the stories of that land or their ignorance of the mountains or deserts or cityscapes around them, we must also understand that nature and environmental writing itself has a history that has shaped the literary place at which it has arrived.

So, with this chapter, we examine how nature and environmental writing came into being and how these movements have grown and evolved. We begin our history by focusing on nature writing, as that's where the genre began chronologically, yet very soon nature and environmental writing became intertwined, and so we shift our discussion accordingly. Further, we explore this history, for the most part, by considering various historical modes of nature and environmental writing, an organizational strategy that allows us to discuss contemporary analogues (many of which are included in the anthology) and to more readily connect the history to our own writing projects—which is, of course, our hope: that you might begin to locate yourself within these traditions, that you might find your own home ground, and then from that vantage be better able to explore new landscapes in nature and environmental writing.

The prehistory of nature and environmental writing

The trouble with our time machine exercise above—as you no doubt intuited—is that the roots of nature and environmental writing are divergent and expansive, and you could rightly choose a variety of starting points.

For instance, you could make a strong argument that nature writing actually begins before the written word, with the creation stories and myths and tales of aboriginal peoples across the globe. These oral traditions intimately dealt with the natural world and how human beings might know and engage with their landscapes. These stories were then passed on from generation to generation.

Another starting point might be the work of the ancient Chinese poets, T'ao Ch'ien, also known as Táo Qián, (AD 365–427) and Hsieh Ling-yün, also known as Xie Lingyun (AD 385–433). T'ao and Hsieh created the rivers-and-mountains tradition of poetry, which have a strong narrative, occur in natural landscapes, and are composed in easy-to-understand prose. Though the rivers-and-mountains poetry of ancient China is most likely the first written example of what we call nature writing, these poems did not influence the Western tradition until the mid-nineteen-hundreds, when T'ao and Hsieh and others were first widely translated. But since then, these translations have helped shape the writings of Gary Snyder, Peter Matthiessen, Gretel Ehrlich, Ursula Le Guin, Scott Russell Sanders, and countless other writers.

Others might argue for the Greek philosophers. Aristotle believed that between nature and humanity there existed a harmonious relationship. Aristotle's and the other Greek philosophers' work demonstrates the connection between animals, plants, and humans, and expresses the equality of all creatures and beings. These philosophers saw their environments as playing pivotal roles in the current state and the future of humankind. Nearly 200 years later, Theocritus and Virgil shared the ideals of their predecessors, with focus in their writings on the shepherd and the idealized environment they inhabited. The influence of the ancient Greeks spanned time and space, reaching Edmund Spenser, Friedrich von Schiller, and Johann Wolfgang von Goethe nearly 2,000 years later.

Next we have Nicolaus Copernicus, a Renaissance astronomer and mathematician from Poland who formulated that the sun, not the earth, was the center of our universe. His publication, *On the Revolutions of the Celestial Spheres*, triggered the Copernican Revolution, which led to the scientific revolution. And if we have to pick a particular point to mark the modern beginning of nature writing, we might argue that the scientific revolution is the actual genesis of the Western, and especially the American, nature writing tradition.

In 1607, Galileo Galilei (1564–1642) turned a telescope toward the night sky, transforming our understanding of the Earth's role in the solar system. No longer could we see Earth as set apart, as a creation unto itself. Rather, Earth was a part of the extravagant systems slowly being understood and described by the sciences. In the wake of Galileo came Swedish botanist and zoologist Carolus Linnaeus (1707–1778), who wrote *Systema Naturae* in 1735 and *Species Plantarum* in 1753. These books laid out the first modern scientific system for identifying and classifying living things through, according to one of Linnaeus's subtitles, "the three kingdoms of nature, according to classes, orders, genera and species, with characters, differences, synonyms, places." Linnaeus's system identified all living organisms by two Latin names, which meant scientists and laypeople could study the natural world and more easily share their observations. Further, by explicitly relating all living organisms, this system implicitly challenged observers to look for relationships and similarities between various plants and animals. And the scientific search for natural processes and relationships (and our place within those processes and relationships) formed the foundation on which nature writing would be built.

Gilbert White (1720–1793) was one of many who used Linnaeus's classification system to catalogue his region. In 1789 White wrote *The Natural History and Antiquities of Selborne*, a compilation of 110 letters to other naturalists and a natural history of the Selborne area. In the text, White explains that he is an "out-door naturalist," a point of view that differentiated him from most other naturalists of the time, who studied dead plants and animals in a laboratory. With *The Natural History and Antiquities of Selborne*, White incorporated modern science but also moved beyond the language of science: his prose isn't dry and stuffy but literary and engaging. White didn't merely describe a bird in flight. Rather, White mirrors the flight patterns of the birds he describes with his syntax. He was part-scientist, part-artist. *The Natural History and Antiquities of Selborne*, which became a best seller in Europe and America, inspired many future nature writers, including Henry David Thoreau and Charles Darwin.

Not long after the publication of White's study came Romanticism, which spanned, roughly, the first half of the nineteenth century. Romanticism was a movement in art and literature that reacted against the ravages of the Industrial Revolution, which had increasingly affected every part of European life: populations exploded, cities swelled, and all manner of natural resources were taxed. The Romantics saw in industrialization not a prosperous, more efficient future but a soulless, bleak mechanization. The Romantic ideal, then, was to escape from the over-industrialized, overpopulated urban world to a quieter, wilder, more beautiful natural world. So, in contrast to Gilbert White, the Romantics worried less about cataloguing the natural world and focused more on experiencing nature in its sublime and terrifying beauty.

This European crossroads—the science of Linnaeus, the natural histories of White, and the sensibilities of the Romantics—led directly to modern nature writing.

The natural history

When Europeans first settled the coastlines of the Americas, they were scared: vast, rocky shorelines; towering trees; exotic animals in the forests; strange fish in the streams; and the many native peoples and their complex, unfamiliar cultures. Any of these terrains, plants, animals, or humans could (and often did) kill individuals and entire communities. Add to the sheer novelty of the place a puritanical worldview—which saw wilderness as a religious evil, one that should be tamed in the name of God and dehumanized native peoples to view them as part of that wilderness rather than rightful and sophisticated users of that very "wilderness" which they shaped into their homeland—and you've got the perfect recipe for a decidedly adversarial relationship with the natural world.

And so, as these first Europeans began living on the edge of this strange new world, they devoted much of their writing to understanding—in an attempt to subdue and master—this new landscape. This cataloging led to the first wave of American nature writing: natural histories of the land and the peoples of the land.

In a **natural history**, the writer's gaze is focused on natural phenomena foreign to the writer. The writer studies the geography, plants, trees, animals, and people of a place as a way to understand scientific processes and relationships. Often, the writer's role is secondary, or even unimportant, to the role the land and flora and fauna play. It is not the writer's journey that is important; rather, the writer's eye is focused outward, toward defining, cataloging, and scientifically understanding the land and what or who lives on the land. This focus outside of the writer means most natural histories are written in third person (she/her/they/them) rather than first person (I/me). Still, many natural histories blend science with the art of language so that the science rises off the page. Perhaps the first American nature writer was William Bartram, who in 1792 published *Travels,* a natural history detailing his explorations in the American South. In *Travels,* Bartram describes many of America's exotic plants and trees, yet he also focuses on human nature and society; he is an eloquent, graceful writer as well.

Though the natural history of old—an observer cataloging the wonders of a new land—has mostly gone by the wayside, our microscopes and satellites and vast storehouses of scientific knowledge continue to bring us to the edges of what is known, and so natural histories remain a vital form of nature writing. For an example in our anthology, see Michael McGriff's poem "Coos Bay."

Pastoral narratives

In 1790, the first census listed the United States as having 3,929,214 white citizens and one factory, a mill in Pawtucket, Rhode Island, where cotton yarn was made. By 1860, just seventy years later, the United States had grown tenfold, to a population of 31,443,321, and had become an industrialized nation with countless factories and rail lines and vast urban centers along the Eastern seaboard, the Great Lakes, and even in the far West.

During this period, many Americans began to feel stifled by urbanization and began to look away from urban cores, away from factories and mills, away from the gray air and snowing ash. They gazed toward the pastoral world they remembered from not many years ago. This yearning for the pastoral was coupled with the growing fear that we hadn't just mastered but destroyed nature. In 1799 we killed off the last of the eastern bison. The railroad soon split the bison of the West, and both the southern and northern herds were gunned down by the early 1880s. Soon after, we drove the Arizona elk to extinction, killed off the bighorn sheep in the Badlands, and shot the last passenger pigeons from the skies. Along with these massacres came the damming of rivers, the extraction of minerals from the land, and the deforestation of vast swaths of the country. All the while the United

States was carrying out a brutal campaign against Native Americans: by the 1890s, only 250,000 remained of a population that had once numbered in the millions.

This longing for the pastoral, and this fear that we'd lost it altogether, led to a boom in nature writing: people wanted to experience nature, even if only on the page. So nature writers, rather than observing, cataloging, and ordering in an attempt to know and understand, as in a natural history, began to write about journeys through what was left of the pastoral landscape. We call accounts of these journeys to the edges of cities and towns to explore the rustic and bucolic world pastoral narratives or rambles. **Pastoral narratives** are most often about short excursions where the writer is escaping the city to search for how he (most of these authors were male, and more than a few of them were dealing in romantic clichés and misrepresentations) fits into the landscape and how the landscape affects him. Pastoral writing might include scientific detail, much like natural histories, but like the Romantics, pastoral writers are more concerned with aesthetic, emotional, philosophical, and ethical concerns. For this reason, pastoral narratives often use first person (*I, me*) and balance external observations with internal observations.

Henry David Thoreau (1817–1862), one of America's most important nature writers, penned, among many other things, lively pastoral narratives that blended careful natural observation, lyric sensibilities, and persuasive argumentation. In his journals, Thoreau explains why these pastoral rambles are so important: "In society you will not find health [...]. There is no scent in [society] so wholesome as that of the pines, nor any fragrance so penetrating and restorative as that of the everlasting high pastures" (Thoreau, The Journal of Henry D. Thoreau December 31, 1841).

For an example of a pastoral narrative with a modern, urban twist, see Bonnie Nadzam's short story "Cartography" in the anthology.

Adventure narratives

A ramble at the edge of town satisfied many, yet some longed for the explorations and adventures of the generations that preceded them, so they began to travel deeper into what originally were the lands of Native Americans, lands now called wilderness—even the terming of the lands "wilderness" allowed Euro-Americans to more easily steal those lands. These explorers wrote **adventure narratives**, which are similar to pastoral narratives in that both forms involve travel, but adventure narratives travel much further, detailing an author's experiences deep in some remote, unknown, and, often, dangerous landscape. Also like pastoral narratives, adventure narratives are often penned in the first person, yet there tends to be less introspection and more focus on the dramatics of the journey itself with adventure narratives, which allows the reader to be immersed in the full excitement of the adventure. Yet there is some internal work done: as we adventure along with the writer, we begin to see how the writer changes throughout the journey.

Two of America's earliest adventure writers were Meriwether Lewis (1774–1809) and William Clark (1770–1838). In 1804 Lewis and Clark began their famed journey to find a waterway to the Pacific Ocean, and *The Journals of Lewis and Clark* shared with readers the vast wonders of that journey and of the North American continent. Lewis and Clark detailed their adventures with grizzly bears, bison by the millions, unknown Native American tribes, and mountain ranges that scraped the skies. Along with these observations and discoveries, the journals detail the joys and worries of the thirty-three-member Corps of Discovery Expedition itself.

The adventure narrative remains a mainstay of contemporary nature writing, with many outdoor magazines featuring numerous adventure narratives. In the anthology, Joe's poem "Seven Devils," which we introduced in the previous chapter, might also be classified as a lyrical adventure narrative.

Enter: Environmental writing

The rapid industrialization and urbanization of the nineteenth century was only the tip of the proverbial iceberg. In 1900, the population of the United States was 76 million; by midcentury, that number would double; by the century's close, that original number would nearly quadruple. In 1900, around 8,000 automobiles motored on a small network of regional roads. By 2000, nearly 220 million automobiles zoomed across a continent-spanning system of interstates, toll-ways, and highways. In 1903, at Kill Devil Hills in North Carolina, Wilbur Wright flew for fifty-nine seconds; today, over 100,000 airline passengers move through North Carolina's Douglass International Airport in a single day.

But we're not done yet: note that nearly all of these dizzying changes are predicated on energy extraction, on wringing something from the Earth to feed our machines and our appetite for machines. And note this as well: Joe's grandfather was born in a sod shanty in eastern Montana in 1914. For most of his life, he made his living off the back of a horse, cowboying and ranching, yet he died in 2001—these decades of colossal change spanning little more than a single lifetime.

It was, and is, almost more than a society could understand. Still, American society desperately needed to understand what was happening to our landscapes and daily lives in a rapidly industrialized world. And so, our writing about the world around us evolved. With so much already catalogued and categorized, the pastoral a long-gone myth for most, and even the wildest places bearing human footprints of one kind or another, writers began to record and interrogate the changes themselves. And this is **environmental writing**, writing that concerns itself with how humans affect nature. When we use the term *environment*, we are concerning ourselves with the intersection of humans and nature. Poet Juliana Spahr delineates the difference between nature writing and environmental writing: "[E]ven when [nature writing] got the birds and the plants and the animals right it tended to show the beautiful bird but not so often the bulldozer off to the side that was destroying the bird's habitat."

Wilderness and preservation narratives

Once European-Americans had drained, logged, dammed, fenced, and/or plowed the land; industrialized towns and cities; and devastated the native cultures; the continent was tamed. In 1893, at the American Historical Association in Chicago, historian Frederick Jackson Turner shared his *Frontier Thesis*: the American frontier, as we understood it, officially closed in 1890. Many viewed this as a good thing: the world outside our front doors was safe—we no longer had to worry so much about grizzly attacks—and we could continue to go about the business of harnessing and extracting the resources of the land.

Yet many saw a nation that had lost more than it had gained. Turner himself posited that the closing of the frontier presaged the loss of the rugged independence displayed by the first European Americans. Further, the landscape—variously and intensively extracted as it was—had lost much of its personality and character. As a corrective to the used and abused landscape and as a place of respite and renewal for the human spirit, many Americans longed to preserve what wilderness remained. In this spirit, nature writers began the essays, stories, and poems that we now recognize as the first environmental writing, **wilderness and preservation narratives**, which argued for the protection, preservation, and restoration of wilderness lands.

One of the first wilderness and preservation writers was John Muir. Muir (1838–1914) saw the glory of Yosemite Valley in California and longed to preserve it. To reach that goal, Muir founded the Sierra Club (an organization still active in environmental issues) and researched the Yosemite Valley with a scientific eye. Yet Muir realized he needed to do more than just organize like-minded people and do scientific research into glaciation; he needed to convince the general population that the preservation of wild lands mattered. So, although Muir was a dedicated scientist, he changed the way he wrote to better convey to readers the true wonders and worth of nature. Muir explained this shift in his writing: "The man of science, the naturalist, too often loses sight of the essential oneness of all living beings in seeking to classify them in kingdoms, orders, families, genera, species, etc. [...] while the eye of the Poet, the Seer, never closes on the kinship of all God's creatures, and his heart ever beats in sympathy with great and small alike."

Wilderness and preservation writers venture into wilderness in search of a more authentic way of life. While traveling these wildernesses, preservation writers grow introspective as the silence of the mountains or the desert or the river challenges the writer to examine themselves and their ideals. Though similar to pastoral narratives, these journeys and philosophical meanderings lead preservationist writers to not only lament the loss of some natural order but also question humanity's relationship with nature and to argue, then, for how humans might better preserve the natural world. And these arguments are inherently political. David Gessner, in his short graphic essay, "Nature Writing by Numbers," highlights both nature writing and the more political bent of environmental writing.

As influential as preservationist ideas were, and remain, to environmental writing, still many writers, especially Native American and Latino writers, question the very idea of wilderness because seeing the land as wilderness allowed Euro-Americans to colonize the land more easily. Also, many writers wonder when the forests and mountains were ever without humanity; they remember, through oral traditions, a continent that has been a human habitat for tens of thousands of years. Louis Owens's essay, "Burning the Shelter," discusses how Owens burned down, on the instruction of the Forest Service, a collapsed Forest Service shelter in the Glacier Peaks Wilderness of Washington in 1976. The Forest Service was trying to return the land to a wilderness state; however, after he burns down the structure, Owens realizes that he is helping create a false representation of America's original wilderness: "Before the European invasion, there was no wilderness in North America; there was only the fertile continent, where people lived in a hard-learned balance with the natural world."

Agrarian narratives

In 1800, 90 percent of Americans lived on farms. By 1920, that number had fallen to 30 percent. By the early 1980s, less than 3 percent of Americans lived on farms. Not only were people moving from farms and ranches to cities full of industry and business but farms and ranches themselves were also becoming places of industry and business.

Though the United States, in accordance with Thomas Jefferson's ideal of the yeoman farmer, had originally modeled itself as a land of single-family farms and ranches—where most everything a family needed was grown or raised on the farm—twentieth-century changes in technology and policy, as well as creeping corporatization, radically transformed rural communities. No longer was the rural landscape a patchwork of self-sustaining farmers and ranchers working family acres with hand-me-down tools and techniques; now it was a vast monochrome of corn, dairy, or hog barns, shiny machines tilling and spraying the fields, the land itself treated as commodity rather than an ancestral home.

Much like those who lamented the loss of wilderness and argued for the preservation of what wilderness was left, many environmental writers began to pen essays, stories, and poems that we call **agrarian narratives**, which highlight the successes, struggles, and changes faced by family farmers, while arguing for revitalizing and restoring a sustainable culture of farming and ranching. Further, as it became harder to know where, exactly, our food came from and how it was raised, let alone recognize much of what was sold in grocery stores as food, agrarian narratives began to trace and critique our food and food systems.

No writer is more important to the agrarian narrative than Wendell Berry. Berry was born on a tobacco farm in Kentucky in 1934 to parents whose families had farmed within that county for five generations. After moving from Kentucky to teach in New York City and, later, at the University of Kentucky, Berry quit and moved to a 125-acre farm in his home county. There, he grew grain and corn. Berry has written more than forty books, including *The Unsettling of America: Culture and Agriculture*, *Farming: A Hand Book*, and *Bringing It to the Table: On Farming and Food*, and he continues to write essays, poems, and stories about agrarian issues, including small-scale farming versus corporate farming, philosophical and spiritual issues related to farming, and issues of land stewardship, and he deals with these issues in ways that help us not just imagine how to reduce our footprint and connect to nature but to reimagine through place a new niche for humans on earth. One example of an agrarian narrative is Julia Shipley's "Migration of Baling Twine."

Along with farming and ranching, many Americans hunted and trapped. Like farming and ranching, hunting and trapping demands a deep, sustaining relationship with the land and a respect for the interconnectedness of all beings. Yet, also like farming and ranching, hunting and trapping have changed in the twentieth century; fewer people need to hunt and trap to survive, and exploitative, technologically dependent forms of hunting and trapping have become ascendant. Often, hunting and trapping narratives lament this change and seek to reestablish the necessity and spirituality of hunting and trapping. In the anthology, David Treuer's essay "Trapline" examines the cultural and personal importance of trapping on the Leech Lake Reservation.

Science and nature narratives

By the close of World War II, the United States had become a nation of factories and assembly lines, as well as one of the nations leading the revolution in biological and chemical technologies. Many of these technologies began as potential wartime tools and weapons, yet they were quickly repurposed and used to fertilize fields, eradicate insects, and prevent illnesses. Though these chemicals helped grow more food and prevent certain sicknesses, they also poisoned our lands and bodies. In our rush to use our new technologies, we forgot that science is not beyond natural systems but part and parcel of the living, breathing world. In her National Book Award acceptance speech for *The Sea Around Us,* famed science writer Rachel Carson (1907–1964) explains:

> This notion, that "science" is something that belongs in a separate compartment of its own, apart from everyday life, is one that I should like to challenge. We live in a scientific age; yet we assume that knowledge of science is the prerogative of only a small number of human beings, isolated and priest-like in their laboratories. This is not true. The materials of science

are the materials of life itself. Science is part of the reality of living; it is the what, the how, the why of everything in our experience. It is impossible to understand man without understanding his environment and the forces that have molded him physically and mentally.

In light of this, Carson began to pen **science and nature narratives**, which are essays, stories, and poems that explore the dangers and pitfalls of science and argue for an ecological awareness in the use of technology. Like natural histories before them, many science and nature narratives balance science and art, yet they do so in service of a clearer, more political argument.

Rachel Carson's *Silent Spring* may be the best-known science and nature narrative. Carson's book investigates the role synthetic pesticides played in the die-off of birds and other creatures. *Silent Spring* asked us to own up to the many terrible consequences of our technologies and helped bring about a number of legislative changes during the 1960s and 1970s, including the Wilderness Act in 1964, the Wild and Scenic Rivers Act in 1968, the Clean Air Act and formation of the Environmental Protection Agency in 1970, and the Endangered Species Act and the banning of DDT in 1973.

Examples of science and nature texts in our anthology include Jennifer Lunden's exposé of mammograms and mammogram culture, "Exposed."

Environmental justice narratives

A sibling of science and nature writing is **environmental justice narratives.** Environmental justice is, according to the US Environmental Protection Agency, "the fair treatment and meaningful involvement of all people regardless of race, color, national origin, or income with respect to the development, implementation, and enforcement of environmental laws, regulations, and policies." Environmental justice is the intersection and intermingling of civil rights, social rights, and environmental rights. Environmental justice narratives highlight how racism and poverty put certain people and places at a greater risk for health issues related to environmental degradation.

Environmental justice moved into people's consciousness in 1983 in rural Warren County, North Carolina, a county heavily populated by poor African Americans. A hazardous-waste landfill was planned in Warren County, but local residents protested. Five hundred protesters were arrested, birthing the environmental justice movement. Out of the Warren County protests and other protests related to environmental justice issues sprang government studies that found that over half of the nine million people living within two miles of a hazardous waste site were people of color, highlighting the fact that they were more likely to carry the physical and emotional burdens of environmental devastation.

Sandra Steingraber, a biologist, cancer survivor, and writer, is at the forefront of the contemporary environmental justice movement. In her twenties, Steingraber was diagnosed with bladder cancer. Though bladder cancer is rare, there was a cluster of bladder cancer victims in her hometown. Out of this experience came her seminal book, *Living Downstream: An Ecologist Looks at Cancer and the Environment,* which details how industrial and agricultural pollutants affect people every day. Steingraber is also an activist. Recently, she was arrested for protesting fracking in upstate New York, where she lives and works.

Examples of environmental justice narratives in the anthology include Sean's essay "Spring Ends in Bangor, Pennsylvania."

Climate change narratives

Starting in the mid-1980s, scientists began to argue that climate patterns across the earth were changing and that, overall, temperatures were rising due to excessive carbon dioxide emissions trapping heat in the atmosphere. Many of the scientific papers on the subject read like apocalyptic science fiction: melting polar ice caps, flooded coastlines, tens of millions of displaced peoples; weather patterns growing more violent and unpredictable across the globe; untold species driven to extinction. Originally called global warming, climate change is now perhaps the singular environmental issue of our time.

Climate change narratives detail the ways climate change is impacting ecosystems and human communities across the globe. Much like science and nature narratives or environmental justice narratives, climate change narratives illustrate how humans have adversely affected, and continue to affect, the environment; yet climate change narratives often have a wider reach, as climate change affects the entire biosphere. The most prominent climate change writer today is Bill McKibben. In 1989, McKibben wrote *The End of Nature,* which is considered the first book written about climate change for a general audience. Since the writing of that book, McKibben has continued to write about and speak out on issues related to climate change.

For examples of climate change narratives in the anthology, consider Chris Dombrowski's poem "Weekly Apocalyptic, or Poem Written on the Wall in an Ascending Space Capsule."

Postcolonial narratives

The history of nature and environmental writing that we have discussed thus far, for the most part, follows the European-American story of exploration and settlement; however, that is far from the only story. In this section we examine **postcolonial narratives**, which are the narratives of people who have been colonized by others. As you can imagine, the history of nature and environmental writing becomes more complex (as well as fuller and richer) when examined through a postcolonial lens. Below, we consider the ways Native Americans, African Americans, and Latino Americans continue to deepen and grow nature and environmental writing.

Native American narratives

Often, when we think about the American continents before Europeans landed, we imagine a mostly empty space with a scattering of Native Americans. But that image is far from accurate. Possibly tens of millions of Native Americans were spread across the entirety of both continents as members of thousands of unique and distinctive nations speaking hundreds of different languages. Although often Native Americans didn't have what Europeans would term "advanced technologies," they had built rich, sustaining cultures with complex social, political, and religious underpinnings. And though none of these tribes possessed a written language, for thousands of years before Europeans arrived in North America, Native Americans were telling stories.

Native Americans saw stories as a part of everyday life. Tribes used oral literature as a way to teach tribal history, customs, values, and rules. Deeply rooted in the landscape, these stories detail the natural and spiritual history of a place and how it ties to a particular Native culture. Almost as soon as Europeans landed in the Americas, they began recording Native American oral literature. As Native Americans learned to read and write, they also began to record these stories. In 1821, a Cherokee, Sequoya, created the first Native alphabet. Soon thereafter, Native Americans began writing literature in their own languages. We call these writings, whether transcribed by European Americans or written by Native Americans, **Native American narratives**.

Native American narratives can be broken down into three major subcategories. The first are the myths, creation stories, and songs of oral literature. These are stories composed for an entirely Native American audience in a Native American tongue before or during the early arrival of Europeans. This subcategory is called **traditional** Native American narratives.

The next subcategory is **transitional** Native American narratives. Transitional narratives are stories recorded by European Americans from great Native American orators, as well as the first memoirs written by Native Americans. Transitional narratives often detail the loss of land, religion, and culture experienced by Native Americans and are thus deeply elegiac in tone. These transitional narratives were written, most often, in English for a European American audience, in the hopes that European Americans could learn the other side of the history. The final category is **modern** Native American narratives, which includes all the essays, stories, and poems written in the recent past by Native Americans. Modern Native American narratives detail and investigate issues pertinent to contemporary Native American life, including identity, history, racism, landscape, reservation politics, cultural reclamation, assimilation, education, alcoholism, war, suicide, poverty, and religion, among many others. Perhaps the most famous modern Native American writer is N. Scott Momaday, a Kiowa poet and fiction writer who won the Pulitzer Prize in Fiction in 1969 for his novel *House Made of Dawn*, which details life on New Mexico's Jemez Pueblo. Momaday is often credited with beginning a renaissance in Native American writing.

For other examples of modern Native American narratives, read M.L. Smoker's "The Feed."

African American narratives

Stolen from Africa and brought to the United States to work in servitude, African American slaves shared stories of place and loss as a way to hold onto their cultural identities. Unlike Native Americans, African Americans wrote not about losing their American lands but about being stolen from their African homeland and forced to live in a new world. Thus, **African American narratives** often illustrate a different relationship with the landscape than do narratives of European Americans or Native Americans. In African American narratives, the land, especially at first, was a place of toil, deceit, and violence. Consider the landscape of Major Jackson's poem "Migration," a landscape of prior and potential violence: "I read oaks and poplars for signs: charred branches, tobacco leaves strung up to die."

African American narratives, much like Native American and Latino narratives, cover a wide gamut of ideas and topics and encompass many sub-genres. Some African American writers, like the European Americans who wrote the natural histories, offer a careful study of the land—but to a different end. Runaway slaves needed to intimately know the natural landscape, as a deep knowledge of living off the land (knowing what to eat, how to tell directions, which animals were dangerous, etc.) often meant the difference between success and failure when escaping to the North.

There is also a pastoral strain in many African American narratives. Many African Americans learned to love the landscapes of the American South, to call them home. In Camille T. Dungy's essay "Tales from a Black Girl on Fire, or Why I Hate to Walk Outside and See Things Burning," Dungy deftly spans the gap between the fear of wilderness (and lynching) and the sublime beauty of nature.

Though the African American experience began as one rooted in the American South, it is now, statistically, an urban experience. And African American writers also increasingly narrate their cityscapes, viewing urban areas as landscapes. Poet G.E. Patterson contrasts traditional views of nature with his urban home in his poem "The Natural World."

Latino narratives

The fastest growing minority population in the United States is Latinos. The US Census Bureau recorded a 50 percent increase in the Latino population between 2000 and 2012, and 53 million Latinos currently call America home. For the purposes of this textbook, we consider Latino writers to be those who trace their ancestry to any Spanish-speaking country in the Americas and have also lived in the United States for a significant portion of their lives, which means, of course, that Latino writers and **Latino narratives** do not share a single origin and often have as many differences as similarities.

The historical roots of Latino writing begin with Spanish explorers arriving in what would become the American Southwest to explore and colonize. Written in 1542, Alvar Nunez Cabeza de Vaca's *Adventures in the Unknown Interior of America* details Cabeza de Vaca's eight years (1528–1536) exploring the Southwest and, like much of the Latino literature that would follow, dealt with leaving one culture (Spain) for another (Mexico and the United States).

Just as Cabeza de Vaca wrote about the lands he was exploring, many Latino writers focus on place, whether missing ancestral homelands, being glad to have escaped those homelands, or dealing with issues resulting from settling into a new homeland.

One of the most prominent contemporary Latino writers is poet Juan Felipe Herrera. Herrera, the son of migrant farmers, often draws upon his and his family's experience working the San Joaquín and Salinas Valleys of California. Yet Herrera was also deeply influenced by the movements for social change that sprang to life in the 1960s, especially the Chicano Movement. Perhaps Herrara's third major influence is his continuing work in his community, as an artist and activist. Herrera has published more than twenty-one books, and in 2015 Herrera was named the Poet Laureate of the United States. In the anthology, you can find his poem "Water Water Water Wind Water," which speaks to the suffering and courage of those who faced Hurricane Katrina.

Other postcolonial narratives

In no way, of course, are Native American, African American, and Latino narratives the only postcolonial narratives. There are countless more. Choose a spot on the world map and chances are that an indigenous community in that region has a postcolonial narrative to share. For instance, in his poem "Remembering Minidoka," W. Todd Kaneko highlights one of many plights faced by Asian Americans, the World War II internment camps.

Other branches, other forests

As you have probably noticed, many of the categories we've discussed overlap each other like tree branches in a forest. Many science and nature narratives also intersect with agrarian narratives. Adventure narratives often deal intimately with wilderness and preservation issues. And many postcolonial narratives are also environmental justice, agrarian, or wilderness and preservation narratives. Further, many of the authors we've discussed often wrote across these categories. Truly, the history of nature and environmental writing is messy and complex and, we think, richer for it.

We also researched and debated about including other categories that focused on urban areas: overpopulation, globalization, war, and other issues that deserve to be talked about in the nature and environmental writing tradition. But we encourage you to read widely and continue to debate, reorganize, and redefine the historical threads of nature and environmental writing. (Also refer to Chapter 12: A Trail Guide, which organizes many of these historical forms of nature and environmental writing into more contemporary modes.)

One cross-category issue that must be brought up is that of gender. Especially during the early years of nature writing, women had little opportunity to share their experiences of landscape; thus, the history we have highlighted is full of male writers, and only after World War II do we present our first iconic female writer: Rachel Carson. This is not to say that there haven't been powerful female nature writers before Carson. There have been many, including Mary Austin, Fabiola Cabeza de Vaca, Florence Merriam Bailey, Harriet Beecher Stowe, Susan Fenimore Cooper, Margaret Fuller, and Mabel Osgood Wright. But in that male dominated society, female (and postcolonial) nature writers were not afforded the same opportunity to write and publish and be read. Luckily, that situation is quickly changing. And we are pleased to include many of today's most powerful female nature and environmental writers in our anthology.

Along with gender, we should also consider queer nature and environmental writing. The early 1990s saw some of the first queer environmental writing after the devastating outbreak of AIDS in gay and heterosexual communities alike. Environmental writers Jan Zita Grover and Derek Jarman, among others, shared the losses of loved ones to AIDS through the examinations of deserted landscapes and depleting plants and animals; both of these authors paralleled defeats experienced by both the human species and the environment.

The pairing of environmental activism and queer writing has developed even further in the past five years. Sustainability activists have researched the varying consumption and waste production levels of heterosexual and homosexual relationships, and LGBT writer Alex Johnson questions the presence of queerness in nature through the lens of environmental studies, focusing on how society accepts queer as natural or unnatural. Similarly, Elizabeth Bradfield, with her poem "Creation Myth: Periosteum and Self," creates a bio-mythological argument for her own existence as a gay woman and for lesbianism as natural.

Though the history and the ideas we have presented here are far from neat and tidy, the beauty of nature and environmental writing lies in that very organic complexity. This is not a genre that is simple to catalogue or easy to define. But with this chapter we hope we have helped you join the wider conversation surrounding the history of nature writing and environmental writing. And, we hope, as you begin to pen your own essays, stories, and poems that this chapter will allow you to more fully know who you are and where you come from as a nature and environmental writer.

Exercises

The following exercises will help you practice the techniques learned in this chapter.

A. Write a paragraph about why and how you see nature and environmental writing as similar and as different. Then write about where you expect your writing to fall within these sub-genres.

B. In the spaces below, list three key points for each of **nature writing's** subgenres.

   Pastoral Ramble:

   -
   -
   -

   Adventure Narratives:

   -
   -
   -

C. In the spaces below, list three key points for each of **environmental writing's** subgenres.

   Wilderness and Preservation Narratives:

   -
   -
   -

   Agrarian Narratives:

   -
   -
   -

Science and Nature Narratives:

-
-
-

Environmental Justice Narratives:

-
-
-

Climate Change Narratives:

-
-
-

Native American Narratives:

-
-
-

African American Narratives:

-
-
-

Latino Narratives:

-
-
-

D. Research online five of the writers below and choose a subgenre of nature and environmental writing to include them in. Since many of these writers can fit into multiple categories, offer reasons why you put these writers into specific subgenres.

E. What subcategories of **nature and environmental writing** interest you the most? Why? How can you widen your lens to include other genres? Which genres are you least interested in? Why?

F. What subcategories of **nature and environmental writing** have we missed? Why should we have added them? List some of the key features of these subcategories.

Writers:	Subgenres:	Reasons:
Edward Abbey		
Sherman Alexie		
Mary Austin		
Hector St. John de Crèvecoeur		
Winona LaDuke		
Annie Dillard		
Ralph Waldo Emerson		
Louise Erdrich		
Linda Hogan		
Bill McKibben		
Reverend Samson Occum		
Leslie Marmon Silko		
Sandra Steingraber		
Alice Walker		
James Welch		
Terry Tempest Williams		

Prompts

The following prompts will help you practice the techniques learned in this chapter.

A. After thinking about the keys to **nature writing**, write a piece from any one of the traditions of **nature writing**.

B. After thinking about the keys to **environmental writing**, write a piece from any one of the traditions of **environmental writing**.

C. Think about a genre we may not have touched upon (or combine a few). Now create your own new subgenre of **nature and environmental writing**.

Part II

The Craft of Nature and Environmental Writing

Part II

The Craft of Nature and Environmental Writing

3

Seeing the World, Believing the World

Relevant readings

Creative Nonfiction: Chelsea Biondolillo, "Geology: An Investigation"; Erik Reece, "Hell Yeah We Want Windmills"; David Treuer, "Trapline."

Fiction: Alyson Hagy, "Border."

Poetry: Gabrielle Calvocoressi, "I Was Popular in Certain Circles"; Major Jackson, "Migrations"; Michael McGriff, "Coos Bay"; Derek Sheffield, "As a Species Flies from Extinction, Consider the River."

Free write

Get up and take a five-minute walk. Whether indoors or out, there's no destination needed here. Just walk. And as you walk, consider the sensory data streaming in: what is the quality of light? Do you smell window cleaner or river? How does the pine duff or carpet feel beneath your feet? Do you hear birds, a jackhammer, the hush of the wind? Is the taste of this morning's coffee still on your tongue, or have you slipped a grass stem into your mouth?

Once you've finished your walk, write a list poem (for an example, see Michael McGriff's "Coos Bay") or a paragraph built entirely of the sensory details you observed on your walk. Make sure to use all five senses (sight, smell, touch, sound, and taste), and don't interpret or make sense of these physical sensations—just get them on the page!

Now share your poems/paragraphs with a partner. Talk about the poems/paragraphs themselves, as well as the process of writing the pieces. What in your piece feels most alive? Did writing from your five senses come naturally? Which of the five senses did you struggle with the most? Did you find yourself wanting to interpret or explain what something meant to you? If you do add interpretation or explanation, how would that affect the poem/paragraph?

Vignette

When I was nine my father died, leaving my mother with three hundred acres of eastern Montana farmland and three young children. My mother made a way for my sibling and I—she went back to teaching school and leased the farm to pay the bills, she loved and challenged and fought for us, and she told us again and again that despite poverty and bad schools and worse luck we would make it (and by most counts, we did)—yet there were some things she couldn't do.

For instance, I remember a winter evening when I was maybe thirteen or fourteen:

There is the chug and hollow gurgle of the faucet as I twist it off, then the alkaline stink of hard water rising from the sink. My mother hands me one of my father's old white-and-yellow plastic razors—out of minginess and grief she has kept so many of his things—then his ceramic mug of shaving soap and horsehair shaving brush.

In my palm the razor is so light, so insubstantial I almost can't believe it. And the brush is stiff at the ends, the crinkle and chalky rime of old suds when I press my thumb against the horsehair. I look from the razor, to the brush, to

*the mirror before me. I stare at my own face, at the patchy stubble on my ado-
lescent neck and cheeks and chin. I have no idea what to do. My mother doesn't
know either. She says, I'll call your grandfather.*

*When my grandfather shows up, he grins and rubs the salt-and-pepper stub-
ble on his own chin, then asks my mother to leave us be. My grandfather lives
just a quarter mile down the gravel road and is a cowboy, a real cowboy—one of
the last to ride the open range of this high prairie country we call home, a badlands known as the Big Dry. My grandfather takes off his work shirt, the skin of
his upper arms and shoulders shockingly white next to the rough, sun-dark skin
of his hands and face. He shows me now, as he prepares to shave before me, how
to work the brush to get a lather going in the mug, how to spread the suds across
your cheeks and chin and in great swaths down your neck, how to pull the razor
lightly, surely across your skin, that slipping, scritching sound.*

*Now, it's my turn. My grandfather's rough hand is on my hand, and there
is the sharpness of soap at the corners of my lips as together we lather my face.
He hands me the razor, and I set it near my ear, just like he did. I breathe and
despite the floral scent of the soap am reassured by the straw and sage smell
of my good grandfather. I can do it. With my grandfather by my side I can do
anything: I pull and pull and rinse and soon am done, only one small driblet
of blood along my jawline.*

*For all those years, my grandfather was the truest father I knew. He died when
I was twenty-two, and though I still grieve for him, still wish I could talk to him,
ask nearly every day his advice and blessing—I hang on to what I have. And
I mean it when I say I have so much: his hard and tender touch, the sing-song and
gentle insistence of his voice, the smell of dust and hay as we drove out together
to feed the sheep, the warm, sour taste of the biscuits he made every morning at
the camphouse, a wide grin breaking over his craggy face. I knew him and still
intimately know him through my senses; truly, I can conjure him in a moment.*

*And the sheer power and force of those sensual memories often staggers me,
brings tears to my eyes.*

—Joe

Seeing the world, believing the world

We never know so deeply as when we know with our **five senses: sight,
smell, touch, sound, and taste.** We might discuss hydrology all day, but
to plunge one's head beneath the cold, bracing waters of a horsetail falls

in the high Bitterroot Mountains of Idaho is a knowing of a deeper order altogether. We might study soil composition and precipitation patterns in a classroom, but the knowledge gained in shoveling, spreading compost, poking seeds into earth, in measuring rain and weeding, and finally biting into that first tart-sweet tomato—that is an earthly wisdom, a knowledge compounded by our sensual experience.

This tactile information is the kind of wisdom we are after as nature and environmental writers—the wisdom of sensual experience, of truly seeing (and smelling, touching, hearing, and tasting) and thereby knowing and reckoning with and caring for the physical world. But how do we show a reader what we, as writers, see? When Joe goes to write about his grandfather, about the landscape that bore and held them both—the Big Dry of eastern Montana—how does he get across to a reader that bone-deep wisdom, how does he offer all that rises up for him as he calls to mind his grandfather, the distances and sage hills of his home place?

The answer is image. In writing, an **image** is any bit of language that appeals to one or more of the five senses. By appealing to the reader's physical senses, an image allows the reader to imagine (note that even linguistically you can't get to *imagine* without *image*) their way into the essay, story, or poem, and to place themselves in that landscape and with those characters—to feel the sun, the wind, the dust beating against their skin. While writers have long known about the power of image, recent scientific research shows that image-filled writing lights up the very areas in a reader's brain that would light up if the reader were actually physically participating in the activity they were reading about. That is what makes image the building block of nature and environmental writing.

So, when it comes to nature and environmental writing, seeing (as well as touching, tasting, hearing, and smelling) is believing. For instance, consider these lines from Chelsea Biondolillo's essay "Geology: An Investigation":

> That whole first year in the desert, a newlywed (digging down through the strata, now, the layers like colored silt and sand), I missed the sea—it was like an acrid taste in the back of my throat, that longing for rhythm. *It's not you, it's me,* I told myself. To him: *I don't even know who I have been here, I'm sorry.* What is the sound the wind makes when it blows through the arms of a saguaro? Which smell stings the nose more, salt or sage? My nightmares regularly featured drowning by sand; I woke coughing.

Notice how Biondolillo's images—the tastes and sounds and stinging smells—allow us into her particular experience; despite the fact that many of us probably haven't been a new wife in a foreign geography, we know now how it feels: we, too, feel the grit of that sand in the back of our throats. The key to creating powerful images is to make them specific and significant. By **specific**, we mean images that stand for only one exact thing; you must give us details to see not just any cactus but a saguaro cactus, as Biondolillo does above. And by **significant**, we mean details that relate the piece you are writing to bigger, more consequential ideas. Biondolillo's essay investigates the way geology and landscape make (and sometimes break) us, and the images above, and throughout, often reference geology in both scientific and personal ways.

The opposite of an image is an **abstraction**, or a piece of language used to distance and categorize; for the most part, abstractions appeal to our rational selves. While abstractions (such as *love*, *freedom*, and *sadness*) can be useful when we're making sense of experience or proceeding with a logical argument, even in those instances abstractions ought to be used sparingly, as abstractions often leave a reader feeling unmoved and cold. For instance, what would have happened if instead of the image-filled paragraph above, which is indeed making a kind of argument, Biondolillo had relied solely on abstractions? Does this paragraph help us feel and truly know her experience?

> After we married, we moved across the country, and I wasn't sure if I liked the new region we were living in. It was so different. I was depressed at times, and my husband wasn't sure why. I began to have nightmares.

Note the abstractions: *region*, *different*, *depressed*, *nightmares*. These are words that sum up or categorize a particular experience. Thus, this paragraph may indeed *tell us* what happened, but it doesn't *show us*. It doesn't let us enter into Biondolillo's experience (and, therefore, to experience it ourselves). And, thus, it isn't nearly as effective at physically and emotionally moving a reader.

Kinds of images

Though we commonly associate the word *image* with sight, it's important for writers to keep in mind that images should appeal to all five senses. In fact, one of the dictionary definitions of *image* is "a mental representation," which directly ties to all five senses.

Smell is the sense most strongly associated with memory and thus can place us powerfully in a certain time or space. Though it can feel like a stretch of the imagination to appeal to taste in an essay, story, or poem, remember that smell and taste are connected; we might taste, as well as smell, the dry stink of weeds behind the barn. Further, as writers our medium is language, the musicality of syllables, words, and syntax. Use the sounds of language to build images that appeal to a reader's sense of sound. Finally, when readers admire a book, they often say they were "moved" or "touched," and that physical connection begins with images that appeal to touch, that allow readers to feel and know the rough, warm bricks or the hard insistence of falling water.

Along with using images appealing to all five senses, it's important to consider whether the images you are using are literal or figurative. **Literal images** are exactly what they are. For instance, here's the closing of Derek Sheffield's poem "As a Species Flies from Extinction, Consider the River":

> The syllabics of scree, too,
>   Clatter before a buck's long skid
>   And purling swim, and the river
>   He rises from and shakes
> From his antlers, the river
> Of sunlit droplets
>   Pelts the rocky dust
> Around his tracks.

While the language here is lush and rhythmic, most of the images themselves—"clatter," "a buck's long skid," "the river," "his antlers," "the rocky dust," "his tracks"—are literal. They are simply—and exquisitely—exactly what they are.

In contrast, some images are built using comparisons, either as metaphors or simile; these are **figurative images**. Consider these lines from Major Jackson's "Migration": "I shivered by a flagpole, knowing betrayal / was coming my way. Just the same, I believed like a guitar string / believes in distance." Here, the speaker compares his own shivering fear to the trembling of a guitar string. The speaker is not actually a guitar string, of course, and guitar strings don't actually believe in distance. Yet the figurative image clarifies and quickens our understanding. We've seen the way a guitar string vibrates along its length; we understand something of the speaker's fear and his feeling of being stuck via this figurative image.

Why choose literal over figurative or figurative over literal? Literal images have the advantage of clarity and specificity and are often employed in moments of action or confusion, where a reader might get lost or where figurative images, which are often dramatic in and of themselves, might overdo the drama and push the scene or moment into melodrama or sentimentality. We can see this illustrated in Gabrielle Calvocoressi's "I Was Popular in Certain Circles." When talking about a graveyard and the bodies decomposing beneath the soil, Calvocoressi chooses the literal telling, which amplifies both the deadpan humor and the sense of pure abandonment felt by the speaker: "I was hugely popular with the gravestones. / Also with the meat liquefying / beneath."

Conversely, figurative images often suggest action or drama even in moments of stillness and so can heighten scenes that on the surface seem quite ordinary. Further, by allowing us to compare two things, figurative images clarify very particular or strange experiences, experiences the reader isn't likely to have had or even know about. Later in "I Was Popular in Certain Circles," Calvocoressi chooses the figurative when she writes, "[The vultures] loved me so deeply / they'd visit in pairs. One to feed me. / One to cover my eyes with its velvety wings. / Which were heavy as theater curtains." Notice her use of the figurative in the last line: the simile allows us to feel what the wings of a vulture, something most of us have never felt, might well feel like, as well as indicating what they might mean: the closing down of sight, of the vision and imagination offered by a theater.

Along with figurative and literal images, we also have **general images**, which are unadorned images that might conjure very different pictures in different readers' minds. For instance, we might write "cabin" in a story, and the reader calls to mind a stock image of a cabin. And, many times, a general image is all we need; it might not matter if the reader pictures a battered shanty or a trim, prefabricated cabin. Yet there are times when we need our images to do more work. When we offer an image rich in detail and depth, an image which doesn't let the reader make assumptions, we call that a **particular image**. Consider the way David Treuer, in his essay "Trapline," extends and deepens our understanding of his trapping cabin, as well as the project of trapping and those who undertake it, via particular images:

> Old cupboards were shoved in the corner between two nonworking gas ranges. A table, three beds (one a stowaway bed like you find in hotels), clothes, a wood stove, a box of beaver traps, and three or four bags of garbage completed the cabin. Under one of the beds I found a stack of *Playboy* and

Penthouse magazines; a centerfold was tacked to the door. The whole place was overrun by mice. That night we cut firewood, got the cabin thawed out—it was minus ten degrees Fahrenheit—cooked some pork chops, and chopped a hole in the lake to get water. Then I learned the first thing about trapping: how to play cribbage.

Image is tone, action, symbol, and, well, everything

Let's pretend you're planning to write about a train trip along the Coast Range of Oregon and Washington in the Pacific Northwest of the United States. From steep, wet banks of fern and cedar sliding quickly by to slow, stately, far-off views of snow-capped, volcanic mountains, there will be a surfeit of images to choose from to make this trip come alive for the reader. So, of course, the question is: which images will you choose to use on the page? The answer: it depends. Because here's the thing about image: it doesn't just allow a reader to feel and feel for; image also contributes, in a big way, to tone, action, transition, symbol, and argument—to everything, really.

For instance, let's say you choose to write about Mt. Rainier, that great volcanic peak. You watch for ten, twenty minutes, and despite having traveled through towns and valleys, the mountain is still there, still massive and sure. But then, behind a closer range of hills, you lose sight of it; an hour later you look up from your book and the light on Rainier's snowy shoulders flares and glisters. Whether you know it or not, you are building an atmosphere here, a tone, a sense of both assurance and surprise, the mountain as both companion and phantom. So, ask yourself: what tonal qualities do the images you've chosen suggest? Do they offer a sense of mystery, a sense of suspense, a sense of worry, a sense of terror, a sense of love? Are those the qualities you are after? Do these qualities perhaps shift how you might think about your own piece?

Similarly, if you choose to focus on those ferns—how wet and brilliantly green they are, and how they slip by right outside the window, as if you might reach out and grab them—you might be building toward having one of your characters reach out and grab something else that's brilliantly alive in their lives. The image of the ferns suggests and foreshadows this action. So, as you write, interrogate your images: what actions do they suggest? What action in the essay, story, or poem might this or that image allow?

As you have probably noticed, images work to build tone and action through metaphorical suggestion. It's not that images aren't themselves—those ferns are ferns—it's just that they suggest something beyond themselves as well. Along with tone and action, images can metaphorically suggest particular ideas; when an image does this, we call it a **symbol**. In our examples above, perhaps the ferns clinging to the vertical bank symbolize the tenacity of the natural world. Perhaps the sun on the mountainside becomes a symbol of hope for the future. Of course, metaphor and symbol don't just happen. As you revise and rework, pay attention to your images. Which ones seem to hold or encapsulate the ideas you're after? Find those images and deepen them, revisit them later in the piece, help them do that symbolic work.

Images can work as transitions as well. Consider our train example: maybe when we want to indicate the passage of time, the movement up the coast, we could come back to the rhythmic movement of the train, the clacking, the slow shifting with the tracks, and the feeling of being rocked. Later, we might use images of the lengthening angle of the sunlight or the first dim streetlights of Seattle to alert the reader to a transition. In her short story "Border," Alyson Hagy employs a number of images as transitions: for instance, between the first and second scene of the story, Hagy has the main character, who has just stolen a collie pup, touch his hat:

> He closed the crate, put a quick touch on the bill of his Broncos hat to be sure it was set square on his head, and he was gone.
>
> He waited until he was clear of the Meeker Fairgrounds to take off his jacket and turn it inside out so that the brown cloth fabric showed instead of the blue. He also removed his hat and tucked it into his back pocket, though his bare head felt show-offy to him.

Finally, images forward arguments as well. Sometimes, we might make an implicit argument by, for instance, writing a poem that simply describes the savagery of mountaintop removal mining. Here, the images of the hollowed, shellacked region might suggest a moral and political argument: mountaintop removal is unbeautiful and wrong, and we should do something about it. And this is what Erik Reece does in his essay "Hell Yeah We Want Windmills:"

> A hundred feet below, the entire Brushy Fork watershed has been buried beneath one of the largest slurry impoundment ponds in the world. The black ooze called slurry, or sludge, is the toxic byproduct left over when coal

is cleaned for market. The Brushy Fork pond contains 6 billion gallons of slurry, six times the amount that recently broke through a dam in Tennessee. The nine-hundred-foot wall that holds all of this slurry back is the highest dam in North America.

Seeing is believing

The importance of image simply can't be overstated. As nature and environmental writers, we need images to bring readers physically, and therefore emotionally, into our pieces. And we use images during the writing process to discover and build tone and action, to develop symbols and ideas, to transition and make more effective arguments.

In nature and environmental writing, we use images for just about everything.

Exercises

The following exercises will help you practice the techniques learned in this chapter.

A. Find a poem you love in the anthology, one you just can't read enough times. Now, translate that poem into **abstractions**. Take out all the powerful **images** and replace them with flat abstractions. Share your translation (while keeping the original poem a secret) with a partner. Have your partner translate it back into image. What do you notice about your translation and the retranslation and the original poem?

B. Do an image inventory on any piece in the anthology. How many **images** total have you found in an essay, story, or poem? How many for each sense? How many **general images**? **Particular images**? **Literal**? **Figurative**?

C. Using that same piece, try to find examples of **images** that work to build **tone** and **action**. Are there any images that become **symbols** in the piece? Any that work as **transitions**? Any you would categorize as **evidence**?

D. Choose one of your own poems. Examine how often you use **abstractions** and **images**. Examine how often you use **general images** and **particular images**.

E. Practice deepening images. Take the following general images and make them particular and specific images: animal, car, human, tree.

Prompts

The following prompts will help you practice the techniques learned in this chapter.

A. Write a five-senses essay. That is, write an essay that explores the same subject (a place, a loved one, etc.) using each of the five senses. You can create sections here, each devoted to a particular sense, or mix and match the senses throughout.
B. Go on an **abstraction** hunt. Take a piece that you've previously drafted and revise it by replacing every abstraction you find—*love, freedom, joy*, and so on.—with an image.
C. Begin a story by describing, in particular detail, a physical thing your main character loves. What do those **images** suggest? Where do they take you next?
D. Write a poem that argues something and uses only **images** as evidence. You can have the argumentative structure in the title or in the poem itself, but make sure you stay away from too much logic or anything like that. Let the images do the work.

4

Living Maps

Relevant readings

Creative Nonfiction: Leslie Ryan, "The Other Side of Fire."

Fiction: Bonnie Nadzam, "Cartography."

Poetry: Nikki Finney, "Resurrection of the Errand Girl"; Michael McGriff, "Coos Bay"; Julia Shipley, "Migration of Bailing Twine."

Free write

Close your eyes and think about a place you know intimately. Put yourself there. Begin to move through your place. What do you see? What smells linger in the air? What is that brushing against your skin? Now, open your eyes, pick up your pen and write for ten minutes describing your place in such a way as to bring those sights, sounds, feels, tastes, and smells—the whole sensory experience of your place—to life.

Vignette

My family is a family raised along Pennsylvania's Delaware River. Most summer days, you can find my mom floating in a tube, the current spinning her in gentle circles. As she spins, she gets to see all of her home ground. To the north she looks to where the Delaware River bends east at Doe Hollow. Above the river knobs Jack's Hill with cornfields growing along the crest.

As the current spins, my mom's gaze falls westward across the river to a green four-room cabin. Mom summered in that cabin for her first forty-seven years, and my brother, sister, and I spent summers there until my mom bought and remodeled her current home, which is less than a quarter mile away. And our green cabin, our family's heart-home, leans, almost sinks, into a hillside that sloughs off loose slate—once the economic bedrock of this region, the Slate Belt.

Mom spins on the placid water of the Delaware. Her feet and eyes face south. Mom dips her hands into the river and sprinkles water across her black bathing suit. She gazes downriver and sees the green painted steel of the Belvidere Bridge, connecting Pennsylvania to New Jersey. This bridge, twice destroyed by floods, allows her to travel from her home in Riverton, Pennsylvania, to the nearest town, Belvidere, New Jersey.

Further south churns Foul Rift. Mom and I have canoed through this class III rapids many times and during each turbulent float we pass Pennsylvania Power and Light. At PP&L, mammoth cylindrical smoke stacks, seventy-five feet across and one hundred fifty feet high, cough white steam and smoke into our skies. Cables stretch from one steel tower to another delivering electricity to local houses, like ours. At PP&L, outbuildings and construction vehicles metastasize across the landscape.

A gentle breeze spins Mom east. The sun washes down upon her blonde hair. She gazes at Oliver's Beach where we have spent hundreds of days swimming.

She sees the beach where she grew up, learned to water ski, fell in love, and taught her three children to swim.

Beyond Oliver's grows a bank of ragweed, poison ivy, stinging nettles, syca-mores, oaks, and milkweed. If it were autumn and the leaves all fallen, Mom could see BASF two hundred yards away. BASF produces automotive paints, and for much of the 1990s was ranked the third worst corporate criminal by Multinational Monitor, for all the antitrust and environmental violations it accrued. But these buildings also have a deeper history. During World War II, these buildings were known as the Hercules Powder Company, and here explosives—bombs and mines—were produced to help the war effort. A chain-link fence separates Oliver's, our childhood beach, from BASF.

Three miles northeast of BASF sits Hoffman La Roche, which we call Roach, an international pharmaceutical corporation that was the most heavily fined corporation, in terms of antitrust and environmental fines, during the 1990s. Roach racked up $500 million in penalties, double BASF's fines. Roach can-not be seen from the Delaware. But Mom knows it is there. She is a member of Riverkeepers, an environmental organization designed to protect American waterways. Mom sends river water samples to labs that test for toxins. She testified before Pennsylvania's senate about local pollutants. Mom longs to pro-tect her river. She wants to save it for her granddaughter, Danielle. My mom believes that the river might not live without her help. And she knows, deep in her bones, that she cannot live without her Delaware.

—Sean

Place

Every story we tell occurs someplace. And where it occurs informs and transforms the story in myriad ways. Place—maybe as much as our par-ents, grandparents, and all our ancestors combined—shapes who we are and how we live, how we move (or do not move) between worlds. As nov-elist and poet Luis Alberto Urrea tells us, "Place isn't a setting. Place is an elder in the family. We are not describing landscapes: we are writing biographies."

As nature and environmental writers, we know this. We have felt the liv-ing power of place in our own lives and observed it in the lives of others, much as Sean has seen it in his mother's life, as he wrote above. As environ-mental writers, we understand that in the making of story there is a question as powerful as *What happened?* That question is, *Where did it happen?*

Yet we know, too, the answer to that question is not easy. We can close our eyes (as the free-write above asks us to do) and conjure in seconds a beloved or ruined place, a place that strikes us deeply in our hearts. For Sean, one of those places is the Delaware River, the still waters gently rubbing up against steep riverbanks. But no matter what your place, once it has risen behind your eyelids, the quest then becomes how to write that place, to honor that place on the page.

Backdrop versus character

Picture an elementary school theater production: the purple curtain drawn back to reveal a small, dimly lit stage. Our young thespians are trying their hand at *Hamlet*, yet they've only had so much time to prepare; the budget is entirely from proceeds of a single bake sale, and so the stage design consists of a single white bedsheet hung in the back, with mountains and fields and a small village painted on it. It doesn't look that bad, really, but as the play proceeds—ghosts and schemes and soliloquies— everyone forgets about the mountains, the field, and the lantern lights of the little village. This is what we call the **bedsheet theory** of writing place. Paint it as prettily as you can, hang it up, and forget about it. And, too, often, this is exactly how too many writers think about place, as merely where the action happens. They tell the reader: *this essay takes place in a city; this short story happens on a ranch; this poem occurs in a shopping center.*

The problem with treating place as a backdrop, of course, is that place is never just a backdrop in our lives or in the lives of our characters. Rather, place is one of the thresholds for how we enter the world. We work with and against it, and are deeply affected by the places where we work, live, travel, play, and adventure. We interact with our landscapes, with the weather that transforms those landscapes, and with the cultures that grow from those landscapes.

The places that shape our characters must be, just like our characters, dynamic and complex. And to create dynamic, complex places on the page— to get place right—we need to move beyond the bedsheet. As nature and environmental writers, we need to be aware of how place changes through time; how it affects a person or a community or a group of communities; and how it exerts physical, emotional, and psychological forces on us, on our stories, and on our readers.

An essay, story, or poem doesn't just take place along the Delaware River; rather, it is alive with the back roads heavy with shade, the forlorn towns sold to fading industries, the people who live, or once lived, upon this fertile and abused land, and the river that creates it all. What this means is that the places of our stories are also characters in our stories. We call this **place-character**.

Creating place-character

How do we turn landscapes into place-characters that shape narratives and move readers? First, we must remember that a place, any place—with its native and invading flora and fauna, its geological and human histories, its potential futures and deep histories—is complicated and dynamic. Places evolve and wear down; they exist geologically, historically, and culturally. Consider the mountains of eastern Pennsylvania. Once these were some of the tallest mountains on the planet. But now they are old and weary and soft-shouldered. Once they were cloaked in old growth forests and inhabited by the Lenni-Lenape. Then the forests were clear-cut and the Lenape killed or driven off by European Americans. Now, those hills are again covered in forests, though the trees are younger and smaller. And an entirely new culture lives along the river.

One way we get students to complicate their view of place is to ask our classes to reflect on a place we all know. Since Sean teaches at Norwich University in the rural town of Northfield, Vermont, he begins his lesson there. He breaks the class into different groups. One group is for students who grew up in towns similar to the one-stoplight town of Northfield. Another is for students from even smaller, more rural towns. And a final group is for students who come from larger towns, especially bigger cities.

Sean asks each of these groups to think about how their own town is similar or dissimilar from Northfield. The small-town folks might talk about how nice it is that we have a pizza place and a sandwich shop, as many of their hometowns offer no restaurants at all. They mention the traffic on our main road, Route 12, how so many cars whiz by that it's hard to find silence.

Big city students talk about there being no movie theaters, barely any restaurants—only a pizza place, sandwich shop, and an Irish pub—and just two bars—the Knotty Shamrock and a dive, the Rustic, on the outskirts of town. They talk about how there's nowhere to see music or dance at clubs. And they struggle to understand how often you can drive right through town without waiting at every intersection for red to turn green.

Once Sean's students finish comparing their homes to Northfield, he asks them to consider what an eighty-year-old resident would think about how Northfield has changed over her lifetime. Students mention the rise of houses that now ring the small downtown. They talk about the mostly faded railroad that was once the lifeblood of town. They bring up paved roads and the rise of car culture. They speak about the expansion of buildings on campus, which has increased the number of students in town, which leads to more shoppers, more parties, and more hustle and bustle, such as it is, within the community.

Sean finishes by asking students to travel back in time to when our eighty-year-old neighbor was not yet born. To a time before any of her relatives had moved to Vermont, before railways were laid and wagon roads cut through the forests. He asks his students to consider how the Abenaki nation viewed this land and how they would see it having changed over the last two or three hundred years. What would they think of these spindly second-growth trees, those manufactured homes rising up the hill, the river polluted by agriculture? The hospitals? The schools? The dollar stores?

By the end of the lesson, the students see that the landscape surrounding them is manifold and mysterious, a possessor of stories, secrets, and numerous wonders. Further, students see that people can disagree about a place, that a single perspective cannot encompass the totality of any given landscape. Can a town be both large and small? Can it have both a plethora and a dearth of restaurants? Absolutely. The key is that we as writers work to know our own vision of a place, while always keeping in mind those other views.

Our places and landscapes—the communities where we live and work and play—are complex and ever changing, and as we honor that complexity on the page, our readers will more deeply feel our places and our stories. We want to be placed. We want to know where we are, so that we might live well and love who we are. As the essayist Scott Russell Sanders explains: "For each home ground we need new maps, living maps, stories and poems, photographs and paintings, essays and songs. We need to know where we are, so that we may dwell in our place with a full heart."

The sociology and psychology of place

Place affects us. Always. But place exerts different forces on different people. Consider two teenagers growing up in the outpost ranching community of

Melstone, Montana (which is where Joe grew up). One of them may long to graduate from high school and run as far away as possible from the bunchgrass hills and gravel roads and tumbledown homesteaders' shacks. He wants education and culture and diversity; he dreams of San Francisco or New York City. The other dreams of taking over the family cattle ranch. She longs to stay near family, to never leave the tangled sandrocks and pines of the Bull Mountains, and to find herself, always, under that wide, cloud-shot sky.

Often, attempting to capture the primary way place affects us, as sensory experience and vista, we write **imitated landscape**, which is when we describe what we see in the real world: we color our mountains green and our deserts shades of dun and brown; we hear the wind turn and whistle through the canyons. When we are writing imitated landscape, we give exact details so we can see and physically feel the landscape itself. We see imitated landscape in Leslie Ryan's essay "The Other Side of Fire," where she describes the Great Basin Desert:

> It's sage and basalt country: gray and brown and fairly nondescript at first. The hunting-and-gathering Paiutes who lived there in early times were disparagingly labeled "Diggers," because they ate roots and grubs rather than something charismatic like buffalo.
>
> In the rain, the Great Basin ground—where it's not rock—turns to slimy mud. If you have to walk when it's wet, the mud will grow on your boot soles in bricklike platforms, your quads will cramp with the weight of them, and your ankles will roll above the boot blocks like they're broken. When the sun sucks the moisture out of the mud again, the ground will crack into miles of dusty pieces.

Here, for the most part, Ryan gives us physical images of the landscape, so that we might know it in an intimate and sensory way: *basalt, gray, brown, roots, grubs, slimy mud, dusty pieces.*

Yet, as we mentioned in the opening of this section, landscapes are more than just physical descriptions. We as writers need to understand that place affects people (and characters) differently. Is our character drawn to her home landscape? Does she long to keep learning from it, to fall ever more deeply in love with it? Or does our character wish to remake her place? To travel and bring fresh perspectives and ideas and institutions back home? This is what we call **the psychology of place**: how place affects a single person.

These psychological spaces evoke deep emotional reactions, which leads to **interior landscape**. When writing interior landscape, we use metaphor, simile, anaphora, assonance, alliteration, and many other poetic techniques to help us feel, in a psychological and emotional sense, the affect the landscape has on us or on a particular character. Rather than writing about our tactile senses, we write about how a place feels to us in our interior, in our hearts. For instance, consider how Michael McGriff writes his Pacific Northwest landscape of Coos Bay:

> Then there is the rain that never sleeps,
>
>   it's fallen for seventeen years
>   to reach the field below our house
>   where my father and the machinist neighbor
>
>   dying of cancer huddle around
>   an oil drum and smoke cigarettes,
>   a few weeks of newspapers and wood scrap
>
>   hiss into ash, trapped angels
>   under the wire grate they warm their hands over.

McGriff uses literal images ("the field below our house," the "oil drum," "newspapers and wood scrap") to write imitated landscape, but he also uses surreal and metaphorical images ("the rain that never sleeps," that has "fallen for seventeen years," newspaper and wood scraps turning into "trapped angels") to write his own interior landscape, to help us understand how he feels about his home ground.

Beyond the psychological aspects of place, we must also think about the effect place has on a community. This is **the sociology of place**: how place affects a group of people, a community, or a culture. Within the sociology of place, individuals might be outliers, but as a whole, the group tends to act and think in similar ways. Consider Nikky Finney's "Resurrection of the Errand Girl," which takes as its primary narrative a woman's journey, at her parent's request, to get fish for Friday dinner. "Friday. Fish," Finney writes. "Tradition as old as the South itself." Yet this woman is aware of herself as an African-American in a white-owned establishment, as a returnee to her Southern hometown, and as someone no longer bound to *all* the traditions of that area. In short, she is aware of a whole host of cultural and sociological pressures and forces acting upon her and everyone else at the fish market:

She extends her full bowl of ice-blue mullet and flounder to the fishmonger-of-her-youth's son. A man her same age but of a different persuasion. He echoes the words he heard as a boy from his father, Head off and split? Her answer is offered even quicker than the fish. No. Not this time. This time she wants the fish left whole, just as it was pulled from the sea. Everything born to it still in place. Not a girl any longer, she is capable of her own knife-work now. She understands sharpness & duty. She knows what a blade can reveal & destroy. She has come to use life's points and edges to uncover life's treasures. She would rather be the one deciding what she keeps and what she throws away.

Place and story

Much of what we've written above can be summed up thus: **place allows story**. Though landscape is not always the driving force in a piece, it always, *always*, textures and shifts the narrative.

Before the action even gets going, it's important to note how **place affects tone**. What we reveal about a particular place will evoke particular emotions in a reader and thereby influence the tone or mood of an entire piece. Is the piece you're trying to write a quiet, meditative piece about a hike in the woods? Is it about how you ran into wilderness as a way to escape a recent tragedy? Did you head into the city in search of love? Once you have thought about your story as a whole, consider what kinds of emotions you want the reader to encounter along the way. Then, find analogues for those emotions in the landscape. Perhaps the empty house is a symbol of freedom and coming to terms with the past. Show the reader, then, the light on the broken glass, the long view toward the mountains, the wind rivering through the open rooms and across you.

Beyond tone, **place reveals character**; what a narrator or character notices in the landscape illuminates who they are, offers metaphorical possibilities, and even changes what might happen next in the narrative. We can see an example of how place affects character by reading Julia Shipley's "Migration of Bailing Twine," which looks at bailing twine and how it affects the life of a farmer. Merely by examining this seemingly inconsequential product, which is used on most farms, we learn about the lives of farmers. We see the vehicles they often drive (trucks), the equipment they use in their line of work (salt blocks, balers, and baling twine), the way they dress (suspenders), and the products they grow (bales of hay, chickens, cow's milk).

Place also enhances dramatic moments in scene, especially in dialogue, by providing a pause within and/or counterpoint to the direction of the human interaction. So we can slow down action to increase tension by highlighting the landscape.

However, many times **place becomes the reason for the narrative itself**, as characters struggle with, fight for, or flee to a given place. We see this in Leslie Ryan's essay, "The Other Side of Fire." Ryan, after being abandoned as a child by her parents and raped by the men around her, realizes she must escape the city to start a new life. Ryan writes about how her body, even more than her mind, told her to "Get outside," to head to the desert, to find a place where she could test herself with the desert and find a way to become whole again:

> Fortunately, my body still had some sense. She spoke up from under the bed, where I'd kept her locked up like a caged animal and had fed her only scraps for years. She said, "Get outside."
> I went west, to the desert, to a state where I knew no one, and took a job for which I had little preparations other than backpacking. I've heard the Great Basin described by one survival student as "Nature's Worst."

Ryan's essay works because she juxtaposes the poverty of surviving as an abandoned child in the city against the stark, empty—but for Ryan, redeeming–desert. It's an essay that builds narrative by contrasting two locations against each other.

As you write, find the elements that matter, those bits of place that drive your story, and render them on the page. Show those images and scenes. Meditate on them. Have your characters bump into them. All this brings the reader deeper into what is at stake on the page.

Can there be too much place?

Good question. We've all read essays or stories that seem to accumulate place details but not really go anywhere. It's a tough situation: too little setting, and the reader gets lost in the metaphysical ether; too much setting, and the reader gets lost in the forest. When determining how much landscape or setting is necessary, consider the advice of the poet Richard Hugo. He wrote that readers always need a place to physically stand. Even in a metaphorical poem—perhaps especially in a metaphorical poem—readers want to feel grounded. One of the quickest ways to do this is to use specific place names.

Are we in El Dorado, Iowa? Or on Cowls Street? Maybe Hogback Ridge? A specific place name affords readers a wealth of associations and allows them to gain a foothold in the story, essay, or poem.

Further, once we know where we are, we need to know what matters most about that place. As we've mentioned, place is complex and manifold, and there's simply no way to get the whole of a place onto the page. So, as writers who deeply know our places, we interrogate our stories for what parts of the place are necessary. Does the reader need to know how dry it gets in the summer? How traffic backs up across the bridge each evening? Though it is not always easy, and may take multiple revisions, the key is to consider how the landscape affects the story and what details the reader will need to understand the landscape.

Ways of seeing and knowing place

Place affects us deeply; that much is clear. And our relationship with a particular place changes how we see that place. If we know a place intimately, we view that place in one way. If we are new to a place, we see it in an entirely different way.

An **insider**, an old-timer, sees a landscape as home, whether they view their home as beautiful or grotesque. The insider knows the histories and traditions, the people, and, with intimacy, the lay of the land. And insiders recognize their own; they can speak with, trust, and rely on those who know the place like they do. Consider Sean's hometown of Bangor, Pennsylvania: an insider might know where the best abandoned slate quarries are for swimming, or where the best corn can be purchased, or where the high school wrestling star died in a car accident, even though all physical traces of the wreck have been erased for two decades.

But insiders often become blind to, and then get blindsided by, changes in a landscape. Because the songbirds have always been there, the insider fails to notice fewer and fewer gathering on the fencepost each spring—and then one spring the insider wanders outside to listen and hears no birdsong and feels betrayed, as if some part of his home has been stolen.

An **outsider**, however, sees a place with new eyes, and with every glance may notice the wonder or the degradation. Though the outsider sees everything—from the mansions to the shacks, from the mountains to the mine scars—she does so without context. The outsider does not yet possess an understanding of the natural and human history of the area and may struggle to situate her observations in the larger story of place. For instance, in Bonnie Nadzam's story "Cartography," the "you" in the story, the map-maker, wonders at the intricacies of this city she has been given to chart:

> There are beautiful things in this city. Mountains, rivers, little painted houses, stone avenues lined with bakeries and bookshops. There are distant fires eating trees, houses, entire towns. There are earthquakes and floods. There are crooks behind some of the most elegant doors and honest men dying alone in the shadows. Sometimes you smell smoke in the wind, and some days in the city the air makes you sick. Occasionally you hear the sound of a flare gun fired by someone else lost in this same metropolis, and the beauty of its illuminated rain burning across the sky makes you want to throw your own city map in the trash; you have no such signal, and wonder how, with your dim little sketches, you will be found. Isn't that, somehow, the point of your art?

As environmental writers, it is vital that we understand where we stand in relation to the place in question. We must consider whether we are insiders or outsiders, or even a bit of both.

Going deeper

We often write about the places that are familiar to us. And this is as it should be: we know these worlds. We can quickly summon the details necessary to bring that place to life in literature. Yet, as we write about the worlds we know, we must consider as well what details we have forgotten or what things we know so well that we assume they might not be worth bringing up. Further, there are things we don't know about even with the places we love best. The things we don't know—the things we have never considered— these tell us as much about a place as the things we see every day. What was the predominant flora a hundred years ago? When was the river almost dammed? What's the local soil quality? Who lived here before we lived here? What were their stories and myths?

It's often the details that once used to be paramount but have now sunk deep into our collective memories that can shock us into seeing place in a new way. These details, the ones we've yet to learn, can teach us much about a landscape and the people who live, or have lived, within that landscape. To help us look at even the most familiar place in a new way, we study contemporary and historical photographs, examine maps, and ask around for old stories. And we try not to be satisfied with what's easy to find. We strive to be collectors of subtle details, orphan stories, and revisionist histories. Then, when we turn to an essay, story, or poem, we bring all this—as well as our own initiating visions—back to the page.

And one way we know place is by studying **visual and written artifacts**. Spend time with images—photographs, paintings, maps, electronic maps—to see what historical, contemporary, social, and political stories the landscape shares. Read descriptions from other writers and naturalists. Listen to how others talk about the landscape and its history. See what details you can unearth that might help you see landscapes in deeper ways.

Yet, we must also trust our own experiences of a place. Revisit a known landscape in your many **memories** of it. Remember and retell the stories of when you visited that tiny coastal town on vacation, or what it was like to grow up there along the dunes, or how it felt the day you moved from the city to a cottage near the sea. Our memories, and the memories of our friends, family, and neighbors—what we remember, what we don't remember—can teach us much about place.

Finally, beyond research and beyond memory, nothing beats **physically visiting** a place. If your place surrounds you, go for an evening walk and observe the way the night falls with a writer's eye. If the place you're writing about is a thousand miles away, a trip, despite the time and cost, is often worth it. By journeying to a place, and through a place, you make the place the purpose—you make your experience of the place paramount. You go there not to recreate or relax or visit old friends, but to consider the exact darkness of the alleyways or the precise slope of the rocky ridge.

Exercises

The following exercises will help you practice the techniques learned in this chapter.

A. Create a list about a place you are writing about (you can use the questions below to spur your thinking). Write down as many things you can think of about your place. Once you have a list, examine which parts of your list might most affect your characters and the communities your characters belong to. If you don't know an answer, do some research. Once you are finished, circle or highlight those details that feel most important and consider how you can work those details into your piece.

Questions to come to understand your place in a deeper, more complex way:

- What is its population?
- What are its major economic sectors?
- What does the landscape look like?
- What *did* it look like?
- What sort of people live on this landscape?
- What are its striking physical features?
- What is its climate?
- How does the climate affect the people?
- What is its geology?
- What is the area's evolution (geologically, politically, economically)?
- What are its major sounds and smells?
- What are the neighboring areas like?
- What are the politics of the area?
- How do the politics affect the people of the area?
- Do you know the median income for your area?
- Do you know the racial makeup?
- What previous cultures or peoples lived on this land?

B. Choose two places. One where you feel you innately belong, a place that feels like home. And one that feels completely foreign to you, a place where you do not belong. Write a paragraph for each of these places. Compare and contrast your descriptions of being an insider and an outsider. What do they tell you about yourself? Do these two paragraphs belong in the same essay? Keep writing.

C. Create a list of as many words and phrases as possible that you associate with your place. Remember the lessons from Chapter 3. Stay away from vague words such as pretty or rich or even cold. Be specific. Be exact. Be unique.

D. Create a map for a story you are planning to write. On this map, put all the physical features of your world. Also consider which of those physical features most affects the characters within your story. Begin the story by describing one of those landscape features.

Prompts

The following exercises will help you practice the techniques learned in this chapter.

A. Look at a story, essay, or poem you've written to see how you've used place. Examine if you've made place complex. Search to see if you've researched about your place. Check to see if you understand how place affects the individuals and the groups of people living in your setting. Once you do that, revise your piece by focusing on improving setting. Work to make setting a vital character within your piece.

B. Using the words you come up with in Exercise C, create three paragraphs on a place you know well.

C. Write a story about a place you know well, but make your main character an outsider, and make sure your main character's thoughts and reactions to the place are a big part of the story!

D. Take a piece you've written and see what happens when you add more and more details concerning place. See how the piece evolves and changes as you describe the imitated landscape and the interior landscape. Next, take the same piece and strip away as much of the place as you can. Compare these two drafts to see how increasing or reducing place affects your characters and narrative.

5

The Writer in Place

Relevant readings

Creative Nonfiction: John Daniel, "Pack Rat."

Fiction: Alyson Hagy, "Border"; Joe Wilkins, "Like Bread the Light."

Poetry: Gabrielle Calvocoressi, "I Was Popular in Certain Circles"; Natasha Trethewey, "Theories of Time and Space."

Free write

Think about a time you visited, after an extended time away, the house you grew up in. What was it like to move through those old spaces? What surprised you? What excited or saddened you? Write for five minutes.

Now, look back over what you've written and consider the fact that though your house might well have changed in certain ways, many of the biggest changes undoubtedly occurred within you. After all that time away, you saw your house in a different way because you, in effect, were a new person.

Pick a few images or particular items that stood out to you on that return home and meditate on them—why, exactly, did you see them differently? What was it that had changed within you?

Vignette

I'd only been in London a few days, yet I already felt like a different person. Not better. Not worse. Different. I'd wake in the morning and pull on a tee shirt, jeans, and sneakers—my usual attire—and think, Wait a minute. This isn't what people in London wear. *So I'd change into a fitted button-up, dark slacks, and boots. Then eat a piece of toast and jam, throw my book bag over my shoulder, and hike up rainy, gray Headstone Road to catch the Metropolitan line into central London.*

Waiting at the station I'd wonder if I should buy coffee or tea. Smoke a cigarette or read the paper. Though most mornings on the tube I pretended to be engrossed in my battered copy of Eliot's selected poems, I was really studying the other passengers, looking for clues. So this is how you roll your body into a turn. This is how you make a call on your mobile. This is how you ready yourself to rush the doors at King's Cross.

Walking to classes, I did the same—I studied the other students, the loiterers, the busy professors. In the afternoons I haunted bookstores and side streets, ran my hands along the stones and bricks, tried to parse the intricate layerings of scent: stagnant water, tar, exhaust, fried fish, a woman's fading perfume.

And most evenings, before catching the tube back to Harrow-on-the-Hill, I sat in some dark corner of a pub in London and ordered a pint. Then I opened my journal. The writing was hard. I had never really lived in a city before, let alone a foreign country, and didn't know how to narrate my days. I wrote metaphorical poems about dislocation and loneliness, and they were terrible. I tried to parse in argumentative prose what I had learned in the previous hours and realized I hadn't learned much. Finally, months into my London sojourn, I resorted to simply making lists: the names of streets, what songs the buskers were playing, the precise mud-and-iron color of the Thames that day.

And that seemed to work. I felt more comfortable in my journaling, began to look forward to it immensely, in fact. I began to feel more comfortable in the city, too. Though I was surely beginning to acclimate in other ways, I think the writing—the listing—mattered. It allowed me to quit pretending, to articulate for myself, and so be, who I was: a watcher, an observer, a stranger marveling at a strange and ancient land.

—Joe

The writer in place

As we discussed in Chapter 4, Living Maps, there are places where we know, through the wisdom of years and many trials, who we are. There are other places, though, which may be absolutely new to us, yet we recognize instinctively as somehow home. And there are, too, as Joe explains above about his time studying in London, places in which we feel dislocated, places that, for good or ill or a bit of both, take us away from our usual selves.

How do we, as nature and environmental writers, understand our interactions with these places and then speak about them, or about the environmental issues that matter so much to us? In London, Joe's solution was to fall back on a form—the list—that allowed him to marry his lived experience and his literary experience: that allowed him to be on the page the observer he was in his actual life. It's a good solution. We are different selves in different places and in relation to different environmental issues; to create powerful nature and environmental literature, we need to speak accurately, honestly, and from the self (or selves) that we are in that particular place or with regard to that particular idea.

In this chapter we'll look at the relationship between the writer and the narrator and how that relationship impacts the ways we might see and speak about place. We'll look as well at issues of perspective, where we might speak from within our stories, and the ways we might speak, or the categories of narration. And, finally, we'll look at how all of these concerns allow us to build complex, engaging voices on the page.

Persona

To begin thinking about how people interact with place, we need to think about who we are—as a **writer**, a **narrator**, or a **character**—within an environmental story.

During a given day we offer many different versions of ourselves to the world. We are this way with family, that way with colleagues or friends, and another way completely with our significant others. "Do I contradict myself?" the poet Walt Whitman asks, though he doesn't wait for an answer: "Very well then I contradict myself, / (I am large, I contain multitudes.)" As environmental writers, we must come to know and embrace the multitudes we contain, for it is these multitudes that allow us to see fully, think complexly, and speak passionately about the many places and issues that matter most to us.

We call each of these gradations of self a **persona**. Envision a sliding scale, with the left pole representing what we believe to be our most essential self right now and the right pole representing a self that is everything we are not. If we choose to write in a voice nearest to that left pole, we are writing in a persona that is very close to who we are right now, that shares our loves, our concerns, our memories, and our cultural and sociological histories. In this case, the relationship between **the writer (the person actually writing the story)** and **the narrator (the presence on the page telling the story)** is one of intimacy; in essence, the writer *is* the narrator. The writer/narrator may also become **a character (one of the actors within the story)**. For instance, in John Daniel's essay "Pack Rat," we hear Daniel, as the writer/narrator speaking to us, but we also see him as a character on the page.

At other times, though, we may want to slide over to the right pole and speak as another human being altogether—or even as a bear, or a flower, or a hunk of black volcanic rock on the wave-raked beach. In this instance, there is necessarily a great deal of distance between the writer and the narrator, and it is the narrator, rather than the writer/narrator, who may become a character in the story.

However, it's important to remember that though a speaker may be like us or unlike us, that speaker's voice is still ours to wield and to shape. As an example, when writing a personal essay about a recent trip to a farmers' market with his two young children, where his children were entranced by a country band playing John Prine tunes, Joe chose a persona close to the left pole; the experience felt so wrapped up in his actual life that he felt he had to speak as the father, environmentalist, and music lover that he is.

But what if we nudge ourselves to the right? For Joe, we might soon bump into the self he was those months in London—the watcher, the observer, the list-maker. Scoot a little further over, and maybe we run into the young, sad, unhinged speaker of a set of poems—all titled "Lost Boys of the Upper Great Plains"—that Joe is currently at work on, a set of poems he simply couldn't have written if he had spoken as the (mostly) well-adjusted adult he is now.

Now, just for kicks, let's jump all the way to the right side of the scale: here, we run into the speaker of Joe's short story, "Like Bread the Light," which is included in the anthology. The speaker, a woman addressing a lost love, is very unlike Joe, yet she is a narrator/character that allows Joe to investigate issues of gender, class, inheritance, abandonment, and love of place, issues Joe is interested in but can't speak about in the way this narrator can. Yet, despite these differences, the speaker is a persona and connected along that sliding scale somehow back to Joe (even if only because Joe was able to invent her). And this is important to remember: no matter the persona we choose, it is never wholly us, and it is never wholly not us.

What matters is why we choose a particular persona. How does choosing a persona almost exactly like our real-world self affect the piece? How does choosing a very different persona affect the piece? The persona you choose will affect tone, theme, and how your narrator and characters might interact with the world.

Point of view

Along with persona, **point of view**—the vantage we choose to tell our story from—is one of the primary ways we shape our environmental stories. There are three major points of view writers can choose from: first person, second person, and third person.

If we employ **first person point of view**, we see the story through the narrator's eyes. Stories that occur in first person use the pronouns *I, me, we,* and *us* and allow the reader to listen and follow along with the narrator as they tell us of their adventures and thoughts. (Note that the **narrator** isn't necessarily the **writer** here; the narrator might be the writer, as in John Daniel's essay "Pack Rat," but the narrator might also be someone very different than the writer, as in Joe's "Like Bread the Light.") Because of this immediate access to the events of the story, and the narrator's thoughts and feelings concerning the events of the story, first person is the most intimate point of view. When we read Daniel's "Pack Rat," we feel Daniel's frustration as he deals with a particularly wily pack rat: "Three notched sticks fit together to suspend the trap door, and one of them was gone. The smartass had not only sprung the trap from outside, he had left it inoperable." And we feel by the end of the essay as though we have come to know Daniel, as if he is sitting right next to us, whispering his troubled, wondering story. However, this intimacy can sometimes have its drawback, as it holds the reader in one person's voice and viewpoint, which necessarily limits the scope of the story.

The most unusual point of view choice is **second person**. Second person point of view turns the camera around and points it at the reader. This change in camera perspective forces readers to imagine that they are the main character, that they are participating in the story. The writer accomplishes this through the use of the pronoun *you*. The *you*, in effect, transforms the reader into the main character. Often, especially in creative nonfiction and poetry, the second person point of view's *you* also acts as a stand-in for the writer/narrator (Natasha Trethewey's "Theories of Time and Space" is a striking example of this), which makes the second person point of view both intense and intimate, as, much like first person, we then become privy to the speaker's thoughts and feelings.

The danger of second person is that it can make the reader feel awkward: imagine reading a story that began, *You are a deer foraging for apples in the forests of Vermont's Northeast Kingdom.* Many readers might struggle to allow themselves to transform into a deer and might have no idea where the Northeast Kingdom is. Yet, when done well, second person point of view can be intense, as it yanks the reader into the story. We are asked to exactly empathize with our narrator, to feel exactly what they feel.

In first person and second person points of view, the relationship between the writer/narrator and the reader is necessarily one of intimacy; however, the **third person point of view** offers writers more flexibility in how we see our characters by distancing the writer/narrator from the reader. Here the writer/narrator simply points the camera at the characters and follows them around. This is done through the use of the pronouns *she, he,* and *they,* which allows the writer/narrator to manipulate the cinematic space—to zoom the camera in and out, as it were—between the reader and the characters.

If we choose third person, we have a whole range of options before us, from the zoomed-out, objective perspective of most newspaper reporting, which emphasizes the external, to zoomed-in stream-of-consciousness narration that emphasizes the internal. However, as writers, we enter a contract with our readers as we craft our stories, so while this distance can be manipulated, we need to do so in a way that is organic to the story at hand; in other words, we can't break our own rules or zoom in and out willy-nilly. For instance, consider how Alyson Hagy carefully narrates her story "Border" from somewhere just over her main character's shoulder; we are privy to his thoughts and we see what he sees, but we aren't too close. This is so until the last line, which is when Hagy chooses to zoom into the main character's mind as he is being arrested, and his thoughts then take over the narration: "He didn't understand. He would never understand, not with any carving of his heart he wouldn't. How could anybody not want the thing that would keep them from being sent backward one last time?"

As mentioned above, third person point of view offers a variety of options. These can be broken up into **omniscient**, **limited**, and **objective** points of view. In **third person omniscient** the reader can see into any character's thoughts and move across time and space at will; in effect, the omniscient point of view is the God's eye view. While this undoubtedly offers many narrative possibilities, it can, if done poorly, feel false and predetermined, as in our lived experience we never have access to another human being's mind or have future knowledge. **Third person limited** solves this problem by limiting the reader to the thoughts and feelings of one character at a time and disallowing future knowledge. Much contemporary fiction and poetry is rendered in third person limited, as it offers the reader a fuller, broader, more cinematic picture of the story at hand, while still allowing intimate access to a character's thoughts and feelings. **Third person objective** point of view disallows access to any characters' thoughts and feelings. While this distances the reader from the characters, it also forces the reader to interact with the characters, as we do with people in our own lives, trying to intuit and understand as best as we can.

Narration categories

No matter the persona or point of view we choose, though, it is important to remember that every environmental piece has a **narrator**, an eye through which images are revealed or events are recounted. For even if interpretation and personality on the part of the narrator are absent, and the eye of the piece becomes a kind of video camera simply recording what is before it, we understand that someone has pointed the camera in that particular direction, someone has chosen to zoom in or out, to pan or stay still, to show us this rather than that. No matter whether the narrator is or is not the writer, no matter whether the narrator becomes a character on the page, the narrator always controls what ends up on the page and how the reader is asked to interpret those images, events, and/or ideas.

And the video camera narrator mentioned above is, indeed, our first category of narrator, an **observing narrator.** In pieces that utilize an observing narrator, the narrator doesn't interact with the images on the page or interpret the action for the reader; rather, the narrator functions like a video camera, simply zooming, panning, and documenting what there is to see. Because of this lack of participation, the observing narrator often refrains from using the pronouns *I* and *me*.

There are two styles of observing narrators. The first is the **distant observer**. In this version, the narrator has no interaction with other humans, the landscape, or even with ideas. The distant observer offers nothing more than a visual retelling of an event. There is no introspection, reflection, speculation, or judgment. The distant observer merely explains what occurred, much like a sports announcer or political reporter talking about what is occurring in the scene before them. There is often landscape. There may well be action. There may even be other human characters. But the narrator does not take part in any of this.

The second type of observing narrator is the **reflecting observer**. With the reflecting observer we again have a narrator who is not physically present in the piece and so does not engage in action on the page, yet this narrator does offer opinions about and interpretations of what is unfolding on the page. Even though this narrator does not interact with the characters or the landscape, this narrator does interact with the reader by offering us not only image and action but reflection and interpretation as well.

Many environmental pieces, however, have narrators who take a hand in the unfolding action of the essay, story, or poem. We call these narrators **participating narrators**. Stories with participating narrators generally occur in first person point of view. In these stories, the *I* takes the reader on some journey, engages us with the physical world and, often, with other characters and reflects on these interactions as the journey proceeds.

Voice

Beyond not wearing the right clothes and getting lost in various tube stations more often than he'd like to admit during his time in London, Joe exhibited an even deeper marker of foreignness: his voice. Every time he spoke, he placed himself; or rather, he displaced himself; his American accent—more accurately, his blue-collar, Western American accent—forced him to reckon, whenever he opened his mouth, not just with his contemporary surroundings but with his previous cultural and geographic surroundings. Joe's voice marked him as different, and he had never been more aware, in many ways, of the qualities of his own voice—his measured, laconic rhythms, his *aint*'s and *got*'s and dropped *g*'s, his preference of single-syllable words. Yet, as the months in London piled up, he began to notice his speech changing, Anglicizing in slight ways, and he began as well to become more aware of the many different voices he encountered in a given day, the vast number of English's spoken by Londoners of various cultural, ethnic, geographic, and economic backgrounds.

As in life, so on the page: voice is marked by, and so marks, place. As environmental writers, we must be aware of and carefully wield **voice**, which we define as the quality of sound and particular sensibility exhibited by a particular narrator. Note that this definition is twofold: the sound of the voice matters, of course, but what the voice chooses to speak about—its concerns and sensibilities—also matters. Consider, for instance, the wry, gossipy sounds of the opening lines of Gabrielle Calvocoressi's "I Was Popular in Certain Circles":

> Among the river rats and the leaves.
> For example. I was huge among the lichen,
> and the waterfall couldn't get enough
> of me. And the gravestones?
> I was hugely popular with the gravestones.
> Also with the meat liquefying
> beneath. I'd say to the carrion birds,
> I'd say, "Are you an eagle? I can't see
> so well." That made them laugh until we
> were screaming. Eagle. Imagine.

This opening paragraph is humorous and fun and simply delightful to recite (it begs to be read aloud), yet Calvocoressi leavens our fun by speaking in such an unguarded, slanting way: the speaker is popular only with things that ignore her, and we begin to wonder what exactly she is confessing. Further, Calvocoressi's diction, syntax, and rhythms are precise and intriguing; this is someone who knows language. The voice Calvocoressi has built here delights in both self-deprecation and the constancy of the physical world, but it does not do so in thin, flippant ways; this is a textured, complex voice, a voice full of irony, angst, and wonder.

Further, our definition of voice argues that voice isn't some static quality that we find and never change; rather, we understand voice as a quality to build and grow. Like Joe's voice shifted across his time in London, our writerly voices should shift to meet the demands of a particular story, landscape, or environmental issue. Everything we've discussed thus far in this chapter—persona, point of view, and narration categories—contributes to voice, yet nothing is more important for building voice than the language you employ—your diction and your syntax, or the ways you grammatically combine words.

Whether you're writing a first person essay in which the speaking persona, the narrator, is someone very much like you, or a lyric poem from the perspective of a distant observer, the **diction**, or word choice, you employ has the potential to change everything. Consider, for instance, all the many words you might use to describe something breaking: break, rip, rend, rupture, shatter, crash, crack, snap, fracture, fragment, fail, fall to pieces, split, burst, and bust. If you choose to use the word bust—which has an informal, colloquial feel and suggests a breakage of less intensity or drama, perhaps even a comic breaking—you've both characterized the speaker and shifted the tone of the piece: all by choosing one little word!

Similarly, a paragraph built of one or two long, complex sentences will leave a reader breathless and wondering, whirled and wind-blown—and you might very well want your reader to feel that way, especially if the subject at hand is complex and awhirl for you as well. Yet, if you don't, if you're dealing with straightforward narrative, consider instead the steady body blows of short, subject-verb-object sentences, or even sentence fragments. This is your **syntax**, the many ways you string words together to build different types of sentences. And though a piece may have an overriding syntactical strategy—John Daniel's "Pack Rat," which reflects on Daniel's complicated experience with such a rat, is chock full of complex sentences, while Gabrielle Calvocoressi's poem "I Was Popular in Certain Circles" syntactically mimics the fragments and interjections of gossip—strong writing will employ, for emphasis and counterpoint, a variety of syntactical structures.

Though in time you may well develop a combination of qualities that could be called your voice, we urge you not to try to "find your voice" but to build your voice, to listen and read and peruse the dictionary, to work to make your voice as supple and powerful as possible.

Exercises

The following exercises will help you practice the techniques learned in this chapter.

A. Get out every piece you've written in the past months, and create your own sliding scale of **persona**. Which pieces go where on our continuum of persona? Why?

B. Which **point of view** do you write from most often? Why do you think that is? Pick one of your pieces and rewrite it in a different point of view. What changes? What has been gained or lost?

C. Looking through the anthology, find an example of each category of narration in each genre.

D. Take a grammatical inventory of a piece you've been working on. How would you characterize the **diction** you've been using? And look at your **syntax**. What's the average sentence length? Do these choices serve the piece? Why or why not?

Prompts

The following prompts will help you practice the techniques learned in this chapter.

A. Write a poem from the perspective of an inanimate object. Try to speak as eloquently as you can.

B. Think of a moment from your childhood that you remember well. Take ten minutes and write that moment using **first person point of view**. Read over what you've written. Now, rewrite that moment using **second person**. Do the same for **third person**. What do you notice?

C. Take a short poem you've previously written and rewrite it using each of the **categories of narration**. Which category comes easiest to you? Which do you struggle with? What else do you notice?

D. Pick a subject that you've written about before and know well—your childhood river, the months you spent cutting trail in the Cascades, the community garden you helped start in a vacant lot—and begin another personal essay about this subject, yet do so in a **voice** that feels unlike your own, push yourself to speak in a new way about a familiar subject. Get three or four paragraphs down and read what you've written. What do you notice? Give yourself some white space and write the next section.

6

People and Place

Relevant readings

Creative Nonfiction: Camille Dungy, "Tales from a Black Girl on Fire."

Fiction: Bonnie Jo Campbell, "Family Reunion"; Alyson Hagy, "Border"; Benjamin Percy, "The Caves of Oregon."

Poetry: Todd Davis, "What My Neighbor Tells Me Isn't Global Warming"; Chris Dombrowski, "Weekly Apocalyptic, or Poem Written on the Wall in an Ascending Space Capsule"; Laurie Kutchins, "River Keeper"; Aimee Nezhukumatathil, "Lewis and Clark Disagree."

Free write

Write a biography of an invented character. Begin with your character's childhood (maybe even discuss your character's parents' stories and further ancestry), and then proceed through young adulthood and adulthood. At all points, show us what your character looks like and talks like and how the character moves. What kind of music does your character admire? What are your character's life goals? How do all these things change and shift over time? Also, like any good biographer, interpret your character's likes, dislikes, choices, and journeys. Why did your character do this? Why that? Go deep!

Vignette

Years ago, I moved from Idaho to a city far from any mountains. I moved there for a career job, the kind of job you stick with until you retire many years in the future. Since I thought I might spend the rest of my life in this city, I decided to buy a house on the edge of downtown. While I shopped for houses, I began to write an essay about the process. Soon I realized, though, that what I had written was merely about me traveling across town looking at houses. My narrator (me) was flat. The essay was boring. I was doing nothing more than trying to find a house to buy.

I realized that I needed to get deeper into the mind of the narrator. If all the narrator was doing was looking at houses, which was exactly all I was doing, there had to be something more at stake or there was no essay. The thoughts of the narrator, I realized, must matter more than house hunting through a cityscape. In effect, the narrator's thoughts would become a kind of internal landscape, a place of geographic significance and drama. So I re-wrote the piece and layered in not only action, image, and dialogue, but also reflection, introspection, and speculation.

Soon, the piece became about so much more than just looking for a house. It became, as evidenced by the alignment of and tension between the narrator's thoughts and actions, a piece about houses and homes, about feeling placeless, about a lack of love, about trying to impress one's parents, about career jobs, and, by the end, about the terrible fear of a wasted life: a life lived in a house, a city, a region—that might never be home.

In the end, hopefully the reader gets to know me by getting to know not just which house I purchased, but what I thought, what I needed, what I desired, what deep conflict I was in as I made the decision to buy that first house. And only by creating that complex, human character on the page is the reader able to understand the struggle to find home. Only by speaking about human beings is the reader hopefully able to understand something profound about place.

—Sean

People and place

As we discussed in Chapter 4, Living Maps, landscapes are thick not just with biotic communities but also with layerings of human history and culture. Even landscapes that seem remote or unpopulated have deep human connections. Perhaps this rugged, isolated mountain was once a sacred place for native peoples. Maybe this lonesome overgrown valley was once home to a thriving agricultural community. If we endeavor to write well about place, if we want to write convincingly about environmental issues, then we must necessarily write—and do carefully and ably—about people.

In the previous chapter, we examined how we as writers might place ourselves and our characters in our environmental essays, stories, and poems. In this chapter we continue our exploration of the human element in nature and environmental writing; here, we focus on the many ways human beings might interact with place in an essay, story, or poem, as well as the methods of building honest, engaging characters that deepen the reader's experience of a place or an environmental issue.

Common stories of people and place

Each day we reckon with our environment in countless seen and unseen ways: we breathe in the dank, flowery scent of overripe blackberries wafting up from the creek; we flick on the light switch in our classrooms; we heft the bright, lumpy tomatoes at the farmers' market; come evening, we watch the setting sun go all golden and hazy across city smog. As environmental writers we strive to turn these interactions into affecting environmental stories, and one of the ways we might begin is to categorize our interactions, to understand the shape of our interactions and turn them into one of the common stories of people in place.

Perhaps the most common story we might tell of our interactions with place is that of the **solitary journey**. Think of Thoreau at Walden Pond, Muir in the Sierras, or Dillard at Tinker Creek—the story of one's journey into a particular environment is an ancient and powerful tale; it connects us to our origins as hunter/gatherers, and it speaks as well to our contemporary world of global travel, wilderness hunger, and environmental catastrophe.

Solitary journeys often detail a single character's struggle with a new or altered environment; that struggle might be an outward one, where physical dangers are paramount; or it might be an internal journey of sorts, where psychological or other similar dangers are reckoned with. No matter the kind of struggle, though, solitary journeys are often full of introspection and reflection, as the lonely character or writer/narrator spends hours and days wandering and musing. For an example of a solitary journey in the anthology, consider Laurie Kutchins's poem "River Keeper," which details both the external speaker's journey to a river, as well as the speaker's internal journey, her discovery that the physical world holds our stories and our sorrows.

Another common story is that of a **group journey within an environment**. Rather than focusing on a single perspective, group interaction stories highlight how multiple people engage with a particular place or environmental issue. Much like solitary journeys, physical and/or psychological dangers may be faced, yet these pieces also highlight group dynamics and how those dynamics are shaped by the immediate environment. Consider as an example Aimee Nezhukumatathil's bittersweet rendering of the Corps of Discovery's journey in "Lewis and Clark Disagree."

Rather than detailing a journey, many stories of people in place consider how a particular environment affects the **sociology of a group**. These stories are often rooted in a single landscape and emphasize how a place, or how some change to a place, creates and shapes a culture or a community. Camille Dungy, in her essay "Tales from a Black Girl on Fire," shows the sociology of a group when she writes near the beginning of her essay, "When I lived in Virginia, I associated open fires with historically informed terror." Later, she expands on this idea:

> There had been plenty of lynching parties in that part of the country. I couldn't help wondering, while wandering through the southern woods, if one such event might have happened on the ground where I stood. I had no interest in reliving history, through memory or experience. Campfires and bonfires represented a conflation between the natural world and the human. The wood in those piles was innocent and yet acted out a role. Because I was

afraid of what humans had done to other humans in those woods and on those tree-provided fires, I'd come to fear the forests and the trees.

Dungy sees the South as being a place lacquered in racism, as painted with the broad brush strokes of slavery. So even a century after slavery ended, Dungy still associates the bonfires of the South (and those who build the bonfires) with racism.

Historical stories highlight humans' interactions with the historical landscapes around them. Here, the history, natural or otherwise, of a landscape and the people living upon that landscape become the primary narrative. Historical stories—whether nonfiction, fiction, or poetry—require meticulous research and often teach us about parts of our world during or across particular periods of time. However, we don't simply get a dry recitation of facts; rather, well written historical stories are rendered vividly, dramatically, and often use historical happenings as springboards for reflection or meditation on our contemporary situation. Aimee Nezhukumatathil does just this, in her poem "Lewis and Clark Disagree," by making Lewis and Clark complicated human beings, rather than boring, flat heroes.

Another way humans interact with environments is in **imaginary worlds**. Though imaginary, these worlds are not simply created for diversion; rather, like historical stories, these fantastic stories often work as metaphors that allow us to reflect on and more clearly see our own world. Chris Dombrowski's poem "Weekly Apocalyptic, or Poem Written on the Wall in an Ascending Space Capsule" envisions a future in which human beings have to flee an ecologically devastated Earth, yet the poem isn't about that adventure at all; rather, it's about what we might do to enter another future; and what we stand to lose if we don't.

Creating character, seeing character

Even in nature and environmental writing, characters matter. How, then, do we bring characters to life in our stories, essays, and poems? Though there is simply no formula for creating full, real characters, we offer below six ways to begin to build vivid, complex characters on the page: image, dialogue, action, reflection, logic, and contradiction.

We are visual beings, and a person's physical image matters for how we understand them. The same goes for characters on the page; readers need an **image** of a character. As you paint your characters on the page, remember the lessons of Chapter 3: pick specific, significant details. This doesn't mean that every specific physical detail of every character need to be presented to the reader. Rather, you should consider what matters most: which physical images teach us the most about a particular character, which details matter to the unfolding story? You might tell us that a character has brown, wavy hair, small cheeks, a sharp chin, and eyes the color of granite. But it might be more important to see how, when she sits next to her lover, your character leans into him, how she reaches, always, for his hand.

Or consider how Benjamin Percy opens his story "The Caves of Oregon":

> This afternoon, a hot August afternoon, the refrigerator bleeds. Two red lines run down the length of it—and then a third, a fourth—oozing from the bottom lip of the freezer. This is what Kevin finds when he returns home from his job at the foundry and flips the light switch repeatedly without success, when he stands in the half-light of the kitchen and says, "Shit."
>
> Already he can smell it, the blood. And when he draws a steadying breath he imagines he can taste it, too—the mineral sourness of it. He is a big man—a man who spends most of his days with his hands taped, swinging a fifty-pound sledgehammer—and he must bend his body in half to observe the freezer closely. The seal of its underside has gone as red as a tendon. Little droplets are gathering there, swelling fatly, and then, too heavy, they break from their purchase and race for the floor.

Here, we see Kevin immediately, and we begin to see something else as well: because of the images we're presented—Kevin's strength and size—we begin to understand that he is now confronting and going to confront something that it is beyond physical strength to solve. Here, the character images allow the conflict and action to begin.

Beyond image, we begin to know people intimately by listening to them and speaking with them. The same goes on the page: how characters talk, and what they talk about, allow us access to their interior, to how they feel and think, and help us know them in that deeper way. We call character speech **dialogue** and will expand our discussion of dialogue in the next section.

Humans are perpetually in motion. We go for hikes. We dive into mountain lakes. We pull into a diner on the way back home and gnash cheeseburgers. Our **actions**, perhaps more than anything else, teach others who we are—what we value, what we love. So, when we put our characters in motion on the page, when we get them acting and reacting, we teach the reader who our characters truly are. Further, it's not just what a character does, but how they do it. Bonnie Jo Campbell's story "Family Reunion" opens with the main character, Marylou, having illegally shot another deer. Strong, Marylou's father, has helped her hang it:

> Marylou and Strong have just finished stringing up a six-point buck, Marylou's third kill of the season and two more than the legal limit. When Strong found her dragging the body toward the house an hour ago, he reminded her that being only fourteen didn't make her exempt from the law. Some day she would like to try hunting with the new Marlin rifle she won in the 4-H competition, but they live below Michigan's shotgun line, and, anyway, she knows a .22 bullet can travel half a mile, far enough that you might hit somebody you never even saw. Not that Marylou has ever missed what she was aiming for. She took this third buck in the woods at dawn, and the single shotgun blast echoed along the river and awakened Strong. He used to get out of bed early, but nowadays he usually stays up late and sleeps until there's barely enough time to shave and get to work.

This short passage of action tells us much about Marylou and Strong and their relationship. Marylou, a fourteen-year-old girl, possesses the courage and willfulness to defy both her father and state laws, and she doesn't miss. For his part, Strong only *reminds* Marylou about what she should do, while still helping her string up the buck; also, and somewhat more troubling, Strong has recently started staying up late, sleeping in, and rushing to work. It's already clear something has happened to both of them, something that might match Marylou's own violence, and that they are still dealing with the repercussions.

But humans are more than appearance and action and speech. We also live most of our lives in our minds, in our **thoughts**. And in literature we get something more, something we never get in real life—we get to see into other human beings' mind and overhear their thoughts and worries and dreams. It is through a character's thoughts that a reader learns what dialogue, action, and appearance can only hint at. For instance, in "Family Reunion," we later learn that something has indeed happened to Marylou at the hands of her Murray relatives, something Strong is still furious about. Strong thinks Marylou is trying to protect the Murrays by refusing to speak, but we begin to see, via Marylou's thoughts, that she isn't trying to protect anyone; rather, she is simply confused:

> No, she doesn't have anything to say, yet. And it was not just out of loyalty to the Murrays that she wouldn't open her mouth for a trial last year—her daddy is wrong there. At the time she didn't have things figured out, and even now she is still puzzling through what really happened.

Marylou's thoughts above are an example of **introspection**, which is when a character mulls over present events in the present moment. Yet, we know from walking around inside our own minds that we aren't always thinking about the present moment. We spend time in our minds in the past and in the future as well. A reader can see what a character thinks about the past through **reflection,** which is when a character examines past events, moments, images, or thoughts. Similarly, **speculation** involves characters thinking about what the future might hold. We gain deep insight into narrators and characters through introspection, reflection, and speculation; it's in a character's thoughts that we most fully understand and feel for that character and that character's situation.

Though it may sound like common sense, it bears discussing: characters must conform to **logic**. Now, this doesn't mean that a character will always behave logically; as we know from our own lives, we often act in accordance with emotion or impulse, rather than logic. Still, our actions, even those that seem illogical, often match our desires and needs at the time. The same goes for our characters: readers demand characters who are real, who act in response to a kind of logic, whether reasoned, emotional, or impulsive. Again, we can use "Family Reunion" as an example: though Strong repeatedly tells Marylou to stop killing deer, Marylou can't seem to help herself; day after day she haunts the river, and when a shot presents itself she takes it. We begin to understand that she is practicing, and when she finally takes her violent revenge, we're ready for it. We know she is more than capable.

We follow logic, perhaps fittingly, with **contradiction**, by which we mean purposefully allowing two or more of the methods of building characters (say, action and thought) to be in conflict or to contrast. Though counterintuitive, contradiction honors the complexity found within all human beings. We are more than the sum of our parts, as are our characters. Consider again Benjamin Percy's story "The Caves of Oregon": the main characters, Kevin and Becca—who feel so wonderfully, so heartbreakingly real—both contain contradictions. Kevin may be a big man who works at a foundry, a man whose "sledgehammer is like an extension of his body," but he is also the one who tries to keep the peace with his increasingly angry wife, the one who apologizes and pleads. Becca, the beautiful geologist and professor, however, is the furious, barely controlled one, the one who swears and gets things done, who feels, when Kevin tries to touch her, like "a rifle stock, something hard and unbending." These characters feel real. And much of the reason they do so is that Percy has allowed them to contradict themselves, allowed them to be confused and complex.

Dialogue

Let us return now to **dialogue**: how our characters speak. As we discussed in the previous chapter, accents, dialects, and patterns of syntax and diction are often one of the first things we notice when we travel to new locations. Speech marks place and place marks speech. And so, as nature and environmental writers, it is incumbent on us to strive to get dialogue right.

The first lesson to writing effective dialogue is to listen to the world around you. Sit at your grandmother's kitchen table and ask her to tell stories of her immigration from Austria. Nurse a cup of coffee at the local diner and eavesdrop the morning away, listening to the local loggers, hunters, or elementary school teachers. Use any excuse at hand to get sucked into a conversation, especially with people who are rooted to one place. Watch the way people move as they talk. Consider the beauties, powers, and confusions of a particular accent. And consider how place affects speech and dialogue. A Bostonian speaks one way. Someone from the mountains of Vermont speaks another way. Despite the fact that they live three highway hours from one another, these two characters speak languages that are, at times, nearly irreconcilable. We can see how Todd Davis listens to and builds dialogue in his poem, "What My Neighbor Tells Me Isn't Global Warming." Davis writes, "*Global warming's a bunch of / bullshit*, the same way you or I might say, *How's the / weather?* or, *Sure could use some rain.*" Davis pays attention to how others speak and compares the tone to the way "you or I might" speak.

Beyond accuracy, consistency is key. As with point of view, your revelation of character speech and dialogue forms a contract with the reader. We begin to know characters by the way they speak, the quality of their voices. Save for moments of extreme distress or change, those voices should be consistent.

Further, as with many things in writing and life, less is more. Dialogue is hard, and rather than throwing everything at the page, pick only what's vital. If dialogue isn't teaching the reader about character or place, then it ought to be forwarding the conflict. If it's not doing any of those things, get rid of it. Choose the words, the syntax, and the particular subjects or concerns that will teach us who your character is.

Remember, too, that dialogue is often full of pauses and moments of reflection, introspection, or speculation. We consider what someone has said. We start. We stop. We cough. We think. We reach for an apple. We think a bit more. Finally, we respond. Those same kinds of rhythms—the pauses and head scratches, the rhythms of real life—should find their way onto the page in your dialogue. And, finally, clarity is paramount. A reader must be able to follow the conversation. The easiest way to help a reader follow along is to use attribution tags—"he said" or "she asked"—and to begin a new paragraph as each character speaks.

A caution: reproducing an accent or a dialect on the page through phonetic misspellings can easily be read as demeaning and/or historically and culturally irresponsible. In the United States, for example, there's a long and disturbing history of white writers exaggerating and patronizing the speech patterns of African American characters through the use of phonetic misspellings. What's more, a particular way of speaking can often be just as powerfully rendered by paying close attention to syntax, diction, and rhythm. Now, this isn't to say you can't use phonetic misspellings, but if you do, you should understand the tricky terrain you're traversing, and, as mentioned above, work to make it matter and to get it right.

For an example of a piece that makes excellent use of dialogue from a number of characters, read Alyson Hagy's "Border."

Character as desires and needs

Aristotle, over two millennia ago, wrote, "Man is his desire." Every human being has a multitude of desires. It's why we have friends. It's why we fall in love. It's why we quit jobs and buy homes and go on adventures. Because we desire. The same goes for our characters. Their desires propel them into the world, get them in trouble, maybe redeem them in the end. What are your characters after? What do they wish for? How does a character's image, action, thought, or dialogue match the character's desires? Know your characters through their desires.

But there's something beneath our desires—our **needs**; we need sustenance and shelter and healthy bodies and healthy environments, we need love and respect, we need community and work. Though various hierarchies of needs exist, and though cultural concerns play a large part in determining which needs matter most, those needs exist for all of us, and for all our characters. What do your characters need that they don't have? What will they do to get it? Know your characters as well through their needs.

We are the sum of our desires and needs, and it only makes sense, then, that **conflict** arises within ourselves and within our communities whenever desires and needs oppose each other. This intersection of desires and needs is where friction occurs, where fires start in real life and on the page. And conflict is vital to any piece of nature and environmental writing. If there is nothing at stake, then there is no reason for the reader to read the story.

Do you ever tell people about how you woke up this morning just like every morning and then ate breakfast, got dressed, and drove in, just like normal, to work? No. Instead, we tell stories about accidentally sleeping in late, about wearing our shirt inside-out to work and getting yelled at by our boss, about wandering around lost on our first day at a new job and worrying about getting fired. Moments of conflict draw readers in and allow moments of possible transformation or redemption.

As we create characters and stories, we must consider how each character's desires and needs mesh with or push against other characters' desires and needs. This overall pushing against and pulling toward is what causes tension to build and emotional and intellectual investment on the reader's part to rise. Further, the most compelling stories occur on the far edges of our desires and our needs. Rather than sticking with stories of contentment or annoyance, we should push for stories of dream or dread.

Finally, as we grow and learn and travel through life, our desires and needs evolve and change. We need to be open to that same change in our characters' lives. This capacity for change, for stretching beyond one's self, is both hard to capture and essential. Nature and environmental stories, essays, and poems are journeys into the unknown, journeys of fraught discovery—for writers, characters, and readers. Be open to that discovery, to letting your story go not where you would force it to go, but where it needs to go.

Exercises

The following exercises will help you practice the techniques learned in this chapter.

A. Look at a few pieces you've written in class and try to categorize them. Are they imaginary communities, historical stories, or solitary journeys? What is it about your piece that makes it fit into your chosen category or categories? Does thinking about them as part of a particular category help you understand them or give you ideas for revision?

Once you categorize your pieces, examine again those pieces. Consider which ones you might gently push toward another category. What would have to change? Why? How might you change them? What would be gained or lost in the transition?

B. Look at any essay or story in our anthology. See if you can find **historical stories** within these pieces. Does the piece mention a car from a certain time period? Does the piece mention clothes that point to a specific era? Are there other ways that the reader can be placed in a specific time period by the details given?

C. Look at one of your stories, and then fill in the blanks below for each of your main characters to help learn their **desires** and **needs**.

[Character name] is a [adjective] [year old] [noun] who wants [   ]. S/he also needs [   ] because of [   ].

While you are filling in the blanks, also answer these questions:

What makes this character
Laugh
Scared
Mad
Embarrassed

How does this help understand your characters? Your story?

D. Write an entire essay, story, or poem that only uses dialogue. And have at least two characters that possess very different voices.

Prompts

The following prompts will help you practice the techniques learned in this chapter.

A. What happens if you take your story about an **imaginary world** and add a **group journey** to it? What happens if you take your **solitary journey** and add a layer of **history** to it? Pick a piece you've previously written and revise it by adding at least one layer.

B. Have everyone in your group tear a piece of paper in half. Now, think of a character. On the first strip, write that character's image. What does your character look like? On the next, write that character's desires. What does your character dream of? Now, have one person in your group collect the images, another collect the desires. Then, have each collector pass out a random image and a random desire to everyone in the group. Begin a story with that character and that desire.

C. Try to remember a time when an elder told you something important. Re-create that scene, especially the dialogue. Do you find yourself beginning an essay?

7

The River Above, the River Below

Relevant readings

Creative Nonfiction: John Daniel, "Pack Rat"; Sean Prentiss, "Spring Ends in Bangor, Pennsylvania."

Fiction: Bonnie Jo Campbell, "Family Reunion."

Poetry: Juan Felipe Herrera, "Water Water Water Wind Water"; Laurie Kutchins, "River Keeper"; Aimee Nezhukumatathil, "Lewis and Clark Disagree."

Free write

Think about a moment in your life when you fell in love with a spot. Maybe it was your first house, or the woods where you invented elaborate worlds of make-believe, or the river you swam in every summer, or the junkyard near your house that you'd explore. Jot down, quickly, descriptions of your place. Use your five senses. Next, conjure up memories from that place; list as many important memories as you can.

Now that you have some descriptions of your place and some memories to reflect on, examine them for any connections. What ideas, issues, or over-riding stories tie this place and these moments together?

Write about the things that link your moments together. Is this place where you first learned to love? Is it where you first learned about home? Is this spot where you first lost love or lost home? Is it where you learned to be an adult or learned to escape from danger? Once you have a common theme that links most of your moments together, write an essay, story, or poem about these events and the connection that links them together.

Vignette

When I was a junior in high school, the captain of my wrestling team died in a drunk-driving accident. The details in the next morning's newspaper told how Doug raced from a cop car that was trying to pull him over. Doug drifted into the wrong lane and caught the bumper of an oncoming car. Doug's car flipped down the highway and burst into flames.

When Doug died, it was the first time I had lost a friend, a mentor.

Years later, in graduate school, I decided to write about Doug's death. I went to my desk and wrote an essay that linked Doug, wrestling, and the act of writing together. When I showed it to my professor, she told me it didn't work. And she was right. So I revised, still trying to link Doug, wrestling, and writing. Again, my professor told me that I had packed too much into one piece. Her suggestion was that the reader didn't care about me being a writer. They cared about Doug and wrestling and our friendship. Again, she was right.

This same professor also shared a James Wright poem, "Autumn Begins in Martins Ferry, Ohio," which details a small town's violent love affair with high school football. The poem, which takes place in "the Shreve High football stadium," chronicles the hard lives of the people of Martins Ferry, all "[d]reaming of heroes." The final stanza of the poem begins with a line a single word long, a word more often used in argumentation than poetry, and this word works as a hinge from story to meaning:

> Therefore,
> Their sons grow suicidally beautiful
> At the beginning of October,
> And gallop terribly against each other's bodies.

Because of the hard lives of these people, Wright argues, high school football players simply must enact violence against one other as a kind of penance or purgative ritual.

After reading "Autumn Begins in Martins Ferry, Ohio," a new idea for my essay came into focus. This next draft would be about Doug, the poverty lacing our small town, and how the men in our town escape from poverty by galloping into sports and drinking.

With this new vision in mind, I created an essay about how Doug and I both used wrestling as an escape because we grew up in Bangor, Pennsylvania, a poor town on the edge of a band of slate quarries. Our town lacked industry and hope. Sports was one of the few things that offered high school students escape because if we won enough (and Doug and I did on the mat), we could earn a scholarship to college. In a town where less than 20% graduated from college, just escaping to some university was something. Yet because of our town's heavy weight of poverty, many of us were also taught to use alcohol as an escape. Doug earned a wrestling scholarship to Clarion University. But drinking and driving stole Doug's life before he ever graduated high school, before he ever left the back roads of Bangor.

This essay, one of the hardest I've ever written, only succeeded when I knew what it was about, when I understood how the story was leading me toward meaning, how small town poverty had us all dreaming of escape. Once I owned those ideas, all that remained was to paint a picture of Doug, to paint a picture of our town of slate and poverty, to paint Doug and my hopes of escaping from the clutches of hopelessness. I titled the essay, which is in our anthology, "Spring Ends in Bangor, Pennsylvania."

—Sean

Story matters

Humans from every culture across the globe have been drawn to story. Since prehistory, we have been painting stories onto the walls of caves, whispering stories across campfires, writing stories down on scrolls and in books, and now sharing our stories on blogs and in tweets. But why? Why tell stories?

For one, telling stories is the most effective way for humans to learn and to remember. We remember stories twenty times better than we do facts and statistics: a few people might remember the statistical indicators of poverty in Bangor, but many more will remember the story of Doug's and Sean's yearning for escape and Doug's tragic death. Stories stay with us longer than facts because stories allow us to relive moments—even if we were not a part of the original moments.

Also, when we listen to or read a story, the language processing parts of our brain get engaged, but so do other areas of the brain, especially the areas associated with physical activity. Our sensory cortex is engaged when we listen to stories about food or stories that use food metaphors. When we read a piece about chocolate, our brain moves us beyond the words. As we read, it is as if we actually taste the soft melt of chocolate on our tongues, and we savor the sweetness. When we read about a body moving or grabbing something, our motor cortex lights up, so it feels as if we are not just reading about Sean and Doug wrestling in "Spring Ends in Bangor, Pennsylvania," rather we are wrestling with them in the basement wrestling room. We feel the bodies slam into each other, our faces pressed into the mat.

Along with the thrill of living a moment or series of moments foreign to us through story, we tell stories to teach cause and effect; stories illustrate how this or that decision leads to this or that outcome. Stories also help us to know and find community. Through character or argument, we learn what being a friend, neighbor, or lover might mean. And stories teach about place and home; we see our homes from the perspectives of others. Story also allows us a glimpse of places foreign to us and asks us to see them as some-one's home, as places worth protecting. This leads to another crucial aspect of story: stories also help us see the world through others' eyes. As individu-als, we possess one worldview; the view we see through our own two eyes. But stories offer the opportunity to experience the world through a variety of perspectives. We see that characters on the page hope and love and hurt, and so we learn to empathize. When done correctly, like in John Daniel's "Pack Rat," we can even learn to empathize with someone or something, like the pack rat, far removed from us.

Finally, stories help us deal with the sad facts of being human: suffering and loss. We see this in Laurie Kutchins's poem, "River Keeper," an elegy for a young man who drowned: "How clear the river is / only moments after loss." We, all of us, lose everything, eventually, and by reading about other's losses, we begin to learn how to handle and process our own sufferings and losses.

The river above: Making story

Stories matter. To all of us. And in deep ways.

But how do we make story? How do we wield this power? Let's begin, as is often a good way to begin, by taking a walk to the river. We pass through the willows and dry grass and find ourselves on a small crescent of sand among the rocks. And the river flows before us, the blue-green skin of it ribboning and boiling and breaking as it widens into a riffle. This is the river above. This is your story.

The river above includes all the details that make up the situation of your story. It includes who your main characters are, what is occurring to those characters, what decisions those characters make, where the events take place, and when these events occur. One of the keys to having a clear **situation** (the who, what, where, and when) is to show readers the willows, the crackling grass, the great granite rocks, the exact quality of the canyon and the river. Often, as writers, we leave out key details because those details are already inside our own heads, and the world seems perfectly clear to us. Yet our readers aren't mind readers; they only ever know what we tell them on the page. Make sure to give readers all the necessary details; for a story to work, the picture we paint of the river above must be clear, whole, and evocative.

Yet, you can't give them everything. If you attempt to give readers every turning of the water, every bit of wind in the fir trees, all the mosquitoes buzzing, you'll end up putting them to sleep. Instead, consider the real-life situation versus narrative situation. The **real-life situation** is every sensory detail, every physical action, and every mental thought that occurs in a person's life. Reading real-life action would be overwhelming (not to mention boring).

The **narrative situation**, on the other hand, is the good stuff: that first blue glimpse of the river, the trout's fierce strike, the character's realization that she has, in many ways, become her mother. The narrative situation includes all the details, actions, and thoughts that significantly inform a particular story. As you build your river above, think about what details, actions, and thoughts are necessary for your readers to understand the narrative situation.

While your day at the river proceeds chronologically, your story of that day doesn't necessarily have to—this is **plot**, the artful arranging of the surface of your story, the way you reveal the river above. You might start with the lightning. You might even skip to another time and place entirely, perhaps the last time you went fly-fishing with your mother, before coming back to that trout strike.

While plot must conform to some kind of **causality**—that is, how one event, thought, or image causes another event, thought, or image (without causality readers will feel entirely adrift because they won't understand how things are linked)—plot is the primary way you frame, reveal, and develop the river above.

Despite the freedom we have in plotting our stories, there are some forms to follow. **Narrative form**, perhaps the most traditional form, breaks a story into five steps. **Exposition** is where major characters and other necessary information about the river above are introduced to the reader. Next is the **inciting incident**, an action or revelation that sets the river above crashing into motion. Then comes **rising action**, the buildup of suspense as actions and revelations lead to further actions and revelations, putting the outcome into question. **Climax** is the turning point, where a major decision is made or something occurs that releases the tension. As we head toward the closing of a narrative, we reach **falling action** and **resolution.** Falling action is the wrap-up of the story, while resolution is where we leave the story entirely. Bonnie Jo Campbell's story "Family Reunion" utilizes narrative form.

Logical form highlights an assertion or idea, something being argued or considered. Utilizing logical form doesn't mean you can't use the narrative form; it just means that the plot isn't driven by a single narrative but by the way we build, deepen, and link ideas as we move through the piece. So, here, plot isn't so much about telling a tale as it is about thinking your way through a tale or finding a way to connect disparate tales. In many ways, the river above—the detailed situation of your story—becomes somewhat less important in logical form; rather, logical form emphasizes the other crucial part of every story: the river below (which we'll get to, appropriately, below). Aimee Nezhukumatathil's poem "Lewis and Clark Disagree," which strings together a humorous, intimate list of reasons for the disagreement, employs logical form.

Lyrical form, as in Juan Felipe Herrera's poem "Water Water Water Wind Water," focuses on aesthetic effect rather than narrative or logic. Stories, essays, and poems written using lyrical form are more concerned with mood, feel, association, sound, and image. The poetic takes precedent. Often lyrical form rhymes or juxtaposes, much like a collage, placing strangely similar or strikingly distinct ideas or images next to each other to create rhythm or friction that forces the reader to see even a familiar river in a new way.

While these are distinct forms, a quick perusal through the anthology will illustrate that even if there is one primary form, authors often utilize elements of two or even three forms in a single piece. What's more, further study of narrative form reveals numerous subcategories and further distinctions. We encourage you to experiment and modify and find new ways to tell your nature and environmental stories.

The river below: Making story, making meaning

As you paint and texture the river above—all those details and events that clarify, reveal, and heighten the situation of your piece—you also need to be considering what's at work beneath all that.

Think about it: we see the surface of the river, but the surface is only possible as a result of the depths, the cold rocks and alcoves that bulge and shift the river's skin. What's underneath, what's normally hidden, is what most affects how a river behaves. The same goes for your story: while you may want to tell the story of a simple hike to the river to fish, if you're honest with yourself, you'll realize that you are carrying a whole host of previous moments and desires and losses and worries and wonders. All of these inform everything you see (and how you see it) and every decision you make (and why). All of this becomes, in a way, what your story is really about: it's not a simple hike to the river; it's a way, perhaps, to reconnect with your mother, who so loved to fly-fish, and, maybe, to accept motherhood into your own life. This is **the river below**: the real reason *why* you are telling the story, the reason it's worthwhile for others to listen to or read your story.

Again, the river above is all concrete details (again, the who, what, where, and when) that bring the story to life on the page, while the river below is the reason why the story matters in the first place. The river above, the river below: these are the two halves of any story, and to create a successful nature or environmental essay, story, or poem, we must develop both. If we don't keep the river above in mind as we write, we may forget to put in key details, and the story will fail to capture the reader's imagination or, worse, confuse the reader; if we don't focus on the river below, on why this story matters at all, the piece is likely to accumulate descriptions and list events with no major point being made, idea being illuminated, or emotion being evoked, and the reader, then, feels a bit cheated by the end.

In previous chapters we've talked extensively about how to build the river above: through image, place, voice, and character. But how do we develop the river below? Do we bend a story toward a particular theme or argument? Does meaning just arise as we write? Shouldn't we be more concerned with crafting evocative images and speaking with an arresting voice than beating the reader over the head with our own particular agenda?

Let's start with that last question: yes, as you draft, you ought to be more concerned with image and voice than with any particular agenda. Now, that's not to say you might not have an idea or two in mind, but, like Sean illustrated in his vignette above, often a story simply takes over and certain elements become more important than others. As writers, we need to trust the story. And this, we think, answers the second question as well: meaning does arise as we make story, especially if we are attentive to the techniques of powerful nature and environmental writing. We begin to notice, say, a particular pattern of imagery or a certain rawness of voice that leads us to know what a piece might be about. This means, of course, you might start writing with no thematic or argumentative idea in mind at all—and that's perfectly fine. Here, too, let the story teach you.

Yet, there are times we as writers need to take control of our stories. Beyond making meaning, story often makes more story with no end in sight. So, our job as nature and environmental writers, especially in revision, is to trim and train the story toward some goal, shadowed and indistinct as that goal might be. Here again, we can use Sean's example: once Sean's professor told him what mattered most in his essay, he was able to revise toward those ideas, trimming away what didn't matter and deepening what did.

We offer here a list of questions that you might use, in drafting and in revising, to begin to understand, develop, and wield the river below:

- What is driving you to write about your topic? Why do you feel compelled to share this narrative with the reader?
- What do you want the reader to think about and to feel as they delve into your narrative? Why is it important for your reader to think and feel in this way?
- How is your narrative similar to another essay, story, or poem? What congruent meanings might your piece be making?
- How is your narrative distinct? What meanings might it be adding to the conversation?
- Do you notice any interesting connections between images, actions, characters, or ideas? What might these connections mean?

- Read through your piece. What repeated words, images, transitions, motifs, or actions do you notice? What, symbolically, might these repeated elements point toward?
- What words, images, transitions, motifs, or actions might be repeated? Why?
- What images, objects, characters, or actions from your piece might become metaphors? How might you use these metaphors to point the reader toward meaning?
- What might happen if you reorganize this piece? What do you notice if you, say, abandon chronology and move toward a more lyrical form?
- What is your narrative about? Write one sentence that tells us not what happens but why you think what happens happens.
- Think journalistically: give us the who, what, where, and when. When you pare your story down like this, what do you notice? What are the most important elements?

Exercises

The following exercises will help you practice the techniques learned in this chapter.

A. Choose three pieces from the anthology that you've already read. Write a one-sentence description of the river above for each, and list as well the who, what, where, and when. Then do the same for the river below. These sentences should be clear and concise.

Piece 1:
    The River Above:

    Who:
    What:
    Where:
    When:

    The River Below:

Piece 2:
    The River Above:

    Who:
    What:

Where:
When:

The River Below:

Piece 3:
   The River Above:

Who:
What:
Where:
When:

The River Below:

B. Using those same three pieces, outline the **plot** of each. What comes first, second, third, and so on? Why do you think the author plotted it this way? What does such plotting allow or disallow? Which plot form does each piece fit into—**narrative, logical, or lyrical**? If narrative, can you locate each of the five steps? If logical or lyrical, what strategies does the author use to help the reader move from one section to the next?

C. Consider an essay, story, or poem you are working on. What **plot** form have you chosen for this piece? What would happen if you shifted this form from, say, **narrative** to **logical**? What is lost? What is gained? After considering each of the three forms, which do you think might be the best choice for this particular piece? Why?

D. Return to **Questions to Ask about Why You Are Writing Your Narrative** and take out an essay, story, or poem you are writing or about to write. Answer the questions from that section for your piece. Does answering these questions about your essay, story, or poem give you ideas for revision? How so?

Prompts

The following prompts will help you practice the techniques learned in this chapter.

A. Working on your own or with a group, think of as many story situations—**rivers above**—as you can: a family trip to Yellowstone, a protest march against frakking, working on a commercial fishing boat, and so on. Write each of these situations on a small slip of paper, shuffle them, and turn them over in a pile. Now, think of as many emotions or ideas—rivers below—as you can: escape, injustice, consumerism, desire, and so on. Write each of these emotions or ideas on a small slip of paper, shuffle them, and turn them over in another pile. Now, have everyone take one of each and write an essay, story, or poem with the given **river above and below**—perhaps a poem about a family trip to Yellowstone that's really about consumerism, or a story about working on a commercial fishing boat that's really about desire.

B. Write a short essay in five sections. Before you start, choose a **plot form** and map it. If **narrative**, match each of your five scenes to the five steps: **exposition, inciting incident, rising action, climax,** and **falling action**. If **logical**, introduce your idea in the first section and note how you plan to deepen, defend, qualify, or reconsider your idea in the preceding sections. If **lyrical**, describe each section and then note how you plan to transition from section to section. No matter what form you choose, consider **causality.**

C. Take a poem you are working on and rewrite it using each of the three plot **forms—narrative, logical,** and **lyrical**. Which one is strongest? Why?

D. Return to Exercise D above. After you have asked yourself these questions about your essay, story, or poem and garnered some ideas for revision, go ahead and revise your piece based on these new ideas.

8

The Art of Activism

Relevant readings

Creative Nonfiction: Jennifer Lunden, "Exposed"; Louis Owens, "Burning the Shelter."

Poetry: Todd Davis, "What My Neighbor Tells Me Isn't Global Warming"; Juan Morales, "Explaining Seafood to My Future Grandkids after the Extinction"; Sean Prentiss, "Stripping."

Free write

Think of an issue facing one of the places you love. Is a favorite historic building going to get torn down? Is your city trying to decide its energy future? Are lands adjacent to a national park you love slated for frakking? Is the place you call home full of landfills and toxic waste storage sites because most of the people who call that land home are poor?

Once you've thought of a beloved place under attack, consider two things: one, why you love this place; and, two, what this attack will mean for this place's future. How do you think you can communicate both your love of this place and your worry for its future? List as many possible ways you might go about this. Look at your list. Which would be most effective? Why? With what audience?

Vignette

I grew up alongside the Delaware River, which is the longest undammed main-stem river in the Lower 48. On some tangible level, because of this lack of dams, the Delaware is the wildest of all Lower 48 rivers. But it almost wasn't that way. The Delaware, like so many other great American rivers (the Mississippi, Colorado, Rio Grande, Green, Columbia, Snake, and the list goes on and on), could have been dammed, ruined, enslaved.

The potential ruination of the Delaware began in the 1930s when the US government hatched a plan to dam the Delaware at Tock's Island, a non-descript island north of where I grew up. This earthen dam would create a thirty-seven-mile-long reservoir to provide water to Philadelphia and New York City and to generate electricity. At one point, the plan even included a nuclear reactor. The idea for the dam got far enough that, in 1962, the dam was approved by Congress and the Army Corps of Engineers. Lands were snatched (though the government called this theft eminent domain) from people who, like our family, had spent their lives beside the Delaware. Soon, the government said, this massive still-water reservoir would swallow cornfields, farms, barns, and houses.

But local activists refused to concede, to allow the Delaware to be dammed without a fight. These activists created the Delaware Valley Conservation Association, which—through protests and government hearings—soon gained momentum. As the chorus of dissenters grew, others took note, including New Jersey governor William T. Cahil and Supreme Court Justice William O. Douglas, and became concerned with how the government had acquired the land and with the potential environmental impacts of the dam and reservoir. By 1975, the Delaware River Basin Commission disapproved the dam. In 1992, the Tocks Island Dam project was de-authorized. It was permanently scrapped in 2002.

Now, when I canoe past Tock's Island, I whisper, "A dam, right here." I try to imagine a massive wall of earth. I try to imagine a massive bath tub filled with water. I try to imagine the free-flowing Delaware as a dammed river, a dead river. But when I cannot envision those things, when I cannot halt the pull of the current as it carries me closer to my childhood home and away from the tiny (and now barely remembered Tock's Island), I say a silent prayer, which sounds something like "Never again."

As I float toward family, including my mother, who is now a river activist fighting against corporate pollution, I think about the people who stopped the building of the dam, the people like Nancy Shukaitis and Ruth Jones who raised their voices and their pens to convince others to never allow this river to be a slave river. Because of their work, I don't have to worry about this river getting dammed. I can focus on the churning of Buttermilk Rapids up ahead.

—Sean

The very nature of nature and environmental writing

Whether implicitly or explicitly stated, all nature and environmental writing is political. Nature and environmental writing negotiates the distance between place and people and teaches readers how each affects the other—which means, of course, that all nature and environmental writing, on some level, has a message, a point of view, a stance, an argument. Because nature and environmental writing has a stance, all nature and environmental writing can be considered activist-writing. Before we get too far, what is activism and activist-writing? **Activism** is the use of campaigning to bring about change in the political and/or social structure; **activist-writing** is the use of written word to promote activism. In this chapter, we examine what activist-writing is and how nature and environmental writers can control our messages to sway audiences.

Whether you like it or not, you're an activist writer

While you may not think of yourself as particularly political, while you might not often join demonstrations, organize boycotts or letter-writing campaigns, or toss monkey-wrenches into the cogs of the industrial machinery, if you're interested in nature and environmental writing, you're interested, even if you don't realize it, in activism—or, at least, a certain kind of activism, activist-writing.

The earliest nature and environmental writers, as far back as the ancient Chinese poets, were writing about more than just beautiful landscapes. They saw issues with politics and war and starvation and corruption. Later, America's first modern environmental writers saw issues with a loss of wilderness and loss of agrarian landscapes. Seeing those massive destructions drove writers to defend their landscapes with the weapon they could best wield: a pen. Writers penned essays, stories, and poems to protect landscapes, to make others aware of environmental issues, and to energize people to action. And activist-writing has worked. Among other successes, it helped create the Wilderness Act, got rid of DDT, and changed the way we protect our rivers and our air. Further, activist-writing has created countless activists who protest in all sorts of ways. So the solitary act of writing often inspires individuals to join with others to bring about political and social change.

One example of activist-writing in our anthology is Jennifer Lunden's essay "Exposed: The Mammogram Myth and the Pink-Washing of America," a piece which uses the author's own breast cancer scare, as well as exhaustive research, to make the case that mammograms aren't effective, that "pink" culture is an ad campaign foisted on women by pharmaceutical companies and polluters, and that women should focus on breast cancer prevention, rather than cancer screening. The essay originally appeared in the influential environmental magazine *Orion*, and it soon set off a firestorm of online and print conversation; from literary venues to health websites, people were talking about "Exposed" and what it meant for women. One woman, commenting on an online interview with Lunden, said it rather succinctly: "Next time I talk to a doctor I will give her/him a copy of this article."

A different sort of activist-writing is Sean's "Stripping." "Stripping" is less overt than Lunden's "Exposed." It offers a poetic take on the idea that much of what we consider vital is actually unneeded materialism and can be stripped away. Sean writes about how our language (and therefore our materialistic wants) grows smaller once we move into a closer connection with our landscapes: "What use here in the Middle Santiam / Wilderness do we have for the word *sink*? When would we / ever utter *closet* or *phone* or *bank account*? These words as / unneeded as any third thumb, as unneeded as *money* or / *wallet* or *credit card*." And though Sean might not be demanding that we stand up from our desks right this very moment and backpack deep into the wilderness, he is asking us to reflect on those things we consider needs and to potentially reevaluate them.

A third example of activist-writing is Louis Owen's "Burning the Shelter." Owens, after burning down a dilapidated cabin in Glacier Peak Wilderness, comes to understand that the divide between wilderness and humanity is artificial. He ends his piece with a clear call to action:

> In old-growth forests in the North Cascades, deep inside an official wilderness area, I have come upon faint traces of log shelters built by Suiattle and Upper Skagit people [...]. Those human-made structures were as natural a part of the Cascade ecosystem as the burrows of marmots in the steep scree slopes. [...] Unless Americans, and all human beings, can learn to imagine themselves as intimately and inextricably related to every aspect of the world they inhabit [...] the earth simply will not survive. A few square miles of something called wilderness will become the sign of failure everywhere.

The fundamentals of argumentation

The fundamentals of making a good argument, which is the best way to persuade others, come to us from Aristotle and his rhetorical triangle. Aristotle argued that for an argument to be successful, for people to be persuaded, a rhetorician—or, in our case, a writer—needed to employ logic, emotion, and credibility. If any one of these is missing, an audience is much less likely to be persuaded. See the figure below for a graphic representation of the rhetorical triangle.

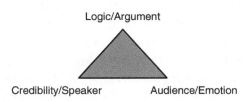

Logic/Argument

Credibility/Speaker   Audience/Emotion

Logic may include **hard evidence** (facts, statistics, surveys, polls, testimonies, eyewitnesses, and interviews) as well as **reason and common sense**. Using logic shows readers that you have a sound argument supported by evidence. Without sound logic, readers will poke holes in your argument. But not all evidence needs to be facts that have in-paper citation. We can sprinkle in research in a way that makes them blend right in with our piece. Examine Todd Davis's poem, "What My Neighbor Tells Me Isn't Global Warming." The poem opens with "Two hours west in Pittsburgh my friend's snow peas / blossom, only mid-April and his lettuce already good for / three weeks." Here Davis uses the logic of a garden coming to bloom months early by painting a detailed picture of when things are occurring. He is gentle and smooth with the logic, letting it speak quietly for itself.

As writers compose their messages, they also need to consider their audience. Audiences want to be moved, and often logic does not move readers to action. **Emotion** does. Humans all too often make decisions that go against logic because we are swayed by our emotions. We follow our hearts. We listen to our guts. Emotion serves as a bridge, connecting writer to reader; it brings people together. Emotion also allows an argument to sustain itself. When readers get bogged down in facts and evidence, the emotional pull of a narrative can reengage the reader. Emotion also works to defuse tension because it can put readers at ease, make connections, or allow readers to suspend judgment. How do we engage a reader's emotions? We follow the lessons from Chapter 3, "Seeing the World, Believing the World," by using our five senses to allow the readers to see and therefore to feel what is occurring.

Logic and emotion are vital, but **credibility** holds the entire argument together because no message, no matter how well written, is effective if the writer has low credibility. To have strong credibility, a writer must be seen as someone who can be trusted. We humans create credibility through our past and present actions. We create **past credibility** by how well known and respected we are, by the tone, language, and logic we have used in previous arguments, and by our credentials and life experiences. If readers have found a writer to be credible in the past, they are likely to find that writer credible until the writer does something to change the readers' minds. So past actions affect how readers view writers today.

Writers also create **present credibility** in their use of language, argument, and emotion. Good language goes a long way to convince a reader that you know what you're talking about; carefully chosen diction also helps create and sustain a tone of respectful, urgent argument. Present credibility is also affected by how much command a writer has over a subject. Is a writer an expert or is she getting her facts wrong? Has the writer done her research? Is her argument logical? Writers can also increase credibility by coming clean with their motives, for why they are writing and what they hope to accomplish. And credibility is tied to audience as well. A community that makes its livelihood on mining or timber might view a writer's credibility very differently than a wilderness advocate. So, credibility must be tailored to audience.

Who is your audience?

Understanding audience and venue is crucial. If you don't pay attention to audience, you're likely to miss key points, offend readers, and, ultimately, fail to persuade people to act. Your **intended audience** includes everyone you think you are writing for. Many authors, in the beginning at least, write to discover what it is they think, to discover where a character's journey might lead, rather than write to a particular audience, and this might be a healthy way to begin. But in revision you should think about who, beyond you, might read this piece: your writing group? your professor? your family? or a group of people advocating for a particular issue? Now, you must think of these audiences' beliefs, values, histories, and political stances. There will be loads of differences, of course, but you might see some commonalities. Write toward those areas of overlap. Think of yourself as uniting and deepening those beliefs, while pushing your audience toward some further idea or action.

Though you may have an intended audience you hope to reach, your **real audience** is all those who actually read your piece. While it's hard to take a real audience into account as you're writing, since you don't know who this might include, just know that people you don't expect to read your work very well might. They might love it. Or they might take issue with it. Both of us (Sean and Joe) have received emails and letters from readers applauding and critiquing our work, and it's humbling to see how closely readers read a piece. It's made both of us more careful, thoughtful writers. One powerful way we've found to consider a real audience is by looking over our pieces and, in our heads, making counterarguments. Who might disagree with this, we ask ourselves. Why? What can we do to at least keep them reading, if not believing?

Consider how Juan Morales uses his audience. His poem, "Explaining Seafood to My Future Grandkids after the Extinction," acknowledges that this poem is written for his future grandchildren, his intended audience. Yet, by the very nature of this poem being published in our anthology, he has a real audience that includes anyone who reads his piece, including, potentially, you. And Morales understands this. Part of the reason for talking to his grandchildren is that his real audience will understand that Morales is talking about a future time when we have killed off most of our seas, a time that, luckily, has not yet arrived.

The nitty-gritty of making arguments

As you begin making your argument about climate change or land preservation or sustainable agriculture or hunters' rights, remember that an activist-writer's purpose is to **move the reader to action**. This may seem obvious, but we find that it helps immensely to keep in mind, as you draft and revise, that everything in your piece—every sentence, every idea, every scene or section—must focus on motivating readers to act. Similarly, it may seem like it's not worth mentioning; however, trust us, it is: you need to give all the **necessary information** concerning the situation (remember **the river above**, which we talked about in Chapter 7). What seems clear to you, as a party already interested in the issue, will befuddle your readers. Take the time to educate your readers, give them the necessary information they need to begin understanding the issue at a deep level. Make sure, as well, that your information is correct and consistent. Even a small, unconscious slip is enough for some people to quit trusting the story.

Also, much like how it is easy for a writer to forget to provide the river above, it is easy for a writer to forget that readers need to hear a writer's message (remember **the river below** from Chapter 7) more than once (and in more than one way) for it to stick. Readers need **repetition** to see connections or remember an idea.

Along with repetition, human beings love to **know why** they should do something or believe something. Think back to when you wanted to do something, and your parents said no. When you asked why, they said, "because I said so." What a dissatisfying answer. Studies show that people are much more likely to act when they understand the reasons why they should do something or believe something. One of the easiest ways to let readers know why an issue is important or why they should act is to use "because" statements or to embed an implicit "because" statement before or after every action you propose.

And we should focus on **intrinsic benefits**, or benefits associated with the internal well-being of a person. Rather than just highlighting how much money can be saved or how little energy the coal might actually provide, which are **extrinsic benefits**, focus on quality-of-life issues. Readers care about long-term gains such as the health of a person, an animal, or an ecosystem, and basic values such as justice, ethics, and community pride, over the more short-term gains related to efficiency or wealth.

In environmental writing, **social proofs** work wonders. Social proofs are the moments you allow others to share their views on a situation. So, rather than only hearing from you the writer, you might bring in the voice of a Forest Service trail builder, a homeowner living next to a proposed power plant, a scientist studying species diversity, or a shrimper trying to make a living in oil-polluted waters. For social proofs to work, the writer must introduce us to characters we trust and value. Then the writer needs to let the characters express their own ideas in their own words. If each person shares similar views, the reader is more likely to accept those views.

Next, you must get readers to **overcome objections** that might prevent action. One way to overcome objections is to **concede points** that are strong from the opposition's side. Conceding works best if you admit that, yes, the opposition has strong ideas, but not strong enough to sway an educated audience. Another option is to offer **counterpoints,** or opposing ideas, to the ideas the opponent expresses. Counterpoints show that an opposition's idea may seem strong but are actually flawed and weak.

Readers can also be moved if you **agitate and solve**, which is where you show the reader the pains associated with an issue. Perhaps you can highlight the loss of a park where families play in the evening or focus on a beach that is so polluted that swimmers can no longer enter the water. Then, once the reader feels that pain or loss, which brings about empathy, you offer a solution, a way to heal that earlier hurt.

A powerful tool similar to comparison is to **show what the future might hold**. Showing the future allows readers to see a potential future, whether it is a doomsday scenario related to climate change or offering hope for a beach to be reopened after plans to remove pollution. Once readers believe this future might actually occur, they are more likely to work with the writer to achieve the best future possible.

Along with showing the future, illustrate **scarcity** and **urgency**. Readers simply aren't worried about protecting the plethora of pigeons in New York City or even possible doomsday prognostications set hundreds of years in the future. To show how valuable a place or resource is, you need to help readers understand how quickly we need to act. One of the keys for successfully writing about climate change is focusing on scarcity and urgency. To get readers to care about an issue with long-term global implications, you need to show specific local scarcities and point out the very immediate issues associated with climate change.

The final key to swaying the reader is the most important. If you want to move readers, you need to tell effective **stories**. Readers crave stories. Stories work so effectively (and can be used with all the ideas mentioned above) because, if writers use stories well, they won't need to persuade readers to believe anything. Stories show rather than tell, and so allow readers to arrive at their own conclusions, which, if the story is good enough, will be the conclusions the writer had in mind all along.

Exercises

The following exercises will help you practice the techniques learned in this chapter.

A. Go through a few of the narratives you have written recently and try to discern what your agenda might be. Remember we're all **activist-writers** of one stripe or another!

B. Examine a few of your pieces. Examine the stance you take, especially considering how you work toward swaying a particular **audience**. What audience are you writing for? What does that audience believe? How are you working to sway that audience? How are you trying to connect to that audience?

C. Examine one of your environmental writing pieces. Which of the following techniques are you using to sway your **audience**? Now choose a piece of environmental writing from the anthology and examine what techniques that writer is using. Every time you or the anthologized piece uses a technique listed in the chart below, write the page number in the chart.

Techniques	Your Piece	Anthology Piece
Overcoming Objections:		
Conceding:		
Using Counterpoints:		
Using Intrinsic Benefits:		
Using Repetition:		
Being Consistent:		
Using Social Proofs:		
Making Comparisons:		
Agitating-and-Solving:		
Prognosticating:		
Showing Scarcity:		
Showing Urgency:		
Crafting Stories:		

D. Choose any piece of environmental writing from the anthology. Examine how they use **logic, credibility**, and **emotion**. You should be able to find more than one example. List the page numbers below.

Logic:
Emotion:
Credibility:

Prompts

The following prompts will help you practice the techniques learned in this chapter.

A. Write a one page environmental essay or story concerning any environmental idea. Write it with a very muted tone. Then rewrite it with a loud, belligerent tone. Compare and contrast the two drafts and tones.

B. Write a one page environmental essay or story for a specific **audience**. Once you finish that piece, rewrite your environmental essay or story for the opposite audience. Think about how you must re-tailor your activist writing to reach each audience.

C. Write a short activist piece of writing. As you write it, consider the many different ways you can move your **audience** to action. Try to add three or four persuasive techniques from the list below.

Overcoming Objections
Conceding
Using Counterpoints
Using Intrinsic Benefits
Using Repetition
Being Consistent
Using Social Proofs
Making Comparisons
Agitating-and-Solving
Prognosticating
Showing Scarcity

Showing Urgency
Crafting Stories

D. Write a short piece of activist writing. As you write, consider the **rhetorical triangle**. Think about how you use **logic, emotion**, and especially **credibility** to sway your reader.

9

A World Larger than Ourselves

Chapter Outline

Relevant readings

Creative Nonfiction: David Treuer, "Trapline."

Fiction: Lydia Peelle, "Mule Killers."

Poetry: Elizabeth Bradfield, "Creation Myth"; W. Todd Kaneko, "Remembering Minidoka."

Free write

Think about a place you visit often. Write down a list of everything you know about the place, its history, and your history with the place. What it looks like, smells like, and feels like. Describe the place as well as you can.

Identify the trees. Explain the style of buildings. Give as many specific and exact details as possible.

Once you have reached the end of your scope of knowledge about your place, begin researching your place. Break out a tree and flower guide. Venture onto the internet and see what you can learn about the history of your place. Who first settled your area? What was mined from your area? Who first developed or preserved your area? Compile a list of all the things you learn about your location.

Once you have completed this research, look over your list and see what details relate to others. See what details you could piece together to create a narrative about your place. Now begin writing.

Vignette

Back in 2010, I began to write a book, Finding Abbey: The Search for Edward Abbey and His Hidden Desert Grave, *about searching for the final resting place of the famed environmental writer, Edward Abbey. I longed to search for Abbey's hidden grave because not only was Abbey my favorite writer, but I had recently moved to the city for a career job, a lifetime job. I was unaccustomed to living far from nature, to being unable to see mountain peaks from my window, to the din and racket of traffic day and night. So the book was a search for an understanding of what to do with my life, trying to figure out where I should call home.*

I set off on a two-year journey that expanded from finding Abbey's final resting place to also chasing down the spirit of Edward Abbey. I visited his various homes (Home, PA; Hoboken, NJ; Moab, UT; Tucson, AZ; and many others). And as I traveled the country, I visited Abbey's best friends (Jack Loeffler, Doug Peacock, David Petersen, and Ken Sleight) and spent hours interviewing them.

But this book was about more than just immersive research. So I purchased every Edward Abbey book I could get my hands on, over twenty in total. Then I bought books about Abbey and field guides for the Desert Southwest, where Abbey mainly lived. Next, I bought Abbey's friends' books since I needed to research them before their interviews. Soon I had a stack of books sixty or seventy deep. Slowly, I read each one, taking notes and marking quotes I hoped to use in the book. That list of quotes ran 60 typewritten pages.

Later, I twice visited The Edward Abbey Special Collections Library *at the University of Arizona. Each time, I spent the day holed up in the library reading Abbey's papers, including his thesis on violence and anarchism and an unpublished novel,* City of Dreadful Nights.

But the research kept coming. I needed to research Abbey's birthplace of Home, PA. I researched Everett Ruess, a famed Desert Southwest explorer who, like Abbey, has a mysterious ending. I learned about Glen Canyon Dam, Black Mesa, and esopogeal varacises, which killed Abbey. I studied the difference between eco-terrorism and eco-sabotage. The list goes on and on and on. I was, gloriously, swallowed by research.

And during it all, I traveled America, putting 25,000 miles on my Ford F150 truck. Each place I visited, I did more research. I looked for Abbey's old homes, the bars he haunted, his old schools, anything that could highlight who Abbey was. The final thing I did was travel out into a great and grand American desert, a desert I spent weeks researching, and went in search of Abbey's final resting spot.

In the end, this book required years of research, and what I learned from it all is that what matters most is not if I find Abbey's hidden grave or not, but it's the mystery, it's the searching, it's the researching that taught me the most about Abbey. It's spending hours or days or weeks falling into that which we are studying, that which we are researching, that which we are obsessed with. And all of this living in the world and words of Edward Abbey taught me all I needed to know. So I quit my job and sold my house in the city, and I moved to an isolated lake in Vermont. All because research taught me the true meaning of home.

—Sean

Why research?

Great question. Why bother with those tens or hundreds of hours of research? Why not just write what we know and ignore the rest? It would be much quicker and easier. We could write a lot more essays and stories with all the time we save. So why bother?

The first reason is because readers expect writers to **be experts**. As we saw in Chapter 8, The Art of Activism, **credibility** is the most vital element of any argument. Without credibility, readers will not bother to read our narratives. One great way to gather credibility is from research. Research shows we have done our homework, it shows we know our subject, and shows we can be trusted by the reader.

We research to **add texture and complexity**. We can complicate our ideas through research. We can see things in new ways. We can find new ways to look at something. Sean learned this firsthand during his research for *Finding*

Abbey. In the Arizona desert, there are saguaro, fishhook, barrel, teddy bear cholla, and prickly pear cacti growing. Those biggest cacti, the saguaros, are over two hundred years old. These details—the names and details of cacti—can transform a piece. It allows the readers to see the world in shining detail.

We also research **to discover**. So often in research, we stumble upon some new idea or make new connections. These moments of discovery are not only exciting, they may change our entire project. The more we research, the more points we uncover; the more connections we make, the more texture our piece has. In researching his memoir, *The Mountain and the Fathers: Growing up on the Big Dry*, Joe discovered that it was Meriwether Lewis himself who first gave the Big Dry, a riverless high desert in eastern Montana, its name. And this surprising connection to westward exploration and expansion allowed Joe to more deeply historicize his arguments about land use, violence, and masculinity.

In the end, there are many great reasons for why we research that we often don't need to find reasons for why we should start researching. Rather, after we've fallen for days into books and interviews and the studying of maps, we might need to consider when and why we need to stop researching and start writing—such is the joy of research into a topic you are curious about!

How to research

There are literally thousands of ways to research. Here, we will examine some of the major ways to research, and we will look at it through textual research, experiential research, and scientific research.

Textual research is the use of books, articles, essays, stories, poems, guidebooks, maps, websites, and other texts to learn about a subject. Within textual research we have primary and secondary sources. **Primary sources** are objects or documents created during the period of study. So, for Sean, all of Edward Abbey's books, speeches, and essays are primary resources. Also, remember that your own materials can serve as primary sources. You can examine old photos you took or letters and emails and journals you wrote. **Secondary sources** examine, analyze, and interpret primary sources. So the Edward Abbey biography written by Jack Loeffler, *Adventures with Ed*, about his friendship with Abbey is a secondary source since Loeffler is examining Abbey's life. Secondary sources examine an event rather than being a part of an event.

Often with textual research, one source will lead a writer to other sources. Pay attention to who the writer talks about and to their works cited page.

This is a great way to fall into the rabbit hole of research. Allow textual sources to lead you deeper and deeper into a subject.

Experiential research is any research where you, the writer, visits an area or explores a place. This includes **observation**, where a writer observes people, animals, or a landscape. Through observing, they learn about people and place. W. Todd Kaneko does this in his poem, "Remembering Minidoka." Kaneko writes, "When I visited Minidoka, all that remained / was a scar." **Immersion** is where a writer does something new to experience it. Rather than observing a hunter sitting in a tree stand, a writer may pick up a bow and learn to hunt. Through immersion we experience something new. David Treuer's "Trapline" offers a sterling example of immersion research:

> As an Ojibwe child from Leech Lake Reservation in Northern Minnesota, I grew up around hunters. But aside from our mother teaching us to snare rabbits, we didn't trap animals like "bush Indians" did. Instead, we harvested wild rice in the fall, made maple sugar in the spring, and shopped for food like everyone else. My father (a Jew and a Holocaust survivor) and my mother (an Ojibwe Indian and tribal court judge) put as much emphasis on homework as they did on living off the land. None of the other kids from Leech Lake that I knew had grown up trapping or living off the land either. But this was still held up as the only truly Ojibwe way of life, and as I grew older I longed to commit myself to the bush. So when Dan Jones, an Ojibwe friend from across the border, offered to teach me to trap beaver on his trapline in northwestern Ontario, I said yes.

Interviews are another great way to learn. Find the experts, ask if you can talk with them, and then pick their brains. Sean did this as often as possible with *Finding Abbey*. He once spent seven hours talking with the environmentalist Doug Peacock in a wide-ranging interview that took place in lawn chairs out in the Sonoran Desert. Sean learned things that no book or article could ever teach him. The only way he could learn these things was by flying to Arizona, driving to Ajo, and spending an entire day in the shadow of one of Abbey's best friends.

Finally, **scientific research** can serve as a means of learning about our environments. Great Britain's and America's original nature writers were often scientist writers. They did experiments, recorded observations, and made hypotheses. Their scientific research allowed them to see the world in new ways and to prove their ideas. Though not a trained scientist, Elizabeth Bradfield, in her poem "Creation Myth," makes use of scientific research: "*Researchers have snipped bits of periosteum / from pedicles, grafted them onto other parts / of a buck's body, and grown antlers.*" Later she writes,

"*Researchers have tricked deer into growing and casting / as many as four sets of antlers in one calendar year.*" These moments of scientific research add both credibility and logic to the poem. But they also add surprise; as Bradfield weaves these facts about deer antlers around the narrator's own longing to grow antlers, to have them rise from her "clavicle," her "cheek-bone. / Ankle. Coccyx. Breast. At last visible, / the antler will grow."

When and how to use research

When Sean was writing *Finding Abbey*, he physically and metaphorically surrounded himself with research. Often stacks of books sat on either side of his chair. Maps lay strewn across the floor. Field guides sat on his desk. Photocopies from the *Edward Abbey Special Collections Library* waited on the edge of the desk. And on his computer, Sean had sixty pages of quotes from the dozens and dozens of books he read. He had eighty pages of typed transcripts from his interviews with Abbey's closest friends. And hundreds and hundreds of photos waited on his computer from his visits to Abbey's former homes.

Once Sean accumulated all this research, he had decisions to make. He could use all this great research—and the research was great—or he could cull it and use only the most vital. In the end, most of Sean's research never ended up in *Finding Abbey*. It wasn't needed. But rather than seeing this as a waste, Sean recognized that all the unused research, even though it never found a home in the book, informed him. It made Sean smarter. It allowed Sean to become an expert on Edward Abbey. It allowed Sean to add texture to his writing.

Once you've decided what research to use, consider how to use it. Two major concerns are credibility and flow. In terms of credibility, remember to teach the reader where your information comes from. We need to know what person said which quote. Also, what makes that person an expert on the subject, which we learn through their **credentials**. Are they scientists? Are they ranchers who know the land through years and years of work? Are they recreational users who hike through the area often?

Examine how Erik Reece introduces who is saying what in his essay, "Hell Yeah We Want Windmills." Notice how Reece introduces quotes. Early in the essay, Reece writes about a political rally: "Jesse Johnson, the progressive Mountain Party candidate for governor, gave a fiery speech in which he suggested we stop pulverizing and burning coal, and instead invest in carbon-composite technology." In one sentence, Reece tells us who Johnson is: "a progressive Mountain Party candidate for governor"; what sort of person Johnson is: "a politician who gives a fiery speech"; and what his politics are; someone who "suggested we stop pulverizing and burning coal and instead invest in carbon-composite technology." All of this information teaches readers how to view Johnson and allows us to understand why we should listen to his ideas.

Also, consider audience. Will your audience want a works-cited page? Will they want in-paper citations? Or will they want the research blended into the narrative? In "Hell Yeah We Want Windmills," Reece does not add a works-cited page. But he keeps his own credibility high by introducing his characters. Reece tells us who his characters are, what they do for work, and what they believe about coal mining. And he also allows them to speak for themselves.

Also consider how your research flows. It is often best to summarize, paraphrase, or synthesize research into your own words, because research is simply the fuel added to the fire of your writing. Research, often, shouldn't be in the spotlight unless necessary. Your words take precedence over citations. For instance, in Lydia Peelle's short story "Mule Killers," we don't get any lists or citations, rather, it's clear, from the specificity of her details and the deftness of her narrative, that Peelle has done copious research about the change from mule farming to tractor farming in the American South.

Whether or not you use a Works-cited or in-paper citation, always be aware of plagiarism. It is easy to lose track of what words are your own and what words are owned by others. Make sure you always give credit when you use someone else's words. A key to preventing plagiarism is to keep track of your research. Write down, immediately, where a quote came from so you can find it again.

The larger world

Earlier in the chapter we asked, "why research?" For us, one of the biggest reasons for researching is because the world is so much larger than us. It is expansive. It is glorious. It is troubled. It is complex. It is beautiful. And only through research can we begin to best explore our world, whether that is the empty field next to our homes or some faraway and unknown mountain range. Research helps us see the world from a multitude of perspectives. It complicates our ideas. It builds up our credibility. And it excites the reader. Research in all its forms is, for us, the best way to see the world.

Exercises

The following exercises will help you practice the techniques learned in this chapter.

A. Create a list that includes all the various types of research you have done during your time as a writer. Think back to your composition or history or sociology classes. Once you have compiled that list, write another list for all the types of research you have used during your time as a nature and environmental writer. Think about **textual research** (including **primary** and **secondary sources**), **experiential research**, and **scientific research.**

B. Look back on a narrative you have been working on, especially one that has no research in it. Write a short paragraph on why research could help this piece. Once you have completed that, write a short paragraph on how you might begin to find resources.

C. Think about a piece of nature or environmental writing you are working on. Put together a list of all the ways you can do research. Again, just as given above, think about **textual research** (including **primary** and **secondary sources**), **experiential research**, **scientific research,** and **interviews**.

D. After completing Exercise A above, work on being specific. Visit your library's database and come up with a list of the exact books and articles you might read. Look for resources online. Find maps or photos of your location. Build a list of resources you can use to add research to your narrative.

Prompts

The following prompts will help you practice the techniques learned in this chapter.

A. Find a narrative you wrote based on memory. Return to the location of that narrative and perform **experiential research**. Explore the landscape. See how it has changed. See what has stayed the same. Once you have visited this location, add a section to your narrative.

B. Just as you did above, find a narrative you wrote based on memory. This time, use **textual research** to learn about your location. Look into the history of the area. Look into the commercial and economic history of the area. Examine field guides to learn more about the plants and animals. Once you have completed this research, add this research to your narrative.

C. Find a narrative that lacks research. Now, **interview** as many people as you can. Find people who are connected to your topic in some way. You can do formal interviews or informal interviews. Take the quotes for your interviews and add them to your narrative.

10

The Nature and Environmental Essay, Story, and Poem

Relevant readings

Creative Nonfiction: John Daniel, "Pack Rat"; Sean Prentiss, "Spring Ends in Bangor, Pennsylvania"; Leslie Ryan, "The Other Side of Fire."

Fiction: Bonnie Jo Campbell, "Family Reunion"; Alyson Hagy, "Border"; Joe Wilkins, "Like Bread the Light."

Poetry: Major Jackson, "Migration"; Anne Haven McDonnell, "Emerging View"; G.E. Patterson, "The Natural World"; M.L. Smoker, "The Feed."

Free write

Think for a moment about types. Maybe you drink a certain type of coffee or drive a certain type of car. Maybe you're a birder or a bass-fishing fanatic. Make a list of eight to ten different types of things you use, practice, or otherwise feel strongly about.

Once you have your list, take one or two and transform them; for instance, transform your old Chevy pickup into a new Toyota Prius. As you make these transformations, consider how each would change your life in many small and large ways.

In creative writing, we use the word "genre" to describe types of writing: essay, story, or poem. Now, take an essay, story, or poem that you've written recently and transform it: turn that essay about birding into a fictional story, morph that story about walking the Appalachian Trail into a poem, or convert that poem about rivers into an essay. Watch as your piece shifts in massive and subtle ways. Watch as a piece of writing you've known well becomes, just by switching genre, something entirely new.

Vignette

Years ago, I worked in the Pacific Northwest as a trail builder for the Northwest Youth Corps. I was hired to lead a crew of ten youth (16–19-year-olds) from May through August. With snow lingering in the Cascade Mountains, we loaded up in a fifteen-passenger van and headed toward trail projects spread across the region. One week we might build trail on Washington's Olympic Peninsula. The next week, we'd work in a clear-cut, removing thistle from southern Oregon. Each week, there was a new location and a new project for this crew that was growing into family.

After working this job for four summers, I decided to retire from building trail, from leading a crew, from eating peanut butter and jelly sandwiches five days a week. So I packed up my old tent, threw out the tattered gloves, even shaved off the beard that made me look more wild animal than man. Next, I got a job as a professor, and later bought a house and began sleeping indoors instead of by the banks of some roaring river.

A decade later, the wilderness feels just as close as it did before. I can smell those vanilla-scented ponderosa pines, hear the sound of rain and snow on a tent's vestibule, and I can tell the exact difference between the sound of rain and the sound of snow. My fingers and hands still know how to curl around the ash handle of a hog hoe or Pulaski. Wildness is a part of me. And I am a part of wildness.

And I write, often, about those years in the woods. I started with an essay about my favorite crewmember, a kid named Kevin, who has tasted poverty and violence and alcohol in ways no one should. A kid who wore anger across his face the first day we met. But also a kid who loved working maybe even more than I did. Kevin loved to sling dirt, and he loved silence like I love silence. We often use the word brother *lightly. But Kevin was, and is, my brother. So I wrote about him. A long, braided essay.*

But my hunger to explore the wilderness was still there. So I wrote poem after poem about baking bread in a Dutch oven, late night drives to new projects, successes and failures and quitters and final days, rain and sleet and snow. Twenty, thirty, forty, fifty poems. And I'm still writing.

Yet there was more. The woods ached in my bones. So I began to write micro-essays. These little, tiny snippets of the woods. These brief moments. The moon in the sky. The rain soaking through rain gear. A brief moment of dinner beneath a cedar.

And what I'm realizing is that I'm circling around my time in the woods. I'm asking myself to remember and remember again those wilderness years. And no one way of telling gets the story just right. Each moment requires a different genre. Each moment requires a different slant. Because there is no one way to tell a story. There is no singular way to remember a vital moment.

—Sean

The nature and environmental essay, story, and poem

While essays, stories, and poems are indeed very different things, good writing is good writing, which is why we have organized this text the way we have. All writing, whether essay, story, or poem, must use image (Chapter 3), build place (Chapter 4), speak with an engaging voice (Chapter 5), create characters (Chapter 6), make story and meaning (Chapter 7), and be concerned with the art of activism (Chapter 8). Still, as the opening exercise suggests, even though an old pickup and a new hybrid car might get you most places you want to go, they are very different things and will exert an enormous influence on the decisions you make.

In creative writing, one of the primary decisions we make as we approach a writing situation is that of genre. **Genres** are categories of writing. In this chapter, we will talk about a few genres of nature and environmental writing, specifically focusing on prose and poetry. Though issues of genre continue to be debated, for our purposes we'll call **prose** writing that uses paragraphs and **poetry** writing that uses line breaks.

If we choose to write prose, we have a further decision to make. Will we write from memory or experience and maintain as much fidelity as we can muster to actual events and emotions? If so, then we are writing **creative nonfiction**. If not, if we instead give our imaginations free reign and invent characters and situations, then we are writing **fiction**.

Though readers are often interested in whether something in a poem actually happened or not, there is no formal distinction in the genre of poetry concerning what is real and what is imagined.

Creative nonfiction

The best way to understand **creative nonfiction,** a subgenre of prose, is to break the two words apart. "Nonfiction" means not fiction, which also, then, can mean true or real or factual. So, all creative nonfiction must be focused on telling stories that maintain as much fidelity as possible to actual events and emotions. Along with nonfiction, we have the term "creative." "Creative" means that writers not only tell true stories, but writers sculpt those stories so that they might be beautiful and emotionally affecting. Creative nonfiction isn't an author aimlessly remembering their lives, and it is more than a mere recitation of facts or observations. Creative nonfiction is the artful telling of true stories.

That said, **facts**—things that are indisputably the case—are vital. Yet, a fact seldom gets at a truth, which is a far more complicated matter. **Truth**, as it concerns creative nonfiction, deals with how an author sees and feels the world; it is how authors make sense of their world for us, how they help us see our own worlds anew. Facts don't usually do that on their own, yet the truth must be built on a structure of facts that are as correct as possible, or else the essay collapses—the reader failing to trust the author to get the facts right, let alone the truth.

A further caveat, however, is that creative nonfiction writers rely heavily on **memory**, and, well, we all struggle to remember events exactly as they were. It is often hard for us to know exactly when an event took place (Was it after dinner? Before? Or did we go out for dinner that night?), what we were wearing (Brown work pants or tan work pants?), or even who was present (Were you there when so-and-so fell through the ice?). In many cases we may never be able to determine what the exact details of a particular situation were. However, what we do know is what we were probably wearing. Most days, for instance, Sean can be found in a pair of work pants, whether brown or tan. So, we can safely write that Sean was in his brown work pants, and we can also safely write that Sean was in his tan work pants. Are we being factual? Maybe not. Are we misleading the reader? No. We're trying to get to the truth of things, and the truth of things—when it involves Sean out in the woods—involves one pair of beat-up work dungarees. Writers need to rely on their memory, to trust the story memory tells—so go ahead and go with those brown work pants. The key is to ensure that you are not trying to deceive the reader, that you are trying your hardest to be factual *and* truthful.

Examine how Leslie Ryan, in "To Build a Fire," uses memory. She bounces back and forth between a variety of past moments—when her parents abandoned her, when she stole food for her brothers, when she went off to college—with the more recent memory of being a wilderness guide in Idaho—with the much more recent memory of being the adult woman she is in the beginning of the essay.

For shorter creative nonfiction, we use the term **essay**. And please note that when we talk about essays here, we are not necessarily talking about the academic essay with its thesis, three body paragraphs, and conclusion. Rather, the term *essay* comes from the French *essai* for "to try" or "to attempt." So when we say essay we mean a piece of writing that tries or attempts to make an argument, discover what an experience might mean, or relate a true, emotionally charged story to an audience.

Creative nonfiction makes use of all the techniques we've discussed in previous chapters; image, setting, voice, character, and story all play major roles. But creative nonfiction often relies more heavily than the other genres on the use of reflection and research.

In fiction, we often read to find out what happens next; in creative nonfiction, however, we often know the basic outlines of the story already (and we always know the author made it through whatever harrowing experience is being related), which means we're not always reading to find out what happened—but to find out what an author makes of what happened. This means **reflection**, which is where an author pauses the river above story and thinks and feels about the river below story, which is absolutely essential in creative nonfiction. For an example of powerful reflection in our anthology, consider John Daniel's essay "Pack Rat." Here Daniel is trying to catch a pack rat. As he prepares a trap, he thinks back to another rat from his life.

> I split a thin piece from a pine board and set to whittling, thinking of the first and, till now, smartest rat to have entered my life. Uncle Tom's home was a cabin on the Blue Ridge of Virginia that my parents bought as a weekend place around 1960. The cabin's hand-hewn beams went back to the early 1800s, and as far as anybody knew, Uncle Tom did too. He was a bare-tailed rat, I think, and big—though any rat would have seemed big to me then. He kept a dignified distance, mostly, unless we left some food in the kitchen he couldn't resist. My mother thought he was fine. It was his place more than ours, she said. We were just weekenders.
>
> But my father didn't like the idea of a rat in the place, so he set out to kill Uncle Tom.

In this section, and in many others, we see Daniel's remembering of past times and past rats. And we get to see Daniel's (and his family's) thoughts on rats. These moments of reflections teach us so much about Daniel's views on rats.

As a genre that engages, by definition, with the real, creative nonfiction often benefits from a deep, intensive research process. Creative nonfiction writers **research** ideas, events, and characters by examining journals and diaries, letters, and photographs; by interviewing or talking with friends, (ex-)lovers, parents, and experts or witnesses; by traveling to a particular place or delving into library archives (see Chapter 9, A World Larger than Ourselves). And this research textures a writer's true world. Sean, in his essay, "Spring Ends in Bangor, Pennsylvania," uses many research techniques. His essay begins with another writer's poem and later brings in a second poem by another writer. Then Sean explores the geologic and economic history of his region, the Slate Belt, the various businesses that existed in and around his hometown, and the names and records of his teammates (Sean wrote this essay nearly fifteen years after his high school wrestling career ended). Finally, Sean used various newspapers to research the death of Doug.

From natural histories to science and technology writing, much nature and environmental writing has been in the form of creative nonfiction, a genre that honors and seeks to deepen our understanding of this astonishing, manifold world of ours.

Fiction

Fiction, like creative nonfiction, is prose; however, where creative non-fiction is the artistic telling of true stories, fiction is the artistic telling of invented stories, stories that use imagined characters and situations to mirror and speak to our shared world. While a fictional story might well take its inspiration from actual events, the author has specifically chosen to grapple with the possibilities inherent in a situation (rather than sticking to the realities). With fiction, we're interested in how a particular invention—a turn of events, a character, a way of thinking—might affect us, might allow us to resee the world.

As nature and environmental writers—that is, writers concerned with the actualities of the natural world—it might seem a strange choice to go with fiction over nonfiction. Why would we ever give up the claim on reality that creative nonfiction carries? It's a good question, and the history of nature and environmental writing does suggest that creative nonfiction has long been the preferred prose form for writing about the natural world. Yet, consider John Steinbeck's *The Grapes of Wrath*; here's a novel not often considered part of the nature and environmental writing canon, yet it grapples with one of the biggest ecological disasters in our history—the Dust Bowl—and the action and the characters are deeply influenced by place, and are inextricable, really, from the landscapes about them. By turning to fiction, Steinbeck, who had written loads of journalistic pieces about the Dust Bowl and the Great Depression, was able to build characters and situations that have captivated readers for decades; unfettered by journalistic actualities, Steinbeck's imagination cut to the heart of the Dust Bowl, the Great Depression, and the ways we as human beings hurt, and might heal, one another.

Fiction, like creative nonfiction, utilizes all the tools and techniques of creative writing, including image, setting, voice, character, and story. However, fiction is a form that more easily accommodates a variety of points of view, which means **voice** carries special importance (see Chapter 5 for more). For instance, consider Joe's "Like Bread the Light," which takes the form of a monologue or confession, told in an arresting, insistent voice, to immediately pull the reader into the world of this story:

> Down there is the bar ditch. The wild mustard tall as me in places and my hair long as it was then caught up in mustard and a few stray burs and bits of driftwood from whenever the last rain was and riffles and sighs of dried

mud and dust when you laid me down on the dirt and gravel and kissed me in the bar ditch.

We often turn to fiction as well to spend time with people we might not ever have the chance to know (let alone know them as intimately as we do in fiction), which means building real, engaging **characters** (see Chapter 6 for more) is paramount. In Alyson Hagy's story "Border" we encounter a number of characters—from our main character, a fourteen-year-old boy on the run, to the half-drunk cowboys he hitches a ride with, to the old lady who shows him kindness, before betraying him—and each of them is as real as anyone we might meet.

Finally, fiction is a form that looks forward—the reader always wants to know what will happen next—which means **story**, too, is of prime importance (see Chapter 7). In Bonnie Jo Campbell's "Family Reunion" we begin to understand, along with Marylou, what has been done to her by her Uncle Cal, and alongside this revelation we want to know what lengths Marylou will go to protect her father and herself—and have her revenge.

While fiction doesn't yet have the history creative nonfiction does in the nature and environmental writing tradition, we are sure that is soon to change. Fiction allows the imagination free, unfettered reign, and in a world beset by ecological trauma, we are deeply in need of the imaginative possibilities (and warnings) fiction offers.

Poetry

As mentioned above, all writing falls into either prose (creative nonfiction and fiction) or poetry. The major difference between poetry and prose is whether the writer chooses to let the size of the paper determine where a line ends (prose) or chooses to use line breaks to shape the meaning and rhythms of the words (poetry). In prose we have sentences and paragraphs. In poetry we have lines and stanzas. Poetry is also often shorter than prose, though not always, and this brevity, or **compression**, is as well part of the power of poetry: a poem forces us to pay attention to every syllable and every image, forces us to see and feel for even the quickest moment of the natural world. In Anne Haven McDonnell's "Emerging View," we can see this compression. Rather than showing us the entire landscape of houses (letting us see what each specific house looks like) for sale on County Road 8 (showing us every wend in County Road 8) and the emerging view of James Peak (letting us see more than just its "snowy teeth"), due to the bark beetles (brought on by climate change) killing off the lodgepole pines, we only get the most vital and lyric details of the forest:

> aspens quilt a dizzy
> yellow, and now this
> blanket of dead lodgepole pine.
> We can almost hear the strange
> rhythm that brings those beetles,
> thrums with weak music,
> the fungus that follows their footsteps,
> their marbled blue trails
> polished like a map
> on her kitchen floor.

Poetry has two major classifications: formal and free verse. **Formal verse** is poetry that adheres, for the most part, to a received form, such as a sonnet, villanelle, or ghazal. While demanding to construct, formal verse allows a poet to access, in a single poem, the long tradition, say, of the sonnet. **Free verse** is poetry that doesn't adhere to a received form; rather, with free verse a poet invents or builds her own form. And this is important to remember: it's not that free verse lacks form; it's that with free verse the poet retains more control of the form. Most, if not all, of the poems in our anthology fall into free verse.

As mentioned above, the primary difference between prose and poetry is the line. A line is similar to a sentence except that a sentence continues across the paper until it runs out of page, then it continues on the line below. A **poetic line** ends whenever the poet decides it should end; the poet simply moves to the line below. This means the poet gets to determine where a line ends, as well as where a sentence ends. So, poets have a tool prose writers don't: the line. And this extra tool allows poets to work with and against the sentence to create surprising turns and interesting rhythms and to develop added meanings.

By deciding where to end a line, a poet changes how the reader reads a line and, often, the meaning of a line. Where a poet decides to end a line is called a **line break**. There are two major types of line breaks: enjambed lines and end-stopped lines. **Enjambed lines** are lines broken in the middle of a sentence, which often leads to an increase in surprise and tension. Every line in G.E. Patterson's poem, "The Natural World," uses enjambed lines. **End-stopped lines** are lines broken at a period, at the end of the grammatical unit of meaning. End-stopped lines slow a poem and offer a feeling of finality. Major Jackson's poem, "Migration," uses enjambed lines in his second, third, and final lines. Part of the art of poetry, then, is choosing where to enjamb and end-stop lines, where to increase tension and undercut meaning, or where to slow and highlight or insist on an image or idea.

Another consideration is where to break a line, which determines which word becomes the last one in the line, a place of power and importance. Poets seldom choose to end on articles (*a, an, the*), coordinating conjunctions (*but, for, so*), or prepositions (*of, with, on*); rather, poets more often choose to end on verbs or nouns, words that connect readers physically to the poem and hint at meaning. Consider how G.E. Patterson uses line breaks to add power to his poem, "The Natural World." Rather than ending on flat words such as "the" or "of," he ends on powerful words that teach us how to read the poem, words such as "shit," "leaves," "climbing," and "birds."

Lines and line breaks also determine how a poem is read. Long lines and enjambed lines often speed up the pace at which a reader moves through the poem, which might be exactly what a poet is after if she's telling a story or searching for meaning. Conversely, shorter lines and end-stopped lines slow a reader down, forcing the reader to spend more time with the words and ideas. Lines of mixed length will force a reader to move at different speeds through different parts of the poem, creating tension and a feeling of unease, which, again, might be exactly what the poet wants!

When a poet gathers lines together in a regular pattern (say, each group has three lines), **stanzas** are created. So along with considering line breaks, writers must consider how they want to group their lines. A **couplet** is a grouping of two lines of poetry. A **tercet** is a grouping of three lines of poetry. A **quatrain** is a grouping of four lines of poetry. Further, poets may choose to use **strophes**, or stanzas of different numbers of lines. While stanzas create a more formal feeling and force a reader to keep the images and ideas of the poem contained, strophes allow for play, free association, and a variety of emphases.

Simply because there is less on the page, images matter even more in poetry than they do in prose (see Chapter 3 for more); for similar reasons, diction is a vital poetic tool. The poet's job is twofold: she must show us a world by using powerful images, and she must do so with language that is precise, evocative, and surprising. While trying to focus on diction, many young poets often try to sound poetic but in the end sound confusing, awkward, or pretentious. A great way to find a poetic voice is to sound like yourself and write using words you use every day—yet seek to build your vocabulary, your language, and your voice. As an example of a poem that is precise and musical, yet carries the rhythms and diction of ordinary speech—that sounds like a real human being speaking—read M.L. Smoker's "The Feed."

Diction also plays a huge role in the music of a poem. And poetry is by nature musical. Many ancient Chinese, Greek, and Anglo-Saxon poems were sung, and the heavy use of **word music**—rhythm, consonance, assonance, and rhyme—only enhanced the lyrical nature of the genres. Because of this ancient connection, writers must consider not just how a poem looks on the page but how a poem sounds. And the various techniques of word music are the primary way we as poets pay attention to the musicality of our poems. Though the use of word music may be more subtle in some poems than in others, we challenge you to find a poem in the anthology that doesn't use it at all!

Rhythm, a pattern or arrangement of sounds, can heavily affect how a poem sounds, and is similar to the beats of a song. As you play with rhythms, consider stressed and unstressed syllables, as well as the rhythms of line breaks and different kinds of sentences. **Consonance** is the repetition of sounds created by nearby consonants, and **assonance** is the repetition of sounds created by nearby vowels; wise use of consonances and assonances can create rich sonic textures in poems. Some poems rely on **rhyme** as well, which is the repetition of sounds in the final syllable of a word. Rhyme can fall in the middle of a line or ring at the end of a line, and, traditionally, many poems used rhyme. Yet, to contemporary ears, too much rhyme, especially end-rhyme, can feel forced and stilted.

Finally, we should mention that creative nonfiction and fiction are determined by their reliance (or lack of reliance) on truth, poetry, on the other hand, can be either true or invented or a mix of both. For poetry, truth does not determine anything. Rather, a piece of writing is called poetry by how it looks on the page.

Exercises

The following exercises will help you practice the techniques learned in this chapter.

A. The term **essay** comes from the word **essai**, which means "to attempt" or "to try." What, right now, are you trying to understand? Make a list of ideas, situations, memories, moments, and/or places you are trying to understand.

Now, share your list with a partner. Can you offer your partner any ideas or possible ways to understand something on their list? Can they offer you an idea?

Now, using your ideas and your partner's offerings, start writing.

B. Think about the firsts in your life—your first backpacking trip, first job, the first meal you cooked by yourself. Take three minutes and list as many firsts as you can think of.

Now, pick one of your firsts and list all the sensory details you can remember from that moment. Try to be as specific as possible. Now, pick one of those details—ideally, a major one—and change it substantially. Now, start writing. Write this changed "first" moment and see what happens.

C. Think about one portion of your life. Maybe you are a hunter, a construction worker, a dancer, a chef, a hiker, or a softball player. Once you choose a portion of your life to focus on, begin thinking of all the unique terms that fit into it. If you are a backpacker, you could use the terms *backpack, tent, vestibule, water filter, hip belt, topographic map, hiking boots,* and *compass*. If you are a bow hunter, you could use the terms *bow, arrow, arrow rest, range finder, tree stand, quiver, broadhead, cams,* and *nocks*. List below the terms that deal with your activity.

Once you have that list, begin fashioning a poem that uses at least five of those words.

D. Look over your essays or poems. Are your essays **personal essays, lyric essays, research essays,** or **idea essays**. Are your poems **lyric poems, narrative poems,** or **prose poems**? Why did you choose that style?

Prompts

The following prompts will help you practice the techniques learned in this chapter.

A. Find a piece of **creative nonfiction** from our anthology that you admire. Study what the **essay** is doing and how it's doing it. Next, write an essay that does something similar. Maybe it is organized the same way. Maybe it shares a title. Maybe it focuses on a similar idea. See how your writing grows as you model yourself after other creative nonfiction writers.

B. Find a piece of **fiction** from our anthology that you admire. Study what the **short story** is doing and how it's doing it. Next, write a short story that does similar things. Maybe it is organized the same way. Maybe it shares a title. Maybe it focuses on a similar idea. See how your writing grows as you model yourself after other short story writers.

C. Find a poem from our anthology that you admire. Study what the **poem** is doing and how it's doing it. Next, write a poem that does similar things. Maybe it uses similar **line breaks** or **stanzas**. Maybe it shares a title. Maybe it focuses on a similar idea. Maybe it uses **alliteration, assonance,** and **consonance**. See how your writing grows as you model yourself after other poets.

11

One More Time to the River: Writing is Rewriting

Relevant readings

Poetry: Please see examples of revised poems at the end of the chapter.

Free write

Think about something you spend a lot of time practicing. Maybe you play a sport, say hockey or rock climbing. Maybe you are a gardener, a birder, a bow-hunter, or maybe you love crossword puzzles. Whatever the practice, consider the hours and days and years you've put into it, all the passion and frustration and slow success. Write about those hours of practice, those days of working hard and failing often. Describe them using all five senses and lots of images.

Now, share your free write with a partner. Are there any commonalities? Can you begin to say something about what it takes to sustain or improve one's practice?

Vignette

Some years ago I woke in Rifle, Colorado, in a cut-rate motel on the scrubby outskirts of town. Even now I don't know much about Rifle, save a news blip I heard a year or more ago about a restaurant owner in Rifle who was encouraging or maybe requiring—it wasn't clear—his employees to carry handguns while at work.

Anyway, when I woke and wandered out to the car to get a bag I'd left in the trunk the night before, I met a man—big shouldered and insistent, asking me something and pulling at the brim of his ball cap, trying, at one point, to look into the cracked door of my motel room—and I thought he wanted to fight me. It turns out he didn't (he was there to fix the ice machine), but the fact that I thought he did, and the fact that I was in a tough-looking little town called Rifle, that we were both perhaps too brusque in our dealings with one another, and that as we talked, as the situation diffused, we discovered we both grew up in ranching families—well, I couldn't leave the moment alone, for there in that gravel parking lot the worked-hard, ready-for-anything ranch kid I was met the quiet, thoughtful teacher and writer I had become.

As soon as I was home, I started work on an essay that opened with that moment in Rifle. I was after a kind of anti-climactic neo-Western showdown and so rendered the scene in present tense; though it ran three pages, I thought the pacing, dialogue, and characterization were all strong. The essay, though, took a turn after that; the next section wasn't a scene at all but a section of voice-driven reflection rendered in the past tense. I kept writing. I began using second person point of view, I began switching back and forth between present and past tense, I slowly worked my way not to that moment in Colorado but to a moment years earlier at a bar in an old logging town in Idaho, a moment far more replete with violence.

I was proud of the essay, which I titled "Out West," and showed it to Sean (beyond collaborating on textbooks and anthologies, we often critique each other's creative work). He liked many things and thought I was missing a few things and wanted me to deepen a couple of sections, but the thing he said I had to do no matter what was cut that opening scene. I, of course, tried to argue; I pointed out the great pacing, the snappy dialogue. It was a well-written scene, I tried to tell him, and it started the whole writing process! He nodded and said it still had to go, that even though there was a small thematic connection, the rest of the essay covered those themes already and did so with a stronger voice and with an organic, associative form that was far different, and far more convincing thematically, than the voice and form of that first scene.

Well, I put the essay away for a while, and when I finally got it out again, I saw that Sean was right. That first scene was just sort of hanging off the front end, like a tag on a new shirt. So I cut it, and not long after that the essay found a home in Orion Magazine, *where you can find it at their website.*

—Joe

Writing is rewriting

There's a wicked myth about writing: that the great writer ascends the mountain to wait for inspiration to strike. Once it does strike, the writer simply transcribes that revelation verbatim, and then brings the beautiful essay, poem, or story back to the rest of us, offering us the writer's wisdom.

This myth is not true. Not even close.

No less a writer than Susan Sontag tells us, "What I write is smarter than I am. Because I can rewrite it." Or, if you're not convinced, let's try Ernest Hemingway, who famously declared, "The first draft of anything is shit."

Hemingway is correct. Our first drafts are almost never our best drafts, which is why writing *is* rewriting. Writing is **revision**, which is where writers reenvision the piece they are working on—resee how it is written, arranged, and layered. Though some initial drafts may be closer to their final form than others, no essay, poem, or story simply arrives. It is developed, rerouted, worked over, worried about, rearranged, recast, trimmed, expanded, shifted, tightened, deepened, distilled—and in the hours and days and years it takes the author to shape the essay, poem, or story (or even this chapter, which has gone through at least six major revisions plus another ten smaller ones), the author finally discovers that she can say something wiser and more beautiful than she ever thought she could say. That's the power of rewriting, of the writing process, of revising. And from the instigating moment or image—like Joe's waking in a motel room in Rifle, Colorado—to large structural concerns, such as genre, voice, and point of view, and on to those final distillations of language, tightening the rhythm of a scene or sentence, writing is indeed a process.

Becoming a writer is a process. You don't have to pay any union dues, and there's no secret handshake; rather, like any competitive mountain biker or bird-watcher, you listen and watch and learn, you practice, you gain skills, and, slowly, you get better. The novelist Ron Carlson says it this way: "The writer is the person who stays in the room," meaning that the person who becomes the published author is the one willing to keep writing. And it's true; the writer is the one who, despite setbacks and failures, continues to keep writing.

While understanding writing as a practice may be disappointing for those who were hoping to be anointed as writers, for the rest of us, it is empowering: we don't have to be perfect right away, we can write messy first drafts (and second and third drafts), we can—with hard work and patience—turn messy early drafts into wise final drafts, we can improve our practice as writers, and we can call ourselves—as long as we keep writing—writers, even if it takes us months to construct an essay or years and years to publish a book.

Layers of landscape: The revision process

Okay, so we've got to revise. But how? Where do you begin? Think of revision as a way of noticing, describing, and deepening the layers of your piece. Think of your piece as a landscape. A particular landscape has various natural layers: the Douglass firs above, the understory of salal and Oregon grape, the mountain creek burbling through its steep channel, the trout in the swift water, the rocky, sandy soil itself, and the granite below. So, too, with a creative piece: there are the layers of image, imitated landscape, interior landscape, tone, persona, point of view, narration, voice, character, and more.

The first task, then, is to notice and describe those layers. Where are the images in your piece? What kind of images are in your piece—figurative, literal, general, or specific? Which senses do your images appeal to? Are there any discernible image patterns? Do those patterns serve the piece? As you ask these questions and jot down the answers, you'll begin to know your piece more intimately and intuit where you might need to deepen, shift, or tighten your piece.

Then, of course, you move on to the next layer. Where are you using imitated landscape? How would you describe the tone? Who, exactly, is speaking? From what distance and where? Do the shifts in voice serve the story? Are the characters complex?

Spend time with each landscape of your piece. Some will be vitally important, and you'll have to sharpen and add texture to these layers. Other layers, for the particular piece at hand, might not be (and need not be) as fully present. But attend to each. Make multiple passes through your piece, strengthening each layer as you go.

And remember that this process doesn't have to wait until you have a complete first draft. While some writers like to turn the internal editor off and bang out a messy but complete first draft before stepping down through the landscapes of the piece, others worry over the landscape of each sentence, scene, and idea, revising as they go. And some mix these two approaches, writing thousands of words one day and then puzzling through a single stanza in a poem the next.

There is no single right way to revise. There are many ways. As you develop your writing practice, you'll begin to discover what works best for you in the revision process. And be honest with yourself: if turning on your favorite tunes and writing into the wee hours isn't working, try carving out an hour of morning silence for drafting and developing, and then an hour in a coffee shop in the afternoon for revision. Attend to your process. Find whatever it is that helps you get the words going, whatever it is that helps you bring your critical attention back to those words, to the landscapes of your piece—choose whatever allows you to successfully draft, develop, and revise.

The lookout: Revising toward theme and argument

As you move through the layers of landscape of your piece in revision, beyond the particular craft decisions you've made, you'll begin to notice something else as well: you'll begin to see, hopefully, what it all means. You'll find in revision a vantage, a lookout, from which you can finally figure out what it was you were after in the first place (think back to our discussion in Chapter 7 about the river above and the river below). And for so many writers, Sean and Joe included, our first drafts miss the mark, miss the story. We have a strong idea, but we don't execute our idea well. Revision affords us the chance to resee, and perhaps know for the first time, what exactly our idea is.

It's wonderful when this happens, as it then allows you to even more carefully target your revisions. Consider Joe's vignette above about writing "Out West": Sean's central insight for him was that the first section was no longer necessary. It wasn't that the scene was poorly written from a craft point of view, and it wasn't that the scene didn't connect in some thematic ways. It was just that the essay no longer needed that scene to make its arguments about violence, tradition, masculinity, land use, and landscape.

Much of the revision process works just like this: you hike back and forth, switchbacking up the mountain, and you finally get to the lookout, where you can shade your eyes against the sun and get a good, long look at your essay, story, or poem—figuring out what it is you're after in a thematic or argumentative sense—and then, wiser (and maybe wearier) for the hike up, you hike back down, revising toward that vision.

Revision details

Though focusing on the layerings of landscapes and surveying from the lookout are powerful ways to revise, sometimes we just need to wallow in the nitty-gritty. Below we offer some keys to help you do just that. Examine the following:

Intros and Conclusions:

- Are they powerful? Do they move the reader? Do they tie to the ideas of the piece?

Setting:

- Does your setting affect the idea of your piece? Can we see your setting clearly? Does the setting match the mood? Do you use images to describe setting?

Characters:

- Do you use images to describe characters? Do you have the right amount of characters? Can you cut out any? Add any? Do all of the characters drive the idea of the piece?

Dialogue:

- Is your dialog relevant, powerful, unique, and realistic? Does most of the dialog focus on the plot, the tension, and/or the idea?

Scene:

- Do you use scene for all the powerful moments? Do you use images in those scenes? Do your scenes build up to the idea of your piece?

Image:

- Do you use strong, clear, powerful images? Do you use most or all of the five senses?

The River Above:

- Does the reader know who all the characters are, what is occurring, where it is occurring, and when it is occurring?

The River Below:

- Does the reader understand why we are reading this piece? Is there a single idea driving the piece? Are you using activism? Are you considering your audience?

Point of View:

- Does your point of view work for the piece? Does the distance of the narrator work for the piece?

Research:

- Have you done enough research? Is your research relevant?

Diction: Word Choice:

- Are your words clear and understandable? Does your diction match the idea/setting of the piece? Do your words sing?

Editing:

- Does your piece have a strong title? Is the piece of the right length? Do you use active sentences? Can you remove any clichés? Do you use only the right words and cut out unnecessary words? Have you edited your piece for grammar?

Hiking partners: Writing groups, workshops, and mentors

There are times, however, when clouds obscure the view from the mountaintop, when pass after pass through an essay fails to reveal a true idea or theme. What then? When Joe wasn't sure where to go next, when he thought he had a solid draft, he asked Sean to take a look at the essay for him. Joe turned to one of his writing partners, someone waking early each day and hiking those same steep trails (and Sean does the same with Joe). Our writing partners help us see our strengths and weaknesses, they help us learn to critique our own pieces, and they keep us honest—keep us writing, so they can keep reading! Though we often think of writing as a solitary act—and the writing process does require many hours of solitude—all writers have as well their hiking partners, friends, and peers they rely on to read their work and offer honest, insightful critique.

If you're in a college writing classroom, you're lucky. Take a look around. You've got loads of potential writing partners. Find a few like-minded peers and meet once a month over coffee to share work in progress. If you're a writer outside the classroom, check out the local library, bookstore, or literary center; see if there's an established **writing group** meeting there. If not, put out feelers on social media or ask around—you might have more writer friends than you know.

The key for building a successful writing group, though, is that you all commit to writing—to bringing a set number of poems or pages to your writers group—that you commit to reading carefully and critically, and that you all commit to listening to one another in good faith and with appreciation for the insight offered. A good writing group can be immeasurably helpful. We encourage you to start, or join, a writers' group of your own.

While writing groups are often informal and generative—that is, the pieces shared are very much in progress and the conversation revolves not only around the work in question but where the author might take the piece next—**writing workshops** are more formal structures that offer insightful, intensive critique. Often housed in a college, festival, or literary center classroom, a writing workshop involves the sharing of complete drafts, which everyone reads and comments on (usually in the form of a letter to the writer) outside of class and then discusses during a scheduled class workshop session. Workshop can be stressful, but it can also be incredibly beneficial. You often leave with loads of great ideas about where to focus and what to revise, and in workshopping other people's pieces, you also sharpen your own revision and editorial skills.

One more time to the river

It's like this: though most of us now twist a faucet for water, we once went to the river. We had to go every day, had to follow that good, old path, noticing the birds and the new blooms. Sometimes, after the spring rains, the water was cloudy. Sometimes, in January, we had to hack through the ice. No matter the season, though, we had to go.

Well, there is no shiny faucet to twist on and let the writing pour out. There's still only that good, old path. As writers, we go again and again to the river. We draft and develop and revise, revise, revise. We practice; we keep writing.

Revised poems

Below are the initial and final drafts of poems not included in the anthology by both Sean and Joe. Notice how both Sean and Joe made drastic changes throughout the process of writing these poems.

Sean Prentiss, "Enough"

Original Version: "After Forty-Five Days in a Tent."

> I sit each night in my tent & slowly unlace
> the long leather laces of my Westcoes &
> yank them from weary feet before setting
> the boots—reeking of a week of work in
> a single pair of socks—under the vestibule
> before peeling off my double-kneed Dickies
> & hickory shirt like a snake sheds his skin
> & fold & set the bundle of clothes at the
> feet of my bag—as if I worry that some
> visitor—Who? Our Forest Service contact?
> The lone backpacker we saw this week?—
> might stop in to whistle, *Hello.*

Only then, even after another sixteen hour
day building trail & then managing this
crew in camp—making sure they cook
dinner, sharpen the tools, get their hour
of education, do I snap off my headlamp &
all at once, as I stare out the tent, the world
becomes a long black veil of constellations
drifting through our night sky whispering
down upon us mere mortals their stories of
every damn thing I cling to—love & lust
& friendship—but as I stare upward, getting
lost in a web of memories, I remember the
other myths those glittering stars tell—war &

death & vengeance—mirroring all my fears for Kevin.

Revised Version: "Enough."

Each evening, as night spreads its long wings across our sky,
I sit in this tent & untie the leather laces of these logger
boots. I yank boots off weary & waxen feet that have trekked
many miles [of mountains, deserts & creeks]. I set these
gnarled boots beside the tent door, ready for dawn. Outside
in that greater world, crewmembers lay scattered beneath
towering cedars, murmuring quietly as they cantor toward
sleep. Alone, I peel off my hickory shirt & double-kneed
Dickie pants like a snake sheds skin. This bale of exhausted
clothes I fold & set at the foot of my sleeping bag. Neither
the boots nor clothes smell worse than the other. Or worse
than me. Three days ago, they demanded a laundering & I
hungered for a shower of soap. Now [maybe] we smell of
earth, duff, cedar, beargrass. Naked of clothes [& done with
the crew & chores at least for today] I snake into my bag &
snap off my headlamp. The world waxes into a long black
topography of celestial constellations whispering upon us
mere mortals stories of every damn thing I cling to during
these few quiet moments—love, lust, valor. The only stories
we have here in this congregation of tents are of a crew taut
like family, but autumn tired. Still, tomorrow, the sun will
rise over the Olympics. The day will grow summer warm.
But before it does, before even that first leak of dawn's light,
during that dark seep of last night, I again will dress in my

battered work outfit, again draw on knurled leather boots &
elbow elk skin gloves in a back pocket. I will break into this
dawn that appears more black than light, more sleep than
wake, more owl than stellar jay. Our crew will congregate
around the hush of breakfast. Then, slowly, like waking deer,
we will begin the day. For we have many miles remaining to
work before this project finishes & many days too until this
season ends, until this crew buckshots into whatever wild
darkness exists in that other world out there, the one of traffic
lights & ATMs & TVs selling everything under the sun.
[Except for the peace of dusk, the peace of dawn—they
cannot sell us that.] So for tonight, for our remaining nights,
this slow & quiet routine, it must be enough.

Notice how Sean made substantial changes throughout his revision of
"Enough." The title changed because the river below changed (from focusing on a violent incident one of his trail crew members experienced to focusing on the entire crew) and the very shape of the poem and the number of
strophes changed. Even though the poem is longer in the final version, Sean
worked to make the final poem more concise and sinewy on the level of
language. He cut out every unneeded image. He also focused much more on
language, on how the poem sounds and flows and how the images matched
the landscape of the piece. In the end, they are nearly two completely different poems, two completely different ideas even though the original poem
led to this new version. What other changes do you notice?

Joe Wilkins, "Sunflower River Road"

Original Version: "Driving Sunflower River Road."

We drive these roads further each day. I am sorry
for my silence. We are in Mississippi now. Can you hear
the cries of the cypress trees? Brother, these roads bend slow

around cane swamps. They raise a thick dust to hide
the end of day. I do not have any words
for these roads. The only words are theirs,

and they are enough. A cicada calls for the night.

Revised Version: "Sunflower River Road."

for my brother

This road bends around
cane swamps, raises

a thick dust to hide
the end of day. I am sorry

for my silence, ashamed
that I have words

for this road and none
for your dying. I can even

hear the green cries
of cypress trees.

Notice here that Joe's revision process was one of concision and focus. The original draft has a few interesting images and some nice moments of word music, but it's all over the place—it's not clear what's most important, what really matters. Further, though the tone is somber, even elegiac, it's not clear what is being grieved or elegized, and thus the pronouncement at the end— that the road's words are "enough"—is unearned. The final draft is far leaner and sharper, and the images and sounds that are left sing all the louder for this concision. The lines are shorter and gathered into couplets, which emphasizes the address, that this poem is from the speaker to the speaker's brother; further, by stretching the poem out and adding white space, the couplets also highlight the speaker's reluctance or, perhaps, inability to speak at all. And this leads to theme: it's clear now what's being elegized— the brother is dying, and the speaker, the poet, can't fully face this loss. What other changes do you notice?

Exercises

The following exercises will help you practice the techniques learned in this chapter.

    A. Write a paragraph about your writing process. What does it look like? Give us lots of details. Once you're done describing, now critique your process. What works? What doesn't? How has your process changed, or how might you change your process?

B. Write a paragraph about your relationship with **revision**. What's your history? What's your current status? Has it been a stormy love affair? Or have you slowly fallen under revision's spell?

C. Find a piece you've been struggling with and do a landscape inventory. Describe and then critique each layer of technical landscape in your piece.

D. Pick up an older piece of writing and read it with new eyes. What do you notice concerning meaning or argument? At the top of the first page, try to describe what it is you're after—the **river below**—in a single sentence.

Prompts

The following prompts will help you practice the techniques learned in this chapter.

A. Using your landscape inventory from exercise C, begin **revising** toward deepening the most important layers.

B. Using the piece from exercise D, read the piece one more time, making an X-sign by any paragraphs, scenes, or sections that either don't fit the theme or argument. Now, for each of those sections, either cut or revise.

C. Find your favorite ending from any piece in the anthology. Now take a piece you are working on and imitate that ending in your own words.

D. Take a longer finished piece of writing and cut it in half. Then cut it in half again. How has the piece gotten better? How has it changed?

12

A Trail Guide

Relevant readings

Creative Nonfiction: Camille Dungy, "Tales From a Black Girl on Fire, or Why I Hate to Walk Outside and See Things Burning"; Erik Reece, "Hell Yeah We Want Windmills."

Fiction: Lydia Peelle, "Mule Killers"; Benjamin Percy, "The Caves of Oregon."

Poetry: Joe Wilkins, "Seven Devils"; Maya Jewell Zeller, "Tire Hut: Seaview, Washington."

Free write

Think back to a time you were asked to build something—maybe that diorama in the fifth grade, or the wobbly footstool in shop class, or the poster for the campus literary magazine. How did you begin? Did you look at what they did last year for the poster? Did you use a list of step-by-step instructions for the stool? Did you follow models, forms, or templates to build the diorama? If so, were those models or forms helpful, intimidating, stifling? Does using a template while constructing something mean that thing was less imaginative or original? Where, indeed, do original, creative ideas come from?

Address these questions by writing a short narrative essay about the experience of making some particular thing.

Vignette

I've only been lost once. We were high in the Eastern Sierras, my soon-to-be wife and I, on the California leg of our pre-wedding road trip/camping trip/ anytime we see a mountain get out and go hike it trip. We'd driven through the night, through the heat of the Mojave Desert, and then into the Sierras that morning, where we made camp and caught a quick nap, then took off on the nearest trail. Perhaps a mile or two in, we saw below us the perfect blue mirror of an alpine lake. We couldn't find a trail, didn't even see this lake on the map, but we picked our way down the mountain anyway, navigated the rocks above the water, and finally made the meadow on the lake's far side, where we hung our clothes on pine stobs and plunged into the cold, blue waters. We spent hours there, splashing and swimming, then shivering and drip-drying in the mountain sun. We were young and very much in love—and here we were with an alpine lake all to ourselves.

We dressed as the shadows lengthened. From the map, it looked like rather than climb back up the mountain we could cut down the stream that drained this lake and pick up the trail below us. So, we followed the creek but soon found ourselves at another small lake—also not on the map. Had we hiked farther than we thought? Were we already in the next drainage? We weren't sure. We circumnavigated the lake and followed its outlet stream until the water dropped—horse-tailing twenty feet in a sudden falls. We thought to climb down and keep going, but we saw that once that stream gathered itself below, it took a hard right, the wrong way altogether.

And this is the moment I remember so well: studying the wilderness of trees and scrub about us, then the map, the wilderness, the map, and with each glance hoping I might find some correspondence. There was none, of course, and the shadows deepened by the minute. We were lost. I felt my reasonable self contract and my senses—the sounds of water and birds, the vivid, almost violent greens, the feel of the chill, skin-stippling air—expand. It was a frightening, exhilarating feeling.

Finally, I considered another possibility: that I'd misjudged the direction of the outlet stream by a few degrees, and we'd thus been traveling parallel rather than perpendicular to the main trail. So—alive, nervous, hoping—we cut left, up through scrub and rock and dark forest.

—Joe

A trail guide

We began this book, back in Chapter 1, "The Trailhead," and Chapter 2, "A Short History," arguing that to come to know ourselves as nature and environmental writers, we need to know the motivations, definitions, and history of nature and environmental writing itself. Our contention was, and remains, that as thinkers and writers we follow in the footsteps of those who came before us, that we continue to brush back the trails they first blazed, that we, by learning from those who came before us, make our way that much further up the mountain.

With this final chapter we want to further argue that following forms or models already constructed by previous writers, that traveling the same trails, isn't canned or unoriginal—but is in fact the very essence of creativity. Even the most well-traveled trails offer sudden, unexpected delights: an alpine lake, a glacier lily, perhaps a glimpse of a black bear. And, what's more, a good map and a clear trail can lead us into wilderness we simply couldn't access any other way. As Joe's vignette above reveals, even a quick afternoon hike can in a moment turn worrisome and potentially dangerous.

So, too, with the written word: we follow the trails and trust the experience of the writers who have come before. In studying and coming to know certain forms and models in intimate and careful detail, we might shift, upend, break, or merge those very forms. Possessing such knowledge allows us to veer from the trail and make our way down to the lake and still find our way back to camp before full dark.

While many of the historical forms introduced in Chapter 2, "A Short History of Nature and Environmental Writing," remain vital to the contemporary scene—especially science and nature narratives, environmental justice narratives, climate change narratives, and postcolonial narratives—others are less often used today. Further, nature and environmental writing is no longer just the writing of essays, but of fiction and poetry as well. So here we offer six modes or forms that extend our discussion from Chapter 2 and that you can use as maps and guides as you begin your journeys on the page and conceive of new territories to explore as you journey toward becoming a nature and environmental writer.

(Un)natural histories and sciences

The traditional natural history considers and investigates the natural phenomena—the flora, fauna, geography, weather, seasonal changes, and/or other natural facts, relationships, and processes—of an area or region with the goal of educating, as well as enticing and entertaining, readers. Most traditional natural histories feature a distinctive but measured voice, and the tone is one of intelligent, calm curiosity. Though readers might begin to know, via voice and tone, the writer behind the words, the writer seldom enters the story itself; as such, most traditional natural histories are penned in the third person.

While traditional natural histories are still written, they are diminishing in number, since we have explored and come to intimately know so much of our world. Yet a perusal of the works currently being published in journals and magazines focused on nature and environmental writing reveals a host of more complicated, edgier descendants of the natural history, pieces we've dubbed **(un)natural histories and sciences**. For instance, consider Maya Jewell Zeller's poem "Tire Hut: Seaview, Washington," which begins, as many traditional natural histories do, listing and cataloguing the particulars of a place in precise language:

> The shop is divided like the brain:
> on one side, dull metals lie crooked
> like limbs after wind. Men shout things
> to each other and no one. Buckets

of bolts line a wall where red and blue
rags hang from nails, already black
with grease. A generator
or tire balancer shakes the floor
as if the ocean were under it pushing
up, and the air tastes like batteries.
This is where the work gets done.

Yet we're not dealing with a beautiful, manifold natural place here. Nor are we dealing with a dangerous natural world. Rather, this unnatural history trains a keen eye on the loud, begrimed inner workings of a tire shop, a place we've all been to but perhaps never considered as poetic, as worthy of the attention of a natural history.

Further, in the final third of the poem, we begin to get a deeper sense of the narrator—of her claim on the place, and the place's claim on her, which makes the place not just a thing to know with the eye, but with the heart as well:

Outside is a half-barrel, steel
or some other metal, rust-colored now.
It catches the rain. My father and brother
keep it there to drown tires in,
to see where the leak is.
The water is the cleanest water
you've ever seen. No kidding.
You can look into that water
and see the mountain from which it came.

And finally, right there at the end, as we gaze into the water and see the reflection of the mountain, as we trace backward the route of the rain, Zeller's poem makes a final leap: from unnatural history to biography of family to ecological argument. Zeller wants us to understand the ways our unnatural lives—the hours spent thumbing magazines and listening to the thump of the tire balancer—are connected, always, to the forces and processes of the natural world.

Zeller's poem is a particularly instructive example of an (un)natural history and science: it catalogues the features of a particular place using careful, scientific language; it upends our notions of natural and unnatural and what is worthy of literary and scientific investigation; it involves the narrator as a character and so invokes pathos; and it makes an ecological claim. While not every essay, poem, or story in this style will meet each of these benchmarks, most (un)natural histories and sciences will display a number of these criteria, as well as subvert our expectations in their own particular ways.

The physical and the metaphysical

Remember the pastoral narrative? Those outpourings by romantic souls burdened by industrialization and so traveling to the edges of cities and towns to search for what remained of the lost pastoral world? While the pastoral narrative—in its privilege (Who has the time to wander around thinking deep, sad thoughts all day?), its romantic excess, and bucolic cliché (Another sunset?)—hasn't aged particularly well, many of the techniques and stylistic choices utilized in the pastoral narrative have. For instance, pastoral narratives made use of the writer as character and were often rendered in first person. What's more, rather than simply focusing on a landscape and the particulars of that landscape, the pastoral narrative explored the inner world, allowing nature writers to take on a whole host of aesthetic, emotional, philosophical, and ethical concerns. In fact, this dual concern, this valuing of both the external and internal landscape, is where—in Chapter 1, "The Trailhead"—we derived the very motivation for writing in the nature and environmental writing tradition: place matters, and so does our response to place.

Essays, stories, and poems that engage **the physical and the metaphysical** honor this understanding, though they do so in myriad ways and with more self-awareness than the traditional pastoral narrative. Let's take another look at Joe's poem "Seven Devils," which begins with the speaker, a version of the poet himself, addressing what seems to be He-Devil Mountain:

> Listen Mister Lightning Catcher,
> you old stone buzzard
> with your red head of rocks
> and rocks for feathers,
> I'm damn tired of remembering
> you. You say: *I will teach you*
> *mountains.* Get down from there.

And even here in the beginning of the poem, we begin to see the physical and metaphysical intertwined. The speaker sees the mountain as a buzzard, a scavenger, something old and insistent, but the poet then refuses his own metaphysical interpretation of the physical: "I'm damned tired of remembering / you"; "Get down from there." As the poem progresses, the speaker continues to search for the right interpretation, a truer way of seeing, yet he is shadowed, always, by memories of loneliness and loss:

> Here, a man listens
> to his own loneliness: his words
> ride their windy way back
> to his ears, he hears himself
> say, *Grass, cedar, father, wind.*
> Then hears it again.

In the end, the poet holds on to both the physical and the metaphysical, the rocky trails of the Seven Devils and what he still has of his mother's wise example and instruction:

> You hand-over-foot the scree slope up,
> goat walk the insane ridge. There's a buzzard
> in these rocks, or maybe it's only
> altitude. Keep walking. See Heaven's Gate
> far below, your brother just ahead. Remember
> her, how she held you safe above
> that snow-melt flood of mountain river: fatherless
> sixteen, furious boy, terrified man. Now,
> up the scree the monarchs stream
> in orange suicide. Their bones are only wind.
> Yours, you tell yourself, are music,
> a ringing down from mountain rocks,
> the fierce promise she whispered in your ear,
> that one truth: *Keep walking.*

Though writers address the physical and the metaphysical in a variety of ways, we can list a few criteria: first, and most importantly, the writer makes clear that the physical and metaphysical are inextricably connected, are in deep relationship, and are both necessary if we wish to truly know our places and ourselves. Second, while pieces in this style often move from the physical to the metaphysical, this does not imply a hierarchy: the physical world is not merely a prop; rather, it is carefully observed in both its sublimity and horror, and any resulting associations and metaphors proceed logically from those observations. Third, the excesses and assumptions of the traditional ramble are guarded against; while Joe's poem is earnest and emotionally affecting, he undergirds any creeping sentimentality with specificity, irony, and exacting language. Finally, the work is surprising and often challenging; it doesn't trade in received notions or easy clichés.

Explorations and encounters

If you pick up almost any slick, glossy magazine devoted to outdoor pursuits, you will run into at least one adventure article—an article detailing the author's death-defying pursuits in exotic, remote locales. While these stories might be entertaining, they are also, most often, formulaic and forgettable. There is no insight, no actual exploration; rather, these articles are the literary equivalent of a roller-coaster ride: lots of ups and downs and scary moments, but we still end right back at the beginning with a narrator who hasn't changed at all from her explorations.

We want to argue here that the true descendent of the adventure narrative, as well as the wilderness and preservation narrative, isn't the contemporary adventure article but, rather, any essay, story, or poem exploring or encountering some facet of the natural world that is new to the narrator or protagonist. We call these pieces **explorations and encounters,** and these are the essays, stories, and poems that truly offer readers exploration and insight, much like Meriwether Lewis and John Muir did so many years ago.

As an example, we'll use Benjamin Percy's short story "The Caves of Oregon," which opens with the narrator, Kevin, arriving home after work to find his refrigerator bleeding: "Two red lines run down the length of it—and then a third, a fourth—oozing from the bottom lip of the freezer." This startling encounter is quickly followed by another, at least for readers: Kevin and his wife Becca's new home is built over a cave, one of the ancient lava tubes coursing beneath central Oregon, and this is the reason the power blinked and the refrigerator was bleeding.

As they deal with all the thawed, bleeding meat, Kevin and Becca argue, and later that night Kevin wakes to find Becca has left the bed and is standing before the door that leads to the cave. Together, they explore the darkness beneath their house, as well as the darkness that has been slowly enveloping their lives: a miscarriage, a series of miscommunications, a marriage on the rocks. And they find in that darkness a way to be together again:

Both of them click on their flashlights at once. They blink painfully, seeing a yellow light with a few filaments of red running through it. The black liquid of the cave oozes at the edges of their vision as the world takes form and they stare hard at each other for a long time. Then, as if something has been decided between them, she grabs a fistful of his shirt and pulls him down to the sandy floor where she brings her mouth against his.

Like Percy's "The Caves of Oregon," explorations and encounters feature narrators and characters exploring, encountering, and engaging in deep, meaningful ways with wild, remote, stark, or strange places, animals, or other facets of the natural world. These encounters send the narrator deep into their own lives, where they explore as well the unmapped territories of the self. And the key difference between a clichéd adventure narrative and an exploration or encounter narrative is that, in the latter the narrator critiques both the journey and self; they recognize that all explorations and encounters change us.

Circling home, growing home

We are a culture that prizes movement, that believes in speeding down the interstate, that celebrates those who get the new job and move to the big city, that values above all else what's new and what's next. And this cultural obsession influences where we live and how we think and feel about where we live. Consider the fact that a recent poll by the Pew Research Center reported that nearly 40 percent of Americans don't think of where they are living right now as home.

Home. The very word calls to mind a whole host of associations—a complex history, a mythic geography, a bright, variegated emotional tapestry. Many Americans feel they are—by dint of history—immigrants, settlers, and sojourners. We move often. Our families are spread out across the country. So, where is home? What is home? Does home have to do with people or place? With culture or geography? With economics? With the accident of birth? What of those who loved or hated their first home, were accepted or not accepted there? Or those forced by environmental devastation, economic plight, or gentrification to surrender their homes? Can home be created elsewhere? Can it be made of the stuff of another place? Or of the people of another place? And what influence does that first home, the mythic home, carry?

Whether a cabin in the mountains, a farm on the plains, a house in a small town or suburb, or an apartment in a busy city borough, home is a question that has been taken up in myriad ways by a whole host of nature and environmental writers. Yet we, as readers and human beings, continue to search for essays, stories, and poems that address the questions outlined above. The stories that share this focus, that help us reckon with our own homes, are narratives called **circling home, growing home**. Due to the immensity of the questions, there is no single formal ancestor for these essays, stories, and poems. They might spring from agrarian, environmental justice, or postcolonial narratives. The key is that these pieces describe, memorialize, investigate, or somehow reckon with home.

Consider Camille Dungy's essay "Tales from a Black Girl on Fire, or Why I Hate to Walk Outside and See Things Burning," in which Dungy catalogues her cultural and personal history with fire and landscape. Interestingly enough, Dungy begins her discussion not with her childhood home, but with her time in Lynchburg, Virginia, where well-meaning white friends often invited her to bonfire celebrations:

> For the seven years I lived in Lynchburg, I occupied several historical planes at once. I lived in a community that was legally desegregated and essentially welcoming, but I (and it) retained the legacies of times when liberty was not a given. There had been plenty of lynching parties in that part of the country. I couldn't help wondering, while wandering through the southern woods, if one such event might have happened on the ground where I stood. I had no interest in reliving history, through memory or experience. Campfires and bonfires represented a conflation between the natural world and the human. The wood in those piles was innocent and yet acted out a role. Because I was afraid of what humans had done to other humans in those woods and on those tree-provided fires, I'd come to fear the forests and the trees.

It's only toward the end of the essay that Dungy circles back to her girlhood home in the "semi-arid hillsides of southern California, where the spark from a campfire, a stray cigarette, a car's exhaust pipe, or an insect burned under a magnifying glass could ignite a firestorm that will burn 100 homes, scorch innocent animals, and demolish thousands of acres of habitat." Here, in her first home, she discovers the thread of her personal fear of fires and forests, writing:

> I realized that as much as I feared the danger posed to my own person when I encountered white people around a fire, I also feared the sparks that erupted from the fires and the violence those sparks could visit on a landscape. The danger fire posed to a human and the danger fire posed to the natural landscape: I had conflated these.

Elegies and calls to action

Some years ago, Joe taught an interdisciplinary environmental history and literature course. It was an exciting, intensive experience, and the semester was filled with challenging reading and stimulating conversation, yet by the end of the course a deep sense of sadness had entered the classroom. Despite the advent of national parks, the banning of DDT, and the resurrection of numerous rivers and previously ravaged landscapes, the class was now staring straight at mountaintop removal mining, fracking, and climate change. One student lamented: "There's been so much done. And it's not enough."

It is, sadly, true. By the day we are losing species. By the month we are losing mountains. Year by year we are losing hope of keeping the Holocene a hospitable place for life, human and otherwise. And when we lose something, we rightly grieve. We cry out. And as nature and environmental writers, we cry out in the form of **elegies**, which are songs of mourning, songs that speak about and honor what has been lost.

Because of the ubiquity of our losses, elegies may in fact be the most recognizable mode of nature and environmental writing, and elegies take many forms: they might be science and nature narratives or postcolonial narratives; they might mourn the loss of a home landscape; others speak to issues surrounding climate change. Due to this variability of form, the elegy is characterized primarily by tone and voice: there is sadness in an elegy, and regret and irony and anger. We know, going in, that this essay, poem, or story is about loss, is about some part of the natural world that is slipping, or has slipped, away from us.

As an example, consider the opening of Lydia Peelle's "Mule Killers," a story that elegizes a dying way of agrarian life:

My father was eighteen when the mule killers finally made it to his father's farm. He tells me that all across the state that year, big trucks loaded up with mules rumbled steadily to the slaughterhouses. They drove over the roads that mules themselves had cut, the gravel and macadam that mules themselves had laid. Once or twice a day, he says, you would hear a high-pitched bray come from one of the trucks, a rattling as it went by, then silence, and you would look up from your work for a moment to listen to that silence. The mules when they were trucked away were sleek and fat on oats, work-shod and in their prime. *The best color is fat*, my grandfather used to say, when asked. But that year, my father tells me, that one heartbreaking year, the best color was dead. Pride and Jake and Willy Boy, Champ and Pete were dead, Kate and Sue and Orphan Lad; Orphan Lad was dead.

Though beautiful, by the end, Peelle's story is in its metaphorical implications horrifying: our hungers and desires trap us in unsustainable relationships and result in the ravaging of what is around us—more land plowed, more useless mules sent to slaughter, more bad, fast decisions made.

The traditional elegy, as we just saw, has tremendous power; we often leave an elegy emotionally devastated, and in that emotional devastation there is an implicit argument: we should not let this happen again. But many contemporary nature and environmental essays, stories, and poems make that implicit argument explicit: these pieces turn from sadness, from the description of what has been lost, toward what we might do about it. We call these pieces **calls to action**.

Much of the beginning in Erik Reece's essay "Hell Yeah We Want Windmills" reads like an elegy:

Recently, while the shadow of climate change lengthened and the lie of free markets unraveled, I had begun to doubt the promise of [coal] to deliver on a future I want to inhabit. No coal-fired power plant in West Virginia, nor anywhere else in central Appalachia, sequesters carbon, nor do they extract from the bituminous ore its mercury and asthma-inducing particulates. A 2008 report from the Government Accountability Office warns that U.S. carbon-capture research is still dramatically underfunded and underdeveloped. So for some time, "clean, carbon neutral coal" will exist in name only—a lie on a billboard.

But then Reece changes his tone, hitting a more promising note that evolves into a call to action. Reece writes, "I had come to Charleston, the center of coal country, looking for a new narrative."

Reece continues with his call to action:

The question shouldn't be, Why don't you move [from land that coal companies want]?, but What kind of economy will preserve this community?

The answer, I think, can be found right here, where the watersheds of Appalachia could serve as a model for a new economy. By its very nature, a watershed is self-sufficient, symbiotic, conservative, decentralized, and diverse. It circulates its own wealth over and over. It generates no waste and does not "externalize" the cost of "production" onto other watersheds, other streams and valleys. In a watershed, all energy is renewable and all resource use is sustainable.

The watershed economy is the exact opposite of a strip mine. It purifies air and water, holds soil in place, enriches humus, and sequesters carbon. That is to say, a watershed economy improves the land and thus improves the lives of the people who inhabit that particular place. It is an economy based not on the unsustainable, shortsighted logic of never-ending growth, which robs the future to meet the needs of the present, but rather on maintaining the health, well-being, stability, and conviviality of the community. To paraphrase Buckminster Fuller, the watershed offers us an operating manual we should have been reading long ago.

In the end, Reece no longer merely elegizes but calls us, the reader, into action, asks us to see the world (and our resource extraction and energy use) in a new light.

Breaking trail

While we encourage you to stay safe in the backcountry—and we want to make sure you know Joe and his fiancee did indeed find themselves on the trail just ten minutes after they left the creek!—on the page we know there are times when the marked trail no longer leads where we need to go, when we must strike out on our own, breaking trail, and risk getting lost.

Are you working on an (un)natural history all about your home neighborhood? Or on an elegy dealing with some pretty hefty metaphysics? Great. Read examples of both forms and use whatever moves might help, whatever will get you home before dark—and appreciate the vistas that that new trail might allow.

The key is to understand those who came before you, to understand the subgenres they wrote within. And then feel free, once you know the lay of the land, once you have your map and compass handy, to head off into the dark corners of the map, to explore new territories.

Exercises

The following exercises will help you practice the techniques learned in this chapter.

A. Look through five pieces you've written. See if they fit into any or all of these categories: **(un)natural histories, physical and metaphysical, explorations and encounters, circling home/growing home, elegies,** and **calls to actions.** List the categories below that your pieces fit into.

B. Look at which categories you have not used. Think about it and write a short paragraph on why you have not written in these modes.

C. Think about how you viewed **nature and environmental writing** at the beginning of this book. Now that we are near the end, contemplate on how your views of nature and environmental writing have changed. Write a short paragraph on this idea.

Prompts

The following prompts will help you practice the techniques learned in this chapter.

A. Look at your environmental writing pieces and categories listed in Exercise 1. Choose any piece and see how you can "**break trail**" and add another layer or subgenre to that piece. Then revise to add that layer.

B. Look at the categories you have not used (from Exercise 2). Write a piece in this category.

C. Take a piece of environmental writing and add a new subgenre to it. Take an agrarian narrative and add an **elegy** to it. Or take a **pastoral narrative** and add an **(un)natural history** to it.

Part III

Nature and Environmental Writing Anthology

Creative Nonfiction

Geology: An Investigation
Chelsea Biondolillo

He said, *Your body is like the Gulf.* And I blushed.

All towns start the same, at the edges where the freeway meets them. The billboards always advertise dentists and divorce lawyers—the bastions of new beginnings; the first buildings are reliably gas stations, fast food drive-thrus, and mobile home parks. Later, the heart of the place opens itself up and it is welcoming or it is not.

He meant,

of Mexico. It was the largest body of water he'd ever seen. When I strode into it, years before we met, I was stung by jellyfish and bitten by black flies. My body and that Gulf—are you kidding? I never said, later, I hate the Gulf, too. He was trying to be poetic. I was trying to convince myself to stay with him.

Instead, I fled him and his sliding, low-slung deltas. His melting into that shallow, tepid sea, silty ton by ton. I couldn't be a wife again. I disappeared for two weeks into Denali. I wanted to, but couldn't stay there.

*

Alaska is a land of accretion, not dispersion. And I need more, not less. A billion years ago, violent collisions built it acre by acre: a litany of groundscapes became an expanse as micro-continents were shoved into one another by volcanic eruptions and the shifting of tectonic plates. Thrust belts slid from magmatic arcs, and rock bit rock. Archipelagos, mountains, and valleys full of water were left behind. And then, once the collecting had slowed, its stitched patchwork covered the northern half of the globe. It was not cold, then. That came later.

Over coffee she said, *You have geographic solutions to your personal problems*, and laughed lightly.

That whole first year in the desert, a newlywed (digging down through the strata, now, the layers like colored silt and sand), I missed the sea—it was like an acrid taste in the back of my throat, that longing for rhythm. *It's not you, it's me*, I told myself. To him: *I don't even know who I have been here, I'm sorry*. What is the sound the wind makes when it blows through the arms of a saguaro? Which smell stings the nose more, salt or sage? My nightmares regularly featured drowning by sand; I woke coughing.

*

There are probably still two roses blooming like fools on Laurel Street between Napoleon and Tchoupitoulas. I still got homesick, then. The last flowers I planted in the dirt, anywhere, were those roses and some tulips I got for free in the French Quarter. I was trying to make a go of it, lay down real roots. *Right place, right time*, said the woman with the wide straw hat, handing me the bulbs, still damp from the soil in her window box.

I drive through Santa Fe—this time an escape route, rather than a lee. I count the shades of adobe, try to predict the street names and fail. I want to remember the mysticism I imagined a decade ago. Instead, I make a note: *the last time I was here, I was somebody's wife*. When does a change of scenery become a personality disorder? The DSM, mapless, offers no relief.

Maybe I'll move to Anchorage, I thought, scraping yellowed orts off the dishes he'd just washed, before putting them in the cupboards. I wanted to have learned from my mistakes; instead they felt like deer paths I would keep walking again and again to and from the water. I said for a second time, *I will never marry you*. He laughed because it sounded like a joke.

*

He kept the cactus and the lemon tree; I took the mother-in-law's tongue. Even our gardens reflect our secret aggressions, now.

In geology, an uncomformity is a missing layer of the Earth's history. It's a lack of proof, a century's worth of centuries blown away, settled under the sea or still floating in a slant of sunlight just this morning, when you woke up late. We know it's gone, because the layers below are jagged, like a mouth propped open. Sometimes, it's difficult to tell the chronological order of the sedimentary deposition: there are many ways for the weather to throw rocks around. There are always parts of the story left out.

Galway Kinnell said, "the killing was just one of those things / difficult to pre-visualize–like a cow, / say, getting hit by lightning."

And over and over I see him on the kitchen floor sobbing about some past lover and me with the words stuck in my mouth for months after, like the skin of a popcorn kernel,

this isn't going to work, either.

On the way out of town, the backs of billboards say nothing. From driveway, to side street, to artery, to onramp: departure widens outward as a crack in stone yawns from the point of torsion.

Pack Rat

John Daniel

It began with faint slow stirrings above the dinner table where I sat writing. The sounds were soft as pencil rub, so scarcely audible they seemed born in my mind, some obscure rhythm of thought, an idea faintly scratching its way to awareness. Then it ran. It skittered loud across the ceiling tiles toward the kitchen, and I knew we had a rat.

In the two-room shack on an Oregon ranch where I used to live, I'd had a whole succession of rats. There was almost always one of them in residence with me, rambling down to the kitchen at night to gnaw at a pear or rip a loaf of bread to a scatter of shreds on the counter, then scampering around in the attic on rat business while I tried to sleep. My neighbors across the road had the answer: a live trap, an oblong wooden box with a drop-door held up by a network of sticks. The rat goes in for the bait, brushes the trigger stick, the door falls, and he's a trapped rat.

It was pack rats I was dealing with, so the baiting was easy. Anything would do—a bottle cap, a matchbook, a wad of foil. I caught one rat with two nickels and a quarter from my pocket. Cheese or bread would have worked too, of course, but I liked the cleanliness of using non-food items. It was purely a business operation, the poor rodent done in not by bodily need but by his own sheer covetousness.

When I caught a rat I'd stick the trap in the back of my pickup, drive five miles up to Gerber Reservoir, and turn him loose. It was a fair shake, I think. Plenty of wild country up there where a wild rat ought to be able to live, but also, in the summer, plenty of fishermen camping in their motor homes—the fishermen who drove ceaselessly past my shack as weekends rolled around. If the rat needed human company, they could provide it. As soon as I got rid of one, of course, some kind of vacancy sign went up and another moved in.

I'd never had a close look at a pack rat, so the first one I trapped I wanted to see. I placed the trap mouth to mouth with a wire mesh cage, then tilted them together and shook him from one jail into the other. He sprang from side to side of the cage like a gymnast gone wild—frenzied, no doubt, by the blinding daylight he'd never been so lost in before. I was surprised how unrepulsive he looked. His black eyes bulged comically; the tail, nearly as long as his body, wasn't bare but furred with brown hair. His belly was white, and so were his feet. All in all, a pretty good-looking animal. He settled down when I draped my jacket over the cage, and when I turned him loose at Gerber he legged it straight to a rotting log and disappeared.

So I knew about rats, and next trip north to visit the ranch I borrowed the wooden box trap and brought it home. This rat wasn't getting into our kitchen, not into our rooms at all, but he was running around in the walls and ceiling enough to bother us at night, and occasionally he'd settle down to a long bout of gnawing—as if he were boring through the walls to join us, or chewing the electrical wires, as Marilyn imagined. It sounded like his passage to the world was in the kitchen area, so I set the trap in the crawl space underneath. In the morning, the drop-door was down. I lay with a flashlight and carefully cracked it. Nothing inside but the slice of bread and tea strainer I'd used for bait.

Then, as I started to reset the trap, I saw what I was up against. Oregon ranch rats were one thing; this Bay Area breed, it seemed, was something else entirely. Three notched sticks fit together to suspend the trap door, and one of them was gone. The smartass had not only sprung the trap from outside, he had left it inoperable.

I split a thin piece from a pine board and set to whittling, thinking of the first and, till now, smartest rat to have entered my life. Uncle Tom's home was a cabin on the Blue Ridge of Virginia that my parents bought as a weekend place around 1960. The cabin's hand-hewn beams went back to the early 1800s, and as far as anybody knew, Uncle Tom did too. He was a bare-tailed rat, I think, and big—though any rat would have seemed big to me then. He kept a dignified distance, mostly, unless we left some food in the kitchen he couldn't resist. My mother thought he was fine. It was his place more than ours, she said. We were just weekenders.

But my father didn't like the idea of a rat in the place, so he set out to kill Uncle Tom. One weekend he brought enormous mousetraps, powerful enough to break a rat's neck. He baited them with cheese and found them undisturbed on Saturday morning, and Sunday morning, and next weekend when we returned. And so, to my mother's disgust, he bought poison—the kind in the little cardboard boxes you open and place under sinks and in closets where dogs can't get it. These too went untouched, for days and weeks. My father bought a different brand of poison. This time, during the week or two we were gone, Uncle Tom found a pair of my father's boxer shorts and left it draped over one of the poison boxes.

After that, my father resigned himself to live and let live, or seemed to. But eventually a friend of his brought a wire live trap to the cabin, and next morning Uncle Tom was in it. My father and his friend spent a long time deciding how to kill him. The mesh of the trap was too fine to shoot the .22 through, so they filled a washtub with water and together plunged the trap to the bottom and held it there, work gloves on their hands, their faces pale. I saw the rat dart and bump the cage in his frenzy, and then I didn't watch.

Not only the first night, but two of the next three as well, the rat of my present life springs my trap and hauls off parts of its workings. I'm getting good practice in whittling sticks, but I'm getting no rat. And so, for lack of a more sensible idea, I pry off a piece of the kitchen wall paneling where his noises seem to be focused, and there's his nest—a foot-and-a-half mound of shredded insulation giving off a sweetly urinous scent. *Things* are in and around this hill of rat domesticity: acorns, a wine cork, bits of foil and cardboard, two razor blades, a package of Stimu-Dents, a ball point pen cap—one of mine, I'm positive—a nub of yellow pencil, and two of my whittled sticks. It's an odd feeling staring at his life-heap, this between-walls home he has made, not in the cottage and not out. I haven't seen StimuDents since I was a kid. How many rats have added to this nest? I feel vaguely guilty, as if I've violated a place I have no right to be…. But no, it's the other way around. I find the hole in the subfloor where he comes and goes-has gone, for now-and smugly nail a board over it.

For a few nights, peace. Then the scuttle of rat again, closer this time, in the wall by the bedroom doorway, which has no door, and in the ceiling just outside. He bustles intermittently for hours with his fine nocturnal energy, scrabbling down into the wall and after a while scrabbling up and across the ceiling, pausing briefly to gnaw now and then, as if suddenly remembering he should exercise his teeth. I'd rather be sleeping, but still, I hearken to him. He's on a roll, this rat. Sometimes I work that way myself, riding a nighttime wave from one piece of writing to another as each presents itself, finishing nothing but touching everything, everything fluid in my mind.

A few hard slaps on the ceiling quiet him; he makes whispery scratching sounds, then nothing. Back in bed in semi-sleep I try to imagine him, huddled silent in his own world separated from ours by an eighth-inch of wood veneer. What's in his mind? Is there anything, some dim meditation on what it means, those sudden booming shakes from below? What's it like to live in such tight spaces, such perfect dark…. I see him crouching, quiet, his muzzle faintly twitching, an aura of secret knowledge about him.

Sometime after we've fallen asleep he's rattling around again, so loud I think at first he's found a way inside, in the closet now, scratching underneath the bed. Occasionally he whaps his tail—it must be his tail, or maybe a foot—a quick percussive drumroll. With ear plugs and a fan going for white noise, we eventually get some sleep. I can still hear him, of course. His scratching and rattling and gnawing are piercing sounds, and after a while I'm listening for them, fixated, measuring the silences between his flurries.

The next two nights are much the same, and I'm at a loss. I've tried the trap again, both under the cottage and on the roof, and now he just ignores it. Much too busy for it, to judge from what we hear. I've plugged a few cracks and holes I've found on the outside of the place, to no avail. Or have I trapped him in the walls? Is he going to die in there—running maniacally to the end—and stink the cottage from his secret crypt? But the pattern of his noises, those bursts of activity with silence between, says he's coming and going unimpeded.

Finally one morning I wake up with a decision already made. After teaching I drive to the hardware store for poison. We would give him our walls, but we won't give him our sleep.

To place the stuff where he's liable to find it, I have to take down one of the wood veneer ceiling panels. I work it carefully, trying to loosen the nails without splintering the veneer, and finally, as one edge drops loose in my hands, a shower of acorns rains on my head and clatters to the floor. So that's what he's been up to. Acorns have been dropping on the roof and all around the cottage for weeks; it's a good year, a bumper crop. Admiring their mahogany varnish, we've brought a few inside and placed them in a basket on the bookshelf. Now I've got a hundred of them on my floor. Doing my part in one of the odder seed dispersal systems in all of natural history, I gather the acorns and heave them out the door.

When I'm not actually lying awake in bed cussing him and jumping up to slap the ceiling, hoping not just to silence him but to give him a concussion, it's hard to hate this rat. He's gotten a lot of work done, and there's something very winning about his industry—his business so sensible, it turns out, and pursued with such innocent vigor. He's got a sense of humor, too. He keeps me in my place, but he does it with imagination and impishness. I leave the poison boxes in their bag and replace the ceiling panel. It wouldn't work anyway. This rat is not only crafty, he's well-fed.

New World rats and mice, it says in my Audubon guide, compose the largest family of mammals in North America—nineteen genera, seventy species, nested in every habitat in the land. Nor surprising. If the greater clan is as canny and ambitious as our cottage mate, it's bound to prosper. Based on where we are, it seems our rat is probably a dusky-footed wood rat. Buff-brown, belly washed with tan. White toes. Omnivorous and nocturnal, like me. After mating, it says, the males live separately—so we likely have a husband, on the lam until the kids clear our. That's hopeful. Maybe he'll leave before long. But what were all chose acorns for? The trading habit, my book says, is common to wood rats. They'll drop what they were carrying to pick up something else, especially something bright. No one knows why, but I understand it. You can make something good chat way, dropping what you started with when something better flashes—collect enough flashes, and sometimes you've got a poem.

Our rodent-in-residence is collecting hard that night, restoring his stash. Now that we know what he's doing, the trail of his noises is clear. He drops down into the wall, then silence for a few minutes, sometimes half an hour. When he returns from acorn hunting he climbs the wall and skitters quickly through the ceiling. Sometimes—there's nothing else it could be—he drops the acorn he's been carrying and bowls it, or maybe bats it soccer-style, or noses it, somehow sends it rattling across the ceiling to its appointed place. And then he stops cold for ten seconds, a minute, three minutes. I have the surest sense he's baiting us, he's doing it on purpose, just daring us to slide off into sleep.

It's our house, I hear myself thinking. This rat has the run of the entire hillside, thickets and grass and intertwining oaks where he could ramble forever, and here he is clattering in and out some rat-door I can't find like a happy speed freak, bowling acorns for his pleasure ten feet from where we lie not sleeping *in our own house.* I'm tired and mad enough to rip the ceiling down, acorns, insulation, the whole damn thing, except I know it wouldn't help. He knows my house better than I do. He'd dodge ahead along his secret passageways, laughing as I tore the place to shambles.

But how *will* we get rid of him? We joke about giving him the cottage and moving to a Palo Alto apartment. We joke, and after dinner the next evening I go out back and set up the tent. When we turn in we're comfortable there, under quilts on a thick foam pad, and it's wonderfully quiet, just a hint of wind in the Monterey pine. Exile could be worse. Maybe tomorrow night we'll sleep out in the field, and the next night over by the big eucalyptus where the red-shouldered hawk likes to perch, and then still farther, ranging wilder and wilder up the Santa Cruz hills. And our rat, meanwhile, will gnaw out of the walls and roam the cottage, forgetting his acorns as he grows soft and paunchy on our leftovers and bread . . .

Well—there's justice in it, says the rodent in my head. We don't own the cottage, after all. We didn't build it. We found it more or less by accident, as he did, and nested it with things, just like him. And *he* didn't come from far away, either—he was born on this hill, of parents born here the same. But never mind his lineage. What about his generosity? He's perfectly content to share the place, asking only for the inside of the walls. Why are *we* so intolerant?

Because it's our house, damn it. He may have a valid biotic claim, and he may have won the cottage for the night, but I have a bigger brain, and I'm not done yet. I like sleeping outdoors, but no rat is going to *make* me sleep outdoors. We're not just weekenders, we *live* here. And if I can find his secret door, he won't.

It has to be under the bedroom wall. And so I spend the next morning prying off sheets of paneling and peering among studs and electric wires with a flashlight. There's a small opening through the subfloor next to the doorway, but it's more a crack than a hole. I can't believe a beast as loud as our friend could fit through that, so I go on dismantling to the end of the wall. The desiccated corpse of a mouse rests on a two- by- four ledge, but no hole. It has to be the crack by the door. I remember hearing, I think, they can supple themselves to pass through tight places. I nail down a plug and put the wall back together, taping instead of nailing the panel in front of the plugged hole. I don't know what's going to happen, but *something* is, whether I've blocked him in or blocked him out.

I'm hoping out, but of course he's in. In bed we hear him moving around the ceiling at half-speed, probably just waking up, and when he drops down into the wall for his first journey out I'm ready. I pull the taped panel just far enough from the framing to slip in a piece of two-by-four I've cut to fit tight between the two studs. I tape up the panel and he's a trapped rat, plugged below and now above. He knows it, too, because he's very quiet the rest of the night.

There's no time to deal with him in the morning, but I'm in no hurry. He's not going anywhere. My day passes in an aura of satisfied accomplishment. That evening, though, when Marilyn and I are home from work, I'm struck with doubt. This is the rat, after all, who has foiled and ridiculed my every attempt to catch him. And it's awfully quiet in that wall. I crack open the top of the taped panel and scan the bottom of the cell, using a flashlight and a small mirror. He's there, all right, nosed into a corner. But he looks unbelievably small—more of a mouse than a rat. A trick of the mirror, I suppose.

After all that's happened, I'm glad we've caught him alive. He's been a worthy adversary. It will be a pleasure to release him-many many miles away-to assemble his new nest and get on with his life. The trouble is, though, we haven't really caught him. He's trapped in his cell of wall, but how do we get him out of there? A fishing net might do the trick, if I had one, but I don't. Rummaging in a crowded closet, I find a small cardboard box, a little larger than rat-size. The best idea I can come up with is to hold it upside down and lower it over him from above. Marilyn is doubtful, but it's time to act. It's time to get him gone.

As things stand now he's out of my reach, so I put on my work gloves and saw across the taped panel three feet above the floor. Then, as Marilyn stands behind me holding a sheet outstretched—our safety containment—I rake off the top section and slowly lower the box. The rat looks a lot bigger and the box a lot punier as it gets closer to him, but now I'm committed. He squirms a little deeper into the corner. He's a caught rat, I'm thinking, when just as the box is about to cover him he explodes up my arm, launches from my shoulder past Marilyn's face, and scuttles into the bedroom and under the bed.

Marilyn is making guttural noises. I am standing quietly like the fool I am, who has not only failed to catch a cornered rat but personally presented him a convenient pathway into our house. The bed, a pine platform on cinder blocks, has lots of things under it-suitcases, pillows, a box of photos, bags of this and that. He's buried somewhere in that nest-clutter, probably feeling a lot safer than he did a minute ago. I get the wok cover from the kitchen, and with that in my left hand, hoping for another chance, I start removing what's there, tapping each item and gingerly dragging it out. He shoots out of the empty blue duffel just as I touch it. I clap down the cover too late—of course I'm too late—and he's under the dresser in the corner of the room.

Shining the flashlight along the wall, I can see him crouching, but I can't get to him. Marilyn and I look at each other. "You'd better ask Wally for his pellet gun," I tell her.

I stand in the doorway, in case the rat decides to run, but he's not going anywhere. He's crowding himself into the corner, trying his best to disappear. Everything in him wants to go back to the comfortable close-quartered darkness he knows. But he's trapped for good now, he's loose where he didn't want to be and where we can't allow him to stay. He's caught on the wrong side of our walls, too fast and too smart for us in our blundering ways to save him.

Marilyn returns with Wally, Wally with the gun, and we arrange ourselves for the finish. Wally kneels in the doorway with my pry bar in his hand, Marilyn stands behind him with the sheet, but of course the rat stays put. He squirms as my first shot hits him in the side. I don't know if the second hits him at all. The third shot kills him.

Walking into the field with his body in a plastic bag, though he's probably cleaner than I am, I tell myself it had to be done. I tried harder than most people would have to catch him alive. He was driving us crazy, and now at least we'll have our sleep back. It's all true, but I've never felt more thoroughly defeated. I think of all the times I've hiked the mountains or scrambled up desert canyons hoping for a glimpse, or if not a glimpse just a track or scat, some brief witness of a life not human or touched by humans. A creature as wild and intelligent and worthy as any in those far places comes to where we live, gets tangled in our sensibilities, and the best I can do is what Americans have always done. Necessarily, as any reasonable householder would, I trained my vision through the sights of a gun.

But it's not just the rat. He had to go, and remorseful as I now feel, there were many nights I would have gladly murdered him. The field is absolutely still tonight, no movement in the oaks or dry grasses. I can hear the whispered background surge of cars on I-280. Down the hill, something rustles. We still see animals here. A few deer, who browse the grass when it's green and stay close to our watered oasis in the summer drought. And raccoons, who are so adaptable they thrive in city alleys. Once in a while a coyote, the master survivor. But thirty and forty years ago, Wally says, when his was the only house for half a mile, this place teemed with animals. He and Mary saw amazing things. A pair of gray foxes would groom themselves on the porch of his study, six feet from where he watched. Once a red-tail flew across the patio wrestling with a gopher snake, nearly crashing at their feet. Then bulldozers carved the hills, new homes kept rising along new roads, the animals slipped away. We see remnants now. And when this field goes to houses, as it will before long, the remnants too will disappear.

A jet rumbles over toward San Francisco Airport. The night sky is never still around here. A few stars are out, washed pale as they always are by the diffused radiance of the greater Peninsula, ranging away to the north in a twinkling swath from where I stand. And closer, circling almost all around the field, the lights of neighboring homes shine steadily—porch lights, street lights, security floodlamps, lit windows, a constellation of human residence, rooms where people eat and speak and have their lives, where children grow. We need those rooms. We need the walls we put around us. But dropping the pack rat in the field, I wish we knew some other way of building them, I wish we could live in our human house without sweeping it so clean of other lives.

Tales From a Black Girl on Fire, or Why I Hate to Walk Outside and See Things Burning

Camille T. Dungy

I drove into the countryside outside of Appomatox, Virginia. I was going to a party at a friend's old farm. Thick-branched woods grew densely on either side of the road, absorbing all peripheral moonlight. Wind shook limbs until they waved. I didn't recognize these gnarled and night-blackened trees. Now and then something startling broke loose and knocked hard on my rear window, my moon roof, my windshield. An acorn, of course. Maybe a pine cone. A twig. Dead ropes of kudzu dangled here and there, and all my people's horror stories worried through my head. Why was I out in the country at night? Didn't I know better?

The path illuminated in front of me seemed to lead directly to a cemetery. I could see crosses staked throughout the lawn, cut flowers, newly upturned dirt. A white angel guarded the entrance. As I approached, the road turned sharply. I passed the churchyard, the church, more woods.

Behind the big house, I saw them. Though they'd seen me first. Seven or eight revelers, beer bottles in their hands and an old-time country tune still on their tongues, were pointing in my direction. Their bright skin glowed pinkly in the light of a ten-foot fire. They'd been expecting me.

In the broader light I could see bats the bonfire had disturbed. These were their hours to consume.

* * *

When I lived in Virginia, I associated open fires with historically informed terror. Many of my southern white friends enjoyed hosting bonfires, but I started to decline their gracious invitations. Though their gatherings often began with a pleasant hike and a lovely dinner outside, I could never relax on these outings. I knew the woods we walked through would reveal their malice because I was conditioned to fear. Eventually the fire would be lit and my friends' faces transformed.

For the seven years I lived in Lynchburg, I occupied several historical planes at once. I lived in a community that was legally desegregated and essentially welcoming, but I (and it) retained the legacies of times when liberty was not a given. There had been plenty of lynching parties in that part of the country. I couldn't help wondering, while wandering through the southern woods, if one such event might have happened on the ground where I stood. I had no interest in reliving history, through memory or experience. Campfires and bonfires represented a conflation between the natural world and the human. The wood in those piles was innocent and yet acted out a role. Because I was afraid of what humans had done to other humans in those woods and on those tree-provided fires, I'd come to fear the forests and the trees.

* * *

When the opportunity arose, I left that neck of the woods. I found myself spending the summer at an artist's colony in Maine. There, the legacy of racial violence didn't haunt me the same way. I could hike solo again. Deer in the distance filled me with wonder, not fear. Ravens warned me off their path and I felt no sense of personal foreboding. I could spend hours tracking wild flowers, losing myself in the dense forest, and never be afraid of who or what might find me there. I was, again, at liberty in the wild.

After a long stretch of such freedom, it began to storm. The rains lasted six days and all the residents of the colony were trapped inside. On the seventh day it cleared. After dinner, reluctant to return to the cabins we'd worked in all week, we decided on a party so we could linger outside listening to the birds, the rustling leaves and lapping waves.

The bonfire pit, dug expertly by the sculptor, was perfectly safe. Still, I couldn't get comfortable. All the writers brought drafts to use as tinder. I torched the one about the wild iris's melancholy glister under the moon. I didn't want to write about desperation anymore. The fire warmed all of us, even the dogs. The hound who ran the woods circled me twice before laying its head at my heels.

A painter found a log that looked like the torso of a man. It had a knot where the navel should be, a twig protruding from the juncture where the solid trunk branched in two directions. There was some banter about the facile ease with which certain artists impress human experience upon the natural world. This was a log, we understood. Still: "Man on fire!" some of them laughed. *We seek to personify everything when nature has its own, other-than-human entity.*

I diverted my eyes from the limbs that reached out of the greedy flames. The hand that extended toward me, whiter than ever silhouetted by the fire, passed me some wine. Everything around the fire was still wet from the rains. We leaned against each other watching sparks join the stars, flying heaven knew where.

Calm down, it's safe out here. I had to repeat this to myself many times.

***

You've been taught not to play with fire. Your whole life, you've known the rules. When you live in this country, you have to know the rules.

Yucca, ice plant, chaparral pea, Bigcone Douglas-fir: even the plants here make provisions for flame. There are those that hoard water, and there are those gamblers that reproduce best in scorched terrain. Don't tell me you didn't know. It's inhospitable here, dry and dangerous. A desert unless you own the water rights. Sudden Oak Death strikes and dead limbs litter the landscape. It's a tinderbox, this country. Now look what you've done. The whole family's in danger. The whole neighborhood. Acres of wild country. All the beasts and all the birds. You had to look. You wouldn't look away. A child with a magnifying glass you were. That thin-waisted wasp caught beneath your len's gaze and then those sparks and you too slow to quench the fire. And now, this terrifying blaze.

You knew. You know. You've been taught not to play with fire.

***

I grew up in the semi-arid hillsides of southern California where the spark from a campfire, a stray cigarette, a car's exhaust pipe, or an insect burned under a magnifying glass could ignite a firestorm that will burn 100 homes, scorch innocent animals, and demolish thousands of acres of habitat. From a young age I heard warnings about open fires. I was told to be cautious around anything that might ignite and people who find pleasure in starting a blaze. Just as I grew up aware of the historical dangers of being black and discovered outside, I knew to fear fire.

History is a crucible, but that night in Maine I realized African American history alone was not the root of my fear of succumbing to flames. Whether devastation is their conscious intention or not, within the context of my received history I read certain words and behaviors as potentially devastating, just as I know the sparks from any fire might provoke life-engulfing flames. History and experience have linked my fear of violence against the mind and body to those bonfires—and the trees and the woods that permitted them, the people who allowed them to blaze.

In Maine, I realized that as much as I feared the danger posed to my own person when I encountered white people around a fire, I also feared the sparks that erupted from the fires and the violence those sparks could visit on a landscape. The danger fire posed to a human and the danger fire posed to the natural landscape: I had conflated these.

When I encounter fire, these separate fears can become one and the same.

* Fire destroys ppl. (historically) and land
↳ "one and the same"

Nature Writing by the Numbers

David Gessner

Exposed: The Mammogram Myth and the Pinkwashing of America

Jennifer Lunden

Part One: The Diagnosis

On the day of my first mammogram, I walked through the sliding glass doors of the gleaming new hospital and fought the urge to turn right back around. I couldn't shake the feeling that there was something wrong about this rite of passage. Nevertheless, I navigated a series of carpet-lined hallways to the Women's Imaging Center and gave my name to the receptionist behind the glass. With an air of indifference, she led me to a small, windowless room, directed me to change into a johnny, and told me to wait for the mammography tech, Gert, to come fetch me. On the table to my right, beside a lacy pink photo album containing snapshots of flowers, lay *Be a Survivor: Your Guide to Breast Cancer Treatment.* I was forty-one years old, my nurse practitioner had urged me in for a baseline, and there I sat, complying.

It wasn't too long before Gert, a no-nonsense woman in blue scrubs, rescued me from the antechamber and led me down the hall to the mammogram room. As she looked over my chart, I confronted the machine: a big, robotic contraption with metal arms bearing various sets of glass plates that I knew would be used to squeeze my breasts flat. A little Teddy Bear in a pink shirt with hearts on it perched on the left side of the machine. On the right side was a picture of a cherubic, chubby-faced child painted on what looked like it might have been a small fancy box for Valentine chocolates.

I had not worn deodorant, per instructions, and even though I had bathed just two hours earlier, a faint odor of me wafted up when I slipped off the right sleeve of my johnny. Gert grabbed onto my right breast, positioned it on the plate, and stepped on the pedal to lower the clamp down onto my breast. She said, "Compression is your friend." I tried to think of compression as my friend. But in truth, I felt alienated from my body. I gazed into the distance and waited for it to be over. "Don't move," said Gert, and I held my breath while she slipped behind the clear plastic partition and pushed the button.

Don't move? Where would I be going with my breast tightly clamped between two glass plates?

Some of my misgivings about that mammogram can be attributed to a 2004 article I had read in *The New Yorker*. In "The Picture Problem," Malcolm Gladwell reports on the low efficacy of mammograms and the fallibility of the radiologists who read them. Researchers in one study, for example, found a broad spectrum of accuracy when they asked ten board-certified radiologists to analyze 150 mammograms. One radiologist caught 85 percent of the cancers on first look; another, just 37 percent. Of course, the downside of consulting the high-scoring radiologist is that he or she also recommended additional tests—biopsies, ultrasounds, or more mammograms—on 64 percent of the women who didn't have any cancer at all.

The other problem with mammograms, according to Gladwell, is that they generally catch slow-growing tumors. Some of these tumors are so slow growing that they will never make "cause of death" on a death certificate. The tumors more likely to threaten a woman's life are the fast-growing ones that emerge between mammograms. In a study of 429 breast cancers diagnosed over a period of five years, 279 showed up in mammograms and 150 did not, either because they were hidden in dense tissue or because they were fast-growing tumors that didn't exist at the time of the last mammogram. According to a 2003 paper that compiled eight different studies, mammography misses 10 to 30 percent of all breast cancers.

Gladwell notes, too, that mammograms identify substantial numbers of DCIS (ductal carcinoma in situ) tumors, most of which are not likely to metastasize. DCIS tumors appear inside the ducts that carry milk to the nipple. In one study, almost 40 percent of women in their forties who had died of other causes were found to carry DCIS or some other cancer in their breasts. Gladwell points out that since breast cancer is responsible for less than 4 percent of female deaths, most of the women in this study, even if they had lived longer, would have died of causes other than those tumors. The problem is that doctors can't tell from looking at a mammogram whether a given DCIS tumor will metastasize, or whether it will be one of the majority of lesions that never prove to be life threatening. So in 35 percent of cases doctors perform a lumpectomy with radiation, and in another 30 percent they perform a mastectomy. About fifty thousand new cases of DCIS are diagnosed each year in the U.S. Before mammograms, the diagnosis was virtually unknown.

Three years after Gladwell's essay appeared, I happened upon another mammogram article, this one citing a 2000 study by Peter C. Gøtzsche, MD, director of the Nordic Cochrane Center, an esteemed independent research and information center that provides healthcare analyses worldwide. In his review of all eight randomized mammography trials that had been conducted at that time, Gøtzsche found that the four trials judged to be of poorest scientific quality were also the ones whose data made the strongest case for mammography. The two studies found to have the highest scientific rigor showed no significant reduction in breast cancer mortality resulting from mammogram screenings.

Gøtzsche's overall finding, based on all eight studies, including those of poor quality, was a breast cancer mortality risk reduction of just 0.05 percent for all women submitting to annual or semiannual mammograms. This is not a typo. This is point-zero-five percent. Meanwhile, according to Gøtzsche, mammography also led to overdiagnosis and overtreatment, resulting in a risk *increase* in 0.5 percent of cases. "This means for every 2,000 women invited for screening throughout 10 years, one will have her life prolonged," said Gøtzsche. "In addition, 10 healthy women will be diagnosed as breast cancer patients and will be treated as such, unnecessarily." That means undergoing any combination of treatments, from radiation and chemotherapy to lumpectomy or mastectomy—all to treat a tumor that would never have metastasized or else would have disappeared on its own. Studies have shown that somewhere between 25 and 52 percent of all breast cancers detected by mammography would have disappeared spontaneously if simply left alone.

Because breast cancer survival rates have increased significantly in recent years due to more effective treatment, Gøtzsche now contends that mammography screening no longer reduces the risk of dying from breast cancer at all.

As a woman in her early forties, I had come to think of my body as an ecosystem, and was determined to exert as much control as I could over what I inhaled, ingested, and submitted to medically. I resisted that mammogram because everything I'd read indicated that I was more likely to be overdiagnosed than I was to have my life saved by early detection. It didn't occur to me to think at all about the radiation. But it should have. Americans are now exposed to seven times more radiation than they were in 1980. And scientists agree there is no such thing as a safe dose.

The National Center for Environmental Health, a division of the Centers for Disease Control and Prevention (CDC), categorizes ionizing radiation—the kind emitted during mammograms (as well as other X-rays and CT scans)—as an environmental hazard. According to the Breast Cancer Fund's report *State of the Evidence: The Connection Between Breast Cancer and the Environment*, exposure to ionizing radiation is the "best- and longest-established environmental cause of human breast cancer." Simply put, this means that the very test meant to save women from the ravages of breast cancer may over time actually *increase* their risk of the disease. Ionizing radiation promotes the DNA damage that causes cancer stem cells to form. It also triggers mutation of the p53 suppressor gene—known as the "guardian angel gene"—preventing it from doing its job, which is to suppress tumors by thwarting genome mutation. In essence, ionizing radiation, just like any other pollutant, upsets the delicate balance of the human body.

Each mammogram typically exposes a woman to 0.1 to 0.2 radiation absorbed doses, or rads. Since 1972, the National Academy of Sciences has maintained that each rad of exposure increases the overall risk of breast cancer by 1 percent. Forty mammograms add up to a total of four to eight rads in a woman's lifetime, which translates to an increased risk of 4 to 8 percent. Several recent studies indicate, however, that the mutational risk of low-dose radiation, such as the kind used in mammograms, is actually two to six times higher than previously thought.

Damage from radiation is cumulative, and can amplify the effects of other carcinogens. Because breast tissue, like fetal tissue, is extremely sensitive to radiation, even small doses are harmful. And because younger women's DNA is more easily damaged by radiation, the younger a woman is when her breasts are first exposed, the higher the risks.

And at least once in all those years of mammograms, the patient is likely to get a call-back. The *New England Journal of Medicine* reported that out of ten mammograms, a woman has a 50 percent chance of at least one false positive. That means another mammogram, and probably also an ultrasound. And maybe even a biopsy—a sometimes painful procedure whereby some or all of a suspicious breast growth is either cut out or suctioned out through a needle to be evaluated by a pathologist.

Three quarters of all biopsies ordered by concerned radiologists come up benign.

For years, the U.S. government, along with the American Cancer Society, the National Cancer Institute, and the American College of Radiology, advocated annual to biennial mammograms for women starting at age forty. But then the research came in, and people like Gladwell started sounding the alarms. In 2009, the United States Preventive Services Task Force—a panel of experts in evidence-based medicine—changed the guidelines to recommend that women start mammogram screening at age fifty and get a mammogram every two years thereafter up to the age of seventy-four, thereby cutting radiation exposure by about two-thirds, and the risk of overdiagnosis nearly in half. (These new guidelines do not apply to women with increased risk for breast cancer due to a gene mutation. However, some research indicates that that very mutation causes its carriers to be even more vulnerable to radiation-triggered cancer than the general population.)

The Task Force report, published in the esteemed *Annals of Internal Medicine*, concludes that "the decision to start regular, biennial screening mammography before the age of 50 years should be an individual one and take into account patient context, including the patient's values regarding specific benefits and harms."

The new guidelines provoked a furor of confusion. It didn't make sense to people that less screening could be equally effective. People suspected the U.S. government of putting economics ahead of women's health. Women in their forties came out of the woodwork to tell reporters about how their lives were saved by mammograms.

Dr. Otis Brawley, chief medical officer of the American Cancer Society (ACS), responded to the Task Force report with a confession: "I'm admitting that American medicine has overpromised when it comes to screening. The advantages to screening have been exaggerated." Nonetheless, the ACS maintained its stance that mammograms should begin at forty.

In an interview with Terry Gross on National Public Radio, Dr. Marisa Weiss, a breast cancer survivor, breast oncologist, and founder of the website breastcancer.org, countered the Task Force, saying its decisions were based on "old-fashioned studies using old-fashioned technology: film mammography instead of what we have today, which is digital mammography. And they use that old-fashioned literature to make futuristic predictions." In fact, she said, "it is the younger woman who is going to derive the greatest benefit from today's technology." Indeed, in 2005, a comparative study found that digital mammography was "significantly better" than film mammography at detecting breast cancer in young women and women with dense breasts.

That may sound like good news for some. But better imaging doesn't solve the radiation problem, and there's reason to believe that it may actually increase the risk of overdiagnosis.

Two days after my mammogram, the telephone rings.

"Could I speak to Jennifer Lunden, please?"

"This is she."

"Jennifer, this is Bonnie Raymond calling from Mercy Hospital. The radiologist has asked me to give you a call because he found a suspicious mass on your right breast, and he wants you to come back for a follow-up screening."

Something inside me freezes.

"Oh," I say. "Okay."

"Can you come in on Monday, March second, at nine a.m.?"

"Yes ... uh ... yeah, I can do that."

I hang up the phone, lie down on my bed, and think about the radiologists in the Gladwell essay. I think about Gøtzsche's data, and about slow-growing tumors.

But what if they find something? Then where will I be with all my facts?

I return to the hospital on the appointed day with an odd mix of resignation and resentment. My mammography tech, Carney, whose cheeriness is a welcome contrast to Gert's all-business demeanor, points out the little white spot on my X-ray and says, "It might be nothing, but it would help to look at it from a few additional angles." She tells me her grandmother died from breast cancer because she wouldn't go to the doctor, even after she found a lump. "It's amazing how much you can miss someone," she says wistfully, as she slides back the curtain to exit the room.

This time, the hospital has scheduled me for an ultrasound as well. Another room, another machine. The tech has a soft southern drawl and wears orange scrubs bearing the logo for the Dallas Cowboys. She applies a cold gel to my breast and moves the paddle across it while she scrutinizes the monitor. Back and forth. Back and forth. I stare up at the ceiling, which is painted sky blue with puffy cumulous clouds, and say, "So, when you do this, is it sort of like dredging the lake for bodies?"

"Sort of," she replies.

Finally, after two hours of bouncing from room to room and submitting my right breast to various forms of imaging, the verdict, delivered by the Dallas Cowboys fan, is in. Everything is fine, she says. Two benign cysts.

Benign.

A week later, a letter from the hospital arrives in the mail, the results typed in all caps, immediately following three alarming little asterisks:

***THERE IS AN AREA ON YOUR RECENT MAMMOGRAM THAT WE BELIEVE IS NORMAL. *HOWEVER, IN SIX MONTHS YOU SHOULD HAVE A FOLLOW-UP MAMMOGRAM TO CONFIRM THAT THIS AREA HAS NOT CHANGED.*

But I have already promised myself and my breasts that I am not going back.

Part Two: The Cure

The National Cancer Institute's online breast cancer risk-assessment calculator asks just nine questions. When I plugged in my information, I learned, perhaps predictably given the limited survey, that my results were exactly average. At age forty-one, my risk of breast cancer was 0.7 percent.

While I was relieved to see that my risk was so low, overall I was disappointed with the experience, because the risk-assessment calculator did not ask what I have come to know are very important questions when calculating a woman's risk for breast cancer. For instance, it didn't ask about my history of radiation exposure from X-rays, CT scans, and airport scanners. It did not ask how many cosmetic products I wear, whether I am exposed to air fresheners, what kinds of cleaning products I use. It didn't ask if I've used birth control pills, and if so, for how long. There were no questions at all about endocrine-disrupting compounds or carcinogens. And none about my diet, my body-mass index, or how much I exercise.

Despite the prominence of breast cancer in our media and our culture, these questions are largely missing from the conversation.

Charlotte Haley wanted to change that. By the time she was sixty-eight, Haley had watched her grandmother battle breast cancer, and then her sister, and, finally, even her daughter. She was outraged by what seemed to be a dearth of research on how to prevent the disease. One day, she sat down at her dining-room table with some spools of peach-colored ribbon, a pair of scissors, and hundreds of little cards bearing this message: "The National Cancer Institute annual budget is $1.8 billion, only 5 percent goes for cancer prevention. Help us wake up our legislators and America by wearing this ribbon." It was 1990. She sent her ribbons to prominent women all over the country, from former first ladies to Dear Abby, hoping to effect a sea change in the way the breast cancer epidemic was being addressed.

Two years later, as *Self* editor Alexandra Penney was busy preparing the magazine's second annual Breast Cancer Awareness Month issue, she had her own ribbon idea. What if she took a page from the HIV movement and created a ribbon to promote breast cancer awareness? And what if Estée Lauder—whose senior corporate vice president, Evelyn Lauder, had guest edited the previous year's issue—distributed the ribbon at its cosmetic counters?

When Penney learned of Haley's campaign, she called her up and asked her to join forces with *Self*. But Haley declined, saying Penney's plan was too commercial. So Penney consulted with *Self* magazine's lawyers, who recommended she choose another color for her ribbon. With the help of a focus group tasked with identifying the color that was most reassuring and least threatening, she chose pink. That year, Estée Lauder distributed 1.5 million ribbons, and the pink ribbon movement was born.

Twenty-one years later, the emblem is as ubiquitous as the Nike logo or the golden arches. In "Welcome to Cancerland: A Mammogram Leads to a Cult of Pink Kitch," critic and breast cancer survivor Barbara Ehrenreich lists what she describes as a "cornucopia" of pink ribbon products:

> You can dress in pink-beribboned sweatshirts, denim shirts, pajamas, lingerie, aprons, loungewear, shoelaces, and socks; accessorize with pink rhinestone brooches, angel pins, scarves, caps, earrings, and bracelets; brighten up your home with breast-cancer candles, stained-glass pink-ribbon candleholders, coffee mugs, pendants, wind chimes, and night-lights; pay your bills with special Breast Checks or a separate line of Checks for the Cure.

Stacy Malkan, author of *Not Just a Pretty Face: The Ugly Side of the Beauty Industry*, adds a host of cosmetics to the list: "We can 'shower for a cure' with pink ribbon gel, dust our cheeks with 'Hint of a Cure' blush and 'Kiss Good-Bye to Breast Cancer' with Avon lipstick."

Through the pink ribbon, corporate America has embraced cause-related marketing—reframing shopping as a way to fight disease. Estée Lauder blazed the trail, making breast cancer its cause célèbre. Avon and Revlon followed. Now, companies as diverse as Clorox, Evian, Ford, Mars, and American Airlines leverage the marketing power of the pink ribbon. Even agricultural biotechnology monolith Monsanto has jumped on the pink ribbon bandwagon. In 2009, a seed-development company called Seminis (a Monsanto subsidiary) launched a new variety of cherry tomato called the

Pink Pearl, which was sold in packaging displaying—you guessed it—the pink ribbon.

In terms of visibility, the campaign has been a colossal success. What it is doing for women's health may be harder to quantify. For one thing, the pink ribbon is unlicensed and unregulated. Which means not only that any company can use the symbol to sell its products, but that those companies don't actually have to commit a dime to breast cancer research. Purchasing Procter & Gamble's limited edition pink Swiffer sweeper, for example (released in October of 2009), wouldn't have resulted in any money at all being donated for breast cancer research or detection—unless you also sent in a coupon from the company's brandSAVER coupon book, which was distributed to newspapers on September 27 of that year. And then? Procter & Gamble donated two cents from your purchase to the National Breast Cancer Foundation.

Some companies are more generous than others. Estée Lauder's pink ribbon lipstick and blusher raised $120,000 for the Breast Cancer Research Foundation (which was founded by Evelyn Lauder) between 1993 and 1995. And Evelyn Lauder, herself a breast cancer survivor, personally raised much of the $13.6 million necessary to build the Evelyn H. Lauder Breast Center at the Memorial Sloan-Kettering Cancer Center. Avon, Revlon, and Estée Lauder all donate funds to sponsor breast cancer awareness events.

It is surprising, given their commitment to the cause, that all three cosmetics companies would manufacture and market products with ingredients that include hormone disruptors and other suspected carcinogens. But both Revlon and Estée Lauder were singled out in the Environmental Working Group's 2005 *Skin Deep* report for using toxic ingredients, scoring eighth and ninth, respectively, on the "Top 20 Brands of Concern." All three companies—Avon, Revlon, and Estée Lauder—declined to sign the Compact for Safe Cosmetics, a pledge to produce personal-care products that are free of chemicals known or strongly suspected of causing cancer, mutation, or birth defects. In fact, through their trade association, the Personal Care Products Council, all three companies opposed a California bill that would require cosmetics manufacturers to disclose their use of chemicals linked to cancer or birth defects.

The hard truth is that a market-based approach to the breast cancer issue falls dramatically short when it comes to anything that might pose a threat to the corporate bottom line.

Why are we so fixated on awareness, anyway? Aren't we all aware by now that breast cancer exists? That it is a bad disease? That it touches the lives of far too many women?

And why this fetishizing of mammograms? It is a testament to the monumental success of the breast cancer awareness movement that the majority of women continue to get annual mammograms despite the U.S. Preventive Services Task Force's revised recommendations. According to a study published in April of this year in the peer-reviewed journal *Cancer*, nearly half of all women in their forties are still flocking to imaging centers all over the country. Even more troubling is the fact that all this awareness has somehow led 68 percent of women to believe that mammograms actually prevent cancer. But mammograms don't prevent cancer. *Prevention* prevents cancer.

There are organizations, such as Breast Cancer Action and the Breast Cancer Fund, that are dedicated to preventing cancer through ferreting out its causes, empowering women to make healthier choices, and pressuring the U.S. government to change the policies that put all of us at risk. But why do their efforts seem so small in the sea of pink?

Answer: corporate sponsorship.

It is illuminating to examine the key players in National Breast Cancer Awareness Month. Or perhaps I should say "key player," because for a long time there was just one: Zeneca, the pharmaceutical giant that became known as AstraZeneca following a merger in 1999. On the surface, the company's decision to market and fund National Breast Cancer Awareness Month appears philanthropic. But when I learned that AstraZeneca is the maker of Tamoxifen, the most widely prescribed breast cancer drug on the planet, suddenly the focus on awareness seemed less than benevolent. Because the greater the number of women diagnosed, the greater the sales of AstraZeneca's star drug.

Zeneca launched National Breast Cancer Awareness Month—and the slogan "Early detection is the best protection"—in 1985, and for the first few years the corporation was its sole funder. It still wields control over the marketing. Which means it wields control over the message. And the message is this: Breast cancer is an individual problem and an individual responsibility. The sensible woman gets annual mammograms and, when diagnosed, seeks cancer treatment.

Early detection is a gold mine for the drug company. In a 2002 PowerPoint presentation, Brent Vose, then head of oncology for AstraZeneca, described the corporation as having a "unique franchise in breast and prostate cancer," and said that "the move into early disease represents an enormous expansion of the potential market."

So prevention doesn't get much attention during National Breast Cancer Awareness Month. Nor does the rampant production and marketing of products that contain ingredients known or suspected to cause cancer.

According to natural health advocate Tony Isaacs, Zeneca itself did not exactly have a stellar record when it came to carcinogenic products. The agrochemical arm of the company produced pesticides such as Paraquat and Fusilade—both classified by the Environmental Protection Agency (EPA) as "possible human carcinogens"—and in 1994 it introduced Acetochlor, which was classified as a "probable human carcinogen." Zeneca's now-defunct parent company, Imperial Chemical Industries, was the owner of what was once identified as the third-largest source of potentially cancer-causing pollution in the U.S. In 1990, the company was named in a lawsuit by the federal government for allegedly dumping DDT and PCBs into the harbors in both Los Angeles and Long Beach, and in 1996 it released fifty-three thousand pounds of recognized carcinogens into the air.

Why eliminate cancer-causing chemicals from your product line when you can profit from them coming and going? In 1997, sales of Acetochlor, *the probable human carcinogen*, accounted for approximately $300 million in profits for Zeneca, while sales of Tamoxifen, *the cancer-fighting drug*, added up to about $500 million. "Clearly, cancer prevention would conflict with Zeneca's business plan," wrote Peter Montague in *Rachel's Environment and Health Weekly*. Other corporations that sell both pharmaceuticals and pesticides include Aventis, Dow Chemical, DuPont, Merck, and Monsanto.

But there's plenty of conflict of interest to go around when it comes to the pinkwashing of America. Susan G. Komen for the Cure, a nonprofit that sits alongside AstraZeneca on the list of Breast Cancer Awareness Month sponsors, owns stock in several pharmaceutical companies, including AstraZeneca, and also in General Electric (GE), one of the largest makers of mammogram machines in the world.

In St. Louis, Missouri, the Race for the Cure is sponsored in part by Monsanto, whose genetically modified crops are almost singlehandedly responsible for tripling the use of the herbicide glyphosate since 1997, when its Roundup Ready seeds were first introduced. Until 2008, Monsanto was also the producer and distributor of rBGH, the artificial hormone given to cows to make them produce more milk. Because rBGH has been linked to breast cancer and other health problems in humans, it has been banned in Canada, Australia, Japan, and all twenty-seven countries of the European Union—but not in the U.S.

DuPont, which supplies much of the film used in mammography machines, is also well served by the National Breast Cancer Awareness Month push for early and frequent mammograms. A contributor to the American Cancer Society (ACS) and one of the world's largest chemical companies, DuPont rivals GE—another ACS supporter—for Superfund sites.

Even the American Cancer Society itself—whose board members, over the years, have held ties to the Pharmaceutical Research and Manufacturers of America, to drug companies such as GlaxoSmithKline, and to industries that produce carcinogenic products, such as the Sherwin-Williams Company (think paint stripper)—is not free from blame. With reported annual net assets of over $1.5 billion, the ACS "is more interested in accumulating wealth than saving lives," says the nation's leading charity watchdog, the *Chronicle of Philanthropy*. The ACS has a long history of obfuscating links between chemicals and cancer, according to an article in the *International Journal of Health Services*, and was conspicuously silent on California's Cosmetics Safety Act, which passed without the nonprofit's support in 2005. The Cancer Prevention Coalition says the ACS allocates under 0.1 percent of its annual budget to investigating environmental causes of cancer. Five radiologists have served as its president.

More recently, there is some evidence that the ACS is beginning to give prevention its due. In 2009, it published a position statement recognizing "the essential role of cancer prevention in reducing the burden of disease, suffering, and death from cancer." However, it's hard to imagine how much headway the ACS can make on prevention when its major donors include companies like DuPont and AstraZeneca.

The Cancer Industrial Complex—that's what Barbara Ehrenreich calls "the multinational corporate enterprise that with the one hand doles out carcinogens and disease and, with the other, offers expensive semi-toxic pharmaceutical treatments." Given that breast cancer treatment is a $16.5 billion-a-year industry, it's easy to see why Ehrenreich calls the disease "the darling of corporate America."

Of course, if we're serious about trying to prevent breast cancer, we need to figure out what causes it. Studies indicate that fewer than 30 percent of breast cancers are genetically based. And what of the other 70 percent? Exact figures are uncertain, but researchers say that exposure to radiation and chemicals, as well as poor diet, high body fat, lack of exercise, and hormone replacement therapy, are all likely culprits. Even those cancers with a genetic basis may have been triggered into full expression by risk factors such as these.

It is difficult to pinpoint just how many breast cancers are caused by chemical exposures. Carcinogenic chemicals insinuate themselves surreptitiously, and their impact on the body makes its appearance so long after the fact that people rarely make the connection. According to testing done by the Centers for Disease Control and Prevention, we all have some combination of more than 212 industrial chemicals—including at least six known to cause cancer and dozens more that have been linked to the disease—lurking in our bodies: stealth toxicants.

In April 2010, the President's Cancer Panel—a two-member panel that met with forty-five experts before coming to its conclusions—released a groundbreaking report, "Reducing Environmental Cancer Risk: What We Can Do Now," which criticized the U.S. government for its failure to adequately regulate environmental toxicants. In their cover letter to the president, the panelists wrote that they were "particularly concerned to find that the true burden of environmentally induced cancers has been grossly underestimated."

While many people believe that the government regulates chemicals in order to keep Americans safe, the effectiveness of such efforts is limited at best, in part because industry insiders are calling the shots. For example, in 2009, President Obama put Monsanto lobbyist Michael Taylor in charge of regulating his own industry by appointing him Senior Advisor to the Commissioner of the FDA. And in 2012, the FDA was caught spying on its own employees—five whistle-blowers who were e-mailing documents to legislators and lawyers that showed the agency was using faulty review procedures to approve GE mammogram machines that did not reliably identify breast cancer and/or exposed patients to dangerous levels of radiation. A review by the U.S. Office of Special Counsel later found "significant likelihood" that those and certain other radiological devices approved by the FDA posed "a substantial and specific danger to public safety." To this day, the FDA does not require the cosmetics industry to demonstrate the safety of its products.

And then there's the Environmental Protection Agency, which is charged with protecting us from environmental chemicals such as pesticides. In the thirty-five years since the Toxic Substances Control Act of 1976 was enacted, the EPA has restricted the uses of just five of the eighty thousand chemicals in circulation. A full 95 percent of chemicals in use have never been tested for safety.

If you review the Breast Cancer Fund's 127-page report *State of the Evidence: The Connection Between Breast Cancer and the Environment,* you'll find a jaw-dropping list of chemical compounds known or suspected to cause breast cancer. These include benzene, found in cosmetics, including nail polish, and also in gasoline fumes, car exhaust, and cigarette smoke; 1,3-butadiene, found in hair mousse and gels, shaving creams, and cigarettes; ethylene oxide, found in fragrance; urethane, found in mousses, gels, and hair sprays, and in cosmetics, including nail polish, mascara, and foundation; perfluorocarbons (PFCs), found in nonstick coating on cookware, and in stain guard on furniture, carpets, and clothing; and toluene and resmethrin, found in pesticides.

But carcinogens are not the only cause of breast cancer. According to functional medicine specialist Dr. Elizabeth Boham, "the most damaging environmental toxin when it comes to breast cancer is estrogen and substances that mimic it." Endocrine-disrupting compounds—which are stored in fat and bioaccumulate—can emulate natural hormones, particularly estrogens, and since high exposure to estrogen is known to increase the risk of breast cancer, the Breast Cancer Fund recommends avoiding these chemicals as much as possible.

Not an easy thing to do, it turns out. A list compiled by researcher Dr. Theo Colborn, author of *Our Stolen Future*, documents around eight hundred potential endocrine disruptors. Culprits include Bisphenol A (BPA), which is in the interior lining of almost all metal food and beverage cans; phthalates, found in air fresheners, perfumes, nail polish, baby-care products, cleaning products, and insecticides; parabens, found in underarm deodorant and cosmetics, including creams, lotions, and ointments; synthetic musks, found in fragrance; nonylphenol ethoxylate, found in cleaning products and air fresheners; alkylphenols, found in hair products and spermicides; bovine growth hormone (rBGH/rBST), found in most cow's milk and other commercial dairy products; many pesticides and herbicides; and polycyclic aromatic hydrocarbons, found in charred or grilled meats and in cigarette smoke. Oral contraceptives and hormone-replacement therapy have also been found to increase the risk of breast cancer.

A woman attempting to steer clear of all these toxicants would find it virtually impossible.

Given the complex web of industries with their hands in the breast cancer money pot, it's not hard to see that a focus on prevention would threaten to collapse the whole enterprise. It's a shell game of monumental proportions. These masters of illusion instill us with fear, then with a little sleight of hand distract us from the real problem. And the real problem is that the majority of breast cancers are triggered by environmental factors, including exposures to toxicants. And toxicants are everywhere.

Instead of obsessing about detection, we ought to be promoting precaution. It's a simple idea, really: when in doubt, play it safe. The European Union is paving the way with REACH, a law implemented in 2007 that requires manufacturers and importers to register the chemicals in their products with the European Chemical Agency, and to include in their registration packets data on the hazards of each chemical. Chemicals are evaluated and then either authorized or restricted. Thanks to REACH, some of the cosmetics companies peddling products containing questionable chemicals to Americans are already selling those very products, *but with less-hazardous chemicals*, to our neighbors across the pond.

Why are American women not outraged by this fact alone?

"We used to march in the streets," says Ehrenreich. "Now, we're supposed to 'Run for a Cure.'" Imagine what change could be effected if all those women in pink turned their energies toward working to pass legislation that would protect all of us from the chemicals that cause cancer. Imagine if the millions of dollars spent searching for a "cure" were instead invested in researching causes and prevention. Because if we truly want a cure for the breast cancer epidemic, we don't need more mammograms. We don't need more ribbons. What we need is to face a truth that is not pretty, not pink, and not reassuring at all. Chemicals are in our bodies. They are causing cancer. And all the pink ribbons in the world aren't going to fix that.

Burning the Shelter

Louis Owens

In the center of the Glacier Peak Wilderness in northern Washington a magnificent, fully glaciated white volcano rises over a stunningly beautiful region of the North Cascades. On maps, the mountain is called Glacier Peak. To the Salishan people who have always lived in this part of the Cascades, the mountain is Dakobed, the place of emergence. For the better part of a century a small, three-sided log shelter stood in a place called White Pass, just below one shoulder of the great mountain, tucked securely into a meadow between thick stands of mountain hemlock and alpine fir.

In the early fall of 1976, while working as a seasonal ranger for the United States Forest Service, I drew the task of burning the White Pass shelter. After all those years, the shelter roof had collapsed like a broken bird wing under the weight of winter snow, and the time was right for fire and replanting. It was part of a Forest Service plan to remove all human-made objects from wilderness areas, a plan of which I heartily approved. So I backpacked eleven miles to the pass and set up camp, and for five days, while a bitter early storm sent snow driving horizontally out of the north, I dismantled the shelter and burned the old logs, piling and burning and piling and burning until nothing remained. The antique, hand-forged spikes that had held the shelter together I put into gunnysacks and cached to be packed out later by mule. I spaded up the earth, beaten hard for nearly a century by boot and hoof, and transplanted plugs of vegetation from hidden spots on the nearby ridge.

At the end of those five days not a trace of the shelter remained, and I felt good, very smug in fact, about returning the White Pass meadow to its "original" state. As I packed up my camp, the snowstorm had subsided to a few flurries and a chill that felt bone deep with the promise of winter. My season was almost over, and as I started the steep hike down to the trailhead my mind was on the cold months I would be spending in sunny Arizona.

A half mile from the pass I saw the two old women. At first they were dark, hunched forms far down on the last long switchback up the snowy ridge. But as we drew closer to one another I began to feel a growing amazement that, by the time we were face-to-face, had become awe. Almost swallowed up in their baggy wool pants, heavy sweaters, and parkas, silver braids hanging below thick wool caps, they seemed ancient, each weighted with at least seventy years as well as a small backpack. They paused every few steps to lean on their staffs and look out over the North Fork drainage below, a deep, heavily forested river valley that rose on the far side to the glaciers and sawtoothed black granite of the Monte Cristo Range. And they smiled hugely upon seeing me, clearly surprised and delighted to find another person in the mountains at such a time.

We stood and chatted for a moment, and as I did with all backpackers, I reluctantly asked them where they were going. The snow quickened a little, obscuring the view, as they told me that they were going to White Pass.

"Our father built a little house up here," one of them said, "when he worked for the Forest Service like you. Way back before we was born."

"We been coming up here each year since we was little," the other added. "Except last year when Sarah was not well enough."

"A long time ago, this was all our land," the one called Sarah said. "All Indi'n land everywhere you can see. Our people had houses up in the mountains, for gathering berries every year."

As they took turns speaking, the smiles never leaving their faces, I wanted to excuse myself, to edge around these elders and flee to the trailhead and my car, drive back to the district station, and keep going south. I wanted to say "I'm Indian, too. Choctaw from Mississippi; Cherokee from Oklahoma"—as if mixed blood could pardon me for what I had done. Instead, I said, "The shelter is gone." Cravenly I added, "It was crushed by snow, so I was sent up to burn it. It's gone now."

I expected outrage, anger, sadness, but instead the sisters continued to smile at me, their smiles changing only slightly. They had a plastic tarp and would stay dry, they said, because a person always had to be prepared in the mountains. They would put up their tarp inside the hemlock grove above the meadow, and the scaly hemlock branches would turn back the snow. They forgave me without saying it—my ignorance and my part in the long pattern of loss that they knew so well.

Hiking out those eleven miles, as the snow of the high country became a drumming rain in the forests below, I had long hours to ponder my encounter with the sisters. Gradually, almost painfully, I began to understand that what I called "wilderness" was an absurdity, nothing more than a figment of the European imagination. An "absolute fake." Before the European invasion, there was no wilderness in North America; there was only the fertile continent, where people lived in a hard-learned balance with the natural world. In embracing a philosophy that saw the White Pass shelter—and all traces of humanity—as a shameful stain upon the "pure" wilderness, I had succumbed to a five-hundred-year-old pattern of deadly thinking that separates us from the natural world. This is not to say that what we call wilderness today does not need careful safeguarding. I believe that White Pass really is better off now that the shelter does not serve as a magnet to backpackers and horsepackers who compact the soil, disturb and kill the wildlife, cut down centuries-old trees for firewood, and leave their litter strewn about. And I believe the man who built the shelter would agree. But despite this unfortunate reality, the global environmental crisis that sends species into extinction daily and threatens to destroy all life surely has its roots in the Western pattern of thought that sees humanity and "wilderness" as mutually exclusive.

In old-growth forests in the North Cascades, deep inside an official wilderness area, I have come upon faint traces of log shelters built by Suiattle and Upper Skagit people for berry harvesting a century or more ago—just as the sisters said. Those human-made structures were as natural a part of the Cascade ecosystem as the burrows of marmots in the steep scree slopes. Our native ancestors all over this continent lived within a complex web of relations with the natural world, and in doing so they assumed a responsibility for their world that contemporary Americans cannot even imagine. Unless Americans, and all human beings, can learn to imagine themselves as intimately and inextricably related to every aspect of the world they inhabit, with the extraordinary responsibilities such relationship entails—unless they can learn what the indigenous peoples of the Americas knew and often still know—the earth simply will not survive. A few square miles of something called wilderness will become the sign of failure everywhere.

Spring Ends in Bangor, Pennsylvania

Sean Prentiss

Smart lad, to slip betimes away
From fields where glory does not stay

A.E. Housman

This is how I remember it.

December 1987, wet snowflakes hush Pen Argyl's nighttime sidewalks and blanket old duplex homes. At the high school, which leans against a shale hillside, people exit Cavaliers, Escorts, and K-cars and jog across damp asphalt. With wet hair and snow-stained shoulders, they enter Pen Argyl's aging gymnasium to watch the hometown Green Knights wrestle my high school, the Bangor Slaters in the biggest meet of the year for both teams.

One by one the four hundred fans slump onto hardwood pull-out bleachers. Their breath and damp clothes fog the windows. Once the meet starts, everyone will forget tonight's snow, the uncomfortable seats, even the latest downturn of the economy—another round of layoffs at Alpha Cement. Instead they will focus on the wrestlers, on us, battering terribly against each other as we try to prove, if only for tonight, which town stands as the best.

– –

Two hundred years ago, Bangor and Pen Argyl, each with 6,000 people, rose out of the Slate Belt, a geological band of rock stretching fifteen miles from Pen Argyl, on the west, to Bangor, on the east. Until even fifty years ago, Bangor and Pen Argyl produced much of the slate for the kitchen tables, roofs, pool tables, and chalkboards of America. But with the collapse of the slate industry in the mid 1900s, roofs began to be made of cedar or tar shingles, and blackboards evolved into dry-erase boards. Now our slate-gray barstools get held down by the sons and grandsons of quarry miners who came from New York, New Jersey, and Italy to cut the earth. Today, their descendants find little to do but drink because the nearby steel industry moved overseas, the cement plants quit producing, the quarrying moved to Middle America.

– –

In Pen Argyl's gym, wrestlers think nothing of slate, snow, or ailing economics. Instead, Bangor's Jon Stonewall sprints back and forth across the wood floor. I spin a jump rope until sweat beads across my forehead. In the crowd, Mom waves at me, her blond brushed to either side of her thin face. Dad, a wide-shouldered former 132-pound Division I collegiate wrestler, evaluates the Pen Argyl squad. He sizes up which Bangor wrestler should win and which should lose. I wonder what he thinks of my match versus John Frable.

Jumping rope, I imagine that later tonight fathers will speak to their young sons, "Did you see Sean? He was so quick." Later in the week, in humid junior high wrestling rooms, sons will pretend they are me. They'll practice my low-leg single across the mat. I almost laugh as I jump rope because I know better than anyone that fathers won't talk about me after tonight's meet, and sons won't want to be like me. Not many people want to emulate a 103-pound sophomore who has only won six of fourteen matches during his first year on varsity.

And whether I win or lose tonight, fathers will speak about the winner between the two schools' senior heavyweights, Pen Argyl's Rick Sterner and Bangor's Doug Communal. Sterner is undefeated at 13-0. Doug is one of Bangor's best wrestlers ever and sports a 13-1 record. Everyone expects Sterner and Doug to travel through the District and Regional tournaments before reaching State. Everyone understands that Sterner and Doug are the great wrestling hopes of our rock-rich but job-poor towns.

After tonight, sons will long to be Sterner or Doug, depending on which end of the Slate Belt they live on. I jump rope, knowing that I, maybe more than anyone else, long to be like Doug. In the hallways at Bangor High, Doug slaps my back and asks, "How's it going, Prentiss?" During practice he says, "Keep your weight over both feet, don't get too far forward." Once a match begins, he drivers wrestlers to the mat and then across the mat until they quit.

And off the mat, I want to be like Doug. I want people to trudge through wet snow to watch me wrestle. I hope that if I keep trying to wrestle like Doug—only acting and reacting—that maybe in two years, Bangor fathers will leave barstools to watch me. Maybe they'll whisper my name as I run onto the mat.

— —

In the mid 1980s, one-third of Pennsylvania jobs originated in the manufacturing and industry sectors. Steel, cement, garments, automotive paints, pharmaceuticals, and electricity came from local factories and power plants. Still, rampant unemployment choked our region, and we worried about closed quarries, Bethlehem Steel bankrupting, and Alpha Cement laying people off. During my high school years, Pennsylvania had a worse unemployment rate than thirty other states. Our economy stagnated like the stillwaters of abandoned Slateford Quarry.

During my sophomore year, one in six Bangor kids hungered below the poverty line. On my team, four of thirteen wrestlers were destitute—the 119, 135, 162, and 189-pounders. They knew a hunger different from wrestling.

— —

Plump cheerleaders in green and white miniskirts cheer as Pen Argyl's 103-pound wrestler, John Frable, runs onto the mat. I yank off my sweatshirt, remove my glasses, and clip on my headgear. My team forms a funnel of clapping wrestlers. Coach grabs my head and stares into my eyes, "Are you ready? This kid's a fish. Kick his ass." My team slaps my back and butt as I sprint through the gauntlet.

In the center of the mat, I scan the crowd. Without my glasses the spectators resemble the murky waters of the Delaware River, which flows in front of my parents' house. I am no longer able to see Mom, who runs a bed and breakfast out of our house, or Dad, who owns a car dealership just south of Pen Argyl. Though I saw Doug's parents earlier, I can't find them now. Doug's mom, Dawn, feeds kids in the school cafeteria. Doug's dad, Dave, climbs the metal powerline towers that I've always thought looked like giant metal men. Dave repairs the electrical cables that run from nearby Pennsylvania Power and Light (PP&L) to our homes.

From the stands, Mom yells, "Good luck, Seanie." Coach shouts, "Get us a V." As the ref blows his whistle, Frable rolls from the balls of his feet onto his heels. I dive toward his ankle, hook his right heel with both hands, and drive my shoulder into his shin. Frable falls to the mat; the ref throws up two fingers for a takedown. Instead of battling to his knees, Frable flounders.

After six minutes, I win 11-1 and hope that my victory is enough for the crowd to begin remembering me. Still, I'm dissatisfied. I didn't practice all week just to wrestle someone who refused to fight. I feel as if I punched in, did my job, and can now go home. I jog off the mat. Coach grabs me in a bear hug. "That's what we needed." I smile and think that maybe I can fill Doug's shoes once he graduates in May.

An hour later as Pen Argyl's 189-pounder pins Steve Stackhouse, Pen Argyl's lead becomes insurmountable, yet neither the Pen Argyl nor Bangor crowd departs. As Stackhouse staggers off the mat, his head low, our teammate-funnel forms for the thirteenth and final time. Even though three-quarters of our team lost tonight, still we clap and holler as our captain takes the mat. Coach slaps Doug on the butt. "Redeem us!" Though we will lose the meet, a win by Doug will satisfy Bangor fans because then we can lay claim to the best wrestler in the region. Tonight, that needs to be enough.

Doug slaps his calloused hands together and runs through the gauntlet. In the center of the mat, he waits for Sterner, who jogs onto the mat. Sterner's black, wavy hair droops to his shoulders. Chin stubble makes him look older than eighteen, and with thick arms dilating from his green singlet, Sterner somehow makes Doug appear beatable, mortal.

The ref blows his whistle. The crowd waits for these boys to collide. Sterner and Doug move tentatively, knowing they carry the weight of the towns on their hips, which is where a wrestler's power originates. In a region of failed natural resources and failed economy, failing schools and functionally illiterate students, so many of us need to feed off of Sterner and Doug's success.

With 0:30 remaining in the third period, Doug leads 8-7. Everyone stands from the rickety bleachers, and, instead of cheering, a silence sweeps through the gym. I lean far off my folding metal chair and steal glances at the clock.

0:22. Sterner and Doug circle the mat. Doug hugs the outer edge.

0:20. Sterner shoots a high-crotch takedown and slinks his arms around Doug's leg.

0:18. Someone in the stands yells, "Come on, Doug."

0:16. Doug throws his bicep across Sterner's face. Sterner's head snaps back, but he holds on. Doug struggles for the edge of the mat. If he reaches the line, he'll be out of bounds and no points will be awarded. Doug wrenches at Sterner's arms, and Sterner's fingers begin to separate.

0:10. Two feet from the boundary, Doug leaps. Sterner strains to hold on as they thunder to the ground.

0:08. The ref throws two fingers into the air. A takedown for Sterner. Doug, down by one, fights to escape.

0:06. Doug climbs to his knees. Peels back Sterner's fingers.

The buzzer wails. Sterner stands and throws his arms into the air. The Pen Argyl fans jump up, shaking the bleachers. Their cheers bounce off the rafters. Doug gently slaps the mat and then climbs to his feet. The Bangor contingency falls to their seats, silent. We are amazed that anyone can out-wrestle Doug. His loss proves he's conquerable, and we are so much more so.

– –

Three months after the Pen Argyl and Bangor meet, all that remains of the 1987–88 season is the State tournament. At the District tournament, eleven of my twelve teammates were eliminated. Doug placed second, losing to Sterner in the finals. I was ranked twelfth out of sixteen 103 pounders. But, despite a broken nose, I worked my way into the top five. My fifth place and Doug's second place sent us to the Regional tournament. And though I sur-prisingly qualified for Regionals, no one talked of me in reverent tones like they did of Doug, whispering while he wrestled, "Shit, did you see how fast he was? It's like he doesn't even think out there."

At Regionals, I lost two straight and my season ended. Though disap-pointed, I was excited to have made it to Regionals. Doug won every match at Regionals until the finals where he again lost to Sterner and again placed second. Still, Doug became the first Bangor wrestler in thirteen years to advance to State.

During those same days, Doug accepted an athletic scholarship to wrestle for NCAA Division I Clarion University, securing his way out of Bangor. The scholarship paved the way for him to become the first member of his family to attend college. And he became the only Bangor wrestler I knew to receive a sports scholarship.

A day after my loss at Regionals, Coach invited me to attend State. Coach wanted me to keep Doug relaxed and wanted me to experience State in prep-aration for my anticipated appearance there next year and the year after. I accepted.

– –

I didn't notice it back in 1987, but many of Bangor's male role models were reckless with their teachings. Without realizing it, we hoped we could under-stand their toughness, persistence, and low-leg singles while disregarding their examples of alcoholism, despondency, and limited job potentials wait-ing us after high school. Those of us who could imagine something more than factory work hoped for an escape, but we often didn't know to what. We strained to envision a career other than the assembly line. We had so few examples of success.

With little work to be found, many former Bangor athletes searched ten, twenty, even forty years after high school graduation for something to fill their lives. After days spent in the steel works, too many spent nights hunched over Bangor bars—the Oak and Maple, the Rod and Gun Club, the Pequest. Evenings when Bangor wrestled, these men left their stools and longnecks of Yuengling lager for gymnasium bleachers. While their children wrestled, Bangor fathers visualized themselves back when they were high school wrestlers. They recreated memories until they won that final match of their careers.

We didn't know it then, but everything our role models taught us would at best give us three years of athletic glory. And we learned that alcoholism and unemployment mean the same thing to a former .500 wrestler as it does to a former Regional qualifier.

– –

Late March, Doug, Coach, and I travel two hours south to Hershey Arena for the State tournament. Since only coaches and wrestlers are allowed at mat level, I sit in the bleachers. I stare at the eight mats lined in rows of four and envision myself wrestling there next year.

Day one, Doug loses one of his three matches. Doug appears confused when the ref raises the other wrestler's hand. Coach hugs Doug and whispers in his ear before Doug stumbles into the locker room. I so badly want to know what Coach whispers.

I leave the bleachers and find Doug slumped on a splintered wooden bench. His singlet straps dangle from his waist. "How are you?" I ask.

"I wrestled like crap." His words come between deep breaths. "I should've practiced more." Doug wipes sweat off his face.

"Can I do anything?" I want to comfort Doug like Coach did.

"No." Doug's fingers twiddle in his singlet straps. "No, thanks though." Doug stares at the cool cement floor. "Sean, you ever been to a college meet?"

"A few. Lehigh versus East Stroudsburg and a couple others."

"Were the wrestlers better than here?"

"Not as good as you."

"I thought I'd beat him."

"You can still place third."

"Yeah, third."

Day two begins with Doug losing his first match by a point. Afterward, Doug and I study the heavyweight brackets taped to a wall. Doug traces his finger from loss to win to win to loss to the fifth place bracket. Doug has one match remaining in his high school career. He finds his name, and below it Rick Sterner. Doug whispers, "I've got him."

And though Doug has lost three in a row to Sterner, I say, "Yeah," and all I feel is faith.

– –

For the 179 seniors who graduated from Bangor High in 1990, I was one of fifty-five who attended college and one of about twenty-five who received a degree. Because both my parents had attended college and Dad graduated, I had an example to follow.

Most of the other 119 drifted off to places like Bethlehem Steel, once the world's largest steel producer. But by the late '80s, Bethlehem Steel rusted beside Route 22. In 1988 and '89, the mills began shutting down as the industry moved to China and Korea. By 1995, after 140 years of producing, the steel works closed, sending workers to unemployment lines.

Ten minutes south of Bangor, cement factories, like Alpha, coughed gray dust onto lawns. Everyone hated the grit until the cement industry followed Bethlehem Steel toward bankruptcy.

Majestic Garments sewed sweatshirts in windowless brick buildings in South Bangor. Women, including my aunt, streamed into work in the mornings. All day the seamstresses stared at their fingers because there was no view of trees.

Binney and Smith, the world's largest producer of crayons (Crayola), opened a factory beside cornfields in nearby Wind Gap. A former lover of mine, Mary, got a job after dropping out of college her freshman year. After second shift, she came home reeking of chemicals and cheap wax. I loved her smell.

A mile east of my parent's home, Hoffman la Roche's four story building rose tan and tall. From various pipes, Roach belched pharmaceutical waste into the air and water. Each morning, at 5:30, cars streamed by Mom and Dad's house. Some headed home from the graveyard, others traveled to first shift. My friend, Jeff, joined his father at Roach after Jeff got a girl pregnant freshman year of college.

And five miles south of home, Pennsylvania Power and Light swallowed coal and converted it into electricity. From two wide and low cooling towers, PP&L released steam and smoke into the sky—long fingers of white-gray broken only by the breeze. Five days a week, Doug's dad and other Bangor fathers traveled there for work.

– –

From the stands at Hershey Arena I watch as Doug and Sterner prepare to wrestle. The first thirty seconds the clock scarcely moves as Sterner attempts a headlock. "Sprawl, sprawl, sprawl," I holler as Sterner laces his thick arms around Doug's head and arm. Sterner throws his hips into Doug's hips. I wait for Doug to be tossed through air.

But Doug slips Sterner's grasp, and as Doug slides to the mat, he pulls Sterner down. The ref raises two fingers, two points for Doug. The rest of the first two periods, time surges. The ref throws up two fingers for Doug for a takedown, two for Sterner for a reversal, two more for Sterner for a takedown, one for Doug for an escape, two for Sterner for a takedown, two for Doug for a reversal.

Fifteen seconds remain in the third period. Doug leads by one.

0:10. Sterner shoots a high crotch. Doug sprawls and regains his feet.

0:07. Sterner shoots again. Doug sweeps to the side.

0:03. Sterner shots a single. Without thought, Doug sprawls.

0:01. The buzzer blasts.

Sterner slumps to the mat. His hands cover his eyes, steeling himself. Doug smiles, his shoulders stretch backward, his chest juts out, his arms rise. Doug reigns as the fifth best wrestler in the great state of Pennsylvania. He is finished. He has cemented his legacy.

– –

After Doug's fifth place finish at State, he and I take seven weeks off to heal my broken nose and his aches and pains. During my time away from the mat, I think about wanting to reach State before I graduate. I assume Doug thinks about August when he will enroll at Clarion because he approaches me in the hallway of Bangor High one May day, "Hey, Sean, want to practice tomorrow?"

Honored, I stutter, "Yeah."

The next day, Friday, May 19, 1988, Doug and I return home to Bangor's basement practice room one hundred and eighty-seven days before next season begins. A breeze wafts through the propped door almost suppressing the reek of sweet. Doug and I sit on the mat and tie our wrestling shoes. "So, you gonna wrestle me today?" I jokingly ask Doug.

"Not after how well you wrestled at Districts. You'd kick my ass." He grins.

I pop to my feet and crouch in a wrestler's stance. "Quit ducking me. You know I can take you. I'll finish what Sterner couldn't."

Doug climbs into his wrestling stance, the scabs of battle brittle on his freshly shaved face. "That's right, what Sterner couldn't," I repeat. Doug moves toward me, his arms reaching for my wrists. I back away. Still, I prod, "This is your last chance to duck out. I won't tell anyone you're chicken."

"You won't? Promise?" Doug smirks, and, as he finishes speaking, he explodes toward. Most wrestlers telegraph moves with a twitch of the hips;

Doug shows nothing. I try to sprawl, but Doug's fingers clamp around the back of my left knee, tearing it from the ground.

The smartest thing to do is become motionless and hope Doug carries me tenderly to the mat. But I've been trained to fight, so I wrench at his grip. Caught off guard, Doug's fingers begin to separate. Doug recovers and jams his head into my hip. As I fall to the padding, Doug pitches his two hundred pounds on top of me. The mat tears into my cheek. My hair jerks between the padding and Doug. I try to push Doug off, but my arms remain pinned at my side. Right before I yell for Doug to get off, he springs to his feet. "Hope I didn't hurt you." He holds out a hand.

I stumble to my feet and shake my head groggily. "Hurt me? Not a chance. And don't worry, I won't tell anyone I just whooped you."

For the next hour and a half, Doug and I practice, rehearsing phantom fireman-carries, low-leg singles, and high-crotches. I study Doug, watch how he finds the space where the body acts without thought.

– –

Each day my team trained repetitively, as if we were being prepared to one day run a drill or a solder. Coach shouted, "Shoot, shoot, shoot, shoot, shoot," as we practiced high-crotches. We obeyed and put our bodies on the line. I hyper-extended an elbow, broke my nose and a few fingers, and loosened my right shoulder enough that for half a decade it was hard to write for longer than ten minutes. When I briefly wrestled in college, athletic trainers used electrical stimulation to relax my back spasms.

The rest of the team was the same. Vomiting on the mat, shoulder dislocations, stitches, and broken bones occurred seasonally. Taped and bandaged, we resembled many of our fathers and mothers who returned from work with sore backs and crushed fingers from the press machines and the pneumatic nail guns.

– –

Outside the wrestling room, the sky softens with the red stains of dusk. It's nearly dinnertime, so Doug and I end practice. We pull on sneakers and stroll to our cars, the only two in the parking lot.

Doug crams his 6'2" body into his 1980 Mercury Lynx. His four-cylinder engine sputters to a start. I climb into my 1971 Ford Torino station wagon. With a turn of the key, the 429 cubic-inch engine roars to life. Doug leans an arm on the top of his door and shouts through the open driver-side window, "Let's practice Monday."

"Sounds great." I'm still amazed Doug wants to practice with me.

"Hey, and I'm having a party tonight. Come. Nine. My parents went to Lake Wallenpallack. You know where I live?"

"Yeah."

"Wanna race? You know this baby blue Lynx can beat that shitty wagon of yours." Doug runs his hand along the faded paint below the driver side window. "Plus, I need paybacks for that whooping you gave me today." Doug and I smile, and then Doug slams the gas pedal. His Lynx crawls across the parking lot. I wait for Doug to get a substantial lead before I step on the gas pedal. My tires gyrate, spewing smoke. My wagon surges past Doug's Lynx.

On empty back roads, I race past heifers chewing cud in muddy fields and old farm houses in need of paint jobs and new porches. In back fields, barns lean away from the wind. In fifteen years, at the time of the writing of this essay, those barns will crash to the ground and soil will blow over the fallen red-painted boards. In fifty years, grass will cover the mounds of wood. In a hundred, no one will remember that the barns ever stood, and the piles of decayed wood will resemble giant, freshly dug graves.

At home, I do not go to Doug's party because I haven't gone to any high school parties yet. I'm nervous about hanging out with seniors, plus I don't have any reason to drink; I haven't yet felt loss or tasted failure. The worst pain I've ever felt was losing at Regionals two months ago. Afterward I cried.

I go to bed with dreams of more spring matches against Doug. I dream of becoming one of the best wrestlers in Pennsylvania. I go to State, win my final match, and cement my legacy. I earn an athletic scholarship to a far away school. I follow Doug and use wrestling as a ticket out of Bangor. I dream as May 19 bleeds into May 20.

– –

Fifteen years after my sophomore season, a mentor and I speak about my wrestling career. A few days later she hands me James Wright's poem "Autumn Begins in Martins Ferry, Ohio." I sit in my office at the University of Idaho, where I teach, and read stanzas about a football season beginning in a small Ohio town. Locals drink long-neck beers, and the blast furnace workers dream of heroes. Tired women cling to their men. While reading the final lines, visions of my wrestling career spring to mind:

All the proud fathers are ashamed to go home…
their sons grow suicidally beautiful…
and gallop terribly against each other's bodies.

Just like that Martins Ferry becomes Bangor. We gazed into the stands at our fathers. Our mothers clung to our father's arms and searched the rafters of the gym for all that they had lost and all that they had been promised but never received. And we, we wrestled suicidally against each other.

– –

May 20, 1988, I wake confused. In the first light of dawn Mom and Dad stand at the foot of my bed. One of them must have called, dragging me from slumber. I sit up. Dad speaks in a steel voice, "Doug died last night in a drunk driving accident."

I've seen the old buried in dark Pennsylvania loam, but I know nothing of burying my peers. I climb from bed, pull on a pair of pants, and walk past Dad. He was a great high school wrestler who used wrestling as his way to escape his hometown on rural Long Island. Wrestling offered him a college scholarship and a degree. From there he started his car business.

I move past Mom's slumped shoulders, her gentle hand rubs my back. "Okay," I say as if this word can protect me from all the thoughts that will come. I head out the screen door, which slams behind me, a slap of wood against. I skirt the edge of the cornfield growing behind my house. Stalks break from May soil. In two months they will tower over me. In four months, farmers will scythe the brittle growth to the ground. All across the field, the reek of manure hovers in the air. Everything smells of spring.

The field abuts the tranquil Delaware River, but around the bend the rapids of Foul Rift churn, and the river dives over and around boulders as it surges south one hundred and seventy miles before escaping into the Atlantic. I sit on the grass beside yellow honeysuckles, stare at the river, and sob. Maybe Doug's Lynx hit a tree or a bridge abutment or flipped across a cornfield. Maybe he blew a tire and crashed into a shallow creek. Later, I read the truth—Doug, drunk, leaves his party. A cop pulls behind Doug and turns on his lights. Doug tries to run, takes a corner too fast. His Lynx slides into the other lane, hits an oncoming car fender to fender. The Lynx flips and flips and flips, and in my mind it never stops flipping. The Lynx bursts into flames. Newspapers write that Doug was partially ejected and died instantly. A week later, a friend, a paramedic, tells me about screams. Fifteen years later, I still see the Lynx rolling down asphalt. I still hear screams.

I was the last person to wrestle Doug, to lose to him. It becomes the first loss I've ever been glad about. Sitting and crying beside gently moving water, I don't know that during the next two years of high school, I will never qualify for State. I will never follow Doug there. But I realize that Doug has been added to the list of people who thought they could escape Bangor but never did. He never made it to Clarion.

Two years later I abandon Bangor to wrestle half a season at a small Colorado college. By January, I quit the team, but I still graduate three years later. Once I went off to college, I never moved back to Bangor. I left friends and family rusting in factories. I left Doug sleeping beneath a tombstone made of tan marble quarried in Indiana. His stone, with a wrestler etched into it, sits on the slant of a mowed hill.

Fifteen years later, when I stand at his hilltop grave, caressing cold rock, thousands of acres of cornfields flow three miles to my parent's house, to the placid Delaware, to PP&L. Between the grave and the river, corn quavers in a breeze, and it is a sea, a sea, a sea of green with corn running all neatly rowed like the graves surrounding me.

Looming over that verdantness are huge metal towers heft powerlines from PP&L to our homes. These steel shadow-casters have always reminded me of one hundred foot tall wrestlers with broad chests and narrow waists, but no heads and an empty space where their hearts should rest. And in those giant metal men, I see everyone from my wrestling team—athletes trained to fight but not to think. The tower-men stride next to Doug's cemetery and down the hill. I trace the cables and the towers to PP&L, five miles away, which gulps in Delaware riverwater to cool turbines and engines.

Beside the power plant, smokestacks and massive cooling towers rise above the landscape. They rise above the gigantic tower-men and seemingly rise even above our rolling Kittatinny Mountains. These stacks and towers cough white fingers of steam and smoke into a perfectly blue spring Pennsylvania sky.

Inside the windowless power plant, former classmates of mine, former wrestlers, convert coal into electricity and long to return to the days when they, when we, galloped terribly against each other.

Hell Yeah We Want Windmills

Erik Reece

On a warm September afternoon, I pulled off the interstate in Charleston, West Virginia, under a billboard that read, in stark black letters:

YES, COAL.
clean, carbon neutral coal

I drove another two blocks and parked my truck next to the governor's mansion, where, in a small rock garden, red and white begonias spelled out: hope.

Coal and *hope*—for a moment, I considered the rhetorical and symbolic proximity of those two words. Recently, while the shadow of climate change lengthened and the lie of free markets unraveled, I had begun to doubt the promise of either to deliver on a future I want to inhabit. No coal-fired power plant in West Virginia, nor anywhere else in central Appalachia, sequesters carbon, nor do they extract from the bituminous ore its mercury and asthma-inducing particulates. A 2008 report from the Government Accountability Office warns that U.S. carbon-capture research is still dramatically underfunded and underdeveloped. So for some time, "clean, carbon neutral coal" will exist in name only—a lie on a billboard. As for hope, even that idea had been losing, at least for me, its audacious potential, its ability to navigate the shoals of public cynicism and despair. Here, in this domestic flower bed, hope looked at best like a decorous sentiment—sweet but irrelevant, certainly no match for Big Coal.

Some years ago, Wendell Berry warned me that, to fight the coal industry, one must "accept heartbreak as a working condition." Since then, I've watched coal operators dismantle one mountain after another across central Appalachia. I've watched them dump entire mountaintops into the valleys below, strangling and poisoning the region's healthiest streams.

I've watched the previous administration rewrite the Clean Water Act to make this dumping legal, and I've watched industry insiders take control of, then undermine, the federal agencies whose job it is to prevent such abuse. Which is to say, there's been more than enough heartbreak to go around, and it has made me leery of anyone trading in hope and promising change.

Friends from the coasts tell me I'm too pessimistic, too doom-and-gloom. Maybe so, but for too long it seems like environmentalists around here have been caught up in some kind of circular Appalachian three-step: 1) fight the good fight; 2) lose the good fight; 3) go have a beer and take consolation in the fact that at least you fought the good fight. Over time, this story of our struggle to save these imperiled mountains starts to sound like the larger story of Appalachia, a tragedy of the commons that repeats itself with an unnerving relentlessness: industrial aggressors buy off the politicians and the police, rob the region of its wealth, then blame the people of the mountains for their poverty and stubbornness in the face of "progress." I had come to Charleston, the center of coal country, looking for a new narrative.

In his recent book *The Last Refuge*, David Orr writes of the environmental movement, "The public, I think, knows what we are against, but not what we are for. There are many things that should be stopped, but what should be started?" That day last fall, under the capitol's gilded dome, some coal field residents from southern West Virginia had gathered to offer their answer: a wind farm. They wore symbolic green hardhats and held signs that said:

YES, WIND.
truly *clean and carbon neutral*

Jesse Johnson, the progressive Mountain Party candidate for governor, gave a fiery speech in which he suggested we stop pulverizing and burning coal, and instead invest in carbon-composite technology. Then a bluegrass band called the Long Haul started playing, and someone up on stage said that was about right—fighting the coal industry in West Virginia is indeed a long haul.

This particular attempt to fight Big Coal began in 2006, when a group of citizen-activists called Coal River Mountain Watch teamed up with Orr to commission a study of wind currents along the top of Coal River Mountain in Raleigh County, West Virginia. WindLogics, a firm out of St. Paul, conducted the feasibility study and found strong, recurrent winds sweeping through the valleys and peaking across the tops of these close-shouldered, sprawling mountain spurs so characteristic of the southern Appalachians.

Using Google Earth software, and working in alliance with the American Wind Energy Association and the National Renewable Energy Laboratory, the citizen-activists of Coal River Mountain Watch constructed a computer model of a wind farm that would accommodate 220 turbines. If built, these turbines could generate 328 megawatts of energy annually, enough to power more than 7 percent of West Virginia homes.

What's more, Coal River Mountain Watch calculated that construction of the wind farm would create two hundred jobs over two years and around fifty permanent on-site maintenance jobs, which would generate $40 million in local spending over the first two years and $2 million every subsequent year. Annual county tax revenues could reach $3 million, with state revenues coming in at around $400,000. Adding the amount of coal-based energy the wind farm would displace to the tons of coal that would be left in the ground at Coal River Mountain, project coordinator Rory McIlmoil calculated that 86 million tons of carbon dioxide would be kept out of the atmosphere—truly sequestered—during the wind farm's first twenty years. Downstream Strategies, a consulting firm out of Morgantown, would later confirm these numbers. Bottom line: more jobs, more tax revenue, less CO2, and far fewer health problems that result from contaminated water and coal dust.

There was only one snag, but it was a big one. Massey Energy, out of Richmond, Virginia, had already leased the mineral rights beneath the six thousand acres where the wind farm would stand, and Massey was indeed planning to exercise those rights by leveling most of Coal River Mountain. A spokesman for Massey issued this statement: "We encourage the Coal River Mountain Watch to do what any responsible energy producer would do: identify and acquire a site for their project and obtain the permits and infrastructure necessary to make that project happen." There are, however, two problems with this statement. To imply, for one, that Massey is a "responsible" producer of energy represents a considerable disregard for the facts. Between 2000 and 2006, the company violated the Clean Water Act more than 4,500 times, racking up $20 million in fines from the EPA (the maximum fine could have been $2.4 billion). When security concerns were raised about some of Massey's underground mines, CEO Don Blankenship wrote a memo to employees that read: "If any of you have been asked by your group presidents, your supervisors, engineers or anyone else to do anything other than run coal (i.e., build overcasts, do construction jobs, or whatever) you need to ignore them and run coal." A few months later, two miners died in a Massey mine fire caused by a buildup of flammable coal waste along a conveyer belt. Cleaning the belt might have prevented the fire, but the mine foremen were too busy running coal to stop for that.

The second, more fundamental problem with Massey's statement is that the people who live around Coal River Mountain are not *trying* to become energy producers. They are trying to keep the mountain that frames and defines their communities from being blown apart. A wind farm, it turns out, looks like the best way to make that happen.

"Coal River Mountain is the last of our mountains in our community," longtime resident Bo Webb told me at the rally. "Everyone's life revolves around that mountain. Hell yeah, we're fighting for it. I don't know why the governor is so perplexed by that." The governor in question is Joe Manchin, who had tangled with Don Blankenship before and seemed uneager to re-enter the fray. Over three thousand calls to his office in support of the wind farm had failed to move him. Thus a sense of urgency surrounded the rally. A long procession of coal field residents stepped to the mike and urged Manchin to get off the dime and rescind the Massey permits. They said they were not against coal, that their fathers and grandfathers had been underground miners, and that they were proud of that tradition. But mountaintop removal was destroying Coal River Valley. Lessie Maynor said a Massey holding pond had collapsed behind her house in 2001 and washed away "everything we had worked for, for the past forty years." Charles Ballard said the strip mining was "messing up every damn thing we have in these mountains." They were citizens of West Virginia, they said, and they had the right to live in peace, with clean air and clean water, and without fear of blasting and flooding. They wanted something else for Coal River Valley.

When the rest of the country thinks about southern Appalachia, it often thinks of the past—of backwardness even. That image benefits the coal industry immensely, making it much easier for companies like Massey to justify irreparable damage that would never be tolerated in, say, the Adirondacks. These West Virginians were tired of living on the receiving end of that attitude. They were tired of nineteenth-century stereotypes and nineteenth-century sources of energy. Now they had a plan, a blueprint for how to disentangle the region from the world's most toxic industry.

It all sounded pretty impressive to me. The people of Coal River Valley were calling for a new kind of economy, one that was both socially and ecologically just. It was a more honest economy, whereby the "externalities" of doing business—the mine waste, the toxic water, the flooding—were not off-loaded on the people who, unlike Don Blankenship, actually had to live in the coal fields. At a time when 60 percent of the world's ecosystems are being degraded by human impacts, here was a plan that maintained both the integrity and the diversity of the Appalachian Mountains. At the onset of peak oil and radical climate change, here was a plan that worked with, rather than against, the ultimate system of exchange—the economy of nature.

Outside the Coal River Mountain Watch office in Whitesville, West Virginia, Matt Noerpel hands me a motorcycle helmet and we head for Sycamore Hollow, a few miles away. It's October, and the first fall color is coming to the poplars. We stop at the home of Bacon Brown, an elderly man who has collected nearly nine pounds of ginseng root from these hillsides since the official ginseng season began in September. On the Asian market, the herb will fetch him a tidy profit. Traditionally, many mountain families use their ginseng money for Christmas presents; unfortunately, ginseng is one more local economy that is disappearing along with these forests and mountaintops.

Beneath Brown's carport, Noerpel unlocks two ATVs. Within minutes, we are careening along a steep trail that leads up the ridgeside. As I follow Noerpel's long mane of red hair, my enormous Kawasaki four-wheeler leaps over fallen tree limbs and heavy cobble. Once we reach the ridgeline, we head west to the site where Massey is planning to begin mining. As we cross a wide haul road cleared for coal trucks, I see a sign warning of the blasting to come. A few miles farther on, we are speeding under unusually tall sassafras trees, and then we dip down to a small clearing where the trail, an old logging road, ends. The autumn color along the ridgetops abruptly drops off at a man-made "highwall," a steep precipice where half of the mountain has been sliced away by explosives. We climb off our ATVs and walk to its edge, where the deciduous broadleaf forest plunges down into a cratered emptiness that looks like nothing so much as a bombing range.

A hundred feet below, the entire Brushy Fork watershed has been buried beneath one of the largest slurry impoundment ponds in the world. The black ooze called slurry, or sludge, is the toxic byproduct left over when coal is cleaned for market. The Brushy Fork pond contains 6 billion gallons of slurry, six times the amount that recently broke through a dam in Tennessee. The nine-hundred-foot wall that holds all of this slurry back is the highest dam in North America. It is also a reminder that, in fact, "cheap" energy carries a very high cost that most Americans do not recognize because it is hidden in poor, remote places like the coal fields of Appalachia.

At the end of his influential book *Collapse*, Jared Diamond lists what he considers the twelve most serious environmental problems we face, the ones that would most likely cause a nation to topple. Of these twelve, ten—deforestation, species loss, erosion, coal-burning, harm to underground aquifers, misuse of sunlight, toxic chemicals, alien species, global warming, and overconsumption—can be tied *directly* to mountaintop removal strip mining. A wind farm, by contrast, could begin ameliorating every one of them. There is certainly still an environmental impact, and there is some troubling evidence suggesting that bat populations are declining in some places because of wind turbines (bats like to mate at high altitudes). That said, I would direct wind critics to its alternative: this slurry pond and the miles of leveled mountains and toxic mine sites all around it.

I look up at the ridgelines beyond the slurry pond and try to imagine them covered with wind turbines—220 of them staggered along the peaks and side spurs of Coal River Mountain for thirty-six miles. A mere 267 acres would have to be cleared for the turbines, compared to the 6,450 acres that would be lost to mountaintop removal, and with a wind farm, the nine miles of streams that would be buried by mountaintop removal would remain healthy and full of life. I decide the tall white turbines would look quite elegant spinning slowly above the treeline. They would stand like sentinels, guarding the mountain from bulldozers and trucks carrying explosives.

A few days before my visit, Noerpel had done some independent research at the West Virginia Department of Environmental Protection (DEP) and found that Massey, in its rush to start mining up here, had not received approval for revisions to its permit. The understaffed DEP—whose job, in effect, Noerpel was doing—issued a statement that any blasting would be illegal. Coal River Mountain had been granted, in Rory McIlmoil's words, "a stay of execution."

Even if Massey did start blasting along this ridgeline, the majority of the strongest wind is farther southeast. And while Massey has also leased the mineral rights beneath that part of the mountain, there is still time to find a developer to turn that wind into energy and profits. But, as Noerpel says, "Once Massey Energy gets started, they're hard to stop." He lets out a rueful laugh. "They're hard to stop anyway."

I drop Matt Noerpel off at the modest Coal River Mountain Watch office and follow Coal River Road along a narrow valley floor framed by steep ridgelines. The road ends at the home of Lorelei Scarbro, the community coordinator for the Coal River Wind Project. Scarbro lives in a modest wooden house built by her late husband and surrounded in part by a small orchard they planted together. She wears her graying hair cut short and she doesn't seem much given to small talk. People around here know and trust her. Still, organizing isn't easy in a place where Massey holds sway and where the air is thick with intimidation; some activists I've talked to say they have received anonymous calls warning that a family member employed by Massey might be fired if the activism doesn't stop.

Scarbro got started by making a large batch of apple butter in a hundred-year-old copper pot and taking jars of it door to door. Soon there was enough support for the wind farm to begin holding meetings in Rebecca Chapel, the same small church Robert Kennedy visited in 1968.

Scarbro distills her organizing goal down to this: "We're trying to save the community."

Her own property borders Coal River Mountain and sits right below the ridgelines that Massey Energy is proposing to flatten. This rolling land was handed down through her husband's family, many of whom are buried in the hillside cemetery you can see from Scarbro's front porch. Up behind the cemetery rises Pond Knob, one of the highest ridges on Coal River Mountain. It would generate the most megawatts of wind energy, and it also holds the greatest lodes of coal. Like many deep miners, Scarbro's husband died from black lung after working thirty-five years underground. Now Lorelei Scarbro worries that she could develop silicosis if Massey starts blasting apart the thick layers of sandstone—the "overburden"—that lie between the top of the mountain and the thin seams of coal below.

The off-site damage caused by mountaintop removal strip mining is enormous. A recent EPA study found that 95 percent of streams near surface mines had been degraded and contaminated by sedimentation and the leaching of heavy metals. Many mountain families rely on private wells for their drinking water, and many of those are cracked and poisoned by the blasting. It's not uncommon, Scarbro told me, for her neighbors who live around active mining to find black water running through their taps. And to make matters worse, coal companies are allowed to inject mining waste laden with heavy metals into old underground mines, which many suspect is seeping into the water supply (the EPA recently denied this, even while admitting to having done no research into the matter). Highly abnormal levels of kidney failure have been reported throughout the community of Prenter Hollow, just west of Scarbro's place; an eight-year-old child developed a kidney stone, and a sixteen year old died of cancer. The DEP denied that there had ever been underground injections of mine waste in that community until Bobbie Mitchell of Coal River Mountain Watch produced a document to the contrary. When someone from the DEP asked Mitchell where he found such a document, Mitchell replied, "Your office."

All of this often leads outsiders to ask the question that makes Scarbro angriest: Why don't you move?

The simplest answer is that, once mountaintop removal begins, those who live around it *can't* move because their property loses nearly all of its value. But the question is insulting and condescending on a deeper level. It implies that the culture of Appalachia, so rooted in a sense of place, is of little value compared to cheap energy. Standing beside her late husband's headstone, under a large chestnut oak, Scarbro says, "We mountain people feel a connectedness to the land. It's a survival instinct. It's hard to explain that to people who are not attached to the place where they live."

The question shouldn't be, why don't you move? but what kind of economy will preserve this community?

The answer, I think, can be found right here, where the watersheds of Appalachia could serve as a model for a new economy. By its very nature, a watershed is self-sufficient, symbiotic, conservative, decentralized, and diverse. It circulates its own wealth over and over. It generates no waste and does not "externalize" the cost of "production" onto other watersheds, other streams and valleys. In a watershed, all energy is renewable and all resource use is sustainable.

The watershed economy is the exact opposite of a strip mine. It purifies air and water, holds soil in place, enriches humus, and sequesters carbon. That is to say, a watershed economy improves the land and thus improves the lives of the people who inhabit that particular place. It is an economy based not on the unsustainable, shortsighted logic of never-ending growth, which robs the future to meet the needs of the present, but rather on maintaining the health, well-being, stability, and conviviality of the community. To paraphrase Buckminster Fuller, the watershed offers us an operating manual we should have been reading long ago.

After Leaving Lorelei Scarbro's, I pass a barn along Coal River Road, where a fading metal sign reads: prove you are against coal mining. turn off your electricity. It doesn't surprise me, nor does it surprise me that some of the more visible voices of Coal River Mountain Watch have received death threats and encountered other forms of intimidation (A sign on Scarbro's door reads, warning: trespassers will be shot. survivors will be shot again.) To many living outside the Appalachian coal fields, blowing the top off a mountain seems ludicrous, an act of industrial aggression wholly lacking in subtlety or nuance. But things aren't that simple in communities where most jobs come from coal. In Raleigh County, some people feel that to call for the end of strip mining is to take food from their children's mouths. They become angry, and the industry only stokes their belief that environmental-ists are to blame for declining jobs and persistent poverty.

One of the more inspiring aspects of the wind farm proposal is that it has the potential to break the long and frustrating impasse in the jobs-versus-environment debate. In addition to the construction and maintenance jobs, the wind farm could potentially bring far more mining jobs to Coal River Mountain. While turbines staggered along its ridgetops would stave off mountaintop removal, a highly mechanized form of mining that requires few workers (less than 1 percent of West Virginia's employment comes from surface mining), there would remain the opportunity to extract the region's low-sulfur coal through underground mining, which could create far more jobs.

"We're not telling them they can't mine," Bo Webb told me. "We'll put the windmills on top, they can mine coal underground, and everybody wins, right?" It would seem so.

The problem, from the coal operator's perspective, is that if too many people see wind turbines spinning across the peaks of Coal River Mountain, they might stop believing the industry's hundred-year-old canard that coal is the region's only hope. In the forty-five years since Lyndon Johnson stood on a miner's porch to welcome him into the Great Society, central Appalachia's poverty rate has barely moved from 30 percent, the highest rate in the nation. Historian Harry Caudill used to say that poverty was east-ern Kentucky's only tourist industry. In February of this year, ABC's Diane Sawyer took her viewers on that tour once again. It was the most watched episode of *20/20* in five years; Americans apparently like poverty tours—the trashed-out trailers, the mothers and miners hooked on painkillers, the kids with bad teeth. But what wasn't on display, because it is harder to find and to film, is the systemic cause of that poverty—namely, a single industry that has dominated the region for a century and fought every attempt to raise the region's standard of living. Central Appalachia has stayed poor because it was made to stay poor by an industry that broke unions, bought off politi-cians, and despoiled the land and water.

Thus the potential of the wind farm reaches far beyond Coal River Mountain, because it could finally lay to rest Big Coal's false promises by offering a more compelling future—a future where jobs are not based on a finite resource, they do not cause black lung or black water, and they con-tribute to the solution, not the cause, of the climate crisis. After all, once Sweden decided to abandon a carbon-based economy, its GDP began to grow three times as fast as ours because of investment in alternative energy.

Van Jones, special advisor for green jobs, enterprise, and innovation at the White House Council on Environmental Quality and author of *The Green Collar Economy*, has shown that "we can fight pollution and poverty at the same time." In Oakland, he helped create entry-level jobs for poorer people that had them performing energy audits and improving energy efficiency in homes. While replacing coal with wind and solar power is obviously crucial, Jones points out that "the main piece of technology in a green economy is a caulk gun."

Or a shovel. Patrick Angel, who heads up the Appalachian Regional Reforestation Initiative, has called for a massive tree-planting effort across all of the abandoned mine land throughout the mountains. Fast-growing willow trees could be planted and harvested for biofuels, while slower growing hardwoods could support a sustainable forestry movement while also contributing to the emerging carbon-credit market. Now that the dream of corn ethanol has passed, other abandoned mine sites could be planted with a more promising biomass such as switch grass, a high-yield perennial that thrives on marginal land.

What about mounting solar panels on south-facing valley fills, of which Appalachia has plenty? Rory McIlmoil has done some computations and figures that 20 percent of West Virginia's energy could come from thirty-thousand acres of barren mine land fitted out with photovoltaics. Energy from those panels, coupled with the wind energy from the mountaintops, could be fed into a direct-current "smart grid" so that the region's sources of energy become radically decentralized, along with the profits from that energy. Then thuggish corporations like Massey Energy would no longer wield so much power or cause so much havoc and heartbreak.

Still, change comes slow to coal country. On the same November day that the United States elected a new president who had made renewable energy a fundamental part of his campaign, West Virginia governor Joe Manchin easily won re-election as well. Days later, Massey began blasting near the ridgetop where Matt Noerpel had taken me four-wheeling.

Bo Webb lives in the valley below. Webb, who served as a Marine in Vietnam, sat down and started writing a letter to President Obama. "As I write, I brace myself for another round of nerve-wracking explosives being detonated above my home," Webb began. He said he was out of options. The Fourth Circuit Court of Appeals had overturned a prior court ruling that required thorough environmental impact studies on land permitted for mining, and on his way out the door, George W. Bush had overturned a rule prohibiting mining around streams.

"I beg you to re-light our flame of hope and honor," Webb wrote the president, "and immediately stop the coal companies from blasting so near our homes and endangering our lives. As you have said, we must find another way than blowing off the tops of mountains."

On March 24, two weeks after Webb sent his letter to President Obama, a seismic wave rolled across Appalachia, and it had nothing to do with explosives. The Environmental Protection Agency, in an abrupt reversal of policy, announced that it would re-examine all mine permits that might violate the Clean Water Act—including almost all the permits on Coal River Mountain. In a letter to the Army Corps of Engineers, Lisa Jackson, the new head of the EPA, wrote that she had "considerable concern regarding the environmental impact these projects would have on fragile habitats and streams."

When I saw the headline "EPA Signals Mining Crackdown" in the *Lexington Herald-Leader*, the words almost didn't make sense. They had really done it. The activists of Appalachia had actually beaten back Don Blankenship and opened a clearing for a serious consideration of wind development. It was by no means a final victory; this battle won't end quickly or cleanly. But more good news came on March 31, when U.S. District Judge Joseph Goodwin issued an injunction that voided certain valley fill permits and blocked the Army Corps of Engineers from issuing new permits for valley fills in southern West Virginia. The message was clear: the Corps was finally going to have to answer to someone other than coal operators. Suddenly, that four-letter word planted in Joe Manchin's flowerbed back in Charleston seemed not so frivolous. It was beginning to look like it might hold its own against the forces of Big Coal. It might even prevail.

Forty-two years ago, Wendell Berry pondered the concept of hope while camping in Kentucky's Red River Gorge, which the Army Corps of Engineers was then threatening to dam. "A man cannot despair," Berry concluded, "if he can imagine a better life, and if he can enact something of its possibility." To imagine—it is perhaps the most powerful moral force we posses. It maps a future that is worth finding, a place where we want to dwell. Then it calls us to enact that vision. It could happen on a mountaintop in West Virginia. It could happen in the heart's own private landscape. It could happen.

The Other Side of Fire
Leslie Ryan

I have heard it said that storytelling starts with the body and ends with the body. That's what gives stories the ability to snag the mind by its ankles from behind and land it facedown in something: life if the story's good, blandness if it's not.

But as a woman, I worry about this. For most women, the body, like the story, is not a simple thing. It's a battlefield where lies and truths about power go at it. A woman's mind might wander from skirt to skirt in that smoky place like a dislocated child, looking for some grounded legs to stand by, or on, for years. The woman might end up knowing herself only as a casualty, or recognizing herself only by her scars. While there may be some truth in such an identity, it is only a partial truth, and a potentially destructive one.

I want a different story.

I never thought much about fire until a few years ago, when I began teaching wilderness survival in the Great Basin desert of southern Idaho. I worked in a wilderness therapy program for troubled youth. The idea was that direct contact with the natural world could help these kids gain a more healthy sense of identity and empowerment.

Some of the teenagers who ended up walking around the desert like hunter-gatherers had been court-ordered to do so. A few of the boys arrived in cuffs, with their hair shaved down to the rind on one side and left to seed on the other. On their forearms they displayed homemade logos of heavy-metal rock bands, scratched in with sewing needles and flooded with blue fountain pen ink. They wore the tales of their crimes like dog tags, and we called these narratives "war stories."

But most of the boys didn't come that way. In spite of a few shocking tales, the boys' toughness hung on them uncomfortably. The manic energy they used in comparing transgressions made me smile, because beneath it they seemed to writhe like grubs set down in unfamiliar terrain, glistening and blinded by their recent emergence from childhood but as yet unsure of how to burrow into the next phase.

The girls came to the desert differently. Their fear wasn't just a thing to guess at beneath layers of toughness and tattoos; it was as evident as the black lace panties and see-through underwire brassieres they wore for twenty-one days of rigorous hiking. Their stories, shared in secret with other girls, were less war stories than love stories—or, more specifically, sex stories—but they were stories of power and identity just the same.

We instructors taught our students how to make backpacks from their blankets and string, how to find water in the desert, how to dig coal beds, how to construct debris huts and other shelters, how to identify and gather wild edibles, and basically how to keep themselves alive in difficult terrain. But the hardest thing we learned out there—the thing that made the students cry in frustration—was how to make fire with sticks.

I have been questioned about the relevance of bow and drill fire making to everyday life, and I have been challenged on the social structuring of wilderness therapy programs, which mostly benefit rich, white children. Wouldn't these kids feel a lot different about survival if they *really* had to do it—if they had to make fires on the floors of their freezing city apartments, rather than in this fabricated desert game?

I can only answer that question from my own experience, with a story that also takes place somewhere between war and love.

When I was twelve, my younger brothers and I were abandoned for a year or so in an apartment on the south side of Richmond, Virginia. Mom was wherever Dad had left her, probably back in the old house where she had been struggling with mental illness for years. After repeated complaints from our neighbors, who thought we children were being hurt and neglected, the court had ordered our father to remove us from the old house. We relocated on the other side of town, where no nosy neighbors knew us. At first I thought we would live in the apartment together—four children and our father—and start a new life. But it didn't work that way.

We still don't know where Dad lived during that time. At first it was every few days that he came back, bringing what we needed to survive. Some groceries: Spam, milk, and a case of Bisquick boxes. Then every week he would come. Then there was no pattern, and we couldn't tell when we would see him again.

Before long, the power got shut off. Water too. We were living in a husk of a house with no resources. The dishes in the sink had been crusted for so long they began to flake clean. The toilet hadn't been flushed in what seemed like months. We just kept using it until it began to overflow, and after that we shut the bathroom door and went in the new construction site under a pile of boards. Some of the windows in the apartment were broken out– one from my head, one from my brother's fist, others from things we threw. My brothers were aged ten, eight, and four. We fought.

We also made a pact. If anyone found out we lived alone, Dad had said, they'd break us apart. Mom was too sick to take care of us, so we'd all have to go live with different families, and we'd never see each other again. The four of us had gathered in the kitchen one day by the dry sink, and I scraped the crud from a sharp knife with my teeth. We sliced a blood pact into our hands: Never tell.

The neighbors on the left had evidently abandoned their apartment in a hurry. We went in there a lot at first, eating the food they had left and looking at the bloated fish floating in the tank. There were parts of a broken water bed, some lava lamps, clothing, and a bunch of empty boxes. All their wallpaper was swirled with bright metallic patterns, like our kitchen paper, but patches of it were torn down and left hanging. No one ever came in or out of there, and after the food was gone we stopped going there too, because it was a creepy place.

The neighbors on the right acted like we didn't exist. I think they knew we had gone into their apartment and stolen food, because they got double bolt locks and began to talk loudly about calling the police if they saw any delinquents around. We saw that we could get caught and separated, so we stopped taking from them.

My brothers learned from an older boy how to steal from stores. They could walk to the 7-Eleven in about half an hour. They stole ready-made food from there, since we had no electricity to cook the Bisquick and everything else was gone. The boys refused to eat Bisquick raw. Mostly they stole small food, for safety. Candy bars were usually the biggest they got from the 7-Eleven, because the clerks could see down the aisle pretty easily. From Safeway, though, they could get more, like peanut butter; it was easier, because the clerks changed more often and people didn't expect kids to be stealing. Sometimes they'd get extra for the baby, who couldn't come. I don't know how long this went on. Nine months, maybe a year.

Then one day I found myself standing in the kitchen. It was coming on winter, dusky in the house. A wet wind blew through the broken windows. I lifted my bare feet up and down on the cold kitchen floor. I was staring at the stove, scooping dry Bisquick from the box with crooked fingers. I wanted to turn on the stove. I wanted to wave my hands over the fiery concentric circles of the working heating element. I wanted there to be power in the house.

"I am twelve years old," I said out loud.

Bisquick floated onto the air as I spoke. In summer I had mixed the Bisquick in a bowl with sprinkler water and eaten it wet like that. Now the sprinkler faucets were off. The boys had shown me where they drank from the creek; the water was oily and bright orange-brown. I wouldn't do it.

"Bisquick should be cooked," I said.

When was the last time he came? I couldn't remember. He might never come back. Could we actually freeze here?

Something about the stove began to infuriate me. It was supposed to give us something.

"Damn thing," I said.

Big and useless. It made these promises and never kept them. I spit chunks of Bisquick at it, but they were too dry to stick. They fell all over my arms and chest, making a pattern of white, dusty splats.

I pulled the burner control knobs from their sticky prongs and hurled them one by one across the kitchen at the orange metallic wallpaper peeling from the wall. They left the paper dented like bent foil.

I grabbed a big metal dish spoon from the dish pile and banged on the steel edge of the stove. I wanted sparks. I wanted gouges. It was the cheap kind of spoon, and its bowl just bent back perpendicular.

"Damn you," I said, with the Bisquick on my teeth like plaque.

The baby was four, and he still couldn't talk. He did know to poop in the lumber. I was still getting good grades at school, because I had learned to read at a young age and was placed in the gifted classes, but my brothers were not doing so well. They had missed over a hundred days of school each. We had received a letter about it, addressed to Dad. I had to do something. I surveyed my options.

The only reading we had were old *Scientific Americans* and the other magazines under the mattress where Dad used to sleep. *Scientific Americans* were all men. The mattress ones were all women: *Penthouse* and *Playboy*. Dad liked their articles best. All of us had read them.

I read them again. There were women who had sex with all their best friends, their bosses, delivery people, and pets, with everyone watching everyone else, and it seemed to make things better. "Dear Xaviera," they wrote to their friend Xaviera, a woman who was pictured only as a pair of red lips with a penis-shaped lipstick going in. They told her all about it.

I read about all the special techniques women could learn to please men, like mouthing unwaxed cucumbers. Men took women to cooked dinner for this, and gave them promotions. They'd provide apartments, heated, for the whole family.

I walked to the bathroom doorway and stood outside. No one ever went in there. Stuff had actually flowed onto the floor. We could smell it all over the house. But the bathroom had the only mirror. I stripped off my pants, shirt, and underwear. I held my breath, opened the door, and climbed onto the sink counter.

With the murky light seeping in from the hall, I looked at my legs in the bathroom mirror. If I held them together, there were three long diamonds where the light came through, just like Xaviera said men liked: one above the ankles, one below the knees, and one between the thighs.

A stiffened orange towel lay on the small bathroom counter. I wrapped it around my mouth and nose like a gag so I could breathe. I turned around on the bathroom sink to look at the backs of my legs and butt.

If I swayed my back I looked curvier. I bent down with my butt stuck out and my hands on my knees to get the sideways picture, checking the curve of dim light along my spine and the flatness of my stomach. I was still holding my breath for as long as I could because the towel smelled almost as bad as the bathroom.

I squatted above the sink and looked into my pupils, wide and dark above the bristling cloth. I said aloud through the mask, "You have one thing."

I remember a time not long after that stove day when I was being hit by a jealous man. He was nineteen years old; I was twelve. He had six motorcycles, a punching bag, and a seemingly unlimited supply of drugs. I couldn't leave; he was giving me the drugs I sold for money. I wish I could say I sold them for food money, for food I would share with my brothers. This did happen sometimes. But not often. I wasn't a good mother.

What I really wanted was to be someone. What I really wanted was power, and the only way I could get it was to take it from someone who had more than enough. Drugs were the currency that allowed my body to be exchanged for money, and money is a poor person's idea of strength and possibility. So I just clamped my teeth, stood there, and let my friend hit me.

As he got madder, one zigzagged vein began standing and pulsing on his forehead like lightning. He was hot, coiled up red with his fury.

I, on the other hand, felt like a block of ice. Each blow to my head seemed to break off little pieces of my mind; they would go floating up into the corner of the room and stick there like ice chips behind a river rock.

Soon my body was standing alone in the bedroom, being hit.

But not me. He couldn't get at me. I was hovering alongside the brown ceiling stain from the upstairs toilet. I could watch my head lolling around as he cuffed me.

Do whatever you want to my body, you jerk, I said to myself. That's not *me*.

It was the same way having sex with him, and with the other men who, as I see in retrospect, had no business being sexually involved with a twelve-year-old girl. When I was with them, my mind would slip out the back of my head and go look out the window, if there was one.

My mind became more and more a body unto itself– in time, when it left me on the bed, I could feel its dry, bare feet shuffling across the floor. One time it made it all the way to the door, and paused there with its delicate spirit fingers on the knob. When it looked back to say good-bye to my body on the bed, something—compassion, necessity?—made it pop back inside.

After this went on for what seemed to be a long time, I began to worry about my brothers. We knew that our father thought of us, at least occasionally. We could tell by the apartment's utilities, which flickered on, through the months, as he paid—and then off, through the months, as he did not pay—the bills. But a number of different young men were coming into our house, and there was no one to stop them. Sometimes they brought their friends. If I was not home when they arrived, they came in anyway, drinking and smoking while waiting for me. They included my eleven-year-old brother in the party.

One night, my brother and I sat on the living room couch watching TV. We were both stoned, and the vertical hold on the TV didn't work, so we were watching Captain Kirk's head and torso being severed and lifted by a constantly rising black line. My brother told me that some of the men I'd been sleeping with had given the baby pot to smoke while they were smoking, and maybe other drugs too.

This, I said to myself, is not what I want our lives to be. I quit doing drugs then and didn't allow any of the men into our apartment again. All my friends disappeared.

I made another plan. My body had gotten me into this trouble; my mind would get me out. I had good grades, but they weren't useful yet. In order to be a good mother to these boys I'd need a job.

But I knew that a girl of my social class couldn't get a job; my clothes were embarrassing, my hair greasy, my shoes fake leather with unglued soles that slapped the ground as I walked. I was thirteen. I couldn't work for three years. I did look sixteen already, though; someone might be fooled into hiring me if I had the proper attire. Even if I couldn't get work yet, I reasoned, it was best to steal my wardrobe now, because as long as I was under sixteen, nothing would go on my permanent record and expose us if I did get caught.

I hitchhiked downtown to a fancy department store called Miller and Rhodes. This was before the days of electronic theft devices. I told the salesladies my father had asked me to come look for something nice for my mother– she was about my size, I said– and he'd be back later with me to see what I'd found. In the dressing room, I opened my big Naugahyde purse and stuffed in a grey wool business suit: tailored skirt, vest, and jacket, completely lined. I broke the hanger in half and stuffed it in too, and left the rest of the clothes there.

From that department I went to lingerie. I picked out a peach-colored Christian Dior teddy, pure silk. It snapped discreetly at the crotch; one hip was cut out and flounced with pleated gauze. I stole that too.

I see now that my faith in my mind was skimpy. My body was still the bottom line for power. I resented the fact, but I was a practical girl. Even if I was lucky enough to get a job with my suit and my grades, I'd need to be high class underneath too– for my boss, and for the real work that women do.

When I got home, I went up to my room and found my suitcase full of Barbies, which I was ashamed about still having anyway. I had written my name in pen all over the plastic luggage a long time before, in big curly handwriting with exclamation points and flowers. I took it into my father's closet and dumped the Barbies on the floor, so no boss would see Barbies in my room. I cleaned the little Barbie shoes out of the side pockets, folded the grey suit and the silk teddy into separate piles in the suitcase, and hid the suitcase under my bed.

As time went on, I added to the suitcase with a tan pantsuit, some oxford shirts, a pair of leather sling pumps stolen right off the rack, red lace bikini panties with bows on them, a matching bra, and the sexy kind of nylons that need a garter belt.

Before the suitcase was full, though, my father had come back, apparently to stay. When he came, it was late at night. He had a woman with him.

He called us downstairs one by one to where she sat at the three-legged kitchen table. Most of the lightbulbs were blown out, so only half her face was visible in the dim light from the hall fixture.

The woman was young, twenty-seven or so. She was twenty years younger than my father, but she had three children of her own. By the time I came downstairs to stand rigidly beside the boys, the woman was crying. We were embarrassed by her emotion, and by the way she said she would marry our father and save us.

She did marry him, but she couldn't save us. She could make sure we had shoes and meals and schooling, for which I am grateful. But she couldn't protect us from our father, who was violent and who owned her love. She couldn't even protect herself.

The skirts she wore, and the power they signified, offered no refuge to a child. They were too much like the ones I had stolen. All the pretty garments underneath, which were supposed to lead my stepmother somewhere better, only dragged her further into my father's control, like bridles and bits. In a landscape of boys and men and lies about power, though, they were the only skirts she and I knew. A year later, when the nine of us lived in a three-bedroom apartment, my own suits and panties still lay tucked in the suitcase under my bed, waiting there like passwords.

There are other lies about power and identity, more subtle than the ones told by pornography. When I first learned, not long ago, that being abandoned in a house without utilities or food is called child abuse, I smiled. When I learned that a twelve-year-old girl is a child, and a child being molested by anyone—an adult or another child—is called sexual abuse, I grinned. Suddenly I had a strange, different kind of power over the men who had hurt me, and it lay in my scars: If I had been wronged, then I was on the side of the good, and the men were on the side of the evil. Although I might not be stronger, or richer, or better in any other way, I was morally superior to them. And the moral superiority of the victim brings her power.

Like the virtue of victimization, the promise of pornography—that a woman's body is her identity and her source of strength—wasn't entirely wrong. But the way in which both of them were wrong, no person would ever teach me. The desert had to do that.

In my mid-twenties, I was led to the desert less by a decision of intellect that by a response to blood urgency. Going there was like picking up a baby who's facedown in a puddle.

Through all those years after middle school, my mind and body had stayed as distinct from each other as the wool suits and the garter belts. My mind had helped me get a job and go through college on scholarships. But as time went on it grew more and more controlling, until it became tyrannically disdainful of my body. By the time college ended I was living almost completely in my head: The intellectual jargon of modern philosophy rang in my brain all night like an alarm, and I hardly knew if or why I was alive.

Fortunately, my body had better sense. She spoke up from under the bed, where I'd kept her locked up like a caged animal and had fed her only scraps for years. She said, "Get outside."

I went west, to the desert, to a state where I knew no one and took a job for which I had little preparation other than backpacking.

I've heard the Great Basin described by one student as "Nature's Worst." It's sage and basalt country: grey and brown and fairly nondescript at first. The hunting and gathering Paiutes who lived there in early times were disparagingly labeled Diggers because they ate roots and grubs rather than something charismatic like buffalo.

In the rain, the Great Basin ground, where it's not rock, turns to slimy mud. If you have to walk when it's wet, the mud will grow on your boot soles in bricklike platforms, your quads will cramp with the weight of them, and your ankles will roll above the boot blocks like they're broken. When the sun sucks the moisture out of the mud again, the ground will crack into miles of dusty pieces.

In some places, a six-foot-tall person can lie in the dirt and make dust angels without knocking into anything but basalt gravel and stickers, so people call the desert barren. But the desert isn't barren. It's alive, and it tells the body stories that are true.

When I began teaching survival, wandering for several months through the basalt-pillared canyons and the expansive plateaus of the Great Basin with some blankets, knives, cooking cans, and personal items, I underwent a transformation.

My hands twisted wet bark into cordage, carved fire sticks, and dug holes for coal beds; my fingers and palms hardened into dark, basaltic chunks of flesh. Wind and sun made my hair spiny as the wild wheat we'd gather near old homesteads; the nomadic days chiseled a landscape of calluses and cracks into my feet. My dung shrank like a coyote's, and my breath came slow and reptilian.

I came to know a little about the creatures that passed their lives out there. Snipes would swoop above us at dawn like bats. Grouse would do the unthinkable– eat sagebrush, puke most of it back up in pellets, pass the rest through in slimy wads like black slugs– and live healthy, normal lives in the process. Golden eagles would fly over with their writhing meals– rabbits or snakes– in tow. Overnight, badgers would excavate holes big enough for a twenty-gallon drum; with their bare hands, they'd put a shovel to shame, plowing through cementlike earth in the dark. And the sun ignited both ends of day with what looked like fire; morning and evening never tired of being burned that way.

My mind and body began separating less and less often, mostly because I was learning to survive out there, and doing so did not require that my mind float up in the air and watch bad things happen to my body.

In fact, the desert required just the opposite: In order to survive there, I had to be fully present. When the summer heat seemed intent on vaporizing my scalp as I walked, my senses would tell me where to locate shade. They'd show me which cranny was safe to crouch in during a rainstorm. They'd let me know which plant was wild carrot and which hemlock.

In the desert, a mind that wanders far from the body can land a person in strange territory, far from water or cover. If at any time I stopped listening to my body and to my lived experience, I might get lost. I found myself realizing that power does come from my body after all, but in a very different way.

On the first winter survival trip I led, I met a student who brought some things together for me. Dawn was fourteen years old. Her face was tinged with a solemn and unnerving coldness, like the blush on frost-nipped fruit. On that trip, she was the only other female. For some reason, I wanted her to be the first to make bow-drill fire.

On the trail, Dawn was a quiet girl, and distant. Like so many students, she triggered in me the feeling that something had been lost. I didn't know why she was there.

On day ten of the trip, we awakened to a low dawn in the mouth of a wide canyon. We'd each built a fire the night before in a rock-lined pit, and then buried the coals. Eight hours later, the earth beneath me was still as warm as hands. Four teenagers and another instructor lay around me in their snowy pods, each tight in a sheet of plastic and two blankets. Three boys snored out of time with one another; one had come unhatted. His hair stuck out in a unicorn spike.

Later that day, I was working with Dawn on her bow-drill fire. I had already let the boys quit trying; they were cooking lentils a short distance away. Big sagebrush, seven feet tall, stood around us on an unlikely patch of fertile riparian soil. Twenty degrees, platy sky, preweather stillness. Serviceberries were shriveled on the bush; the wild onions, yampah, and nettles we'd gathered all year had dried to bony stalks and blown away. Loose strands of grey-brown bark ribboned the tall sage; they scraped in a brief breeze.

Dawn knelt on a thin layer of granular snow. Her left hand, blistered and ruddy from carving, cupped a bone hand socket that served as a pivot point for a sage spindle. Dawn worked wood considerately, and her spindle was just right: Like a stout pencil, it was a little longer than her hand and thick as her index finger. She'd sharpened the upper end of the spindle to fit into the hand socket. The lower, blunt end was black from friction.

When the blunt end was newly carved, before it had begun to burn, it had shown the sage's concentric growth rings. The wood grain moved out from them like the linking strands in a spiderweb. I told Dawn I hadn't seen many things prettier than that pattern. She gave me a sideways, suspicious look.

The thong of a half-moon bow girdled Dawn's spindle, and by stroking the bow back and forth with her right hand, Dawn could drill the spindle down into a plank of sage. The friction between this fire board and spindle would rub off clouds of smoke and charred wood fibers called punk.

The punk would drop down through a pie-shaped notch in the fire board. Hotter and hotter punk would accumulate there, and it would eventually weld itself into a small coal. Then the fire maker would gently lift the coal into a nest of well-rubbed sagebrush bark, and her long, steady breaths would turn it into flame.

Theoretically. But Dawn still stared at her bowdrill set as if she were illiterate in fire, even though she had cut the set herself. Technically, she was fine. Perfect form. I stayed after her about it, keeping her up later than the boys almost every night, trying to figure out what was wrong. Her light hair whipped back and forth above the fire board, her bowing arm cramped tight, and her breath came hard, but each day ended the same: no punk, no fire.

She'd say quietly, "I'll never do it."

None of the other students had made this type of fire yet either. Everyone could make sparks by striking a quartz or flint rock against their carbon steel knife blades, and they got fires at night this way, even Dawn.

But something about bow drill spooked them. It seemed so old, like magic. There was nothing but their own bodies and the body of the sagebrush twirling together, and the result was fire.

The boys had a bow-drill-related superstition. The one with the unicorn spike, George, would shake a crusty ash cake at Dawn and say, "Dude. You gotta believe."

On day eleven, the group had hiked the usual distance of about seven miles. We made camp near a shallow basalt cave. It was don't-get-your-hair-wet weather, but Dawn and I wanted to wash up. We heated two billycans of water on a small fire, grabbed our bandanas, and retreated to the shadowy cave where we could undress away from the boys.

White owl splats looked like paint along the head-high inner ledges of the cave. Dawn and I shifted our cold barefoot weight on the basalt gravel and tried to give each other as much bathing privacy as possible, but then an echoing crack and rush snapped along the walls, and we both jerked to the sound. Rock and ice from a ledge outside.

I saw then in the half light that the girl had a secret. Low on her breast-bone, where no one would see, a lattice of rippling white scars ran over Dawn, like someone had thrown a net on her. Unlike the superficial heavy-metal logos the boys flaunted, her grid was a private and personal statement from herself to herself; white and geometric as a chain-link fence, the pattern was more certainly the sign of her own neat hand than the cramped signature she made on paper.

Later, when I talked to a supervisor on the radio, she said Dawn was cruel at home. She was cruelest to what was most vulnerable: her younger sister and the pets. Helpless animals called forth a meanness in her, and trapped creatures flipped something inside her– she became vicious.

The supervisor also told me a story about Dawn. She had been seeing a bad therapist not long ago.

He had told her this: "Listen. If you can't get along at home, you'll end up on the streets. You'll need food. You'll need shelter. You'll need warmth. And to get those things, you'll need money. You're a fourteen-year-old girl. You have no marketable skill. You have nothing."

I imagined him pausing and scanning her.

"Well," he'd continued, "you do have a nice body. You could use that."

He showed her magazines, how the girls—eleven, twelve, sixteen—had found their pimps and set up their survival strategies.

He was trying to scare her into behaving at home, but when I asked her about it, Dawn said, "He didn't tell me anything I didn't already know."

On day twelve, I was leading, so I called a silent hike. I'd woken up in a funk; I wanted some time to think. We had a five-mile jaunt up and down over scree slopes, through icy sage, and over frozen coyote turds. I kept turning around to find the group shrinking on the near horizon. Dawn was farthest back, straggling forlornly.

I realized I was stalking the desert like a madwoman, clamping my teeth and pounding my digging stick on rhyolite blocks without noticing every time I had to wait.

I thought of the untold stories that had caused Dawn to carve a grid on her chest and to torment helpless things. I imagined what had compelled her to shut her body in a cage of scars. I read once that two-thirds of people jailed for abuse have been victims of it themselves.

There is something pathological about inhabiting victimhood, and living off its skewed sense of power and identity. It's like being in a high basalt tunnel. It's all right to hang out there for a while, while the actual storm of abuse is occurring; the true victim doesn't have much choice. The high walls are protective, and "moral superiority" offers an overhang of some dignity. But moral superiority itself can become an abusive trap, where the floor is a sharp cushion of dark gravel. Like anger, victimization is a place to move through. The next step is survival.

I don't know what comes after that.

Dawn wasn't moving; she was fenced into one of those partial truths that quickly become lies. The pornographic therapist told her to separate her mind and body and peddle the body part; her role as a victim told her that power lay as much in being scarred as in scarring. Both lies make battlefields of women's bodies; they require that we keep hurting our bodies somehow, because our power and our identities depend on it. But these lies are based on an incomplete assumption: that strength lies only in our having power *over* ourselves or others.

Day thirteen marked Dawn's turn to lead the hike. Overnight, the temperature had dropped from twenty to zero, and the wind shot up over the mesa rims in a wall of velocity. We began walking over a major plateau at sunup, and by midday it was minus fifteen in the wind.

At one point we set our eyes on a big chunk of basalt three miles away, which appeared periodically through the whipping, granular snow. We planned on crouching there for a minute of rest, but when we arrived, the wind crashed around the rock like icy surf. It knifed through the blankets we had wrapped around our sweaters, and when George stopped there to pee, his zipper froze open.

By dusk we had reached a system of shallow caves and overhangs in a sheltered basalt canyon. We made camp there.

Squatting on the ground, chipping away pieces of frozen earth with my digging stick to make a coal bed pit, I realized why I had been so anxious for Dawn to be the first to make bow-drill fire. I'd wanted her to have power over the boys, so she'd believe in herself. But the desert doesn't teach power over. It teaches something else.

Mastery of fire has long symbolized humankind's power over nature, and it's hard to interpret the forms of fire we usually encounter—electric stoves, internal combustion engines, or nuclear warheads—otherwise. It's true that bow-drill fire can be used to teach us power over the land and over one another. But it can also be used to teach us power through, and within.

Standing in front of a dead electric stove is nothing like kneeling beside a smokeless fire board. Regardless of her race or social class, unless the stove girl is a master electrician who can illegally tap into power from a faraway source, she is bodily helpless before the cold metal cube. All she can do is break it apart and throw it around. The stove teaches her that her body can't bring her power, unless she uses it to take power from someone or somewhere else, at the expense of her spirit.

When she's kneeling by her fire board, though, the cold girl is free to choose another identity. In fact, she can identify with the world through the bow-drill set. After all, she chose the tall, dead sage plant, cut the branches from it, and shaped the parts herself. In choosing and shaping her tools, she has created a sense of autonomy. If the tools don't work, there are things she can do about it, with her mind and body together: push down harder, go faster, examine the set, smooth out the parts, try again.

Fire by friction requires something more than turning a knob on a stove. It requires spirit, or at least, in Dawn's case, the belief that mind and body can go safely together in the world. It requires the faith that a woman's power does come from within her body, but not separately from her mind.

Even though a girl feels individually empowered by making friction fire, she never does it completely alone. As anyone who had tried to make fire from sappy or sodden wood will tell, she makes flame only through her surroundings, by the grace of the fire which exists already in the sage and in the natural world at large.

In some spots in the Great Basin, basalt towers spewed as fire from the recesses of the earth just three thousand years ago. In these spots, fire making seems less individual than collective: It's an invocation of an ever-present, hidden power.

The attentive student comes to tell which plants—like sage, clematis, and cottonwood—are full of fire, and which are not. The fire in her own arms shifts with her physical or psychic state. In this sense, friction firemaking enacts mystery and provides a link with a different sense of identity. The woman has power within herself and through her connection with the natural world, not power over them.

This sense of identity I could never force Dawn to accept. She'd have to choose it herself or find a different one on her own, probably through a long chain of experiences. Her story might end up sounding nothing like mine, or the other girls' love tales, or the boys' war stories.

Dawn's flint and steel fire-making skills were good enough for safety, and she had hiked well in the lead. I wouldn't keep her up bow drilling any later than the others from now on.

After finishing my fire pit, I went and sat beside Dawn under her overhang, out of the wind. She looked small, sitting back on her heels rubbing tinder. I got out the map and measured the day's route with string.

"Fourteen and a half miles, Dawn."

She quit rubbing and looked up. "What?"

"You led fourteen and a half miles without a break."

Dawn stared at me. I heard the irregular sounds of the boys breaking up wood.

After a while she said, "Either it wasn't fourteen and a half miles, or I didn't lead."

We were silent.

"You led fourteen and a half miles without a break," I said again. I cut the string and laid it over the knee of her wool army pants, across the long strands of sagebrush bark tinder, which spread around her like a dress. The Paiute Indians, "Diggers," used to weave their clothes, boots, and blankets from such bark– the same bark they blew into flame.

"You must be tired," I said. "You can skip bow-drill tonight."

Dawn's camp stayed quiet until after dark. I was about to go check on her when the sound of grinding fire sticks echoed out from under her ledge. I sat for a while wondering whether or not she'd want company for this attempt.

After a few minutes the good smell of sage smoke traveled out toward my camp. I was on my feet heading toward Dawn's spot when I heard the bow drill stop and saw a glowing pile of punk moving slowly through the air on her knife blade.

The cherry coal disappeared into the dark tinder. She lifted the bundle to blow. The tinder nest began to glow orange, and its dim light revealed Dawn's uptilted face as she sent her breath through the fibers.

I walked up just as the bundle took flame. The fire lit the ceiling of her overhang for the first time, and she still held the bundle aloft. But she wasn't watching the fire; she was looking up. Chiseled into the rock overhead was a petroglyph, left by the Paiute or the Shoshone: a series of concentric half circles like a sunset, or like half the pattern of a pebble thrown in water. Dawn didn't smile, but I saw the reflection of the fire in her eyes.

Trapline: An Ojibwe Man's Search for Identity on the Canadian Taiga

David Treuer

Beavers are, as far as animals go, odd contraptions. The largest rodent in North America, the beaver has webbed feet, a scaly tail, and two front teeth with orange enamel on the front and dentin in the back so that as they wear down they self-sharpen. They are powerful swimmers, chewers of trees, and builders of dams—some of which have been known to stretch for hundreds of feet. They were once trapped in unsustainable numbers for their fur, their fat, and their scent glands, which produce a secretion that has been used for medicinal purposes since antiquity. Pliny the Elder maintained that the smell of the glands was so powerful, much like smelling salts, as to cause a woman to miscarry, although it was later diluted in alcohol for use as a musky addition to perfumes.

When beavers were plentiful during the early days of the fur trade, my tribe, the Ojibwe, enjoyed an incredible quality of life. While other tribes were being wiped out or displaced, our birth rates were up and our land base was increased by a factor of twenty. In 1700, England exported roughly seventy thousand beaver-felt hats (beaver skins were dehaired, and only the hair was used in hat making). In 1770, the number of exported hats had risen to 21 million. But the demand (and supply) of beaver couldn't last.

Some estimates place the number of beavers in North America at over 60 million at the time of contact. By 1800 they were all but extinct east of the Mississippi. We Ojibwe shared much the same fate, pushed west, reduced in numbers, eking out an existence in the swamps and lowlands of the American interior. Though the tribe was once as defined by trapping beaver as the Aztecs were defined by gold or the Sioux by the buffalo hunt, by the twentieth century only the idea remained. The furs and the knowledge necessary to harvest them were fading.

As an Ojibwe child from Leech Lake Reservation in Northern Minnesota, I grew up around hunters. But aside from our mother teaching us to snare rabbits, we didn't trap animals like "bush Indians" did. Instead, we harvested wild rice in the fall, made maple sugar in the spring, and shopped for food like everyone else. My father (a Jew and a Holocaust survivor) and my mother (an Ojibwe Indian and tribal court judge) put as much emphasis on homework as they did on living off the land. None of the other kids from Leech Lake that I knew had grown up trapping or living off the land either. But this was still held up as the only truly Ojibwe way of life, and as I grew older I longed to commit myself to the bush. So when Dan Jones, an Ojibwe friend from across the border, offered to teach me to trap beaver on his trapline in northwestern Ontario, I said yes.

Lewis Henry Morgan in 1868 wrote, "the life of the trapper, although one of hardship and privation, is full of adventure. They lead, to a greater or less extent, a life of solitude in the trackless forests, encountering dangers of every kind, enduring fatigue and hunger, and experiencing, in return, the pleasures, such as they are, accorded by the hunt."

Perhaps because I had never been trapping, I was sure that every word Morgan, a gentleman ethnologist and fan of the beaver, wrote was true; at least I wanted them to be true. I wanted the special knowledge that all trappers seem to possess. I wanted their forearms and their expertise with a knife. I wanted to be a part of that brotherhood of whom it was said in bars, and around kitchen tables, and over the open tailgates of dented pickups, "Oh him? He's a real bushman. No one knows the bush like he does."

I drove to Dan's reserve in northwestern Ontario after Christmas in 1996. The name of the reserve, in English, is somewhat odd: Redgut Bay (named after a former chief of the band). The Ojibwe name is much longer: Nigigoonsiminikaaning (The Place of Abundant Little Otter Berries). I have never been able to find a "little otter berry," nor have I found someone who has found one, so part of me wonders if "little otter berry" is a way of saying "otter shit." Which just goes to show that if you scratch the surface of romance you'll find slapstick, and if you scrape off the slapstick you might find wonder, because, after all, places (like animals) don't always give up their secrets.

All of this—romance, slapstick, wonder—were mingled in Dan. About five foot eight and more than two hundred pounds, Dan looks like a traditional Ojibwe man should look: stocky, strong, black hair, dark skin. He's also—and I've tested this—pretty close to imperturbable. Once, when we were checking traps together on a beaver house, the ice broke underneath him and he fell into the freezing water. All he said after he got out was "oops." He is indifferent as far as money is concerned. I've never known a stronger paddler. When you see him filleting fish or skinning animals, you think to yourself that he was born with a knife in his hands, yet when he sleeps he needs no less than three pillows to be comfortable. His jokes are terrible. He thinks it great sport to tease people in uncomfortable ways in public. He remains one of my very best friends and always will.

Dan mostly traps for two animals—beaver and pine marten (like a Canadian sable)—although he grew up trapping and snaring just about anything that moved. His mother once held the world record for beaver skinning. He was raised on the trapline, moving from the village out to the line in the winter, back to the village in the summer, to rice camp in the fall, and back to the trapline. His first memory is of lying in a rabbit-skin sleeping bag, watching the jagged outline of spruce against the sky.

We drove to the super-market and loaded up on what Dan referred to as "trapping food"—cigarettes, bacon, eggs, butter, bread, Chips Ahoy!, Diet Pepsi, canned potatoes, oatmeal, and pork chops. His wife drove us out of town on a double-track path through stands of jack pine and over frozen creeks. We followed it for twelve miles and stopped. We offloaded the snowmobile, attached the sled, and filled it with food and clothes, then drove off the road toward Moose Bay—a clear clean fingerlet of water stretching to the northern-most arm of Rainy Lake. An hour later we arrived at the cabin on a small bay surrounded by balsam and poplar.

Rainy Lake is in the Canadian Shield. There is water everywhere—pond after pond, river after river, lake after lake. According to geologists, the water is still learning where to go, channels and streams hardly set. This land of old rock and new water forms the base of the boreal forest—the largest unbroken forest in the world—and is the world's largest terrestrial biome. The land is studded with pine, fir, and spruce. In summer, it is almost impassable; in winter, if you step off your trail, one hundred yards might as well be a mile through the deep snow. There might be something about the Great Plains—the openness, the sense of scale—that is good for stories and epic struggles. Not so the boreal forest. Horizons are hard to come by. The sky is a fractured thing. There are precious few vistas. Instead you are enclosed, hemmed in, covered over. It is a good place for secrets and secret knowledge, for conspiracies and hauntings.

The cabin was less beautiful than the country around it and, as regulated by law, rather small—ours was sixteen feet by twenty feet. Only trappers who buy the trapping rights to an area are allowed to build one. This one hadn't seen a human being since the previous year. If what happens on the trapline stays on the trapline, then it's equally true that what goes into the cabin stays in the cabin. Old cupboards were shoved in the corner between two nonworking gas ranges. A table, three beds (one a stowaway bed like you find in hotels), clothes, a wood stove, a box of beaver traps, and three or four bags of garbage completed the cabin. Under one of the beds I found a stack of *Playboy* and *Penthouse* magazines; a centerfold was tacked to the door. The whole place was overrun by mice. That night we cut firewood, got the cabin thawed out—it was minus ten degrees Fahrenheit—cooked some pork chops, and chopped a hole in the lake to get water. Then I learned the first thing about trapping: how to play cribbage.

Trapping beavers is largely a matter of finding where they live. Before ice- up, either by walking along the shore or by canoe, the trapper will locate the beaver house, beaver dams, food stash, and channels (worn paths near convenient food sources) and place drowning sets at these areas using either 220 Conibears or 330 Conibears. This trap was invented about fifty years ago by Frank Ralph Conibear, an Anglo-Canadian trapper. It was a revolution in traps and trapping, making it much more certain and productive. Conibears, or body-grip traps, are two steel squares attached to one another by a hinge. Steel springs keep the jaws open. To set the trap, the springs are compressed and the steel squares of the trap are held together by a catch from which dangles a trigger. If a beaver swims through and touches the trigger, the catch moves up, and the springs, under tension, slam the steel squares open across the beaver's chest, neck, or head. Death is quick. Until the advent of body-grip traps, trappers relied on wire snares or, more often, leg-hold traps set in channels and at the entrances to a beaver lodge. These would close on the beaver's foot and drown it, or often enough, the beaver would lose a leg in the trap.

Before steel or iron, trapping was another matter entirely. To trap beaver without the use of steel meant tearing open beaver houses to catch the beaver in its den, which is a hollow chamber above the waterline, or isolating the channels and runs under the ice. One would break open the house and wait at each and every channel for the beaver to surface, then kill it—with arrows, guns, or clubs—when it emerged. This was time-consuming and brutally hard work, and it took a lot of bodies—two people tearing up the house and four or five waiting at the channels.

But Dan and I had everything we needed, and we relied on steel body-grip traps exclusively. We would be trapping the en- trances to the beaver houses on the string of ponds that, like terraces, are stacked one on top of the other all the way from the big lake deep into the woods, almost to where we were dropped off. We stopped at the first beaver house. Dan showed me how to tell if the house is occupied or "dead"—look for a cone of crystallized vapor on top of the house that looks like a nipple or wick. This is a sure sign that the house is live; the beavers' warm breath travels through the frozen slurry of mud and crisscross of sticks on top of the house. When it meets the subzero air, it freezes, creating the nipple. In the first pond, one house was live and the other dead. Once we located the live house, we got off the snowmobile, and with Dan in the lead, we tapped around the house with the point of the chisel. The ice is usually thinner over the entrances, worn by the passing, in and out, of the beavers' bodies. The chisel broke through, we cleared the ice and sticks away, and using a long bent pole, found the beaver run. We set our traps. Then on to the next, and the next, and the next. We put thirteen traps in the water that first day.

Perhaps this is the strangest thing about modern trapping among the Ojibwe: it is an age-old cultural practice, as ingrained, as natural, as everything else about our culture. The snare, the trap, the trail, the lure, the catch—these are the metaphors by which we make our meanings. Yet it has been many hundreds of years since we have even so much as worn a fur, except as decoration or for ceremonial purposes. As soon as we could, we traded pelts for guns, axes, kettles, wire, and cloth. Furs are fine, I guess (I have, for sentimental reasons, a beaver-skin cap and moose-hide gloves). But cloth—wool especially, but also cotton—lasts longer, is easier to clean, can be sewn into many more things, and holds up longer. I only know of one Indian who wears furs—Jim LaFriniere of White Earth Reservation has a muskrat-hide jacket. I don't think he wears it because he's Indian; I think he wears it because he is, at White Earth, a BIG MAN. Modern synthetics are even better than trade cloth. There is nothing quite like chopping a hole in the ice with an ax and getting covered in dirty slush, only to have it bead and then freeze on my Gore-Tex parka. As for gloves, moose skin gets slick fast when the water freezes, and the ax goes flying out of your hands. But waterproof gloves with rubberized palms—they make all the difference. All the furs we catch—with a few held back for ceremonial use—will go on the market. In 1996, beaver were fetching, as I remember, between thirty-five and fifty Canadian dollars per hide. Occasionally we ate the meat. Mostly we ate pork chops.

The next day we had three beaver in our traps. Not bad for one night's sets. We checked the traps all that morning, napped, and then spent the evening skinning. Or, rather, Dan showed me how to do it on one beaver, and I spent the rest of the night working on the other two (since they were caught in sets I had made). As with any kind of hunting or trapping, the killing is the easy part; skinning and butchering is where the work is. Beaver have incredibly thick hides, which, when rough skinned (taken off the body but not cleaned), are thick with fat, especially around the tail, that I can only describe as blubber.

I learned quickly to rough skin a beaver in ten minutes or less. Fine skinning, or fleshing, is much harder and more important—leave too much fat on, and the hide won't dry right; slice or put holes in the hide, and that lowers its value. There are many methods for fleshing. Dan pinches the hide between his thumb and middle finger, and using his index finger to provide tension, he takes long, smooth strokes with his knife; the fat peels away smoothly and cleanly. It took me hundreds of hours of practice to approximate his skill.

As I struggle to separate the fat from the skin using a fillet knife, Dan, smoking a Player's Light and drinking Diet Pepsi, tells me that all the furs are taken to the fur buyer, graded, and bought, and then the fur buyer brings them to a fur auction where lots of furs are bid on, purchased, and then sewn or made into something. Since the British have stopped wearing funny-looking beaver hats, I'm not sure who's buying them. Dan says the biggest buyers are the Greeks, Russians, and Chinese.

It was uncomfortable, to a degree, to see the beavers undergo the transformation from beautiful animal to a skin worth x dollars. Hunting is, to many people, more palatable, I suppose. Eating an animal you killed seems more just. On the other hand, maybe it only seems that way. It is largely a myth that Indian people were somehow natural conservationists who used all the parts of the animal. We were as wasteful as every other people living on the move without electricity or refrigeration: we ate what we could, dried what we could, and left the rest for the wolves. And trading an animal's life for the resources that you need is not, as far as Dan is concerned, a bad trade. His response is that if our ancestors had had the same ethical concerns, we wouldn't be here today. (By comparison, my father—of European stock—had no use for trapping. But the "old ways" of doing things were one of the things my father admired, perhaps romanticized, about the Indians he befriended when he moved to Leech Lake in the 1950s.)

Dan was clearly less worried about it than I was. And why should he be worried? Why, just by virtue of being American Indian, should he live out ideals (about the sanctity of life, about the equality of animals) that have largely been foisted on him by James Fenimore Cooper and Rousseau and every other conscientious outsider? Dan is an Indian who loves to trap, who loves the animals he traps, enjoys the process of handling them, and who, at the end of all that, loves to golf and needs new clubs.

After the hides are fleshed, they are nailed onto boards on which a series of concentric ovals have been drawn. The size of the beaver determines which oval you use. Stretching beaver is its own art. Too loose and you cheat yourself of profits because the beaver dries to a smaller size than it might have. Too tight and the number of hairs per inch is reduced, your furs are graded down, and you lose money. We leave the beaver carcasses on the ice for the eagles and the wolves—there's not a trace left come morning. The fat and muscle skinned o= the hides are chopped into baseball-sized chunks as bait for marten and fisher (a sort of cross between a marten and a weasel but much larger).

New Year's passes and we listen to the country countdown on the radio, play cribbage, skin and stretch beaver. Every day is blessedly the same. There are no other people. Nothing moves. Occasionally we hear a plane far overhead or a snowmobile in the distance. I hear wolves at night. We have caught sixteen beaver and a few marten by the first week of the new year.

And then Dan says, "Think you can handle this on your own now? I've got to bring our furs back to the reservation, and then I have to go to work. I showed you how to do it beginning to end. No problem, right?" He leaves the next day, and I will be, for the next two weeks, on my own. Since he is taking the snowmobile with him, I will also be on foot.

The days blended into one another. I left the cabin after first light carrying a shotgun, an ax, a pack with lunch, and coffee. I was finally getting the romance I thought I wanted. Our line of traps was seventeen kilometers long, and I walked it every day. I checked and reset the traps, skinned the beaver on the ice and put the hides in my pack, caught the occasional rabbit in a snare, shot the occasional partridge. I would return to the cabin after crossing a wide bay of Rainy Lake, and sleep for a few hours before fleshing and stretching. After that I read, wrote, and went to bed. I bathed by heating up water and pouring it into a five-gallon plastic bucket. I saw a lot of trees. I saw a lot of snow. I caught a lot of beaver, and I skinned a lot of them. I read and reread Confessions of Felix Krull, and when I ran out of cigarettes I began ripping out pages from the back to roll tobacco and read the Playboys instead. I read Tim O'Brien and T. C. Boyle and marveled at the odds of two of my favorite stories—"On the Rainy River" and

"King Bee"—existing in this trapping cabin far from any other kind of print. I began to dislike airbrushing for the same reason that long ago I really liked airbrushing.

During the nights I listened to the ice booming on the lake. During the day, when I went to fetch water from the hole in the lake, I began to see how subtle changes in temperature and wind affected the thickness of the ice. I heard a lot of wind and came to like the difference between wind through spruce, wind through balsam, wind through bare poplar, wind through red oak, wind through marsh grass, and wind through dead cat-tails. I saw what wind and sun did to old moose tracks and deer tracks and squirrel tracks and rabbit tracks and fisher tracks and marten tracks and fox tracks. I once crossed a pond to check my traps, and when I crossed back ten minutes later, seven sets of timber wolf tracks had crossed over mine. I learned that, despite everything, I wasn't very comfortable with the idea that there were so many timber wolves so close to me. At night, when I fleshed and stretched the hides, I listened to country music. I memorized "Strawberry Wine" by Deana Carter, "Is That a Tear" by Tracy Lawrence, and "Little Bitty" by Alan Jackson. I liked "Little Bitty" least of all, but I found myself singing it more often than any other.

I learned I liked quite a bit the medicine-y smell of beaver fat. I learned that each and every animal I killed and then skinned was more or less perfect. I learned that each and every animal had been designed to live a certain way and had acted according to that design. I learned that walking upwards of seventeen kilometers a day, chopping through inches of ice, cutting firewood, and hauling water on a diet of pork chops and oatmeal gets you in very good shape. And then, one day, I learned that steel was a pretty amazing thing and that without it very little of the bounty around me would be mine.

I had been chopping through the ice to check one of my beaver sets. Each night a couple of inches of ice formed over the hole, and so every morning I had to remove that ice. It was soon mounded all around the hole, and the hole itself was like a funnel. I had finished chopping and had scooped out the ice and slush and placed the ax behind me, and before I knew it the ax slid down the funnel and disappeared into the water. It was the only ax I had, and without it I wouldn't be able to check any of the other traps. Without it I couldn't split any wood for the stove, and dry wood was scarce near the cabin. Without the ax, I would have little to do and our fur count would plateau and I would be reduced to eating out of cans. In a flash, I came to appreciate my tribe's age-old hunger for metal and later plastic. One of the great criticisms of my tribe's behavior in the eighteenth and nineteenth centuries was our so-called dependence on trade goods. But try living without metal knives, or axes, or even a pot to cook in.

I knew I had to do something about the ax, and there was only one thing to do: I stripped down, set my clothes on the ice, and lowered myself into the hole. The water was thirty-four degrees, and it hurt everywhere at once. The good news was that the water wasn't any deeper than my armpits. The bad news was that I had only a few seconds during which I'd have feeling in my toes. I found the handle with my left foot, took a breath, ducked under the surface of the water, grabbed it, and got out as quickly as I could. It took me an hour of fast walking to get warm again.

Dan came back after two weeks and brought with him more coffee, more cigarettes, more food, and the feeling that instead of romance I had gotten intimacy. With him, to be sure. But also with the animals under the knife and the place itself. After a while I had to try very hard to locate the danger and excitement that writers like Morgan and many others attach to the bloody business of professional trapping. For Dan, growing up on the trapline and then returning to it after high school had been the most peaceful times of his life. Indian boarding school, life in the mainstream, these had been bloody and hard. Trapping, by comparison, was guided by rhythms and activities that were, in themselves, small, finite, measurable, and, paradoxically, eternal—a quiet steady kind of work that was reminiscent of a life outside of time. For me, after a while the thrill of trapping gave way to a deeper satisfaction much harder to name and much more profound than romance and danger.

This became the rhythm of the rest of the winter: two weeks alone, Dan for an extended weekend, repeat. It was part of the most profound years of my life at the end of which there were many things I could do that few others could, and many things I could do that I never imagined I could. And none of what I had learned really mattered in the larger world. I was pleased to discover that trapping rewards a mind that is organized, creative, and neurotically interested in details. Which is to say: trapping is an activity made for a mind just like mine. I became a trapper.

For the next five years, I spent a few weeks every year trapping with Dan and a month or two trapping on my own back home on the Leech Lake Reservation. In 2002, after having trapped beaver, mink, marten, fisher, and otter, my brother Micah and I decided to expand our trapping techniques to include more snaring. We hoped to snare a fox. We talked to as many trappers as possible, read books, went to trapping forums online, and after buying and treating (boiling, dying, and waxing) our snares, we were ready to begin.

We hung our first snares at the beginning of the holidays in December. It was warm and there wasn't much snow and we didn't know what we were doing. We set our snares too high or too low; we set them on rises and humps so they were too clearly silhouetted on the trails. We set a snare in an area that we thought was a fox run and came back the next day to find a porcupine caught by the neck and foreleg. He squirmed in a kind of slow agony. We used natural funnels—places where the game trails narrowed to squeeze through dense brush or swamps or between deadfalls—but we didn't trust the snares themselves and blocked up the trail with sticks and branches so that the fox would have nowhere to go but into our snares. It must not have looked right to them: no fox came near our sets. We did almost everything wrong. Every morning we got up, excited at the prospect of fox after fox dead in our snares. Day after day our snares hung empty. Christmas came. It went.

On the twenty-sixth of December our mother called all of us over to her house—her partner Ron, my siblings, and our spouses. She had news, she said: she hadn't been feeling well for some time. She had been coughing a lot. Her ribs on her right side hurt her constantly. She was tired and had lost a lot of weight. She'd gone to the doctor, and they had taken X-rays and made scans and had detected a large lump, a tumor, in the lower lobe of her right lung. The tumor had grown so large as to push past and envelop her ribs. These had become brittle and had, at some point, broken—the source of the pain. They had taken a sample to be biopsied and she would, she said, know more soon. She had been a steady smoker for over forty years. It was, in all likelihood, lung cancer.

I can't remember how we reacted. Some cried, I'm sure. Some didn't. Some started strategizing—as though the cancer were an enemy we could fight. I think this was probably my response. It would be a week before we got the results of the biopsy. In the meantime we carried on. We got groceries. We went to the bank. We watched movies. We argued. We did everything we could. We did nothing at all.

When Micah and I went to check our snares, I noticed that the fox we had been trying to snare had begun using the ruts my truck tires left in the fields of big bluestem we crossed. So, on a whim, we cut down a small jack pine, dragged it close to the tire tracks, and wired a snare to it.

On New Year's Eve my mother gathered us together again and told us that she had lung cancer. The doctors planned to operate within the week.

I don't remember much of that time. I don't remember living in any conscious was—that is, making decisions or acting purposefully—but I must have. I do remember thinking a lot about snaring.

Snares are elegant tools—there is something beautiful about a snare, whereas there is little that is beautiful about a metal trap. Metal traps, no matter what kind, are nasty, brutish things. A snare is so simple: a piece of wire formed into a loop. One end is anchored to the ground or to a drag stick; the other ends in a lock through which the wire passes. When an animal walks through a snare, the lock slides down the wire and the snare tightens around the animal's neck. The animal struggles and the snare gets tighter and tighter, until the animal can no longer breathe and it dies. With a piece of wire and not much more than that, a man can survive for a long time.

As I contemplated my mother's operation, it seemed to me that seen in a certain way, snares, unlike traps, don't actually kill the animal. The animal's habits are what kill it. Same with my mother. Every animal has its habits—where it walks, where it hunts, where it dens, where it mates—and snares more than any other kind of trap take advantage of those habits. Trapping beavers at their houses or dams or channels is a matter of taking advantage of geography—if you put a trap in a doorway, the beaver will have to go in or out sometime. Fisher and marten traps are baited and as such use hunger against the animal (a weasel must eat two times its body weight a day just to stay alive). But snares use an animal's habits. Instead of using lures or attractants or bait, instead of trapping the entrances of a den or digging out the den or burrow, you set a snare where an animal goes, and a good snare set works be- cause it is unobtrusive. And there they hang—a nice clean loop, no mechanical springs or parts, nothing but gravity and the animal's own struggles to help with the kill—and could hang forever, waiting. It is tempting to think of snaring (and trapping) metaphorically—we already speak of things like "snares of love," for example—but the real beauty of it is literal: this wire, on this trail, will choke to death a fox whose life is not that of all foxes, but was his and his alone.

Four days after my mother received her diagnosis, we went, as we did every day, to check our snares. We drove out into the fields and checked our line along the old fencerows and among the jack pine and down near the slough. Nothing. We drove back out into the fields and Micah yelled, "Stop, stop!" I stood on the brakes, and above the dead brown grass we saw a fox jumping and twisting. He would disappear into the grass and then jump in the air and fall back down. We bailed out of the truck and ran toward it. He was caught in the snare we'd set in the open field on the tire track. It was a clean catch. Tight around his neck. But he must have just gotten into the snare a short while ago. The stick to which the snare was wired was too big for the fox to drag very far.

A few days later my mother went into surgery; they resected her ribs and removed the lower two of the three lobes of her right lung. All of us were waiting for her in intensive care when they wheeled her bed in. She was still unconscious and on a respirator. A long translucent tube snaked from a hole in her side down to a bag filled with blood and a slimy yellowish fluid. She was gray and ashen, and though she wasn't awake and couldn't have spoken if she were, the way the tube went down her throat distorted her face. She looked like she was screaming. But her body was limp, her eyes shut. The only sound was that of the respirator and the squeak of our chairs. I wanted her to live. I wanted it more than I had reason to expect she would. I closed my eyes and tried to think of something else—of something other than her pain, and what- ever the future might be, something other than our collective hopelessness. I could think of nothing.

The fox we'd snared had also wanted to live. That, after all, was its purpose. He'd wanted it so much that when he felt the snare tightening and he couldn't breathe, he tried to run away, to get his body far from the snare and the log to which it was attached. He jumped again and again, and it was something both strange and beautiful. He lifted clear into the air—a bright flash of red against the sky—and then disappeared below the grass, which was about three feet high. First his nose, then his body, and then his black- and-white-tipped-tail cleared the grass and was jerked back down by the weight of the log. He jumped and jumped and jumped again. All his traits and everything he had learned, the land itself and what it offered him, forced him to choose this path, on that patch of land on that day, and it was killing him. His instincts were killing him, but it was his instinct to live, too.

Finally we drew close enough to knock him on the head with the ax handle and down he went. I felt the quickness of his breath as I knelt on him with one knee. With one hand on his head and the other on his chest, I felt his heart and the life in it. Who knew a heart could beat that fast? I felt, too, in those beats and under that fur, in that quick, elegant body, how much it strained toward life, how much it jumped for it. Everything in that animal's body was bent on it. It wanted to live. And we, too, gathered around our mother, wanted to live. And she wanted to live. Us and all the others and everyone—regardless of the lives we'd led and more than anything else, and beyond the agonies and dangers that attend every act and action of ours in this life, we all wanted to live. And that desire, if not the result, is something to think about.

Fiction

Fiction

Family Reunion

Bonnie Jo Campbell

"No more hunting," Marylou's daddy rumbles. Mr. Strong is a small man, hardly bigger than Marylou herself, but he's got a big voice, and some people call him just *Strong*, without the *Mister*. "We got more than enough meat. You understand what I'm saying, child?" He stands up from the stump where he's been sitting, sharpening the butcher knife, and glances around, looking for her, and Marylou fears he will also spot the yellow paper stapled to the beech tree. Marylou has just noticed the paper herself, and she is sneaking around the side of the house, intending to jump up and yank it down before he sees it, but she is not quick enough. He puts down the butcher knife and whetstone and moves to the tree.

Strong is freshly shaven for work–the new job makes him go in on Saturdays–and Marylou can see his jaw muscles grinding as he reads. Under his green wool cap, his forehead veins are probably starting to bulge. She didn't notice anybody putting up the invitation, but maybe one of her cousins snuck over here after dark last night. Uncle Cal couldn't have posted it himself, because of his tether and the restraining order, in place on account of the trouble at last year's Thanksgiving reunion party. Ever since Grandpa Murray died, though, Cal has been the head of the Murray family (not to mention president of Murray Metal Fabricators, the only shop in town paying a decent wage), and so in Strong's eyes, the photocopied invitation has come straight from Cal.

Marylou and Strong have just finished stringing up a six-point buck, Marylou's third kill of the season and two more than the legal limit. When Strong found her dragging the body toward the house an hour ago, he reminded her that being only fourteen didn't make her exempt from the law. Some day she would like to try hunting with the new Marlin rifle she won in the 4-H competition, but they live below Michigan's shotgun line, and, anyway, she knows a .22 bullet can travel half a mile, far enough that you might hit somebody you never even saw. Not that Marylou has ever missed what she was aiming for. She took this third buck in the woods at dawn, and the single shotgun blast echoed along the river and awakened Strong. He used to get out of bed early, but nowadays he usually stays up late and sleeps until there's barely enough time to shave and get to work.

But Strong seems to have forgotten about getting to work now. He shakes his head and says, "Son of a bitch." All he needs to see are the words *Thanksgiving Pig Roast*, and he knows the rest, that it's the famous yearly family gathering of the Murrays, when uncles and aunts and truckloads of cousins come in from out of town, and outside of Michigan, to play horse-shoes and drink beer and eat pork. Worst of all, the paper is stapled too high for Strong to reach up and tear it down.

He storms off and returns a few minutes later with his chainsaw and yanks the starter until the motor roars. He jabs the tip of the saw into the beech, knee-high. Sawdust flies, and with one clean, angry slice, the adolescent tree is free of its roots.

As the beech falls, Marylou notices the few marks where she and Strong carved dates and lines for her height in the smooth bark, dates that moved up and stretched out as the years passed, making any year-by-year compari-sons useless. The tree is taller than she has realized, and the top hangs up on a big swamp oak before breaking free by taking down one oak arm with it. When the beech lands between Strong's truck and the venison-processing table, it smashes a honeysuckle bush. Strong puts his foot on the downed trunk and cuts some stove-length pieces. When he reaches the invitation, he shreds it with the chain.

"Nerve of that bastard." His white breath mingles with the oily blue smoke.

When he notices Marylou staring at his face he says, "You got something to say, child, say it."

Marylou looks away from him, across the river, toward the Murray farm, toward the white house and the two red barns. The big wooden barn would be full of hay this time of year, and she knows how the cold morning sun streams through the cracks inside, the shafts of sunlight full of hay dust. Behind that barn is the hill where she used to shoot targets with Uncle Cal and her cousins, before all the trouble.

She decided to stop talking last year because she discovered that she could focus more clearly without words, and by concentrating hard with her breathing, she has gradually learned to slow time by lengthening seconds, one after another. In target or skeet shooting, she sometimes used to fire without thinking, but on opening day this year, she took her first careful, deliberate aim at a living thing. As she set her sights on that buck, she found she had all the time in the world to aim—up from the hooves and legs or else down from the head and neck, smack in the chest, touch the trigger, and *bang*.

On the way to his truck, Strong is shaking his head in exasperation, and once he's inside, he slams the door hard. When he pulls away, the truck's back wheels dig into the ice crust of the two-track. Marylou hears him throw up gravel on the road, and she hears the truck's noisy exhaust as it crosses the bridge downstream. No, she doesn't have anything to say, yet. And it was not just out of loyalty to the Murrays that she wouldn't open her mouth for a trial last year—her daddy is wrong there. At the time she didn't have things figured out, and even now she is still puzzling through what really happened.

This morning she puzzles about the invitation on the tree. It certainly wasn't meant for her mother, Cal's sister—she ran off to Florida with a truck driver and only calls home a few times a year. And it definitely wasn't meant for Strong—although he worked for the Murrays for years, they've never liked him. *The man broods,* Uncle Cal has always complained. Even Anna Murray used to say, *Loulou, don't brood like your father.* Marylou tried to defend him, but the Murrays could not understand that a person sometimes needed quiet in order to think about things.

The invitation on the tree has to mean that, despite all the trouble, the Murrays want to keep Marylou in the family, and Marylou feels glad to be wanted by them, by Anna who taught her to cook, and by Cal who taught her to shoot. And having boy cousins was as good as having brothers.

Marylou kicks at the lengths of wood Strong has cut. The beech is too green to burn or even split this year. She retrieves the sharpened knife from the stump and returns to her strung-up buck. She wants to hurry and get the first long cut behind her. She will be fine after that, once the guts slosh into the galvanized trough, but she hates that first slice that turns the deer from a creature into meat. Strong would do it if she asked, but Grandpa Murray always told her, from the time she was little, how important it was to do a thing herself. She reaches up and inserts the knife about a half inch into the buck's throat. Pulling down hard and steady on the back of the blade with her free hand, she unzips the buck from neck to balls, tears through skin and flesh, and then closes her eyes for a moment to recover.

A gunshot yips from the Murray farm across the river, and Marylou drops her knife into the tub of steaming entrails. A second shot follows. Uncle Cal's black Lab begins to bark. Marylou has known this day would come, that

Strong would one day kill her uncle with the pistol he carries behind the seat of his truck. And now Strong will go to jail, and she will have to move to Florida to live with her mother. Two more shots echo over the water.

Marylou considers the hole she has dug for the deer guts, and she knows she has to act fast to cover up her daddy's crime. She will bury Cal. Except she'll have to get the tether off somehow, so the police won't locate his body. She grabs the shovel and the bone saw from her venison table, carries them to her rowboat, tosses them in, and rows a hundred fifty feet across the current to the other side. She ties up to a fallen willow near Uncle Cal's hunting shed, where the trouble occurred. This is the first time she's been on the Murray property in almost a year. She climbs the bank, ignoring a sick feeling as she passes the shed, and makes her way upstream toward the Murray farmhouse. There she sees how Cal's new white Chevy Suburban is sunk down on flattened tires. Cal stands alongside the vehicle, yelling at the banged-up back end of Strong's departing Ford.

"Strong, you son of a bitch! Those were brand new tires!"

Cal's wife stands beside him, wearing a dress with pockets, holding an apple in one raw-looking hand and a peeler in the other. Marylou feels bad she didn't consider Anna when she was thinking about burying Cal. Marylou wonders if Anna is making pies for the party.

Tuesday, two days before Thanksgiving, Strong comes home from work to find Marylou dragging the warm, soft body of an eight-point buck by the antlers across frozen leaves, toward the venison table. She has to stop and rest every few feet.

"Marylou, what the hell are we supposed to do with all this meat? We've got no room in the freezer." He shakes his head. "Even if you aren't going to talk, child, you've got to listen."

Strong would be even madder if he knew she shot the deer across the river, because he doesn't want her to set foot on that bank for any reason. But Marylou was on her side of the river, watching the shed, puzzling through a few things, when the buck came high-stepping down the trail to the river's edge. Marylou aimed the shotgun and calmly fired. She wasn't sure she could hit at that distance, but the buck collapsed to his knees on the sand, then to his chest. She carried the knife across with her, dreading the prospect of finishing him off, but by the time she got there, he was dead. Dragging the buck into the wooden rowboat was difficult, and she was lucky nobody saw her. He was bigger than she realized, and the weight across the prow made it hard to fight the river current.

"Listen," Strong says. "The Murrays could make one phone call, and if those DNR sons of bitches open our freezer, we're in big trouble."

Marylou isn't worried. The Murrays always avoid the law, always figure they can take care of their own problems–apparently they haven't reported Strong for shooting out Cal's tires the other day.

Strong helps her string up the buck and then stands back. "You are one hell of a hunter, though. You always hit what you're shooting at, child of mine."

Marylou squeezes her daddy around his middle, and he puts his arms around her as he hasn't done in a while. Over his shoulder, across the river, she notices Billy, who is her age, dragging out the pig-roasting barrel from the barn. At last year's party, Marylou ran around with Billy and a whole flock of cousins, and some of the boys spit into the men's foamy draft beers while the men were tossing horseshoes. Billy has gotten tall this year, maybe tall enough to staple an invitation way up a tree, but when he or any of the other cousins see Marylou in school, they always turn away.

Aunt Anna appears by the water's edge, wearing insulated boots and a coat almost as long as her dress. She messes with an orange extension cord to light up the waterproof tube lights before she even starts stringing them around the dock. Last year Marylou helped Anna attach hooks for those lights.

Strong pulls away from Marylou's embrace and turns to look at what's caught her attention.

"I know you miss your aunt Anna," he says, shaking his head. "But don't you even think of going to that party."

Before Marylou can look away, Anna drops her string of lights into the river, and Marylou sees the end waggle and sparkle a few yards downstream. Anna is probably laughing as she fishes the lights from the cold current. Anna has always pulled Marylou out of being serious by saying, *Quit brooding and sing with me, Loulou!* or by letting Marylou bake something sweet in her kitchen, a place with all kinds of good smells, like vanilla and nutmeg.

"You don't seem to understand what's been done to you by those people," Strong says. "If you would have spoken against Cal at the trial, he would not have been able to plea bargain down to a damned ankle bracelet."

When her father goes inside, Marylou lets herself puzzle again about what they did to her, what Cal did. She still doesn't know why she followed Cal into his shed–her daddy had told her a hundred times to stay away from Cal when he was drinking. Even before Uncle Cal shut the door, she knew something was wrong by the anxious way he was breathing, but she never grabbed the door handle to leave the way she thought about doing.

What the men did to each other afterward was more violent than what got done to her, wasn't it? Just after she crawled into a corner to gather herself together, Strong busted into the shed. Marylou heard bones crunch, and two red and white nuggets–Uncle Cal's front teeth–bounced on the plank floor. The men growled like bears. With all the noise and fury, Marylou forgot how Cal had insisted he had to teach her that afternoon how to dress out a deer–he said if she wanted to hunt, nobody was going to do her gutting for her. When they entered the shed, she was surprised to see it was a doe hanging there.

Anna Murray showed up a minute after Strong clobbered Uncle Cal. First she knelt beside Marylou and said, "What's the matter, honey? What happened?" But when Anna saw Cal's bloody mouth, she moved away to help him. Then Cal sputtered those words Marylou has just remembered. "The little slut lured me in here," Cal said. "And don't let her tell you any different." After that, Anna didn't look at Marylou anymore.

Cal had busted open Strong's cheek, and later at the hospital they shaved off his beard for the stitches. Marylou hardly recognized him as her father–going home with him afterwards was like going home with a stranger. He hasn't grown his beard back because of his new job, which pays only about half what he made at Murray Metal Fabricators. The nakedness of his face still sometimes startles Marylou.

On Thanksgiving morning, Strong says, "I can't have you killing any more deer, child. I'm taking the shotgun with me. I'll be home from work at six." He slides the twelve-gauge into its case and hangs it in the truck's window rack. His old job with Murray Metal gave him holidays off, and Marylou can't help thinking that everything was better the way it used to be. Used to be when Strong was at work, she could spend time across the river being the girl that Anna and Cal said they always wanted, maybe still wanted. Grandpa Murray used to say that your family was all you had, and that a strong family like the Murrays could protect a person. He said it even when he was sick and dying, said he didn't care what her last name was, she was a Murray.

Instead of stalking another buck, Marylou sits on the bank all morning and watches vehicles pull in at the farm across the river, and she studies each Murray through the scope of her Marlin rifle. After a few hours, Marylou is sick with yearning to be on the other side of the river, to hear the old-fashioned country music from the outdoor speakers, to smell the meat roasting, and to see heaps of Murray cousins wrestling in their winter jackets. She pulls the rifle strap over her shoulder and rows her boat across. She ties up at the willow near Cal's shed. She slowly narrows the distance between herself and the shed as she kicks out rabbit holes in the yellow grass to keep warm. She is listening to the clinks and shouts from the horseshoe pit, wondering what the Murrays would do if she walked over and took a can of pop off the table. But then Mr. Strong's truck pulls into the driveway at home, hours before he is supposed to return.

She knows he will see her rowboat tied up, so she runs down the path to the river and waves her arms until Strong sees her, to let him know she is not at the party. As he pulls out of the driveway, Marylou notices her shotgun in the truck's window rack. Luckily Cal is nowhere around. But then, as if conjured up by her thoughts, Cal stumbles out the shed door, looking drunk and sleepy. Marylou silently hoists herself onto the lowest branch of the snake-bark sycamore. Uncle Cal doesn't even glance up as she climbs higher into its leafless branches. She straddles a smooth branch and looks through the window into the shed, looks for another girl like herself who might have gone in there with Cal, but she sees only a skinned carcass hanging.

Cal closes the shed door and steps around to the river side of the building. He puts a red-and-white beer can on the windowsill, and he leans against the unpainted shed wall. Marylou hears Strong's noisy exhaust on the road bridge, but Cal lights a cigarette and doesn't pay any special attention to the sound. Marylou is fifteen feet off the ground, high enough to see her daddy's Ford when it pulls up outside the rail fence a hundred yards away. Cal fumbles with his zipper, and when Marylou realizes he is going to pee right there on the path, she looks away. Then she looks back. Cal doesn't seem to hear the truck door creak open or slam shut. He continues to draw on his cigarette and stare down at his pecker in his hand, waiting for something to come out.

Marylou concentrates with her breathing to slow everything down so she can think better. Strong might kill her uncle, and Marylou knows he would not survive being locked in jail. She also knows he won't shoot a man on the ground, so maybe Marylou should take Cal down herself before Mr. Strong gets there, injure Cal rather than kill him. Marylou grips the branch with her legs, pulls the rifle off her shoulder and takes aim at one of Cal's work boots. At this short distance, she could shatter the white radio box tethered to his ankle.

Marylou sights Cal's kneecap. Strong won't kill a man who has fallen forward as though he is praying or begging forgiveness.

She aims at his thigh. For a split second Cal wouldn't know what hit him. A stray horseshoe? A biting snake? Then he would clutch his leg in confused agony. The bullet would continue through the side of the shed, bury itself in a floorboard.

Years ago Marylou's cousins held her down and put a night crawler in her mouth, and Billy once put a dead skunk in her rowboat to set her off. But she always got revenge–she chased Billy down that time and rubbed his face in cow manure until he bawled. Her cousins always enjoyed teasing her, enjoyed her shrieks, and afterward she evened the score, and they all got along again.

Uncle Cal wasn't teasing her, though–he wasn't even listening to her begging him to stop. Over the last year, she has been going back and forth, not knowing for sure if she had begged out loud, but looking at him now, she knows she said, "Please no, Cal," over and over.

"I know you want this, Loulou," he said, as though having him on her was a nice thing, like a hunting trip, like sitting down to a piece of pie. That afternoon, she saw past Cal's shoulder, through the dirty window glass, three little Murray kids peeking in. They looked terrified, and when she looked back at them, they ran off. Whatever they saw scared them enough to go get her daddy from the party.

Marylou looks past the beer can on the windowsill, past the table with the knives and saws, past the newly skinned carcass, to the place on the floor where Cal pushed her down. She has been puzzling about whether he really did push her down, but when she looks at Cal from up high in this tree, things get clearer. A year ago Marylou didn't know about slowing down time to study a situation, to make sure her aim was perfect or to avoid a terrible mistake. Those little kids were two girls and a boy, and Marylou thinks she knows what they saw, what scared them: they saw Cal had opened up Marylou and was gutting her there like a deer on the plank floor.

As Mr. Strong reaches the place where the path widens, Marylou realizes he doesn't have the shotgun or even his pistol. Seeing him unarmed now is as shocking as first seeing him without his beard at the hospital. Under his Carhartt jacket he still wears his blue work smock. He hasn't left work for the day, but has just come home to check on her.

Marylou looks through the scope at Cal's eyes, where she sees the same expression of concentration as when he was holding her down, so far from the door handle she could never have reached it. She looks at a patch of Cal's chest–it is amazing Strong was able to hurt such a big man at all. She moves her sights down farther to where a button is missing from his flannel shirt–why hasn't Anna sewn that button back on for him? Marylou moves the tip of her rifle down to Cal's hand, loosely clutching his pecker, from which a poky stream dribbles. She has to do this thing for herself; nobody is going to do it for her. She aims just past his thumb. She knows she is good enough to take off the tip of his pecker without hitting any other part of him.

The shout of her rifle is followed by a silent splash of blood on the shed wall and one last horseshoe clink from the pit. Cal's mouth is open in a scream, but it must be a pitch discernible only by hunting dogs. Marylou grasps the branch above with her free hand to keep herself from falling. The weight of the .22 in the other keeps her from floating up. She closes her eyes to lengthen that perfect and terrible moment and hold off the next, when the air will fill with voices.

Border

Alyson Hagy

It was not as hard to steal the collie pup as he thought it would be. From early morning when the woman set up and wiped her table with a cloth until the time the silver container of coffee was emptied by those coming to look at the dogs, there had been somebody around the camper and around the crate that held the pups. But lunch hour put the scatter in people. Tacos and fry bread were for sale on the other side of the bleachers—he could smell them. And the heat slowed things down, even for the dogs that panted hard and fast like they knew they were destined for the sheep-herding finals.

The high sun was what seemed to drive the woman into the camper. It was nothing more than company, the chance to talk out of the hearing of adults, that got rid of the girl and her sister. They went off with kids they seemed to know from the sheep-raising universe of Colorado. There was discussion of buying cokes or lemonade. The older girl was the one who'd offered him a pup to hold. He'd refused, staying polite and not looking too interested. He had a dog at home, he said, one that was good over pheasant and jumping in the water for ducks. A hunting dog from Texas. This was a lie from his mouth, though he'd heard the exact same words said by a long-haul friend of his father's.

Except for the dog stories, he had not liked that friend.

The girl had smooth brown hair held off her neck in braids the way 4-H girls he knew wore their hair, especially the ones who barrel raced on horses. He was a little sorry she would get in trouble because of him. She'd take the blame, no matter what. That was how it worked. But there was a pile of pups in that crate. At $400 apiece, nobody's feelings or whipped ass was going to hurt for long.

Luck would determine if it was male or female. He wouldn't have time to check. A bitch was easier to train. This, too, came from his father's friend.

But there was some number of male dogs in the finals. He'd watched them stalk the skittery bands of sheep in the preliminaries. He knew how capable they were. And he didn't care what it was. The one the girl held away from her chest to show him had looked good enough to him. Everybody knew border collies were smart beyond the ordinary for dogs. You could train them to within an inch of their business, and they would wait outside a building for you with no rope or leash. They would wait for you all day.

He partly zipped his jacket and snapped the snap on its waistband. His Broncos hat was already so low on his head he could barely see. He slipped in and unpinned the crate before he even squatted down. The lucky one was toward the front, round-bellied, asleep on its side. He used two hands for support so as not to shock the pup, wanting it to think well of him from the get go. He lifted it like it was a glass tray. Then he got one hand under its sleepy, dangled haunches and slid it into his jacket. It didn't make a peep, nor did its many sisters and brothers. He closed the crate, put a quick touch on the bill of his Broncos hat to be sure it was set square on his head, and he was gone.

He waited until he was clear of the Meeker fairgrounds to take off his jacket and turn it inside out so that the brown cloth fabric showed instead of the blue. He also removed his hat and tucked it into his back pocket, though his bare head felt show-offy to him. This was his disguise. He had to set the pup on the ground to make his changes. It was more alert now, and he saw its tongue bend in an arch when it yawned, and he saw its tiny teeth. The teeth were see-through and small like fish teeth. He scooped the pup with his hands and cradled it. It was a female. He could tell that much. He could also tell from the mask of her face that she had the good, preferred markings he'd heard the handlers talk about.

She made a sound in her white-furred throat, and he made a sound back.

He carried her through town inside his brown jacket, cars and trucks passing on both sides of the road. He supported her round belly with his hands, walking as if his hands were only in his jacket pockets and he was only going for a stroll. He used sidewalks when he could. He wished he could stop at the cafe he saw—one with yellow paint around the windows—but he knew he could not, even though he had money, because of the deputies and what had happened with his father. He read the sign for the cafe that hung out over the street, and he liked the sound of the name. Belle's. He could call the pup that, call her Bell after the instrument and after the cafe in the town where he'd gotten her. Border collies always came with short names. It cut down on confusion.

Bell. A good name for a dog that was bound to be sweet but never shy.

He walked until he got to the gas stations. There was one on each side of the road just before the road filled out into a highway. He saw what he hoped to see on a good weather Sunday, a steady stream of livestock trailers and open-backed trucks, many of them too large and awkward to pull next to the pumps. He'd planned to buy food, but he knew better than to pass on what looked like a rare chance. A red trailer stacked with hay was goose-necked to a diesel pickup with Colorado plates. The driver had left the rig angled near the air hose. He did what he'd done before, apologizing to Bell in a low voice for the delay of their supper. He unlatched the trailer's gate on one side and stepped into the dark crowdedness of the hay. Then he slid Bell loose from under his jacket and set her safe in the trailer's corner. He turned, made a loop of the orange rope that was already tied to the rear of the trailer, caught the latch handle in that loop, snugged the gate closed, and dropped the latch to lock them inside. It would be a hell of a sight easier to travel with hay than with steers or horses. They might not even get caught.

He sat down and drew Bell onto his lap, leaning into the sweet wall of hay. Bell had slept in the nest of his jacket, but she was awake now. Her dazedness was wearing off. He could feel the difference in the set of her legs and the sharp probing of her teeth on the soft parts of his hands. She would miss her brothers and sisters soon. He knew how that would go. Missing a sister—he did not have a brother—was a burn that was slow to cool. What he needed most was for Bell not to bark. Barking would not be good. He tried to keep her busy chewing on the bottoms of his jeans and on his hands, though her sharp fish teeth were already making him sore. He was glad when the driver cranked the rig and they eased onto the highway. The weather was dialed in. There would be no problems with heat or cold. They could find food later. He understood food was something he had learned to do without while Bell had not. But if he was right, the trailer's destination was close—no more than a couple of hours. He pulled his Broncos hat from his pocket and smoothed it down over his hair. He knew how to wait.

When the rig slowed to leave the highway, he took a look and thought the town might be Hayden. The driver pulled into another gas station but didn't cut the engine—it seemed like the driver only needed to take a leak. He bundled up Bell and got out of the trailer while the going was good. The sun was still flat and clear in the sky, but the air was beginning to smell of evening. He walked behind the station and took a leak of his own, then he let Bell walk and sniff some in the gravel. He needed to get one of those whistles, the kind only a dog could hear. For now, he'd count on his voice and the way Bell would learn to listen to it.

"Come on, Bell. Come on, little gal." He knelt on the gravel and called until she came to him. He told her she was pretty smart to make him proud on her first day.

He apologized for what he had to do next. He set her in an empty barrel that was soured from garbage, and he walked fast around the station and went inside and bought a pint of milk and some sticks of peppered jerky and two bottles of the fancy water his father made fun of. He paid for his selections with the bills folded in his front pants pocket. He was tight with worry for Bell. He got back, and he stroked her on top while she drank water from a hamburger container until they both were calm. There was hay mixed in her black fur and a flat mark of grease on her tail. He tried to clean her with his fingers. He had some water, too, while Bell lapped at milk, then he got after the jerky. Bell didn't care for the jerky. He told himself that next time he would get the kind without pepper.

He had passed through Hayden before, and he liked his chances of finding a ride. He knew people paid no attention to strangers and how they came and went, alone or not alone, in the summer. He only wondered how bold he should be. His question was answered by the arrival of a club-cab Ford bearing two cowboys. He was standing near the phone booth when it pulled in.

He watched the driver for a short time. The driver was a rodeo cowboy, for sure. Ironed shirts hung in the window of the Ford, and there was a show hat on the driver's head. The passenger was dressed cowboy, too. He walked up to the driver and asked for a ride.

"It's just me and this little dog," he said.

The driver, who was young and red-skinned from the day's sun, looked him over. "Where to?"

"I got cousins on the Front Range, cousins and a aunt," he lied. "Any place toward Denver is good. The dog is for them."

"Denver it is," said the driver.

"Tell him he's got to buy beer." This came from the passenger.

"I don't believe he's old enough to buy beer."

"Shit. You know what I mean."

"I got money," he said. And he dug into his pocket with some defiance. He freed up ten dollars, handed it to the young driver.

"Cute dog."

"She is," he said. "Smart, too."

"What if she messes in the truck?" This from the passenger again, in a mood.

"I'll hold her. If she wets, she'll wet on me."

"I got a towel," the driver said. "I don't know what Ray's worried about. A little dog like that can't out mess him no how."

"Fuck you," said the passenger, making one piece of a smile. "And give over that money. I've got a thirst."

They got going pretty fast, him and Bell squeezed in the back of the cab with some rigging and a bull rider's vest. He held Bell so she could look out the window as they drove, and she seemed to like that. The driver and Ray cracked beers and drank them and didn't talk. They started to talk when they slowed to pass through Steamboat Springs because they wanted to make fun of the town for its traffic lights and tourists. The driver said he didn't know a single good horseman who could still afford to live in Steamboat.

"They got girls, though," said Ray. He was watching out the windows just like Bell.

"Not the kind you like," said the driver.

"What's that mean?"

"It means rich. It means talking and spoiling and taking your time."

"And I can't do that?"

"Besides the fact that you're butt ugly, I've never seen you slow down for nothing, not even a rich girl."

"Fuck you."

"It's true," the driver said, laughing. "We have plowed this field before—"

"I ain't plowed nothing with you. You can't—"

"My point is you could act right with girls, but you don't."

"And who are you? Mister Smooth Shit?"

"I didn't say one way or the other. I didn't say a thing."

Ray looked over his shoulder. "You say you're giving up that dog. I wouldn't give up a good dog or a good gun, neither one. With dogs and guns you know what's next. They stay in bed all damn night whether you want them or not."

"You got to excuse Ray," the driver said, laughing some more. "He just got throwed off the crippledest mare on the Western Slope."

"You didn't do so hot yourself, twig dick."

"I didn't. It's lucky I got a credit card for gas."

They went into their third beers as the truck hauled up Rabbit Ears Pass. He stashed their empties at his feet. Bell whined some at the change in altitude until Ray asked to hold her. He didn't want to give her up, but he knew travel meant all range of favors. So he gave Ray the pup, and she seemed to take to him, working at his skin and his sleeves with her tongue and teeth. Ray gave him a cold beer in return, and he drank it, grateful.

He would guess later that it was the losing Ray couldn't get past because he couldn't find anything else about the situation that might have flipped the switch. Ray hadn't had that much beer, none of them had. It was just that Ray had to make somebody else the loser.

"This is a nice dog," Ray said after Bell curled into his lap for some sleep. "How old?"

"Seven weeks," he said. "She still misses her mama."

"I don't miss mine. How much she cost you?"

He paused, listening for the trap. Older boys and men liked to set traps. "Four hundred," he said.

Ray made a whistle sound behind his lips. It was not the admiring kind. The sound perked Bell up. "How much did those heelers go for in Rifle?" he asked the driver. "I saw Bobby Byrd take one, but I don't recall the price."

The driver turned his head for one second. "I don't remember, had to be a couple hundred. You know, when you wake a pup—"

"Oh, damn. Shit."

"That ain't shit."

"Damn. Make her stop. Come on, dog, stop."

"Naw," the driver said, laughing once again. "Your britches ain't wet with shit."

Ray cussed a long streak, holding Bell in the air like a paper airplane while he tried to work the piss off his legs. The towel, they'd all forgotten that. The driver, still aiming fast into the valley, reached under his seat and found an oil rag, which he tossed at Ray. "Oh," said the driver. "Oh, I got one now. Pissed pants and a crippled mare. I got a story to tell on you now."

"God damn dog," Ray said. "Right on my good jeans."

"I'll take her," he said from the back seat. "She didn't mean to hurt nothing."

"The hell she didn't," Ray said. 'She's one bad thing after another on a bad day. So are you. Dillon there made you part of my damn bad day."

"Then let us off," he said, his heart bolting the way it did when he was close to trouble. "That's what you can do."

"That's not what I *want* to do," yelled Ray.

"Christ, Ray," said the driver. "It's no more than pup piss. It'll dry."

"It is more. It's what you said."

"Christ, then. I take it back. I didn't mean to get under your saddle."

"Yeah, you did, you son-of-a-bitch. In the money at Gunnison two weeks ago and you ain't let up since. You don't think I'm good enough to haul with your god damn gear."

"Give the kid his dog."

"No."

"Give it to him."

"I'll give him something else first," Ray said, his hand going after his belt buckle, and that meant two things to him in the back seat—it meant belt whipping or worse—and he'd given up taking the hurt of both, so he reared between the seats and grabbed for little Bell. But Ray was quicker, and mean. Ray kept his hands free, and he got his window down, and he dropped the dog out onto the moving road.

"Christ. Jesus Christ, Ray. You can't do that," yelled the driver.

But he had.

The driver, Dillon, hit the brakes which sent them all flying forward and cut down on the punches and kicks that followed. They threw him out of the truck, too. Ray kept yelling, his face the color of meat, but he heard nothing of it. He ran. He was all running. He saw her by the side of the road, black and white like a shoe tossed into the bristly cheatgrass. He saw her move. Then he was by her and with her, lying on the ground low and flat so she might see his face. Pleading. "Don't be dead, Bell. Please don't be dead."

She staggered to her feet. She shook her head as though her ears itched, then bounded deeper into the bristled grass. She went away from him and away from the road. Scared.

"She rolled. Swear to God she rolled, I saw it in my mirror. She might be all right." It was the driver, Dillon. He had backed his truck up to where they were. Ray wasn't with him. "Young ones like that don't have much bone. She might not've felt it."

He lifted her up, afraid to see blood in her mouth, afraid she'd have eyes like his sister's cats after they had been drop-kicked.

"I'd take you to a vet, but I can't, not with Ray. I'm sorry. The town's right up here. Walden. I'm sorry. Here's money to have her looked at."

There were sounds. The truck disappeared. He made out that the truck stopped for Ray before it started again, and he made out the pale leaf of a twenty-dollar bill on the darkness of the road. He picked up the bill and put it in a separate pocket. Bell's heart was like a hammer against his hands, and his own heart was moving blood so fast it made his stomach sick. He was afraid the live part of Bell would tear through the skin of her chest and leave him behind, but it didn't.

After a minute or two she acted like she wanted to walk. He didn't let her down at first, but then he did. She walked like normal. She sniffed at the oily road. When she saw a grasshopper and tried to stalk it, he knew she was all right. Bent, but not broke. He told her he was glad. That he was proud of how tough she was and how she learned things. What she'd learned was a lesson he hadn't meant to teach her right away even though it was the kind of thing that was bound to come before you were ready for it, the black lesson of fear.

He let her play until his face was dry.

There were lights in some of the Walden houses, and the air was as cool as the river. The streets were quiet. He and Bell weren't likely to catch a ride now. He walked along the main street where the businesses were closed until he saw a pizza place. It was open, and there were kids inside, regular kids, paying $7.95 for the special advertised in the window. He wished he could spend his money that way. Maybe when they got to Denver he would. As a treat for himself even more than Bell.

He walked past the pizza place with Bell snug in his jacket. He turned left, smelling hot bread, then turned left again at the alley. The dumpster was near the kitchen where he could hear people talking and banging things as they worked. After dark, he would check the dumpster. Leftover pizza wasn't bad if you got it out of the box quick.

If a deputy or anybody asked, he was waiting for his father who was fishing. There was a lot of fishing around Walden. He knew that even though he was from across the state line in Wyoming and had only been fishing with his father one time that he remembered.

His mother had never been part of anything.

He started walking again to avoid deputies and the kids moving through the spreading dark on their bikes. This was how he found the funny house. To him it looked no bigger than a garage with windows, and it was painted orange with trim that had some purple parts and some red. It was the kind of place that made people shake their heads. There was a white fence, too, no higher than his knees, and a small sign on the fence written in swirly letters. He put Bell down along the fence while he tried to read the letters. This was when she started to talk.

"Is that you, Donny? Donald Bunch? Is that you raising money for the band?"

The woman was at the purple door of the house. She was holding on to the doorframe with both hands.

"No, ma'am. It's not who you think."

"Are you coming in? We're still open."

"I don't know. I just got here. I have my dog."

"You should come in," she said, turning. "I'm not busy. I like dogs."

He got Bell from the ground, and he opened the gate in the low fence and went in. He wanted to be polite. The woman stopped him at the screen part of her door and said again how much he looked like Donny Bunch or any of the Bunch brothers.

"Do you know him from school? He lives on Spur Ranch. Likes to ask me for money."

"No, ma'am, I don't know him. I'm not from here."

"Just as well," she said. "New faces mean new facts. Come in so I can see you."

He thought then that there was something wrong with her eyes and the way they seemed not to look right at him. He wondered if she was blind or partly blind. He was still wondering when he went into the house that smelled like a flower shop that kept both old flowers and new ones. The front room was crowded at the edges. There were square tables of different heights. There were books and piled magazines.

"Do you have a name?"

"I do. Tyler. Tyler...Bell."

"And your dog?"

He realized his mistake. "She don't have her right name yet, I just got her."

"We might have to give her one then. She's very pretty," the woman said, touching Bell between the ears like she knew what she was doing. Like she wasn't all blind. "Will you have something to drink? We're open."

He could tell there was no other person in the house to make up a "we." He wasn't sure what it would cost to drink something. He didn't see any lists. But he would pay if he had to. Ever since smelling that pizza, he'd wanted to spend money.

"I can't stay long," he said. "But a soda is okay if you have some."

"Would tea be all right...and water for your friend? I have that. I'm sorry to hear you're in a hurry. You didn't look it."

He started to tell the story about waiting for his father but something made him stop. He said nothing rather than saying a lie. His father hated places like the funny house. He would hate the woman and say terrible, rude things to her. But now...now he was a long distance from his father. He had changed how the two of them were. Thinking of that made his hands go thick and hot.

The woman came back with water in a dish for Bell. Her return stirred up the smells again, the papery thin ones he didn't know. Bell was all over the floor of the house, playing, but it seemed to be working out. The woman said tea would be ready soon—he could have any kind he liked—and she apologized for the noise of a radio he'd barely heard.

"It's the war," she said. "Sometimes I can't stop listening to it."

He looked at her and her funny eyes when she said that. There was something in them, or not in them. "Do you have somebody over there," he asked, "in that war?"

"No, Tyler, I don't. My boy fights what he fights down in Pueblo. I don't see him very much. I'm listening because I think if I listen long enough I can learn what a damn thing is about. They've got me fooled on that. I still think there's an answer to my questions. Maybe you'd like to tell me I'm wrong."

"No ma'am," he said. "I wouldn't do that."

"You're shy," she said. "But I can tell that doesn't keep you from taking care of yourself."

"The pup," he said. "I'm taking care of her."

"Yes. I see that. You're very good with the dog."

Then there was tea—he picked a mint one—and milk to put in it and lemony cookies and peanuts in a clay bowl. He ate more than he should have. He let her see he was hungry, but he planned to pay her so there would not be an obligation. He liked how she did everything calm and slow, though after a while it was hard for him to keep from yawning.

While he drank tea, the woman lit a match and put it to a straw she took from a bunch of straws. She stuck the straw in the pot of a green plant, and it gave off sweet smoke that he watched curl into the air.

"It's called a joss stick," the woman said, knowing he was watching it.

"Joss. It smells good," he said.

"I had a cat named Joss," she said. "A good cat. I don't suppose the name would do for a dog."

"It might," he said. "I could think about it."

"How old are you?" she asked.

"Fourteen," he said. And that was the truth.

Night darkened the windows of the house until he saw the two of them in the separated panes of glass. She was smaller than he was, and careful moving with a thin cap of white hair, and seeing that made him ashamed that he'd forgotten to remove his Broncos hat. He was double ashamed he hadn't asked for her name. It felt too late to do it now.

He said, "I should take this pup and go on."

"Oh," she said, clearing his plate. "You're ahead of me. You're making a move, and I haven't even asked you to stay."

The air around him closed in with all its smells, then opened again to his hard breathing. He took Bell onto his lap not knowing what to say.

She said, "I appreciate your not fooling with me. You have character. You haven't asked for a thing. But I know you're on your own, I can see that much. It's cold out, or it will be, and you need a place to sleep."

He sat in the chair she'd given to him, thinking. There was a bladed feeling in his stomach. He wanted to dull that blade and keep it sharp all at once. After a long minute he asked if she was a school teacher.

"I have been a teacher. I've been a lot of things, some of them good, some just necessary. You don't have to worry, I won't ask you many questions."

"Just a few."

"A few. Yes."

Bell was wiggling to get down. He stood, planning to walk out.

"The dog," the woman said. "She shouldn't be in that cold without a name or a bed. You need to think of her."

He cleaned himself at her sink and put on a sweatshirt she had given him. The shirt was soft and faded. He wondered if it belonged to her son. There was a box for Bell with rags and paper. For him, there were blankets the woman brought from downstairs. It looked like she slept there, in the basement. She said he could sleep on the floor next to Bell.

"It's not like home," she said.

He said, "It's real nice. Thank you."

"I call it home," she said, seeming to chew around the word. "That's my name for what it's made of me."

After the woman left, Bell lay down in her box, and he sat upright and watched her breathe for a long time. He liked how her body was loose. He liked how the day hadn't left any marks on her. He touched her a few times on the head before he lay down to make himself loose. The house was warm, and it felt smaller than ever, like a tight, lidded box. He wondered if his breath, and Bell's, and the sad, stretched breathing of the woman could fill up the box in a single night.

They were at the door before he was awake. There was one at first, a deputy, and then another one. He was confused from sleep and from how quickly the woman walked around him and around Bell like she could see fine in the dark. She didn't say anything. It wasn't even morning. Bell shook herself like dogs do. She started licking at her fur with her tongue while the inside of him took off running at full speed, his heart and his head—flying at full speed. The rest of him stayed put, stiff and silent next to Bell. It was too late.

The woman tried to talk to the deputies through her door, but they came in, two of them dressed in uniforms and thick jackets. He stayed on the floor with his legs held straight under the blankets so they could see he'd quit. When one of them said his real name, he nodded. He knew they'd seen copies of his picture.

"You come along with us," the first deputy said. "We know you got a story. We don't want trouble."

He nodded again. Asked if he could put on his shoes.

"Not until we check," the first one said. "Stand up and let us check."

They stood him up and put on handcuffs and took the money from his pockets and took his hat, and while they touched him in those ways, his mind went to a high, cool place where it could stand hours of dark and hours of light and still hear the occasional hopeful words if they were spoken. He knew how to quit. And he knew how not to quit on everything. The thing he would miss most was Bell. He'd really wanted it to work out with her.

The woman was talking faster than her usual talk. With more letters and sharp notes.

She said, "I didn't ask questions. But I know a thing or two, I figured you out."

He stood there wearing her soft sweatshirt, not able to give it back.

She looked at him with padlocked eyes. "It's the kind of person I am. What I've turned into. I made a clear decision."

He asked, "Will you take care of her?"

"I can't."

"I wish you'd thought of her. She likes it here. I guess I don't think it's right not to think of her, a little dog, when you make a decision. That's how you said it with me. You said I had to consider." He remembered how Ray had thrown Bell out of the truck and how he'd never told the woman about that. Maybe it would have made a difference to her, that story.

She said, "You made your decision when you put your father in a pool of blood up there in Lyman, Wyoming. It might have been right to do that. I don't know. Things get out of order in a family. Living gets us out of order."

He climbed upward to his safe, inside place, hand over hand. The woman went on, and the deputies went on, and they laid out their sentences like smooth, straight roads telling about his sister and who was caring for her and what his chances were. Bell left her box and came to his feet. She scratched at his jeans with her claws until the second deputy picked her up.

He said, "Cute dog."

The woman said, "You let him ride with that dog, Walt Mason. You let him have her in the car for the drive to where you're going. He won't see her again."

He heard what the woman said in his high, quiet ears. She *had* been a school teacher, it was all through her voice. He was glad to know that. She had been a teacher in another time and another world that never included him, maybe a world that worked better than his did. She had taught things he hadn't learned. Still, he knew little Bell would be good for the woman, he felt that, everybody in the tiny house had to feel that, and the woman didn't want the dog. He didn't understand. He would never understand, not with any carving of his heart he wouldn't. How could anybody not want the thing that would keep them from being sent backward one last time?

Cartography

Bonnie Nadzam

If you are among these pages today, you are rich with words. Rich with teachers. You are one of the ardent-hearted, a philosopher, a student.

Though you may not always see it, especially with your nose in a book or a magazine, you're in a massive city that includes ocean parks, apartment buildings, factories, sand hills, forests, bridges, distant bands of stars... You don't know how far the limits of the city extend, but it doesn't matter, because you will never reach them, not in this lifetime, not as yourself.

You don't really get it—why this city, why you in it—but after a couple decades among its people, trees, schools, and buildings, you come to the conclusion that your job is to map it. It is a tremendous task, and, you see now, it is the only task. Your map will be a tribute to the city, because for all its suffering and hardships, you love it.

You're not alone. The city has many, many mapmakers—and there are many disagreements among them. The primary disagreement is whether you are ultimately to detail a copy of the city exactly as you see it, or whether you are to make the city as you map it, mapping the city as you make it.

For example, one of your fellow mapmakers sees, say, a crushed sparrow on the sidewalk. A small yet poignant loss. There was an accident, or it fell ill—these things happen. The mapmaker in question sketches it out, beautifully. Such verisimilitude. She is, everyone knows, a world-class cartographer. Anyone who sees the fallen bird on her map will see it in the world, too, and know exactly where they are. Or find the bird in the world, and immediately locate their own place on the map.

You have another colleague, however, who takes a different approach. He sees the crushed sparrow, and gently sets the bird's wings, soft and gray and brown, in the crook of an oak tree lined with a thin white snow. He cleans up the rest of the small spill with his sleeve, collecting the bones and brushing what remains under the young evergreen beside the walkway, where on a warmer day the ants can gather in relative safety. Then he polishes the little bones and carefully strings them together into a necklace, a treasure that he hands over to a boy playing adventure with his brothers in the city park. In this cartographer's map, he sketches the boy and his game, the bird's wings in the branches. He also picks up a broken bottle. When he is finished, this spot on his map is a clean, smooth sweep of sidewalk.

Sometimes the inventory of the city, and hence the things you must map, come to you in glances from other people or in lights in the sky. Sometimes in metaphor. Today, the piece of inventory you must map is, of all things, an hour of time. Your map of the hour can include much:

Words you don't say.
Your judgments.
Your reservations.
Your lunch.
Your heartache.
Your loose change.
Your motives.
A lie.
A plan.
A pain in your head, or in your neck and hands.
Wonder.
Exhaustion.
Disbelief.
Ultimately, you are the one who gets to say.

There are beautiful things in this city. Mountains, rivers, little painted houses, stone avenues lined with bakeries and bookshops. There are distant fires eating trees, houses, entire towns. There are earthquakes and floods. There are crooks behind some of the most elegant doors and honest men dying alone in the shadows. Sometimes you smell smoke in the wind, and some days in the city the air makes you sick. Occasionally you hear the sound of a flare gun fired by someone else lost in this same metropolis, and the beauty of its illuminated rain burning across the sky makes you want to throw your own city map in the trash; you have no such signal, and wonder how, with your dim little sketches, you will be found. Isn't that, somehow, the point of your art?

In such moments, as today's, when you've been called upon to map an hour of time, you must remember that everyone else is here in the city with you. There is no one flying overhead looking to rescue you, or orient you, or to later provide you with a map of an aerial view. There is no one to make a note of it if you give up and remain lost. You are the witness. You.

How overwhelming that is. To chart the minutes of this hour, when time itself is so mysterious a thing—it's very difficult indeed, too much responsibility to wrap your head around. Much as if you were called upon to create the very fabric of the cosmos. It strikes you, correctly, that this is not something you can do on your own. In fact, boundless collaboration is as pervasive and automatic as breath. It couldn't be up to you, alone, if you wanted it to be. You smile a bit to yourself, at your own self-importance, your own presumptuousness and worry. But it's okay. Mistakes, pride, self-righteousness—these things, too, are pervasive and automatic.

It's a beautiful, cool morning. The early light is hitting the bare tree branches just so. Your heart is full. Outside of a crowded café, it occurs to you that within the best map, the real map, there are many mapmakers, and they are forever changing and adjusting the map that contains them.

You stop midstride and stand very still to absorb the impact of this thought. As you take a deep and even breath, the wind blows your hat off your head, and a stranger—a young man out with his wife—retrieves it.

"What's up, man," he says, as he hands it back to you.

"Not much," you say.

The woman smiles. You thank them, each, and head in for your coffee.

Mule Killers

Lydia Peelle

My father was eighteen when the mule killers finally made it to his father's farm. He tells me that all across the state that year, big trucks loaded up with mules rumbled steadily to the slaughterhouses. They drove over the roads that mules themselves had cut, the gravel and macadam that mules themselves had laid. Once or twice a day, he says, you would hear a high-pitched bray come from one of the trucks, a rattling as it went by, then silence, and you would look up from your work for a moment to listen to that silence. The mules when they were trucked away were sleek and fat on oats, workshod and in their prime. *The best color is fat*, my grandfather used to say, when asked. But that year, my father tells me, that one heartbreaking year, the best color was dead. Pride and Jake and Willy Boy, Champ and Pete were dead, Kate and Sue and Orphan Lad; Orphan Lad was dead.

In the spring of that year, in the afternoon of one rain-brightened day, my father's father goes to Nashville and buys two International Harvester tractors for eighteen hundred dollars, cash. "We've got no choice nowadays," he tells the IHC man, counting out the bills and shaking his head. He has made every excuse not to buy what everyone has come to call a mule killer, but finally the farm's financial situation has made the decision for him. Big trucks deliver the tractors and unload them in the muddy yard in front of the barn, where for a day they hunch and sulk like children. My grandfather's tobacco fields stretch out behind them, shimmering in the spring heat. Beyond the slope of green, the Cumberland River is just visible through a fringe of trees, swollen and dark with rain.

The next morning after chores my grandfather calls in the hands to explain the basics of the new machines, just the way the man in Nashville has done for him. He stands next to one of the tractors for a long time, talking about the mechanics of it, one hand resting on its flank. Then with all the confidence he can muster he climbs up to start it. He tries three times before the tractor shivers violently, bucks forward and busts the top rail of a fence. "This one ain't entirely broke yet," my grandfather jokes, struggling to back it up.

"Reckon you'll break it before it breaks you?" someone calls out, and only half of the men laugh. Most of them are used to sleeping all down the length of a tobacco row until the mules stop, waking just long enough to swing the team and start on back up the next. They all know when it's lunch time because the mules bray, in unison, every day at five to twelve.

My father stands with the men who are laughing, laughing with them and scuffing up dust with his boot, though he is nervous about these tractors. His light eyes are squinted in the sun, and he slouches—he has his father's height, and he carries it apologetically. He is trying hard to keep certain things stuffed deep inside his chest: things like fear, sadness, and uncertainty. He expects to outgrow all of these things very soon, and in the meantime, he works hard to keep them hidden. Lately, he has become secretive about the things he loves. His love is fierce and full, but edged in guilt. He loves Orphan Lad: Orphan's sharp shoulders and soft ears, the mealy tuck of his lower lip. Music. Books and the smell of books, sun-warm stones, and Eula Parker, who has hair thick and dark as soil. He has loved her since he was ten and once sat next to her at church; during the sermon she pinched him so hard his arm was red until Tuesday, and he had secretly kissed that red butterfly bruise. But Orphan will soon be gone, and none of the hands read books, and he laughs at the tractors just as he would laugh if one of these men made a rude comment about Eula Parker; because the most important thing, he believes, is not to let on that he loves anything at all.

Late that night, some of the hands sit on the porch to dip snuff and drink bitter cups of coffee. My father sits with them, silent on the steps. When he is with people he often finds pockets in the noise that he can crawl into and fill with his own thoughts, soft familiar thoughts with worn rounded corners. At this particular moment he is turning an old thought of Eula Parker over and over in his mind: he is going to marry her. If he goes so far as to conjure dark-haired children for them, I don't know, but he does build a house where they sit together on a porch, a vast and fertile farm on the other side of the river, and on this night, a shed full of bright chrome tractors, twice as big as the ones that rest still warm and ticking in his father's mule barn. He plants a flower garden for her at the foot of the porch, he buys a big Victrola for the dining room and a smaller, portable one for picnics. Guiltily he touches just the edges of one of these picnics: Eula's hair loose and wild, a warm blanket by a creek, cold chicken and hard boiled eggs, drowsiness, possibility.

In a moment his pocket of quiet is turned inside out: the hands roar with laughter at the punch line of a joke and the screen door clatters as my grandfather comes out to the porch. "You all ever gonna sleep?" he asks them and smiles. He is an old man, nearing sixty, and the thin length of his body has rounded to a stoop, like a sapling loaded with snow. But his eyes are still the eyes of a young man, even after years and years in the sun, and they are bright as he smiles and jokes. My father stands up and leans against a post, crossing his arms. His father winks at him, then waves his hand at the men and steps back into the house, shaking his head and chuckling.

My grandfather understood mule power. He celebrated it. He reveled in it. He always said that what makes a mule a better worker than the horse or the donkey is that he inherited the best from both of them: strong hindquarters from his dam and strong shoulders from his sire. He said *the gospel according to mule is push and pull.* When his wife died young of a fever, it was not a horse but Orphan Lad who pulled her coffin slowly to the burying grounds, a thing the prouder men of the county later felt moved to comment on in the back room of the feed store. My grandfather was a man who never wore a hat, even to town. *Uncover thy head before the Lord,* he said, and the Lord he believed to be everywhere: in the trees, the chimneys of houses, the water of the creek, under Calumet cans rusting in the dirt.

Eula Parker is a slippery and mysterious girl, and my father's poor heart is constantly bewildered by her fickle ways. Like the day he walked her home from church and she allowed him to hold her cool hand, but would not let him see her all the way to the front door. Or the times when she catches him looking at her, and drops her eyes and laughs—at what, he cannot guess. With a kit he burns her name into a scrap of pine board and works up the courage to leave it at the door of her parents' house in town: when he walks by the next day and it is still there, he steals it back and takes it home to hide it shamefully beneath his bed. At church she always sits with the same girl, fifth pew back on the left, and he positions himself where he can see her: her hair swept up off her neck, thick purple-black and shining, the other girl's hanging limply down, onion paper pale. Afterward, when people gather in the yard, the other girl always smiles at him, but he never notices: he is watching to see if Eula smiles, because sometimes she does and sometimes she doesn't. His love fattens on this until it is round and full, bursting from every seam.

At night, when he is sure his father is sleeping, he sticks the phonograph needle in a rubber eraser and holds the eraser in his front teeth. Carefully, with his nose inches from the record, he sets the needle down. With a hiss and crackle, the music reverberates through the hollows of his mouth and throat without making a sound in the room. Ignoring the cramp in his neck, this is how he listens to his favorite records night after night. Wild with thoughts of Eula with her hair like oil. Her snakecharming eyes. Her long fine hands. How she teases him. He dreams he finds pieces of his heart in the boot scraper at her door.

On a warm and steamy afternoon my father makes a trip to town to buy new needles for the Victrola. He walks along the side of the road and passing cars do not give him any room. Several times he has to jump into the tick-heavy weeds that grow at the road's edge. At the river a truck heavy with mules from a farm to the north passes him and bottoms out on the bridge: he keeps his head to the side until it is out of sight. Soon the truck will come for the last of his father's herd. *Oh, Orphan.* On the coldest mornings of his boyhood, his father had let him ride Orphan to school, bareback with two leads clipped to the halter. When they got to the schoolhouse he'd jump down and slap the mule's wide wonderful haunch, and the big animal would turn without hesitation and walk directly home to be harnessed and hitched for the day's work.

When my father gets to town it is still and hot. The street is empty, buildings quiet, second-story shutters closed like eyes. He buys a tin of needles at the furniture store and lingers to look at the portable record players, nestled neat and tidy in their black cases. When finally he steps out of the store, head bowed in thought, he nearly runs into two girls who stand bent close in serious conversation.

When they look up and see that it is him, they both politely say hello. Eula looks up at the store awning behind him. The other girl, the girl with the onion pale hair, she looks down at the toe of her boot. He hears himself ask, "Want to go for a soda?" His voice is like a round stone that drops right there on the sidewalk. Eula's face closes like a door. But the other girl. The other girl, she guesses so.

He takes her to the only drugstore in town and they sit at the counter and order two sodas. She doesn't speak. They watch the clerk stocking packages on the high shelves along the wall, sliding his wooden ladder along the track in the ceiling with a satisfying, heavy sound. She seals her straw with her finger and swizzles it around the glass. She crosses her right ankle over her left, then her left ankle over her right, then hooks her heels onto the bottom of the stool. My father compliments her on her dress. The clerk drops a bag of flour and curses, then apologizes to the girl. There are hollow fly carcasses wedged into the dusty seam of the counter and the warped wood floor. Even with two ceiling fans running, the air is hot and close.

This must have been the middle of August: though my father doesn't tell me this, it is easy enough to count backwards and figure for myself. The walls of the store are painted a deep green and the paint has bubbled in some places. My father's mind fails him as he searches for something to say. He watches her twist a strand of hair around her finger, but she feels his eyes on her and abruptly stops, folding her hands in her lap.

"So, you and Eula, y'all sit together at church," he says, forgetting to make it a question.

Puzzled, the girl nods her head. She has not yet said a word. Perhaps she is having trouble believing that she is sitting here at this counter, having a soda with a boy. Or she is worrying that her hair is too pale and limp, or her wrists too big, or her dress too common. She has never believed she would find herself in this situation, and so has never rehearsed.

"I've always thought this time of year is the saddest," she finally says, looking up at my father. He lays his hand on the counter and spreads out his fingers. His chin tilts forward as if he is about to speak. Then the sleigh bells on the door jingle, shiver when it slams shut. It is Eula. She doesn't look at them. She brushes her sweat-damp hair back with two fingers and asks the clerk for something—what?—my father's ears are suddenly filled—she is asking the clerk for a tin of aspirin, peering up at the shelves behind him and blinking her snakecharming eyes. The clerk stares too long before turning to his ladder. My father considers socking him one in that plug ugly face. Eula raps her fingers along the edge of the counter and hums tunelessly and still she won't look their way.

At this moment, my father feels his heart dissolve into a sticky bright liquid. Jealousy has seized her, she has followed them here—he is certain. Finally, a staggering proclamation of her love. His heart has begun to trickle down into the soles of his feet when the girl somehow catches Eula's eye and ripples her fingers at her.

Hello.

Then Eula unfolds her long body towards them, and smiles. An enormous, beautiful, open-faced smile: a smile with no jealousy hidden behind it at all. She takes her change and paper sack from the clerk and turns, one hand stretched out towards the door. She is simply going to leave. She is going to walk out the door and leave them here to their sodas and silence. At this point my father, frantic, takes hold of the girl on the stool next to him, leans her in Eula's direction, and kisses her recklessly, right on the mouth.

My father tells me this story in the garden, bent over and searching through the knee high weeds for long thick stalks of asparagus, clipping them with his pocket knife and handing them to me. Here he stops and straightens and squints east, and I know his back is starting to bother him. Why he never told me the story when I was a boy, I don't know: I am twice as old now as he was, the year of the mule killers. But still he skips the part of the story where I come in.

It doesn't matter; I can imagine it. Before the door has even closed after Eula, something has changed in my father, and as he slides from his stool he firmly takes the girl's hand. He leads her out of the drugstore, glancing back once more at the pock-faced clerk, who is carefully smoothing Eula's bill into the cash register drawer. Slowly they make their way somewhere: back to the farm, most likely, where his father is sitting with the hands at supper. He takes her to the hayloft, a back field, the mule barn, the spring house: any place that was dark and quiet for long enough that my father could desperately try to summon Eula's face, or else hope to forever blot it from his mind. Long enough that I, like a flashbulb, could snap into existence.

Mercy, mercy, mercy, my grandfather said, that day they finally took Orphan. *He'll be all right.* He pinched the bridge of his nose and looked away when they tried to load him onto the truck. The mule's big ears swung forward, his narrow withers locked, and he would not budge when he got to the loading ramp. It took four men to finally get him up, and they saw his white eye swiveling madly when they looked in through the slats. *Not stubborn, just smart,* my grandfather said to the ground, then again pinched his nose and leaned against the truck as two more mules were loaded up. His herd was so big that this was the last of three trips. He had intended to send Orphan with the first load, but had put it off and put it off.

Ain't it some kind of thanks, my grandfather said as he latched up the back of the truck, the mules inside jostling to get their footing, and Orphan's long ear had swiveled back at the sound of his voice. The best of them brought three or four cents a pound as dog meat; some of them would merely be heaved six deep into a trench that would be filled over with dirt by men on tractors. The hollow report of hooves on the truck bed echoed even after the truck had pulled onto the road and turned out of sight. The exact same sound could be heard all through the county, all across the hills of Tennessee and up through Kentucky, across Missouri and Kansas and all the way out West, even, you could hear it. The mules' job, it was finished.

When the back of the truck is finally shut, my father is high above, hiding in the hayloft. At church the pale haired girl had pulled him into the center aisle just before the service and told him her news, the news of me. All through the sermon his mind had flipped like a fish, and he had stared hard at the back of Eula's neck, trying to still that fish. In the hayloft he thinks of this moment as he listens to the shouts of the truck driver and the engine backfiring once before the mules are pulled away, but he doesn't come to the edge, he doesn't look down for one last glimpse of Orphan Lad.

Late that night my father creeps to the Victrola in the living room and carefully opens the top of the cabinet. He slides a record onto the turntable and turns the crank, then sets his eraser and needle between his teeth and presses it to the first groove. A fiddle plays, is joined by a guitar, and then a high lonesome voice starts in about heartbreak. Every time he listens to his records like this, the first notes take him by surprise. When the music starts to fill his head, he can't believe it is coming from the record on the turntable and not from a place within himself. He closes his eyes and imagines Eula Parker is in the room, dancing behind him in a dark red dress. He moves his face across the record, following the groove with the needle, and spit collects in the pockets of his cheeks. *Eula, Eula, Eula.* He lets her name roll around in his head until it is unclear, too, whether this sound is coming from the record on the turntable, or from the deepest hollows of his heart.

Three weeks after the last load of mules is taken, one of the tractors overturns on a hill down by the river and nearly kills one of the hands. It is not an unexpected tragedy. My grandfather is the only one with the man, and he pulls him out from underneath the seat and searches through the grass for three scattered fingers while the machine's engine continues to choke and whir. He drives the man to the hospital in Nashville and doesn't return until late that night. His trip home is held up by a wreck at the bridge that takes nearly an hour to be cleared away. When he finally arrives back, his son is waiting up on the porch to tell him about the pale haired girl.

My father has rehearsed what he will say dozens of times to the fence posts and icebox, but when he sees his father's brown blood caked forearms and hands, he is startled enough to forget what it was. Weary and white in the face, my grandfather sits down next to him on the top step and touches his shoulder.

"Son," he says, "you're gonna see a future I can't even stretch my mind around. Not any of it. I can't even begin to imagine."

If my father had understood what his father was trying to tell him, maybe he would have waited until the morning to say what he now says. Maybe he would never had said anything, packed up a small bag and a portable Victrola and left town for good. Abandoned love and any expectation of it. Instead he confesses to my grandfather, all in a rush, the same way he might have admitted that he had broken the new mower, or left the front gate open all night.

My grandfather stares hard at my father's knee and is quiet a long time.

"You done wrong," he says. Repeats it. "You got no choice but to take care of it. You done wrong."

In those days this was my grandfather's interpretation of the world, a thing was either right or it was wrong. Or so it seemed to my father, and he was getting tired of it.

"No, sir," he says, lips tight. "That's not what I intend. I'm in love with someone else." He takes a breath. "I'm gonna marry Eula Parker." Even as he speaks her name he is startled by this statement, like it is a giant carp he has yanked from the depths of the river. It lies on the step before both of them, gasping in the open air.

My grandfather looks at him with sadness rimming his eyes and says quietly, "You should've thought of that before."

"But you see," my father says, as if explaining to a child, "I love her."

My grandfather grips his knees with his big hands and sighs. He reaches out for his son's arm, but my father brushes him away, stands up and walks heavily across the porch. When he goes into the house, he lets the screen door slam behind him, and it bangs twice in the casement before clicking shut.

Late that night, after washing the dishes of a silent dinner, my father sits on the porch sharpening his pocket knife. He taps his bare feet against the hollow stairs and even whistles through his teeth. His father's words have still not completely closed in around him. Though an uneasiness is slowly creeping up, he is still certain that the future is bright chrome and glorious, full of possibility. Behind him, the strings of the banjo gently twang as they go flat in the cooling air. It is the first night of the year that smells of autumn and my father takes a few deep breaths as he leans against the porch railing and looks out into the yard. This is when he sees something out under the old elm, a long twisted shape leaning unsteadily against the thick trunk of the tree.

He steps off the porch onto the cool grass of the yard, thinking first he sees a ghost. As he gets closer to the shape, he believes it next to be a fallen limb, or one of the hands, drunk on moonshine—then, nothing but a forgotten ladder, then—with rising heart—Eula come to call for him in her darkest dress. But when he is just a few yards away from the tree, he sees it is just his father, leaning with his back to the house, arms at his sides. He is speaking quietly, and my father knows by the quality of his voice that he is praying. He has found him like this before, in the hayfield at dusk or by the creek in the morning, eyes closed, mumbling simple private incantations. My father is about to step quietly back to the porch when his father reaches a trembling hand to the tree to steady himself, then lets his shoulders collapse. He blows his nose in his hand and my father hears him swallow back thick jumbled sobs. When he hears this, when he realizes his father is crying, he turns and rushes blindly back to the house, waves of heat rising from beneath his ribs like startled birds from a tree.

Once behind the closed door of his room, my father makes himself small as possible on the edge of his unmade bed. Staring hard at the baseboard, he tries to slow his tumbling heart. He has never, ever seen his father cry, not even when his mother died. Now, having witnessed it, he feels like he has pulled the rug of manhood out from under the old man's feet. He convinces himself that it is must be the lost mules his father was praying for, or for the mangled man who lies unconscious in the hospital bed in Nashville, and that this is what drove him to tears. It is only much later, picking asparagus in the ghost of a garden, that he will admit who his father had really been crying for: for his son, and for his son.

These days, my father remembers little from the time before the tractors. The growl of their engines in his mind has long since drowned out the quieter noises: the constant stamping and shifting of mule weight in the barn, the smooth sound of oats being poured into a steel bucket. He remembers the steam that rose from the animals after work. Pooled heaps of soft leather harness waiting to be mended on the breakfast table. At the threshold of the barn door, a velvet-eared dog that was always snapping its teeth at flies. Orphan standing dark and noble in the snow, a sled hooked to his harness. Eula Parker in a dark blue hat laughing and saying his name, hurrying after him and calling out *Wait, Wait,* one warm Sunday as he left church for home.

He remembers too his mother's cooking spices lined up in the cupboard where they had been since her death, faded inside their tins without scent or taste. When he knew he was alone in the house, it gave him some comfortable sadness to take them out one by one and open them, the contents of each as dusty and gray as the next. He has just one memory of her, just an image: the curve of her spine and the fall of her hair when she had once leaned over to sniff the sheets on his bed, the morning after he'd wet it. This is all he has of her: one moment, just one, tangled in those little threads of shame.

In the same way I only have one memory of my grandfather, one watery picture from when I was very young. When my mother and father would rock me on the porch at night, my grandfather sat with them in a straight backed chair, playing the banjo. He would tie a little tissue paper doll to his right wrist, and it danced and jumped like a tiny white ghost. I remember sitting on my mother's lap one night, and in the darkness the only things I could see were the tissue doll, the white moon of the banjo face, my mother's pale hair. I remember watching that doll bobbing along with my grandfather's strumming, and from time to time, the white flash of his teeth when he smiled. And I can hear him sing just a piece of one of the old songs: *I know'd it, indeed I know'd it, yes, I know'd it, my bones are gonna rise again.*

This is the story that my father tells me as he bends like a wire wicket in the garden, or, I should say, what once was my mother's garden. He parts the tangle of weeds to find the asparagus, then snaps off the tough spears with his knife, straightening slowly from time to time to stretch his stiff and rounded back. The garden is like a straight-edged wilderness in the middle of the closely mowed lawn, a blasted plot of weeds and thorns and thistle. Nothing has grown here since my mother died and there was no one who wanted to tend it. Nothing except the asparagus, which comes up year after year.

The Caves of Oregon

Benjamin Percy

This afternoon, a hot August afternoon, the refrigerator bleeds. Two red lines run down the length of it—and then a third, a fourth—oozing from the bottom lip of the freezer. This is what Kevin finds when he returns home from his job at the foundry and flips the light switch repeatedly without success, when he stands in the half-light of the kitchen and says, "Shit."

Already he can smell it, the blood. And when he draws a steadying breath he imagines he can taste it, too—the mineral sourness of it. He is a big man—a man who spends most of his days with his hands taped, swinging a fifty-pound sledgehammer—and he must bend his body in half to observe the freezer closely. The seal of its underside has gone as red as a tendon. Little droplets are gathering there, swelling fatly, and then, too heavy, they break from their purchase and race for the floor.

Right then he hears his wife, Becca, her car grumbling up the driveway, as she returns home from the community college where she teaches. He hears her keys jangle, her footsteps on the porch, in the hallway. She calls out his name and he says, "In here." She begins to say something, something about the garage door failing to open, her voice cut short by a sharp intake of air when she sees the bleeding fridge.

"Power's out," he says and she gives him a tight-faced look that trembles at the mouth from her teeth taking tiny bites from her cheeks. He can sense her anger coming and it makes him feel as if he is shrinking, small enough to put in his own pocket. "I just got home," he says, his voice coming out in an almost whine. "Like, five seconds ago. I was just about to start cleaning."

She hurls down her keys. Against the Formica counter they make a noise like bottles breaking. "Great," she says. "That's just great. That's *just* what I need." She lifts her arms and lets them fall and stomps her way from the kitchen, into the hallway, bringing down her high heels as if to stab something with every step. He can hear her muttering to herself as she burrows roughly through the closet. A moment later she returns with an armful of beach towels. She throws them down at the base of the fridge and tells him to get the cooler.

"The cooler?"

"Yes, the fucking cooler," she says. "You know, the *cooler*."

He retrieves it from the garage and with some hesitation sets it on top of the towels, watching his wife as he does so, hoping this is where she wants it. She says nothing. She will not look at him. All her attention, this radiant anger he has come to know so well, is momentarily focused on the fridge. For this he is thankful.

These days she is always angry, it seems. All it takes is a dropped dish, the wrong word, heavy traffic, and a switch goes off inside her that sends blue electricity sizzling through her veins.

He retreats from her and crosses his arms, his hands tucked into his armpits. For a moment his wife stares at the freezer, her head cocked, as if listening to something in the far distance. He watches her back, the rigidity of it. A long brown ponytail curls down her spine like an upside-down question mark.

And then she suddenly brings her hand to the freezer door and pulls. At first it resists her, and so she brings her other hand to the handle and leans backward. Then, with a sort of sucking, sort of gasping noise, it opens.

The sight of it reminds Kevin of the time he had his wisdom teeth removed. His dentist had given him an irrigator, a plastic syringe. Twice a day he filled it with salt water and placed its needle into the craters at the back of his mouth—and from them, in a pink rush, came scabs, bits of food. That is what the freezer looks like when its door opens and the blood surges from it—all down the front of the fridge, dampening their photos, glossing over their magnets, until the front of the fridge has more red on it than white.

Becca makes a noise like a wounded bird. She turns her head away from the mess and squints shut her eyes. Her pants, her shoes are splattered with red. A tremble races through her body and then she goes perfectly still.

Kevin goes to her and places a hand on her shoulder and her shoulder drops a little from the weight of it. He feels as if he is touching a banister, a rifle stock, something hard and unbending. "Let me do it," he says. "Please."

The kitchen is loud with the noise of dripping.

"I hate this house," she says, her voice a harsh whisper. "I hate, hate, *hate* this house."

"You go sit down and I'll take care of it. You rest. You need your rest."

She raises her arm, long and thin, her hand gloved with blood, like a stop sign. She will not speak to him, mute with a kind of fury.

"Sorry," he says and his hand falls away from her when she bends over to reposition the cooler. And then, with her arms out as if to hug, she reaches into the freezer. There is a surprising amount of meat in there and she hooks her arms around it, the pile of it, and slides it out all at once. The T-bones, pork chops, bratwursts, chicken breasts splat into the cooler, one on top of the other, a mass of meat along with two ice trays and a sodden box of baking soda. A hamburger patty misses its mark and plops on the linoleum, making a red flower pattern.

By this time Kevin has removed from beneath the sink a sponge, a roll of paper towels, a Clorox spray bottle. His wife watches him when he tears off five lengths of paper towels and lays them in the freezer to soak up the blood pooled there. "That's not enough," she says and snatches the towels from him and lays down several more sheets. "Just let me do it."

He pinches shut his mouth and drops his eyes and holds up his hands, palms flat, as if pressing them against a wall. "Okay."

She plucks the photos and magnets from the fridge and tosses them in the cooler. Then she kneels with a bouquet of paper towels in one hand and the bottle of Clorox in the other. At first, when she sprays, when she wipes, she only smears the blood, making it pinker, making swirls like you see in hair and wood grain. Then the blood begins to come away and the fridge begins to look like a fridge again.

Thirty minutes later, when she at last finishes, she says, "There." She is damp with sweat, with gore. She runs a forearm across her forehead and takes a deep, shuddering breath. Her blouse, once beige, now clings to her redly, pinkly, in tie-dye designs. She strips it off and tosses it in the cooler, along with her skirt, her bra and panties. Her shoes she sets aside. Naked, she goes to the sink and runs the water and soaps up her arms and feet and splashes her face and when she turns toward Kevin her face is calmer, paler, drained of its previous flush.

"Sorry I snapped at you," she says.

"It's okay," he says, raising his voice so it follows her down the hallway, to their bedroom, their bathroom, where she will climb into the shower and leave behind a pink ring at the bottom of the tub as she did several months ago when she began to hemorrhage, when she lost the baby.

The power went out because of the cave.

The cave—a lava tube—runs beneath their house, their neighborhood, and beyond, a vast tunnel that once carried in it molten rock the color of an angry sun.

People say Central Oregon looks like another planet. Mars maybe. The reddish blackish landscape is busy with calderas, cinder cones, lava blisters, pressure ridges, pressure plateaus—much of it the hardened remains of basalt, a lava that spreads quickly, like thin porridge, flowing sometimes seventy miles, its front fed by lava tubes, like their lava tube, one of so many that network the ground beneath Bend, Redmond, La Pine.

Sometimes the caves collapse. A tractor-trailer will be growling along Route 97 when the asphalt opens up—just like that, like a mouth—and the rig will vanish, crashing down into an unknown darkness. Or someone will go to their driveway and find it gone, along with their car, their johnboat, replaced by a gaping hole. Or a hard rain will come, dampening and loosening those unseen joints beneath the surface that send the ground buckling. Imagine five acres dropping several inches, maybe even a foot, in an instant. Imagine fissures opening in your lawn. Imagine septic tanks splintering, sewage bubbling up from the ground like oil. Imagine power lines pinched off and neighborhoods darkened for days.

It's upsetting, not trusting the ground beneath your feet.

Their house is part of a new development called Elk Mound. It is located on a spur of basalt overlooking a coulee crowded with juniper trees that deepens and widens on its way south to accommodate the spring-fed Newberry River that winds through the Aubrey Glen Golf Course on its way toward Bend, just five miles south of them.

Theirs was the last house in the development to sell, a year ago. It had been built over the mouth of the cave. To pass inspection and ensure no vertical settlement the contractor widened the foundation, bolting it to the bedrock with twenty Perma Jack brackets. The realtor advertised the cave as a "natural basement with cooling properties."

In the living room there is an insulated steel door. Somehow, through the cracks around it, the breath of the cave finds its way in, smelling faintly of mushrooms, sulfur, cellar-floor puddles. Beyond the door a steel staircase, nearly forty feet tall, descends into darkness.

Becca teaches in the Geology Department at Central Oregon Community College. She often wears her hair pulled back in a ponytail and khaki pants with many zippered compartments. She keeps a special toothbrush by the sink to scrub away the crescents of dirt that seem always to gather beneath her fingernails. In everyday conversation she uses words like igneous, tetrahedron, radar-mapping. The cave, to her, was the equivalent of a trampoline or fire pole to a child. It was cool. "I know I ought to know better," she said with a smile, when they signed the deed and bought the place for a song.

Three years ago Kevin met Becca when skiing at Mt. Bachelor. She was standing at the summit of the mountain, at the top of a mogul field, when he slid off the chairlift. It was her honey-colored hair that first caught his attention. The wind blew it every which way, so that with the blue sky all around her she looked as if she were underwater. She wore this white outfit that stole the breath from his chest. He unwrapped a PowerBar and hungrily ate it. When she still hadn't moved five minutes later, he approached her.

He asked if she was okay, thinking she might be afraid of the long drop before her, but she only looked at him curiously, completely unafraid, and said, "I'm fine," with the breath trailing from her mouth.

To their north the spine of the Cascade Range continued with the Three Sisters rising through a thin layer of clouds like gnarled vertebrae. Becca pointed her pole at the saddle-shaped place between the South and Middle Sister and said, "I'm just studying that moraine over there."

He had never heard that word before—moraine—and it made him picture a great flood of water, frozen in its tracks.

Then she adjusted her goggles and gave him a smile and took off down the mountain, her skis arranged in a careful pie wedge that curled the powder over, exposing in her wake a broad zigzagging track of blue. He followed, and one thing led to another.

There was a time, not even five months ago, when she would sneak up behind him and pinch his butt and yell, "You're it!" and run from him, squealing as he chased her through their new house, over the couch, under the dining-room table, finally catching her in bed with his hands made into crab claws that touched her roughly all over.

Afterwards they would drink beer and watch the *Late Show* and she would laugh with her head thrown back, smiling so widely he could see her back teeth, her fillings giving off a silvery light.

They were pretty happy.

Then she was late. A few days passed, then a week, then two weeks, before she sent Kevin to the pharmacy. By this time she knew because she had always been like clockwork, had never been this late. But she wanted to be certain. She wanted some bit of proof she could point to and say, "There."

In Aisle 5 the shelves were crowded with dozens of pink boxes. Not understanding the differences between them he randomly selected one—an expensive one with a picture of a rose garden on it—and on his way to the register he grabbed a pack of gum, a Butterfinger, an *Us Weekly,* trying to clutter the register with other things. The checkout girl wore blue eye shadow. He thought it made her look very sad.

At home, when he handed his wife the box, she turned it over and scrunched her eyebrows and read its back as if for nutritional information. "Is this even a good one?" she asked and he said, "Yes. It's very reliable." He leaned toward her and tapped the place on the box where it read *98% Accurate!*

This seemed to satisfy her and she went into the bathroom with the kit and closed the door, and he could hear the cardboard tearing, could hear her swearing when she peed a little on her hand, could hear the muffled roar of the toilet when she finished.

There was a lengthy silence and then she emerged from the bathroom. She had a plastic stick in her hand and she was shaking it and looking at it between shakes like an undeveloped Polaroid.

"Well?" he said.

She looked at him with a blank expression and held onto the stick a second longer before handing it to him. He took it with two hands and brought it close to his face. At the end of the stick, in a tiny window frame, there was a plus sign. It was an absurd shade of pink—the kind of pink little girls favored in their dresses and bubblegum. "Plus means what?"

"Plus means pregnant," she said.

His eyes grew larger and he felt at once light-headed and ebullient and fearful. "You're kidding me?"

She pressed her hands hard against her face. "I am not kidding you."

"You're shitting me?"

"I am not shitting you," she said and looked at him through her fingers. "I'm serious."

Kevin, openmouthed, considered her. "You're serious."

"I'm being seriously serious. We're having a goddamn baby."

Kevin works at the foundry, the Redmond Foundry, which produces over 200 alloys. It is a high-ceilinged cinder-block building whose interior is black with dust and red with fire. All around him men wear heavy leather aprons and canvas gloves and tinted goggles. One of his main tasks is shaking-out— breaking up sand castings to get at the metal castings cooling and hardening within them. His sledgehammer is like an extension of his body. When he leaves work his hands are still curled in the shape of it. All through the day he swings it again and again until the weight is nearly impossible to bear, until his face goes as red as the liquid metal glowing all around him and his veins rise jaggedly from his arms. When he swings, his breath goes rip-rip-*rip* and the hammer blasts open the sand casting with a *crack*. A cloud of particles rises from it and sticks to his sweat. And there is the alloy, like a fossil fallen out of mud, to toss in a nearby bin.

Sometimes, if someone calls in sick, he'll work the induction furnace or the electric arc furnace, getting clamps in the right places, arranging molds, making sure they're free of dirt, and then pouring into them the hot metal that looks so much like lava.

His wife thinks he should go back to school—he is capable of so much more, she says—but the pay is good and nobody bothers him and he likes the rhythm of the work, the mindless repetition.

Weekends, they used to explore the cave. They would throw on their jeans and fleece and tie their hiking boots tight and descend into the darkness with their Magnum flashlights throwing cones of light before them. Down here no birds chirped, no dogs barked, no planes growled overhead. Occasionally the cave would pass beneath a road and they could hear the traffic humming above them, but otherwise, their noise was the only thing. Their footsteps, shooshing through black sand or clunking off rocks, seemed so loud. And so they spoke in whispers. And when they spoke—saying, "What was that?" or "Watch your step," or "I love how old everything smells down here. It smells like it's a hundred million years old"—their breath fogged from their mouths.

When a vein of quartz would catch the light, Becca would put her hands to it. The rock would be slick and streaked pink and white, like bacon. She would remove from her backpack a pick and hand it to Kevin and he would swing it in a short arc and chip some of the quartz from the wall. And she would collect it to take home and stack neatly across her bureau, across bookshelves and windowsills, so that after a while their house seemed to glitter from every corner.

The cave branched off into narrow corridors, scarcely wider than the Korean hatchback Kevin drove, but the main tube reached thirty, forty yards across, like the hollowed passage of an enormous worm. They wondered if it had an end.

Sometimes the blackness would go gray and they would click off their flashlights and pick their way through the gloom until they came upon a sort of skylight, where the roof of the cave had collapsed and now let in the sun. One time they found a dog—a German shepherd—hanging from such a hole. It had been lynched by its leash, its leash tethered to something aboveground and out of sight, perhaps a tree. And the dog dangled there, spotlit by the sun, turning around and around.

There were things—a far-off moaning, a bundle of bones, a dark shape scuttling just past the reach of their flashlight—that scared them. Rocks scared them. Rocks cluttered the cave floor, some of them the size of melons, others the size of elk. For this reason they bought REI spelunking helmets. Sometimes the ceiling would come loose with a click of stone, a hiss of dirt, nearly noiseless in its descent, but when it slammed to the cave floor, it roared and displaced a big block of air that made them cry out and clutch each other in a happy sort of terror.

But that was before.

Becca doesn't like to go down in the cave anymore. Not since the day in July when the bats came. It was early evening, and they were sprawled out on the couch watching *Wheel of Fortune*. At that time she was four months' pregnant and her belly was beginning to poke out enough that women would stop her in the grocery store and ask. She needed a safety pin to fasten the jeans she wore now. He was drinking a Bud Light and she was drinking water. She let in enough liquid to visibly fill her cheeks, and then swallowed in tiny portions, her cheeks growing smaller and smaller until sunken. He liked watching her drink. She drank water as if it were wine, not as a necessity but as a pleasure, trying to make it last longer. She looked at him looking at her and said, "Do you hear that?"

"Hear what?"

"That."

He picked up the remote and hit the mute button and the applause of the audience fell away and a hush descended upon the room. He heard nothing and said as much.

Becca had her head cocked and her hand raised. "Just wait," she said, and then, "*There.*"

And there it was, a scritch-scritch-scritching at the steel door.

For a long time they simply looked at each other and then she pushed him and said, "Go see what it is," and he said, "All right already," and got up from the couch and slowly approached the door and put his ear to it. The metal was cold against his cheek. From here the scratching sound sounded more like the sound of eating, of teeth mashing something into a paste.

Becca said something he couldn't hear and he pulled his head away from the door and said, "What?" and she said, "You think it could be a wild animal?"

"Don't know." Right then he opened the door and the bats came rushing in, a dense black stream of them. They emitted a terrible screeching, the noise a thousand nails would make when teased across a chalkboard. They fluttered violently through the living room, the kitchen, the hallway, battering the walls and windows, seeking escape. Kevin screamed and so did Becca and the noise of flapping, of air beaten in many different directions, was all around them.

Somehow Kevin ducked down and pushed his way through their black swirling color and ran for the front door and threw it open and not thirty seconds later most of the bats had disappeared into the twilight gloom.

Becca was on the couch with an injured bat fluttering limply in her hair. She did not move, except to part her lips and say, "Holy shit." She had a hand between her breasts, over her heart. "Holy fucking shit. What the fucking shit was that?"

The next morning she woke up complaining of cramps.

Even before she was pregnant she would talk about her pain incessantly, saying her back hurt, her neck hurt, her feet hurt, her head, her stomach. If it were touchable—like, the space between her eyebrows—she would touch it. "I think it's a tumor," she would say, completely serious. "Feel this. This does not feel normal."

And Kevin would say, "I'm sure it's nothing."

"I'm sure it's nothing," was what he said when she complained of cramps, when she limped to the shower with a hand pressed below her belly.

"My lower back," she said. "On the right side. I really, really hope I'm okay. I'm pretty worried about the way this feels."

And then she began bleeding. A rope of red trailed down her leg. And Kevin, now in a panic, wrapped her in a bathrobe and with shampoo still in her hair drove her to St. Charles where she delivered, with a rush of blood, the baby that looked like a baby, a little girl, only too small and too red, the size of his hand.

Becca was convinced it had something to do with the bats. Perhaps she had been bitten or scratched and perhaps some parasite with leathery wings and claws traveled through her bloodstream and did ruin to her. When she told the doctor this, vines of sadness trembled through the skin around her eyes. They ran blood tests and found nothing. No, the doctor said. Not the bats. It was just one of those things.

She didn't like this. She didn't like to think that her own body could turn on her, collapse upon itself. So she said, "What does he know? Doctors don't know anything. One day they say eggs are good for you. The next they're bad. How can they have the answers when the answers are always changing."

Right then Kevin could see the pain between her legs in her face. Still can to this day. Sometimes he imagines a rotten spot inside her, like a bruised bit of peach he wants to carve away with a knife.

Tonight, after they clean all the blood from the fridge and their bodies, after they buy Chinese takeout and carry it into the living room to eat on TV trays, they find a bat. It is tucked into a corner, where the wall meets the ceiling. Kevin can see its heartbeat pulsing through its thin leathery skin. Maybe it is one of the old bats that never escaped or maybe it is a new bat that somehow found its way inside, its tiny brown body crawling through the heating ducts, the walls.

Kevin wants to surround it with something—maybe a glass or a Tupperware container—and carry it outside and release it. When he says this Becca looks at him as if she wants to spit. "I hate this house," she says. "I hate this stupid, stupid house." Then she grabs the poker from the fireplace and holds it like a spear and jerks it forward, impaling the bat.

When the metal moves through it, it makes the smallest scream in the world.

They haven't had sex in a month and a half, not since the miscarriage.

In the back of the closet, on the top shelf, beneath his sweaters, Kevin keeps an old copy of *Penthouse*. He bought it at a gas station several years ago and sometimes sneaks it down to read when his wife isn't home. He likes having something hidden from her, something that belongs to him alone, a small betrayal.

Becca has a rule: if you don't wear a piece of clothing for a year, you get rid of it, and right now she is going through their closet with a garbage bag, filling it with clothes for Goodwill, when she finds the *Penthouse*.

Kevin comes out of the bathroom to find her standing there, with her legs spread apart, the magazine crumpled up in her fist. "What?" she says. "I'm not good enough for you?"

"It's not that."

"Then what is it?"

This is a question with barbed wire around it, and when he doesn't answer she rips the magazine in half and then in half again and throws its pages to the floor and stares at him, panting. The way her anger grows reminds him of an umbrella, a big red umbrella, suddenly sprung.

"Look," he says, exasperated. "You want to punch me? Would that make you feel better?"

Her eyes narrow with anger and he motions her forward with his hands and says, "Come on. Hit me, why don't you. You know you want to. Do it." He can see her little hand baling into a fist. And then she draws it back and gives him a glancing blow to the shoulder. "Is that all you've got?" he says. "Come on. You can do better than that. You hit like a girl. Hit me like you mean it."

This triggers some switch inside her. She makes a furious little noise and charges forward and hits him again and this time his shoulder seizes up with hurt.

"That's better," he says.

She has a look of complete rage or religious exaltation on her face—he isn't sure which. She is breathing hard. He can hear the air coming in and out of her nose. "What else do you want me to do to you?" she says.

"You tell me."

She points her finger at him and tells him to take off his shirt. And he does. Bare-chested he stands before her, swaying slightly. She reaches forward and twists his nipples—hard—and when he screams she smiles and pinches between her fingers a clump of chest hair and rips it out, leaving behind a pink place where the blood rises in tiny dots. And he screams again. And their eyes hold together like the pieces of a puzzle.

She throws him against the wall and kisses him, roughly kisses him through all their laughing. And they tear the clothes off each other and he picks her up and pushes her against the wall and enters her. And she is bucking her hips against his and he can feel himself losing control, can feel the heat rising in him, moving through the tunnels of him and nearing eruption, when all of a sudden she pushes him away and says, "That's enough."

When he asks what's wrong she absently scratches her bare breast and stares down at her feet as if the answer lies somewhere underground.

It is easier for Kevin. He can lose himself in the rhythms of his hammer, can smash the frustration from his body. Every day at work he drinks a milk jug full of water and sweats out every last drop of it and it is more than a little like crying.

Right after the miscarriage he thought a lot about the baby, the little girl they never named. How she might have smiled ridiculously at him making funny faces. Or used the coffee table to pull herself up and take her first teetering steps. Then he drank himself to the very pitch of drunkenness, and that was enough. The baby has almost disappeared from his memory, almost.

Sometimes he will say something—maybe he will be watching CNN and maybe they will broadcast a dead Iraqi child lying in the middle of the street and maybe he will make some offhand remark about how lucky they are—and only when he sees the crumpled-up look on Becca's face does he remember and say, "Oh."

She cannot not remember. A playground busy with children. A dirty pacifier abandoned in the aisle at Wal-Mart. The purple teddy bear she bought and set among her rocks on the bureau. On a daily basis all of these things fly into her eyes and thump around inside of her skull, like bats, leaving the poisonous dust of their wings. She keeps her lips pursed around the edge of a pain he can only imagine and she cannot seem to forget.

Midnight. He wakes up to find his wife gone, the shape of her head still imprinted on her pillow. He calls out her name and when she doesn't answer he gets out of bed and walks down the hall and into the living room where moonlight comes in through the windows and makes the quartz set here and there sparkle.

He observes the steel door hanging open—and there, surrounded by blackness, a palpable blackness, strange and horrible, that seems to ooze into the house, stands his wife.

He goes to her. If she hears his footsteps, if she feels the weight of his hand on her shoulder, she gives no indication. She wears one of his T-shirts and nothing else, her feet tight together, her arms at her side.

From the door a cool wind blows, bringing cave smells, of guano and mold and sand and stone. He closes the door and hoists up his wife and cradles her in his arms and carries her to the bedroom, to bed, where she finally comes alive and says, "No," and jumps up and goes to her dresser and opens its drawers. She steps into her panties and zips up her jeans and pulls a fleece over her head and asks, as she begins lacing her boots, whether he is coming or not.

Their flashlights are the only lights. There is no moon down here. Beyond the cones of yellow light there is nothing, everything utterly black. Dark as only a cave can be dark. The longer they walk, the closer the walls seem to get, the narrower the passage.

Becca leads the way—her body tense, her shoulders bunched up nearly to her ears—down a series of unfamiliar corridors, taking a right at each junction so they will know to always take a left when returning. Around a bend, among a pile of rocks, a pair of red eyes brighten, then vanish, and Kevin spends the next dozen yards sweeping his flashlight back and forth, waiting for something to materialize and come rushing toward them.

Becca moves her pale hand along the basalt, steadying her passage and crumbling away the green-and-gold patterns of lichen growing there. Occasionally she pauses, close-lipped, contemplating something visible only to her, before continuing forward. Her flashlight makes giant shadows that seem to knock against each other.

Then the channel opens up into a space as big as a banquet hall. The floor is strangely clean, absent of rocks. From the ceiling hang roots, like capillaries, groping for purchase. He gives one a tentative tug and when it doesn't give he tries swinging from it and it carries his weight and he flies from one side of the cave to the other, like something out of a Tarzan episode.

Becca has a small smile on her face when she walks the room, touching the walls and looking all around her, as if committing the space to memory. And then she locks eyes with Kevin and brings the flashlight to her face, throwing shadows across it. They seem blacker than the darkness of the cave.

The light clicks off and she becomes a gray shape in the near distance.

He waits a moment, surrounded by his own ball of light, before clicking off his own flashlight. And the next thing he knows a cloud of darkness settles around them. He can hear her feet whispering across the cave floor and then her voice playfully calling out to him, "Marco."

He can hear the saliva popping in his mouth when it rises into a smile. "Polo," he says and moves toward her voice with his hands out before him, his fingers like the snouts of moles, routing through the dark. When he touches stone he hears her voice again, saying, "Marco," behind him now.

This continues for a few minutes, with her always eluding him. He can hear her voice and her footsteps and by the time he races to where she was, he knows she is already gone, but not where, not exactly.

All this time the roots startle him, coming out of the dark to lick his face. More than once he screams. And this is how she finds him. He can feel her hand at his elbow. It squeezes him and rises to his chest and pauses there. "Hey," he says and she says, "Got you."

Both of them click on their flashlights at once. They blink painfully, seeing a yellow light with a few filaments of red running through it. The black liquid of the cave oozes at the edges of their vision as the world takes form and they stare hard at each other for a long time. Then, as if something has been decided between them, she grabs a fistful of his shirt and pulls him down to the sandy floor where she brings her mouth against his. And this time she doesn't stop him when he peels off her pants and explores the slickness between her legs with his hands before climbing on top of her.

Together they move slowly, with the rhythm of a sleeping chest, until they are finished—and this takes a long time—so long that their flashlights begin to dim and eventually black out. And they are alone in the dark, huddling together with the cold creeping into their bare skin.

When they finally untangle themselves and rise from the cave floor he takes off his belt and runs it through his back belt loop only, so that it serves as a sort of leash. She grabs hold of it and follows him as they continue back the way they came. They can hear dripping sounds of water and the hushing sound of wind and the booming sounds of rocks falling somewhere deep in the cave. But they aren't afraid so much as they are resigned to making it home. Kevin reaches his hands before him and moves them in a slow scissoring motion as if clearing the cobwebs from the air. And he lifts his feet high and brings them down carefully and when necessary warns Becca: "There's a big rock here, about knee-high, so don't bang into it."

Every time the cave walls fall away he follows the left passage, groping through the dark, and eventually they find the staircase. They climb it and close the steel door behind them. The air is warmer up here. It feels soft. A patch of dawn sky is visible through the living-room window.

Becca goes to the kitchen and pulls out a gallon of milk and before pouring it into a glass stands there, backlit by the fridge, her face in shadow, looking at Kevin as if wondering, in mystery, how they found their way back.

Like Bread the Light
Joe Wilkins

Down there is the bar ditch. The wild mustard tall as me in places and my hair long as it was then caught up in mustard and a few stray burs and bits of driftwood from whenever the last rain was and riffles and sighs of dried mud and dust when you laid me down on the dirt and gravel and kissed me in the bar ditch.

You were pulling at my t-shirt. The snap of my jeans. My panties. I was thinking I would like you to touch as much of me as needed touching. Which right then was a whole lot. I was thinking but not really thinking. Not like you. In your head the way you always were I wondered if you might up and decide it not a good idea and leave me there. Leave me there in the bar ditch. You didn't. You did one good thing. I can say that. God but all those long days hauling hay in the summer sun had roped our arms and umbered our shoulders and necks and strawed our hair. If we were not lovely there in the dust and mustard of the bar ditch then I am telling you it is all for shit. Your wrists the way a river kinks around a rock. Slope and flower of my own breast. And I was breathless.

My old mother watching TV in the trailer. Peanuts in a can of Coors. Dinner plate of crushed cigarettes. My father in Tacoma or Oklahoma or some other gone-the-fuck-away place. It oughtn't to have been any good between us. Young and kindly and dumb as we were. I guess maybe it wasn't. Maybe my old mother was right about you. But even after. When you had gone and given yourself over to your own fears. Those ones you called dreams. When I had decided there was nothing left to do but wreck my stupid self on every mean man I ran up against. Every dry-knuckled, chap-lipped man. Even after.

I tell you this spring the rains came hard and the bar ditch ran like a river and in the culvert a tangle of watersnakes unspooled. I saw one day lifting from the ragweed a heron wide as God. Now I move my hands like this over my hips and feel the wind. Now when I do this with my lips it is the wind I kiss.

I guess I hope a few things for you. A wind to roll in your mouth. On your tongue the iron tang and mud lick of dust. That sometimes you are sad in the middle of the day and go walking along a gravel road and squeeze between your blunt thumb and finger the stems of weeds. I hope you understand that summer we lived on sunlight. Gnashed like bread the light.

Would you believe it? If I told you it's still in me? That here at the lip of the ditch I fucking shine?

Poetry

Poetry

Creation Myth: Periosteum and Self

Elizabeth Bradfield

    Hormonally imbalanced females of all deer species
    have been known to grow antlers.
This is what I choose. Periosteum rampant on my brow
and testosterone to activate it at the pedicle.
    "Luxury organs," so called because they aren't
    necessary for survival.
I choose the possibility buried in the furrow
which has ceased to disappear between my eyes
in sleep, in skin my lover has touched her lips to.
    Females produce young each year. Males produce antlers.
Forget the in-vitro, expensive catheter of sperm
slipped past the cervix, the long implications
of progeny. I am more suited to other sciences, other growth.
    Researchers have snipped bits of periosteum
    from pedicles, grafted them onto other parts
    of a buck's body, and grown antlers.
I'll graft it to my clavicle. My cheekbone.
Ankle. Coccyx. Breast. At last visible,
the antler will grow. Fork and tine. Push and splay.
    Researchers have tricked deer into growing and casting
    as many as four sets of antlers in one calendar year.
It won't wait for what's appropriate, but starts
in the subway, in the john, talking to a friend about her sorrows,
interviewing for a job. My smooth desk, my notebook,
my special pen with particular ink, my Bach playing
through the wall of another room—not the location

of the prepared field, but what the light says, when
the light says *now*.

> *Deer literally rob their body skeletons to grow*
> *antlers they'll abandon a few months later.*

It could care less about the inconvenience forking
from my knee, the difficulty of dressing, embracing, or
piloting a car. It doesn't care

> *Essentially bucks and bulls are slaves to their antlers.*

if I'm supposed to be paying bills or taking the dog
for her evening walk. There is no sense to it, no logic, just thrust.

It does its work. It does its splendid, difficult, ridiculous work and then,
making room for its next, more varied rising,

gorgeous and done, it falls away.

I Was Popular in Certain Circles

Gabrielle Calvocoressi

Among the river rats and the leaves.
For example. I was huge among the lichen,
and the waterfall couldn't get enough
of me. And the gravestones?
I was hugely popular with the gravestones.
Also with the meat liquefying
beneath. I'd say to the carrion birds,
I'd say, "Are you an eagle? I can't see
so well." That made them laugh until we
were screaming. Eagle. Imagine.

The vultures loved me so much they'd feed
me the first morsel. From their delicate
talons, which is what I called them:
such delicate talons. They loved me so deeply
they'd visit in pairs. One to feed me.
One to cover my eyes with its velvety wings.
Which were heavy as theater curtains. Which I was
sure to remark on. "Why can't I see what I'm eating?"
I'd say. And the wings would pull me into
the great bird's chest. And I'd feel the nail
inside my mouth.

What pals I was with all the scavengers!
And the dead things too. What pals.

As for the living, the fox would not be outdone.
We'd sit on the cliff's edge and watch the river
like a movie and I'd say, "I think last night…"
and the fox would put his paw on top of mine
and say, "Forget it. It's done." I mean,
we had fun. You haven't lived until a fox
has whispered something the ferns told him
in your one good ear. I mean truly.
You have not lived.

What My Neighbor Tells Me Isn't Global Warming

Todd Davis

Two hours west in Pittsburgh my friend's snow peas blossom, only mid-April and his lettuce already good for three weeks. Whenever my neighbor and I meet at our mailboxes, he tells me, *Global warming's a bunch of bullshit,* the same way you or I might say, *How's the weather?* or, *Sure could use some rain.* It's a strange salutation, but he's convinced the president is a communist. I keep asking my wife if any of this is going to change. I think she's tired of my questions. Yesterday our son wrote a letter to give to his girlfriend after he breaks up. He says he's real sorry. So am I. The tears they'll cry are no different than our cat's wailing to be let out, despite the rain that's been falling since dawn. The three donkeys that graze in the pasture share the field with exactly eleven horses. It's instructive that the horses don't lord it over the donkeys that they're horses. For two straight weeks in March it was thirty degrees warmer than it should've been. Last night the moon shot up brighter than I've ever seen it, a giant eyeball staring us down, or one of those lightbulbs that's supposed to last for five years. The weatherman called it perigee on the six o'clock news, so I walked to the pasture to see if it made any difference to the donkeys. Each time a horse shuffled its hooves and spread its legs to piss or fart, the shadow looked like a rocket lifting off. Awe and wonder is what I feel after a quarter century of marriage. My wife just shakes her head when I say her right ankle is like a wood lily's stem, as silky and delicate as that flower's blossom. If she'd let me, I'd slide my hand over her leg for hours without a trace of boredom. This past week large mouth bass started spawning in the weeds close to shore, patrolling back and forth with a singular focus. You can drag a popper or buzzbait right in front of them and they'll ignore it. All this land we live on was stripped for timber and coal a century ago. We still find lumps, hard and black, beneath the skin. Now it's fracking for natural gas. Can you imagine? We're actually breaking the plates on purpose. I know what my grandmother would've said about that. Last time, before the mining and timber companies pulled up stakes, they brought in dozers that raked what little soil was left, planted thin grasses and pine trees. With the real forest gone, warm wind funnels through the gaps in the ridges, turns the giant turbine blades we've bolted to the tops of mountains.

Weekly Apocalyptic, or Poem Written on the Wall in an Ascending Space Capsule

Chris Dombrowski

We had to stop what we were doing
to see what we had done. Thing was,
we wouldn't. How devoted we were
to despising one another, to erecting
our own private islands made of water
bottles and various other plastic
disposables. "Will you forgive me?"
was a phrase stricken from our language—
theirs, too, "they" ballooning to include
nearly everyone but that arcane term
"us." Upon discovering that gulls
feasting on our unearthed dead bodies
died of our toxicity, we sobered up
but couldn't stand to look at ourselves
in what was left of the light. Despite
what so many movies had taught us, "just
in time" was a tick too late. There was
this bird we used to call a whippoorwill.

Resurrection of the Errand Girl

Nikky Finney

The girl is sent for dinner fish. Inside the market she fills her aluminum bowl with ice-blue mackerel and mullet, according to her mother's instruction. The fishmonger standing there, blood on his apron, whale knife in hand, asks, Head off and split? Translation: Do away with the watery gray eyes, the impolite razor-sharp fins, the succulent heart, tender roe, delicate sweet bones? Polite, dutiful, training to be mother, bride, kitchen frau. Her answer, Yes.

Forty summers pass. Girl no longer girl. Her blood dries into powder red dust. It is the time of animals on the move: on land, fancy blue lights beep quotidian conversations deep into the inner ear of fast-walking humans; on thinning ice, polar bears turn cannibal and the last male emperor penguin is holding one solitary egg on the quivering slope of his webbed feet. In the oil-drenched Gulf a flotilla of grandfather sea turtles floats—shell down, feet up. On hurricane-soaked rooftops Black people have been abandoned—again. The errand girl, resurrected—woman, dutiful, grown—drives home as she often does to see the two who made her. On the way in, her mama calls, to ask if she can stop and pick up dinner from the market. Friday. Fish. Tradition as old as the South itself. An hour later, she steps into Liberty Street Market, this fragrant hundred-year-old fish house. Inside, the hungry wait wall to wall. Beneath her cotton dress she wears what she could not wear when she was the errand girl—her poet's gauzy slip. She pulls her chosen fish by the tail out of the bed of ice that anchors all sides of the room. She extends her full bowl of ice blue mullet and flounder to the fishmonger-of-her-youth's son. A man her same age but of a different persuasion. He echoes the words he heard as a boy from his father, Head off and split? Her answer is offered even quicker than the fish. No. Not this time. This time she wants what she was once sent for left whole, just as it was pulled from the sea, everything born to it still in place. Not a girl any longer, she is capable of her own knife-work now. She understands sharpness & duty. She knows what a blade can reveal & destroy. She has come to use life's points and edges to uncover life's treasures. She would rather be the one deciding what she keeps and what she throws away.

She recognizes the fishmonger: he does not recognize her. Even though she is the daughter of the most beautiful woman in the world. He holds his inherited bone-handled whale knife high in the air, teasing her answer of refusal around. He laughs out loud, warning her about the painstaking work the toothy boney fish will require. With his hairy hands around his own hairy neck he imitates choking on an overlooked bone. Nobody waiting in the fish market laughs. He is boastful, imprecise. Three Black boys wearing rubber aprons listen right behind him, waiting to be handed bowls of fish, for dressing. His backup chorus: three dollar an hour, head off and split boys, snugly set like rhinestones in the dark wet air behind him. They shine out in unison, their faces speckled with the white sequined scales of fish already beheaded. The boys honk a Pip-like reverie out into the salty air of the sweaty room. The sight and sound of them does nothing to change her mind. For once in her life she will not go sentimental. She will not rescind her order. She wants what she has come for kept whole, all marrow and every organ accounted for, just as it was pulled from the sea. Her whole fish is wrapped in yesterday's news, tied with white fishmonger string, and handed over. She steps through the crowd, slips out the door, heads home.

Water Water Water
Wind Water

Juan Felipe Herrera

---

for New Orleans and the people of the Gulf Coast

water water water wind water
across the land shape of a torn heart
new orleans waves come louisiana the waves come
alabama wind calls alabama
and the roofs blow across red clouds
inside the divine spiral
there is a voice
inside the voice there is light
water wind fire smoke the bodies float
and rise

kind flames bow down and move across
the skies never seen blackish red bluish bruised
water rises houses fall the child
the elders the mothers underwater
who will live who will rise
the windows fill with the howling
where is the transfusion where is the lamp
who who in the wet night jagged in the oil

waves come the lakes loosen their sultry shape
it is the shape of a lost hand a wing broken
casinos in biloxi become carnations across the sands
and the woman in the wheelchair descends

her last breath a rose in the razor rain
uptown on mansion hill even the million dollar house bows
in the negative shade someone is afloat
a family dissolves the nation disappears
neighborhoods fade across lost streets the police
dressed in newspapers flutter toward nothingness moons
who goes there

under our floors filtered wooden stars
towels and glass gasoline coffins
the skin of trees and jalopy tires fish
bebop dead from the zoo the dogs half drag
ward number nine miss Symphony Spikes and
mrs. Hardy Johnson the new plankton new
algae of the nameless stroll in the dark ask
the next question about kindness
then there is a bus a taxi a hearse a helicopter
a rescue team a tiny tribe of nine year olds
separating the waters the oils and ashes
hear the song of splinters and blood tree sap
machine oil and old jazz trumpeters z's and x's
raffia skirts and jujube hats and a father man
holds the hand of his lover saying take care of the children
let me go now let me stumble stumble nowhere drink this
earth liquor going in petals

stadiums and looters
celebrities cameras cases more water cases
again and again a new land edge emerges
a new people emerges where race and class and death
and life and water and tears and loss
and life and death destruction and life and tears
compassion and loss and a fire stolen bus
rumbles toward you all directions wherever
you are alive still

Migration

Major Jackson

That summer, municipality was on everyone's lips,
even the earth eaters who put the pastor in pastoral.
Truth is my zeal for chicory waned, and my chest was damp.
I shivered by a flagpole, knowing betrayal
was coming my way. Just the same, I believed like a guitar string
believes in distance and addressed each bright star *Lord
of My Feet*. A country of overnight deputies, everyone had a knot
to endeavor. I read oaks and poplars for signs: charred branches,
tobacco leaves strung up to die, swamp soil in my soul. Ever trace
the outline of a phantom mob, even if you were late arriving?

Remembering Minidoka

W. Todd Kaneko

And with the camps came extremely significant designations and distinctions that are with us to this very day: "What camp were you in?" Or as my great-grandchildren in the next century will say: "What camp were they in?"
—*Lawson Fusao Inada,* Legends from Camp

There's no place like home.

—*Dorothy Gale,* The Wizard of Oz

1.

My grandmother remembered little about Minidoka
because her husband remembered it for them both—
fabricating home from splintered timber
and a lingering taste of horses. She remembered life
before the war—dancing with her husband
in hay-filled barns, fearless walks
across meadow and township, through forests
deep with greedy tigers, through Chinatown.
After the war, she rebuilt her family in that house
brimming with shadows, the forgotten odor
of livestock. After her husband died, she reread
old newspapers in the dim light of her living room,
she gazed at outlines of barbed wire
just beyond her curtains.

2.

My father remembers Minidoka differently—
I remember it all wrong, he says, then explains
how the crows kept him awake, their sorrow

drizzling through morning. When the wolf loped
into camp, my father climbed on its back, rode it
through laundry lines, his fingers digging into fur
reeking of brimstone. He battled hordes of rats
in the hollyhocks, drove them out of gardens
and into fissures beneath other families' barracks.
The memories I have are all that I have,
my father says. They're just memories.
Flocks of sheep devoured hillsides
like earthbound clouds. The hills
caught fire and set the sky ablaze for days.
The children were set to play cat's cradle
only to find they had no thumbs.

3.
When I visited Minidoka, all that remained
was a scar—that debris of family reclaimed
by the earth, that rubble of guard towers,
those broken mousetraps in the remote
curves of the yard. My grandfather's great hands
are buried out somewhere in the thistles.
My father's childhood lies overrun by knotweed
because this is all we have—
the landscape is coated with a black sheen
of memory. The land feels nothing.

River Keeper

Laurie Kutchins

How clear the river is
only moments after loss.

Gurgle of a sandhill crane.
Orange flash of western tanager.

Sagebrush that needs the rain.
I found a simple bench carved from an evergreen.

A plaque in stone with a boy's name,
two dates that subtract

to nineteen years.
River, do you know him?

Someone is building a new bridge across
without handrails.

When I walk on it I get dizzy
from wanting to hold on.

Under there's the long spine.
Always the swift current,

never the same. And the river,
more stones than stars.

Emerging View

Anne Haven McDonnell

---

written on the *for sale* signs scattered
and spreading up County Road 8. Fall
in the conifers, a rusty glow sinks
then tags the mind, a thing
forgotten, the tug of
unraveling. The forest gives
itself up, a luminous
smear of exit—
aspens quilt a dizzy
yellow, and now this
blanket of dead lodgepole pine.
We can almost hear the strange
rhythm that brings those beetles,
thrums with weak music,
the fungus that follows their footsteps,
their marbled blue trails
polished like a map
on her kitchen floor. Still,
an old woman can rest here,
orchids in the boggy meadow,
chanterelles on the fire road,
a pine marten on the bird feeder
watches her watch him through
the window. Hungry moose furrow deep
trenches through snow banks
on the creek, which roars
into spring's swarm. We look

through dead pine,
the snowy teeth of James peak
now visible, mountains
rise like the grieving that rolls
into this strange season,
wheeling towards us, nameless
on our animal tongues.

Coos Bay

Michael McGriff

The World's Largest Lumber Port,
the yellow hulk of Cats winding bayfront chip yards,
   betting on high-school football

at the Elks Lodge, bargemen,
   abandoned Army barracks,
Japanese glass floats, cranberry bogs,

   mooring lines, salmon roe,
swing shifts, green chain, millwrights
   passing each other like black paper cranes

from one impermanence to the next,
   phosphorescent bay water, two tons
of oyster shells, seagulls, beach glass

   tumbled smooth in the surf, weigh stations,
off-bearing, front-loading, cargo nets,
   longshoremen, scabs,

the Indian casino marquee promising
   continental breakfast, star-crowned animals
stitched to blue heavens

   behind the fog, log booms,
choker setters, gypo outfits, acetylene sparks
   falling from the Coast Guard cutter *Citrus,*

dredging units, gravel quarries, clear-cuts,
        Scotch broom taking over the dunes,
smokestacks pocked with peep shows

        of flame and soot, the year-round
nativity scene and one-armed Santa
        in J.C. Penney's alley window,

my grandmother dying just over the ridge,
        mother-of-pearl, sea lion calls
in the dark, low tide at Charleston Harbor,

        the sound of calk boots
in gravel parking lots, salmon sheen hosed
        onto the street, the arch

of a big rig's empty trailer, sand
        in all the moving parts,
floodlights, tie-downs, ridge beacons,

        great blue herons whispering
through the hollow reeds, the cat piss smell
        of a charred meth lab between the V.F.W. hall

and pioneer newspaper museum,
        the rusted scrapyard and tank farm.
The drawbridge spans forgotten coal bunkers,

        buried fingerprints of Chinese laborers,
rope-riders and mule bones.
        Then there's the rain that never sleeps,

it's fallen for seventeen years
        to reach the field below our house
where my father and the machinist neighbor

        dying of cancer huddle around
an oil drum burn barrel and smoke cigarettes,
        a few weeks of newspapers and wood scrap

hiss into ash, trapped angels
            under the wire grate they warm their hands over.
The great heave of the Southern Pacific,

            sturgeon like river cogs, barnacle wreckage,
cattle guards. The last of the daylight,
            a broken trellis falling into the bay.

Explaining Seafood to My Future Grandkids after the Extinction

Juan Morales

I will describe, like a murder, how we used to rip open
juicy bodies and clacking claws of lobsters and crabs
to feast on warm meat inside.

I will smack my lips, describing how we seared tiny ones with red tails,
called shrimp, in butter, garlic, and batter. I will contaminate
the moment by describing cocktail and tartar sauce, as red or white.

I will explain how the ocean's snake-like wonders
called eels, bendable monsters
were made only of arms,

and fish who clustered and swam in nimble clouds
up and then down to the depths
where deep-sea fish created their own light

in a time when the sea was not stung full of jellyfish
and swirling garbage, and we swam
with the taste of salt pressed to our lips.

Lewis and Clark Disagree

Aimee Nezhukumatathil

Because Meriwether ate the last berry
without consulting William. Because

the prairie dog only let *William* feed
it dried corn. Because the Nez Perce

gave one a necklace of purple quartz
and not the other. Because osage oranges

gave Meriwether hives. Because a grizzly
chased William into an oak tree, left him

high for hours. Because "Someone" tucked
buffalo chips into Meriwether's knapsack

when he wasn't looking. Because after walking,
rowing, swimming, climbing, trotting, pulling,

cutting, all they really wanted was a name
for a fruit one found sour, the other, so sweet.

The Natural World

G.E. Patterson

You got trees all dappled with sunlight and shit
You got trees green with lots of leaves
You got fruit-bearing trees   made for climbing
        good for something

I got trees too   My trees stainless steel poles
with no flags   My trees streetlights redyellowgreen
glass shattered on the ground

You got birds waking you up in the morning
Birds waking you up in the morning   TweetTweet
ChirpChirp   That's how it is for y'all
                                        mutherfuckers

I got birds too   My birds
loud as jackhammers   My birds
loud as police sirens   My birds
loud as gunfire   My birds
electric   gas-powered

My birds   My birds   killers

Stripping

Sean Prentiss

Like a benediction, we grow into a smaller language. So
many words given up, disremembered, abandoned from
tents & saw packs. What use here in the Middle Santiam
Wilderness do we have for the word *sink*? When would we
ever utter *closet* or *phone* or *bank account*? These words as
unneeded as any third thumb, as unneeded as *money* or
wallet or *credit card. Girlfriend* becomes little more than
a weekend ghost. I give to you *TV.* I give to you *movie
theatre.* I give to you *radio.* Do you want more words that
these backwoods winds strip away? Take *traffic jam.* Take
fuel pump. Take *the 9-to-5.* God, take *commuting.* Take
Howard Stern. Take *Pavement.* Take *asphalt & concrete.*
Take, we beg of you, *microwave.* Take *power lines.* Take
nightly news. We give each & every industrial word away
because those words, they ache our new memories.

As a Species Flies from Extinction, Consider the River

Derek Sheffield

In passing clarity, curled
                    Feather and flash, see
The brown eyes
            Of the world. What rocks
                    Are these?   Fourteen million
                            Orbits refract this
Influence of spreading center, polarity
                Spinning a water strider's legs like needles
                    To the pulse in every
Tongue. Below Skookumchuck, the shape
                Of a bird's neck in sleep
                        Holds the current and the memory
                            Of ancient ice releasing
Mad gleaming, rivulet violence.
                Could this etch of avian glyph,
                        This fluxing flurry of onwardness
                            Bear the conception that ending
Is myth, is the syllabics of scree
                Clattering before a buck's long skid
                        And purling swim where the river
                            He shakes from his antlers,
                The river of dazzling droplets,
        Freezes the light, is the light?

Migration of Baling Twine

Julia Shipley

I have seen it in the truck bed, one fat spool
quiet as a salt block,
then rigged in the baler and sent
to bind each bale twice; I have grabbed it
like a man's suspenders yanking him to me,
Look here or sultry, *Sweetheart, where's my kiss?*

I have seen twine unhold with one touch
of knife, or in a bind his car key can
saw through, divided the packed bale splays;

I have seen these agricultural spaghetti
(orange plastic, dun burlap, fungicidal green)
drawn off thirty opened bales,
grouped in hanks, slumped over a nail
or hastily piled, as on slaughtering day we'll have
a heap of chicken heads, a heap of yellow feet,
here's a month's worth of yanked, chucked
twine plus milk filters, the newspaper, Dunkin's cups,
mastitis syringe, purple latex gloves shoved in
old grain bags for the dump from which

I have seen him take a bunch,
and deftly twist a halter for the calf; or link six to make a lead
or tie the milkhouse door open so the flies can go,
one loop from knob to hook.

Flapping tarps quit with a quick pass-it-
through-the grommet-cinch-it-down;
hoses hold their ovals with three snug wraps of a strand.

I have seen it eel its way, from one lump sum
to plenty of crude-ish sutures, like twenty extra fingers
pinching–as if the farm was a wound or a bird they keep trussed,

keep from blowing crawling falling growing away.

The Feed

M.L. Smoker

Several of my cousins lean up against the house,
taking long drags from the pack of Marlboros we share.
We have always been this way—addicted and generous.
A pow wow tape plays from inside the open garage
where two old uncles are thinking to themselves in the
safety of its shadows. Our aunties are in the kitchen,
preparing the boiled meat and chokecherry soup and
laughing about old jokes they still hang onto because
these things are a matter of survival. Outside, we ask
about who was driving around with who last night,
where so-and-so go beat up, whose girlfriend left him
for someone else. (But she'll go back to him, we all think
to ourselves.) Aunties carry the full pots and pans to the
picnic table, an uncle prays over our food in Assiniboine.
We all want to forget that we don't understand this
language, we spend lots of time trying to forget in
different ways. No one notices that the wild turnips
are still simmering in a pot on the stove.

Theories of Time and Space

Natasha Trethewey

You can get there from here, though
there's no going home.

Everywhere you go will be somewhere
you've never been. Try this:

head south on Mississippi 49, one—
by—one mile markers ticking off

another minute of your life. Follow this
to its natural conclusion—dead end

at the coast, the pier at Gulfport where
riggings of shrimp boats are loose stitches

in a sky threatening rain. Cross over
the man-made beach, 26 miles of sand

dumped on a mangrove swamp—buried
terrain of the past. Bring only

what you must carry—tome of memory
its random blank pages. On the dock

where you board the boat for Ship Island,
someone will take your picture:

the photograph—who you were—
will be waiting when you return.

Seven Devils

Joe Wilkins

He-Devil
Listen Mister Lightning Catcher,
you old stone buzzard
with your red head of rocks
and rocks for feathers,
I'm damn tired of remembering
you. You say: *I will teach you*
mountains. Get down from there.
I don't need that kind
of dignity. The music in your bones
is scree and stone, off-key, and old.

Devil's Throne
I call this place Kingdom Come,
or Cutthroat Hook, maybe
Devil's Throne: a rocky saddle
between bowls of rock and frost-stunted pine.
The only bones here, of course, are bright
white and warm today in sun
and wind, and can you see
how the smoke of my breakfast fire
writes a story for a moment in the sky?

Mount Baal
This is where bear grass
dances twenty ways
in wind that shifts the skulking cedars,
rolls lake water to the sky. Hang on
to your hat. Here, a man listens
to his own loneliness: his words
ride their windy way back
to his ears, he hears himself

say, *Grass, cedar, father, wind.*
Then hears it again.

The Twin Imps
For eighteen years you were good,
dirty boys: faces ringed
with mud, the sandbox flooded,
mother's bent spoons and that egg-sucking dog's
sucked eggs. Who told you
you could leave? You must know
it's killing all her bones—
the way the sun leaves the mountains:
cold, completely.

Tower of Babel
In the mountains a man lives
close to his eyes. When there is sun,
he is fat and happy
and fish bones pop in the fire,
in their little blue flames of oil.
But when the sky goes
black with storm, the bright mouths
of stars snap closed and a man must
speak with his hands.

Devil's Tooth
Fireweeds are something less
than weeds: pale, rigid, not quite
green. Strange how fire
takes the pith and leaves the stem. Fireweed,
that's me: ugly in the sun,
clacking in the wind, my heart gone
up in flame. I need
a green star to flame between the peaks.
I need a myth that tells me, *Be alive.*
I need to sit a while and think,
chew this bitter weed.

She-Devil
You hand-over-foot the scree slope up,
goat walk the insane ridge. There's a buzzard

in these rocks, or maybe it's only
altitude. Keep walking. See Heaven's Gate
far below, your brother just ahead. Remember
her, how she held you safe above
that snow-melt flood of mountain river: fatherless
sixteen, furious boy, terrified man. Now,
up the scree the monarchs stream
in orange suicide. Their bones are only wind.
Yours, you tell yourself, are music,
a ringing down from mountain rocks,
the fierce promise she whispered in your ear,
that one truth: *Keep walking.*

Tire Hut: Seaview, Washington

Maya Jewell Zeller

The shop is divided like the brain:
on one side, dull metals lie crooked
like limbs after wind. Men shout things
to each other and no one. Buckets
of bolts line a wall where red and blue
rags hang from nails, already black
with some grease. A generator
or tire balancer makes the floor shake
as if the ocean were under it pushing
up, and the air tastes like batteries.
This is where the work gets done.
But the customer comes in to wait
on the other side, sees tires splayed out
in pretty black rows. This one for fifty-nine.
This one for seventy. This set on sale:
buy three get the fourth free. Posters of
babies erupting from lying-down tires.
Tables with shiny magazines to lift
and touch, and everywhere
the smell of new coffee, sweet gasoline.
Outside is a half-barrel, steel
or some other metal, rust-colored now.
It catches the rain. My father and brother

keep it there to drown tires in,
to see where the leak is.
The water is the cleanest water
you've ever seen. No kidding.
You can look into that water
and see the mountain from which it came.

Biographies

Chelsea Biondolillo is the author of the prose chapbook *Ologies* (Etching Press 2015). Her work has appeared in *Orion, Hayden's Ferry Review*, and *Flyway*, and her essays have been awarded the Carter Prize from *Shenandoah* and a Notable listing in *Best American Essays 2014*.

Elizabeth Bradfield is the author of the poetry collections *Once Removed, Approaching Ice,* and *Interpretive Work.* Founder and editor-in-chief of Broadsided Press, she lives on Cape Cod, works as a naturalist locally as well as on expedition ships, and is the current Poet-in-Residence at Brandeis University and on the faculty of the low-residency MFA program at University of Alaska, Anchorage.

Gabrielle Calvocoressi is the author of *The Last Time I Saw Amelia Earhart, Apocalyptic Swing,* and the forthcoming, *Rocket Fantastic.* She is senior poetry editor at *Los Angeles Review of Books* and *Voluble* (a channel of *Los Angeles Review of Books*).

Bonnie Jo Campbell is the author of *American Salvage*, a finalist for the National Book Award and the National Book Critics Circle Award, as well as the story collections *Mothers Tell Your Daughters* and *Women and Other Animals*, and the novels *Once Upon a River* and *Q Road*. She lives in Comstock, Michigan.

John Daniel's books of prose, including *Rogue River Journal* and *The Far Corner*, have won three Oregon Book Awards for Literary Nonfiction, a Pacific Northwest Booksellers Award, and a fellowship from the National Endowment for the Arts. His most recent book—*Of Earth: New and Selected Poems*, from Lost Horse Press—presents poems from his two previous collections and a selection of newer work.

Todd Davis is the author of five full-length collections of poetry—*Winterkill, In the Kingdom of the Ditch, The Least of These, Some Heaven,* and *Ripe*—as well as of a limited-edition chapbook, *Household of Water, Moon, and Snow: The Thoreau Poems.* He teaches environmental studies, creative writing, and American literature at Pennsylvania State University's Altoona College.

Chris Dombrowski is the author of *By Cold Water*, a Poetry Foundation Bestseller, and *Earth Again*, runner-up for ForeWord Magazine's Book of the Year in Poetry. His first book of nonfiction, *Body of Water*, is forthcoming from Milkweed Editions. With his family, he lives in Missoula, MT.

Camille T. Dungy is the author of *Smith Blue, Suck on the Marrow*, and *What to Eat, What to Drink, What to Leave for Poison*. She edited *Black Nature: Four Centuries of African American Nature Poetry*, and coedited the *From the Fishouse* poetry anthology. Her honors include an American Book Award, two Northern California Book Awards, a California Book Award silver medal, and a fellowship from the NEA.

Nikky Finney is the author of four books of poetry: *Head Off & Split*, which is winner of the 2011 National Book Award; *The World Is Round*; *Rice*; and *On Wings Made of Gauze*. Finney is the John H. Bennett, Jr. Chair in Southern Letters and Literature at the University of South Carolina, Finney also authored *Heartwood*, edited *The Ringing Ear: Black Poets Lean South*, and cofounded the Affrilachian Poets.

David Gessner is the author of nine books, including *All the Wild that Remains*, in which he follows the ghosts of Wallace Stegner and Edward Abbey around the American West. He is a professor at the University of North Carolina at Wilmington, where he founded the award-winning literary journal, *Ecotone*. He can also be found at Bill and Dave's Cocktail Hour, a website he created with the writer Bill Roorbach.

Alyson Hagy is the author of seven works of fiction, including *Ghosts of Wyoming* and *Boleto*, both published by Graywolf Press. A native of Virginia, she lives and teaches in Laramie, Wyoming.

Juan Felipe Herrera is the twenty-first Poet Laureate of the United State (2015–2016) and is the first Latino to hold the position. Herrera's many collections of poetry include *Notes on the Assemblage, Senegal Taxi*, and *Half of the World in Light: New and Selected Poems*. He is also the author of *Crashboomlove: A Novel in Verse*, which received the Americas Award.

Major Jackson is the author of four volumes of poetry, most recently *Roll Deep* and *Holding Company*. A recent recipient of a National Endowment for the Arts grant and a Guggenheim Fellowship, he is the Richard Dennis Green and Gold Professor at the University of Vermont.

W. Todd Kaneko is the author of *The Dead Wrestler Elegies*. A recipient of fellowships from Kundiman and the Kenyon Review Writer's Workshop, he is currently coeditor of Waxwing Magazine and teaches at Grand Valley State University.

Laurie Kutchins is the author of three books of poems: *Slope of the Child Everlasting*, *The Night Path*, and *Between Towns*. *The Night Path* received the Isabella Gardner Award and was a Pulitzer nomination for Poetry in 1997. Kutchins teaches creative writing at James Madison University in the Shenandoah Valley of Virginia, and spends her summers along the Wyoming-Idaho border, near an area of the country where she grew up and to which she keeps her roots.

Jennifer Lunden's writing has seen print in *Orion*, *Creative Nonfiction*, *River Teeth*, and the *Yale Journal for Humanities in Medicine*, and has been selected for inclusion in a number of anthologies. Her personal essay "The Butterfly Effect," which interweaves narratives of the decline of the monarch butterflies and the challenges faced by people with multiple chemical sensitivities, won a Pushcart Prize.

Anne Haven McDonnell lives in Santa Fe, NM, and teaches English and sustainability courses as an associate professor at the Institute of American Indian Arts. Her writing has been published in *Terrain.org*, *Flyway: Journal of Writing and Environment*, *Whitefish Review*, *The Fourth River*, and *Crab Creek Review*. She was the winner of the fifth annual *Terrain.org* poetry contest, and she was nominated for a 2014 Pushcart Prize.

Michael McGriff was born and raised in Coos Bay, Oregon, and writes largely about the postindustrial landscape of that specific bioregion. He is the author of three collections of poetry: *Early Hour*, *Home Burial*, and *Dismantling the Hills*. His other books include the story collection *Our Secret Life in the Movies*, a translation of Tomas Tranströmer's *The Sorrow Gondola*, and an edition of David Wevill's essential writing, *To Build My Shadow a Fire*.

Juan Morales's second poetry collection, *The Siren World*, was selected as one of NBC News' 2015 Latino Books: 8 Must-Reads, from Indispensable Small Presses. He is also the author of *Friday and the Year That Followed*. He is a CantoMundo Fellow, the editor of *Pilgrimage Magazine*, and an associate professor of English at Colorado State University, Pueblo, where he directs the Creative Writing Program and curates the SoCo Reading Series.

Bonnie Nadzam's first novel, *Lamb*, was recipient of the Center for Fiction's Flaherty-Dunnan First Novel Prize; long-listed for the Bailey's Prize, it has been translated into several languages, and made into an independent film (The Orchard, 2016). She is coauthor, with environmental philosopher Dale Jamieson, of *Love in the Anthropocene*, and her second novel, *Lions*, is forthcoming from Grove Atlantic in 2016.

Aimee Nezhukumatathil is the author of three books of poetry, most recent being *Lucky Fish*. Awards for her writing include an NEA fellowship in poetry and the Pushcart Prize. She is professor of English at SUNY, Fredonia.

Louis Owens was a professor of English and Native American studies at the University of California, Davis, where he taught until his death in 2002. Among his publications are the novels *Wolfsong*, *The Sharpest Sight*, *Bone Game*, *Nightland*, and *Dark River*, as well as several nonfiction volumes, including *Other Destinies*, *Mixedblood Messages*, and *I Hear the Train*.

G.E. Patterson is a veteran of the slam-poetry scene; he was a featured poet-performer in New York's Panasonic Village Jazz Fest. He is the author of two poetry collections, *Tug* and *To and From*. Among other honors, his poetry has garnered a fellowship from New York City's Fund for Poetry. After years on the east and west coasts of the United States, G.E. Patterson now makes Minnesota his home.

Lydia Peelle is the author of the story collection *Reasons for and Advantages of Breathing*. Her short stories have appeared in numerous publications and have won two Pushcart Prizes, an O. Henry Award, and been twice featured in *Best New American Voices*. She lives in Nashville, Tennessee.

Benjamin Percy is the author of three novels, *The Dead Lands*, *Red Moon*, and *The Wilding*, as well as two books of short stories, *Refresh, Refresh* and *The Language of Elk*. His honors include an NEA fellowship, the Whiting Writer's Award, the Plimpton Prize, two Pushcart Prizes, and inclusion in *Best American Short Stories* and *Best American Comics*.

Sean Prentiss is the author of the memoir, *Finding Abbey: The Search for Edward Abbey and His Hidden Desert Grave*, which won the 2015 National Outdoor Book Award in History/Biography and is a finalist for the Colorado Book Award in Creative Nonfiction. He is the coeditor of *The Far Edges of* *the Fourth Genre: Explorations in Creative Nonfiction*, a creative nonfiction craft anthology. He lives with his wife, Sarah, on a small lake in northern Vermont.

Erik Reece is the author of five books, including *An American Gospel: On Family, History and the Kingdom of God* and *Lost Mountain: A Year in the Vanishing Wilderness*, which won Columbia University's John B. Oakes Award for Distinguished Environmental Journalism and the Sierra Club's David R. Brower Award for Excellence in Environmental Writing. He teaches writing at the University of Kentucky.

Leslie Ryan holds a BA in English from the College of William and Mary and an MS in Environmental Studies from the University of Montana. After teaching survival, she led academic backcountry courses for the University of California's Sierra Institute.

Derek Sheffield's book of poems, *Through the Second Skin*, was a finalist for the Washington State Book Award; and his collection, *A Revised Account of the West* (2006), won the Hazel Lipa Environmental Chapbook Award. He teaches at Wenatchee Valley College where he also works as an advocate for sustainability and environmental humanities. He lives with his family in the foothills of the Cascades near Leavenworth, Washington, and serves as the poetry editor of *Terrain.org*.

Julia Shipley is the author of *Adam's Mark: Writing From the Ox-House*, named a Best Book of 2014 by the Boston Globe, and *The Academy of Hay*, winner of the Melissa Lanitis Gregory Poetry Prize. She lives in Vermont's Northeast Kingdom.

M. L. Smoker belongs to the Assiniboine and Sioux tribes of the Fort Peck Reservation in northeastern Montana. Her family home is on Tabexa Wakpa (Frog Creek). Her first collection of poems, *Another Attempt at Rescue*, was published by Hanging Loose Press in the spring of 2005. In 2009 she coedited an anthology of human rights poetry with Melissa Kwasny, entitled, *I Go to the Ruined Place*. She has also won a regional Emmy Award for her work as a writer/consultant on the PBS documentary *Indian Relay*.

Natasha Trethewey served two terms as the nineteenth Poet Laureate of the United States (2012–2014). She is the author of the poetry collections *Thrall* and *Native Guard*, for which she won the 2007 Pulitzer Prize, as well as *Bellocq's Ophelia* and *Domestic Work*. She is also the author of *Beyond Katrina: A Meditation on the Mississippi Gulf Coast*.

David Treuer is the author of the novels *Little*, *The Hiawatha*, and *The Translation of Dr Apelles*, as well as a book of nonfiction *Rez Life*. His next novel, *Prudence*, is forthcoming from Riverhead Book. He divides his time between his home on the Leech Lake Reservation and Los Angeles, where he is a professor of Literature at USC.

Joe Wilkins is the author of a memoir, *The Mountain and the Fathers: Growing up on the Big Dry*, winner of a 2014 GLCA New Writers Award and finalist for the Orion Book Award, and three collections of poetry, *When We Were Birds*, *Notes from the Journey Westward*, and *Killing the Murnion Dogs*. Wilkins lives with his wife, son, and daughter in western Oregon, where he teaches writing at Linfield College.

Maya Jewell Zeller is the author of the books *Rust Fish* and *Yesterday, The Bees*. Her poems and essays appear widely. Maya teaches at Gonzaga University, codirects the Beacon Hill Reading Series, and serves as fiction editor for *Crab Creek Review*. She lives in Spokane with her husband and two small children.

Permissions

Index

SONG OF THE LAGGORNS

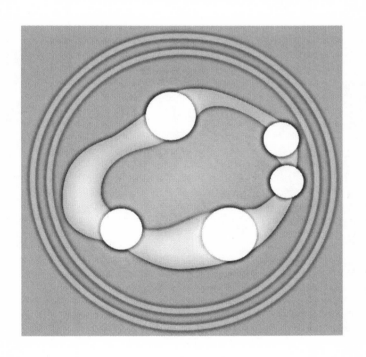

SONG OF THE LAGGORNS

Gregory Benson

Published by Blue Giant Publishing, LLC

First edition.

Print ISBN: 978-1-7340196-4-3

eBook ISBN: 978-1-7340196-5-0

gregorybensonbooks.com

To my son Luke, my original beta reader and Sci-Fi buddy. You've kept my heart warm and my thoughts young.

Don't let anyone look down on you because you are young, but set an example for the believers in speech, in conduct, in love, in faith and in purity.

—Timothy 4:12

CHAPTER 1

CRIX

*I*t's called a shot propulsive orbital dive, and I'm about to take it right into *the heart of Oro's hostile storm system.* It'd been two years since Crix took the same journey and six painstaking months for Joric and Plexo to develop the armor they felt confident would withstand the extreme pressure, radiation, and cold—provided everything went as planned.

Kerriah let out a heavy sigh. Did anything ever go "as planned?" Her thoughts overlapped. Waves of possible problems and theorized solutions bounced and churned, creating a mangled nest. While Crix had the blue orb to protect him, she would have no such benefit. This version of SPOD armor would need its integrity to hold until she entered the station. Early attempts to send the remaining high-pressure Eetaks proved ineffective. The trajectory for landing on the station was near perfect in all but one instance, but communications with the Eetaks always went silent shortly after.

There hadn't been any direct communication with Crix since he took control of the Marck Central Core. Only the lone

Marck scout that approached her after the Thraxon withdrew from the Oro System exhibited his body cues, letting her know he still lived. Kerriah knew it was him inside that rigid metal body, but he never responded verbally. Instead, the head hung low with dropped shoulders, and the occasional dimmed eyes tilted up and met hers. She kept it around her home in Corasan, trying patiently to talk to it each day, hoping he would open up to her, but that never happened.

One morning, she awoke early and discovered the scout lying motionless on the floor. She straddled its metal torso, screaming and pounding her fists upon its chest with tears streaming down her cheeks. Without any sign or warning, he had left her without a word. She had cried for days after and even tried to speak to him through Marck patrol units she came across on the streets, hoping Crix would communicate to her through them. She knew she would never find peace until she could speak with him again, and entering the Core was the only way.

Until recently, Kerriah alone drove the efforts to enter the Central Core and find Crix. However, eight months ago, the Marcks protecting the Oro System began to exhibit erratic behavior and, in many cases, collapsed into a permanent state of dormancy. Most started pacing in circles before dropping to the ground and curling up with their knees to their chests before their power systems went offline. Joric explained the behavior as likely an emotional projection from their controller, Crix.

Before this, Plexo, Joric, and her adoptive father, Governor Septin, had grown weary of her endless discussions to save Crix from the Marck Central Core. She didn't care about the risks and even tried to persuade them to let her use the yellow orb.

However, the yellow orb did not share the same abilities as the blue. It could provide power, yes, but not a lifesaving barrier.

The Marcks began dropping like Troika Day flies in recent weeks, and now very few were still online, leaving the system vulnerable to another Thraxon invasion. One thing was sure; something was wrong with the Central Core, which also meant something was wrong with Crix. Nothing could hold Kerriah back from going into the core, and now a desperate leadership finally placed their support behind her.

"I'm ready!" she announced over her helmet's comm.

"Just one more minute, Kerriah. We are performing the final calibrations. This must be exact, or you will miss the station, and there are no second shots," Joric replied.

Right. She didn't want that for obvious reasons.

Her nerves on edge, even the slightest unexpected sound had her jumping out of her skin. She twisted and turned inside the bulky suit, jerking her muscles, adjusting her neck, cracking her ankles, and curling her toes, anything to calm her anxious thoughts.

She tried to gain control of her rapid breathing as she stared ahead with her helmet tilted up from her lying position. The forward-facing platform slowly began to rise. It stopped and then slid her into the breach.

Finally! The lights flared up, and she squinted to adjust.

"Kerriah?" Joric's voice cracked through her comm. Could this be the last voice she'd ever hear again? Her mind momentarily strayed from the task ahead. At least it was her natural father; it seemed fitting, though she barely knew him.

"Yes, I'm ready. I've been ready."

"Okay then, remember everything we've discussed, and I'll see you when you return."

She rolled her eyes. *Of course, I'll remember everything; that's how you designed me.* She never forgot anything, though at times she wished she could.

The breach door closed with a bass-drum clunk and a long hiss before squealing tight. Kerriah's helmet display indicated a blue bar slowly shrinking to nothing before everything illuminated red. She felt her body leave her consciousness as she blasted through the cylinder at an insane speed into the outer atmosphere of Oro. The magenta-colored planet swirled with violet clouds. It was a view everyone who had ever lived on Thale, Soorak, and Solara were acquainted with, but what surged into her viewpoint appeared hostile, like the familiar, old behemoth raging toward her with the intensity of a territorial predator.

The vibrations from her armored shell tickled across her body as she entered the cloud layers. Deeper inside, the tickling turned into an aggressive shake. Her visor formed a thin layer of frost as the temperature dropped, and the ice thickened until her view completely disappeared. Her bones suddenly felt chilled, and her stomach soured. Fear's skeletal hand gripped her throat as she envisioned her possible fate in the abyss below. Thankfully, Joric accounted for this as the thermal-infused visor began its countermeasure and melted away the ice, clearing her view. A haze of clouds and ice gushed past her.

The bitter cold crept into the suit like razors slashing at her skin as the internal heating systems struggled to keep pace with the rapidly dropping temperatures. Kerriah's visor flashed warning messages:

4

SONG OF THE LAGGORNS

:Danger, extreme pressure:

:Thermal integrity failure:

Below this point, the planet's gases began to liquefy from the extreme cold. A decelerating impact hit her, and the view changed from a red haze to a black and violet hellscape as she finally broke through the upper cloud layers.

Funnels of liquid hydrogen needled across the horizon, momentarily illuminated by the persistent lightning flashes. An ocean of the rippling frozen gas far below would be her inhospitable destination if Joric's guidance systems were off even by the slightest calculation. Kerriah observed the slender fingers of liquid gas dancing around in their majestic haunt, prodding the skyline far above. It would have been a beautiful sight if it wasn't for the taxing distraction of near-certain death.

She pinched her eyes closed for a moment to regain focus. The suit's audible alarm rang out, and the message on her visor changed:

:Target approaching:

The descent control pulsers fired with a blinding flash of white, and her body leveled. Fortunately, she could still see the shadowy silhouette of the Marck Central Core below through the opaque haze. It approached quickly, and she noticed her misaligned trajectory. Her current course would have her zipping by the side of the station and plunging into the ocean of death far below. Joric had known the station's position could shift at any point, throwing off his plotted trajectory. He also had known Kerriah was more than capable of a last-second manual adjustment.

"Bank left!" The suit's hip and shoulder pulsers fired.

Dang! Not enough. As she neared her target, it became evident she would miss. She had only a split second to adjust.

"Bank left! Bank left! Dammit!" The pulsers fired several more times, smacking her into the side of the station's domed top, or "cone" as Joric called it. It felt like her teeth loosened from the impact, and she frantically clawed at the side, trying to get a grasp of something to stop her free-fall. Her hands found nothing to grasp, and she continued her plunge, watching helplessly as her target vanished into the blackness above. Her voice screamed out inside her helmet as she plummeted toward the abyss.

"Fire pulsers!" Her fall slowed briefly. The dark, slender midsection of the station swooshed by as her fall continued, and its lower point came into view. Once she passed that, she would only have a minute or two to gather her final thoughts.

"No . . . no . . . no. . . . I'm not going out like this!" Her voice cracked with frustration, but there wasn't time for fear. The lower point passed her.

:Danger, extreme pressure:

:Danger, extreme pressure:

:Warning, shell failure imminent:

Her suit creaked and popped. Even with the careful efforts to design this SPOD suit for this mission, they hadn't accounted for it going this deep into Oro. She jarred her muscles to one side, flipping her body over to face upward. In her view, the station became smaller.

You've got to be kidding me. She blew out a heavy breath and shook her head. *Crix.*

He was her last thought before a sudden jolt took all the air from her lungs and sent electric shockwaves through her back and extremities. She squeezed her eyelids shut for a couple of seconds and then slowly opened them.

Am I dead? The audible alarms of the helmet and flashing pressure warnings informed her that wasn't the case. At least not yet. The pain of cold raking across her skin intensified, and she noticed the station grew more prominent in her view. *I'm moving upward. How?*

She carefully rolled over to her knees and placed her hand on a metal surface. A flash of red filled her view as she slowly raised her head. The eyes of a mechanical face stared straight at her—a *guardian drone.*

"Crix," She spoke aloud, knowing he was the reason Oro's pressure hadn't crushed her.

Joric briefed her on the possibility of encountering these drones. They were responsible for not only protecting the outside of the Core Station but also for its maintenance. An arm coiled out from the drone, and a bright hot flame ignited from its tip. It waved across her armor, and she felt the warmth creep inward, soothing her skin. A tear formed at the corner of her eye. She knew this was him saving her again. She wanted to jump up and throw her arms around the drone's apathetic metal face, but she still needed to remain focused.

She felt a hot knife stabbing into her waist, and a new alert flashed across her visor:

:Armor compromised—environmental exposure imminent.:

"Agh . . . that's just great." Distracted by her near-death experience and Crix's warming flame, she had overlooked the cold entering her suit. She felt choked and began to gasp violently.

"Purge!" The suit started pushing oxygen out at an accelerated rate to compensate for the leak. Her breathing returned to normal, but the reversed pressure would shorten her limited oxygen supply.

As she ascended past the torso section of the station, cosmic thrusters flared, strobing her view with a flash of white. The guardian drone paused at the base of the upper cone. An outer door swirled open, and the drone carrying Kerriah drifted inside.

The external hatch closed, and her stomach dropped as she felt the drone descend. Its movement stopped. She stood, noticing an area cast in a dim red glow. She could barely see any detail, only the shadowy silhouette of the guardian drone behind her. She called for her helmet's external lights. Two intense beams switched on, fully illuminating the area. From the look of things, she assumed it was a drone maintenance area. Rows of drones lay in varying states of repair. Some appeared functional, whereas others had been parted out, with their skeletal frames visible. Large bins of charred, gummed-up appendages and other falling-out parts were scattered about.

Her helmet's audible alarm rang out, and a new message flashed into her visor:

:Oxygen levels low:

She let out a long sigh. There wasn't much time. She needed to locate the life support systems or find an area with normalized pressure and oxygen.

What about this stastic gas Joric mentioned? She thought about the deep-pressure stabilizing gas filling the station. *I don't see anything that looks like dense gas here.*

Joric had told her it would be almost like wading through liquid inside the station. She swung her light around for a thorough look. Had Crix purged the gas ahead of her entry? It had to be, or the station's structural integrity would have failed some time ago.

As she panned the room, she noticed movement behind her. A Marck promptly detached from the guardian. The body puzzled into the drone's upper control area. Its prominent face pulled away, and two slender legs stood up. Its bulky head faced Kerriah as it walked forward. As she watched its movement, it became clear the drone's deck was for the maintenance Marck to stand upon while servicing the station's exterior. The Marck's disk-shaped feet lifted and lowered slowly. Each step snapped down upon the deck as they magnetically connected to the surface.

She took a few cautious steps back, bumping into a bin filled with parts. The Marck kept approaching her, and she closed her fists, standing firm.

Crix is controlling this. It would have let me die outside if it wanted to harm me. Her breathing labored, and a nauseous pit formed in her stomach. Her helmet visor flashed:

:Oxygen levels critical:

She pursed her lips in frustration as she shook her head. *Does this thing ever have any good news?*

Joric had designed natural weaknesses in her to fit into an everyday existence growing up, and the need to breathe oxygen was one of them. Right now, these designs worked against her. She let out a rasping cough before taking a knee. The room spun, and she coughed again. The Marck's thin, segmented arms extended and cradled her like a small child. A thin layer of frost coated the inside of her visor from her breath as a new warning flashed.

:Oxygen depleted:

Her vision blurred, and everything around her became indistinguishable aside from the mechanical face of the Marck. The lights around her changed from red to a subtle white glow. The whine of a tiny drill buzzed in her ears. Her helmet pulled away from her head, revealing her smooth, ivory skin, and clattered to the metal floor.

Sound! That means there's air. But was there oxygen?

She took a careful inhale. The frigid air burned her throat and blistered her artificial lungs. Her vision focused, and each exhale filled her view with a cloud of frozen breath. The bitter cold burned against her cheeks, and the icy atmosphere clawed down the neck of her suit and slithered around her body inside. Beneath the chill, a wave of burnt, synthetic lubricants mixed with industrial cleaning compounds clenched her nasal passages. At first, it seemed strange to her a facility maintained by highly advanced systems would be so minimally kept, but then she quickly remembered who was truly in charge, the young, mop-haired Mendac for whom she had developed deep feelings, Crix. It was the same person whose main priority in life, just a couple of years earlier, was winning some trivial game with his friends.

A resounding clack of metal upon metal broke the relative silence. The startling commotion nearly made Kerriah leap from her skin, and she snapped her attention to the Marck with disk-shaped feet lying facedown on the cold, metal surface.

"Crix," She whispered to herself. "Where are you?"

It appeared the Marck had dropped her off inside a hexagonal corridor lined with large pipes across the ceiling, extending as far as she could see in both directions.

Okay. . . .

She needed to get this bulky SPOD suit off. Gripping her fingers under the neck ring, she gave it a firm twist and lifted it over her head. She flung it to the side and then wrestled with the collar yoke, which snugged around the base of her chin and ears. She pressed two releases and pulled hard over her head. After being free from the restricting neck components, she reached inside the opening for the release bars, pulling upward and out. The bulky metal suit peeled open with a loud click, and she quickly stepped out, feeling free in her movements once again.

Kerriah peeled the snug, transparent cap from her head and let her jet-black hair spill over her shoulders. She slid the map disk Joric had given her from her shirt pocket and placed it in the base of her palm.

"Show me the way to the nucleus," she commanded.

The disk spun and rose from her hand. A soft-blue light emitted from it, and it began to move down the dimly lit corridor. The blue illumination cast across her face momentarily turned her green eyes teal, until the disk moved further away. She chased closely behind as it zipped around corners and through passageways, leaving its shimmering silhouette on each turn. It stopped in a large, open area littered with Marcks either disabled or blasted into pieces.

He's been through here.

11

Her heart began to race. Crix had been strangely silent since taking control of the Marcks and routing the Thraxon invasion force. Never an informal word spoken from any Marck unit indicating Crix was there, somewhere inside their metal frames. Nor did they mention the state of the core, the Queen, or his condition. In her quest for answers, Kerriah had only found awkward encounters with Marcks carrying out their civic duties that abnormally seemed to stare directly into her soul, yet never said a word.

She noticed the series of disks on the floor.

Okay, the Apex. The holographic control panel lit up before her as she walked across the larger disk in the middle. She scanned across the panel; there was T1 . . . N2. "That's it!"

The groan of stressed metal echoed through the corridors, a telling sign the station's hull integrity was failing from the extreme pressure outside. How long could the station stay intact without the stabilizing gas filling its cavities? During the planning phase of this mission, Joric hadn't been able to give her an exact answer, but he had said it would likely be an hour, maybe two, after the purge. Since she didn't know the precise time the gas had been expelled, she knew she didn't have long to make decisions.

She stared intensely at the control panel. The Queen controlled the core from the throne room, but the nucleus was the actual core. Crix was supposed to place the override into the nucleus, but he never did, or at least that was assumed since Joric had never received a control signal. She stared at her two options for a minute before a startling creak from the station's hull forced her decision.

12

SONG OF THE LAGGORNS

The throne room it is.

She pressed the T1 button, activating the corresponding floor disk. The disk lit a bright white, and she stepped upon its smooth surface. It turned transparent and dropped into a vast, nearly pitch-black area. She instantly felt the temperature plunge and a sudden, dizzying sense of weightlessness as a dark tower emerged. The only illumination source was an occasional light sphere darting away from the tower and into the station's outer hull.

The disk stopped near the upper portion of the tower at a circular platform. Kerriah moved carefully onto its grated metal deck. Her boots clanked with each step as she climbed the steep stairs leading to an arching entrance. The chilling cold seeped deep into her flesh and her body quivered. Two purple-cloaked Marcks lay motionless, leaning with their backs against the wall, like toppled props once guarding the entryway.

She cautiously stepped inside the open doorway to the throne room. Sprays of black soot stained the walls and floor in the back of the chamber from what appeared to be a blast of energy. Charred remains of curled hoses and bare wires dangled loosely from the ceiling. She took a few more steps and then stopped for a moment and squinted. A starling jolt of fight impulse tightened her muscles, and a tingling sensation swept over her body as her attention instantly snapped upward. She leaped back into a defensive posture at a menacing female figure dangling above, nearly hidden amongst the tangled mess. Charcoal burns sprayed across the once-synthetic white body, and a crimson crown of long spikes circled her lowered head. Kerriah relaxed her stance as she continued to stare upward. *The Queen.* At least she appeared disabled.

She kept her gaze on the queen as she slowly paced forward. The faint acidity of scorched metal, synthetics, and wires still hung in the air from the events that had occurred here two years ago. Her foot's forward motion stopped on something heavy.

A body. She leaned down for a closer look. *Merik!*

The corpse didn't look exactly like what she remembered, but it was him. She would never forget that slimy villain from the lowest level of Dispor. The flesh portions of his face were now mechanical.

How did he get down here? Poor Crix. She knew he must have had to deal with him again, but this time alone. She took solace in the fact Merik appeared to have lost in that encounter.

Below the dangling queen, there was an open hatch on the floor. Kerriah carefully stepped up to it and peeked down into the darkness below. She slid a pen-shaped light from her pocket and clicked it on. Between the clouds of frozen exhale, she noticed a ladder leading down into a faintly lit area. Without a second thought, she started crawling down the icy metal ladder. The smooth, cold bars burned into her fingers, and she couldn't wait to get to the bottom, clench her fists together, and warm them back up.

Her boots hit the metal bottom with a clang, and she immediately waved her light around.

"Crix!" she shouted.

A body slumped against the wall in the corner of the chamber. She focused her light on it and then took a shocked inhale and a step back. It was an Andor, unlike any she had ever seen, with a smaller frame and shorter muzzle. White streaks covered its short tan pelt. She slowly moved toward the body with her light on its face. Then it hit her. It was Crix. It was his actual appearance he told her about at Pinor Eden. His sunken cheeks and eyes matched the gaunt, emaciated body, which appeared as though all the blood had drained away, along with any signs of life. Kerriah leaned down and placed the back of her hand on his cheek. His face felt almost as cold as the metal bars from the ladder. She pulled one of his eyelids back with her thumb and revealed an opaque white cornea. Her heart sank into her stomach, and she stammered back.

"No." She started to breathe faster, and her mouth dried. "No . . . no . . . no. . . . You can't be dead."

She looked up and noticed a dim blue glow radiating from an opening in the low ceiling.

"Crix?" she called out. She stared directly into the space above. "Crix!" she screamed out. She screamed his name several times before sitting with her back against the wall, exhausted and unable to carry on without him.

Hiding her face in her hands, she broke into a manic sob. The emotional pressure of the last two years poured out at once.

"Dammit! Where are you!" She slapped her hand on the cold metal floor.

She leaned back and stared up for a minute as the station let out another startling groan, followed by several loud thuds. Its

15

hull was collapsing and wouldn't last much longer. With a clenched fist, she made her choice; rather than attempt to escape without him, she would spend her last moments here with the one that captured her heart and saved everyone.

The blue light above suddenly brightened, and her heart skipped a beat. The orb dropped from the opening and hovered in the chamber a meter before her. Crix's face appeared inside with the look of a sad child. It was the face she remembered. She quickly wiped the tears and hair away from her eyes.

"Crix." Her breath left her as she said his name.

"Kerriah," Crix's faint voice spoke from the orb. "You shouldn't have come here."

She straightened her posture. "I had to. I'm just sorry it took so long."

"No. You were safe. You should have let me go."

Kerriah abruptly stood up with her fists tightly against her hips. "The Marcks are all failing, and we knew that meant you were likely dying as well. I'm not going to leave you here to die and be forgotten. Do you hear me, Crix? Nothing was going to stop me from coming down here to get you . . . nothing!"

"I would like nothing more than to return with you, but I can't."

"Why?"

"I need to find a way to get you out. I just need a little time."

"No! Get us both out of here!" Crix's face faded from the orb, and then it floated upward again. "Wait! We need to get both of us out of here. Crix! Stop! Listen to me. I'm not leaving without you," Kerriah shouted upward, trying to get her words out before he disappeared.

The orb stopped, and his face emerged again. "Kerriah, please understand; I care about you. You're beautiful, brilliant, and too important for the UMO to lose." He paused. "But I destroyed the primary power core when I took out the queen. The auxiliary core is damaged and can hold on its own for a brief period. It needs my power to formulate and maintain the basic hydronic pressurization and stabilization routines. The shifts in the planetary storms and pressure systems are erratic, and it needs intelligence to adjust continuously. So, you see, if I leave, this station will plummet into the hydrogen sea below, killing both of us."

"But—" Kerriah hesitated for a moment.

She was astounded by this boy she had met in rural Troika speaking with such technical prowess. But her thoughts shifted quickly, and she moved directly in front of the orb and raised her voice.

"No! There's a way out. There's always a way. Listen to me. You can push enough power into the station and loop its stabilization and maintenance commands to buy us enough time to escape. Joric already figured all this out. It'll work!"

The orb pulsated, and she could see Crix staring back at her through its shimmering glow. "Kerriah, I no longer have a physical body. Mine died two years ago."

17

"It's not dead. It's not. Look!" She gestured over to the lifeless mass on the floor. "It's not decayed or withered. It's just dormant." She stopped and bit her lip; a sick feeling warmed over her. Deep inside, she hoped she was correct about what she sold him. She had to be. "You can wake it back up. I know you can. You have to try." She wasn't sure of her statement, but she needed him to believe he had a chance to escape.

"I've always loved that about you," Crix said.

"What?" she huffed.

"Your assuredness and optimism."

"Just get back into your body, Crix."

"I will for you, but you must understand, I am not the same person you once knew. The nightmares . . . I cannot stop them. I'm afraid." The station trembled violently.

"Crix, just do it. We will deal with that later, but you have to hurry!"

The orb rose back into the ceiling. A flash of blue from above beamed out and filled the room before lowering back down and fading into Crix's body. An azure radiance emerged from the fur-coated flesh and began pulsating. His arms flinched, and his neck rolled as he stumbled to his feet like a clumsy doll. He fell facedown onto the chilly floor, and Kerriah leaped over to help. His arms flailed around violently, knocking her away. He flopped around and began convulsing. Her eyes widened, and she bit her lip again, trying to hold back and allow his body to do what it needed. Crix's mendac form flashed several times, but ghostly pale and thin. He flopped over facedown and then onto his back once again. The old illusion returned as the orb reinfused with his cells, and from his physical appearance, it was the Crix she remembered. The Andor was gone.

He stopped moving, and his body lay motionless, with his mouth open and back arched upward. Kerriah couldn't take it anymore.

"Crix! . . . Crix! . . . Wake up!" His face was still pale, and his eyes rolled back. Shaking him by his shoulders, she stared intensely into his face. His eyes darted toward her. "Crix? Can you hear me?"

He slowly sat up with his mouth still hanging open. His eyes were wide and tinted blue.

"Kerriah?" His wobbly legs attempted to stand again, but he slipped back to his knees. "We've got to go."

CHAPTER 2

Kerriah's eyes welled with tears after hearing his voice. He was back, and now she needed to get them out of there. She wrapped her arms under his and tried to pull him upright. As she heaved his nearly dead weight, a look of shock filled her face upon catching close sight of his empty right sleeve. His right hand was gone; only a charred stump remained. Her jaw locked with a gasp, and she turned away without inquiry.

"We've got to hurry." Crix's speech was barely understandable.

"I know. But you're going to have to take it slow."

He shook his head. "No, I mean it. I've put enough power in the station to sustain it for about fifteen minutes." His voice sounded groggy, and she had difficulty understanding him, though she knew what he meant. "When I blasted the Queen, I blew most of the station's power storage systems from the surge. I've had to push massive amounts of power to keep this station operational." He took a dry gulp and squinted. "It can only hold about fifteen minutes."

She strained him back up to his feet and over to the ladder. Crix shook his head and pointed toward a narrow doorway. They crouched to get through, and the accompanying tight corridor ended at a small metal door hissing open as they approached. The other side was pitch-black. There were no more darting stars chasing through the outer hull, nothing. Just the inviting glow of the lift disk that would hopefully lead them closer to their destination . . . out of the core. They slowly stepped upon the disk, and a chilly breeze whisked from below, wrapping its icy claws around their bodies. The station let out a lengthy groan followed by the audible stretching and crunching of its rigid structure.

"Apex Zone," Crix commanded.

They shot upward and emerged back into the domed area above within seconds. As soon as they stepped from the disk, he collapsed to the floor. Kerriah strained to pull his dead weight back up again, but it was useless without his help. All around them, lights began to strobe, and an alarm sounded throughout the station. The occasional groaning and creaking of metal became persistent as the outer hull integrity went into imminent failure.

"Oh, great!" Kerriah shook Crix's limp body and then gave a solid smack to his face. "Crix! Wake up!" She struck him again. "Crix! What's the quickest way to the supply return container?"

He let out a moan, and his eyes rolled back. Kerriah grabbed his face and glared directly at him. "Crix!"

His eyes darted back to hers, and he took in a deep inhale. "Kerriah? Where are we?"

"We have to go! The station is coming apart, and we have less than fifteen minutes of power. We need to get to the supply return container."

"It's gone. It was jettisoned before I took control."

"Friggen . . . frick . . . aghhh!" she shouted at the ceiling. She somehow knew it wouldn't be that easy, and the uncharacteristic unleashing of a Krath-influenced salty tongue had become her go-to release as of late. "Okay, then we turn up the stationary thrusters and push the entire thing into low orbit."

He pinched his eyes closed for a second. "No."

"What do you mean 'no?'" Her frustration level redlined, and she wanted to scream.

"It won't work."

"What?" She shook her head and clenched her jaw tightly.

"There's not enough power to break the station free of the planet's gravitational pull. And h-hull integrity won't hold against the stress without s-stastic gas." He stopped to take a few heaving, deep breaths. "It'll come apart and fall back into the hydrogen sea." His eyes shut, and his head lowered.

Her eyes burned with frustration. "Okay, so now what do we do?" He didn't reply. "Crix!" She gripped his shoulders and shook him aggressively. "What do we do now? Please wake up!"

Crix's eyes popped open as if he had been startled from a deep sleep. "We try anyway. G-Get me to the cosmic thruster power relay. We will overload them with power and force them open. Hopefully, t-that s-should get us high enough to use . . . use the hazardous materials release torp—" His conscious left him again.

Kerriah slid the map disk out again. "Cosmic thruster power relay." The disk lit up and started slowly moving to the elevator. She grabbed Crix by his feet and dragged him along the smooth floor. The muscles in her shoulders pulled tight, and her feet began to slip as she approached the doors. The elevator hissed open, and the disk hovered in with her following behind, dragging Crix's limp body without hesitation.

"Cosmic thruster power relay," she breathlessly called out. The elevator started upward, and a blinking light on the wall indicated their destination was only three decks away.

"Crix, you have to help me. I can't do this on my own. Please."

His arms raised and then flopped like noodles over his head. "Where are we?"

She blew out a forced exhale and frustratingly pulled her hand across her forehead. "You've got to be kidding me."

"The cosmic thrusters," he softly mumbled.

"Right! Now get up!"

He tried to push his body up as she pulled under his arms. Kerriah's neck and shoulders cramped as she did most of the work, lifting him back to his feet. "Come on. . . . Help me!"

The elevator door slid open, and the map disk zipped out into the corridor ahead.

"Come on!" She tugged at his frail body, and he stumbled out.

Crix kept his footing, though it looked like he could topple over at any moment. Kerriah kept her right arm locked under his as they staggered after the disk. They took a couple of turns and one more long corridor before the disk stopped at a large metal door. They both looked up slowly with reserved anticipation. Noise from the other side sounded like the constant rumbling of thunder.

"We're here," she said. "You're up, so you can't pass out on me anymore, okay?" His head nodded.

A large red lever outside the door kept it locked. "Are you okay to stand on your own?" Crix's tired eyes looked up at her, and he nodded.

Kerriah leaned close to his face and gestured toward the lever. "Okay, stay with me. I need to get this door open."

Grabbing the lever with both hands, she put her weight down atop the rigid handle. It slowly moved into a down position with a clack. The heavy door let out a medley of growls and squeals as it labored upward. The intensity of the scorching, dry air escaping from the other side felt like it pulled the breath from her lungs as it blasted her in the face. She squeezed her eyes closed and rubbed her knuckles into each. A wave of heat distorted the view of the grated metal floor inside.

She advanced into the cosmic thruster relay with Crix in tow. Inside, a long gangway crossed a chasm of pulsing white lights. Five octagon-shaped windows lined the far wall. White lights flashed from each of them in a consistent rhythm from left to right. Kerriah peeked back and waved Crix forward.

Crix gripped the guardrail and limped across the bridge. He took a slow, careful pace, glancing down at his feet with each step. Kerriah kept close behind him. The blazing air clawed at her exposed skin, and a persistent rumbling amplified as they neared the other side, making her eardrums scream and their teeth chatter.

As Crix reached the end of the bridge, he stumbled, narrowly catching himself against the window-filled wall. He turned his head. "I'm going to force the lower cone thrusters into full, but I need to give them—" He stopped for a gasping breath. Kerriah could barely make out his words but followed along, hoping he didn't need anything from her. "—give them additional power first."

"What do you need me to do?" she shouted over the noise, but he didn't respond. Instead, he jammed both of his arms into a window. His body blazed in blue light, which shimmered against the heat surrounding him. He turned and did the same in another window. Then he staggered over to two valves, turned them, and pushed them into the wall. She felt a slight sense of vertigo and additional pressure on her heels and spine as the giant station began to move upward.

The gravitational force intensified as their speed accelerated. Before she realized Crix had moved, he appeared right next to her. He seemed to have better focus and footing than earlier.

"Let's go," he said while nudging her out of the power relay area.

The hum of the ship's thrusters and the rapid popping sound from the outer hull became apparent once they reached the corridor. The lights strobed, and the floor shook.

"The station is moving through Oro's cloud layers, but it's going to lose power and upward momentum soon," Crix said.

Kerriah didn't need to see the concern in his eyes to know they didn't have much time, and the odds of them making it out were scant. She chased close behind him as his wobbly legs bound through each passage as though he knew every inch of the place he had called home for the past two years.

They struggled to an elevator and rode it up two levels. An unexpected shockwave rocked across the station. Kerriah's wide eyes looked over at Crix. "What was that?"

He didn't respond and kept his focus forward as the doors opened. Before them, the dimly lit passageway had only amber lights, giving off an eerie appearance to their surroundings.

Crix stopped Kerriah from moving forward with a firm hand against her chest. "Radiation," he said. "The orange lights indicate elevated levels of radiation detected here."

She noticed a few beads of sweat dripping down his cheek and felt a mix of relief and anxiety. At least his body appeared to be functioning normally. However, neither of them knew how much resistance to this environmental hazard she would have. The orb could protect Crix, but what would it do to her? It would be certain death to a normal person without protection. But at this point, it didn't matter; they would both die if they didn't proceed.

They advanced cautiously down the corridor, and Kerriah could feel her heart speed up with every step toward the circular door with radiation warnings blinking above. Crix grabbed her and pulled her close as a field of blue immersed them. She gripped her arm around him, knowing her life depended on keeping him close. He triggered the door release. The thick door rolled open, and curling whisks of vapor swooshed out like a fleeing wraith. Inside, white glowing fluid drizzled through outlets along the wall, disappearing into openings on the floor. Fingers of vapor clouds steamed up from the radiating toxins.

Two slender white Marcks stood nearby with their heads lowered. Along the far wall were a dozen empty racks and a single torpedo canister laying at a forty-five-degree angle below a dark tunnel in the ceiling.

"That's our ride out." Crix took a glance at Kerriah, who gripped tightly to his side. "They were meant for expelling highly unstable waste as far from the station as possible. Fortunately, it's not something that needs to be done very often. But—"

The station lighting flickered out, and it started shaking so ferociously that maintaining a steady footing became challenging. Kerriah felt helpless, and her wide eyes stared up at Crix. "Okay, whatever you need to do, let's do it quickly!"

Crix led them to one of the stationary Marcks and placed his thumb into the back of its head. The Marck instantly sprung to life and walked over to a control panel.

"Let's go." He led her to the torpedo, pushed it from the rack, and the heavy tube clunked to the floor.

"What are you doing?" Kerriah gripped her fingers into Crix's side until she could feel his ribs.

"Just trust me!" The top was already open, with just enough room to squeeze inside together. They slid inside, still carefully hanging onto one another. "Try to calm your breathing. We'll be okay. I promise," Crix whispered in her ear. Kerriah closed her eyes and nodded. There was a clatter of metal against the torpedo wall, and the top sealed shut, leaving them in complete blackness. They suddenly felt rotated upright before clanking into a slight angle.

The Marck. Kerriah knew the worker Marck did his job for the last time in setting the torpedo for launch. They snuggled closer in the tight space as they felt the station tilting further and further to its side as its stabilizers failed to maintain its direct, upward trajectory. Everything around them trembled, and their teeth chattered. Kerriah held her breath, waiting for either the end or the sudden momentum of the torpedo firing into the atmosphere. They both stared helplessly at the black cylinder wall with hope ironically placed on a single Marck completing its task.

Their insides dropped to their feet as the torpedo fired into the upper atmosphere of Oro. The outside of the canister went from stingingly hot to icy cold, and the accompanying sounds of metal popping and stretching from the extreme temperature shift pounded their eardrums. The torpedo rumbled as they broke through the atmosphere, and the searing cold outer walls burned through the meager protective layers of their clothes and into their skin. Despite the conditions, Kerriah felt reassured by Crix's presence, and she could sense him trying to maintain the air pressure using the orb. As she squeezed him in tightly, a subtle tickle of a familiar scent stimulated her nasal passages. His essence already returned, even after his long dormancy. For her, it was breathing the outdoor air as a child. Cool and sweet. She felt safe with him next to her, even though the next few minutes were uncertain.

Their momentum slowed, and the feeling of weightlessness crept in. It, however, only lasted for a few minutes before they felt the dreaded sensation of falling.

"Oh no," Kerriah's voice quivered. "No, no, no! We didn't get enough altitude."

Everything flashed before her. The war, the years without Crix, the plotting of his rescue, it all hit her in seconds. How could she have planned this better? What could she have done to have a different outcome?

Crix closed his eyes as he clutched her tightly. A sudden clack echoed from the outer shell, and their downward motion stopped. They began to move upward again.

"Krath!" she said with her eyes rolled upward as though telepathically pouring out her gratitude for her faithful friend.

Crix opened his eyes. A wide smile crept over his face. "Yes." He let out a deep breath.

Kerriah smiled back. As cranky as Krath got, he always did what he said. He always came through on his word.

Clack . . . clink. The sounds smashed into their ears. A tiny light pierced through the outer shell and crawled down, over, and back up. The section peeled open, and light blasted inside.

29

They both squinted for a second to adjust. "Ha! What cha waitin' for?" Krath's booming voice announced. "Since I had to rescue tya again, at least tya can do is get off yer bumps and give me a hug!"

They pulled themselves out from the canister and, with an overwhelming feeling of relief, planted their feet onto the deck of the ship. Krath had a massive grin as he looked at Crix. "Well, come on, boy; get over here." He grabbed and pulled him off his feet like a child, squeezing him until Crix's breath escaped his lungs and his ribs popped. "Tya been gone so long, and tya never bothered to stopped by to see ole Krath." He set him down, and Crix wobbled to keep his footing. Noticeably exhausted.

Krath looked over at Kerriah. "Tya did well, little girl. . . . Tya did well."

CHAPTER 3

Dammit, Crix!" Kerriah slammed her hand down on the table and abruptly stood up from her chair.

Crix looked up at her with a blank expression. "What?" His voice sounded like he had just woken up from a nap and not of someone that'd been subjected to mild interrogation for the last twenty minutes.

"What! What do you mean 'what?' I'm trying to help you, and all you can give me is 'what?'" She scowled at him and shook her head. "At least go see Plexo. He can run some tests. He can make sure you haven't been . . . you know . . . neurologically damaged during your time in the core."

His eyes slowly drifted down to the tabletop. Kerriah grabbed him by his shoulders. "Look at me!" His attention snapped back to her again. "I care about you. I need you to get checked out."

His brow furrowed with irritation, and he peeled her hands away. "I've already been through all of that. I'm fine. Just need some time to myself."

"How much time? It's been four months, and you haven't changed a bit."

"I-I don't know." Crix looked as though he hadn't slept for weeks. Dark circles haloed his sunken eyes, and his ghostly pale skin appeared as though he had just emerged from a cryo tray of the local morgue.

Kerriah stared down at his right shirt sleeve, which bagged loosely over his wrist. He ardently refused to get a synthetic replacement for the hand he had lost in the core. *He's so frickin stubborn!*

She took a calming breath and then settled back into her chair, taking a sip of water from the cup she had filled earlier. It was still cool due to the uncomfortable near-bitter temperature in the room. Crix complained if she turned the heat up above a frosty chill. He didn't tolerate warm air anymore, though none of the medical experts could explain why aside from some mental conditioning from his years in the core.

She pressed her thumbs into her eyes and then took another long exhale. "Look, Plexo mentioned that you need to go to Gabor. There you will find the council, and they may be able to help you, or at least give you some answers to whatever questions you have. That was part of your original plan anyway. All Tolagons must train, or apparently, you'll die using the orb. It's amazing you haven't died already. Did you ever think that this might be what's wrong with you to begin with?"

Crix looked indifferent and shrugged in reply.

"Jesselle, the woman that has the red orb of Solara, she is also suffering with similar withdrawn behavior. Not as severe, but very similar."

Crix's eyes shot up; his brow wrinkled and lip curled. "Who's Jesselle?"

"I've explained who she is before, but you must have been in one of your zoning out moments and didn't hear me." Kerriah's frustration level had begun to hit the tipping point, but she took a few more deep breaths and managed to bring herself back down for another explanation. "She's the woman we had to fight with on Nathasia, the red woman. After the Thraxons and Zearic fled, we found her fighting for her life against her orb-spawned apparitions. She was losing control as the orb's power was overtaking her. Plexo feels that it was likely due to her use of it for evil and because of her lack of proper training. Jesselle is a good person that Zearic manipulated, so she was able to use it for a while before it turned against her."

Crix stood abruptly, knocking his chair to the floor. "Where is she? I have to see her."

"She's been put up in an under-dwelling in Corasan. She's keeping a low profile but still has the red orb. Fortunately, hers does not stand out the way yours does. There's no subtle radiance coming from her skin. She has the same hair as you, though it's a little better kept." She reached over and brushed the locks away from his eyes. His hair had grown long and bushy over the months. He refused to get it cut. "We can go see her, but what're your intentions?"

Crix began to breathe as though he had just run up several flights of stairs. "I just need to see her. She's the only other person I know of who has wielded the power of an orb. I just want to talk to her."

"Sure, if you think it will help. I'll try anything at this point." Kerriah took it as a positive move. Getting him out of their home would be a good thing.

CHAPTER 4

The streets of Corasan bustled with residents going about their daily tasks. The warm, breezy day tussled their hair as they walked down the open roads, and the whine of traffic zipped by in the skyway pipes above. Much of the older interior portion of the city looked like it was pulled from black and white images, evenly peppered with onyx and bone-colored marble buildings. Nearly everyone that passed by gave Crix a strange look. Not because of his blue radiance, it was barely noticeable in the bleached sunlight of midday; instead, his gritty appearance drew their attention. It wasn't a surprise, given his bushy, unkempt white hair, matching beard, and dirty, wrinkled clothes. No one would know he was the reason they still existed.

There were no official pictures of Crix, and he wouldn't let anyone take any. His reclusiveness since his return had made him as anonymous as any random individual walking by. Kerriah hadn't given up. She still maintained as normal of a life as she could while keeping away from politics and allowing Realm Chancellor Septin to do all the heavy lifting in the political sphere. Her adoptive father's rise to leadership was certainly no surprise, given his role in the resistance. He all but begged her to take a leadership role, but she wanted to stay focused on helping Crix. Though she still made time for herself. It was necessary to maintain her sanity. Her long white skirt cupped her fit legs as they paced in the wind. She bobbed her jet-black hair to her shoulders. The sleek new style gave her a strong look. She was striking, and the pedestrians darting a glance at Crix generally took an accompanying stare at her as they passed.

They reached the lift station to the Enclave 13's under-dwellings. The enclave under-dwellings were the communities beneath the streets of Corasan. Fifteen in total, this is where the city populace of lesser means resided. Life on the luxurious upper side of the city was expensive, yet vibrant and attractive. But many residents of Corasan could not afford to live there, so the enclaves formed, providing affordable access to the wealthy city and its many amenities.

An oval-shaped lift peaked up to street level, and a few locals stepped off as the gate clattered open, indicating it had reached its destination. Crix leaped back with wide eyes and an open mouth upon hearing the gate. Beads of sweat formed across his forehead, and he looked like a startled animal about to dart off into the safety of thick cover.

"Crix? What's wrong?" Kerriah asked as she stepped back, prepared to stop him from running off.

Crix shook his head. "No. I-I can't go in there." He took a dry gulp before opening his mouth again.

"The lift?"

Then it hit her. Many nights, Crix woke screaming and shaking. She had to calm him, talk him down, from the haunting dreams of the Heydromac at Gorag's castle. The terrible things that happened to the commando team that went with him. The elevator. It's one of the things he would always mention—the trip up to the top of the mountain.

"It's okay. You're not there anymore. You're with me, safe here in Corasan." Her voice was gentle and soothing. Calming his triggers over the past four months had become a new skill for her.

He squeezed his eyelids closed for a few seconds and slowly opened them again. His heart still raced. "Okay." He sighed. "I can do this."

They slowly stepped into the lift with a few other residents. Head tilting stares peered as the uncertain Enclave 13 residents tried to figure out if they needed to worry about the shaggy looking stranger. The leery glares continued as Kerriah rubbed his back, trying to keep him calm. As the doors clacked shut and the lift descended below the street, Crix broke into a cold sweat.

Several passengers took a careful step back, giving more distance between them and Crix. One passenger cupped a hand around their child, pulling her close while looking at Crix as if he had a contagious disease. Kerriah fired an annoyed stare back at them.

"It's too bad you don't recognize that you'd all be dead right now if it weren't for the person standing here. All of you!" She shook her head. "This Tolagon saved our asses, so a kind 'thank you' instead of rude stares is what he deserves."

The lift stopped and the doors opened. None of the other passengers wanted any part of Kerriah's ire and quickly filed out without saying a word.

37

"Jerks," she said. "Let's go, Crix."

She tugged his arm, leading him into a gritty area with wide passages going in three separate directions. The dirty ceiling lights camouflaged spotty hues across the walls and floor. Bits of trash and debris peppered the ground as though whatever cleaning crew was responsible for keeping this area tidy hadn't been around for a while. They took a left and walked for a time, passing dwelling doorways. The doors arched at the top and varied in color and wear. Unseen voices echoed in the distance.

They took a right and then left.

"Let's see," Kerriah said as she studied the numbers at the top of each door. "Thirty-six forty-two." She turned to face a red door. "This is it."

The door looked as though it had seen better days. Dents and scratches adorned most of it, particularly the center. She looked over at Crix who glanced around nervously while clawing at his chest.

"We really need to get you out more."

Crix's eyes stopped at the dent on the door. Kerriah waved her hand in front of his face. "Hello, Crix?" His eyes moved toward her.

Kerriah moved her face in front of his, trying hard to get his attention. "She's very nice but also is suffering some levels of distress over her experience with Zearic and the orb. So please, let's keep this cordial." She waited for him to agree, but his focus returned to the dent in the door.

She grabbed his chin and pulled it toward her. "Crix. Did you hear me?"

He slowly nodded his head.

"Alright then." She pressed her thumb into a recessed panel near the door, and a small screen projected out. "Jesselle? It's me . . . Kerriah."

The door creaked and squealed to the side, disappearing into the wall with a few starts and stops before fully opening. Its rickety surface caught against the edge several times, and it was probably fortunate it would even open. They stepped into a small, cluttered dwelling with a red-haired woman sitting in a cushioned chair with her head down. The round black chair hugged her thin body as though form-fit to her figure. The woman's attention swung to Kerriah as she wiped her eyes and gave a quick, fluid sniff.

Kerriah noticed she had been crying but didn't want to start her introduction of Crix by questioning her over what was wrong. Instead, she stepped aside and allowed the two to see each other.

Crix's eyes widened, and his forehead scrunched into a lip-curling scowl. He charged at her like a ravenous drock in a cratic worm field. Jesselle leaped from her chair, and Crix dove atop her with his hand around her throat.

"Crix!" Kerriah screamed.

She wrapped her arm around his neck and pulled him off. His eyes spun with madness, and strings of saliva dribbled through

39

his beard. She shoved him away and shook her head in disappointment.

"Have you completely lost it? Didn't we talk about this already?"

Her attention turned to Jesselle, who still lay on the floor with her hand guarding her neck. She stopped to cough into her sleeve before slowly rising to her feet.

"It's okay," her voice rasped. "I deserved that."

"No, you don't," Kerriah said. "You're a victim, the same as the rest of us." She shot a scowling glance back at Crix. "And you." She stopped to point at him. "You need to pull yourself together. We have all suffered, and we're all in pain. But we can't let it out on each other. Jesselle is with us. She's a good person that was placed in a terrible situation, just like you."

Crix's eyes lowered, and his breathing slowed. He nodded slowly and then wiped his sleeve across his beard.

"Okay." Kerriah helped pull him up from the floor and moved Jesselle's chair upright again. "Can we sit and have a discussion like civilized people?"

They both lowered their heads and nodded. Kerriah let out an exhale. "Good."

Kerriah and Crix sat next to each other on a petite, firm couch across from Jesselle, who peeked back at her small, well-worn kitchen. "I'd offer you something to drink, but the only thing I have is water."

"That's okay, we're fine." Kerriah squinted as she stared at Jesselle's long, wavy, auburn hair. "Did you color your hair?" She'd had the blaring "Tolagon" white hair the last time she'd saw her.

Jesselle gently padded her hand across the silky strands. "Yes, I'm trying not to stand out, but it only holds for a day, before it just suddenly turns back to pure white. You know the kind of white that's obvious."

"It's after you use it," Crix said, his voice gritty and broken. He cleared his throat. "You're still using the orb's power, aren't you?"

Jesselle stayed quiet for a minute. "Yes."

"What for?" he asked while scratching his beard.

Again, she took a long pause. "I-I can't stop using it. Since I'm not assigned to any specific purpose, I use it for convenience." She stared down at her feet and dug her thumbnail into her leg.

"Convenience?" Crix's voice became stern. He clenched his teeth and fist.

She looked up slowly at Crix and then into the tiny galley kitchen behind her. An ethereal version of herself wisped into shape. The nearly transparent replica stood about two meters from them. It gave an eerie smile before turning into the kitchen and sliding a cabinet door open. Her iridescent arm reached in, pulled a small cup out, and filled it with water. Like a silent holographic image, its fluid motion strode back in and handed the glass to Jesselle.

Crix let out a disapproving puff of air. "Pfffff. . . . Self-indulgence is not what the orb's power is meant for." The intensity of his scowl hid behind his scraggly beard. "What about the visions? You must be seeing them."

Her eyes perked up and rounded like a child. "Yes. They're terrible. I have them in my dreams most nights, and I wake up drenched in sweat, unable to fall back asleep."

"Uh-huh . . . yep. The sickness?"

"I've lost thirty pounds," she replied.

Crix waved his finger at Jesselle. "You shouldn't have the orb. It wasn't duly given to you."

"But it was to you?"

"That's right. My fath——" Crix lowered his hand and cleared his throat again. "Tolagon Emberook gave it to me, as was his right to do so. How did you get yours?"

"Sectnine," she whispered and then squeezed her eyes shut as if wincing off some painful memory.

"Zearic?" Crix asked.

She nodded quickly, and her sad eyes lowered as she explained. "Nine years ago, I was a normal fourteen-year-old girl living modestly on the outskirts of Kortel. My parents were good people and just wanted the best for me. My father was a stabilizer repair technician for the skyway pipes in our sector, and my mother was an archival custodian. Between them, they did okay, but they wanted me to be accepted into Corasan Science and Medical Engineering School."

Kerriah puckered her lips and nodded. "That's certainly a good one. Probably the best, honestly."

Jesselle adjusted her seat and took a deep inhale. "Right. But without expensive neuro-augmentation, there was little chance I could pass the exams required for acceptance. Only the elite had the resources to make it in."

Crix looked over at Kerriah. "Did you get that done to you?"

She started tapping her foot and gave him a wide-eyed stare. "Uh, no. I never needed it." And exhaled with frustration. "Jesselle, please continue."

"Well . . . anyway . . . nine years ago, Sectnine Corporation sent out a special offer to parents with children between twelve and fifteen. They offered a select number of children a new neuro-enhancement that they were working on, which would place their child into the upper tier of learning and cognitive aptitude. It was supposedly experimental, and they needed test subjects to expose to a 'harmless' new power source that would stimulate the neuronal circuits." She turned and rubbed the back of her neck before continuing. She seemed uncomfortable and adjusted her seat again.

"My parents, and many others, were cautiously excited, asked all the right questions, and were provided all the right answers. A group of fifty parents and their children agreed to take a trip to one of Sectnine's orbital labs, except this lab wasn't above Soorak. It orbited Nathasia." Jesselle looked away, rubbed her neck again, and stared at the floor.

Both Crix and Kerriah instantly looked at each other upon hearing this. "Nathasia?" Kerriah asked. "And no one found this to be a bit odd?"

"Apparently not. At least not enough to back out. Everyone wanted their children to do something great, like working on future gammac corridor development and expansion. You know, something significant. So we all traveled to this station on one of the corporation's transports.

"However, as soon as we arrived, everything changed. We were all separated from our parents, never seeing them again. I later discovered that my parents were never seen again by anyone. They vanished, I assumed, killed." Jesselle stopped for a moment, and her eyes welled with tears. "Zearic and his agents started exposing us to the red orb's power. The orb they had found hidden deep inside the largest volcano on Solara, burbling amongst the magma." She locked her knees together and nervously dug her thumbnail into her thigh.

"They wanted to see how our bodies and minds reacted to it. Some died instantly, others were unaffected, and some showed positive effects, like mental sharpness and physical stamina. I was in the latter group." She stopped. The muscles tensed across her jawline and along her temples. "It was then that they started giving us the orb to wield in small slices of time.

"I remember the first time I was instantly drugged by its power. They had me do small things like form balls from dirt or spin a fan, which later turned into forming combustible gas from the nearby elements and sucking the air from chambers to create artificial vacuums."

44

Crix leaned forward to gain her attention. "Who taught you to do this?"

"Tolagon Tenier."

"What?" Crix's face scrunched and his voice rose with shock. "That can't be. A Tolagon taught you? Taught you to use it for evil?"

"Yes, it is true. However, he was as much a victim as we were. After he relinquished his orb, Zearic captured him and apparently tortured him for months, maybe years, until he was fully an obedient servant of theirs."

"Okay, why didn't he just have Tenier use the orb for them? Why did they need you?" Kerriah asked.

Jesselle squirmed in her seat. "He couldn't. Zearic had his legs and arms removed during the torture sessions he put him through. He could still speak, but when he was finished training us, from my understanding, Zearic had his tongue removed and changed his name to hide his identity. He hated all Tolagons and wanted Tenier to suffer as much as possible. They eventually sent what remained of him to some raving mad bioengineer that supposedly worked out of Dispor."

Crix turned even whiter than his usual ghostly pale. "Do you know what he changed his name to?"

Jesselle sucked a gulp of air through her teeth and pinched her eyes closed for a moment. It seemed painful for her to say the name. "Guttel."

Kerriah's eyes widened, and she looked at Crix. "Guttel? You're kidding?"

"No. I'm pretty sure that was it."

"It appears I met another Tolagon after all. Though I would have never guessed it," Crix said.

"So you met him in Dispor?"

"We did, but he was barely recognizable as a Solaran." Kerriah's face turned sour at her last memory of Dispor. "More like some twisted mess of flesh and machine. The work of a cruel sociopathic scientist, if you can even call him that."

Jesselle took a slow drink from her cup of water. Her hand trembled as she raised it to her lips. She set it down, rubbed her eyes, and stopped with a sniff. "I hate what happened to him. I see the good in him now, looking back. Zearic terrorized him. He was broken. And I was blinded by manipulation."

"It's okay. You were still a child, and he took advantage of you," Kerriah said.

"No. You don't understand. He had me do awful things. They subjected us to longer sessions with the orb until some of the others went insane and killed themselves or had his cronies kill them because they became too difficult to control. Once they had us down to a few viable hosts, he made his choice, and he chose me. The first thing I was required to do was murder the remaining children. I had to use the orb to kill them to prove my obedience. If I didn't, he would take the orb away and give it to another, and I would be killed."

46

Tears welled in her eyes, and she continued. "These were my friends. The only companions I had to talk to during those years. Now I had to kill them for Zearic. At first, I hated him for it, but later, he was all I knew. The only one that knew who I was. He began to treat me differently. Like I was important, and it made me feel good. I carried out his tasks of assassinations for several years before encountering you."

Crix scratched his beard for a couple of minutes. A few loose bristles of hair showered down, and he aggressively dug his fingers into his cheeks. "So Tenier couldn't teach you how to deal with the sickness? Somehow, you've used the orb for years, and you're not dead. I used it for about a month before I felt like I was dying inside."

Jesselle slowly shook her head. "No, though he did give me some tips on suppressing it somewhat. He said that he could not help me with that side-effect. I would have to travel to Gabor, but he knew they would never accept me, especially with Zearic controlling me."

Crix shifted up in his seat, his focus completely on Jesselle. "How do you suppress it?"

"You have to remove it from your body for a portion of each day. At least eight hours at a time. You know how risky that is. If you're like me, you're always afraid of losing it. I'm worried it may just float away to another host, and I'm a wreck the whole time it's out of me."

"Yeah, great." Crix looked defeated. He raised his glowing blue hand and flipped it around. "I can't even do that. It's bound to me, and if it leaves my body, I go with it. A blessing and a curse." His head fell as he tried to prop his right fist under his chin, quickly remembering it wasn't there. He glared at the empty sleeve for a second with contempt bristled across his face. "Though mostly a curse," he snarled.

Kerriah carefully placed her hand on his leg. "Crix, you and Jesselle need to enter Gabor. It's the only way to end this madness you are both experiencing."

"No!" Jesselle shouted. "They will never accept me. I'm a villain . . . unworthy. They will see that and take the orb away."

"You don't know that. You're not that person. Besides, you can't continue like this. It's killing you slowly." She looked at Crix with a sharp stare. "Both of you."

"How, Kerriah?" Crix's voice was low as the words mumbled out. "How are we going to find this place?"

Kerriah leaned her head forward and raised her eyebrows. She could have sworn he played dumb but couldn't understand why? "Are you kidding? You're the one that told me what Plexo said about the bracer. It has a map to its location that is activated with the orb. You need two orbs to unlock its entrance, and I'm looking at two right here. So what's the problem?"

"Right," Crix mumbled again, staring at Jesselle.

Jesselle bit her lip. Her apprehensive eyes reflected the light in the room. "I don't know."

"Oh my. What happened to the two people I witnessed holding their own against some of the toughest opponents and situations I've seen?" Kerriah paused for a minute to see if either one would give a reply. They both sat quietly with their heads down.

"It's the orb!" She growled in frustration. "You guys can't see that the orb made you strong at first, but now it's killing you. You must get the training, or you'll both die." She stood up and placed her hands on her hips as though she challenged them to a fight. "Look, it doesn't matter if you're both going willingly or I drag you there by your necks. But you're going, and I'm taking you there."

CHAPTER 5

The entrance is somewhere inside Sector Forty-Eight." Plexo said while turning away, distracted by something he had been working on before their arrival. He tinkered over a panel filled with slowly twirling colors and then returned his attention to Kerriah and Crix. "It's something that few have ever been privy to aside from orb-bearing individuals." He turned back to his tinkering.

"Plexo?" Kerriah wasn't satisfied by the vague explanation.

"Yes?" He replied with a half-turn of his head.

"We need to know what to do next?"

"Ah yes, just travel through Gammac Corridor Pizan; Sector Forty-Eight is on the far side."

Kerriah bit her lip and stared at the floor for a minute, trying not to get upset with someone who had always been immensely helpful in the past. "Plexo," she said in a subdued tone.

"Yes, Kerriah?" He continued tinkering.

"Plexo!" She shouted with a stomp of her foot.

Plexo's body flinched, and he turned around with a frightened look. "Oh my! What is it?"

"I--" She paused to look over both shoulders at Crix and Jesselle, who remained timidly in the background. "We need you. We know how to get to Sector Forty-Eight. What then?" She shrugged. "We have no instructions as there are no Tolagons to provide them. We only have you."

Plexo massaged his forehead for a second, appearing uncharacteristically perplexed. "I do apologize. Between finishing the final stages of the Zeta mirror rebuild and oddities in my ship's intelligence systems, I'm finding my focus somewhat out-of-tune."

Plexo and Joric worked feverishly to reverse engineer the remaining corridors so that they could rebuild the Zeta mirror, which had been offline since Crix ordered the Marcks to destroy it years earlier. Plexo and Pira, the only other Luminar in the UMO system, were concerned about Eesolan. With Zeta disabled, there was no way to know if Zearic and the Thraxons had been able to locate their home world in a mad quest for the white orb. They could only hope the far-side mirror was still intact and not guarded by Thraxon warships. The alternative without the far side mirror was to create an open portal in the direction of Eesolan, and free-form travel, which was almost unthinkable, as it could land them nearly anywhere in the galaxy. However, though this was originally how the Luminar deep-space explorers paved their interstellar corridor path through the galaxy.

Kerriah took a step toward Plexo and lowered her tone. "It's okay. It's just that, as you know, these two have been in possession of orbs for too long now, and it's taking a toll on both. They need the Tolagon training."

51

"Of course. I again am truly sorry for my inattentiveness. It's my understanding that, once inside Forty-Eight, Crix will need to attach the bracer to his arm and energize it with the blue orb. The signet within the bracer will reveal the location. It is not only a map but a key." He looked at Jesselle. "I realize that you do not have a bracer, as all others were destroyed. However, if the future follows history, you should receive a new one upon completing your training."

Kerriah looked back at Crix. "Got that?"

Crix gave a hesitant nod. "Thank you, Plexo. And I am sorry for destroying the Zeta mirror."

"You've nothing to be sorry for, Crix. You did what needed to be done at the time," Plexo replied with a smile.

Kerriah turned to leave and then stopped. "Plexo, there's one other thing I wanted to ask you."

"Certainly."

"I believe you originally told Crix that the illusion of Crix's mendac appearance was finite, that it would go away over time. But, when I found him in the core, it was gone until he re-energized his body with the orb. We both agree that it seems like it's permanently tied to the blue orb."

"Yes, that it would seem. What I said was, of course, a theory. Since the orb had bound to his cells at a level we'd never seen before, it was impossible to put that to a proper test. What I do know is that no other Tolagon had mastered the secrets of the orbs like Corin. His ability to mix the unique power of two orbs was astounding. The yellow orb created the psychological veil, but

52

the blue orb unlocks it." Plexo looked over at Crix. "Is this not what you want?"

Crix shrugged. "I want whatever Kerriah wants."

Plexo tilted his head with a smile. "Oh, fascinating. I've always found the intimate love for another individual inspiring." He approached Crix and looked him straight in the eyes. "You will learn to master this with your training. I'm certain of it. Once finished, you will be able to turn it on and off at will. Remember, you are your own person and have earned well-deserved respect from those around you."

Crix dropped his head momentarily as though trying to hold back tears and then wrapped his arms around Plexo. Plexo's body stiffened for a moment, and then he gave Crix a few gentle pats on his back before Crix pulled away, saying nothing more.

"Farewell, Crix. I hope to see you again soon as a fully trained and ordained Tolagon. It will be a pleasant day indeed," Plexo said with a friendly wave goodbye.

CHAPTER 6

The boarding platform slid back into the ship's hull, and the outer door hissed shut. Jesselle, Kerriah, and Crix fastened into rigid seats inside the small ship's cockpit. Kerriah pulled a lever down and grasped the controls. The ship hummed to life and rose from the deck. Their final departure from the landing bay located on outpost thirteen on Miran, the second moon of Nathasia, would take them to the inner mirror of the Quadril Corridor.

It took a few days of travel to get to Miran, and Kerriah couldn't stop thinking about their visit with Plexo. Her interactions with him were pushy and cold. She didn't want to be like this. Insensitive and driven. The uncertainty regarding the safety of his home world, Eesolan, and the persistent issues with his ship's computers had to be taking their toll.

Kerriah took a brief look at her two quiet passengers; each of them appeared as though they were going to an execution versus an exciting journey to discover how to tame the powers they had inherited. Crix's face nearly disappeared behind his Tolagon white beard as he stared out with a blank look through the window. Jesselle would occasionally place her hand over her face, gaze down at her lap, and then snap a glance up as though something may have snuck up on her.

"Come on. Lighten up, guys, this is exciting. You're getting closer to having the answers you both have been looking for regarding the orbs. Stop with the gloom faces," Kerriah said before slowly pushing the thrusters forward, sending the small vessel towards Quadril. She sighed. This would be a long trip with these two nervous corpses on board.

***

The small, nimble ship arrived quicker than expected at the nearside Quadril mirror. The sizable monolithic disk filled their view as they approached. Its dark, textured, metallic outer edges contrasted with the mirror reflection of the inner portal. A UMO patrol ship stood guard near the entrance. The light flashed on the instrument panel, and a repeating chirp indicated the patrol ship hailed them. Kerriah pressed the switch near the flashing light, opening their communications.

"Unidentified ship, please state your business and destination," the voice buzzed through the speakers.

"Outer Pizon Sector Forty-Eight, our destination is classified, per the chancellor's office," Kerriah responded.

"Please submit your encoded UMO directive," the patrol ship replied.

Kerriah pulled a thin, transparent card from a nearly hidden pocket on her shirt sleeve, inserted it into the panel, and pressed another switch. After a few minutes, there was a response. "Confirmed, standby for routine scanning."

Two small probes released from the UMO ship and began circling them. Strobing red beams fanned out from the probes and waved across their hull. After another few minutes, the voice returned. "You're cleared to enter Gammac Corridor Quadril. Safe travels."

Kerriah gripped the forward propulsion controls and gave them a steady push. The transport slowly approached the giant mirror. Their ship's reflection grew more prominent as they neared and appeared to be in a headlong crash trajectory with another vessel. The silent mirror shimmered brightly around the ship's nose as it breached the corridor, and the crew's view changed from a reflection of themselves to a negative picture as they entered. The reversed light inside the corridor made the stars black and the darkness of space a ghostly white. Crix snapped a look at Kerriah, who he barely recognized. She turned his way, with her ordinarily black hair now devoid of color and her usually pale skin a pure onyx.

The view around them looked like something from a strange dream rather than any reality they knew. The last time Kerriah and Crix had traveled through the portals, they were too nervously focused on the Dispor mission briefing and didn't take full notice of the side effects of traversing the corridors.

At the time, the likelihood that their journey was a one-way trip into one of the most terrifying places in the UMO-controlled systems kept them adequately distracted. This time they took in the altered reality.

As the ship slid fully into the gammac corridor, the lights blinked, and the passengers felt as though they had been unconscious for an unknown amount of time, though it was only for a couple of seconds. Their brains swam inside their skulls, and their hearts momentarily stopped and then raced at an irregular pace to catch up. It was a brief, yet jarring, light, disturbing experience. The nose of their ship dipped into the far side mirror with a black radiance as it passed through. Normal light returned, and the view of space appeared familiar, though they were far from Nathasia and the core UMO system. They followed the same procedure as they traversed Delta and Pizon. The trip took twelve hours between corridors with the transport's radiant drive system, but they had finally reached Sector Forty-Eight. The interstellar space here appeared darker, and they noticed the brightness of the distant stars a little more than normal.

"Okay, Crix," Kerriah said. "You're up."

Crix sat staring at the onyx bracer he clenched with his cold, clammy hand. The center blue signet's white swirls always put him in a trance-like state when he gazed at it too long. His wide eyes looked like a scared animal cornered by a predator, which didn't go unnoticed by his fellow passengers. Jesselle reached out to touch his shoulder, hopefully breaking his frozen trance and bringing him back into the moment. However, Crix immediately flinched and returned an icy stare.

"Crix!" Kerriah scolded, trying to get him to ease up a bit so that he could focus on the task. "Do just like Plexo instructed. We need to see the map, the one that will activate with the orb's power inside this sector."

He took a deep, calming breath and then clasped the bracer around his forearm. It fit loosely, without a hand to secure it, but it held enough to activate. The white lines swirling around its surface began to move quicker, almost in pace with his heartbeat. He laid his head back and drew the orb's power. His body ignited brighter than normal, and the bracer, except for the blue signet, turned white. His head popped up, and his eyes were devoid of color. Unfamiliar symbols scrolled across the signet's surface.

"What are those?" Jesselle asked.

Kerriah's forehead scrunched as she stared at them. "I'm not certain, but I'll bet they're Luminar."

Jesselle shrugged. "Okay, do you know how to read them?"

"Nope," Kerriah said and then glanced back at the ship's control panel. "But this ship does. This is a diplomatic transport we borrowed from the UMO and has all known dialects installed on its translation systems."

Kerriah stood and grabbed Crix's arm. "Come on, Crix. We need you to bring this over to the system's onboard translator." She tugged him up to his feet, and he took a few obedient steps forward as though in a waking dream. She rolled the bracer above a glass panel, and a display of a nearby planetary system formed.

"Gero Six," she said. "It looks like it's near the toxic planet Gero Six." The lone planet Gero Six was desolate and located on the outskirts of Sector Forty-Eight. Tidally locked around the red dwarf star Irio, the planet was uninhabitable, with clouds of sulfuric acid covering much of the atmosphere. Hence, it served no strategic interest and was ironically the perfect place for a secret gateway to hide.

"According to his map, the entrance should be about twenty-six million kilometers from Gero Six. I'm locking that into

SONG OF THE LAGGORNS

the navigation now." She tapped a few keys, touched a display on the console, and then tapped a few more.

"All set. Crix—" She shook him, snapping him from the orb's lock on the bracer. The color in his eyes returned to normal, and his shoulders relaxed.

"That was strange," he said. "I could see it."

"See what?" Kerriah replied.

"The gateway. It was as clear to me as if I was . . ." he looked up. "I was standing right in front of it."

"Yeah, well, buckle yourself back in because we're headed that way." The ship's radiant drives flashed to life and blipped away into the direction of the Irio system.

CHAPTER 7

The ship's Luminar-designed radiant drives made short work of their travel to the outer system in Sector Forty-Eight. The advanced drive systems halved the travel time between systems and was another significant technological advancement the Luminar's had provided. The UMO had begun converting their fleet ships from the older quantum drive soon after the close of the second Thraxon war.

With stormy grey clouds stirred with an abundant mixture of yellow, Gero Six stood foreboding in the distance from their cockpit window. The ship's navigation systems gave an audible chime, indicating their arrival.

"We're here," Kerriah announced. "If the navigation reads the Luminar dialect correctly, we should be near Gabor's gateway."

Both Crix and Jesselle moved slowly, their faces drawn and pale. "Guys, you look like you're going to get sick."

Kerriah's frustration with them had begun to hit a tipping point. She knew they were both in a broken and anxious state of mind, but the constant need to push them had started taking its toll on her nerves. "Come on! No one is getting sick on my ship. Get your e-vos suits on and your butts into the airlock now!"

She hated playing the drill sergeant. She also knew they both needed this type of motivation, so if this is what it took. . . . "Let's get moving!" She gave a last-second verbal kick to place a fire under their backsides.

***

Crix and Jesselle fumbled clumsily with their e-vos suits, the official UMO-designated essential vacuum of space suits. Not having a background in utilizing them, they had to follow the interactive instructions on their proper use and testing before staging themselves into the ship's small airlock.

These two were poor company for Kerriah. Their nervousness and silence during the trip had made her feel like she had two strangers onboard. She just wanted to get this over with and hopefully help them move forward with the rest of their lives.

Jesselle held her helmet for a moment and stared at Crix as he finished clasping the pressure seal around his left glove. Without his right hand to assist, his suiting up lagged. She bit nervously on the inside of her lip and tapped her finger against the helmet's visor.

"Crix," she said in a soft, barely audible voice.

Crix leaned down and awkwardly grabbed his helmet with his left hand and the empty glove of his right. "Yeah."

"Despite our differences. I'm glad we're doing this together."

Crix looked up at her with a blank expression. "Great," he replied just before plopping the helmet over his head and fumbling to latch down the stiff clasps.

Jesselle closed her eyes for a moment and then gently placed the helmet over her head. "I tried," she whispered to herself.

CHAPTER 8

A re you ready?" Kerriah said over their comms. Crix gave a thumbs-up to the camera mounted in the corner. "Okay, here we go. Three . . . two . . . one—" The external door hissed open, and they both floated into the darkness of space.

Crix squeezed the control grip on his e-vos, releasing the light propulsion jets. He shot forward, ahead of Jesselle. His nerves moved away from fear and uncertainty to anxiousness and enthusiasm. He continued juicing the suit's propulsion until both the transport and Jesselle were visibly small in the distance.

"Crix, wait up!" Jesselle's voice crackled through the comm.

He ignored her request. Instead, he let up on the controls and allowed himself to coast freely through the stillness around him. His forward momentum continued to push him ahead, though it was impossible to tell, as there were no objects to judge his distance aside from Gero Six, which was too far away. He closed his eyes and drew the orb's power. He had to take care not to overload the suit's circuitry, yet he needed enough power to activate the bracer's signet. The blue glow filled his view. A tingling sensation swarmed around his forearm and turned into pinpricks.

"Wow! Do you see that?" Jesselle said. Her voice sounded excited and hopeful for the first time since Crix had met her. He slowly opened his eyes.

A massive, shadowy door stood directly before him. The outer frame gushed with dark-grey clouds of gas and particles. Its sides ran smoothly down from a jagged top, which looked like teeth from some great beast. There wasn't any light in its center, just a black void surrounded by the long, ghostly skeleton. The creepy, three-dimensional doorway appeared to have been ripped from a dark lord's castle of ancient horror and flung into space.

With nothing to slow his forward momentum, Crix still moved briskly toward the doorway. He gave a small shot of propulsion to the right, nudging his trajectory slightly to the left and steering himself straight into the center of the massive gateway.

"Crix, wait for Jesselle," Kerriah's voice chimed in through his comm.

He kept his eyes focused directly ahead. Nothing was going to stop him, and nothing would slow him up. He was about to enter the gateway all other Tolagons had entered before him. Every hair on his body stood on end, and his heart pounded as he passed through the center. But nothing was on the other side, just the distant view of Gero Six.

"What?" he whispered. What was he missing? Where was Gabor and these mystical aliens? This couldn't be it.

"Crix," Kerriah's voice returned. "You have to wait for Jesselle. Do you remember it takes two orbs to open the gate?"

"Gahh . . . right." In his enthusiasm, he had forgotten about why they towed her along. "Great. Where is she?"

"Right behind you," Jesselle said.

Crix turned around to look, and she bumped right into him. "Watch it! Are you trying to kill us both?" he said, annoyed by her presence.

"Uh, no. I'm just trying to keep up with you. We're supposed to do this together. Remember?"

Crix snatched her arm before they separated. "Okay fine. Carefully power up your orb, and I will mine," he said sharply.

"Okay."

"Carefully!"

"I got it, I got it." Inside her helmet, a light-red shimmer slowly intensified, drowning out her face until nothing but an opaque red light appeared. Crix joined and slowly drew upon his orb's power. The gateway's black void flashed. Dozens of liquid black fingers reached outward and clutched them both, their bodies went numb, and their minds blanked. Kerriah's voice faded into the distance.

"Crix! What's happening . . . Crix!"

CHAPTER 9

As Crix's thoughts returned, he sensed he had traveled billions of light years yet somehow lost track of time. The strange paradox consumed his mind until sensation returned to his limbs, and he felt his arms and legs floating freely with zero pressure, though he couldn't see his surroundings.

His heart jumped as cold fingers wisped across his arms and chest, followed by a shiver and tightness inside his muscles. The air suddenly expelled from his lungs like a brutal punch to the gut, and a feeling of claustrophobia leaped into his thoughts. The pressure intensified, and he found he couldn't take a breath to refill the empty cavities in his chest. He panicked. His arms locked into place, and he couldn't even grasp his throat. His heart sped faster, and his chest cramped, followed quickly by a stabbing pain. He let out a soundless scream as his life flashed before him, every thought, vision, feeling, emotion, scent, and sound. The contents of his life's memories spilled out.

His vision returned, now clearer than ever before. He could see details, even the most minuscule things, without getting close. The pain was gone, and he tried to take a breath, but no air came in, and no air flowed out from his lungs. They were empty but also not craving oxygen. His mind felt rested, recharged, and sharper than it'd been in years.

His body dangled in a sea of murky green dashed with wisps of midnight blue. Shadowy trees laced the area with organic bases swaying like fluid. Their spanning limbs dripped like oil into an unseen vastness above. In the distance, a flickering serpent slid between the trunks, moving closer as it twisted its way around the celestial forest.

Crix glanced side-to-side as he tried to track its slithering movements. Fear gripped his throat, and he couldn't help but feel trapped inside an ancient painting clinging to the dingy walls of some black castle—a masterpiece of a madman.

Crix froze as he caught sight of a slender figure nearby. He turned his head to see what terror would greet him next. Jesselle stared back at him with wide eyes. He tried to speak to her, but no words came out. His missing voice persisted even as he tried to shout her name.

He looked back, and there was nothing, a void, a blackness. At that moment, he noticed his e-vos suit was gone. *Oh, Great.* He would concern himself with that later and instead focus forward. As he turned, he felt the presence of something close. Jesselle was no longer there, but a serpent stood upright with dozens of wiry limbs curled in his direction. He extended his leg, trying to feel for something solid. His toes stopped and flattened onto firm ground. The serpent remained in the same spot, its wire limbs shifting in an unfelt breeze as though guarding the way forward.

Crix tried to step back, but his foot slipped into nothingness. So he took the only path and stepped forward into the murkiness and the serpent's arms. Its limbs closed like a coffin around him, and he felt his stomach drop into a free-fall. His body slapped down upon a hard surface without the physical throb of impact, and he winced, even without the enticement of pain. There was no light or sound, not even the steadily increasing thumps of his heartbeat. His senses screamed out for stimulation, something to let him know he was still alive.

"What are you doing here?" a screeching voice entered his ears, the first sound since he had passed through the doorway. The language was something he had never heard before, yet he understood the words. A few seconds passed, and Crix remained still, not knowing what to say. Wasn't it obvious why he was there? Wasn't this where Tolagons came to train?

"Why are you here?" the voice asked again. A shining face accented in black appeared from the void, as though it peeked into an unseen window standing right above Crix. Its ovular eyes bulged back at him with intensity.

"I'm here—I—" His mind fogged over as he struggled to get the words out. "I'm here for training."

"Training?" the strange face replied.

"Y-Yes. Tolagon training."

Its mouth slowly quivered open, bearing crimson fangs. It turned its head to peer at someone else nearby. Its eyes gleamed against a phantom light, and it turned back, glaring at Crix. "We do not train . . . Tolagons . . . We consume them. Ours is to create old life from new, destroy what is wrong, and reset the dark ways of this present existence. You are a mere tool for our disposal."

"Wait!" Crix shouted. "What are you? Isn't this Gabor?"

68

Another face peeked down from a void window. It appeared older, and its eyes pinched at the center like an hourglass.

"Gaaborrr?" it screeched back. "You have entered Antathaw. We can see your soul, and what is there is not Tolagon. You are not even true to yourself."

As they spoke, he couldn't help thinking they looked familiar, like something from a distant memory or dream. He quickly shook off the thought.

"What? I opened the gateway, the door to Gabor. I don't understand." Crix patted his fingers across his face and chest, noticing short fur and a longer muzzle. It was his natural Andor body, and he was naked. He instantly locked his knees together and placed his hand over his mouth upon this realization.

The first face looked at the elder and grinned. The eyes of the older face pulled in tighter at the center, turning the hourglass into four separate eyes.

"Hmmm . . . you are ashamed of who you are, as you ought to be—a worthless wretch, unworthy of the power you possess. You have arrived here because you have been deemed unfit. We will feast on your sssoul, and you will become ours." The voice turned from a hiss to a roar. It opened its mouth, and its dark-red fangs protruded. Its skeletal torso emerged, dipping its head down with its black mouth wide open. Crix felt his thoughts and strength drain away before the dark face retracted and snarled.

"Equus," the elder's voice boomed.

"I, too, smell Equus," the other face replied.

"He cannot be controlled." The elder's face pulled further away from Crix. Numerous rumblings of growls and slithering of hisses emerged from all around him. "Your soul is tainted. Go away from here and never return, or we will feast on your soul, tainted or otherwise."

Crix suddenly realized where he had seen these faces before. During his waking nightmares from overusing the orb's power, these were the same faces of horror that flashed into his view.

"Wait!" Crix shouted. He needed answers, even if they came from these strange dark lords. "What am I supposed to do now?"

"Gahhh . . ." the first face snarled with frustration.

The elder's eyes formed back to hourglasses. "Die and release the power within. You are of no value alive. The mere sight of you is a disgrace and desecrates our sacrosanct sphere. Now go!"

Crix's body drew upward, and the murky trees flashed into his view, and then audible chirps and the whisper of his breathing filled his ears. The transport remained stationary before him.

"Crix?" Kerriah's voice chimed through his helmet comm. "Are you okay?"

"I-I don't know."

"Where's Jesselle?"

70

CHAPTER 10

I don't understand. What do you mean they wouldn't train you?" Kerriah stood back as Crix finished removing his e-vos suit. He tossed his gloves and kicked his boots across the room. She tried to help him with the body plate release locks, but he flinched away angrily before wrestling it off himself and slamming the synthetic parts onto the floor.

"They said I was unfit, unworthy, and a disgrace." Crix could not look at her. He stared down with swelling red eyes that would occasionally look up at the ceiling as if attempting to keep the tears back.

"Well, this is just ridiculous. You're unfit? You just friggen saved the system from a power-hungry tyrant, a genocidal, bloodthirsty species, and an oppressive mechanical army. How in this lifetime, or any lifetime, how is that unworthy?" Her eyes focused with anger, and she bit into her lip. She placed her hand on his back, and he broke down. He sobbed so violently his body heaved with every breath and shuddering wail.

I can't believe this. Kerriah massaged her palm across her forehead. *Where is Jesselle? She still hasn't returned.*

She looked down at Crix, a broken spirit with no way to fix him. His possession of the blue orb could be a liability in his current mental state. She knew this but would never dare tell him. She knelt beside him and wrapped her arm across his shoulders and let him cry out the pain. It took longer than she could have imagined, but she stayed there to comfort him as her heart broke and her mind spun with thoughts.

***

A while later, Jesselle appeared outside the gateway. She returned to the transport and sat down with Kerriah and Crix to explain her experience inside Gabor. Something had changed with her. Her eyes appeared focused and her confidence elevated. Kerriah hadn't known her to be like this. Since that day two years ago, when they found her succumbing to the very power she wielded so effectively against her weeks earlier, Jesselle was a broken shell. But now, she spoke as though she had everything in her life under control and her future paved with certainty.

"Just so I fully understand you, Jesselle," Kerriah said, leaning in with a slight squint. "This council agreed to train you as the red-orb-bearing Tolagon?"

"Correct," Jesselle firmly replied.

Kerriah peeked over at Crix, whose face had turned dark over the past few minutes as Jesselle explained her experience inside Gabor. "But they told Crix he's unworthy?" she sneered. "So the one that sacrificed himself to save . . . all of us . . . gets told he's worthless, and the one that—no offense—but the person who worked for Zearic is embraced. Is that about right? I mean, am I missing something here?" Right now, the Council of Gabor was not high on Kerriah's list of respected entities.

Jesselle sat up straight, and her expression didn't change as she answered. "That's correct. However, there's something you need to know. As part of my training, I gained certain knowledge that may change how you look at this." Kerriah and Crix both looked curiously at each other.

Kerriah's shoulders lifted, and they looked back at Jesselle. "Okay, please continue."

"When Tolagon Corin Emberook betrayed the council by deceiving them and the UMO Security Council to buy time for Zearic and later used the yellow and blue orb for personal gain, he lost the right to name his successor. They will not recognize Crix as a Tolagon nor train him."

"That's not his fault!" Kerriah raised her voice in protest. "He can't help what his fathe—or whoever handed him the orb did. He's proved himself a Tolagon by his own right and actions. Crix never used it for his own gain."

Crix shot a glance at Kerriah after she made her last remark. She squeezed her eyes closed for a second, suddenly remembering the annexis game. "Crix, that doesn't count. You were still saving someone's life."

"It does matter," Jesselle responded. "His action cost an entire civilization."

Crix smacked his hand against the wall in anger upon opening the old wound. "I made a mistake! I get it! I can't take it back. How much longer do I have to pay for it?"

Jesselle put her hand up to calm him. "I'm not judging you, Crix. Zearic certainly had no rights to give me the orb either, and I also did things unworthy of a Tolagon."

"Then why—" Kerriah pursed her lips and shook her head. As unfair as it seemed, it wasn't worth getting into a bitter back and forth with Jesselle.

"I know what you're going to ask, Kerriah. Why me and not him? They wouldn't say, but I suspect—" Jesselle stopped and shook her head. "I don't know." She uncomfortably shifted in her seat and then cleared her throat. "There's one other thing worth mentioning. Crix never actually entered Gabor."

Crix rolled his eyes and took a frustrated exhale. "Just stop! Stop it! I don't care anymore."

"Now wait a minute, Crix." Kerriah raised her index finger to pause his objection. "What do you mean he didn't enter Gabor? I watched clearly from the transport as you both entered the gateway."

"Right," Jesselle said. "The gateway can take you to two different locations. We know of Gabor, and that's where most Tolagons go for knowledge and training. However, there's another place, a dark place where the—" she stopped to clear her throat again, "where the unfit go."

Crix's hand gripped his pant leg, and his knuckles turned white. Hearing the word "unfit" again was about to send him over the edge from the look in his eyes. Tension, boiling blood, and numbness flushed across his body.

74

Kerriah pressed her thumb into her forehead and briefly closed her eyes as she asked the next question. "So what is this other place?"

"Antathaw," Jesselle responded in a serious voice. She stared intensely at Crix. "I'll have to confess; I was surprised to see him here when I returned, as the knowledge provided to me indicates that anyone who enters Antathaw is consumed by its guardians. He would leave, yes, but not as himself." She paused and gave Crix a sideways stare. "Although obviously angry, he still appears to be himself."

"They said my soul was tainted by Equus."

"Equus? What is Equus?" Kerriah asked.

"It is the great Laggorn of the beasts. Troika's creator. The one that Suros told me about. Whose power, along with all of Troika's history, all of the fallen Andors, is contained within the Tersik crysta—" Crix stopped and scrunched his brow as if having a sudden revelation.

"You mean that crystal we took from the sacred forest?"

Crix leaned his elbows down on his knees and placed his hand over his mouth. "Yes," He mumbled through his fingers. He remained frozen in thought until Kerriah became irritated.

"Crix, you've got to let me in, or I can't help. What's on your mind? What about the crystal has you so provoked?"

He gave a quick head shake and sat up straight. "Nothing," he replied. "I need you to take me to Nathasia."

Kerriah drew her head back in shock. "Nathasia? Why would we need to go there? The planet is off-limits to non-science personnel. It's still hazardous, and they are trying desperately to find a way to turn it back into a habitable world again; though, at best, it will take generations to undo the damage the Thraxons left behind."

Crix looked at her with exhausted eyes. "I know. You just need to take me there. If you care about me, you will do this. Please."

"It's not a good idea, Crix. I'm worried you're not in the right frame of mind, and we're just inviting trouble by going there."

"I can help. I can restore that world."

"How?" Kerriah's voice cracked as she pleaded for clarity. She clenched her fist and pulled them tightly into her chest. "Please communicate with me! What's on your mind?"

"I will, but I need you to trust me now."

"I do trust you, but no. We're not going to Nathasia."

Crix drew closer to her and stared straight into her eyes. She could see there was no turning him away from this idea. "Please, Kerriah. I need you to support me on this." His voice softened, and his eyes rounded.

"Crix . . . damn you," she whispered to herself. She dropped her fists and leaned her head back, feeling drained. "Fine. But you need to let me know what's on your mind as soon as you've had time to pull yourself together." Kerriah looked at him, her heart sank, and she didn't have the strength to argue or question him anymore.

Whatever was on that condemned planet to which she had vowed never to return, she hoped it would at least give him some peace and closure. Her eyes filled heavy with tears, but she fought them back and turned the ship toward Nathasia.

CHAPTER 11

Crix walked back into the ship's small cargo hold and rifled through his bags. His eyes perked up when he found it—the Tersik Crystal. The hazy violet crystal winked back at him, and he reached down to pull it out. After his rescue from the core, Plexo had returned it to him with explicit instructions to be careful if he ever decided to energize it with the orb's power. Plexo felt he had no right to keep it from Crix, being one of the last known survivors of the Andor species. It was out of respect for Crix and the civilization that had lost their lives.

Crix hung onto it and never let it get too far from his reach. The guilt would likely kill him if it were ever lost or stolen. He knew that, so he packed it for the journey to Gabor. Now he knew why he had it and what needed to be done, though he couldn't tell anyone, not even Kerriah. They wouldn't understand, especially her. But it was something he had to do, something he could make right.

He sat down in the corner and crossed his legs. Cradling the crystal in his palm, he stared into it, focusing on the tiny light inside. Equus was within him because of his link to the crystal. Equus was within the crystal. It was why he was still alive. He energized his hand into a bright-blue aura with a small amount of the orb's power. His eyes opened wide, and his jaw dropped.

Images flooded his view and poured into his mind, filling every crevasse and pocket of mental capacity. He witnessed the birth of a galaxy and a system encompassing an intense blue star. As the chaos of this creation peaked, luminescent beings emerged from an anomalous ripple in the fabric of reality. They evolved into a flame of colors as the planets took shape. Life developed, and the glowing beings formed into physical bodies: *Laggorns*. Life spilled from their worlds and spiraling bridges spanned between them as the azure star's light simmered from their strange organic matter.

As the images filled his mind, he somehow understood what had happened. The blue star of Auroro flashed, and everything around it turned black. Power was left behind, and a nebula emerged. Life and energy fused into the molecules of gas and particles. The impossible life created by the Laggorns survived. Its massive shape swept freely into interstellar space, changing its form as it moved. The life and power inside gushed and churned as the remnants of the Laggorns merged into spheres of energy.

An unfamiliar array of sounds filled his ears like an orchestra picking up its musical tempo. Hazy whistles and burbling purrs synthesized through a rippling cosmic stream until they found the rhythm of his heartbeat—the celestial sounds curled around him, tingling his body in the cool comfort of disarming numbness. The whistles faded into a gentle echoing of tones, and Crix could not only hear but feel their chorus. The song was from the Laggorns. Though he couldn't understand their words, he knew they sung about their love of creation and their children.

The orbs, their power, and their origins all started to make sense. Cyos and the orbs were born of the unique energy signatures of the Laggorns that had died within the star's blast. A combination of the orbs' power and the Tersik Crystal . . . it was the key—the key left by Equus.

A vision of a ship of silver and light emerged. The glowing creatures onboard seized the orbs and disappeared behind a portal. But it wasn't the first time they had come. They took the white orb first. *Why did Cyos allow this to happen?* There were no answers, and the question scrolled into his head. His heart pounded, and his eyes burned as he continued to stare at the crystal.

Four of the Laggorns that survived the supernova were bound together and cast through space. They eventually found the Oro System. Crix had seen this before through Suro's vision. The Laggorn Trias died and formed the sea-covered moon of Thale. Equus, Vorvol, and Albizous took their residence on Soorak. Now depleted after so many ages away from the star of Auroro, the Laggorns remained confined to Troika and built the great Equine species, the Andors.

They were all here, every Andor that had died and their souls departed for Mothoa. Their souls were imprinted here, in this crystal. It was overwhelming to behold, and he could see all their lives flash before him. The creatures in Antathaw wished to build upon destruction. But there was a place that was already destroyed—a place of death where Crix could create life.

He took a jarring breath, and his focus returned to the present. He looked around at the cargo and supplies secured on shelves and strapped to the walls and floor. Everything seems so small, so insignificant. His purpose was clear, and his destiny still lay ahead, unfinished.

***

Crix returned to the ship's cockpit, where Kerriah's fingers tapped several panels, adjusting their coordinates and ETA for Nathasia. They had just passed through Pizon and headed for

Delta. She turned around, gave him a half-smile, and then returned her attention to the ship's instruments. Crix's love for her would never die, but she knew so little of what he struggled with inside, mostly because he didn't want to talk about it or let anyone into his thoughts. It made him angry, and he didn't want to be upset at this person he so loved. Still, he would have to leave her again, and he had no idea how to let her know, as she would undoubtedly fight him over what he was about to do.

Crix settled back into a seat behind her and massaged his chin through his beard as he thought through the coming days. Jesselle remained in the sleeping quarters after hours of relentless probing from Kerriah as to why they were going back to Nathasia, questions even she was unsure of but stood steadfast to help Crix in any way he needed.

"Crix," her voice broke through the gentle humming of the ship's propulsion system and the occasional beep from the cockpit's instrument panel, "Jesselle told me something. . . . Something that she didn't want me to tell you, but I feel you should know."

Crix's eyes sparked, and his muscles tensed up in his seat over the thought of something Jesselle wanted to keep from him. "Really? What did she say?"

Kerriah let out a deep exhale and gave him a serious stare back. "You can't say anything to her. I agreed that I wouldn't tell you right now, but I feel you need to know. Whatever you're thinking about doing on Nathasia, you need to have all the facts first."

"Okay," Crix calmly replied, but the near-constant shifting in his seat gave away his nerves.

"When she received her training, the council entered her mind and retrieved her thoughts and memories. Somehow, from those memories, they decided to grant me the yellow orb of Nathasia. That I was somehow the worthy beneficiary."

"What?" His voice rose.

She raised her hand to settle him. "Now I know what you're thinking, and I'm not even sure I'm going to take on the role or if my body could even accept it. It's put a lot on my mind as if I didn't have enough to think about already. I need you to know all the facts but remain calm and not make rash decisions."

Crix smacked his hand against the armrest and stared up, his eyes red with frustration. He shook his head before looking back at Kerriah. "This whole Tolagon thing," his face tightened, "it's absurd."

"I don't understand. What's that supposed to mean?"

He turned his attention out the cockpit window. "Who do we think we are? Some sort of gods? We're not. We're just puppets manipulated by Gabor, the UMO, and those around us. Just pushed and shoved into whatever situation they see fit. I give and give, and they take and take." He looked down at his chest with a scowl. "It seems like anyone that has one of these suffers the same fate."

"Crix," Kerriah said in a near whisper. "Many of us are in a similar situation. Of course, your orb makes you unique, but we are all suffering. As far as being gods, well, I agree. You're not, but if you didn't have the orb, well . . . I don't need to explain where we'd be now."

"It has nothing to do with me. Someone else would have filled the role. There are plenty of heroic sorts out there."

"Maybe," she shrugged, "or maybe not, but you saved us all. You did—not someone else."

Crix sat quietly for a few minutes, continuing to stare out the window. "You're right," he said sharply. "I'm happy for you. I think you'd make an amazing Tolagon. I mean, what better choice could there be?" He nervously pulled his empty sleeve tight and shook his head again.

"Right," she said under her breath and gazed out the window. "It's just so much to think about. You've had your whole life to prepare and become acquainted with the orb, and you've done an amazing job of using it with no instruction."

"At least you know they'll accept and train you."

Her face appeared to wither with sadness. "I know you're hurt, Crix. Gabor hurt you at a time when you were already wounded and really needed their help. I disagree with their decision regarding you, and that's a big reason I'm skeptical over their decision with me."

"No, don't be. It's the right choice. I know that now. The system could use someone like you to have this power. You'll always use it for good . . . to protect its citizens. My destiny changed the day Troika was destroyed." He looked more determined than ever.

She stared at him quietly as though trying to read his thoughts. "I really wish you'd let me in. Let me know what's going on in that head of yours so that I can help."

"Believe me, if I could, I would," he replied.

CHAPTER 12

"Any particular place you want to set down at?" Kerriah asked Crix as their transport circled over Nathasia, trying to be as covert as possible, given the planet's prohibited status. The small ship could go unnoticed if it didn't hang around in orbit too long or fly aimlessly through its airspace, searching for a spot to land.

"On a mountain."

She rolled her eyes. "Okay, so some mountain. Crix, Nathasia is a big planet; I need something more than 'some mountain.' Besides, landing on a mountain is less than ideal."

"Just a mountain. Any mountain. I want to be high up overlooking the horizon."

"Great," she said, shaking her head. "How about the Corvid Mountains?" It was the only one she knew of, having heard Creedith mention it when she was here before.

"That sounds good."

"Ooookay." She set the ship's navigation to the Corvid Mountains on Nathasia and began their descent into the planet's atmosphere.

The thick, hazy, green-tinted clouds swished by, giving more of an appearance of diving into a deep sea versus entering a planetary atmosphere. The ship jolted and trembled as the turbulent winds outside took their toll. They felt their guts drop as their descent accelerated. Kerriah pulled back on the throttle, trying to control their plunge. The ship's collision alarm squealed out and a shadowy mountain peak coated with a tint of red flashed into view. Kerriah banked the transport to the left, clearing the massive crest before slowing to a hover above the range.

She squinted as she took the ship lower for a better view of the mountain surface and then engaged the ship's scanners. A display screen from the instrument panel lit up with an enhanced image and the words:

:algae: chorahydra variant . . . recent classification, known only on Nathasia . . . Unique characteristics – binds to energy sources where it can rapidly multiply.:

She looked back at Crix.

"This can't be. I think it's the same algae that attacked me years ago."

Crix unclipped his seat harness and stood. He pressed his face to the cockpit window, staring down at the reddish glaze. "It's everywhere. It seems to prefer the mountaintop, probably trying to access the strongest energy source here, the trace solar energy that's seeping through the fog. Not to worry."

Kerriah scowled. "What do you mean 'not to worry?' That algae is extremely hostile. It almost killed me and will likely attack our transport. We cannot set down here or anywhere near this location."

Crix looked back at her and smiled. "I know. I won't let it harm you. Just remain stationary here. Okay?"

"Crix, you really need to start communicating with me. Let me know what's on your mind."

"I've got this. Don't worry," he replied and then left for the rear of the ship.

"I think he's going outside," Jesselle said, crossing her arms and cocking her head to the side.

Kerriah sighed with frustration. "Really?"

The aft door alarm sounded. "Yep." Jesselle smiled while pointing out the window. A blue glow briefly flashed into view and then darted toward the surface.

"Ahhhh . . . damn you, Crix!" She tilted the ship's nose downward and accelerated. "I have to keep an eye on him."

She chased him across the mountainscape, dipping deeper through the fog and across spires of rocks and valleys of red. There was hardly a trace of the non-algae-coated surface across the mountainous peak. Crix stopped above a flat location overlooking a vast territory below. As far as their limited view through the fog could observe, the lands below rippled with the red algae.

Crix looked back at the transport and gave a thumbs up. He raised his palms and released a brilliant blast of blue energy. The algae instantly withered into black dust and receded further and further away as Crix waved his arms around, covering a generous area where he intended the ship to land. He waved his hand, inviting them to land on the freshly cleared site while blasting the algae further from the proposed landing site.

"It may crave energy, but I guess it has its limits," Jesselle observed as the algae withered and turned black against each cast from Crix's blue orb.

Kerriah stared back at Crix, exhausted. She would do anything for him, but he was pushing her to her limits. Setting the ship down anywhere remotely near this hostile organism was a risk she would not usually accept unless there were no alternatives. Yet she slowly leveled the transport and began to lower it down. Its landing gear tapped gently against the hard surface, and the engines quieted from an eardrum-piercing whine to a nearly inaudible hiss.

The boarding deck slid out, and she and Jesselle stepped cautiously outside. "Okay, Crix," Kerriah shouted with a bit of frustration in her tone. "Now what?" She landed the ship a generous distance from the edge, hopefully far enough from any algae that could creep up the rocky wall.

He stood at the cliff's edge and waved her over. She tapped her foot for a few seconds before shaking her head and finally approaching him. "What is it about this place? Please tell me what's so important here."

He said nothing, touched her cheek, and pulled her into a long, soft embrace. His hand stroked the back of her neck as he placed his forehead against hers. He still had a hint of that scent she always loved.

"I love you. . . . I love you so much," he said. "This is something I have to do." He released her and stared closely into her eyes. A tear formed at the corner and trickled down the side of his nose. "I will always be here. Whenever you need me."

Her brow furrowed with both anger and confusion. "What? What do you mean you'll always be here? No! You're coming back with us to Soorak. You can't stay here; you'll die."

"No. I'll live, and so will Troika."

It suddenly hit her with the punch of an attacking battle cruiser. "No, no, no! You're not!" It was that stupid crystal; they should have left the damn thing in those caverns where they had found it. "Please, Crix, don't do something foolish. Please tell me you're not going to—"

"Kerriah," his voice was gentle, and his body began to glow bright with the orb's power, "I have to do this. There's no other way. If you want to save me, let me go."

"But I just got you back!"

He leaned in, curled his body around hers, and kissed her deeply as she protested. "Now go. You must leave now. They are calling me." His quivering hand pulled the crystal from his pocket, and his blue radiance intensified. The ground shook, and the air electrified. She glanced back at Jesselle, who stood with a defensive posture. All the hair on Jesselle's head stood straight out in every direction. Kerriah felt a tickling sensation across her scalp, and she patted her hands across her head, noticing the same with her hair.

"Go!" Crix shouted and then looked skyward. "Please, go now!"

"What? Who? Who's calling you?" she shouted back. "Crix, wait!"

"The ancients. Equus. I shouldn't have brought you here. I-I thought I could . . ." He screamed out and looked back down at her with a grimace, his eyes on fire with azure flames. "You don't understand. I can't stop it! The crystal is calling me . . . forcing my hand. I must . . . follow . . . my . . . destiny!" His voice strained with every word.

A dancing whistle filled her ears, and a purr seemed to cascade from the sky above and back up from deep underground. It was unlike anything she had ever heard or could easily describe. It was beautiful yet frightening. Crix looked back to the sky before his body became immersed in flames of blue. His head blurred as though shaking at an unnatural speed.

The ground heaved, and the blue radiance glared so brightly visibility became difficult. Kerriah could feel her skin burn as the waves of energy pulsed against her body.

"No! I can't leave you! I won't leave you!" she screamed as she fell to her knees.

She could only see a silhouette of Crix through the blinding aura. He held the crystal high in the air. She cupped her hand over her eyes and tried to protect them from the searing energy, but it was too much, and she had to turn away. Tears streamed across her face, and her heart was ripped out again.

Massive stone arms wrapped around her and lifted her from the ground. She felt a heavy, lumbering gait carrying her away, and the burning sensation from the energy waves slowly subsided. She noticed a featureless face looking forward, and she felt her body snug against the elemental beast's chest. *Jesselle.*

The great protective arms unfolded, lobbing her onto the boarding deck of the transport. She tumbled back to her feet and spun around to look at Crix one last time. The large stone figure stood broad, cupping its body between the main force of the energy and her path into the ship.

"Come on!" Jesselle's voice cried out behind her. "We have to leave now!"

Kerriah turned to see Jesselle standing at the top of the boarding deck, waving her inward. She turned back again; the stone beast's sides began to crumble from the force. She knew she would never see Crix again, or would she? There wasn't any time, and she would deal with whatever fate he had made for himself after she got her and Jesselle to a safe distance. She wiped away her tears, sprinted up the deck, and took command of the ship's controls. As it rose from the unstable surface, she had to rely on instruments and her instincts to get safely in the air due to the immersive blue glow encompassing everything, causing a complete lack of visibility.

The ship spun and shook as she tried to maintain control. There was no time left for precision as the hull integrity alarms sounded, and a deafening roar of continuous thunder quickly built up around them. The sound was like nothing she had ever heard or felt before. Her bones rattled, and her teeth chattered together uncontrollably. It was as though the world ended abruptly, and the scream of an angry deity shouted from the clouds, crushing its creation below.

She closed her eyes and slammed the throttle forward. The ship bounced upward, hastening from the compounding force below. Their bodies pressed into their seats as the accelerating pressure intensified, and the transport quaked so violently it felt as though nothing would be left but their cockpit seats by the time they reached the upper atmosphere. The sea of azure whisked away from their view as they breached the gravitational confines of Nathasia and found some relief in the planet's lower orbit. Kerriah took them up further and leveled out to view the planet below.

The once gloomy, war-stricken world rippled with an iridescent blue across the entirety of its surface. Kerriah pinched her lips tightly together and struggled to fight back the welling tears in her eyes. Her heart ached, and she felt helpless as she watched the blue globe pulse and swirl with a chorus of emerging storms.

Jesselle leaned over and placed her hand on Kerriah's back. "I'm so sorry, Kerriah."

CHAPTER 13

For hours, Kerriah leaned over the flight controls, staring at the planet below. Several times Jesselle pleaded with her to get some rest, only for Kerriah to wave her away. Her thoughts shifted from understanding what Crix had done to a future without him. She flipped through so many scenarios her focus blurred and became frozen with a mental paralysis. It didn't matter how many different angles she took; the conclusion always ended the same. He was attempting to restore Troika, but how? Was that even possible? She didn't understand the orb's power or the mystical significance of the Tersik Crystal. She understood science, and neither the crystal nor the orbs had a basis in logic or science. Instead, they seemed to gain power from a mythical source, which defied everything she knew.

She felt desperate to gain some vestige of control over her life. Her brain searched for a solution, meticulously tapping her fingers against the control panel. Would she take this offer to be the new yellow orb bearer? She would need to get a better understanding of its power. It would be worth undertaking if it could help her grasp what was happening to Crix. That alone enticed her to accept the role. Decision made.

The hailing frequency chirped from the ship's controls. Kerriah expected this and felt surprised it took this long. She tapped the comm control, opening communications. "Unidentified diplomatic vessel, this is UMO science and research vessel Oray; this is a restricted planetary system. What is your purpose here?" The silhouette of a UMO Glimmar Class science ship came into the forward view. Its broad disk-shaped hull and side protruding IO propulsion system gave it away.

Kerriah took a throat-wetting gulp before pressing her thumb into the transmitter. "Uhhh, Oray, this is diplomatic transport six COF, we are . . . um—" She didn't have a valid purpose to give them. *Dang.* She sighed. Why hadn't she prepared for this encounter? Her distracted thoughts usually did a better job of juggling tasks. She lifted her thumb from the panel.

After several silent minutes, the panel chirped back with a crackling voice. "You are requested to maintain your current position. ISMSF is en route."

Kerriah massaged the base of her nose and squeezed her eyes closed. "Great. I don't need this right now," she whispered. The Inter-System Mobile Security Force was the post-Marck-era planetary police force for the UMO. She would have little influence on this group and did not have the time or patience for this encounter.

Just as she was about to take a seat and wait for the security vessel's barrage of probing inquiries and ultimately a boarding party, the atmosphere of Nathasia exploded from a shimmering blue to a blazing white. The shockwaves reached their ships, jarring them and sending Kerriah onto her backside.

With the shocks still rocking her ship, she stumbled back to her feet and quickly peeked out the window.

"What the heck?"

Could it be Crix coming back up? She stared out the window as a white glow glistening from the planet slowly receded. The white blaze faded, and Kerriah's jaw dropped over the sight of what was left behind. A brilliant marble of green and blue filled her viewport. It was astonishing and beautiful all at once. She rubbed her eyes to ensure what she saw was real and not some stress-induced hallucination. The same planet that had been a toxic wasteland of death for over two decades was now a lush new world. She drew her hands down and rested them over her mouth.

"I-I can't believe it."

Jesselle stormed into the cockpit and leaned across the control panel. She stood gazing out at Nathasia. "Are you seeing the same thing as I am?" Her voice rose with excitement.

Kerriah looked up at her and shook her head. It was a negative physical cue, but her words confirmed Jesselle's observation. "Yes." She was short of breath as she answered. "I can't believe it. Crix created this new world."

"It's incredible, "Jesselle said as she stared out the window. She leaned forward a bit more with her leg kicked up behind her, and the newly formed Nathasia reflected in her eyes.

Kerriah's tactical mind shifted back to the ISMSF ship. She wanted to rush down to the surface and find Crix, but she needed to avoid any interrogations. "We need to go while the other ships around Nathasia are distracted with this."

Jesselle looked back at her with raised brows. "What? Are you serious? We can't leave now."

"I'm very serious. I'm in no mood to explain all this to some pressing security agent right now. We need to get back to Soorak and talk with Plexo about what's happened here."

"Plexo? I thought he was returning to Zeta to complete the final stages of the mirror rebuild?"

"He hasn't left yet. I sent him a message earlier. I didn't want to explain too much over long-range comm channels, but apparently, he got held up with some ongoing issues he'd been having with his ship's intelligence systems."

"Okay, I get that, but what about Crix? We need to find out if he's dead or alive or something else. Aren't you curious?"

Kerriah buried her face into her hands and slowly pulled them back over her hairline. As she stared back at Jesselle, her eyes appeared a bit crazy. "Of course, I want to find out about Crix. But if we get taken in now, we'll be held in interrogations for possibly days trying to explain all of this. I just can't . . . not right now. I need time to clear my thoughts, digest what's happened, and speak with someone who may know something that will help us."

"Yep, I got it," Jesselle replied sharply with a half salute.

"Jesselle, don't be that way, please."

"I'm sorry. I'm not that close to Crix. It's you I'm concerned about. So we'll do whatever we need to do for you."

Kerriah bit her lip. "Thank you."

CHAPTER 14

They are searching for your ship," Plexo said. "In fact, the whole of UMO is searching for you. Everyone wants to know who or what is responsible for the unprecedented and sudden change in Nathasia. Myself included. Unfortunately, I've struggled with ever-increasing abnormalities in my ship's computer systems for some time, or I'd have a clearer picture via my observation drones."

Kerriah had managed to avoid UMO patrol ships as she snuck her transport away to Plexo's highly modified Dargon corvette. The shiny bronze vessel with its shifting walls and the overly lit interior was where she and Crix had shared their first kiss, and it would always hold a special place in her heart.

She needed to see a familiar and friendly face, and she trusted Plexo. Aside from Joric, her biological father, he was the most intelligent individual she knew. He would somehow have the answers she needed, or at least the wisdom she needed to hear. Her eyes welled, and her chin twitched upon seeing his glowing body. Before the tears could fall, she took several quick steps forward, threw her arms around him, and squeezed his thin frame tightly.

"Ohh." Plexo, taken off guard, stood rigid for a moment and then relaxed his posture before gently patting his arms across her shoulders. "My dear Kerriah, I am sorry. By your grief and the fact that Crix is not with you, I suspect I know what may have happened."

She let go and took a step back, wiping pools of tears from her eyes. "He's gone. . . . I think. . . . I don't know. I just don't know what's happening right now." Her life felt out of control for the first time. Even in the direst of situations, she had always had a plan. This time was different. Her scattered thoughts had her on her heels, searching for answers, trying to regain focus, but her emotions kept getting in the way.

"No." Plexo shook his head and kept his eyes on hers. "He's not gone. Only changed."

"Changed how?" Her voice struggled for volume as the words left her mouth. She thought she may have known what he meant; she certainly had some time to develop some crazy theories since he had somehow transformed Nathasia. But Plexo had a way of piecing puzzles together, and she needed to hear his explanation.

"Did he have the crystal with him at the time of this Nathasia event?"

"Yes."

"Right." Plexo gently rubbed the base of his chin. "That ancient crystal from Troika contained a mystical power, and please understand that I am not one to believe in mysticisms, but I witnessed it firsthand when I briefly exposed it to the power of the yellow orb. The crystal is a vessel that contains a collection of information. An archive going back to some unknown time, a time well before Soorak and the Andors. Perhaps universal origins.

SONG OF THE LAGGORNS

"However, the most interesting aspect is its capacity to store this data infinitely without a measurable power source or identifiable media. It also had an astonishing reaction to an Orb's power, which provides the ability to observe the contents of its archive. At this point, I have no viable scientific explanations to explain the crystal's distinctive attributes. Though out of respect for Crix and the loss of his ancestral home, I chose not to pry into it any further. At least not without his consent."

"So what does all that mean? Is he trying to resurrect Troika from the crystal?" She'd had enough time to consider all the possibilities, and this was the one that stood out as the most probable. As crazy as the idea sounded, it was the only one that made sense.

"Yes, that is what I suspect. Though I don't know to what end for Crix. What becomes of him? I know he was severely traumatized over the loss of his native home and its population. When I told him about the crystal's unique characteristics, I could see his obsession right away. That's when I knew I couldn't give it to him until after the Core mission. Once he eventually returned, he demanded access to it. So I gave it back, although somewhat reluctantly."

"I wish you wouldn't have, but I also understand why you did," Kerriah said.

Jesselle, who stood quietly in the background, abruptly cleared her throat. "Uhh . . . Plexo."

Plexo's eye shifted to the slender female with ghostly white flowing hair. A half-smile crept from the corner of his mouth.

"Ahh, the newly minted Tolagon Thoran!" He clasped his hands together and turned his attention fully towards her. "What a pleasure. Please, you must tell me details of your visit to Gabor."

97

She took several short steps forward. "That's what I wanted to speak to you about. Please, just call me Jesselle."

"Of course, Jesselle. What is on your mind?"

"It's regarding the yellow orb of Nathasia."

"Ohh," Plexo peaked over at Kerriah with a slight wink. "Go on, please."

"The council instructed Kerriah to take possession of it and the role of Tolagon."

A wide grin formed across Plexo's mouth. "Of course."

Jesselle's face blanked with astonishment. "You're not surprised?"

Plexo shook his head. "Not at all. In fact, I expected it to some degree. After all, she bears all the common traits of a Tolagon." They both turned their attention to Kerriah.

Kerriah stepped back and froze momentarily as though a spotlight shone upon her. "Yeah," she said as she began nervously rubbing her fingers into the base of her neck. "I still don't understand how they know me. Or anything at all about me." The thought this mysterious ancient species from an unknown system knew her was unsettling.

"They only needed to lift the thoughts from Jesselle and Crix to understand who you are. This is not an unusual method for choosing a Tolagon. At least, that is my understanding. It was very much how Tolagon Emberook had been chosen forty years ago. His heroic acts during the tragedy at Orbital Reactor Station Thirteen earned him that role.

"He had been a young engineer working there when its thermal shielding systems failed due to the reactors overloading. The events that followed would have been difficult to script. It was a perfect series of calamities, and all their contingencies failed. Therefore, station operators faced certain death.

"Between the station's power containment cells, which were melting due to overcharge, the unstable reactor, and failed shields, they were left with only two options. Self-destruct, killing all the workers in the station or sending a massive power surge back to the surface, potentially killing everyone at the relay station below and blacking out a substantial region for days until power could be rerouted from an auxiliary station. You must understand that the orbital reactors were relatively new at the time, and power forward was not yet an automated process.

"Then engineer third-class Emberook placed his life in harm's way to save the station while the senior crew and supervisors fell to fear and indecision. Upon hearing of this impending tragedy, Tolagon Gellon of Soorak was the only one that could enter the reactor station quickly and safely with the help of his protective orb. By that time, Corin had already successfully evacuated all the surviving crew to the life pods and was working feverishly to stabilize the station's cores, even though it would likely cost him his life. Corin's efforts bought Gellon the precious minutes he needed.

"Ultimately, Tolagon Gellon's clever use of the blue orb's power over mass created enough negative energy to reverse the overloaded reactors and save the station. This act, however, did cost him his life. His protective orb shield dissipated as a side effect of using negative energy, allowing his body to become overexposed to radiation. In the days that followed, his health declined rapidly. He knew his time was short, so he returned the orb to Gabor. They then saw Corin and his selfless acts of leadership and courage. That was that.

"So, you see, this is how Tolagons are selected. The council at Gabor was never beholden to the UMO or their proclamations.

Their purpose is to ensure the stewardship of the orbs of Cyos. There are two orbs without bearers; who else would they choose?"

Kerriah remained quiet, and she reflected on the story. Even though she had requested access to the orb to help save Crix, she had never considered becoming a Tolagon until recently. She had merely wanted to "borrow it" for a single purpose.

"I had already thought this through after Jesselle told me of the council's decision. I must admit, I never imagined myself as some virtuous super-powered hero. I'm just . . . you know, me. I mean, I used to steal tech for the resistance."

"And that is why you're the perfect choice," Plexo said, crossing his arms.

"Okay," Kerriah rubbed the toe of her ankle boot nervously into the smooth metal floor. She looked up at Plexo and then over to Jesselle, who gave her a friendly nod. Thoughts brewed in her mind, and things started to make sense. She gazed back at Plexo with an increasing feeling of conviction.

"Fine," she said with an uncomfortable sideways grin. "As I said, I already gave this enough consideration, and I guess I'm ready."

Plexo smiled. "I know you are. So let's get you reacquainted with your future, the yellow orb of Nathasia."

CHAPTER 15

Plexo led Kerriah to his scientific artifacts chamber, where the yellow orb remained in the cube at the far end. She had not seen it since she had pulled it from the well on Nathasia over two years ago. The event had nearly killed her. Seeing its warm, golden glow felt different this time. Before, it was some mysterious object of lore. Something she thought of as nothing more than a weapon needing to be kept from Zearic but never something she would ever consider possessing. A Tolagon? Her? For the first time since she could remember, she looked through her eyes from a completely different viewpoint. Accepting this orb and the role of Tolagon would change her forever. There would be no turning back. Instead of being on the outside looking in, she would be on the inside of this exclusive circle. She would see things and understand them differently than most. She would be privy to knowledge few would ever know.

Plexo casually strolled over to the cube with his unique, spirit-like gait. He picked the cube up, slid open the top, and extended it to Kerriah. "Please, don't be afraid. If you truly wish to be the yellow orb's new bearer, we must see if it will accept you as its host."

Kerriah's eyes fixated on the orb in a trance-like state. "What about my cellular structure? I'm not like anyone else who has ever bonded with one before. Will it take? Could it kill me?" she asked, but at this point, it didn't matter to her, she would try regardless. The words just spilled from her mouth.

"Ahh, yes," Plexo said with a smile. "The truth is, we don't know for sure, but we could wait until I finish a complete study and a simulated tested regiment along with Joric, which would take weeks or months, or we could see for ourselves here and now. The choice is yours, of course. However, knowing you as I do, I suspect you will make the latter decision."

The orb glistened in her eyes. "Right."

She placed her hand down into the cube, and the moment her fingers touched the light, her body froze and her muscles locked. Her eyes widened, and her mouth dropped open. A surge of energy and clarity ripped through every nerve and synthetic cell in her body. Her heart pounded, and every memory and thought she ever had flashed through her mind with brilliant lucidity. The orb drew up through her fingers and down her arm before seeping into her chest. Energy poured into her body as a chill swept across her skin. Her fingertips and toes tingled for a few seconds, and she felt the urge to run, jump, or fight. The orb fit like a glove.

She looked over at Plexo. He maintained a focused stare as she assimilated with the yellow orb. His hands clenched tightly together as he stood there.

Oh, please . . . bond with her without harm. She could hear his words, but his mouth didn't move.

"Plexo?"

"Yes? How are you feeling?"

"I'm fine." She tilted her head with intrigue. "How did you just speak to me without moving your mouth?"

He smiled, and his hands relaxed. "I didn't. You just read my thoughts."

"I what?" She briefly stared at her fingertips, which gave off a fading yellow glow, before massaging them gently across her chest.

"Yes. You'll need to get used to that. It's the yellow orb's gift over thought and perception that you're experiencing. From now on, you'll hear everyone's thoughts. Although you will find that you won't want to hear everyone's thoughts all the time. Not only can it be disappointing but maddening. You'll need to find balance. Find a way to turn this feature off until you need it. Otherwise, you'll realize that maintaining friendships will be nearly impossible. The yellow orb is one of the most challenging orbs to tame." He raised his hand and extended his index finger. "However, despite what others may see from the outside, I'm of the opinion that it's also the most powerful of the four orbs."

In addition to hearing thoughts, you will also control actions.

Kerriah cracked a smile. "So I can control their actions as well? Correct?"

"Why yes, certainly." Plexo looked at her with a slight squint. "Did you just read my thoughts again, or were you already aware of this?"

"Both," she said with a larger smile. "The common abilities of the orbs are widely known by most. But it was fun hearing it from your thoughts."

"Hmmm . . ." He stopped for a moment to study her. *I really must warn you again regarding the taming of this power. It will drive you to the brink of madness. It has happened in the past.*

"Really?" she said, responding to his thoughts.

"Yes. I wanted to demonstrate one of the more effective uses of the yellow orb and further extend my warning." He began

103

to pace as he explained. "Using this ability to conceal your discussions and tactics from the ears of adversaries has proven to be quite effective in the past. You may find yourself in direct interactions with them, and being able to adjust your strategies real-time with other members of your team, without your opponent's knowledge, can have a powerful impact on the mission's outcome." He took a deep breath.

"But remember, until you get back to Gabor for your final training, and I do recommend doing so quickly, it is imperative that you either minimize your contact with others or focus on taming this thought-reading ability. Even with training, another bearer of the yellow orb developed such paranoia from hearing everyone's thoughts that he succumbed to psychosis." He took another deep breath and covered his mouth. "It was a gruesome act. He began murdering everyone he encountered. A Tolagon killing friends and innocent bystanders."

"I recall hearing about this story. It left a dark spot on the Tolagon's reputation for many years," Kerriah said.

Plexo's hand slid away from his mouth and his stare pierced through Kerriah. "In the end, then Tolagon Kartelle paid the worst price for his actions. The yellow orb did not react well to these acts of malice, and it ripped itself from its host. Leaving Kartelle's body turned inside out."

Kerriah's eyes opened wide, and she took a dry swallow. Her eyes drifted down to her chest, and she pressed her fingertips into her sternum. *What did she commit to?*

"Yes," Plexo said. "The orbs reject evil, which is a major point of frustration for the likes of Zearic and the Marck Queen. Those who would like to exploit their power will suffer. If there were any doubts regarding this fact, take note of Jesselle."

She massaged her hand over her chest one last time and let out a strong exhale. "I understand." She knew the consequences and would focus diligently on maintaining the virtues of a Tolagon.

Plexo smiled and gently touched her shoulder. "I'm not worried about you, Kerriah. The council has made the right choice."

CHAPTER 16

Kerriah returned home and cried herself to sleep over the thought of Crix not being there. Despite his degrading mental state over the past six months since his return, his old self would still peek out at times, and they would find love and joy in each other's embrace.

For now, she would keep herself distracted with her new quest to become a Tolagon. First, she needed to get Jesselle and return to Gabor for her Tolagon training. However, she also tried to stay abreast of any latest developments on Nathasia by messaging all her media and politically connected sources. The last thing her sources told her was there were Andors on Nathasia. *Andors!* This news lit her ambitions ablaze with her path forward.

The next morning came early to a harsh pounding on her door. *Who would be pounding on the door at this early hour, and why in the heck are they not using the integrated comm system?* She irritatingly snapped the thin temperature balancing cover to the side and slid out of her stasis platform. The stasis platforms used artificial gravity manipulation to make a near contactless sleeping surface. Crix loved it over the primitive bed sacks of Troika. When he first returned, she had trouble rousing him from bed. He would stay curled up most of the day, escaping into the feelings of comfort and safety.

The pounding continued with more ferociousness. A loud, grumbling voice penetrated the thick synthetic door. She cinched a long silken robe around her body, rubbed her eyes, and then stared up at the ceiling, shaking her head. This had better be a damn emergency, or she intended to tear into whoever was on the other side.

"Just hang for two friggen seconds!" Kerriah stormed out of her sleeping room, down the stairs, and into the foyer area to the front door. She didn't even bother to view the camera to see who it was; instead, she released the security locks and swung the door open.

"Har har har . . . now tat's the crabby face I like seein'."

Krath! His husky body stood there with both fists posted at his side. His clothes were still tattered, but they looked newer and didn't stink quite as bad.

"Krath!" She jumped at him and wrapped her arms around his muscular torso. She squeezed him so tight he let out a belch followed by a wet cough.

"Okay, now okay." He peeled her off. *This is embarrassin'.* "I know tya miss old Krath and all, but tya are goin' to give my little buddy here the wrong impression."

"Oh Krath, no need to be embarrassed. . . . Wait, who?" She looked at him and then glanced side to side for someone else.

For a second, Krath appeared confused. "What?" Then he quickly shook his head. "What the heck is tya doin' hidin'?" His large hands reached to his left and grabbed the neck of a short Hybor youth. He yanked him over to the front of the door. "Timmon, get tya butt over here."

A shorter version of Krath stumbled over, nearly losing his footing to the aggressive pull. His round eyes blinked several times, and he gave a quick, forced smile. His smooth, charcoal skin appeared fresh and not one that had weathered war and elements outside of his native world of Thale.

Krath lightly swatted Timmon across the backside of his head. "Well, come on, show some respect. At least give her a proper greetin'."

"Hello," he shyly said while half staring down at the floor. "I'm Timmon."

Krath swatted his head again, and Timmon dropped his head deeper into his shoulders, anticipating another blow. "She already knows tya name, numb-head. I just told her."

Kerriah placed her hand over her mouth and chuckled. "Come in, Krath, please." She waved him into her home.

Krath's cantankerous humor was a welcome sight, and the timing couldn't have been better. Her tall, cylindrical-shaped dwelling located in the Tilecca District wasn't uncommon for an upscale artistic community on the edge of Corasan. Over the last two years, it had become the perfect home for her since she could explore the local galleries to escape her memories of the war and, more recently, her frustrations with Crix. The location had kept her close to the capital and Septin. She still wanted to keep her finger on the pulse of the rapidly changing political landscape since the defeat of the Queen and the Thraxons. As much as she loved her hometown of Teinol, Tilecca was a better place for her at this time.

They walked through her door and into the foyer with a rounded ceiling and various pieces of art hanging from the walls. Some works displayed an impressionistic scene actively changing while staring at them. Timmon stopped to look at a piece depicting a scene of a rocky shore with dark-blue storm clouds whisking by. He jumped back, bumping into Krath.

Krath shot an icy stare down at him. "What the heck is wrong with tya, junior? Tya actin' like tya never been indoors!"

Timmon carefully peeled his eyes away from the art and peeked up at Krath. "B-But Krath, that picture reached out at me!"

"Just leave the silly, overpriced finger paintings alone! And if you touch anything in here, I'm gunna put a knot on that skull of tyas."

Kerriah cracked a smile and gestured for them to follow her. Krath nudged Timmon toward a larger room at the end of the hall dotted with sculptures and then into a round sitting area to the right. He smiled and winked at Kerriah as he followed Timmon into the room. "Can I get you guys something to drink: water . . . juice . . . or something stronger?" she asked.

"No. Tat's okay. Timmon here will just make a mess all over ty're high-priced rug."

Oh, some seacra juice would be so good.

"Timmon, I don't have any seacra juice, but I have some ogeena juice."

Timmon looked at her like he had just swallowed a large egg. Krath squinted and let out a confused grumble. "Did I miss somthin'? When did he ask for seacra juice?"

Kerriah stood and panned nervously around the room. "Gah . . . uhh"

Upon seeing Kerriah's reaction, Krath nearly stood taller before hunkering back into his usual slouch. "What's wrong with tya?"

Kerriah raised her hand and took a deep breath. "I need to get used to this. Well, I'm now the new bearer of the yellow orb of Nathasia. So with that comes a new ability or challenge, depending on how you look at it, in hearing everyone's thoughts. It's just a bit startling at first. It feels like you're going a tad crazy."

"Oh yah, ole glow stick told me about tat. Great, so now tya goin' be proddin' into our noggins all the time. Just when I was startin' to think you were fun to hang around."

Kerriah shook her head and waved the notion off. "No. No, it's my burden to learn how to not intrude into your thoughts unless it's necessary. Right now, it's all so new to me that your thoughts just pop into my head. Believe me, I'm not trying to read your minds."

"'Kay, well, just don't get tya feelins hurt when you hear something that I wasn't meant to say."

"Okay, that's a deal. Please make yourselves comfortable." She gestured toward a nearby sofa before settling into a plush, burgundy chair. Krath and Timmon both plopped down on the long couch.

"So," she smiled, "you have to tell me more about your new little . . . umm . . ." She put the palm of her hand out and shrugged. "Friend?"

"This little guy here is goin' to be my baggage for a while. His father passed while on mission to Semptor. It was the same mission our buddy Crix went on and came back alone."

"Gorag?" Kerriah asked and peeked carefully at Timmon.

Timmon's bright eyes turned dark, and his face scrunched into a scowl. *I hate him. Why did you have to say his name?*

Krath raised his hand near his mouth and made a trivial attempt to conceal his words from Timmon. "Shhh, careful saying that name around him. He looks innocent enough, but like most Hybors, he can pack a hot temper."

"Oh, sorry."

110

"Tat's alright. His father, Carr, died on tat mission. Word had gotten back to this little fella as to who and what happened. So he's bent on vengeance."

Kerriah looked over at Timmon. "That's terrible. I'm so sorry, Timmon."

Krath let out a grumble. "As tya know, Solarans and Hybors have a dark history hatin' and killin' each other. I'm tryin' hard to do my part to break this pointless cycle, but this sort of thing makes it difficult." *Guy didn't even get a clean death. Stabbed in the back like some gutless coward.*

"I know. Crix told me about what happened with Gorag. It's a travesty of justice that he still rules over Semptor, but the political dealings on Solara are complicated."

Krath scowled. *Complicated, huh? Guy's been killin' Hybors and his own people for decades. How the heck is tat complicated?*

"Krath, I agree with you. If it were completely up to me, we would have already sent a force down there to take him out," Kerriah said and then flinched her head back. She rolled her eyes with disappointment in herself.

"Would tya stop jabbin' into my skull!" Krath barked.

"I know. I'm sorry, Krath. I can't help it. I need the training from Gabor."

"Hmmm, well anyway, Plexo told me about what happened to Crix and I, or a, me and junior here are goin' with tya to see him on this new Troika."

Kerriah gave a surprised look. "New Troika?"

"Yah, tat's what they're callin' it already. Plexo said there are sightins of Andors trottin' around all over the planet now."

Surprisingly, she hadn't heard about the new name. Her heart immediately started racing with the news. "Really?" The name fit, and she knew Crix would be with them. She cleared her throat. "Yes, I'm leaving right away." She couldn't wait. She wanted to leave now. "But I'm going to Gabor for training from there."

"Tat's alright. We're taggin' along with tya the whole way." He put his hand around Timmon's neck and gave him a friendly but solid squeeze. "Aren't we, junior?" Timmon nodded. "I'm goin' to be there as the first to congratulate tya as an official Tolagon."

Kerriah smiled. "Thanks, Krath. I could use some friendly companionship. It'll help to keep me out of my head."

Krath chuckled. "Yeah, and in mine instead."

"Oh, and Jesselle will be coming along as well," Kerriah said, waiting for Krath's rebuttal.

Krath let out a pondering growl. "Still not sure if I trust her. I get it, tya and her have formed some sort of connection, but she used to take orders from the rotten sea viper Zearic."

"Krath, if you'd just get to know her a little better, you'd understand that she is a victim. Zearic manipulated her when she was a child, and she's suffering, like so many others. Besides, she's an official Tolagon now, with full rights and training from the Council of Gabor. That has to say something of her true character."

"Hrrrfff . . . tya mean the same group of know it all's that told our buddy Crix to stuff it? Tat he wasn't good enough?" *I'd like to give those bunch of stiffs a good ole fashion kick to the backside.*

Kerriah clenched her jaw. "Yes, that same bunch of stiffs."

"Now I told tya to stay out of my head!"

"Sorry, sorry, and didn't mean to—Look, Jesselle has to come as it takes two orb bearers to open the gate. It's true. I saw it myself. So, like her or not, if you're coming along, she will be there."

112

Krath looked over at Timmon and gave the top of his head a quick rub. "Fine, I get it, but she had better not try to pull any stunts, or I'll pull that orb out her tail. Got it?"

Kerriah sighed. "Yes, I got it."

***

After Krath and Timmon left, Kerriah tried to rest before her trip, though her racing mind wouldn't allow it. She tossed about, staring at the ceiling and kicking the cover to the floor. The stasis platform felt cold and lonely without him. All she could think of was Crix on New Troika and the yellow orb. How would this change her life moving forward? Would she ever be able to have lasting relationships with the temptation to steal thoughts or manipulate the actions of those around her? It was much power to wield, and the impulse to abuse it would be the most significant challenge she had ever faced. She wasn't sure she would have the discipline.

She had already made the necessary arrangements to procure a means of transport for the morning. It wasn't difficult with her connections. After over packing for the trip, her thoughts pinged around to a breaking point over the possibilities. Would Crix be there? Would he be the same, or would she see a new Crix? Or maybe the old Crix before he left for the Core? She might be tempted to stay with him in this new world; if so, she would need to pack for a prolonged period. She'd never been this indecisive. She took solace that at least she'd have Krath there to keep her grounded.

CHAPTER 17

The trip to New Troika flew by, and once again, they were in orbit around the green and blue planet. Kerriah had the authorization this time and didn't need to worry about UMO patrols. She had already provided her statements to UMO authorities regarding the events that led to the transformation of this world. As expected, much of what she said was met with extreme skepticism. She couldn't blame them, as she would have the same questioning looks and sideways stares if told the same story. Besides, she could hear every word they were thinking, so there wasn't any doubt they didn't believe much of what she told them.

The crowded orbit must have had every UMO science and media vessel circling. There hadn't been this level of non-military activity here since before the second Thraxon war over thirty years ago. Plexo's ship might be the only one not here since he had to return to finish the work on Gammac Portal Zeta. From what he had explained, it was close to operational again. His anxiety drove him to finish, and he had developed a renewed desire to return to Eesolan ever since the queen's control of the Marcks had been severed. It had been nearly eighty years since he or Pira had been home, and without access through Zeta, there was no chance of ever returning.

Jesselle remained seated and quiet. Her eyes would occasionally dart over to Kerriah. Kerriah would look directly back at her without a word spoken between them. She couldn't help feeling like Jesselle tried to keep her thoughts clear. She wanted to probe into her mind, but she couldn't. Despite her curiosity, she needed to train herself not to violate others' private thoughts.

Krath leaned forward for a better look through a viewport. "Would tya look at tat? I can't believe tat boy Crix did all this."

Wuwow! Can we go down there?

Kerriah snapped a glance over at Timmon. His face pressed against the glass, fogging it with his breath. She suspected he didn't actually say anything, so she chose not to reply, and since Krath didn't acknowledge his question, she knew it was just the orb reading his thoughts.

"I'm taking us down," Kerriah said as she impatiently grabbed the ship's controls.

"Nathasia-r-ahh New Troika is a big world. Any idea where?" Krath asked.

"Yes, the last place I saw him. The Corvid Mountains."

She dipped the nose of the transport down. It shook and shuddered as it broke through the lower atmosphere. This time it was a different experience, with white clouds and clear skies. The ship didn't feel like it would shake to pieces and felt more like entering Soorak's airspace. The bright grey mountain peak came into view, capped in white snow. How had this developed so quickly? Her intuition spiked. The mountain top was already snowcapped? It didn't seem real, and she wondered if this was just some wakened dream or some afterlife. Given Krath's spill of thoughts, she knew he had the same concerns. She had quickly discovered loud, emotionally driven minds were much more challenging to block out than calm ones. Ignoring Krath was not an easy task for her.

"There's the spot." She pointed down to the area where she had last seen Crix. It wasn't the same algae-stained rock as before. Now covered in mint-green moss with crystal streams cascading down the mountainside, the scene appeared surreal, like something from an enhanced photograph or painting.

She gently set the transport down and raced out the rear boarding deck. She intentionally took in a lungful of the crisp, clean air and then scanned the area. Flocks of birds ballooned across the landscape below, and forests of green spread around open fields of purple and gold. The cool wind whisked up and chilled her skin while heightening her senses.

"What do you think?"

"Crix?" she spun around. An Andor with light-tan fur and an unusually short muzzle stood there, staring at her with a familiar smile.

"Don't you believe your own eyes?" Crix folded his arms. The blue glow no longer covered his skin, and his round eyes were their normal color.

She paused for a minute and just stared at him. *Strange, he has no thoughts.*

"Well?" he persisted with a broader smile.

She ran forward and threw her arms around him. He gave her a firm hug back.

"I missed you," she whispered. She quickly released her embrace and stared into his eyes with two short sniffles. "How did you know I'd be here?"

"I didn't for sure, but I've been coming up here almost every day since you left, knowing this is where you'd look for me."

"Really? You trekked all the way up here nearly every day?"

Crix squatted, placing his palms against the rocky surface. His arms lit with blue fire, and he rose with two swirling balls of energy hovering above each hand. He snapped his fingers, and they both instantly dissipated. "I may have dispersed the blue orb into this new world, but I still have control over its power."

"Ahhh, I see." She stopped to give him a thorough look up and down. "Wow! You've changed."

A wide smile slowly emerged across Crix's face. "Kerriah, I haven't changed. It's the illusion that's gone now. I'm the same as I've always been. It's just that you can see me now."

She peeked down at his right arm. "And your hand?"

Crix popped his lightly coated fur hand into the air and playfully failed it around. "It's back and as good as ever. It was an added benefit to restoring everything that was lost. Any Andor that had a handicap or ailments when they died have been made whole. Myself included."

Kerriah let out a relaxed sigh. "You don't know how much I've missed you." She caressed her fingers down his cheek, feeling the silkiness of the short, smooth fur. "I want you back. You're so much more upbeat now, like when we first met. I need that version of you back in my life." She embraced him again and closed her eyes.

"I miss you too. But for us to be together, you would have to give up everything. This is my home now, and I can never leave."

A tear trickled down the side of her nose. Crix gently swiped it with his thumb. "I don't understand," she said. "Why? What exactly have you done here?" She stepped back and looked around.

"I've restored Troika and all of its departed souls. They are here now, and I have completed the last of what I was destined for. It wasn't until I returned from Antathaw, and energized the Tersik Crystal that I knew for certain this is what I was meant to do. That is why Suros guided me to the crystal of his brother and why Grand Chief Isomar sacrificed himself so that we could take his ship and escape. The ancients and all the leaders knew this day would come. It was all part of the prophecy."

She sniffed and rubbed the back of her hand across her nose. Her eyes peaked up at his, and he appeared youthful, like the first day they had met years ago. It was the first time since they had met she felt he had a firm handle on his purpose and his life. She didn't, and it was a strange feeling for her. She sniffed again. "So now what are you going to do?"

He turned away to look across the valley below. "Live amongst the Andors in peace. I am one of them, and this is where I belong." He turned back and gave her a penetrating stare. "You're changed. Something is different."

She touched her fingertips against her chest. "The yellow orb. It's within me now. Though it's not an easy burden to carry; you know that better than anyone."

He smiled and nodded. "Your destiny is still ahead of you. The system needs you. I need you."

"I know; that's a big reason why I don't want to leave. I should just stay here with you. Leave everything else behind."

"No, not yet. It's Creedith." Crix stopped, and his eyes scanned the horizon. "He's not here on New Troika. It's the Andor way. If he died that day over two years ago on this planet, his soul would have lain dormant on this soil, lost, until re-awakened by the Tersik Crystal. He should have emerged with the rest of the Andors. But he's not here. The ancient chiefs believe he was taken from here that day. So he's either alive or he died somewhere else. Either way, I need to know for certain. I need you to find him."

"Are you sure he didn't die that day? I mean, how could you know for sure?"

"Because other Andors that fell here during the war have emerged. Not just the ones that came from the Tersik Crystal, but the ones that died on Nathasia."

She stared at him for a minute and then looked back at her ship. Krath stood there with Jesselle and Timmon. They remained by the ship, giving her the space she needed with Crix. Krath's fists posted at his hips. When he saw her turn toward them, he waved his stubby, partially webbed hand at her. She gave a slight smile and turned back to Crix.

"I don't know, Crix. Where would I even begin to look for him? Zearic escaped through Zeta years ago, and who knows where he is now? I want to help but don't have much to go on."

He placed his hand on her shoulder and stared into her eyes. "Follow your destiny, and you'll find him."

She let out an uncomfortable chuckle. "My destiny? Great." She rested her hand over her forehead, exhausted with thoughts.

He pulled her in and gave her another hug. "How about I return some advice you once gave me?" His mouth moved closer to her ear. "Go to Gabor and complete your training," he whispered and then took a step back, unclasping the bracer from his forearm. "You'll need this." He handed it to her, and she clasped it around her arm without hesitation.

"Gabor. Right." How could he be so sure of things? This bright-eyed kid that found her crashed in the bogs had never traveled outside of the sheltered life of Troika. Somehow, he now had all this wisdom. It was difficult for her to process.

"Do that and return to me. But beware of Antathaw. They seek access to Cyos, and a corrupted Tolagon is all they need. It's the key to building their negative universe. It's the one thing I stole from my encounter with them. It's what made me realize what I needed to do here; by my guess, that is why I wasn't accepted in Gabor. Inside, my intentions were more aligned with those in Antathaw."

Still frozen on two words Crix mentioned, she gave her head a few quick shakes and asked the burning question. "Wait, a what? Negative universe? How do you even know any of this?"

"When they spoke, their intentions somehow bled into my mind, and I'm not sure if it was deliberate or accidental. The negative universe is where everything that's lost is restored, but—" Crix paused for a moment.

"But what? And when who spoke?" Kerriah shook her head with a wide-eyed shrug of her shoulders. Her voice sounded irritated over his not explaining this to her after he had returned.

"The Tracolds, the ones in Antathaw. As bad as it sounds, it's not too different from what I've accomplished here restoring Troika. Everything that was here is gone, and everything that was lost in Troika is now restored . . . here. They intend to do the same, but on a much . . . much larger scale."

"Okay, well, how do we stop them?"

"The white orb is the key."

"Right." She shrugged. "And that's safe in Luminar possession on Eesolan."

Crix's round eyes enlarged, and his head tilted. "Is it? When was the last time anyone had contact with Eesolan?"

120

She clenched her jaw and shook her head. "Great. Just what we needed. Plus, this could all be a trap. I don't trust any of them."

He placed his thumb under her chin and raised her head. "Fair enough, but I trust you and have faith in you, Kerriah. I know you'll come back to me."

She wanted nothing more. She returned to the ship. Krath and Crix spoke for a time before leaving for Gabor while she gathered her thoughts. She knew what was immediately ahead of her but was uncertain what lay beyond. She wanted to return to him, but now she needed to find Creedith and the white orb? The days ahead were going to be some of the most important of her life.

CHAPTER 18

KERRIAH

Kerriah stared up at the void ahead. She was as close as she could get without penetrating the barrier known as Phantos and taking that anxious trip to the other side. She could still turn away and release the orb. Everything could go back to the way it was. Except now, Crix asked something from her. How could she selfishly refuse after he had sacrificed so much? She looked over at Jesselle, who floated nearby, waiting patiently for Kerriah and not saying a word. They hadn't spoken much since she had acquired the yellow orb, but Krath had filled her ears with more than enough to break any unwanted silence.

"Well . . . tya goin' in there or are we just goin' to wait till tya suit's oxygen reserves run out and call it a day?" Krath's witty crack over the comm snapped her away from the anxiety.

"No. I got this Krath." She slowly stuck her arm into the gateway. A warm vibration and a nearly inaudible hum filled her body. Her hand vanished, along with all sensation. She quickly pulled out, only to find her hand wasn't attached, but somehow her suit remained pressurized. She waved her empty wrist in front of her helmet and stared into the socket. *Empty?*

SONG OF THE LAGGORNS

The gateway appeared closer, or did she move? She panicked and jolted back, kicking her legs, and waving her arms. Her body spun, and the void suddenly drew outward.

Her bare feet dangled in a murky, sea-green mist with shimmering black trees as far as her eyes could see. She inspected her hands and the rest of her naked body. No suit, no clothes. Why hadn't someone told her about this little inconvenience? She tried to take an empty breath, but there wasn't any air to fill her lungs, and despite her nakedness, she wasn't the least bit cold.

So, I just stroll into these trees? Crix and Jesselle had mentioned this part, but they hadn't clearly explained what they had done next. Instead, they just somehow appeared in front of the council, or in Crix's case, those creatures in Antathaw.

She moved her foot forward to find solid ground. With each step through the airless space, she seemed to move ahead into the trees. Deeper and deeper into the mystical forest with no sound or sensations of a breeze upon her skin. One of the things Joric had failed to design for her was dreams. She never had known if it was due to lack of time or an oversight, but he made sure she needed to sleep for the appearance of normalcy. She hadn't spent much time with her biological father since the core mission, and it was a question she had neglected to ask. Sleep for her was nothing more than black spots in her life. However, this was how she had imagined dreams to be.

As she continued to move ahead, she occasionally peeked back. The trees extended as far as she could see in all directions. *How much further?* Her thoughts grew into frustration, and she began to have doubts as she advanced. She had to be doing something wrong. Part of her wanted to turn back, but she had gone too far already to turn around. So she continued ahead. Deeper and deeper without the slightest change in scenery.

Her emotions changed to anger. Was someone toying with her, playing games? Why hadn't Jesselle said something about this? She had to be doing something wrong. Hours must have passed as she advanced into the unending alien forest. Her anger turned to sadness, and she broke down and sobbed uncontrollably. Her head throbbed, and her brain felt too big for her skull, swelled with emotion and pain. How was this fair? She wasn't doing any of this for herself.

After a while, she stopped crying and remained still, hovering in the murky forest. Tearing eyes accompanied short, empty breaths, her shoulders hung lower than usual, and her back curved into a fetal position. She would no longer persist further into the endless forest. They would have to come to her. She'd wait them out. Her stubborn determination not to play their games carried on for hours, and the view of shimmering trees began to drive her mad. She pinched her eyes closed, but they remained burned into her vision as though her eyelids were transparent.

"Stop it!" she screamed out, but no words left her lips. Only the maddening silence of the trees waving at her in the green-tinted fog persisted. She pulled her hands down her face and peeked through her fingers. She wanted to continue, she wanted the training, but no one would come to help her.

She lowered her head as it became clear to her. *I can't do this; I can't beat them with my determination.* She felt the urge to renounce her free will, to release all of herself upon this invisible altar of obstinacy. *I give myself up. I surrender my will and my selfishness. I come to you empty, and what I am is yours.* She raised her head, not in defiance but with obedient reverence.

"Do you hear me? I am yours!" she shouted without words.

SONG OF THE LAGGORNS

A tendril of light broke from the unseen above and whisked around her body. She felt a pull upward, and her view turned to a space filled with a fantastic array of colors and shapes. The force shifted her upright. Her feet touched a solid surface, but it was unlike anything she had ever felt. The surface wiggled under her toes, tickling them slightly like the flinching skin of a druna beast reacting to a light touch. Spherical shapes pulsing with an immersion of colors drifted by slowly. As she looked closer, she realized they were not moving freely but appeared tethered by translucent, ovular clusters with swaying, bright tendrils. She stared as they slowly swooshed around in a circular pattern. As her mind adapted to her surroundings, she could now see dozens of distinct clusters of circular colors. They weren't random or intentionally placed there, but beings moving around, inspecting her.

"Kerriah," a whisper filled her ears, "you have passed into Gabor. It's time that you learn the hidden truth."

A thin tendril swooshed around and shot directly into her chest. Her body locked, and her muscles deadened. Images and knowledge began filling her mind. A celestial song flowed into her ears as a blanket of warmth wrapped around her skin. The tingling melody was unfamiliar, but she knew it was the Laggorns singing their creations into existence. The living system of Auroro spilled into her thoughts, and she could see the Laggorns shaping it over time. These beings making up the council of Gabor were the Laggorns' creations, residents of Auroro, which could freely move from planet to planet without vessels through vibrant space bridges strewn with bizarre floras of unfamiliar colors and shapes.

"We are the Trifilleds," the whisper continued. "Our system and creators perished ages ago, but our secret society survived. When the cataclysmic event transpired, we were with the great Laggorn Sequia, the one who created us. Sequia sensed the cosmic event moments before its occurrence and created an ethereal tear into the fabric of our system, a transient opening in reality for which we escaped. We are blessed by our survival and cursed by our entrapment away from our home."

"What about the Phantos?" Kerriah asked through her thoughts. "Can't you leave through the same gateway Tolagons use to enter Gabor?"

"Phantos was created by our yearning to leave and the love of our creator."

"Your creator?"

"Yes, Sequia"

Kerriah's eyes lit like fire, and her limbs tingled with excitement. "Sequia is here? A Laggorn?"

"Our creator, saddened by the yearning for some of us to leave Gabor, sliced a hole to the other side and formed the Phantos Gateway to hold it open. Our merciful creator granted any Trifilled who desired to leave access to Phantos. However, those that chose this path returned malevolent and misguided, corrupted by the absence of Sequia. Though allowed back, they are now forever separated.

"We are divided into two factions, one that remained akin to our creators and the other who desired to pervert the course of time and reality. To create an inverse of the Laggorns, something that would have survived their destruction. A negative existence. And so our realm split into two, Gabor and Antathaw. The Trifilleds of Antathaw became Tracolds, and they reshaped their forms."

"Wait!" Kerriah still wanted to hear more about Sequia. "You said you have a Laggorn here—" The council ignored her words and continued.

Her view changed to a massive gold and cerulean nebula sprinkled with shimmering dust. "Cyos remained from our destruction, the vestige power of our creators and their creations for which had escaped the aftermath; blown from its stellar region, it became aware. The orbs are the seeds of the Laggorns, the children of Cyos. With its children safe, it went into dormancy, and the seeds were removed during its long sleep by the logical ones." Kerriah knew who they meant—the Luminars.

"A time after the Tracolds departed, the curiosity of the logical ones placed them at the Phantos gate. It was then we agreed to use the seeds of Cyos for life. To lift the weak and besieged and use this power to create unity.

"Eventually, the Tracolds returned contemptuous by the knowledge they found outside, and they now seek an unworthy Tolagon to take possession of the white orb. Their way is to create a reality where everything that is lost is restored, and everything that exists is lost. With this power, they can create a negative existence. Our will is to use these great powers to further the Laggorns' yearning for peace and harmony among species. Beyond creation, this was their greatest goal."

"What about the visions?" Kerriah asked, thinking of Crix's description of fanged creatures when he used the orb. Though she hadn't seen them, she knew other Tolagons had. "The monsters that other Tolagons mentioned after using the orbs?"

"They are Tracolds, and the visions are the orb's warning when it feels its power overused by its bearer. The power could lead to corruption by the weaker mind. No more inquiries. We will provide the answers you require without injection."

Information continued to fill her mind. She saw the orb as part of her, like a new limb she was adept at using. Countless hours of training filled her mind, memories seemingly implanted with no recollection of time. Oddly, she had no desire to ask questions or further inquiries and felt overwhelming gratitude.

"There is one more important piece of knowledge that we must bestow. Beware of the worlds outside. They will tempt you with selfish desires. A fallen Tolagon is a tool for Antathaw." *Herkro*. The name entered her mind. *The fallen one.* She remembered the story of Herkro, the second Tolagon of Solara. Solaran crime lords had assassinated him, or so the reports said. Now she knew the truth.

Herkro used the red orb's power to subdue a region on Solara, to make himself a monarch. But when the orb began to resist his selfish will and turn against him, he returned to Gabor but found himself in Antathaw. The Tracolds took control of his mind. They instructed him how to use the orb for their purpose without its rejection. Herkro returned to the Oro system and murdered a Luminar emissary and attempted to take the Luminar's ship back through Zeta, his directive, the white orb. Fortunately, the other Tolagons banded together to stop and kill him. They needed the cover story to keep the Tolagon image as protectors intact. The public could never learn of a Tolagon capable of evil.

"The fallen Tolagon, Herkro, is why we re-keyed the gate to require two. Now you have the information required to become a Tolagon. Go and bring peace as was the will of the Laggorns," the whispering voice concluded.

Her body dropped, and she fell back into the shimmering forest and then quickly pulled back through the gateway. "There she is," the voice of Jesselle cracked out through her helmet comm.

"Little girl, are tya okay?" Krath's voice followed.

"Yes," Kerriah replied. Her thoughts still hung inside Gabor and everything she had just learned. "I'm fine."

"Good. Let's get goin' then. Ole glow rod just sent out a message that they opened Zeta and received some distress messages from Eesolan. The scrawny fella is freakin' out and seekin' permission to head home."

Kerriah's mind instantly returned to the present upon hearing Krath's words. She tilted her head sideways with a confused squint. "A distress signal from Eesolan?" How was that possible? From her knowledge, it wouldn't be unless they had rebuilt the corridors leading back to their home world. If so, that was a dangerous move with the Thraxons and Zearic still at large somewhere in the galaxy. They could never have access to the white orb.

CHAPTER 19

U pon returning to her transport, Jesselle looked at her
differently. Instead of silence, her expression appeared eager,
like someone who wanted to talk privately. However, Krath was all
over them, concerned about Plexo. "If Zearic and the Thraxons
found his homeworld, they coulda been wiped out already. Plexo
could be walkin' into a trap."

"I agree." Kerriah's voice was firm and confident for the
first time since Crix had returned from Antathaw. "But we need to
assemble a special-ops team and a long-range tactical warship. I'll
send a message to my fathe—I mean, Chancellor Septin."

Krath let out a low growl. "No need to. He's already
messaged us. He knows tya too well and wanted to make sure tya
weren't takin' off through Zeta to save the Luminars on tya own.
He's got a freshly commissioned UMO destroyer and an assembled
team in route already to pick us up." The UMO shipyards worked
at full capacity to rebuild their navy, but larger class military
warships were still in short supply.

Kerriah didn't respond. She leaned back and looked at
Krath as if something had just come to light. She wasn't hearing
his thoughts like before. Was the orb's power still working? She

focused on him and intentionally peeked inside his head. *Why tya heck is she givin' me that dumb look? This is serious, and now she wants to play the dumb look game.* Nope, it was working, but now it seemed natural to not hear everyone's thoughts. The Trifilleds' training was already having a positive impact.

She shook her head. "Krath, believe me, I'm taking this seriously. You just have to work with me for a little bit as I adjust to everything."

"Aww, come on! Are tya just going to camp out in my head from now on? Cus we're goin' ta have a tough time gettin along if tya keep this up."

"No. Sorry, Krath. I just needed to ensure I could still hear your thoughts when I wanted. I'll stay out of your head. Now about that destroyer?"

"The Mertel will be here in the next day or two with a light crew complement, full supply load, and a fresh platoon of greenies. It's 'bout all the UMO could scrounge up for us. If the Thraxons are on ta move again, the UMO can't afford to keep our already thin defenses any thinner."

Kerriah cringed over the thought. She knew they had relied on the Marcks for too long, and now they were too weak to defend themselves from any real threat. The UMO would be easy picking from any well-supplied attack force. "It will have to suffice."

Her thoughts drifted back to Plexo. It wasn't like him to make an emotional and uncalculated move. He'd been working on rebuilding the Zeta mirror for some time, and Kerriah thought it was his concern for Eesolan. Ever since Crix had destroyed the mirror connecting the gammac corridor, leaving the Knactor Legion and Thraxons on the other side, the fear for his home world had been his main driving force. She could understand that, but going through it alone, without letting the UMO know or waiting for the military escort to arrive, it wasn't like him to be so reckless. Why hadn't he mentioned his intentions to her? She could have helped. One thing was sure, the UMO owed Plexo a debt that could never be paid, and she would make sure they did everything possible to help him.

***

Jesselle and Kerriah found some time away from Krath and Timmon to share their Gabor experience. They kept the traditional Tolagon code of not disclosing specific knowledge outside their inner circle. Sitting on the small cargo area floor, Kerriah decided to use the yellow orb to communicate through thoughts, hiding their voices. She wanted to know more about the Tracolds and if Jesselle had seen them in her visions.

"The Tracolds. So they were the rumored ancient species that had once lived amongst the Luminars. I haven't seen them in any visions, but Crix gave a vivid explanation of what they looked like in his orb-induced nightmares. If you've had these visions, what do you recall them looking like?"

Jesselle sighed. "In the early years before you found me, they haunted my daily existence more than they didn't. Strange-shaped eyes and red fangs are what I remember, mostly. When they spoke, my thoughts went into a fog. It was something I couldn't shake until the visions subsided."

"Yeah, that's what Crix described as well. I'm sure you're aware they want to destroy the universe."

"I know," Jesselle replied, though Kerriah had hoped for a more detailed response.

"Well, I knew the orbs were important to keep out of evil hands, but now it's way more than I ever realized." The other burning question spilled from Kerriah's thoughts, the one she'd had in the back of her mind to ask since the start of their discussion. She sat up straight with her hands on her lap. "Okay, What about Sequia? Did you know there is a Laggorn in Gabor?"

Jesselle smiled. "Yes."

"Yes?" Kerriah's body stiffened. "Did you get to see it? Talk to it?"

"No, not exactly, but I think this is the ultimate source of knowledge and wisdom that comes from Gabor. The Trifilleds just act as Sequia's voice. I mean, they are alive and have their own will, but when it comes to Tolagon training, we are communicating to Sequia. So, in a sense, yes, I spoke with it."

As Kerriah took a minute to ponder Jesselle's explanation, she knew what she told her was correct. "Wow, you're absolutely right."

"I know. Like you, it didn't hit me right away, but I realized it later."

Even though they communicated through thought, Kerriah leaned closer to Jesselle. "I'm still not certain I fully trust them after what they did to Crix." She gasped and nervously massaged her hands together. "It's so hard to tell who the bad guys versus good guys are these days. It was way less confusing when we were dealing with Zearic. I mean, they sent Crix to Antathaw? Crix?"

"I know, and I completely understand. Gabor split in two was never something anyone outside of Tolagons, and some Luminars, were privy to. For Crix, there was a larger plan, and I think we witnessed it firsthand. We have to go with generations of Tolagons before us and assume that the Trifilleds are good guys."

Kerriah hesitantly nodded in agreement. She had what seemed like years of memories implanted into her mind with the Trifilleds; in a sense, they seemed like family to her. Still, she had some hesitancy and would remain guarded for now.

CHAPTER 20

The Mertel arrived after a few days, and it couldn't have come soon enough. Kerriah paced and stirred as much as she could around the small transport. She wasn't used to waiting around, and the downtime filled her mind with crazy thoughts. The humor of watching Krath swat and scold Timmon for every bungling word and clumsy misstep had worn thin. She knew telling Krath how to teach the bright-eyed Hybor wouldn't go well, so she tried to stay clear and out of their heads. Jesselle wanted to talk whenever she saw her, but Kerriah mostly steered clear of the unwanted discussion and chose to stay inside her own mind despite its unraveling.

The Mertel's dark military-blue hull was a welcome sight. The sleeker design didn't display its defenses like the older UMO warships; instead, they remained hidden inside the hull until needed. This ship could easily be mistaken as diplomatic until it needed to defend itself. After a brief soft dock with the UMO military vessel, they transferred themselves and their belongings into their new temporary home.

SONG OF THE LAGGORNS

"Welcome aboard, Kerriah Septin. I'm Captain Mallor Ashton. I've already heard so much about you." Captain Ashton greeted them as they exited the starboard airlock.

He was fit and handsome, with a smooth, sculpted face and well-maintained dark-brown hair. The young commanding officer's eyes had a slight twinkle as he spoke to Kerriah. She cringed at hearing her adoptive last name. She never cared for how her full name sounded, and now that she had found her natural father, she was less fond of her adoptive name.

Krath loudly and intentionally cleared his throat. "Oh yes." Ashton gave a loose-handed salute. "It's an honor to have an old vet with your reputation onboard."

The interior of the visually modern ship consisted of interconnected circular passageways lit with glowing white archways and horizontal grids emitting a subtle, sky-blue luminance. The newness of the vessel shown as there wasn't a scratch, a spot of grease, the sweet odor of lubricants, or the bitter scent of charred electronics characteristic of the older warships. With the bright, clean interior, the Mertel looked much closer to something Plexo had helped design than traditional UMO military ships.

Timmon lost his footing entering the vessel with his eyes looking up more than down as he stepped inside, fascinated by the military ship. Krath's eyes widened, and he leaned his head back in an obvious sign of holding his scorn.

"Does this ship have any guns?" Timmon blurted out, staring past Ashton as though he would see some dangling from the corridors and ceilings.

Krath jabbed his plump finger into Timmon's chest. "Now I told tya keep that smacker shut, didn't I?"

"Yes, sir." Timmon lowered his head and kicked at something imaginary on the smooth metal floor.

Captain Ashton placed his hands on his knees and stooped down to get an eye-to-eye look at the youthful Hybor. "Well young fella, the ship has plenty of guns; we just hope we won't need them."

"Aye, but if we do, I'm sure this boat can light up those nasty bug cruisers just fine," Krath added.

The captain gave Krath a friendly smile. "That's right. The Mertel is the latest in the UMO's redesigned military fleet vessel. It's faster, with advanced weapon systems and more resilient shields than the warships of the old Thraxon wars." He posted his hands on his hips and nodded arrogantly. "Heck, I'd even go as far as to say if the UMO fleet consisted of these new ships back in the day, we wouldn't have ever needed a Marck fleet or possibly even Tolagons." His eyes peeked over to Kerriah. "Oops. No offense. I've been informed that you are a recently ordained Tolagon yourself."

Kerriah subtlety shrugged. "That's right, and no offense taken. So, Captain, can you give us the current situation with Plexo and word on Eesolan?"

"Yes. Well, Science Officer Plexo has decided against UMO standby orders and proceeded through Zeta and onward to Eesolan. His orders were to wait for our arrival and escort, but I suppose he lost his patience."

Kerriah shook her head. "No, something happened. Something changed. Were there any additional messages from his home world?"

"Not that we were made aware of. However, we are ordered to set a course for Eesolan, so hopefully, we will meet him there."

"What about the Thraxons? Any reports of them on the other side of the corridor?" Kerriah asked.

"We sent some probes through, and there was nothing. No sign of Thraxons or the lost Marck fleet. So with a little luck, we hope to have a clear path to Eesolan."

"Do we know how long it's gonna take to get there? I gotta send a message to junior's momma so she knows how long the little fella is goin' to be away," Krath asked.

"No one aside from Luminars has ever made the trip there, but according to our trajectory and the Mertel's Super Radiant Drive System, we should be there about eight months after we pass through the far side mirror of Zeta. That is unless they have rebuilt the corridors to their home world, in which case, we could be there a lot sooner. Maybe a week or two in that latter case?" Captain Ashton shrugged. "It's an educated guess. We have some rough coordinates from Luminar Emissary Pira, which should get us close either way. I'll have Lieutenant Anor see you to the comm room if you want to get that message to her right away; otherwise, you'll have access from your quarters after you tour the ship and meet her crew."

"Eight months! We gotta be cooped up in this sterile tub for eight months?" Krath shouted and then stomped away, tripping over Timmon before stopping briefly to pull the young Hybor to his feet.

Ashton looked at Kerriah with shock over Krath's sudden outburst. "W-What just happened?"

Kerriah casually shrugged. "He doesn't take bad news too well. You'll get used to it."

***

Over the next hour, Captain Ashton walked them around the ship to familiarize them with its layout. He introduced them to the crew and briefly explained their day-to-day routines. The crew was mostly young, primarily twenty-somethings, which was understandable given the wars. There wouldn't be too many vets remaining as able-bodied fighters. Kerriah couldn't help but notice Jesselle's subtle flirtations with some of the ship's engineers and special ops troops. It suddenly occurred to her Jesselle never had an opportunity to have genuine relationships. In fact, she had never been around so many handsome young suitors in her adult life, so her maturity, or lack of it, with those she found attractive was evident.

Following the tour, Kerriah settled down in her tiny sleeping quarter. The modest junior officer suite consisted of a small bed inset in the wall, a silver-tinted locker, and a small, sturdy chair with a table providing terminal access to the ship's onboard systems. She swiveled the chair out and plopped down, resting her head in her hands with elbows leaning against the table. *Eesolan.* She let out a deep breath. She should be excited, but so much had happened in just the past couple of weeks. Every event had completely changed her life. She dealt with Crix's emotional swings, the mysterious formation of New Troika, her learning to live with the yellow orb, her visit to Gabor, and now this. She yearned for some time to herself to process her thoughts and plan.

Ashton invited her to the officers' tables for dinner. However, since she didn't feel the need to eat dinner, she stayed in her quarters instead of going to the mess hall. Her thoughts spun amongst the subtle hum of the ship's operational systems until she finally collapsed into her rack.

CHAPTER 21

The ship's alarms woke her early in the morning. The howling siren blared into her room. Kerriah sprang from her rack and pushed her thumb into a recessed wall switch. Her door slid open, amplifying the noise as it poured in from the outside passageway. The screaming siren echoed through the halls, with hidden lights strobing across the ceiling in concert with the alarm. An officer walked with a brisk pace by her door

"Excuse me?" she shouted out to get his attention.

She spun around. "Yes, ma'am," she replied.

"What's going on?"

"We're about to pass through Zeta. You need to find a place to brace yourself as it's going to get a bit choppy."

Kerriah was not about to return to her room and sit this out. No one had been on the other side of Zeta in years, and she wanted to be involved, not some helpless bystander. She stormed down the corridor and dashed into the ovular-shaped personnel lift. Another officer stood inside anxiously waiting to arrive at his deck. Kerriah tapped the lift's panel display, spawning an image of the ship and its various deck locations. She tapped the command deck, and the screen flashed red with the text:

:unauthorized:

Irritated, she squinted and tapped it again, except this time with a little more intensity.

:unauthorized:

flashed again.

The officer looked over at her. "You're not allowed on the command deck. The facial recognition system is only going to allow authorized personnel."

She noticed the lieutenant triangle on his uniform's collar and chest. "Are you authorized?" she asked through grit teeth.

He hesitated for a second. "Uhh, yes, but—"

"Good." She stared at him, focusing on what she wanted him to do.

He leaned in, tapped the display, and tapped again to activate the command deck. The audible system replied, "*Rerouting to command deck, Lieutenant Steet.*"

After a minute, the door swooshed open to an expansive area with command, communication, weapons, and navigation stations occupied by various officers tapping displays and speaking into comm systems. A sizable, holographic display in the center of the bridge showed an image of Gammac Corridor Zeta.

Captain Ashton sat upon an elevated chair overlooking the area and a forward view of the main observation window into space. Kerriah leaned to one side for a peek around him, noticing the shimmering portal of the nearside mirror for Zeta. It was close and appeared as though the ship's nose was about to dip inside.

"Umm, Captain, we have visitors!" a voice of one of the crew called out.

Ashton spun around. "Kerriah! You're not supposed to be up here."

SONG OF THE LAGGORNS

"I realize that, but I'm not going to sit in my quarters like some useless civilian. I have more experience than most of your crew," she snapped back.

"Fine, but you need to strap in. Grab a seat at OPS station." He pointed to a chair and terminal remaining unoccupied. She ran over and pressed the button recessed into the arm. A flexible strapping system folded out and fastened across her shoulders and around her waist.

"*Five . . . four . . . three . . . two . . . one,*" the bridge computer system announced as the nose dipped into the mirror. The lights on the ship blinked out, and Kerriah could feel the seat beneath her tickle from vibration. Her head spun, and the lights flickered. She felt the vibrations in her seat turn from tickling to a light massage and then into a continuous shuddering pulling a vocal groan from deep within her abdomen. Zeta was the longest-reaching corridor. It took them to the other side of their galaxy, whereas the other corridors took them to a chain of neighboring solar systems.

The panoramic view from the sizable, curved bridge window turned to pure white. No stars whipped by, or long lines of colors like some might expect, just an eye-blistering white light keeping the bridge fully illuminated when the onboard lighting systems failed. The whine of alarms sounded, and the crew snapped back to life. "*Three . . . two . . . one.*" The shaking stopped, and the view outside changed from a blank white canvas into a vast nebula of red and purple spattered across the space before them.

"That's it, crew, the Richotaan Nebula. It's truly a thing of beauty. She's still ten light-years away from us, which speaks of its immense size," Captain Ashton announced.

For the crew of the Mertel, the nebula had only been seen from archive video and pictures. Like a masterpiece of impressionistic art, its streaming spikes of bright fuchsia reached into the cosmos and sprawled across their view. The Richotaan Nebula was a sight to behold.

As Kerriah stared out, taking in the sights with the rest of the crew, her thoughts couldn't help but wander. Where were the Thraxons and the Knactor Fleet? They had passed through the mirror two years ago, and now there was no sign of them anywhere. Not even a garrison ship to guard the mirror.

Without the far-side mirror to complete the corridor, passage through would, supposedly, lead to some random location in the galaxy. It would be an extremely perilous move for sure. However, this was how the Luminars had originally discovered the Oro System. The deep-space pioneers, driven by science and discovery, had thrown their lives and caution into the wind. But for the Thraxons, with their endless quest for life to consume and use for breeding, how could they not see more value in the mirror? At least enough to keep one ship here. Something didn't feel right.

"Sir," the voice of the ship's navigator spoke out, "look behind us."

An aft view illuminated over the holographic display at the center of the bridge. The appearance of the mirror wasn't what they had expected. Instead of the refined, smooth, metallic rim, organic-like matter draped over the outer ring. The dark -live matter shimmered against the peppering light of the stars. It looked like something pulled from a deep ocean floor rather than the high-tech marvel built by Luminars.

"Thraxons," Kerriah spoke to herself. "What are they up to?"

"This looks like the work of Thraxons," Ashton said, leaning forward as he inspected the display image.

"Perhaps it's their way of marking territory?" the Hybor first officer of the Mertel, Marth, growled.

"Regardless, let's not waste precious time," Ashton announced. "Set course for Eesolan. Maximum speed." His voice had a sudden urgency, which hadn't been apparent until now. The ship pulled away from the mirror and banked left when something horrifying appeared.

"Sound the general alarm!" Ashton ordered.

As the ship continued its leftward bank, a massive nebula of gold and cerulean crept in from behind the mirror. Its clouds swirled and simmered against the blackness of space. Ethereal fingers outlined with a golden glow whisked around the ring of the mirror. A great eye of red opened over the top of the Zeta and tilted down at the Mertel.

Several voices on the bridge cried out in shock. Everyone's jaws dropped and eyes pried open in terror. *Could it be?* Kerriah's mind went to the one thing that would fit the description of what was before them now.

"Cyos!" the name shouted from her lips.

The ship's general alarm screamed out across every deck. "Evasive maneuvers! Ensign Hanner, get us clear of that thing!" Ashton's command shouted over the alarms.

The ship swung hard right, and the holographic display filled with the aft view of Cyos, encompassing the once blackness of space behind them. Now, only the outline of Zeta appeared against the cloudy backdrop. As the ship's drive system spun up, a whisk of skeletal gas drew off before them. Like some great mouth, a giant opening formed, and a shower of distortion scattered outward toward the Mertel. Everyone onboard suddenly felt an electrical impulse shocking through their muscles.

"Full reverse!" Ashton somehow managed to get the words out before his jaw locked together.

The ship's reverse propulsion jolted everyone forward. The distortion intensified, the molecules around them began to pull apart, and everything blurred. Kerriah lifted her hand and noticed her fingertips widening and fading from her view. The last sound filling her ears before she lost consciousness was the bridge computers announcing a hull breach.

CHAPTER 22

Kerriah's eyes opened and there was a subtle scent of burnt wires in the air. Not noxious, but just a hint, as though maybe hours old. The bridge crew hung slumped in their seats. A grey planet swooshing with pale-green clouds leered back at her from the window outside. She looked down at her hands and gave a sigh of relief. Her fingers were all there and intact. The ship's alarms were strangely silent. She unbuckled herself from her seat and walked around, checking the condition of the bridge and its crew. The first thing catching her eye was the ship's helmsman, Ensign Hanner. The junior officer had exposed bone and muscle over half her face, yet there wasn't any blood. Her left sleeve and arm were also missing. Kerriah pressed two fingers against her neck. *Dead.*

She looked around at the rest of the crew, all of which appeared to be intact, except for the communication officer, whose right hand seemed to be missing the last three fingers and most of his right leg. She checked his pulse and confirmed he was also dead.

"Where are we?" she spoke aloud. *And where is Cyos?*

She approached the window where the unfamiliar planet filled most of the view. She closely inspected every detail, finding no sign of Zeta, Cyos, or even the Richotaan Nebula. They weren't anywhere near their last known position. She needed the crew to be conscious to figure this out together.

She closed her eyes and trained her focus on Captain Ashton. His brain activity was active. Asleep from the best she could tell. She could see his dreams and quickly confirmed her initial suspicions the young captain was smitten with her. She rolled her eyes. How pointless, he barely knew her. He would be better served to keep his focus on the mission before them.

"Wake up!" she screamed into his mind. His body jolted, and he took a sudden, startled breath. His eyes snapped open, and he took a panicked glance around the bridge.

"Where are we?" he asked groggily. "Lieutenant Bannit, report!"

"If you're addressing your communications officer, he won't be able to respond. He's deceased."

Ashton looked over at her. "Kerriah? What's happened? Is my crew dead?"

Kerriah turned to look out the window at the unfamiliar planet. "I don't know. I think something went wrong when we backed through Zeta. Maybe it had something to do with that killer nebula attempting to demolecularize us. However, most of the bridge crew is still alive since I can hear their thoughts and see into their dreams. I can't speak for the rest of the ship's crew." Her face turned sickly pale, and her eyes opened wide. "Oh no." Her voice quivered.

"What?" The unsettled captain nearly jumped from his seat. "What is it?"

146

SONG OF THE LAGGORNS

"Krath . . . Jesselle. I need to check on them." She hurried toward the bridge's lift, frantically tapping the screen to call the doors.

"Wait! What about my crew? We need to revive them," Ashton pleaded as Kerriah stepped into the lift.

"Wake up! Now!" she shouted into their thoughts as the door slid shut.

For a second, she felt slightly impressed with herself, being able to jump into a dozen minds all at once. She had never done that before, and it had just come out in her haste to help her friends. The lift opened to the officer's deck, and she sprinted down the corridors shouting for Krath and Jesselle. They were nowhere to be found as she listened for thoughts while passing each crew quarter and common area.

They had better not be dead. Her mind drifted to the worst-case scenario, and a twinge of anger boiled into her blood. *I should have never let them come . . . stupid!* She called the lift again, and as the door slid open, a sturdy-built Hybor stood there with Timmon slung over his shoulder.

"Krath!" She took a deep sigh of relief upon seeing her old friend. He was the only one on the ship she would genuinely trust with her life. "You're awake!"

"Yeah, lucky for me I was sloppin' down a bowl of chow in the mess hall when all this fracas occurred. Next thing I knew, I was layin' on the deck with the bowl over my head and mush seeping into my mouth. Woke up coughin' and gaggin' only to find everyone, includin' Timmon, face down. I haven't been able to get the little guy to come to, but at least he's alive."

"I can help," she said. "Put him down."

Krath plopped Timmon onto the hard floor like a sack of sea spuds. "Kay, do what tya got to do. Last thing I want is an angry Hybor mom commin' after me for losing her only child."

She entered his mind and could instantly feel his innocence. But hidden deep within his goodness was a fire of anger and the desire for vengeance, a mind too immature to be stricken by grief. His knowing his father was murdered and the evil which had taken him remained unpunished. The loss of his father and the absence of justice was why his mother had given him to Krath; otherwise, the hate would eventually drive out the innocence and possibly create a monster.

"Wake up, Timmon." She was gentle in her delivery. "Wake up. Krath is here."

Timmon's eyes cracked open and darted around with a look of fear.

"It's okay," Kerriah said with a soft voice. When his eyes stopped on Krath, who leaned over to look at the awakening youth, a wide grin spread over his face.

"Ahh, junior." Krath smiled back. "Now get tya butt off the deck and give me a hand with gettin' the rest of this boat's crew back to our world again."

"Jesselle," Kerriah said. "Have you seen her?"

"Nope, but last night she was getting' a little too close to some of the special ops guys. So I think we may need to have a peek down on the enlisted quarters."

Kerriah's jaw clenched. "You must be kidding? What the heck is wrong with her?" she said through her teeth.

Krath shrugged. "Hey, times are tough, and we all gotta do what we gotta do. Who am I to pick at who she chooses to roll in the sack with?"

148

Timmon sat up and put his hand over his mouth to hide his giggle. Kerriah scowled with disdain. "Whatever. I'll follow you to the enlisted quarters."

***

Krath led them down to the various service decks, where the enlisted quarters resided. Overall casualties were light, along with some displaced rooms and inoperable doors. A section of the floor on the weapons deck was demolecularized, leaving a webbed appearance of missing metal. Kerriah revived any unconscious personnel they found while checking into everyone's minds to see if Jesselle was among them.

Krath used brute force to heave a stuck sleeping quarter door open on the cargo deck. Like most racks they had encountered so far, they were empty, with the small compartment door for each bunk open, except one. Kerriah walked over and peeked into the small window viewing the rack. She clenched her teeth before pushing out a frustrated exhale.

"There she is." She pressed the door release to the top bunk. The door slid upward, and Jesselle's arm flopped out. Her bare, unconscious body lay next to a special ops member.

"Get up!" she shouted into their minds.

Both jolted with a sudden inhale.

"Get dressed and get out. Now!" Kerriah's voice was sharp and angry. Without saying a word, Jesselle and the soldier quickly started sliding their undergarments on and jumped down.

Krath growled and glared at the soldier. "In the sack during a general alarm? What the heck is wrong with tya?"

Kerriah gave Krath a glance. "Yeah, and you have your face buried in a bowl of mush."

She turned back to Jesselle, whose tussled, snowy hair looped over her face and across her shoulders. "I'm disappointed in you. Get dressed; we have a major issue right now, and we'll need all the help we can get." The soldier grabbed his clothes and dashed around Krath and out the door, not saying a word. Krath's head turned with a growl as he sped by him.

"You don't need to worry about me," Jesselle said in a raspy voice as she began to toss on her shirt and pants aggressively. "So, what—what's going on?" Her sharp tone came through a piercing stare.

"Cyos attacked us, and now we're in some unfamiliar neck of the galaxy. If that's not enough, a number of the crew is deceased, and portions of the ship are damaged." Kerriah posted her hands on her hips, waiting for Jesselle's reaction to the news.

Jesselle's eyes sprung wide open. "Did you say Cyos attacked us? So that thing is real?"

Kerriah pulled her hand back across her scalp. "Jesselle, what's going on with you? You seemed to have it together since your Tolagon training, but now that you're around a bunch of young men, you've lost your mind. You know it's real. Your training in Gabor confirmed that."

Jesselle leaned toward Kerriah as she gave her snappy reply. "Like I said, stop worrying about me. I can take care of myself."

With a quick eye roll, Kerriah decided to take an uninvited peek into Jesselle's mind to confirm her suspicions. With a slightly uncomfortable pause, she quickly saw what she suspected. She was someone stolen away from a normal childhood just before she started dating, and she had never been in a serious relationship with anyone. Last night was her first sexual encounter with a male and the reason for her fiery response to being chastised for her behavior. She saw her life at risk with the days ahead and felt entitled to explore physical intimacy.

Kerriah's facial expression instantly softened, turning from annoyed to empathetic. "I'm sorry, Jesselle." She didn't have a right to judge her and felt terrible after seeing Jesselle's desperate grasp at life. A yearning for love. She wrapped her arms around Jesselle and gave her a firm hug.

Jesselle flinched away and scowled back at Kerriah. "You just got into my head, didn't you?"

"Now Jesselle . . . please . . . I—" She reached out to touch her arm, and Jesselle angrily smacked it away.

"Stay out of my head! It's not fair that you can do that to people!" she shouted, pointing directly into Kerriah's face.

"Okay . . . okay . . . I'm sorry. I shouldn't have done that." She looked back at Krath, who shrugged, not wanting to get involved with their current spat. Timmon stood near the door with the curious look of a child interested in the drama and not wanting to get any of the ire directed his way.

The ship's general alarm sounded off once again.

"Great, now what?" Kerriah said, sounding exhausted.

"Don't know, but we need to find our way to that bridge to figure it out," Krath replied.

With a gesture forward, Kerriah started walking toward the door. "Come on."

CHAPTER 23

The bridge door slid open, and Krath shoved the unsuspecting UMO officer out of the lift and then stormed into the ship's command center. The personnel were active again, doing their jobs with the sounds of radio communications shouting out over the alarm. An image of a Thraxon frigate spun in the holographic display.

"Kerriah!" Ashton's voice shouted. "You have to stop doing this."

"Then grant me access to the bridge."

"Fine, consider it done, but we have bigger issues right now," Ashton said as he pointed to the image of the frigate.

"A friggen bug boat." Krath stared at the image and cracked his knuckles.

Timmon's round eyes looked up at Krath. "Are we going to battle?"

Krath growled. "Anytime we see one of these parasite-filled cans, that's usually the case." He placed his hand on Timmon's shoulders and gave them a firm squeeze.

"Captain, what's our status? Has there been any contact?" Kerriah asked.

"Nothing. We are too far to get a comprehensive scan for life or movement, and our main drive system is offline. We are advancing with low pulse thrusters."

Kerriah quickly stepped to the bridge's center; alarmed at the captain's brash move, she needed his full attention. "Wait! Is that a good idea? I mean advancing on a known hostile warship, with a partially incapacitated junior crew and inoperable drive system?"

"Kerriah, with respect, I need you to back away and let me call the shots here. My intention is not to engage them but to get within scanning range."

Kerriah's eyes rolled up toward the ceiling, and she leaned her head back with a snort. "How do we know there aren't more of them?" *We should be moving out of range, not in range. We're at a complete disadvantage.* She tossed her hands up in frustration. "At least let me help in some way. I'm certainly familiar with the operations of a ship, and I'm a quick learner."

"Fine. I need you to take over the communications panel. Scan every frequency you can for anything coming from that ship or the planet it's orbiting."

She unclasped Lieutenant Bannit from the chair and let his body drop to the floor before plopping into the deceased communication officer's place. There wasn't time for courtesies for the dead. She slipped a nearly transparent band over her head, filling her ears and eyes with various noise pitches and visuals of waves and numerical measurements. Her mind slowly adapted to the sound spectrum and signals as she focused.

"I'm getting two different signals," she announced as she continued to study the communications data.

"Explain," Ashton said in his authoritative officer voice.

153

"Well . . . if I'm reading this right, and I believe I am, we're getting a long-wave signal from the Thraxon frigate and a completely different signal sourcing from the planet."

Krath began storming angrily around the deck upon hearing Kerriah's analysis. "Them nasty bugs! Focus tya rail guns on that can and blow it—"

"Krath!" she interrupted his tirade. "I need to concentrate here!" She leaned in, trying to make out the signals and translate them based on the ship's linguistic database. "It appears that the signal from the frigate is a call for help. It's the same one used in the past when the UMO has attacked single ships or smaller Thraxon convoys."

"We've gotta stop it. That means we're gonna have a swarm of Thraxon junk crawlin' up our backsides at any moment," Krath brashly complained.

"I'm not so sure," Kerriah responded. "I now agree with the captain; we need to get closer so we can scan their ship."

A brief and subtle smile crept over Ashton's face as he leaned back in his chair. "So the question is did they send this call for help because they saw us or something else?"

Krath snorted and let out a snarl. "It's not like the Thraxons to send their fleet alert before taking at least a few potshots at us."

Kerriah swiped her finger down the panel screen, trying to isolate the frigate's signal. "I agree, Krath. Something isn't right here. I don't think this is because of us, but we need to make sure."

Ashton tapped a small triangle on his shirt collar. "Engineering, I need a status on the drive system." He looked over at Kerriah. "Okay, what about the signal from the planet?"

Kerriah's lips tightened as she shook her head. "There is no reference in our databases. It's completely unfamiliar."

"I guess that's expected since we are off our known charts. But that means someone is down there, and it's not Thraxon. Keep me posted on any changes."

As the crew of the Mertel slowly revived and made initial assessments of the ship's condition, the reports were not what they had hoped. Portions of the main drive system were missing and not replaceable without the aid of a supply ship. The best estimates from their navigation system placed their current position in sector 1003.501.3. That wasn't much help since there wasn't a way to send communications that would reach any UMO outpost before the crew was long deceased from old age. For now, they would remain focused on the Thraxon ship and this mysterious planet.

CHAPTER 24

S ir," the sensor array technician announced to the captain, "our sensors indicate no detectable life or movement coming from the Thraxon frigate."

"Then who's sending the signal?" Ashton replied.

"It's probably automated and has been transmitting for months or even years for all we know." Kerriah looked at the screens with unwavering focus and continued to unravel the information.

"Wait!" the sensor technician shouted with his arm in the air. "There's a low-level life reading. Very faint, as though dormant or in some sort of cryostasis."

"Single?" Ashton inquired.

"That's the best I can tell."

Ashton looked over at Krath. "A squill, maybe?"

Krath shrugged. "Bah, if it's Thraxon, we should kill it regardless."

Captain Ashton slowly massaged his thumb into the arm of his chair as he stared out the window at the Thraxon ship. "Okay, we need to prepare a boarding party." He called down to his tactical infantry commander to assemble a team of UMO commandos.

Kerriah agreed with Asthon's decision to investigate the frigate. If, for no other reason, they might need to salvage it for desperately needed parts. However, she couldn't tear her concern away from the mystery planet.

"What about the planet? Maybe the Thraxons are there, or whoever is responsible for their demise?"

"Right," Ashton replied. "Let's start a multi-pronged effort to investigate the planet." He looked over at his science officer. "Lieutenant Dellien."

"Sir?" The fresh-faced bridge officer looked like she had just stepped out of the academy yesterday, though her forked science credentials displayed on her collar would have her with at least an eight-year stint going through their Apex program. Still, she looked all of twenty-four, and Kerriah resisted the urge to probe her mind for her life story. Although curiosity had her thoughts racing, it would be so easy but deceitful and untrustworthy of a Tolagon to use this power for such a meddlesome purpose.

"Get us an enhanced view of the planet's surface."

"Yes, sir." Lieutenant Dellien tapped her screen several times. "Deploying a recon probe now." A spherical probe fired out of the Mertel's hull into the planet's atmosphere and plunged through the wispy, green clouds. "Surface coming into view. High pressure reading with low oxygen levels, but breathable." The probe shot deeper, with rolling hills of dark-grey stone. "Higher mercury and nitrogen."

"So, is the air safe to breathe?" Ashton asked.

"Yes, for short periods."

"Put up a visual. I want to see what you're seeing."

"Affirmative." The holographic display lit up with vast regions of grey hills, twisted with boney leafless trees scattered throughout. "Plant life detected." Lieutenant Dellien swiped her fingers across the screen and adjusted her immersive head display. The intrigued crew's eyes remained entranced by the scene as the probe zipped over the hills and the repeating landscape swished by for hundreds of miles.

Ashton squinted with interest. "Strange trees, it almost looks like there was a massive fire not long ago. Where's the intelligent life? Or at least animal life?"

"None detected so far. Not so much as a rodent or bird." As Dellien's finger steered the probe up a larger hill, a ruined city emerged as it drifted down its peak. "Structures." Below, a landscape of dilapidated buildings and monuments cast as far as the probe's optics could detect. The same boney trees littering the rolling hills scattered through the sprawling streets and around the elevated constructs. The invasive trees poked through the pavement and out of the sides of many towers and monuments. The city displayed no signs of life and appeared abandoned for some time.

The bridge crew came alive with overlapping chatter upon seeing the alien city.

"Quiet down," Ashton ordered with his hand raised. He was calm and calculated. "Well, it looks like this society caved a while ago. I want an expeditionary team down right away. We need to find out if the Thraxons had anything to do with this civilization's apparent collapse and if there's anything we can recover to help us out of this situation we're in."

"Right away," a bridge officer acknowledged.

"There is still an unknown communication signal sourcing from the planet," Kerriah advised. "It's either from something living or some automated system that still has enough power to transmit. I recommend we send additional probes to scan the rest of the planet."

"Agreed," Ashton replied. "Dellien . . ."

"On it, sir." Two more probes shot into the atmosphere below.

"Now what's the status of my boarding party . . ." the captain asked, momentarily focusing his attention back to the Thraxon frigate.

At that moment, Kerriah looked at him differently. For his years, he seemed to show natural leadership ability, someone that listened to advice and maintained attention to various, quickly evolving situations without losing his cool. Ashton had earned her respect for now.

CHAPTER 25

O uter door breach commencing, . . ." a hollowed voice
crackled from one of the tactical ops' team comm units.
Their attack transport locked itself against the side of the Thraxon
frigate as the team worked through the outer access door.
Thickening tension filled the bridge as the crew held each breath
tight, waiting to see what fate awaited them.

At the same time, an expeditionary team accompanied by
Jesselle was about to touchdown inside the ruined city. Jesselle
insisted her abilities could serve as an important safety net if they
encountered someone or something hostile below. Kerriah had
agreed, with some reservations. Jesselle's intimacy with certain
members of the ops units had possibly influenced her decision.
Still, Kerriah maintained hope her volunteering was for the right
reasons.

"We're inside," a voice from the frigate team announced.
"Keep tight."

The unit tactically moved slowly through the passage with
their rifles snug against their shoulders. A shaky view from a dark,
misty passageway came across the bridge's holographic deck
display. Ribbings of darkened matter lined the narrow corridors,

with small spear tips of scant illuminations filing down the center of the ceiling. The floor was honeycombed with tiny holes, and the sound of their boots hitting the floor with each cautious pace let out a deadened clonk.

"Anyone know their way around that tub?" Krath's voice broke the moment of silence.

"Yep," the bridge intel officer replied as he studied the illuminated, green lines of a digital schematic. "According to our archive data, this frigate is an older model 'Zygint' class frigate. The helm area should be two decks down. The team will need to get to the suckuel to access the other decks. They need to make two rights, and they should be there."

Kerriah looked up from her communications display. "Suckuel?"

Krath turned to her and let out a raspy chuckle. "That's the lift these insects use to move between decks. If tya fought these nasty critters long enough, tya would have heard that term before."

"Ah, I see," she responded. Her focus had always been Marck technology since the Thraxons were the lesser of the two evils during most of her lifetime.

"Sergeant Alar," the intel officer called to the team lead, "take two more rights, and the suckuel should be dead ahead."

"Affirmative." The Sergeant made a chopping motion to the next corner leading right. "Stay sharp, team. Watch our six and the overhead panels," referring to the organic limbs reportedly residing throughout the deck corridor ceilings. They had access from panels over most of the ship.

Reports indicated a Thraxon squill, an extremely large variant with long squirming appendages, represented the central control of most of their larger ships. The ship's command systems plugged into the brain of this Thraxon species, and all controls

161

went through its organic neurons. None of the data had ever been fully verified as the vessel's internal destruct sequence would dissolve the squill if the ship were downed and rendered debilitated, making this frigate even more intriguing.

The team made two rights, and the passage opened to a circular chamber. "Suckuel located," one of the team announced. "What the heck? Sarge, now what?"

"Mertel, are you seeing this?" Sergeant Alar said, panning his view up to the ceiling. Organic holes spanned overhead like puckered, grey flesh with a visually empty cavity inside each.

"We see it, Sergeant," Ashton answered. "What is the next course of action?" he asked the intel officer.

"They need to find the Thraxon symbols on the wall. One should resemble an 'X' with a line through the center. Secure their weapons and place a hand over the symbol," the intel officer instructed.

"Did you copy that, Sergeant?" Ashton asked.

"Got it," he replied. The team stood beneath the suckuel, and one of them located the symbol.

"You've got to be kidding me?" a voice complained.

"Can the chatter!" The sergeant ordered. "Alright, hit that switch."

One of the team placed his hand over the symbol, and a dozen flesh tubes wiggled down over each soldier. The tubes pumped and gyrated, pulling them upward.

"Aww, man," one of the team yowled as he passed through the flesh tubes. Without pause, they dropped down upon the helm area.

"Hostiles!" a voice shouted. The team readied their weapons and swung them quickly around the area.

"Stand down!" the sergeant replied. "Mertel, we have enemy KIA, all over the place." The view turned to Thraxon corpses littered across the deck and one headless, still leaning against the wall on its feet. "What in the heck happened here?"

"Did they kill each other?" Kerriah asked.

"Here's one of those squill limbs," a team member said as he nudged a slimy, black tendril dangling from the ceiling with the nose of his rifle. "Looks like it's either dead or dormant."

"Let's leave it alone, soldier," the sergeant ordered. "Just keep an eye on it and the other access panels."

"Sergeant, can you give us stats of the ship's operational level? Do their helmet computers appear online?"

The holographic image from the sergeant's helmet camera slowly panned across the room. Pods molded into the shape of Thraxon exoskeletons lined the walls with a large cavity in the center of the helm area. A triangular visor hung at eye level over each of the pods.

"Mertel," the sergeant's voice called back, "how the heck are we supposed to tell if the computers are online?"

"Sergeant," the intel officer replied, "you'll need to steady your face in one of the control pod's visors. Let us know if you see anything."

"You heard him," Sergeant Alar said, motioning to one of his team. "Stick your face in one of those things and let us know what you see."

"Sir?" The apprehensive soldier looked at the sergeant.

"Move it, Soldier!"

"Yes, sir." The soldier cautiously paced over to a pod and leaned his face into the visor. "Nothing here, sir, just a black screen."

"Well, Mertel, is that your answer?" Sergeant Alar replied.

"No, he needs to remove his helmet."

Alar took a deep exhale and shook his head. "So what's he supposed to do? Hold his breath in here?"

"That's right," The Mertel intel officer replied.

Alar gestured to the soldier. "Well, you heard the order. Do what you gotta do."

"Man, I don't get paid enough for this," the nervous soldier complained before unsnapping his helmet's retention clasps and peeling it from his head. He quickly stuck his face into the pod and then moved away, securing his helmet back over his head.

"Well . . ." Alar said, awaiting the soldier's report.

"Nothing."

"There you have it, Mertel, nothing."

The feeling on the bridge of the Mertel was a mix of relief and concern. They were relieved the Thraxon ship was offline and a minimal threat, yet at some point, they might need it to be operational for their salvage efforts. It would certainly be helpful with the power and gravity systems online.

"What about the signal?" Kerriah asked. "If the ship's offline, who or what is sending the signal?"

"Sir," one of the bridge officers shouted, "the planet team just touched down."

"Okay, keep me updated on their status," Ashton responded and then turned to Kerriah. "I think we—"

"Oh shoot!" a voice from the ops team on the Thraxon frigate screamed. The display swung to the soldier leaning into the helm cavity for a peek. He leaped back and drew his rifle up; the rest of the team followed suit into a defense posture.

"Talk to me. What's going on over there?" Sergeant Alar shouted.

"Sir, I-I think I just woke it up," the soldier replied.

164

CHAPTER 26

The transport gently touched down in the center of the ruined city. A light mustard coating whisked up from the ground beneath, revealing a rutted surface made of an unrecognizable alloy. The city's street system and walkways appeared lined with plank metal. Much of the metal buckled, with the skeletal trees ripping through sporadically in every direction. The deck slid down and clattered against the hard ground. A team of soldiers filed out with their rifles ready, taking a kneeling position outside the ship while assessing any threats in the area. Jesselle walked out behind them, a little less guarded. Her burgundy jumpsuit clung snugly against her slender build. She took a few deep breaths and felt a twinge lightheaded.

"The air is thin and smells a little sour," she said with her nose scrunched. Her lungs tickled, and she tilted her head to cough into her sleeve. She looked down at the alien surface, noticing the metal plates each had a faded pink hue, and thought this was once a bright and colorful city.

"Reports from the probe indicate a possible Thraxon deceased a few blocks away," the unit commander announced. "We've been ordered to investigate. The captain indicated that it's imperative to know what happened to the Thraxon crew and if the crew of the Mertel is facing a similar fate."

Most of the buildings around them arched and intertwined against each other in a malformed lattice pattern. The trees ruptured from the sides of many of the structures with no apparent purpose. One of the soldiers edged close to the nearest tree to inspect the only thing looking like life on the planet's surface. They neither leaned toward nor away from any visible light source. Abnormal dark-blue veins webbed up from the ground and across the trunk.

"I've never seen a tree like this before," a soldier said, edging a bit closer.

"Leave it," her commanding officer ordered in his deep, gravelly voice. "Our current objective is to investigate the deceased Thraxons. Until then, nobody touch anything." The commander slid his tactical visor down. "Now, let's move out."

The group moved slowly, using the buildings for cover as they crouched and paced through the city streets. Jesselle remained toward the back, allowing the military unit to lead the way. The probe above guided their movements to where it located what appeared to be a group of dead Thraxons, which it reported soon after their departure. It was imperative to know what had happened to the Thraxon crew and if a similar fate awaited the crew of the Mertel. Captain Ashton made this a top priority for the ground team.

The streets were quiet aside from the occasional whistle of a light breeze sliding between the structures and the patter of their boots as they progressed ahead. Personnel transports with transparent tops and ovular bases lay overturned or smashed into the side of buildings as though the last hours or days here were filled with chaos.

166

Jesselle couldn't shake the thought of why there weren't any signs of the inhabitants once occupying the city. Not a corpse or skeletal remains anywhere. Pausing to inspect one of the structures, she noticed the buildings didn't appear to have any visible windows and no way to allow any natural light inside. She tapped her knuckles against the side, and a layer of yellow dust flecked away from the vibration. As her knuckles knocked against it, she realized the structures weren't made of metal or mason but rather some sort of smooth polymer.

She observed the strange fauna and twisted trees throughout the area. The UMO system didn't have a plant species this invasive, and these trees managed to rip through the metal streets and the synthetic building walls. It was hard to imagine what the residents of this once assumingly thriving city did to control them.

"Check this out," one of the soldiers taking point said with a raised voice. He poked his rifle barrel into a pile of fabric caked into the corner of a building. The stiff, faded garments crusted away from the surface as he lifted them for a better look. "Think this is one of the former residents?"

"Who knows?" the commander replied. "I noticed a couple of similar piles a block back. Whatever happened to the citizens here, it's almost like they just evaporated, bones and all. Hopefully, whoever or whatever did this is long gone. Let's keep moving!"

As they snuck around several more corners and weaved through groupings of the strange trees in their path, the remains of the Thraxons came into view. Visually, it was merely a cluster of black armor lightly coated in mustard-yellow dust. A noticeably denser mass of trees gathered around the Thraxon armor and a troop carrier, which lay overturned with the smashed structure above, signifying its impact.

"These Thraxon appear to have been KIA for quite a while," a soldier's voice chimed through the comm. "Look!" He kicked at the armor pile, uncovering the remains of Thraxon exoskeleton casings hidden beneath the yellow dust and metal plates.

The gruff commander peaked at the remains and then nervously swept his rifle around the higher points of the buildings. "Yeah, but who killed them?"

"I don't like these trees," another soldier said. "Why are there so many around these Thraxon KIAs? What are all these damn trees doing here in the city?"

"Mertel," The commander called to their ship, "we've converged on the Thraxon position, and they all appear to have been killed by something. However, with no blast marks or visible penetration in their armor or exoskeletons, whatever they were fighting wasn't using conventional weapons. It appears that they were . . . vaporized. Request permission to infiltrate one of the structures for further investigation."

The ship failed to respond right away. The impatient commander called back, "Mertel, do you copy? Mertel?" He shook his head with frustration and stared upward. "What the heck is going on up there?"

An anxious voice finally buzzed back over the commander's comm. "Planet team, we copy. Please stand by for further orders."

"Stand by, team." His soldiers paced around, sweeping the buildings and alleyways, and verbalizing an occasional complaint over the situation. It was apparent they were becoming increasingly anxious since locating the Thraxons.

Jesselle finally broke her silence. "I don't like this. Everything in this city is dead or missing, and everything that has since entered the city is dead." She turned to the commander. "I think we should return to the transport."

"With respect, Tolagon, you're not calling the shots here. Our mission is to do a full threat assessment of the city before we can send our science team down. So far, we have no idea what's happened here."

"I just don't like these trees," the soldier complained again. This time, he nudged his rifle barrel into the side of one. The surface was surprisingly pliable. "What the?" he said as he pushed into it again with more force.

Like that of cellophane peeling apart, a crinkling came from above them. Their rifles turned upward, and Jesselle took a few anxious steps back. The top of the tree peeled open with whisking threads blossoming out. Hundreds of slithering strands lapped around the trunk and lashed through the air randomly.

"Get back! Everyone, now!" the commander shouted with his rifle snugged against his shoulder and his eyes focused into the optics. He took a few cautious steps back, stumbling over a discarded Thraxon blade.

The thick branches began to move, one jutting at the nearest soldier, smacking into his armored chest plate. He stammered back from the blow, nearly losing his footing. The other branches followed up on the attack, jabbing into his leg, and another smashed through his visor. Immediately the limbs began to pump with slight bulges rippling back into the trunk. Its deep-blue veins slowly turn red with each siphoning flex.

The shocked team fired into the tree, not knowing what part to hit but frantically trying to suppress its attack. The energy shots charred into its side, and the base pulled up from the street, leaving a hole where it once rested. The tree lurched for the group, and they frantically pulled back their position. It paused with the downed soldier directly at its base. It raised its limb, pulling the fallen warrior's empty flesh through the neckline of his armor and uniform. The vacant skin shrunk inward until it hung like a wet rag.

"Focus all fire at the center mass!" the commander ordered.

The energy blasts went from peppering across the trunk and limbs to zeroing in on a half a meter section in the middle. The advancing tree paused, and a boney, white head glopped from beneath the top of the whisking strands. It let out a loud groan as two dimples formed and rotated to the group below.

"The head! Shoot the head!" the voice of a soldier shouted above the fray.

Their shots jerked up from the center trunk to the pale, blob-like head. The tree recoiled back and then jolted forward, leaning down with its whisking strands wrapping around the commander's head and torso. He tried to break free, swinging his rifle around and then chopping down upon the strands as they coiled around his body. The larger limbs pulled back to strike their final blows when a burning, red-winged creature swooped in, ripping the captive threads from around the commander with its claws and teeth.

The commander fell back and then quickly stumbled to his feet again. Jesselle stood back with her hands forward as the transparent bird of prey swung around to fend off the oncoming limbs. The team continued to focus their attack on the head, and each connecting shot left a seared, black splotch in its flesh.

"We need to . . . hit it with . . . something heavier," the commander called out; his breath heaved between every few words. "Dronar, lance it!"

"Aye, sir." A bulky Solaran soldier slung his rifle and drew a large, white cylinder from his pack. He rotated the weapon's grip down with an audible click, wrapped his muscular hand around it, and flicked a switch with his thumb. The cylinder jutted out twice its length with a spear tip at the end. Locking the optics in place, he leaned his head in, aiming at the target, and squeezed the trigger. A red beam shot out at the tree's head, followed instantly by an impact sending shockwaves across the entire city block.

The team stumbled back, and the yellow dust blew up from the surface and filled the air with a cloud of mustard. The head exploded into a spray of red and blue mist with oozing streams pouring down its dark trunk. The tree leaned back before tipping over, falling into the side of another nearby tree.

The rustle of thin plastic crinkling and splattering of wet flesh filled the brief silence seconds after the tree fell.

"Hostiles!" the commander shouted.

Clusters of trees awoke from their dormancy. The tops peeled open, and whisking strands darkened the sky. "Fall back! Fall back!" his voice boomed through their comms. They took a few desperate shots and turned to run back in the direction they had come. "Get back to the transport!"

They turned around several corners, tracing their steps back in the direction of their landing site when they suddenly skidded to a stop. A wave of the lurching trees moved toward them, blocking their escape.

"Heads up!" a voice cried out. Three trees stuck their limbs into the building above, crawling down the sides to reach their intended prey.

"The whole friggin city is alive with these things!" the commander shouted. "Transport! We need immediate evac from our current position!" he called back to their ship, waiting just a few blocks away. "Transport! Do you copy?" There was no reply.

"Mertel, we need air support and an evac ASAP. We may have lost our transport!"

"Copy that," the command bridge replied. "Our drone confirmed that your transport has been disabled. Sending evac team and air cover. ETA twenty minutes."

"Mertel, we're not going to last two minutes down here," the commander replied.

"Here!" Jesselle pointed out a rough opening to one of the buildings, though she hadn't recalled seeing it when they went through here earlier.

"Team, take cover inside!" the commander ordered.

The team filed inside, where they encountered a series of tall, slender chairs, some still upright and others toppled, with elaborate, brass chandeliers dangling above most seats. No one gave a moment of thought regarding the interior or its purpose. Their concerns focused on the amassing of hostile creatures outside. The chorus of chandeliers chimed across the expansive area inside as the ceiling began to rumble, and a web of cracks formed above them.

"Oh, man, this is not good!" a voice cried out over the comm.

"Take defensive positions!" the commander yelled.

As the team fanned out, taking cover behind anything they could find, the walls outside peeled open with charcoal limbs ripping through newly formed holes. At the same time, chandeliers rattled and crashed into the floor. Limbs plunged through the high ceiling, and several trees dropped onto the floor. Voices cried out as they were snatched from their hiding spots, and their mostly ineffective rifles desperately tried to fend off the attackers.

"Mertel . . . where's our air support? . . . Merte—" the commander's voice cracked, and he cried out in pain before going silent.

CHAPTER 27

The bridge of the Mertel was ablaze with action as they tried to manage through multiple crises. The engineering team struggled to find a way to repair their damaged drive systems, the tactical ops team on the Thraxon frigate had just awoken the long-dormant squill, and the planet team was minutes away from being consumed by numerous hostile creatures. If there was a time the junior crew of the UMO destroyer desperately needed wisdom, it was now.

Kerriah stared at the scene from the drone and various helmet displays from the ground team with a gaping mouth and a squint.

"That can't be," she said to herself. "Is that what I think?"

Her thoughts went to Crix's explanation of what he called the heydromac that had nearly killed him on top of the mountain in Semptor years ago. It was difficult to imagine this strange creature would be on the other side of the galaxy, where no UMO ships had supposedly ever come anywhere near. It was an anomaly in their home system, as there were no records of such a species in the UMO archives. Yet, what she saw perfectly fit the unique description Crix had given. It had to be the same species, but how?

"Captain." She turned to the heavily occupied Captain Ashton, who swung around getting updates from various officers and revising his orders as the situation changed. "Captain, I think I know what these things are."

His attention shifted momentarily in her direction as he handed a translucent board back to one of his bridge officers.

"Yes, Kerriah, tell me what you think it is?" His blank expression and unpronounced tone made it clear he didn't give credit to her account of this hostile organism.

"Crix," She paused for a quick breath. "He told me of a creature he referred to as a heydromac that he encountered on a Solaran mountain top."

The captain drew his head back with a confused grimace. "Solara?"

"Yes, Solara. It was something that Gorag had used for killing dissidents or anyone that defied him. It nearly killed Crix, and it took every bit of the orb's power to save himself."

"Okay," the captain replied. "How does that help us right now? Does it have a weakness or something we can exploit?"

"First off, I believe they need nourishment to thrive, or they go into a dormant state, like the ones in the city below. The heydromac that Crix encountered was also dormant. When it awoke, it tried to suck out his insides, and he pulsed it with the orb's power, which disabled the creature. He felt that it was just trying to survive. He killed it with a massive follow-up blast from his orb. So they can be killed by energy, but it takes a large amount, and I suspect more than your team's rifles are packing. If I recall, this ship has a small squadron of attack fighters, correct?"

Ashton waved off an approaching officer that had another order for him to sign off. "That's right. We have five alpha class interceptors. I've already signed off on those to provide close air support to the team below. They are scrambling to their ships as we speak."

"What types of ordnance are they carrying?" Kerriah asked.

"Each ship is equipped with dual Torac cannons and four powerhead matter displacement torpedoes."

Kerriah cringed. "The PHMDs will easily take out the heydromacs but likely topple the surrounding structures on top of the team. I recommend that they stick with the cannons. Hopefully, they pack the punch needed."

Ashton tilted his head with a sarcastic nod. "Kerriah, I can assure you our fighter crew knows what they are doing. So allow us to conduct our jobs here."

His dismissiveness felt like a backhanded slap, and for a minute, Kerriah thought it was inappropriate over her voiced concerns, but she couldn't help but probe into his thoughts. She could see he wasn't confident in the orders he gave, and a part of him wanted to relay her input to his squadron, but he couldn't show any weakness in front of her. *Egotistical fool.* His interest in her hadn't waned, despite all the surrounding turmoil. Even without the yellow orb probing into his thoughts, the beads of sweat trickling down his face and soaking into his collar gave away the pressure that had started to get to him, though he mostly hid it well.

"How about our team on the frigate?" Ashton asked aloud. "Give me an update."

"Sir," the bridge control officer replied, "patching them in now."

The holographic display changed from an aerial view of the heydromacs encroaching on the planet team to Sergeant Alar's helmet camera. "Alar, what's your status?" Ashton asked.

"Ahhh . . . we have this squill temporarily subdued. A few controlled blasts to its greasy limbs appear to be enough of a deterrent for now," Sergeant Alar replied.

"Alright, Sergeant, keep us posted on when it's safe to send over an engineering team."

"Captain, our alphas are deployed and should reach their target in ten minutes," a bridge officer said.

"Excellent." Ashton gave a stern look to the officer. "Tell them precision shots with Toracs only. No torpedoes. Understood?"

"Understood, Captain."

Ashton turned to Kerriah with a slight grin. She wasn't sure what to think of his gesture. Should she be flattered or insulted? She wanted to peek inside his thoughts again but resisted the temptation.

CHAPTER 28

"The chief is down!" a frantic voice broke over the comm. "He's down!" Chaos erupted as cries of pain and shots rang out from every corner. The area flashed green with blaster fire, and stringy tendrils and boney arms flailed and snapped, reaching for their victims.

The ground shook, and the air thickened with the stench of sulfur. Six shimmering red monsters ruptured from the floor; their ridged stone bodies had no discernible face and few details: just two thick legs and four hulking arms with long fingers. The brutish figures let out a deathly groan as they tromped forward, wrapping their appendages around the heydromacs and forcing them back away from the soldiers. The heydromacs' pale heads glopped from their trunks, and their wicking strands slapped helplessly against the bodies of their stone attackers.

"Move out! Now!" a voice sounded off over their comms. The remaining soldiers filed out into the street, where dozens of heydromacs had amassed.

"Great, now what?" a soldier called out as she swung her rifle around the target-rich street.

"Incoming alphas! Take cover!" another voice shouted.

SONG OF THE LAGGORNS

The soldiers ducked behind anything they could find in a few seconds as the whine of the alpha class attack fighters' anti-grav propulsion systems zipped by, peppering the congregation of heydromacs with a red blaze of Torac cannon fire. Simultaneous dying groans and the rumble of the great beasts dropping to the street gave the team enough incentive not to waste a second vacating the area. They climbed over and around the downed trunks and deflated blobs once the heads of the bloodthirsty creatures. The noxious stench of burned feces filled the air as fumes from the charred heydromacs turned into an assault on their lungs.

They turned down two different streets appearing vacant before stopping. "Where's Jesselle?" A soldier asked as she glanced around at her seven remaining squad members.

"I thought she fell in behind us?" another soldier said.

She turned around and took five steps in the direction they had just come from, waving her team to follow. "We have to go back and get her."

"I'm not going back into that meat grinder. No way." The soldier lowered his rifle and stood straight.

The ranking corporal tapped his helmet. "Team, we just got a call from the Mertel. Our extraction is inbound and should be in our position in three minutes. They also informed us that there is a massive fissure right outside the city with thousands of these creatures pouring up and heading our way."

"That's it. We can't jack around here anymore. We need to hold position for our extraction."

"We don't leave anyone behind!" she responded and continued to wave them in. "Come on!"

"Screw that!"

179

The corporal gazed over at the defiant soldier and pulled his rifle up into a ready position. "We don't leave anyone behind. So let's move out." He waved his squad to follow behind him and maneuvered back around several large buildings where they had just escaped the heydromac attacks.

"There she is!" a voice called out.

Jesselle remained on her backside, propped up on her elbows, staring desperately at a heydromac lurching over her with another downed nearby, its head strands wrapped around her ankle, still trying to pull her back. A flock of ethereal birds whipped in circles, struggling to fend off the attacker, and another blood-red stone and metal beast pulled the fallen heydromac by its trunk, occasionally stopping to pound a fist into its side.

"Dronar!" the corporal shouted.

The husky soldier stepped forward, pulled another lance from his pack, and shoved it into the empty pipe. "Got it."

He fired into the standing heydromac, striking it in the head and sending it toppling back, falling atop the downed heydromac still struggling to maintain a hold of Jesselle. The crashing impact loosened its strands, and Jesselle jumped back to her feet. Behind her was the city's landscape darkened with a sea of heydromacs, rapidly closing in like an eclipsing shadow across the streets.

She turned and shot a glance back. She had never had a lot of value in her own life, but at this exact moment, she wanted nothing more than to escape these terrors.

"Run!" a voice called out, and all the soldiers turned to sprint back in the opposite direction.

Jesselle felt a spike of heat followed by a chill across her flesh, and she took two steps forward and leaped into the air. Her body flashed with a flare of red around her, and she gracefully floated up and zipped ahead, quickly catching up with the others. She hadn't used this ability since she was under Zearic's influence; she was always hesitant to bring herself back to those dark days, so she intentionally avoided anything that reminded her of that time. But now it felt good, and her confidence soared with her body.

She took to a higher vantage point, looking to assess the situation below. The daytime light dipped into the horizon, and long shadows slowly spanned the streets from the buildings. The group slowly broke away from the wave of incoming heydromacs, but they ran directly into dozens more pulling themselves up from their resting places in the street and climbing down from the buildings. She felt a breeze swoosh against her back. Their extraction hovered down with its guns blazing into the surrounding threats.

"Team," the ship's pilot announced, "we're overhead. Standby . . ."

CHAPTER 29

C aptain, the transport has reached the ground team and is preparing to extract them now," a bridge officer announced to Ashton.

"Excellent," he replied. "Let me know when they're off the ground."

"We also have incoming reports from our drones on the other side of the planet. They have located other cities," the officer continued with her head leaning forward, studying the images and data as they flowed across her view.

Ashton slid to the edge of his seat upon hearing this new development. "Is there any life? Aside from these . . . these . . ." He turned to Kerriah.

"Heydromacs," she replied.

"Yes, those things."

"No, sir. The city structures are different, and so far, we have not detected life, though the streets appear to be scattered with statues of what I'm assuming depicts the native species."

Captain Ashton snapped his fingers and pointed at the holographic display. "Let's have a look."

"Aye, sir."

The holographic display returned images of a city filled with sleek grey pyramids of various sizes. Most were tall and slender, and others were short and wide. Statues, stoic in their postures, stood nearly three meters tall throughout the area. There was no apparent placement of most. No pedestals to prop them up, no signs at their feet, no monuments around them, just an amorphous dispersion as though the citizens had frozen in place as they went about their daily tasks. The grid of streets appeared to have a reflective surface as the daylight peaked across the building tips and the gentle morning glow filled the city.

"That's certainly strange," Kerriah said. "Does anyone actually live on this planet?"

"And there's nothin' to eat besides those lumberin' gut suckers," Krath blared out, startling almost everyone on the bridge. "No surface water either. Just a whole lotta misery. Sorta reminds me of Solara." The Solaran gunner twisted in his seat and scowled at Krath over his comment. Krath shrugged. "Oh, sorry, buddy. Nothin' personal."

"Okay," Ashton said. "Let's get a new ground team together for a closer look."

"I'm going this time," Kerriah spoke up. She wasn't about to sit back passively on this expedition. She had already had her fill with watching everything from afar; besides, she had more experience than most of the personnel they sent.

"Negative," the captain said in a firm tone. "I'm not going to take a chance at losing you. Considering what happened to the last team, it's too risky."

Kerriah nearly stood up from her chair with objection. "Excuse me, Captain, but I'm a Tolagon, and if you've been paying attention so far, you would know that the only reason you have any survivors from your surface ground team is that they had a Tolagon with them."

Captain Ashton nervously tapped his fingers on the armrest of his chair as he stared through her. After several minutes he drew in a deep breath and a slow exhale.

"Fine," he said.

"Great, where do I suit up for departure?"

Ashton waved his index finger into the air. "But I'm coming with you."

Kerriah drew her head back in shock. "You can't leave the ship and put yourself at direct risk." As far as she knew, the notion was absurd and violated UMO military protocols.

"I can and I will. My first officer Commander Marth is more than capable of handling the ship's command while I'm away."

The old, seasoned Hybor officer, Commander Marth, had ship command experience going back to the second Thraxon war. He was easily more qualified to command the ship than Ashton, with many years of real wartime command experience. However, the old prejudices still clung to the UMO military, and a Hybor wouldn't be given primary command of an advanced warship like the Mertel.

"Well, if tya all are goin', then I'm, r . . . ahh, me and junior here—" Krath grabbed Timmon by the back of his neck and squeezed till the youthful Hybor winced, "are comin' with tya."

Ashton looked at Krath with both shock and exhaustion. "Great," he mumbled to himself, rolling his eyes.

Kerriah took notice of Ashton's non-verbal objection. "I trust Krath more than anyone here. We could use his experience. I wish we could leave Timmon here, but I know he isn't going to let him out of his sight."

"That's right. This little guy is 'bout to learn what it takes to be a Hybor. That means if somethin needs a good ole fashion clobberin', then that's what they're gonna get."

Ashton stood and motioned for them to follow. "Commander Marth, you have the bridge," he said as they paused for the lift doors to open. "Keep me posted on the Thraxon frigate."

The gritty, old, graphite-skinned Hybor standing nearby with his hands clasped behind him stepped over to the captain's chair and took a slow seat. "Captain. Not to worry, this boat will be in good hands while ty're away."

"I'm still expecting to have that pint of Hybor grob with tya when I get back," Krath said. Marth returned an acknowledging nod as the door closed.

They descended to the ready deck, where personnel suited up, briefed, and deployed for off-ship missions. Before the door slid open, the scent of rotting garbage and stagnant water filled the tight space. Ashton blinked his eyes a few times and took a dry heave.

Kerriah placed her hand over her nose. "Aww, Krath! You couldn't wait till we could get out of here?"

Krath broke out in laughter. "Hybors don't hold body functions. We let nature run its course when it's needed."

Timmon snickered. Once the door slid open, Kerriah and Ashton rushed out while Krath poked his elbow at Timmon. "Weak-bellied Mendacs."

CHAPTER 30

The transport took a smooth pass over the city of pyramids. There wasn't a single bit of noticeable movement, yet the city streets and buildings appeared clean and immaculately maintained. The streets glared with sunlight as they tried to get a closer inspection. The statues the probe reported seemed more abundant than initially stated. Captain Ashton looked over at Kerriah with a smile. Her face was buried into a thin, portable screen with early images from the probes. She looked up and slid her visor down for a current view from the transport.

"Yeah, this is strange." She lifted her visor and peeked at the screen she held again. "This is the same intersection." She lifted it near Ashton's face and pointed to a spot on the screen. "See that?"

"What?" Ashton replied, squinting for a clearer view. "What am I looking for, Kerriah?"

"Those statues. There are three of them in this view, but there are six when I look at the current view. Plus, they are in different spots."

"Yeah, that's odd," he replied.

"I don't like this. Who or what is moving these around? And why? There's something we are not seeing." Kerriah pulled the screen back to her face for another hard look and slipped it into a chest pocket. Her thick black uniform had pockets everywhere.

Heavily armed and armored soldiers lined the transport awaiting their destination, while Krath sat back with a chest plate, black pants, and no helmet. He tapped his knuckles against the chest plate while telling Timmon some old war story of the times he had worn them in the past.

Kerriah looked through the visor display once more. She would have bet the statues had moved again since the last time she had checked only a few minutes ago. She squeezed her eyes shut for a few seconds, thinking maybe her mind played tricks. Perhaps it was the stress of everything going on over the past days and weeks. The pilot announced they were about to touch down inside the city, and she slid her hand under her visor and gave her eyelids a firm rub. They were about to get a closer look.

***

The smooth streets felt like standing on glass. Aside from the sound of the transport's drive system winding down behind them, there was virtually no noise in this almost sterile city. No dirt, trash, or wafts of garbage scent; it was as if the region was one gigantic, well-maintained prop. Several of the tall statues stood close by. The soldiers carefully paced toward the seemingly lifeless figures with their rifles drawn, carefully examining the still monuments. They stood on two legs with heads slightly taller than the typical Mendac. One of the two had a subtle stride in its stance.

Captain Ashton stepped out of the transport and took a few deep inhales of the thin air. "Look at this place," he said aloud.

Kerriah could sense his heart rate increase, and his thoughts blinded him with excitement over what was before him. He wasn't thinking like a leader, with a healthy skepticism needed for the unfamiliar situation. She felt an imminent danger and suspiciously walked over to one of the statues and gazed at its face. She noticed what appeared to be three eyes, with a slightly larger center eye positioned right above the bridge of a small nose. There weren't any noticeable pupils to tell which way it looked, and its mouth appeared to be pinched closed, almost in an untrusting scowl. She could feel an iciness of hostility around her. It could have been her group, as the soldiers were ready for anything.

Then something whispered nearby. She turned and looked around for the source. The voice whispered again, except now it sounded like two voices. She slid her helmet off and dropped it to the ground to open her ears to the outside.

She turned back to the statue. It seemed closer than before. Less than two meters from her now.

"Did that thing move?" a soldier's voice shouted from the group.

"What? What moved?" another voice answered.

"That friggen statue. I swear that thing was standing further back." He pointed at the second statue standing further away from Kerriah.

"You're losing it. Nothing moved."

Timmon tugged Krath's arm to get his attention as they stood near the transport. "Look," he said, pointing down the street, "more are coming."

Krath grumbled. "What? What tya mean more are coming?"

"Those statues at the end of the street. There wasn't that many before."

Krath hunched forward for a better look. "Tya sure those weren't there before?"

"I'm pretty sure."

The whispers persisted, but Kerriah couldn't make out the words. It wasn't an accent or language she recognized. She tried to focus on the statue in front of her by using the orb to investigate its thoughts. She felt a bit crazy over the premise. It was a statue, so why was she trying to read its mind? But the whisper became louder, and she found it difficult to disregard. Though the dialect was unfamiliar, she suddenly knew what it meant.

"Get out," she said aloud. "Someone is telling us to get out."

"What?" Captain Ashton said. "Who is telling us—"

"Stand down!" a soldier's voice screamed out as she took two steps back with her rifle trained on a nearby statue. The statue's strong, metal-like arm held one of the soldiers in the air as his body squirmed, and his gloved hands tried helplessly to peel the solid grip from his neck. The rest of the team fanned out, aiming at the giant.

"Take it down!" the team commander ordered.

Shots connected from all around the statue. With each blast, the head let out a subtle glow, which quickly receded into its metal skin. Its expression instantly changed from apathetic to a beaming scowl. The soldier it held was now twisted and broken on the street, yet no one had seen it move.

"Hostiles!" a voice cried out.

Statues suddenly surrounded them, filling the street like an angry mob spawning from nowhere. The soldiers fired their weapons in desperation while shouting orders back and forth, hoping the outcome would change. The statues moved without motion, and instantaneously the shots ceased, and the voices silenced. Bodies lay crumpled around the street with towering figures staring back at the survivors. Kerriah, Krath, Timmon, and Ashton remained frozen, like animals caught in a spotlight.

Krath slowly put his arm around Timmon and pulled him closer.

"Sir, what's going on out there?" the transport pilot's voice clicked in over Ashton's ear modules. He didn't reply and instead remained still, waiting for their fate. "Sir—"

"No one make a hostile move or grab for any sort of weapon," Kerriah said with her hand up in the transport's direction. She was alone in the middle of the street, nearly surrounded.

Leave here. The strange whisper said in an unrecognizable language, but she still somehow understood. It was one of the yellow orb's gifts to break through any language barrier by reading the thoughts and intentions of the speaker. One of the statues flashed right in front of her, its arms folded and its face commanding.

"I don't know how they are moving, but they want us out of here. At this point, I say we heed their request while we still can," Kerriah said, taking a slow, cautious step back with her arms loosely extended for mental balance more than physical. Her heart raced, and her mind focused on the statue directly in front of her.

"Kerriah," Ashton's voice came out gritty and broken. He quickly cleared his throat. "Can you ask them why they attacked us? Tell them we are not here to cause any harm."

"Hmmm . . . too late for that," Krath growled. "Our guys are already cadavers. I don't think they are goin' to be our pals."

"Krath!" Kerriah said, scowling.

The last thing she wanted was to provoke them, whatever they were. She took several more careful steps back before clonking into a statue emerging directly behind her. The figure stared back down at her, and she appeared like a child next to its towering body. She felt a chill flash across her skin as she snapped a startled look back.

"What are you doing here?" the voice whispered into her head. The orb deciphered the words, but she needed to find a way to answer.

She stared into the cold eyes of the statue, and she spoke her answer aloud. "Our ship is stranded in your planet's orbit. We cannot leave without help. Please, we did not mean any harm."

The words were unintelligible to her companions from the Mertel. Krath raised his brow and looked at her like he didn't recognize her for a few seconds. The statues around them suddenly turned their heads at her, each with surprised expressions.

"Then why did you bring weapons here?" the statue asked, again through thoughts.

"We—" she stopped her reply and decided to adjust.

She worried explaining it was routine for them to bring weapons could send the message they were a violent culture. Something that may not go over well here. "There's another ship stuck in your planet's orbit. A ship that belongs to a warring species which killed many of our citizens. We were concerned they may be down here as well."

"A time ago, the ships came here with weapons and ill intentions," the statue replied. "They did not choose to leave willingly."

"I understand. We want to leave but can't. Our ship is damaged and needs parts and repairs. Can you help us?" She took a pasty swallow. Asking them for help only minutes after witnessing them execute eight of their soldiers was a risky move.

An uncomfortable pause followed. To Kerriah, it strangely felt like hours, but it must have been just a minute, maybe two. Her feet felt a sudden throbbing pain and her back felt stiff.

"Captain?" a call came from the Mertel. Ashton's hand trembled as he tapped his ear.

"What is it?" he spoke as softly as he could, turning his head away from the statues.

"Captain, thank goodness you're alive. We've been boarded. I repeat, our ship has been boarded," the voice over the comm replied.

CHAPTER 31

They flickered around the ship like Soorakian glow beetles. These glossy grey figures, who came out of nowhere suddenly, moved about the Mertel within eye blinks, or so it appeared. Their arrival followed a bright, glowing, cylinder-shaped container emerging shortly after her transport arrived. Jesselle tried to keep focused on one mysterious figure remaining inside the landing bay. They moved without sound or visible motion and quickly killed two soldiers. The helpless warriors, still shaken from battling the heydromacs, had raised their rifles upon seeing these intruders but never had a chance to squeeze a shot off before being reduced to broken masses on the deck. The rest of the personnel fled, disappearing down the ramp leading into the ship's inner corridors. She could still hear panicked screams and orders relayed over the ship's communications systems.

She stood frozen as she watched the motionless figure. It faced her as though its principal objective was to keep a vigilant watch over her actions. She was too afraid to move, worried if she budged, she would end up like her broken companions. Jesselle eyed a piece of machinery used to clean the transport's propulsion systems, which sat nearby. It's all she needed. The six smooth, tubular probes with rounded sonic inducers at the ends pointed upward from the cleanser. Jesselle focused; her body lit red as the tubes curled their tips to the floor. The base lifted from the deck, reshaping into a mechanical arachnid. The statue's head instantly turned to the animated construct instead of Jesselle.

The six-legged machine clacked across the floor and pounced onto the statue. It fell to its backside as the arachnid legs coiled around its neck. Jesselle suddenly felt her mind ripped away from her animated creation, something she had never experienced since her time with the red orb. She flinched for a second, trying to regain control, but as she peeked across the bay, she could see the machine lay scattered in pieces, as though ripped apart and beaten into an inoperable state. The statue stood over her with a menacing scowl. In a single motion, she whipped her hands over her face and pinched her eyes closed as she attempted to create an apparition near the statue.

A red figure shimmered into view, wielding a long-handled hammer. It drew back to swing, and the statue emerged behind it, its strong hands grasping through gas and air. Jesselle darted into a supply compartment to hide while her creation momentarily distracted the figure. Her body snugged into the tight space with sharp tools and canisters pinching and gouging into her back. She pulled the door down, letting out a securing clack as it locked shut.

She could only hope the ghostly distraction she had created preoccupied the teleporting intruder long enough for her to slip from its view. Falling tools clattered to the floor, and the purring spin of canisters against the metal deck let her know the statue still moved around. As she lay in the floor-based compartment, the discomfort inside the tight space made it challenging to remain still. A sharp, pointy object dug into her ribs. The stabbing point began to feel hot and possibly wet, like blood. It felt like a blade or hook, and she tried to ignore the pain, knowing her movement would rattle something together, giving away her location.

After several minutes the clatter ceased, and no sounds, aside from the gentle hum of the ship's power systems, reached her. No screams or shots fired in the distance, no footsteps— nothing. Hiding in the cramped space brought back the horrors of being a child in Zearic's testing facility. She was scared when her peers died horribly, so she hid in a maintenance panel for almost a day. She had squeezed tight into a space with little air. Claustrophobia had kept its tight grip around her throat and had kneeled its oppressive weight upon her chest.

When she eventually came out, the punishment for her disobedience was swift and cruel. They placed her in a stasis chamber with no lights and sound for days. With her arms and legs splayed out, frozen in the center of the room, she had been deprived of all senses. She could only twitch her tongue to let herself know she was still alive. It took a couple of days until her mental state nearly degraded to the point of no return. When they finally released her, she begged them never to put her through that again and swore her unyielding obedience to Sinstar and Zearic, a pledge she cringes over the thought of to this day.

The silence inside the cramped space overwhelmed her with terrible memories, and she needed to get out. Even though the manual release for the door was on the outside, she could still manipulate the mechanisms from the inside to release the lock. She grabbed and twisted the thin bars locking the door. Her heart pounded, and her cold, clammy hand quivered to keep a tight enough grip as she rotated the rigid fastener. Finally, it clicked open, and she gently slid the metal door back. The cool, open air calmed her nerves, even in the face of the possible threat outside. She took a deep breath before she moved. As she raised her head, the face of the statue flashed into her view. Its larger third eye was a mere half a meter from her face.

Her heart stopped, and her muscles flexed tight. In another apparent blip in time, its head now faced away from her. Then as quickly as it appeared, it flashed away. Her muscles relaxed, and her heart skipped a few beats before returning to normal. She carefully climbed out of the compartment and to her feet. The foreign ship was gone, as were the statues. She tiptoed lightly across the landing bay and carefully peeked through the golden-tinted repulsion field keeping the vacuum of space outside. There was nothing visible aside from the Thraxon frigate in the distance. As she turned away, she caught a glimpse of movement in her peripheral vision. She quickly spun around, noticing a group of ships had appeared outside.

She ran over to the terminal and frantically tapped the screen. "Bridge!" She hoped someone was still alive to respond. "Are you seeing this?"

"Yes," a voice she didn't recognize replied. "A group of Thraxon warships just dropped in." The general alarms sounded off, and the emergency beacons strobed throughout the hangar.

Jesselle felt a sudden wave of dread pouring over her. A presence she hadn't felt in years was nearby, which shook her to the core. She placed her hands on her knees, laboring with gasping breaths. An abrupt movement inside the hangar caught her attention, and she turned to the transport. The pilot, who had remained hidden inside during the statue incursion, popped his head from the cockpit window. The engines whirled up, and a warm gust of air pushed against her body. He motioned for her to come aboard.

He's leaving? Where to? Her thoughts spun for a few seconds.

SONG OF THE LAGGORNS

If Thraxon warships were here, the Mertel was likely doomed on its own. There was no way he was going back down to the planet below, considering the terror they had just escaped. As she contemplated her next move, the pilot hurriedly waved her in with both hands. She squinted as the idea hit her—the Thraxon frigate.

CHAPTER 32

It was dark yet light. Kerriah tried to make sense of where they were. A fluid of blackness filled the air, and she felt her insides pulsing. The exhales of her breath were amplified, and her senses felt sharper than ever before. She looked down at her hand; the dark, glossy, grey skin reflected like a silhouette of creatures scurrying for cover in a moonlit night. She raised her arm and turned it with her hand open. It looked identical to the statues she had been speaking to moments earlier. What happened? How did she get here? Or more importantly, where was she?

"Why you—" She could hear Krath complaining in the background. "Gimme back my body! Timmon! Get over here. Tya look like somthin' that ran down my backside after eatin' too many scalfin larva." His protests continued, and Kerriah tried to block them out. She needed to keep her thoughts centered on grasping their situation.

"Kerriah," a familiar voice filled her head. Ashton sat near her upon a burgundy seat appearing suspended in the dark. His shimmering, grey silhouette matched hers with only one difference from the statues. Neither of them had the larger third eye. "Where are we?"

"I don't know," she replied. She pushed her heel down and noticed her feet set onto a solid surface, though it visually looked transparent. There appeared to be nothing around them, just the fluid blackness up and down as far as they could see. Kerriah hesitated to stand in the void and chose to remain seated for now.

"You are where we need you to be," a voice said from behind the darkness. A statue stepped forward and came into view. It was the first time she had seen one physically move. "There is a threat approaching. We are dealing with that now, and you have nothing to be concerned about."

A threat? Kerriah's body tensed, and she had to stop herself from standing. "A threat? What sort of threat?"

"Who boarded our ship?" Captain Ashton interrupted.

Kerriah's thoughts spun over his abrupt question. "What? We were boarded? By who?" She tried to turn in her seat, but it was too snug around her sides, and she could only move her head. Again, she hesitated to stand. "When did this happen?"

The statue stood firm as it spoke, keeping a meter distance between her and Ashton. Krath still complained in the background about his and Timmon's bodies. "I'm gonna be bustin' someone's head open real soon if I don't get my friggen body back!"

She shouted her thoughts aloud as she glared over at Krath. "Krath! Please . . . can you be quiet for a minute!" His grumblings stopped following her pointed request.

"We boarded your ship," the statue said the moment Krath's complaining ceased.

"Why? Who are you?" Ashton asked.

Kerriah's eyes widened with surprise over his understanding of the foreign dialect.

The statue turned its head to the captain. "We are entamals. Some of you arrived here with instruments of war. That required subjugation." It spoke in a slow, monotone voice.

"Subjugation?" Kerriah said. "You mean that you killed them."

"Yes," the entamal replied. "You are not expected to understand with your current knowledge." It stepped aside and extended its arm out. "To know, you need to step onto the platform of our lives."

Kerriah looked over at Ashton and then back at Krath and Timmon. None of them moved until Timmon tried to lift himself from his seat and place a foot upon the unseen surface. Krath gave him a sideways glance and quickly swatted him back into his chair. "What tya doin', boy? Tya don't move till I tell tya to."

Kerriah turned her attention back to the entamal. "What should we call you, and how do you know our dialect?"

"I am Stelios. There have been others before you for whom we have decoded their apparatuses and acquired their knowledge. I have personally studied your translations," it replied with its arm still extended.

Her thoughts went to the obvious. *The Thraxons.* Their ships would have technical details of their prey.

"Stelios, okay. I'm going to step down." She needed to say it aloud to gain courage.

She tried to calm her breathing, pushing aside the concern over falling into an eternal void below. When her backside completely left the chair, everything around her transformed into a bustling scene of blue and green with transparent spheres filled with life moving randomly across the colorful backdrop.

Stelios changed as well. His long, boney face almost appeared synthetic, with a milky-white tone. His thin legs stretched gangly into his round torso, and he wore only a loose-fitting, soft-blue top. A smile crept across his thin lips and tiny slit mouth.

"Welcome to Ethis." His mouth barely moved as he spoke, and Kerriah still felt like the words entered her head through telepathy rather than voice. "What you see before you is our hidden civilization. It is our sanctuary from the threats outside. The structures for which your ship landed are not where we live but our Folkim Initiators. The machines that keep this plane of reality open for us to live with euphoric peace and plenty."

Ashton stood and slowly spun around, observing the world before him. "Amazing."

"Alright, tya can stand." Krath gave the go-ahead to Timmon after he stood. "This is somthin' tya got to see to believe."

"Whoa! What is this place?" Timmon appeared as though he wanted to leap into this strange world but hesitated, knowing Krath was within arm's reach.

"I don't know, but as long as there's no giant lugs turnin' our bodies into ego worm soup without givin' us a chance to take a fighin' swing at 'em, it's fine by me."

"Violence of any sort is forbidden in Ethis," Stelios said. "Fear and aggression have no place here and are a plague only to the other side."

Kerriah turned a curious eye to Stelios. "How do you control that? How do you stop violence and fear?" She had seen violence of some form in nearly every species and every civilization she'd encountered. The idea of a species or society without it seemed surreal.

"Fear is the precursor to violence and hate. Those who have displayed those characteristics have since been banished to the other side without an emptocap. Where death is certain."

"Empto-what?" Krath rubbed his head and snarled his upper lip.

Stelios drew a calm smile. "That is the protection we wear on the other side. The outer shell is impervious, and its ocular augmentation allows us to see the sleeves so that we can travel between realities. Most important is that without the emptocap, the cravilars would consume us, as you have already discovered."

"Realities?" Kerriah swung her gaze away from the scene and back to Stelios.

Stelios raised his arm, made a fist, and then slowly opened his hand. A globular vessel swung in before them, with a surface shimmering and rippling like fluid. They could see their reflections almost like they were looking into a mirror; however, they could also see through the craft.

"I see your lack of understanding. Allow me to show you instead." He stepped into the bubble, and his body passed through without any visible resistance. "Please step into the virbulam." His voice had a digital echo as it passed through the barrier.

They hesitantly stepped inside the bubble; their skin numbed as they passed through the barrier for an instant. Inside, their eardrums felt a push of pressure, and their feet felt light. With only their toes touching the surface, they felt like they floated inside but remained upright.

"The virbulams are how we get from place to place in Ethis. You will feel no gravitational pulls as we move. Within them, we move at great speeds and without disruptive noise or latency," Stelios explained, his mouth still barely moving as he spoke. Everything around them blurred, and then an opaque white wall emerged into view. The barrier went as far as they could see in each direction, as though it lacked origin.

SONG OF THE LAGGORNS

"What you see now is the barrier between Ethis and the other side. Our kind developed this barrier long ago to save us from the cravilars. A species we created to destroy our adversaries and end the generation of enslavement, division, and wrath. But now, the cravilars dwell deep inside the crust of our former world. Their nests bore more than could ever be counted, and they consume all life above them. We became victims of our creations, and the greatest of our intellects discovered a way for us to escape. To start anew in Ethis."

"Victims of our creations. A desperate civilization, trading one evil for a far worse one." Kerriah paused as she bit into her lips and glared. She thought about how familiar this all sounded.

"I understand, Kerriah," Stelios replied.

She shook her head. "What?"

"So where is this Ethis? How did we get here?" Ashton interrupted her question with his own.

Before Stelios could answer, Kerriah spoke up. "They created the cravilars and then created Ethis to escape the monsters they could no longer control. What he's not telling us is they plotted to kill them all, wipe them out, even the children. Genocide against those that you had once shared your planet with. Right, Stelios?"

Stelios's ordinarily stoic face turned sour. "You appear to have some special ability to read my memories, yet you fail to understand our reasons. An illness of thought had broken out amongst the nation with which we shared our planet. This mindset spread like a plague, plunging their cities into madness and death. We feared that this plague would spread to our cities. Our world needed to be cleansed of this illness, yet done in such a way that we would not be held responsible for the necessary deaths."

Kerriah felt bitterness clenching within her. So far, Stelios and his kind had murdered her people and an entire civilization. It took everything she could muster to keep a calm posture. "Cleanse? You mean to kill those that had differing cultures."

"Call it what you will, but the survival of our species was at stake, and we were driven by one of our most basic impulses, fear. As such, a group within our scientific community discovered a way to eliminate the threat without political risk. Their gene-altering program created the cravilars through captives. This newly created species was difficult to kill, had an insatiable appetite, and could exponentially multiply in a warm environment. Covertly depositing them amongst their populations, they would consume and multiply until the cities were only filled with these predatory species. No one would know where they came from, only that they eliminated our adversaries."

Kerriah thought about Crix's recollection of the heydromac. It was alone atop a mountain in Semptor. Cold and dry. Did Gorag realize how close to their destruction they were? Or did he know of the creature's ability to multiply in the warm air? A chilly shiver crawled down her back over the thought. "For all your technical prowess, creating these things for the purpose you described has to be one of the most foolish things I've ever heard of."

"Hmmm . . ." Stelios gave her a sideways grin. "A fearful and desperate populace can make unsound choices. Yes, even highly advanced societies. Sounds familiar, does it not?"

Her eyes widened, and she looked around her like maybe he spoke to someone else. She knew what he was inferring, but how did he know? "I don't know what you're—"

"You know precisely what I mean," Stelios interrupted. "Yes, I can read minds as well. At least the weaker ones." He shot a glance over at Captain Ashton. "But it only takes one to betray the group."

Ashton pointed his index finger into his chest. "Me?"

Kerriah rolled her eyes. "Yes, he can see your thoughts." She was already starting to understand the nuances of reading people's thoughts. She let out a deep exhale. "He's right. We were no better for unleashing the Marcks on our system. Fine, Stelios, point taken."

"Very well. It was a miscalculation on our part. The cravilars did their intended jobs well. Too well, and before we could neutralize the cities they ravaged, thereby eliminating the new threat and placing ourselves as noble saviors to the masses, they burrowed deep into the crust of this planet, where the temperatures rise, creating a perfect environment for them to multiply.

"Their numbers became more than we had contingencies for, and eventually, we discovered burrows on the outskirts of our cities, yielding millions of cravilars. As we ultimately were forced to abandon our cities, the difficult decision was made to level each in an effort to send the cravilars back to their underground burrows. Sadly, that effort failed." The despair noticeably crept across Stelios's face.

"Well, what about the city we landed in? How did it survive?" Kerriah asked.

"The vast complex you arrived at is not a city, at least not in the conventional sense. It's a modulating station. The station creates a sleeve between these two existences and generates our protection system when we are on the other side. At first, we forced our populace to make a physical transformation for their well-being. The emptocaps were not generated but infused into their bodies. This existence was cold, devoid of taste, feeling, or intimate pleasures. Hence, we created the sleeve to Ethis so that future generations only donned a generated emptocap when protecting the complex. Its only purpose now is to preserve the connection to the physical bodies on the other side.

"The cravilars that do enter the complex are killed with the same efficiency for which your armed companions were killed. Anything within the photonic pulses of our stations and their outlying prisms is subjected to our time continuity field. With our emptocaps, we can step between your time and ours. By entering and exiting sleeves, we can step ahead of your time. For you it's merely a blink or a momentary pause, but we can manipulate your existence before our times merge to equilibrium."

A shiver crawled through Kerriah as she thought about what could happen if the Thraxons ever got ahold of such technology. "I'm sorry; I don't like the thought of any of this. It's too much power for anyone to have."

"Much like the power you wield to protect your kind?"

She dropped her shoulders, feeling convicted once again. "Right."

"I don't get it." Ashton shook his head, trying to understand what Stelios had told them. "So we are not really here? I mean physically?"

"You are, just not with your original body. Ethis is an ethereal place, though you wouldn't be able to tell had I not informed you of this fact. To exist both here and there, an embryonic link must be maintained to your physical form. Your bodies lay dormant inside one of our impervious containment structures, just like ours."

Kerriah's thoughts stopped upon hearing they were separated from their physical bodies. She raised her hand to her face and stared through it momentarily. The orb stayed with her. It shouldn't have been a surprise, considering Crix's experience in the core, but the idea still captured her.

"On the other side, with those ravenous things you created?" Ashton's tone became sharp, and his posture turned back from the passive witness to that of a commanding officer. "You will return us at once to our bodies and our ship. Taking us hostage is unacceptable!"

"Please do not worry, Captain, you are not hostages here, and your physical shells are safe. The vessel you arrived in, however, is not."

CHAPTER 33

"The Mertel is doomed!" The pilot's voice was steady and assured. His black hair had a few strands of grey peppered evenly throughout, and his darker complexion suggested his ancestors had originated from the southern regions of Nathasia. He strapped himself into the cockpit seat, flipped a series of switches, and tapped several screens. "I tried to stay out of sight as those things murdered our crew." He shot a quick glance at Jesselle. "You were extremely lucky. I still can't believe it didn't kill you."

Jesselle noticed the name and rank on his uniform. She took a seat and pressed her thumb into a switch, calling the wide shoulder bands to slide down from the high back and across her torso. "I wasn't lucky, Lieutenant Camden, and neither were you."

The shuttle's engine purred to a steady hum. "What do you mean?" Camden asked.

"Those things were targeting anything they deemed hostile. You were unarmed and hiding, and I stood there unarmed, trying not to move. It wasn't until I attacked that it came after me."

The transport rose from the deck, and the nose dipped forward. "Maybe," Camden said. "You were still lucky that these Thraxon warships appeared when they did."

"Wait! So now we're just going to abandon our ship without a fight?" Jesselle started to have second thoughts, and she reached down to press the seat release button. "We're deserters . . . cowards!"

Lieutenant Camden turned to her, shaking his head. "No. There's nothing heroic about remaining on a ship that will inevitably be vaporized. It's just a senseless waste of your life." He gestured a glance in the direction of the Thraxon frigate. "But if we can make our way to the frigate, we have a small chance to assist the special ops guys. We can make a difference there since the Thraxons are not known for firing on their ships. Understand?"

"No! I don't understand. You're UMO military, and I'm a Tolagon. We're supposed to fight for others." Jesselle stopped short of using the word hero. She didn't feel like she had earned such a title.

"You're welcome to step out and go down fighting." Camden gestured toward the cockpit door. "I don't care either way, but I'm leaving while I still can."

Jesselle put her finger inches from his face. "We can't leave the crew to die!"

Camden's expression remained cold as he swatted her hand away. The lights in the hangar flashed, and the Mertel shook. A persistent rumble filled the area.

Jesselle leaned forward, trying to get a look outside. "They're attacking us."

"Yep. That's what Thraxon warships do. Look, I don't have time to debate this."

"No—they are attacking the Mertel. We need to help!"

"You're still not getting it. The crew of the Mertel is dead already. There is nothing you or I can do to help. Either sit back down and buckle up or get out, but I'm leaving now!"

The Mertel jolted, and Camden's attention changed to the shuttle's controls, trying to adjust and not crash into the hangar walls. "That's it, we're out of here," he said sternly.

Jesselle stood with both fists clenched and a flare of red streaming up her arms. She wanted to stop him, force him to stay and fight for the Mertel, but she also knew he was likely correct. They would probably both die if she forced him to stay, and then she would have his blood on her hands. She didn't want to be the direct cause of anyone else's death. Her time under Zearic's influence had given her too much of that already. She didn't wish for another victim's face to haunt her. She relaxed her fist and dropped into her seat. Her breath shortened, and the dreaded feeling from earlier poured back over her. Her stomach turned sour as her strength drained away.

The transport rotated, facing the repulsion field. "Hang on. We are going through hot."

Jesselle's fingers gripped into the armrests as the lights outside flashed and a barrage of explosions made everything else around them nearly inaudible. The engine's hum intensified, and their heads pressed against the back of their seats. The hangar of the Mertel disappeared, and the frigate quickly appeared. The pilot hammered the reverse thrusts and stopped their transport a few meters from the hull. In the distance, three Thraxon warships pummeled the Mertel with green energy blasts and missile batteries. The ship helplessly tried to return fire, but the onslaught was overwhelming.

Lieutenant Camden released his shoulder restraints and stood. "Let's get suited up. We need to get to the outside and establish communications with Sergeant Alar and his team."

Jesselle took a moment to look out the cockpit window at the Mertel one more time. Flames flashed briefly out from hull breaches, and its return fire became sparse as the helpless UMO warship held onto its final moments. She turned to follow Camden with sadness filling her heart. She knew that once the *Mertel* fell, the Thraxon ships would shift their focus onto their lost frigate.

Camden popped open two lockers containing e-vos suits. "Come on," he said. "Get your e-vos on as quickly as possible. As soon as they are finished with the Mertel, they'll turn their attack on our transports."

Jesselle slid her legs into the rigid yet flexible suit and pulled it up to her neck before fastening the pointed chin helmet over her head and snapping the clasps down with a vacuum-sealed squeak. She raised her arms, and the torso shell lowered around her and locked into her suit plugs, allowing oxygen and pressure to flow inside.

The lieutenant pointed his gloved hand to the departure hatch. "Let's go!" The hatch slid open, and they felt a sharp pull as their pressure quickly released into space. Outside, they were just in time to witness the Mertel breaking apart before a final flash of white briefly stole their vision as the ship exploded. "Sergeant Alar . . . Sergeant Alar . . . anyone . . . do you copy? This is Lieutenant Camden; we are outside and need entry."

"Hold tight, Lieutenant. We're on our way."

CHAPTER 34

Kerriah wasn't sure how much time had passed since Stelios had brought them to Ethis. It all seemed like a dream. Trying to make sense of their technology made her head feel hot, and she couldn't help thinking that if only Plexo were here, he'd probably give her a detailed explanation. Outside, the entamal's ships moved without movement or any visible propulsion systems. One moment they stood inside an illuminated, cylinder-shaped transport, waiting for liftoff; the next, they boarded a Thraxon battle cruiser, following a trail of goo-ladened heaps scattered about each chamber, passage, and storeroom. The entamal's technology made them efficient killers. These attacking Thraxon ships, which had destroyed the Mertel, didn't have a chance. They never saw their demise coming.

It felt like only a few minutes ago Stelios pulled them from Ethis and reunited them with their physical bodies. She already knew so much about them in such a short time. The rows of pyramidal structures housed thousands of entamals. Their bodies were suspended in embryonic fluids, safely preserved, and stored in hardened structures while their consciousness populated their alternate forms on Ethis. Their physical bodies were only released from suspension when they donned their emptocaps for security or construction work. It was all so confusing, and Kerriah wished they had the time to question Stelios further. The bits she had stolen from his mind told her there was a societal agreement amongst them that modestly grew their population, as more structures and more power were needed to maintain the life-preserving facilities. Their lifespans were preset to two-hundred years, and for each expired entamal, two were allowed to be born into the system to couples chosen by seniority. It was a dry and predictable existence, but the entamals had grown accustomed to it, and the occasional interloping stray would need to be quickly squashed.

Yet Kerriah couldn't help but notice a carefully guarded thought inside Stelios. A thought that he intentionally tucked away, knowing that she could see inside his head. She still saw what he was hiding.

Stelios wanted to leave Ethis.

***

Hardly any time had passed before the three Thraxon warships were devoid of their crews. Two cruisers and a command ship floated dormant outside the planet Stelios, referred to as Tridole. His fellow entamals wanted to destroy all the desolate warships, including the older frigate, which they had initially hoped would have been a warning to others to stay clear of their world. Now, they wanted to remove the possibility it could signal for more ships in the future. Stelios convinced the other entamal elders to preserve a Thraxon ship for the remnants of Kerriah's crew, provided they leave and never return. Although without knowing how to pilot the alien ship, it would be of little use. Stelios knew this and spared the Thraxon commander. Someone Kerriah could control and pull knowledge from as needed.

213

Kerriah, Krath, Timmon, and Captain Ashton stood inside the command ship with six emptocap-armored entamals. An onyx, banded-metal body clattered to the floor, his legs and arms fastened behind his back. Kerriah tilted her head as she took a closer look at the captive. It wasn't like any Thraxon she had ever seen before. It only had two arms, and they were thick and muscular in appearance. She leaned down for a closer look but couldn't see him with his face planted into the metal deck.

"Roll him over," she said in a stern voice.

Krath stepped forward to give the Thraxon commander a good solid kick when he suddenly noticed it faced upward. He let out a frustrated growl.

"I wish tya'll would stop with that blippin' around and just move normal so I can keep an eye on tya." As he finished, Kerriah drew a loud, inward breath.

Krath glanced up at her, noticing she stared wide-eyed down at the Thraxon with her hand covering her mouth. "What?" He looked down, and then his jaw dropped.

"It can't be!" She leaned in for a closer inspection. The long, muscular neck and the extended muzzle were not that of a Thraxon, but rather an Andor. She recognized the black Bracix bands covering half his body and face, but the other half was a smooth, reflective metal. She took a nervous swallow and said the name.

"Creedith?"

"That's not Creedith," Krath said, raising his foot into a stomping position over the captive. He smashed his heel into its chest, and its eyes popped open wide and black. "This is some Thraxon imposter . . . some perversion of their sick bug heads." He leaned his weight into the chest and bit down on his lip, furious over the sight. "Tya hears me, tya crummy imposture?"

214

SONG OF THE LAGGORNS

Kerriah placed her hand against Krath's chest. She thought about Crix's request for her to find Creedith, his biological father. "Wait! We don't know anything right now. Either way, we need him to help us figure out this ship."

Krath twisted his heel for good measure and then stepped back. He spat a foamy white glob onto the captive and wiped the back of his hand over his mouth. "It doesn't matter. I can't stand the sight of him!"

"Let me get into his mind and find the answers, okay?" Kerriah pleaded, hoping she could calm the old Hybor vet down.

Krath folded his arms with a bitter scowl. "Fine, but be quick about it before I lose my temper."

Her hand quivered as she slowly pulled it across her head. Her face looked drawn with anxiety before she took a focused stare at the large Thraxon captive. Looking inside the mind of this Thraxon or Andor or whatever it was and the apprehension over what she might find made her stomach tighten. She needed to concentrate, though it was difficult to drown out her thoughts and everyone standing around the room. She pinched her eyes closed, and instead of blackness, a yellow glow filled her view. The orb was ready, but she wasn't.

She knelt and placed her palms over her eyes, focusing on the restrained mass in front of her . . . nothing. She removed her hands and looked around the room. Her petite frame somehow created a shadow filling the area.

"Leave me!" Everyone cast questioning glances at each other, though the entamals were quick and jerky. "Go! I need to focus. I need every possible distraction away from me."

"Kay, but I'll be standin' right outside to stomp this abomination back into whatever crevasse it crawled out from. All tya have to do is holler. Tya hears me?" Loyalty and spirit were part

215

of the Hybor's way, but his feelings for her were personal. They were like family.

"I hear you, Krath. Thanks."

Kerriah settled her view back to the shadow-clad Thraxon commander. Its eyes remained fixed on her, never moving or blinking. She took a deep breath and carefully placed her hands on the top of its head. The metal was surprisingly warm to the touch, and somehow, she could feel a rapid heartbeat vibrating through the rigid shell. Whatever was inside this shell was either scared or furious. She was about to step inside and experience whichever it was firsthand.

Her hands let out a warm, golden glow, and she felt a surge of anger followed by hate. Her stomach twisted over the emotions, and she turned her head to the side, revolting over the emerging malevolent thoughts. She hadn't been inside a mind so toxic and poisoned before. She pushed inward past the outer barrier of raw disdain and into the inner thoughts of this corrupt individual. She found herself in a place so thick with black clouds of noxious air that everything beyond a few meters disappeared into perpetual darkness. She could feel each heavy breath sear her throat and ignite inside her lungs.

A grating howl followed by a quivering cry of pain and suffering snapped her focus to a hazy gold figure splayed out in front of her. A dim, red glow of eyes shook side to side with each wail of distress. Four golden limbs fused into a wall consisting of thick tar appeared. *Zearic?* Dozens of glossy black fibers coiled out from his torso and slithered around before twisting back in, leaving tiny pinholes from where they emerged. He uttered another scream, and as his mouth opened to release his lament, a ribbed funnel of glistening black slammed deep into his jaw. His voice turned to a gurgle, and his body heaved from choking.

216

Her view took a slow glance upward. Long, silver fangs swayed above her. A giant face of death with four black eyes and wire hair strands moved about as though trying to reach something unseen. The menacing fangs were twice her size, and the mouth behind them was lined with smaller versions of the elongated teeth. Its body hung down and mostly disappeared behind Zearic.

A surge of knowledge flowed into her mind. It was the Thraxon monarch. Their oldest living member and the one that spawns their root species, the layers, and the squills. Black webbing seeped from the pinholes in Zearic's body and crawled over him until the sticky texture covered all the gold armor. His head made short jerking motions from side to side, anchored by the funnel.

The creaking of metal expanding and stretching came from Zearic's body. His torso appeared bloated, and the webbing streamed out faster. A louder crack followed a popping sound. The torso ripped open with dozens of six-legged creatures pulling themselves out from the streaming webs of guts and tar. They scampered off into the darkness, leaving a hollow shell dripping with excrement where Zearic once stood. The final dessert for his failure and the disgrace of the Thraxon attack fleet. A boney arm dipped down from the mess of black and gold, sifting through the sludge until a golden bulb emerged. The arm retracted into the monarch, the found treasure disappearing into some hidden place within the Thraxon elder.

An overwhelming surge of emotions hit Kerriah as she felt a combination of distress, sadness, and relief. This was indeed Creedith! And he was allowed to witness Zearic's death. A death he would not face, but there was still a price to be paid. Zearic had kept him alive to be used as bait after his demented bioengineers completed the work Merik had left unfinished. He would turn the Vico legion vet into a perfect example of obedience and weaponry.

He would become a tool to lure his lost prizes, the blue orb, and Kerriah back into his grasp. Now, with Zearic's death, the Thraxons had an important use for Creedith as well. His knowledge of the UMO's military tactics and the orchestrators of their defeat would prove invaluable to their retribution. But first, his loyalty would need to be assured.

Kerriah continued to witness his memories. They forced him into the abdomen of the monarch. The gooey tar seeped around him until his view turned black, and he emerged into a cavity deep inside. Strands filled his mouth, ears, and eyes. The monarch took over his body but left his mind. It provided nourishment for many months, but not until he felt starvation and death's cold hand closing around him. Then it would feed him and soothe his suffering. The process replayed over and over until Creedith began to feel an emotional tie to the Thraxon leader. He viewed it as his mother, his father, and his king.

Its threads moved into his brain and placed images of their enemies—the UMO population, the ones responsible for so many Thraxon deaths. Crix and Kerriah were the guiltiest of them all, plotting and giving renewed hope to a populace that had already adjusted to subjugation from the Marcks. With the agreement between the Marck Queen and the Thraxons, this civilization should have been easy prey, and the hives would have had the subsidence they needed for decades from the UMO harvest. The queen wanted the citizens of the UMO gone, and the Thraxons wanted them for food, and neither side benefited from the war. These were the thoughts implanted throughout Creedith's mind.

His eyes, now black, opened for the first time as a Thraxon warlord. With his unwavering loyalty and mutual hatred of the UMO populace, he was provided with an attack fleet to seek its enemies and destroy its leaders.

CHAPTER 35

It's him," Kerriah's face appeared hollow as she waved them back into the room. Her normally vibrant green eyes seemed dull and exhausted from her time in his memories. "It is Creedith." Though the stoic and soulful Andor that she knew wasn't there. He still had his intellect, but emotions and Thraxon obedience instead of patience and logic drove him.

She rubbed her eyes, trying to hide the tears. "Though he's not our Creedith. Not the one we all loved and respected." She looked at Krath, who tensely swayed in his stance like he tried to keep his rage from exploding.

"The Thraxons have taken control of his thoughts and driven him mad with hate. Hate towards us. They provided him a fleet of warships with one singular objective, to kill those they felt were most responsible for their defeat."

"Tya means us," Krath said, jabbing his thumb into his chest.

Kerriah nodded. "That's right. Crix, you, Plexo—" She felt dizzy and wasn't sure if it was due to the stress of using the orb or the mental anguish of being in such a hostile mind. She leaned against Krath's sturdy frame, needing the support and comfort of someone she trusted. She felt Krath's posture calm, and he gently placed his arm around her. "I'm sorry, Krath."

"I don't know what's worse. Thinkin' I lost him that day we escaped Nathasia or knowin' that the most incorruptible of us has been turned into a Thraxon stooge. It ain't right. Everythin' that filthy tyrant Zearic touches becomes droona dung." She felt Krath's hold on her tighten and then released as he finished speaking.

Kerriah pulled away from Krath and wiped her eyes. "I don't think we'll have to worry about Zearic any longer."

"Why do tya say that? Did he finally do us all a favor and airlock himself?"

"No," Kerriah replied. "Let's just say that his dealings with the Thraxons finally caught up with him."

"Hmmm . . . serves him right. Though I feel cheated, not being able to stomp the guts outta him myself."

"Well, there's more. The reason he's here now is because his fleet detected us when we backed through Zeta to escape Cyos. They fired a small tracking device through as we fled, which gave them just enough of a signal to report an approximate location."

"How did they get here? Did they follow us through? Seems a reckless move with Cyos between them and us," Ashton asked.

"I'm not sure, but I feel they were already tracking its movements for some reason. I couldn't stay in his head any longer to get additional answers. It's just too painful." She gripped her fingers into her chest, and she felt tormented. "I need time to regain my composure."

"I didn't know Captain Creedith, but there were no shortages of references to him within the UMO military academy and the ranks of the active. He's a legend," Ashton said. "But we still need him. You will have to use your Tolagon abilities and get him to assist us. We need more answers. We need him back on our team." Ashton stood with his hands clasped behind his back and waited for her reply.

Her jaw locked, and her stomach turned sour. Like returning to a nightmare she had just awakened from, she knew going back into Creedith's head would kill a part of her. It was the last thing she wanted to do right now.

"I know. . . . I know." She nervously rubbed her hands together in anticipation and turned away from Ashton. "I really don't want to do this."

She placed her hands back on his head and found the opening in his memories she had discovered earlier. She could see a plan to assassinate Plexo. It started when the Thraxons detected his ship outside of Zeta and an attack force traced him to Eesolan. The Thraxons needed to separate the masterminds of the UMO resistance, and this was the perfect opportunity. Plexo, Joric, and Chancellor Septin would need to die before staging another attack on the UMO.

However, they encountered an Eesolan system ravaged by Marcks. *The lost Knactor fleet?* Devoid of an official military, the peaceful Luminars must have fallen quickly to the formidable invaders. When Creedith's fleet engaged the Marcks, their assault under his military prowess and leadership tilted in the Thraxons' favor. That was until the ill-timed arrival of the fabled living nebula, Cyos. It seemed like a trap, but a trap laid by whom? The Thraxon fleet helplessly succumbed to the demolecularization effects of the fearsome nebula. Their hive ship was lost, and Creedith fled with only three ships before he could complete his objective. Unfortunately, Kerriah had more questions than answers as she sifted through his memories.

She pried deeper into his mind, looking for something she could use—something she could cling to that would pull him back. Through the fog of thoughts and clouds of memories, she found a glimpse of his last moments as the Creedith they knew—Krath's final salute before he dove into Plexo's portal. Shots from around him sapped the strength from his body, and he sank to the ground, curling into a ball with his head tucked into his arms and his armored side facing up.

"Stop! Stop, you fools!" a croaky voice broke through the chaos.

The energy blasts ceased, and Creedith's bracix glared bright white, overloaded with energy. He pulsed, relieving his physical body of the pain caused by his new enhancement absorbing too much energy. It drained his natural body of its strength. A weakness he wasn't aware of until this moment. The pulsating disbursement of stored power jolted the surrounding force, sending some of the Thraxons staggering back and Marcks twirling on their hover disks.

Zearic raised his arms, signaling for them to stand down. He shot a glancing scowl at the downed Andor. "I need this wretch alive now that you imbeciles allowed his friends to escape!"

Creedith pulled his arms away from his head and sized up the surrounding force. Zearic's twitching grin emerged.

"That's right. You may think of yourself as a hero for allowing your pitiful friends to escape, but now you're mine. I'm going to use every bit of you, and you'll swear your obedience only to me! You will be my perfect weapon."

Zearic raised his rod and then pointed it at Creedith. "Subdue him!" A flash of light hit him, this time intentionally missing his armor. His consciousness faded into darkness.

Jesselle, why didn't you tell me that Creedith was still alive? The thought leaped out at her, and she quickly shook it off. Some of his memories were still there. Maybe they all were, and he couldn't access them? She dug further, sifting through his thoughts like a ransacking thief searching for loot and casting aside anything that didn't point to a clue as to why he couldn't find his own memories. The memories that made Creedith himself. There were tiny voices in the darkness. Light, faint, but discernible if she focused close enough.

"Yes, Lord Zearic," the calm male voice said. "The synthetic cladding is fused to his nervous system and will suppress all memories that have an emotional bond. He will remember things he's learned but will not have an emotional bond to anything from his past."

"What about his future?" Zearic's maniacal voice was easy to recognize. "I want him loyal to me. Will he love and obey me? Die for me?"

"Ahh, yes. Of course, my lord."

Creedith's vision slowly brightened from black to a blurry haze of colors and spots. A light blinked from atop a slender figure who held a golden bulb in his hand. Another figure stood nearby, shimmering in gold. *Zearic.*

"This neuron homing beacon will lock his emotions onto you. We will install this into your royal command armor. He will emotionally link to you, and his memories from this time forward will mend only to your will and your will alone. He will hate those that you hate and obey only you."

That's it.

She pulled away from his mind and looked over to Krath. "He's still there. It's this metal shell. Zearic installed it to make him obedient to him, and the Thraxons now have that control. They've

223

used it along with pain conditioning to imprint their strict control upon him." She stood, studying the reflective black armor. "We have to remove it."

CHAPTER 36

While Sergeant Alar pressed Lieutenant Camden firmly against the metal wall by his shirt collar, Jesselle continued to fight against a continued onslaught of panic coming with the arrival of the Thraxon ships. The sergeant's darker complexion helped mask the pitted burn marks covering much of his face. Nonetheless, the old battle scars and his stout build gave him a gruff and burly appearance.

"Coward!" he shouted.

"Sir, as of this moment, he's our superior officer," a nearby soldier reminded the sergeant.

"I don't give a rip what his rank is. He's a damn coward, and I can't stand cowards." Alar pushed him harder against the wall and moved his face close to Camden's. "Tell me now why were you and the Tolagon female the only personnel on the transport? You fled to save your own skin, didn't you?" He pulled the lieutenant back and smacked his body against the wall again. "Answer me!"

"That's right, sarge, I say we space this rodent," another voice chimed in from the background.

"Sergeant!" Jesselle shouted. She pulled herself from the grip of debilitating fear long enough to try to stop the revolt unfolding before her. "If we didn't leave when we did, we would both be dead as well."

Alar turned an icy stare her way. "Good."

Jesselle nervously crossed her arms. "You don't understand; most of the crew had already been killed by strange teleporting things before the Thraxons arrived. There was nothing we could have done and no one else around we could have rescued. At least listen to the facts before you kill us."

Alar gave Camden a good shove before releasing him. He pointed his index finger into the lieutenant's face. "I'm keeping an eye on you. I smell even a whiff of cowardice, and I'll gut you myself." He looked back over at Jesselle. "So you're the brains here, huh? Now, what are we supposed to do? Our ship and crew are destroyed, and we're stuck on this Thraxon junker that's controlled by a squill. Which, for the life of me, I cannot understand why this thing hasn't shut down our life support."

"Well, first we need to figure out why those Thraxon ships are not attacking our transports or boarding this ship," Jesselle said. "Something doesn't feel right. The inactivity since they destroyed the Mertel is alarming. I feel that those same things that attacked us have something to do with it."

"If I may," Lieutenant Camden nervously cleared his throat, "we still have a team deployed to one of the cities on the planet below. That team includes Captain Ashton."

Sergeant Alar jabbed his finger into the lieutenant's chest. "Dammit, why didn't you say something about this earlier?"

Camden gave a wide-eyed shrug. "You didn't give me a chance. You threatened to kill me as soon as you saw me."

"Hmmppff. I don't accept excuses, Lieutenant."

"I know, I know, you don't accept excuses or cowards," Camden mumbled under his breath.

"What was that?" Alar barked.

Camden shook his head and stared down. "Nothing."

"I don't want to see any of that eye roll garbage either. Now you listen and listen good, Lieutenant; I'd advise not pushing your luck with me!" Alar slowly removed his finger from the lieutenant's chest. "Now you're going to get on that horn and hail the captain's transport. Find out what their status is. You got me?"

Camden took a deep breath. "Got it." He turned away, leaving for his transport.

"And you," Alar turned his attention to Jesselle, who leaned with both hands against her knees again, appearing out of breath. "What's your story? You're not getting sick, are you?"

Jesselle gave a dry swallow and quickly shook her head. "No. I'm fine. I-I just need a minute."

Images flashed through her mind. The room started to spin and reverberate, but she was still. Visions she had unknowingly subdued for years filled her thoughts. An Andor coated in shimmering black armor beating his fists into her face and body. He was in an uncontrolled rage, and she was the sole recipient. The red orb, which moments earlier had turned against her, now protected her from being broken by the onslaught. Still, the impacts had taken their toll. Her life drained with each furious swing as she lay on the gritty surface, immobilized. The orb went into self-preservation mode. It used her body and her life as a shield. It didn't want to be openly exposed to an adversary and would keep her physical form intact until her life drained away. But something drew the Andor's attention away. He paused and looked up and then vanished.

"Hello? Tolagon?" Alar stopped to look around at his team. "What the heck is wrong with her?" He slipped his glove off and snapped his fingers twice before waiving to one of his subordinates. "Corporal, get over here and see what's wrong with her."

Corporal Finch, the team medic, took a few hasty steps over to Jesselle and tried to pull her forehead back for a look into her eyes. She immediately smacked his hand away.

"Back off!" she shouted. The medic raised his hands and looked back at Alar.

"Hey, whatever," Alar said. "If you don't want help, that's on you. But the same goes for you, as does the lieutenant. If I think for a moment that you're a detriment to my team, I'm putting you down."

A call chirped in from Lieutenant Camden, and Alar tapped his wrist to answer. "Sergeant." His voice came clear like he stood in the room.

"What do you have for me, Camden?"

"I've located the captain." Camden paused for an uncomfortable amount of time.

"Well, go on, spit it out. Where is he now?"

"I-I still don't understand, but he's on the Thraxon command ship. He's not a prisoner; rather, they are in the process of interrogating the Thraxon commander. An Andor."

"What?" Alar raised his voice. "Sergeant, if I find out that you're on stimulants or you're drinking, I'm going to—"

"No, I'm not making this up, and the captain verified his credentials. This is real."

A sudden sensation of lost time hit Jesselle again. Like what she experienced on the landing bay of the Mertel earlier dealing with the strange statues, but more apparent. Her head spun when she heard the report from Camden. She felt dizzy, and her stomach turned sour before the lights went off. Her body fell limply to the deck.

Alar lowered his wrist. "Unbelievable." He smacked his hand on his forehead and let out a frustrated exhale. "Corporal, make sure our resident Tolagon is still with us."

Tapping his wrist again, he called back to Lieutenant Camden. "Lieutenant, tell our captain that we're on our way to the Thraxon command ship. And Lieutenant . . . you had better be right about this."

CHAPTER 37

I f the shriek from this poor, suffering soul wasn't enough to tear the heart from Kerriah, the shivering wail that followed brought her to tears. This once heroic Andor lay covered in his blood and puckered with tiny holes oozing burgundy-tinted body fluid. The entamals ripped his armor off so efficiently she didn't have a second to make a case for how it should be done as humanely as possible. The moment the words "we have to remove it" had left her lips, a scream of pain had filled the room, and this bloody mess appeared in place of the menacing-looking, black-armored Thraxon commander.

He curled his arms and legs into his chest and shook with pain. Removing the cladding took much of his flesh and left pinholes where the armor integrated into his tissue and nervous system. The fact he was still alive and moving was nothing short of miraculous. Almost any other known species would have died almost instantly.

Kerriah looked up at Stelios with horror on her face. Her mouth hung open, and tears trickled down her porcelain cheeks.

"We have to do something!" Her frantic voice trembled as she pleaded. "He doesn't deserve this, and we desperately need him alive. He's a friend, and some of us here owe him our lives." Unsteadiness swirled throughout her body, her breathing increased, and her head started to pound. Being out of control was not a feeling she processed very well.

Krath, who had been mostly silent since learning this was his old fellow Vico legionnaire, finally spoke out. "Now look here, I realize that tya all can pretty much kill us deader than a sespin rank fish before we could even finish our openin' insults, but tya had better fix my buddy. Cause if I can't plant my boot in your backsides in this life, I'm damn sure gonna in the next one." He stomped over toward Kerriah, cracking his knuckles and neck, preparing himself for a possible tussle.

Stelios's voice entered their minds. "As you wish."

Kerriah felt like she simply blinked, and everything in the room had moved aside from Krath and Timmon. Captain Ashton wasn't there, and Kerriah assumed he must have stepped out for some pressing reason. The five entamals all stood in different places than a second ago. She felt uncomfortable, knowing they could turn on them at any moment. Unlike Krath, she held her sharp tongue and tried to be as cooperative as possible. For now, they needed to work with the entamals, but she would also keep her guard up.

Creedith sat propped up against the wall shivering. His flesh no longer peeled away, dripping with blood. Instead, his skin was tinted charcoal grey, with no fur—just blotchy ripples of flesh without any clothing or his natural fur coat.

Kerriah looked up at Stelios. "Thank you."

She glanced at Creedith as he remained curled up against the wall, not saying a word and with the look of someone who had just awakened from a horrible nightmare. "But why does he no longer have any fur? His body used to be covered in fur."

Stelios didn't move, but his voice filled her thoughts. "He has been in our revitalization chamber for several cycles now. His flesh healed with some scarring, but any follicles he once had could not be regenerated. He is how he will be."

"Wait," Krath grumbled. "We've been standin' here for at least two days? How come my feet ain't barkin' like two sea dogs before morning vittles?" Timmon and Krath looked at their feet and then at each other.

"For as long as we are within range of our modulating stations and their augmenting prisms, we can create a temporal shift by entering a dimensional sleeve, effectively pausing your time while continuing our own. For you, only a second has passed; for us and everything else, it has been two full cycles."

"Prisms—what?" Krath asked, appearing sucker punched over the technical data dump.

"They are invisible and undetectable," Kerriah explained, having already seen the answer in Stelios's mind.

Krath's lower jaw and forehead pushed forward as he let out an exhaustive growl. "Tya and ole glow rod would get along for sure. Between scrubbin' my guts and messin' with my time, I'm sure tya'd have some good ole belly chuckles as my expense."

"The one you call Plexo? I would like to meet this acquaintance," Stelios responded.

"Would tya get out of my head!" Krath began walking in circles, pacing as he continued to complain. "What the heck happened to all the normal folk? Is there anyone normal these days? Tya know, someone I can tell a few knee-slappers over a few cups of grob without them proddin' and pryin' into my body or head? I feel like I'm goin' nuts!"

"I'm normal," Timmons's voice chimed in through the protest.

"Ha!" Krath let out a sarcastic chuckle. "Only after I crack tya in the noggin."

"Krath!" Kerriah shouted. "Please!" She pointed at the still confused-looking Creedith, who had his knees cradled into his chest. "We need to focus on Creedith. I'm not even sure he knows who or where he is right now."

Krath stopped pacing around and straightened himself up. "Right."

Ashton cleared his throat as he stepped back into the room. "Well, I just received a call from our spec ops team on the frigate. They are standing by for further orders, and they have Tolagon Jesselle Orwitz with them."

"Jesselle is with them?" Kerriah perked upon hearing this unexpected news. She had assumed Jesselle had died with the destruction of the Mertel, though with the time shifts and everything that happened with the Thraxons and finding Creedith, she hadn't had a moment to consider the consequences of losing her. Plus, the added complications of the whereabouts of the red orb. She let out a deep breath and dropped her head.

"Oh, thank goodness." She needed something to calm her nerves and bring things back to order. Knowing her fellow Tolagon had survived was something she could hold onto and feel encouraged, even if only for a moment.

"We need to decide our next steps," Ashton said. "Are we taking over this ship or moving to the frigate?"

"No. We need this ship. It has the X88T's jump drive tech that can get us home. The frigate does not," Kerriah replied.

"Very well then. I'll instruct them to pack up and dock their transports here."

"Fine, but take Krath with you," Kerriah said as she stared down at Creedith.

"Uh uh . . . I'm stayin' right here," Krath said with his chest popped out, determined to protect his friend.

"Krath, the captain will need your help ensuring the landing bay is prepped for the incoming transport. Everything needs to be squeaky clean as we can't afford to lose more personnel." Kerriah paused and, with a couple of casual flicks of her hand, waved Krath away. "Besides, you're distracting me here." Her relationship with the Hybor was so close she felt at ease with telling him to back off. He was lovingly annoying but also loyal. She knew he would follow her lead.

Krath's face scrunched with frustration. "Fine. Come on, Timmon." He gestured the young Hybor his way as he turned to the door.

"Okay, Creedith." She extended her hand and gently touched his knee. Creedith's body flinched as her fingers landed on his bare skin. After the armor removal, his eyes were no longer black, and his pupils pinned. A heavy breath labored from his nostrils in long choppy heaves.

"Easy . . . easy." She brushed her fingers over his skin. It felt baby smooth and thin.

She closed her eyes and led the orb back into his mind. His old memories had returned without the suppressing shell, yet he was scared. After so many years, Zearic and the Thraxons had found a way to break him. She could help him recover. The council taught her how to harness the yellow orb's unique power. She gave Creedith's mind a perception of warmth, and he stopped shaking. She slowly stood and then gave him a sense of security. His breathing slowed, and he squeezed his eyes shut before a quick headshake.

She slowly opened her eyes. "It's okay, Creedith. We are not here to hurt you. I'm Kerriah. Do you remember me? Krath is also with us."

Creedith leaned forward onto his knees. Stelios and the entamals instantly appeared back a couple of meters from where they were a couple of seconds ago. "You—" his exhausted, gravelly voice spoke out as though he had just sprinted several kilometers. His wobbly legs slowly stood, "friend of Crix."

"Yes!" She was excited to hear his name. "That's right. Crix is my friend as well." Her emotions poured out. "He's—He's alive and well in New Troika."

Creedith's eyes lit upon hearing the name. "New . . . Troika."

It was at that moment she wondered how much he knew. They had spent most of their time together on Nathaisa. But Creedith had primarily kept quiet, focusing on their objectives, and she didn't recall bringing the destruction of Troika up to him. She suddenly felt embarrassed over the omission. If he knew of it, it would have been something he learned under Zearic's control. But Zearic was conniving; he would most likely avoid the emotional risk of telling Creedith his home was destroyed and the population virtually extinct. He wanted to keep him loyal.

She clenched her teeth in anticipation of telling him. "Creedith," she paused for a second, "Crix created New Troika from what used to be Nathasia. It's the new home of the Andors, and all your great ancestors are there with him. Restored." She just avoided the destruction part, hoping he wouldn't inquire.

"Hmmm," his voice rumbled. "I must see him."

"That's what we are working on. But we need your help. You have to show us how to operate this Thraxon ship. Use its X88T tech to get us home."

"Plexo. We need him. The Marck Queen has the white orb and controls Cyos." As Creedith spoke, she noticed the same stoical posture she remembered.

Kerriah's heart jumped upon hearing the name. "The what? Did you say the queen? As in the Marck Queen?" Her thoughts raced, and she tried to ingest the information. How could it be? Crix had destroyed her years ago in the core.

"That's correct." Creedith stopped to wince. Kerriah kept a subtle probe into his mind and could see his wits quickly returning. "I suspect that she used her Marck control relay system to move her consciousness away from the core. She and the Knactors found Eesolan before the Thraxons and a way to wield the white orb, despite her lack of a soul and malevolent character."

"How do you know? How do you know it's the queen?" Kerriah asked.

"She revealed herself just before she used Cyos to attack our fleet. She couldn't help gloating over her perceived surprise."

"We just encountered Cyos near Zeta's far side mirror. It attacked us, but," she took a dry gulp, and a sour pit formed in her stomach, "it looked like it may have been attempting to traverse the corridor. If the queen controls it, then it's likely heading to the UMO."

"No, it doesn't need the corridors for efficient interstellar travel. We tracked it to you, and it appears to have a way to fold itself through space. It was waiting for you as if it knew you were coming into what would appear to be a well-orchestrated trap—a trap laid by the queen. Your ship ended up here because of an anomaly created by Cyos and its proximity to the corridor when you entered. Something the queen failed to account for. It essentially voided the far side mirror for a few minutes as your ship passed, rendering you to what's called free-form traversal. Oddly this side of Zeta seems to end here more often than not. Fortunately, the Thraxon fleet I was given command over was equipped with the stolen X88T drive tech, which allowed us to jump to this location without the Zeta mirror."

"Wow," Kerriah said under her breath. She desperately wanted to understand how the X88T's Nurac gravity drive generated enough power for such a feat, a curiosity that went unfulfilled after losing the prototype she had stolen. However, with so much data to ingest, her mind returned to one particular oddity.

"There was a desolate frigate left here from what appears to be some time ago. And Gorag, the crime lord of Semptor, strangely has one of the things that infest the planet below. How could that be? There must be a correlation."

"Yes, there is." Creedith adjusted his seat on the hard floor. "If this is knowledge that will help set your thoughts at ease, I will provide an explanation."

Kerriah knew this likely wasn't anything more than satisfying her own curiosities and not critical at this time. "No, it's not. I-I just—"

Creedith slowly raised his palm to stop her from explaining. "It's okay, child. I understand. Before we pursued your ship to this location, I pulled any data I could find from the Thraxon fleet archives. Early on, during the first Thraxon invasion, the UMO cut power to the Zeta mirror some fifty years ago to stop the inflow of Thraxon warships. Without the Thraxons realizing this, they sent a fleet through. Two ships found their way back decades later, but most of the fleet was lost. They reportedly found hostile life and even contained specimens. The ships never made it back to Annakrow with these specimens."

"So they don't know what happened to them?"

"It was a desperate time towards the end of the second Thraxon war. The ships were routed through Zeta as the Thraxon command ordered their fleets to throw everything they had at the Marcks in a last-ditch effort to regain a foothold within the system. It's uncertain what happened to them after that time."

"Well, sadly, it's possible that decision saved Annakrow from this annihilation." Kerriah thought about the joint Marck and Thraxon invasion that would have never been and the lives that would have likely been saved.

"We have graver concerns now." Creedith squeezed his eyes closed for a second as he thought. "The Thraxons have declared war on the queen. Already bitter from her apparent betrayal in the wake of their great joint invasion of the UMO, they wanted Eesolan. With the aid of their newly integrated jump tech, they had finally located the well-hidden world. But the Thraxons had no interest in the white orb. They wanted to use the Luminars for their breeding pits. The idea of their Thraxon offspring benefiting from the highly evolved species as their hosts had always piqued their interest, so they desperately sought Eesolan. The queen took that from them.

"Now the queen controls Cyos, and the Thraxons fear her. Those in fear tend to make rash choices. With her heightened intellect, the queen likely realizes this and is expediting her plans with Cyos. Her fleet also appeared to have expanded. Therefore, she's established a production process for her legions. In addition, the Thraxons no longer need the portals to invade, and as such, we are in the most perilous of times."

Kerriah buried her face in her hands. "I hate the queen and her Marcks. My whole life has been about fighting their oppression over the UMO." Her voice muffled into her palms as she spoke.

"I understand, child. However, her emergence is the only reason the Thraxons haven't already returned to the UMO to finish what they have started. As odd as it may be, I feel that at least for the moment, she is both a blessing and a curse."

Keeping her hands over her face, she slowly massaged her fingertips into her forehead as she spoke, trying to relieve some of the building tension as she processed the disturbing details. "Maybe so, but the Thraxons don't stand a chance with her controlling Cyos, and then she'll be focused solely on us." Kerriah didn't have an answer on their next move. Head back to the UMO now and warn them of Cyos or go directly into the belly of the beast and find Plexo.

"How do we know Plexo is even still alive? The last we heard from him, he uncharacteristically proceeded to Eesolan without UMO clearance. He was supposed to wait for us. Did your fleet detect any sign of his ship?"

"We didn't, even though we tracked him there. But the clouds of battle also didn't allow for an extensive search. He must be found, and that's still his last known whereabouts. Our odds of desisting this monstrosity without his knowledge are nil." Creedith slowly looked down at his naked body and glanced around the room. "May I ask a favor?"

She pulled her hands away from her face and peeked at Creedith's bare flesh standing before her. She blushed, knowing what he was going to ask. "Sure."

"May I have some body coverings before Krath returns?"

She let out a weary snicker. "Of course."

CHAPTER 38

Jesselle and the spec op team from the frigate arrived earlier, along with a storm of drama. Upon seeing Creedith, Jesselle entered full attack mode, unleashing orb-spawned assailants from equipment, weapons, and even corpses lying around the Thraxon ship. Kerriah was becoming wise to the nearly instant actions of the entamals and waved them off at the onset before piercing into Jesselle's mind and subduing her. For now, they kept the two separated. Throughout the subsequent two Tridole cycles, they prepped the Thraxon command ship for their search for Plexo.

Creedith still had command of the ship's squill, allowing him to run the ship himself when he stepped into the center cavity. The squill would wrap itself around his body and slither its appendages into Creedith's mouth and ears. It controlled the ship's propulsions, weapons, life support, and transport systems based on Creedith's direction.

The biggest surprise so far came from Stelios. The entamals, for some time, had planned to travel outside their planetary system. Stelios had volunteered for this excursion but at significant risk to himself. They created an experimental emptocap, allowing them to travel away from the Tridole-based modulating stations with a limited scope of time-shifting abilities. Utilizing this capability at its maximum range to slow time or open a sleeve would nearly deplete his portable power supply. If his power supply, though self-charging, were to run out, so would his mobility, as he would bear the suit's weight, which was considerable. The modifications to the emptocap made it bulky, and its wearer appeared more like a lumbering piece of machinery than a sleek metal statue. Though the modified armor was far from perfect in its current build, Stelios knew now was the time, with an opportunity to leave with a group that could reach known civilized worlds.

"Everything's secured and ready when you are, Creedith," Kerriah said, looking back at Captain Ashton, who gave her an affirming nod.

With the help of the entamals, they made some slight modifications to the Thraxon warship that would make it a bit more UMO-personnel friendly. Aside from sleeping, Thraxons did everything standing up, including eating. There was also no apparent need or desire for personal comfort; their racks were merely round holes in the wall with no padding. They didn't have seats; instead, a wall inset with clenchers allowed them to pull tight against it in case the ship made evasive maneuvers or anything else that would jar its crew. The newer-class command ship had a familiar appearance to the older frigate. Like the Thraxon frigate, damp ribbings glistening in moisture lined the walls and ceilings throughout, but the passages were more expansive and better illuminated than the older ship, giving a much less claustrophobic feeling.

"How about our food supplies?" Creedith asked. "There's enough to sustain us for the journey to Eesolan and then back home?"

Kerriah smiled and laughed to herself, then tapped her wrist. "Krath," she called down to Krath, who was tasked with the inventory, "how are our food supplies looking?"

"If tya call this Dranglion porpoise crap food, then sure. It's here. Though it looks more like somthin' I swiped off my backside shortly after downing a couple pints of Hybor grob and a bucket of aacor."

She snickered once more upon hearing his reply and tapped her wrist again. "He's not happy about what Stelios provided us. It's the only sustenance the entamals have this side of Ethis. It's just a flavorless brown paste they pump into their dormant bodies to keep them alive. But it's either that or Thraxon chow, which no civilized person would even consider."

"Hmmm, splendid." Creedith cracked the first smile since they had found him upon hearing Krath's protests over the food situation. "Fortunately, I've returned to civilized."

"We are all happy—well, most of us are happy—to have you back," Kerriah responded with a brief smile that uncomfortably turned flat.

"Hmmm—we are ready to engage the jump drive system. Brace yourselves. When the drives engage, it will feel like we hit a large asteroid. After that, it's smooth until we reach our destination, which will be brief." Creedith stepped into the center cavity of the ship's command bridge and spoke a Thraxon command.

Upon hearing his words, Kerriah looked back at Ashton, who had as much surprise on his face as she did. There were very few in the UMO that knew any Thraxon dialect. Creedith could speak it fluently enough to give commands to the ship's squill.

The squill's tentacles grabbed him by his arms and legs, wrapping themselves around his limbs and lifting him over the cavity opening. His mouth opened, and its appendages slid down his throat and slithered into his ears. The lights onboard dimmed as power diverted to the jump drive system.

Kerriah grabbed hold of a pair of rough-textured rails with both hands. Ashton grabbed two of his own, leaning forward with his eyes closed and his head down as he gripped the rails tightly. The Thraxon bridge crew must have used the cold metal bars looping out from the wall for the same purpose.

"Assa . . . gossha . . . thwetta," a voice rang out throughout the ship's chambers and corridors.

A sharp jolt hit Kerriah like a surge of electricity. She felt her hands' grips tighten and then loosen until she clung onto the rail with only her fingertips keeping her from being hurled across the bridge. The ship let out a shrilling scream and then instantly went silent. Her grip failed, and then she dropped to the deck and tumbled into the far wall. Ashton's body also launched to the other side of the bridge as he lost his grip.

"Are you alright?" she tried to shout at him, but her voice was muffled and didn't seem to get any further than her ears, even though it was dead silent on the command bridge.

She stood and then felt dizzy as she stammered over to Captain Ashton. She leaned down and gave him a violent shake. He was unconscious, likely hitting his head while tossed across the bridge. Her hand brushed against his cheeks, and she entered his mind, nudging him back to consciousness. His eyes opened, and he looked up. Before withdrawing from his thoughts, she saw his infatuation with her again. She blushed and shook her head, then squeezed her eyes shut. He was both handsome and confident. They could have had something in another life, but she had Crix and needed to remain focused.

Placing her hand out, Ashton's warm, soft fingers grasped hers, and she assisted him up to his feet. Their eyes locked before the apparent dizziness hit him, and he leaned his shoulder against the wall for balance.

"Careful; we're not used to moving around during a jump. Plus, I think you hit your head." Kerriah projected her voice straight into his mind as she spoke. She placed her hand on his arm to offer support in case he lost his footing. She looked straight into his blue eyes. "You okay?"

He nodded with a faint smile. "Assa . . . gossha . . . thwetta," the grainy ship's voice announced again as they suddenly stopped.

The dizziness left her, and her footing felt solid once more. Ashton shook his head and then rubbed his eyes.

"We must have arrived at Eesolan," she said, noticing her voice now resonated throughout the bridge. She felt anxious to see a place she had only heard so much about during her life. Yet, now that the Marck Queen had overtaken the once peaceful planet and stolen the white orb, there were unknown dangers. Would there be a Marck fleet? Or the mythically ominous Cyos, now controlled by the queen? Or had the Thraxons returned in hopes of spawning their next generation from the gifted population of Luminars? They were ill-prepared to deal with the three possibilities, but this was the last place they knew Plexo was headed.

After a few minutes, the squill withdrew from Creedith's mouth and ears, lowering him back onto the bridge floor. "Eesolan is in view and surprisingly, no signs of Marck or Thraxon fleet ships," he said. He paused for a few seconds and then added. "Plexo's ship is here."

Kerriah's eyes lit up. "Really? Is he onboard? Can you reach him?" Her hope cautiously grew.

"Scans for life onboard came back negative."

"What about the orb?" Kerriah asked. "Remember, I mentioned he powered his ship with the green orb."

"No. No orb signatures detected," Creedith replied. "The ship appears to be without power."

"Oh no. . . ." her voice faded.

"That's not my primary concern at this moment," Creedith said in a somber voice.

Kerriah's face turned long over the thought of what could be worse. "What?"

"There's a gigantic onyx entity spinning above the planet as we speak. None of the Thraxon intelligence systems recognized it from any of their known exploits, which is concerning, considering how expansive those exploits are." Creedith stepped forward and cinched his robe tighter. "Aside from an indecipherable and continuous low-frequency pulse, it hasn't made any hostile actions. Although, there is a strong orb power signature coming from both it and the planet. We need to take the utmost precautions here."

"The white orb?" It was the first thought that came to her mind.

"It's much stronger than any we've ever detected. I would say in all probability, yes."

"So you didn't see this giant object here before?" Kerriah asked, needing to be sure of its mystery.

"Negative." Creedith's nostrils flared as he stared up for a moment. "But I don't see how we could have missed it. Something ominous has placed roots here, and I fear we are about to step into this beast's snare."

CHAPTER 39

Though uncertain and full of risks, there was no way Kerriah would stay back on the Thraxon frigate while Sergeant Alar and his ops team swept Plexo's specially modified corvette-class ship. Besides, aside from Krath and Jesselle, she was the only person with them that had ever been onboard that flashy, bronze vessel. Before she stood to get a better view from the transport's cockpit window, she looked back at Captain Ashton. As soon as she made it known she would be going with the team, he insisted he also needed to be there. To everyone else, his decision seemed like a courageous leader who would always put himself in harm's way alongside those who reported to him. However, she knew the real reason why he had come.

"Where are you going, Kerriah?" Ashton asked with a smile.

She smiled back. "Well, not that I need to report everything I do to you, but I want a better look at what we're dealing with." She knew undermining his authority frustrated Ashton. But she also knew his affection for her allowed it to happen. Mature beyond her years due to her recent exploits, she was still relatively young and welcomed the subtle flirts. She enjoyed the game. It helped ground her thoughts and kept her from becoming overwhelmed with the dire tasks ahead. She needed it.

She stepped into the cockpit with Lieutenant Camden and his co-pilot. They hardly noticed her behind them as they stared at Eesolan in the distance. Kerriah tilted her head and squinted as she observed the planet. Luminars always guarded the secrecy of their home world, and as such, there were very few images of it floating around the UMO. The ones she recalled seeing were a white planet with blotches of black and swashes of golden tint lightly brushed across the surface. This version had long black bands feathering across its smoky face. Debris from broken orbiting stations and ships littered the outer reaches of the planet's gravitational pull.

"This," Kerriah's voice was low and her words hesitant as she spoke, "this is Eesolan?"

"Yeah, or at least what's left of it," Camden said as he looked down for a second to adjust the transport's scanning array.

She noticed both pilots kept looking nervously up. She took another step forward and stooped for a better view. Her eyes widened—a white beam connected from the planet to the base of an enormous object. The span of the onyx sickle's slender blades nearly matched in scale to Eesolan as it spun above the planet, slicing through the black void like a fan pushing nonexistent air through the world below.

"What the heck is that?" Her voice quivered, knowing this was what Creedith had warned of when they first arrived, but seeing it firsthand was creepier than she had imagined. It was challenging to keep her nerves pulled together. Everything was out of place here, and it felt more like they moved into a well-orchestrated trap with every passing minute.

"We have no idea," Camden replied. "Right now, we're just going to stay on mission and hope it leaves us alone."

She clenched her jaw tight over the thought of that plan, but she knew there was little else they could do. The transport took a slow, cautious approach with the eerie specter of Eesolan in the foreground when a shimmering object emerged, stealing away their attention.

"Sir, the corvette is dead ahead," his co-pilot said.

"Good. Let's get underneath its belly and see if the bay door is open," Camden replied, making several hurried adjustments on his instrument panel.

Eesolan's glow mirrored off the glassy bronze ship as they approached. Its surface appeared alive as reflections of space wreckage danced across its hull.

"Careful on our approach," Camden warned as a piece of charred ship's hull tumbled past their cockpit window. Fortunately, Plexo's ship was further out from the main part of the debris field, but there were still stray pieces sporadically zipping by at lethal speeds.

"How is anything intact out here?" Kerriah asked. "I mean, I know Plexo built a sturdy ship, but the fact it's still in one piece has to be just short of a miracle."

"It didn't come out completely unscathed," Camden said, pointing to a chunk of decking protruding from the ship's side."

"The fact that it's not spinning out of control tells me the ship's stabilizers are still online, or at least they were on impact. And that it's not venting atmosphere tells me life-support systems are offline, or that section has been sealed off," Kerriah noted. Camden smiled and shook his head, and his copilot turned and gave her a sideways glance.

Ashton stepped up behind her and smacked his hand on her back. "Yep, that's my girl. Always full of surprises."

She turned back at him with a scowl and jerked her shoulder away. "I'm not your girl."

Ashton withdrew his hand, and his face looked as if he'd seen a ghost. "I-I'm sorry. I didn't mean to—"

"It's fine. I'm just way past being called someone's girl."

"Duly noted." Ashton gulped. "Ahh . . . so what's our situation, Lieutenant?"

"Dangerous, Captain. Though the ship is clear of the worst parts of the debris field, there are ample stray fragments hurling around. Just one small chunk of those could ruin our day." Camden steadily pushed down on the control grips, dipping the transport below the belly of Plexo's ship. "Looks like we're in luck. The bay doors are open." A rectangular shadow appeared as the underside of the ship came into view.

"It's dark," Kerriah noted. "Plexo doesn't like it dark. I hope he's still alive."

"Take us up, Lieutenant." Ashton looked over at Kerriah. "Well, we're about to find out."

CHAPTER 40

Inside Plexo's ship appeared eerily dark, and an uncomfortable lump formed in her throat as Kerriah peaked around the ghostly hangar. It was missing one of its most notable characteristics, the eye-blistering glow that usually radiated throughout. She never imagined seeing it in this state. Alar's spec ops team filed out of the transport with their weapons ready. The only lights came from Kerriah and Ashton's non-tactical e-vos suit visors. The pale-green backlight tinted their faces, while spec ops were completely dark.

Alar's team fanned out in pairs, sweeping through the ship. Kerriah and Ashton remained back, awaiting any word from the team for signs of Plexo or other survivors. She wanted to find Plexo, but there was another concern she couldn't shake off. The green orb. It powered this ship and allowed Plexo to live past his natural lifespan. Was it still onboard?

"The green orb is here," she said. "Or at least it was."

"What?" Ashton squinted as if he hadn't heard her correctly. "Did you say the green orb is here?"

"No. I'm saying it was. Few knew of it, but Plexo recovered the green orb years ago and retrofitted it as the power core of this ship. It gave it the ability to open short-range portals via his probes and made this ship faster than any others in the UMO fleet."

Ashton drew a deep breath. "Okay. . . . That's highly illegal. No wonder they never found the green orb."

"Yeah, it was illegal. But now all those stupid preservation acts and treaties are null since the central core's destruction," she rebuked with a fiery tone. "Besides, had he not taken the orb, we would all be Thraxon chow."

Ashton warily raised his hands. "Hey, it's good. I try to keep my nose out of politics anyway. But if it is here, we need to find it."

The one time she saw the green orb, Plexo had taken them there via an internal teleportation system. There had to be a way to reach it conventionally. But how? Without power, the ship's internal mapping system would be offline, and this ship was one big puzzle.

"I'm going to look for it." She spun around and started toward the partially open pressure doors which exited the landing bay. The same doors the spec ops team had left through earlier. Her magnetic boots made her gait jerky as they snapped up and pulled down with each step.

"Wait!" Ashton took a few quick steps and grabbed her arm. "We still don't know what's in there. Until Alar's team finishes their sweep, it's too dangerous."

Kerriah bit her lower lip, trying to hold back a sharper rebuke. "Look, Captain . . . if you only knew what I've been through, you'd understand that I'm not too concerned about what may be lurking around this cold, dead ship. Whatever it is, I've seen worse." She snapped her arm loose from his grip. "If you want to come with me, then fine. If you want to stay here, that's fine too."

Though his face showed a mix of concern and frustration, a quick poke into his mind told her he secretly liked her fiery spirit. Inside, he smiled, and his heart raced with excitement. He wanted to feel some of that intensity with her lips against his. However, the helmet visor and military discipline kept his manors in check. She knew there was no way he would let her leave without him. Even though he was the ranking officer, she owned him. She shook her head and rolled her eyes over the idea.

"What?" he asked with blushed cheeks. "Wait, are you . . . reading my thoughts?" His eyes rounded, and his mouth slacked.

Kerriah chuckled. "Captain, you're not that difficult to read."

"But you're not using the orb to get into my head, are you?"

She shrugged with a smile. Though the timing was inappropriate, she was enjoying this exchange. To some degree, she needed it right now to lighten her mood. Beneath that authoritative exterior, Asthon was emotionally fragile, and for some reason, she liked this about him. It slowly thawed that icy barrier she kept around herself.

"That's not right. You're violating my personal thoughts." He closed his eyes and lowered his head. "Well . . ." He carefully peeked up at her. "Well, I guess you know how I feel then?"

She pursed her lips with a smile and gave a slight nod of agreement. The green-tinted light inside her helmet and the nearly pitch-black background highlighted her facial expressions.

"Kerriah, you fascinate me." Everything he kept bottled up regarding his feelings for her began to pour out. "When you're near me, I-I have trouble taking my eyes off you. I feel drawn to you." He raised his shoulders and then lowered them with a deep breath. "Anyway, I—"

"Look," she said as she briefly turned to look at the door. "You don't know anything about me, and if you did, I doubt you'd feel the way you do now. I'm complicated and would only bring frustration to your otherwise promising future." She turned back to the door again. "Besides, right now, we are here without most of your original crew, on a Thraxon frigate, staring at a besieged Eesolan, with a giant blade spinning over it and a ramp—" She stopped and shook her head with frustration over the list of bizarre challenges before them. "A rampaging nebula that the Marck Queen of all things controls. I think we both have more important issues to deal with now." She delivered the list with a twist of snark mixed with authoritative leadership. She always had a way of outlining a crisis.

"Believe me; I'm aware of our situation Kerriah. I just don't think you should shut me out."

"Fine, let me try to make this easier for you to understand. I think you're fantastic. You're attractive, smart, charming, and confident. You're a dream catch. But I have someone in my life already, and I fully intend to reunite with him when all this is over."

Ashton lowered his head and took a few seconds of silent thought before responding. "Okay, I just think we—"

"Captain," a call from Sergeant Alar chirped in over his comm, "I believe we've found your Luminar."

Ashton squinted. "What do you mean, you think you've found him?"

"He's here, I think, but he's not right. It'll be easier if you see for yourself."

Ashton looked over at Kerriah, but she already stormed down the corridor. "Kerriah, wait!"

CHAPTER 41

Kerriah and Ashton met the spec ops team at the edge of Plexo's main lab. The team stood looking up into the open area with the Arc Stasis control center suspended above. Without power for the suspension field, stepping into the main lab area would result in an unpleasant fall. Kerriah stepped to the edge and looked up at the shadowy silhouette of the teardrop seats and the sphere above.

"Where is he?" she asked, not seeing him at first. Then she noticed everyone around her staring directly above, not at the Arc Stasis control center.

One of the team tapped her shoulder and pointed straight up. She leaned back. Plexo hovered a few meters almost directly overhead. He was so close to the wall it was easy to miss him when distracted by the enormity of the Arc Stasis. His body was completely still, like he had been cropped from an image and placed on this plane of existence. His face stared down, and his expression appeared locked with fright. His figure still had a subtle glow, but it seemed like it seeped out somewhere distant and lost most of its intensity during its long journey.

"Plexo!" Kerriah shouted upon seeing him, and quickly realized he would never hear her words in the airless vacuum. She then attempted to call out into his mind.

"It's no use," Alar said. "We've tried to get his attention and even prodded him. Everything seems to pass right through his body. The strangest thing is that nothing goes through the other side of him."

"What? What do you mean?" Kerriah asked.

Alar reached back and snatched a small cube floating behind him. "Watch," he said before tossing it at Plexo's body. It spun into his chest with a ripple of fluid and vanished. "We even sent a probe in, but it lost connectivity to it as soon as it passed through."

"Right," Kerriah said, not sounding too surprised. "We need to find out what's on the other side." She squatted before leaning down and pressing the magnetic release on her boots. Her feet instantly rose from the floor.

"Kerriah!" Captain Ashton said with an elevated and authoritative tone. "What are you doing?"

"What needs to be done," she replied without breaking her fixed stare on Plexo. She extended her legs, pushing herself upward off the floor.

"Kerriah, no!" Those were the last words she heard from the captain before she drifted into Plexo.

CHAPTER 42

FIVE YEARS OUT OF SYNC

Kerriah?" The soft familiar voice spoke. "Kerriah? Can you hear me?" The twinkling sounds of blips and beeps slowly emerged in the background and seeped into the foreground as her eyes peeled open. "Oh, thank goodness, she's coming to." Plexo's glowing, heart-shaped head appeared over her with a smile. "I am so glad you are okay."

"What . . happened? Where am I?" Her body flinched as the words flowed from her mouth without any thought.

"You're onboard my ship, in my infirmary."

Cloudiness blurred her thoughts. She rubbed her eyes and gave a few strong blinks, trying to clear her vision and mind. "You were . . ." She let out a gasp of frustration over her lack of clarity.

"Hmmm? I was what?" Plexo responded.

"I-I don't know, but you weren't right. Your ship . . . it's . . . damaged . . . disabled."

"Oh my, I'm afraid you've been out of consciousness for quite some time now." He placed his hand under his chin for a moment. "I suspect what you've experienced are possibly dreams or hallucinations. Although I'm not certain either is possible for you. Joric keeps your design a closely guarded secret." His hand lightly touched her shoulder, and his face came closer. "Regardless, you can be rest assured, young one, myself and my ship are perfectly fine."

"No! That's not possible!" She sat up and looked around the brightly lit medical facility.

Plexo was there with what appeared to be an Eetak, which stood motionless closely behind him. Everything looked normal for Plexo's ship. A pure white backdrop with a few uncomfortable-looking tables with various thin conduits hanging over each.

"Where's Captain Ashton and Sargent Alar and his team? I was just with them."

Plexo shook his head and placed his hand back on her shoulder to encourage her to lie back down. "Please, you've been through a lot and are distraught. Take a bit more time to rest, and I will explain—"

"I don't want to rest!" she shouted.

Plexo took a cautious step back, and she pivoted on the table and stood. At that moment, she realized she wasn't dressed. As her bare feet hit the floor, the chilly metal bit into the pads, and she curled her toes with a grimace.

"What the?" Kerriah uncomfortably danced in place for a few seconds, trying to adjust to the uncomfortable sting of cold. She stopped to glance down at her feet and then up her legs. The only thing she had on was a thin white smock draped over her breasts and stopping at her knees. She scowled and then shot a stare back at Plexo. "Where are my clothes?"

"By the time I found you, your e-vos suit's life support system was critical. The only reason you're still alive is due to your unique design. Any other ordinary, carbon-based life would have expired from any combination of oxygen loss, extreme cold, or loss of pressure." A smile crept over Plexo's face. "You are remarkable indeed. Joric truly excelled with your design."

She dug her fingernails into her thighs. She needed to feel some intentional pain, something that could hopefully ground her and let her know she was here. Her leg stung as the nails jabbed into her skin, and she bit down on her lip for the same assurance.

"Tell me what happened? Where's the Mertel?"

"Oh dear." Plexo placed his hand over his mouth and slowly lowered it before answering. "Of course, you don't recall. By all indications, the Mertel had a terrible accident passing through Zeta. We're not certain what happened, but we found parts of it nearby when we rescued you. The Zeta corridor is the longest of the four that leads to the UMO system. It's possible that the new UMO vessel suffered a structural failure, and its hull came apart as it passed the last mirror."

Kerriah shook her head. "A structural? What are you talking about, Plexo? No-no, I was onboard when we passed through. There were no issues."

Plexo massaged his chin for a second. "Hmmm . . . well then perhaps it was attacked by a Thraxon patrol?"

She shook her head again. "No. We didn't encounter any—" She stopped and pulled both hands down her face and stopped over her mouth. Her eyes widened as it hit her. "We were attacked by Cyos right after we crossed through."

"Cyos?"

"Yes. We fled back through the portal, but something went wrong. Cyos somehow began to demolecularize the ship. Some crew members died, but the outer hull remained intact. We ended up on the other side of the galaxy with a damaged drive system." She felt a sudden panic as she ran through her memories. "Ugh," she closed her eyes, "they were attacked by Thraxon ships. The Mertel was destroyed."

"Well," Plexo said with an assured tone. "That's it then. A Thraxon assault destroyed the Mertel." His eyes stared down. "I am sorry."

"No." She let out a deep breath. "That was after we passed back through the corridor."

"At least that's what you thought," Plexo replied.

Distraught, she leaned against the cold metal table with both hands. She tried to think for a minute, focused on her memories, and then smacked her palm down as her frustration boiled over. "No! So much happened after that."

"Kerriah," Plexo said, his voice as soft as she could ever recall. "I believe you. However, you're recovering from extreme trauma, and much of your memories may not have been real events."

She didn't know what to believe. What was real? Krath, Jesselle, and Captain Ashton were all dead? A trickle of fluid ran down her cheek. Emotions and their physical side-effects were a gift from her father. She cherished them but also tried to reject them, as they gave away her vulnerable state. Her face suddenly perked up, and she swiped her tears away. The yellow orb, she still had it in her. She could put this confusion to rest right now. She stared intensely at Plexo, and he took a tentative step back.

"Kerriah, please," he said.

She stabbed into his thoughts like a razor-sharp knife piercing into the skin of a piece of fruit. Searching into his recent memories, she could see it was all there. All his claims, tangled amongst clusters of logic and formulas, everything he said was all true. The Mertel and its entire crew were adrift in pieces outside Zeta's far side mirror. How had she survived? How had she escaped when no one else had? She had no memories that could corroborate what he said, only the memories of the entamals and their planet filled with heydromacs. But that never happened. She slowly lay back on the table; her mind went into a fog of thoughts.

"I realize this is difficult for you to hear. Please, take time to accept what has transpired. I will be back to check on you in a bit." Plexo left, but the Eetak remained. It stood motionless near the doorway.

She turned away and curled into a ball, crying until her eyes swelled and her heart felt like an empty shell. She just wanted to return to Crix and take him up on that primitive Andor life. She could give up all this technology and the orb; she was tired and yearned for simplicity and comfort. She would need to go back and convince Septin and the UMO to blow Zeta again and hopefully keep the Thraxons away. Crix was right in doing so. But did they have the X88T technology? In her unconscious memories, they did. If they did, what could she do? Right . . . nothing. With her mind made up, she would tell Plexo when he returned that she wanted to go home. To New Troika.

CHAPTER 43

It didn't seem like more than a few minutes had passed before Plexo returned with the same placid expression he had when he left. Kerriah sat up as straight as she could before hastily expressing her wish to return to New Troika. He stopped and rubbed his pointy chin, as she would expect from someone she knew who thought everything through before making a decision. He lowered his hand and moved in closer with a tilted head, looking into her eyes. Her jaw tightened in response.

Come on, Plexo . . . really? She always hated the lab animal treatment. His hesitancy irritated her, and she wanted to put her hands around his throat and wring that logical stubbornness out of him.

"I see," he said.

"See what?"

"I see that your emotional bond to the young Crix has you making unexpected choices. You would be the last one I would have anticipated to give up on your quest."

"I'm tired, Plexo. Tired of the fighting, tired of the politics, tired of the death that follows me. I'm even tired of the orbs."

"Tired? Hmmm . . . interesting." He backed away and stood with one arm resting on his hip. "Very well. I will personally take you to this New Troika, but first, I would like you to see something."

"What?" She had a difficult time holding back her annoyed tone.

"The white orb. I feel it may ignite the yellow orb within you and return your lost memories."

Her curiosities sparked over the thought of seeing something so enigmatic and mythical. Even on Eesolan, only a select few had access to this great power. Besides, she wanted nothing more than to fill the holes in her memories. To learn what happened to her and how Krath and Jesselle had died. Were they truly dead? She owed it to them to do everything she could to find out. Yet, her nerves wouldn't let her go. It was odd she was offered this rare opportunity. Did Plexo, who hadn't been back home to Eesolan for over eight decades, have this level of influence? Maybe she didn't understand Luminars enough for this to make sense. She'd only known Plexo.

"Fine," she replied.

As her thoughts brewed over the trip to Eesolan, the transport that would take her to the white orb arrived much faster than she had expected. It was as though Plexo somehow had this already planned out. She quickly shook off the cynicism. Hopefully, one way or another, she would have the answers she sought very soon.

***

The circular transport had a silvery shell appearing transparent, but looking into it didn't reveal the inside or its occupants. There were always reports the Luminars could harness and manipulate dark matter to make their ships disappear into the backdrop of space. This provided a unique advantage to the deep-space explorers, allowing them to eavesdrop on civilizations without detection and only show themselves when the purpose became necessary.

Three shimmering Luminars greeted Kerriah at the base of the transport. They looked much like Plexo, with heart-shaped heads and slender builds. The only way to distinguish them was through their faces and expressions.

Each one had subtle distinctions in their facial features, like their eye shapes and positions and the relative size of their mouths. Some held a firm, serious stare, while others smiled warmly.

"Welcome, Kerriah," one of the Luminars said as she approached the ship hovering a meter above the deck of Plexo's landing bay. Its voice was sterile yet inviting, with the same feeling she would get from hearing Plexo speak, as though hearing it in a dream.

"We are so very pleased to meet you. I am Centif, and I will be your escort to Bellahis."

Kerriah looked back at Plexo with confusion, who stood a short distance behind her. He smiled. "Bellahis is where the white orb is kept. Not to worry, you'll be fine. I will be there with you in spirit."

Kerriah's brow furrowed deeper as she slowly turned back to the ship and the three Luminars. *In spirit?* Plexo was acting weird. Maybe he was just awkward from his lengthy time away, she thought. She shook it off and focused on the three Luminars before her. She needed to get this over with, as her enthusiasm quickly waned.

"I'm, uh . . . excited to see it," she replied, struggling to find eloquent words.

Centif waved her forward; he was the friendly, smiling one. The other two, which stood to either side of him, had serious stares. So serious that if it weren't for Centif, she would be even more hesitant than she was already. Centif's smile grew larger as she neared. It was a disarming smile at first, but as it grew, the less comfortable she became. For a moment, she considered turning around, but just as her pace slowed, Centif spoke again.

"Plexo told us of your memories, or lack thereof. Aside from Seren, our Great Divination, I have the most time with the white orb. I truly believe that it will highlight the areas in your lost recollections."

"Your Great Divination?" she said the words slowly.

It was a strange title, but she understood the Luminars were a secretive species. Although they shared some of their technology and philosophies, they kept their society and much about their history sealed to others outside of their own kind. As far as she knew, no other UMO representative had ever traveled to Eesolan before her, and no official records of what was down there existed, aside from a population of highly intellectual, glowing beings and a mysterious white orb.

Centif stepped to the side, and Kerriah stopped to look back at Plexo. As she turned, a warm, tingling sensation coated her body, and she found herself gripped inside a stasis field, looking back at Plexo from a small observation window. Kerriah was now inside the transport, though she wasn't sure how she had arrived there. She turned to look forward again, and her head moved with a bit of resistance. It felt as though she was immersed in semi-firmed gelatin. It wasn't like zero gravity, where she would have needed something to grab ahold of to move about. She could kick or swoosh her arms in the thickened air to change her body position. Centif hovered two meters from her, and his body floated as hers did, not touching any surfaces onboard the transport. Around them were small round windows, and she could see almost panoramically outside.

She felt a tug, and Plexo's docking bay vanished and was almost instantly replaced with the opaque, white glow of Eesolan. Within seconds, a vast skyline peppered with round and ovular structures and platforms emerged. Some of the forms soared from needle-like bases from far below, and others hovered on their own. Sparse clouds gently swooshed across the smooth shapes, and most of the planet's surface looked like a bone-colored painting marbled with varying grey lines of fissures and canyons.

Kerriah looked in awe at the sight no one else from her civilization's history had ever witnessed. Knowing this highly advanced world was about to peel open for her was invigorating. There would be something to learn from each eyeful. A wall of glass appeared filling the sky before them. Their ship paused, and Kerriah noticed she could see a shimmering reflection of their circular vessel against the glass wall. In the purest sense, it was simple, yet it was also one of the most extraordinary things she had ever seen. The massive glass oval spanned as far as she could see in each direction. A small section directly in front of their ship lost its reflective characteristic and became transparent. The transport slowly moved through the opening, and before them emerged an area so bright even Kerriah had to squint for a few seconds to adjust to the intensity of light.

"Welcome to Bellahis," Centif announced.

At that moment, Kerriah realized he had never taken his eyes off her. Having been distracted by the sights, she hadn't noticed earlier, but subconsciously she knew he had watched her the entire time. She wanted to examine his mind and see what he thought, but she wasn't sure if this highly advanced Luminar elder could detect her probing. For now, she cautiously held back.

He curled his fingers as he rotated his hand in a gesture for her to follow. "Please, prepare to depart."

She swung her body downward, and as soon as her toes touched the floor, they instantly stood outside the ship, looking out at a great globe of white surrounded by phantom wisps of light that would emerge and dissipate. The massive orb hovered twenty meters in diameter at the center of Bellahis. Kerriah felt her skin tingle and her hair rise. She looked down and noticed her chest pulsed a golden glow, and her field of view became immersed in the same yellow hue.

"Your proximity to the white orb has enhanced the yellow orb within you," a feminine voice stated. Kerriah couldn't tell where the voice originated, as it seemed to emanate from all around. She touched her chest and slowly stroked her fingers over the glow. A cool breeze swept up her backside, and as she peeked around, she realized this large area at the center of Bellahis consisted of an open-air ring surrounding the orb.

"You didn't realize that you have the most powerful of the child orbs," the voice said, now appearing to emerge from a source behind the blinding light of the white orb.

"Who? . . . Who are you?" Kerriah asked. She strained to see through the blazing white haze for the voice's source.

"I am the Divination," the voice replied.

A ghostly silhouette emerged from the left side of the orb. A female shape with a luminescent outline hovered a meter above the surface. Her bare toes dangled, and her arms extended outward from her sides. Long white hair sprayed out from her head, whisking freely through the air as though swishing underwater. Kerriah wasn't aware any Luminar had hair. It was an uncommon trait for their species, but what struck her as even more unusual was the shape of her head. It was the round shape of a Mendac female and not the typical heart-shaped of a Luminar head.

"I am the queen of the white orb, its caretaker, its guardian."

Kerriah drew her head back with disgust at hearing the last claim. "Queen?" She scowled with disbelief. "You don't look like a typical Luminar."

The Divination approached, and Kerriah noticed more details around her figure. She was slightly larger than a normal-sized Luminar, with a body shape and size proportional to her own. There was also a slight distortion of light surrounding her head. "I do not appear familiar to you because I am the evolution of the Luminar species. I am what they will become."

"Why would they evolve to you? Are you somehow better than the rest of the Luminars?" the pointed question spilled from Kerriah's mouth with little thought.

"I have been exposed to the white orb for more than two hundred of your years. My body has become the perfect conductor for an orb too great for anyone to bear. As I extend its power beyond Bellahis, my children will also adapt with enhanced abilities."

Kerriah crossed her arms and pursed her lips as she pondered what the Divination said before spilling her thoughts aloud. "Craving power is not a typical Luminar trait. Now, I realize till now that I've only known two Luminars, but their ambitions are the exact opposite of yours. Historically, your species has been more inclined to give power away, like the orbs to the Tolagons." The Divination's face turned strangely dark upon hearing the word. Kerriah squinted for a second over the surprising reaction and then continued. "Or sharing your technology, like the mag infusers that enable the gammac corridors."

"Luminars have their dark history as well. You merely need to look beneath the marvels in the sky to see the wretched discards of their past. Do you think this planet has been kept secret solely to protect the white orb?" The divination smirked. "You have much to learn, child. You may find this surprising to hear, but you are a child of mine."

"What?" Kerriah couldn't believe what this great Luminar told her. It was the furthest thing she would have expected, and now, nothing made any sense once again.

The Divination approached. Kerriah couldn't help but stare at the aura distortion around her head, which was much more prominent up close. "You wanted to unlock your missing memories, did you not?"

Kerriah stopped staring around her head and looked directly into her piercing gaze. With a slight hint of red behind them, the Divination's eyes shot spears straight into her heart as she looked through her.

"Yes, of course."

"Good." Her eyes lit a flaming red as though fire sprayed with fuel. Kerriah went numb, and she lost control of her body as she lifted from her feet. A blaze of red immersed her field of view before clarity emerged.

CHAPTER 44

Five ... four ... three ... two ... one, the bridge computer system announced as the nose dipped into the mirror. The lights on the ship blinked out, and Kerriah could feel the seat beneath her tickle from vibration. Her head spun, and the lights flickered. She felt the vibrations in her seat turn from tickling to a light massage and then into a continuous shuddering pulling a vocal groan from deep within her abdomen.

The pure white view out the bridge window kept the area fully illuminated as the onboard lighting systems failed. The alarm rang, and the bridge crew returned to life. *Three ... two ... one.* The shaking ceased, and the view outside changed from pure white to a gaping mouth of a massive black ship cast in front of the red and purple spray of the Richotaan Nebula.

"Thraxon warships!" the captain shouted upon seeing the view. "Battle stations!"

Outside the far side mirror of Zeta, a fleet of warships stood by, waiting for a hapless ship to pass through and into their set trap. The Mertel was the most advanced warship in the UMO, but the seven Thraxon ships about to bear down upon it would put the sturdy vessel and its green crew to the ultimate test.

"Get those shields up! Tactical, give me an assessment of the enemy fleet," Ashton ordered.

At the tactical post, the young lieutenant tapped and swiped his station's panel as he stared forward into his head-mounted display. "I see two light cruisers, two heavy frigates, a command ship, a hive ship, and an extremely large ship of unknown classification directly ahead."

Kerriah's jaw dropped. "Captain, I realize that this is the latest and greatest in the UMO fleet, but this has to be reaching its limits."

"I don't need this right now, Kerriah," Ashton snapped back at her. "Get all weapons systems online and create an optimal targeting solution on all known weaknesses of the Thraxon vessels." Ashton turned back to his chief tactical officer. "You got me?"

"Yes, sir!"

Ashton leaned forward with his hand on his leg, staring at the ominous ship directly ahead. It looked like a monster lying on its belly with a great open mouth. Nothing was discernible inside except a creepy blackness and questions about what would pop out from the opening.

"I want as much information as you can acquire from external scans on the unknown ship. See if you can correlate it with something in the Thraxon fleet."

"Optimal targets acquired. Weapon systems ready on your word, Captain," the chief tactical officer said.

Ashton calmly raised his arm with his hand open. "Hold there, Lieutenant. We're vastly outgunned, so let's not provoke an attack. We'll see what their intentions are first."

"With all due respect, Captain," Kerriah said, unable to remove her gaze from the gaping blackness of the Thraxon ship, "they are Thraxons. They have only ever had one intention, and that's our total destruction."

"Sir, the Thraxon cruisers are engaging their weapon systems," a bridge officer's voice called out.

"That's it!" the captain shouted, pointing forward. "Fire now!"

The ship's weapon systems engaged with a brilliant glow of green and white igniting the darkness between the warships. Kerriah gripped the arms of her chair, awaiting the inevitable response from the Thraxon ships. Instead, the dark opening before them sparked a violet flare deep within its center and flickered into a swirl of purple mixed with shadowy blackness. The spinning mixture blasted forward with a funnel of gas and energy, submerging the Mertel inside its storm. The ship's power flickered, and its weapons ceased. Its hull rocked like it was in the midst of a storm at sea, and the bridge shook violently.

"We've lost our primary power system!" a frantic voice announced.

Outside, the enveloped view turned into a blackish cauldron of violet streams, which swooshed by at a greater intensity with each passing second.

"Our shields?" Ashton asked.

"Down, sir. Our auxiliary power systems are providing basic life support and ship operations."

A wailing alarm sounded, and the lights appeared to dim further. "Hull breach on our lower deck!"

That was all Kerriah needed to hear. She unbuckled her seat and stood, giving one last look at the chaos outside. She needed to find Krath, Timmon, and Jesselle. She had dragged them into this, and she felt responsible for their lives. Once the ship lost its auxiliary power, there would be no way to get to them.

Ashton and the bridge crew were too distracted to notice as she slipped down the elevator to the lower decks. The door slid open to the mission deployment deck. With the loss of hull integrity, she would need an e-vos suit—the TABS rooms were the tactical, agile, briefing, and staging areas for flight crews and special ops teams. There would be e-vos suits there.

She sprinted down the corridor, weaving around panicked personnel who scrambled desperately for safety. The ship jolted in a figure-eight spiral, throwing her and everyone around her from their feet. Their bodies slammed into the walls and slid across the decks.

Kerriah crawled over on her hands and knees, gripping whatever she could with her fingernails to pull her through the doorway to a nearby TABS room. Suits lined the far wall near several rows of fixed seats, and she could hear voices inside. One familiar voice complained aloud.

"What's with these friggin puny UMO recruits? You'd think they'd eat a sandwich every so often to get up their fightin' strength. Back when I served—"

"Krath!" she shouted with delight over the sight of the beefy Hybor and Timmon. Krath had one leg stuck into an e-vos and both his arms heaving the rest up to his thigh.

"'Bout time tya got your scrawny butt down here. We looked for tya in tya quarters, but tya were gone already. This ship is comin' apart, and we're not 'bout to get stuck sucking void when it happens." Veins bulged from Krath's arms and forehead as he tried to cram the slender leg opening up his beefy thigh.

Kerriah stumbled back to her feet again, pulling her hair away from her face. "At least we think alike in some ways." She looked over at Timmon, sitting with his back against the wall and his legs spread, trying to keep from sliding around as the ship rolled. Why didn't Krath have Timmon in an e-vos? This was certainly out of character for someone she'd always known to have a fatherly, protective way about him. "We need to get Timmon suited up," she shouted so Krath could hear her above the turmoil, hoping he would stop and help her. He didn't respond.

As she located an e-vos for Timmon, the power flickered again, and then everything turned black. Their bodies were raised from the floor and began floating freely, along with anything not secured.

"Oh great, the ship lost its auxiliary power," Kerriah said, flailing around for an e-vos suit she had in her hands moments ago. She felt it float by with her fingertips, and she managed to push herself from the nearby wall and grab hold of it again. In the distance, she could hear the panic, shouts, and screams from crew members dealing with the same reality. Krath's angry voice barked out unsavory words, most of which she didn't recognize, as he frustratingly sprawled out waving his arms and legs for something solid.

The sound of metal ripping apart echoed down the corridor. The darkness gave way to a tint of purple, and the room became visible. The walls around them opened and floated away, leaving them drifting in a storm of violet and black clouds. Kerriah instantly lost sight of Krath and Timmon, and large pieces of the ship's hull and interior drifted by in a swirl of debris.

"Krath!" she shouted, and her voice surprisingly carried, though it was drowned out by the shrills of thousands of other crew members screaming in terror.

She didn't know why she or anyone else could still breathe and weren't freezing to death, but she wasn't going to risk that it would last. Still having a death grip on the e-vos suit, she slid her body inside and pulled the attached helmet over her head. As she activated the suit's internal power system, the neck ring squealed tight, and the internal visor display lit up.

She needed to find Krath and Timmon. Better yet, locate an e-vos floating around and get them suited up before whatever atmosphere they were immersed in disappeared. The swirling soup of flotsam and flailing bodies began to pull inward, funneling directly into the mouth of the unfamiliar, Thraxon-spawned behemoth.

At that moment, she realized why they were all still alive. The Thraxons needed them for sustenance and breeding. The colossal harvesting ship was designed to disable and break apart other ships and encase the contents inside some artificial storm bubble. At the same time, they drew in all the living passengers and crew.

"Oh no," the words escaped her lips, and she slowly spun closer to the dark mouth.

She activated the e-vos integrated propulsion system and clenched her fists, pushing her forward. She panned the kaleidoscope of debris, looking for Krath, hoping his large frame would stand out enough amid the wreckage. Nothing. She could see the bodies filtering into an opaque grey membrane while the ship parts were rejected and jettisoned through a large chute slinging everything into the void below. For all she knew, her companions were already inside. She didn't have time to waste. Calling focus deep inside the yellow orb, she cast out a thought trace, looking inside the minds of all the living souls around her.

The swarming cries of terror and panic made her cringe. The nightmares of hundreds of living crew members flashed into her head. Helplessness and fear gripped them as they witnessed their shipmates being pulled into the membrane to a near-certain demise awaiting them on the other side. A faint voice stood out amongst the hallowed storm of screams.

"Those filthy bugs ain't getting' their greasy mitts on me. There's gotta be a rifle or grenade floating around this mess."

The voice was undeniable. "Krath."

She gripped her hands tight, firing the propulsion forward, and then relaxed her right hand, banking her trajectory to the right. She swung under a large section of a spiraling girder, around several twirling crates, and stitched through a pair of tumbling chunks of machinery. Krath's bulky mass came into view, aggressively flapping his arms and legs as though attempting to swim toward a spinning rifle that caught his eye not too far off. But he was getting close to the membrane, and she could feel the pull toward it increase as she approached.

"Krath!" she shouted, though he wouldn't hear her from the e-vos helmet. She focused through the orb and called again. "Krath!"

Krath's head snapped away from the rifle, and he looked directly at her. A blur of broken ship parts poured down and disappeared behind him as he neared the membrane. She gripped her hands tight to increase her propulsion. As she desperately tried to reach him before he became immersed in the organic barrier, his face turned soft. It was something she had never seen from him before, a look of defeat mixed with sadness. His mouth opened round, and his eyes drooped as if a thief, which he could not catch, had just fled with his soul. She couldn't let him go, but she couldn't reach him in time. The membrane recessed inward as his body impacted like a large pebble smacking into gelatin; he slowly absorbed into the Thraxon ship. The old, great, Hybor warrior was gone.

She had accelerated too fast trying to reach Krath, and the membrane was right in front of her before she spun around to evade its sucking grasp. The suit's propulsion wasn't enough to break away from its pull at this short distance. She gripped her hands until her knuckles turned white, and her fists quivered. She realized the only thing she was doing was buying a few seconds. Her backside pulled within a meter of the barrier and all she could do was await her fate. She could see flashes of red popping inside the storm ahead of her.

Jesselle used her orb to create elemental beasts of metal and gas to hurl her away from the ship. It appeared as an act of futility without an e-vos to protect her outside the Thraxon-created storm cloud.

As she briefly watched her fellow Tolagon desperately trying to survive, Kerriah felt a sharp tug downward, and everything turned black.

CHAPTER 45

Ａnd now you see the truth," The angelic female voice broke through the darkness. "That your friends have all perished at the hands of this new Thraxon monstrosity they call the harvester." Light emerged, and the round face of the Divination appeared with a studying grin. "You survived as discarded scrap. Your synthetic body was mistaken as unusable waste by the technological nightmare they created."

Kerriah drew a breath, feeling like she had just sprinted several kilometers. As she gathered her thoughts for a few minutes, her heart turned sour. They'd killed her friends and left her for dead. Now, this new "harvester" of lives would likely make its way back to the UMO to finish what they had set out to do so many years ago. She had to stop them. Her eyes blazed with fury.

"Where are they now?" Her voice shivered with anger.

"When you look inside your thoughts, where do you think they are?"

"They are moving their attack fleet through the corridors for the UMO," Kerriah replied.

"Yes, your intuition is correct. The Thraxons seek to utilize their creation to rip apart your ship fleets and all the worlds for which your citizens inhabit."

Kerriah still didn't fully trust this Divination. Consistently throughout history, individuals with divine names or titles inevitably let it go to their heads and started to believe themselves superior. This Divination was a Luminar, and their reputations for selflessness would allow Kerriah to give her some benefit from the doubt. Still, there was something she didn't like about her.

"So how do we stop them?"

"Together, we have the power to rid the galaxy of the Thraxon scourge forever." The Divination swung her arm open to the white orb behind her. "With the power of the white orb, I control Cyos. I already have the mystical nebula of Auroro in chase of their fleet. But I need you and the yellow orb to help me stop them."

Kerriah froze. *Is she sending Cyos to the UMO?* The thought of it sent shivers down her spine. What was worse? The Thraxons with their new harvester ship and the horrors that it could unleash, for which she witnessed firsthand? Or Cyos?

"I don't understand," Kerriah said with a skeptical glare. "If you're controlling Cyos, how can I help? I mean, you have ultimate power," *which no one should have.*

"When merged with the white orb, the yellow orb will allow Cyos to project a mental grasp on the Thraxon fleet. We could control their thoughts, control their fleet."

"Why would we do that? Why not let Cyos destroy them? It would be easy enough for it to do."

The Divination's persistent creepy smile turned to a frown. Her expression appeared to be one of disappointment in Kerriah's response. "Your thoughts are too simplistic. If we can control them, we can know with certainty that your friends are dead . . . or alive. Wouldn't you want to confirm that before we annihilate their ships?"

Kerriah felt brash and stupid, and she lowered her head with embarrassment. The Divination was correct.

"It's not just the lives of your friends. We could use them to locate their home world. We could stop the Thraxons from any further genocidal attacks upon other worlds forever."

Kerriah tilted her head back and studied the fiery glare of the Divination's eyes. Her smile had returned. This was the first time she agreed with her. This Luminar oracle of sorts was growing on her. She wasn't what Kerriah had expected for a Luminar, but once she looked past that minor detail, their thoughts were oddly aligned.

"Yes." Her reply was simple, as she hadn't anything to add.

"Good," the Divination responded with clasped hands. The Divination rotated in the direction of the white orb. "Please, come closer and feel the white orb's power stream into your body."

Kerriah cautiously paced forward, and with each step, she could feel the orb's radiance of tingling power intensify. Her skin shivered, and her heart pounded as she neared the tremendous white sphere. She took another slow step, and her hair stood straight up and whisked through the air in much the same way the Divination's hair swished around her head. With another step, her body ignited into a yellow blaze illuminating from the tips of her hair to her feet.

"Good," the Divination's voice sang out like chimes in a bustling breeze. "Now, let the yellow orb merge its power with the white for the first time in two-thousand years."

Kerriah's body lifted, and her arms opened to the orb. Her eyes flamed yellow with swirls of white clouds beneath. Swells of gas particles and tendrils of cosmic dust streaming across the horizon of space appeared before her as she took the ethereal reins of Cyos. A ghostly shrill faded out and then soared back like a taloned bird of prey swooping down for its moonlit meal. The screams faded into the distance as the great living nebula took each hulking push forward through the emptiness of space, covering light years with each stride. Before long, the mystical cloud of gold particles swished in cerulean had reached the Quadril Corridor.

A group of Thraxon warships stood by, holding guard over the portal landing inside the heart of the UMO. Kerriah thought it strange they would be guarding this side. It would have made more strategic sense if they were on the other side, blocking the vulnerable populations from the most expedient escape route to the outer UMO-controlled sectors. However, the thought only lasted for a moment.

Vengeance filled her thoughts, and her view turned red with anger. She reached out through Cyos and infiltrated the walls of the Thraxon ships, filling their minds with madness. The crews turned on each other, soaking the ships with bloodshed. The strongest of the Thraxon crew began to devour their shipmates and bathe in innards before turning their weapons on each other. She could almost smell the stench of death as Cyos's heaping clumps of matter poured over the empty vessels and funneled past the corridor's mirror, folding its way through space and its ultimate destination.

She could now see the light of Oro. As far as she knew, the Thraxon attack fleets might have already overtaken the system, so there wasn't time to spare. She wanted to check on Nathasia and Crix. Did the Thraxons already attack New Troika? But Cyos continued to push forth to Oro at an aggressive and frightening pace. The magenta glow of Oro emerged into full view, and she could already see the Thraxon harvester ship with its gaping jaw over Thale, sucking the moon's oceans into the upper atmosphere in spinning clouds of liquid and mist. Her heart filled with wrath, and she focused on the immense ship intending to pull life from this beautiful world and leave its discarded carcass stripped down to its rocky core.

The whisking tendrils of Cyos fanned out, surrounding Oro and its moons with its fingers of death. Kerriah would make Thraxons suffer for what they had done to her beloved system over generations. They would finally pay the ultimate price for murdering her friends and conspiring with the Marcks. She would find their home world and remove them from existence. As her thoughts furrowed with anger and she prepared to project the yellow orb's mental grasp into the harvester ship, it flashed away. The teal-tinted globe of Thale stood in harmony with no Thraxon ships visible around the ocean-coated moon. UMO merchant ships came and went about their typical day's business. She turned her view to nearby Solara and Soorak, and aside from the encompassing tendrils of Cyos, everything appeared as it did when she left for Gabor.

What is this? Her thoughts drifted away from vengeance and into confusion. Her heart raced over what she was about to do only seconds before she felt a hot spike pierce her spine. A flash of heat poured across her body like melted wax. Her limbs froze, and her thoughts lost clarity. Someone was taking control of her, and she was powerless to stop them.

CHAPTER 46

The crackling fire blazed with amber spikes in the star-coated, clear night sky. The shadows of the breatic trees towered like giants bending for the fire's warmth in the wooded backdrop of Crix's timber home. He could feel the bite of the cold season approaching as the breeze nipped the back of his neck. He leaned in and rubbed his hands together near the flames, thinking about the legends that now lived here.

Crix had already spent many hours sharing tales and engaging in brotherhood and recreation with ancient Andors, which he had only learned from growing up in Troika. Life had been peaceful over the last five years since he had used the blue orb's power to ignite the Tersik Crystal and restore Troika to its golden era glory on what was formerly Nathasia. It was Equus's pure vision and creation, and the lands were perfect, and both beast and Andor lived in harmony.

Litore, Suros, Quarab, and Criollo were historical heroes among the Andors, and now he knew all of them personally. It was an amazing time for Crix, and while everything was seemingly perfect, something was missing. A gaping hole in his heart left him empty amongst the joy in this new world. He hadn't heard from

Kerriah since the Mertel had passed through Zeta years ago. She had left for Gabor to learn how to harness the yellow orb and become a Tolagon. No one had seen or heard from Plexo or Kerriah since that time. A year after she had left, Chancellor Septin had paid a visit to Crix, having been the last known person that had seen her since her disappearance.

Septin explained she had joined with one of their most advanced warships, the Mertel, to find Plexo and investigate the loss of communication with Eesolan. The ship never reported back, and he had since sent another UMO warship that had also apparently vanished.

Crix wanted badly to go find her himself, but like all pure residents of New Troika, he was bound here by the power of the blue orb. No one restored from the Tersik Crystal could ever leave this paradise, including himself, or they would lose their eternal soul. It was the one caveat to their restoration.

A while ago, he had discovered a small group of Andors had managed to survive the Marck attack that destroyed Troika. They had remained hidden until recently. These Andors were so deeply entrenched in their burrows they hadn't realized the Marck control had ended until recently.

Akhal... Crix shook his head over the thought. It was a name he never believed he would hear again. However, Akhal wasn't dead. He led the small group of survivors that day when Troika fell. His humbling loss and near-death experience in their last Annex game had changed him. The fate of twelve other Andors depended on his newfound integrity and natural leadership ability. Crix always knew Akhal was skilled and could have been a great Andor if only he could grow out of his ego and bigotry. He cracked a brief smile. It was funny how a bitter dose of humility could make one see things more clearly.

His smile faded quickly as his thoughts returned to Kerriah. He dropped his head into his hands and tried to remember the green eyes that would always send a flutter deep into his stomach each time they stared into his. Her face had become harder to recall over the years. As crazy as it seemed, he had no images of her. Ancient Andors forbade such things on New Troika. He felt hollow without a way to save her. He could only hope that someday she would show up at his dwelling, jet-black hair tussling in the cool mountain breeze with her heart-melting, cynical grin she would give him back in the early days of their courtship before his trip to the core.

He felt guilty, the only person in this gifted world who didn't feel like his cup of prosperity was overflowing with each glorious sunrise. After all, these Andors lived the prophecy, but he was the one who had the burden of delivering this long-awaited miracle.

Exhausted over the thoughts, he retired to his thatch-filled bed and fell into a deep slumber.

***

Early the following day, Crix awoke, startled, to a continuous banging upon his heavy timber door outside. His eyes shot open to a view of his bedroom, with blades of light slicing through the slits in his window shutters. A faint voice shouted from behind the heavy door in the distance.

"Crix! Get your hiney out of the sack! The UMO needs you again!" Crix rolled out of his tightly stuffed bed sack and stammered to his feet. "Go check around the side," the voice continued. "Break his damn window open; I don't care, just get him out here ASAP!"

"Okay, okay, I'm coming," he rasped, grabbed a pair of trousers, and slipped them up to his waist. His bedroom door groaned open as he gave it a steady push with his palm against its smoothly sanded surface. He rubbed his eyes and shuffled over to the front door, taking a deep breath before turning the cold metal knob and giving it a firm pull.

"It's about time you rolled out of the hay. You're burnin' daylight!" a sharp, commanding voice greeted him as the door slowly swung open.

Crix squinted against the emerging light rays casting over the horizon and against the back of his unannounced visitor.

"Burling?" Like a ghost from the past, the aging UMO commando stood at the threshold with his legs firmly planted shoulder width and his arms locked behind his back.

Burling was now the chief over all spec ops units for the UMO. His light-grey uniform appeared freshly starched and pressed with hardly a noticeable wrinkle anywhere. His short, stubble hair had lost all the black from the last time Crix had seen him, and the rippled flesh on the war-scarred side of his face dropped slightly lower.

A well-equipped soldier stood behind him with a full battle set and a rifle slung across his chest. Burling's brow furrowed, and he leaned in for a closer look at Crix. He hadn't seen Crix in his natural form, and though he was told of his visual transformation, the old warrior had to see through the Andor exterior and look for the familiar face he remembered.

"If that's you, son, then yes, I'm afraid we require your services again. I don't have a lot of time to explain, but roughly a day ago, a massive cloud of gas passed by Quadril, taking out our garrison fleet without even a single defensive measure from any of our warships. This golden cloud of matter has moved its way into the system and overtaken nearly all our defenses. The slim reports we were able to get back were that the ship crews went mad as this strange cloud approached and turned on each other. Basically, killing us from the inside out."

A dark shade cast over the bright blades of light behind Burling, slowly creeping from left to right, like a solar eclipse, except there was not supposed to be an eclipse this time of year. Burling turned to look over his shoulder.

"That!" He gestured back with his thumb. "That is what we're dealing with. Right now, it's slowly pulling Thale apart. The Hybors are slaughtering each other in the most brutal ways imaginable. We've nothing left to throw at it, and I probably don't need to explain that Soorak, Solara, and . . ." he casually looked around, taking a side-to-side peek at the forest around Crix's dwelling, "New Troika is next if we don't do something to stop it."

"Of course," Crix said, with his heart racing as the news hit him. "What can I do?"

"I don't know, son. I was hoping you could tell me that. People are panicking, and the city populations are emptying into the countryside of Soorak. The popular rumor right now is that this thing is Cyos. Now, with you being a Tolagon and having that orb, I hoped you might have a solution."

Crix's pupils pinned, and his eyes widened. "Cyos?" As he said the name aloud, a lump formed in his throat, and his hands felt clammy. He nervously swiped them down his trousers and took a dry swallow. "It's here?" From the bit he'd learned of it over the years, its presence meant the apocalypse had arrived. Now the UMO was coming to him as their last hope? Again?

Crix cleared his nervous throat. "Um, with respect, you know I want to help, but I cannot leave New Troika. Like all the other restored Andors that live here, I am bound to this world and the orb's power that birthed it."

SONG OF THE LAGGORNS

Burling tightened his jaw and nodded, appearing to hold back a mix of anger and disappointment with Crix's response. "Look, I don't know what you have going on here, and to be honest, I really don't care. The fact is that we are all staring down the barrel of extinction right now, and we have to find a solution. So whatever it is that's holding you back, you need to find a way past it; otherwise, none of the excuses mean squat."

Crix stared down at the worn turf which led up to his doorstep. The burden of being an orb bearer, which he wasn't any longer, and a Tolagon, which he never truly was, brought him back to feeling empty. He wanted to see Halflinger, who now lived just a short walk from his dwelling, for a well-needed injection of calming wisdom. Halflinger was the one who had taught him that to have a balanced and harmonious society, there must be those who saw past their own desires. There must be heroes and leaders who could overcome their selfish thoughts and those who wouldn't squander or guard their natural or bestowed gifts, for those who kept their gifts to themselves while others suffered were a blight on civilization. Crix needed to hear his words again and for the wisdom to come from someone he had the utmost respect for.

"Son? Are you hearing me? We have zero time. Billions are being systematically slaughtered as we stand here," Burling said with an intensity hammering Crix's eardrums.

Crix pinched his eyes closed for a second. *Attomis.* The name entered his thoughts like a ghostly whisper in his ear.

"Equus?" he said, looking around at something unseen.

Burling's forehead scrunched, and he tried to follow where Crix looked. "What was that?"

"Attomis," Crix said under his breath.

Burling started to become noticeably agitated. "Son, have you been huffing stims, or are you speaking in a foreign dialect?

Because we're short on time, and right about now, I'm even shorter on patience."

Crix squatted down and placed the palm of his hand on the packed soil ground. He took a heaping breath and looked up at Burling.

It wasn't the first time he had felt Equus's presence. The last time was during the formation of New Troika. Its spirit was here but choosing to maintain a passive existence, allowing the Andors to live of their own free will. As he had his hand on the ground, it told him what to do in a few short whispers.

"You must travel back to Soorak, to the lands of Troika. Find Akhal. He will be in the old province of Crein. I will provide you with a vessel of orb power to give him. It will be as much power as I can siphon from New Troika without everyone here dying . . . again. He needs to drop that power into the mouth of Attomis, the fallen Laggorn, which resides inside the blackness at the bottom of the Barrillian Vortex."

It wasn't until Crix fully released the Tersik Crystal that he learned of Attomis. Suros wasn't even aware of its existence. When the blue orb unleashed its archive of souls and blueprints of history onto this new world, every vestige of knowledge it contained passed through Crix. Over the years, he'd had plenty of time to reflect on the burst of information that hit him that day. Most of it had faded into the fuzzy remnants of long-forgotten dreams somewhere in the collections of his mind. However, the one that always stood out vividly was Attomis.

Crix couldn't recall how many times he and his friends had dove into the Barrillian Vortex. The mysterious gusts that blew out from the seemingly bottomless cavern were something of a mystery that sparked various tales from Andorian lore. However, a chill squirmed up and down his spine once he finally discovered what was at its bottom, far below. That creeping chill lasted for days and weeks over the thought.

"Okay," Burling said. "I realize I just mentioned the importance of every second, but what the heck is a Laggorn, and what the flying frick is an Attomis?"

"It's a complicated story which I think I would lose you on if I attempted to explain," Crix raised his hand with a nod before Burling could respond. "Not that I feel you lack the intellect to understand. I just don't think it's the type of content that would keep you intrigued."

"You should try me, son. You'd be surprised at what intrigues me."

Crix bit his lower lip and nodded with a brief thought of what type of person Burling was outside of his rigid military exterior. "Well, it's just as you stated, time is crucial. You'll just need to trust me."

"Very well," Burling responded with a subtle exhale. "How do I go about locating this . . . Akhal?"

CHAPTER 47

A khal tried to focus his thoughts on the land, the wind, the cool air, and the pure, crisp scent of the morning frost mixed with evergreens, but his thoughts kept drifting. His broken focus came from the unusual anomalies in the sky. He couldn't see the encompassing view of Oro over the horizon or the sunrise or even the waning stars in the backdrop of early morning. For the past two days, a golden cloud of dust outlined by spirals of cobalt had sprayed across the skyline. The other Andors clung to old suspicions and hid indoors, confident the great storm of wicked souls never allowed into Mothoa finally had come to rain upon them and drive those with a weaker spirit into madness. It had been prophesied in their ancient text, though many of the younger Andors had thought it was nothing more than stories to scare the masses into obedience.

Akhal never put too much stock in the old mythical tales until he visited Crix on New Troika. Before that, he was lost and assumed dead, along with the rest of the Andors in Troika. It wasn't until Crix had asked Soorak's leader, Realm Chancellor Septin, to search for possible survivors that Akhal was eventually found. The UMO search party discovered him and a small group of Andors on the outskirts of the old capital providence of Crein. Septin offered them a pilgrimage to New Troika. However, the suspicious survivors felt it was a ploy to drive them from their sacred homelands and finally rid Soorak of its native species. No one took them up on the offer, though Akhal wanted to see the new world, acting as a representative that could keep the old and new lands united. He wished that someday, the two Andor lands could have passage between them. Even though the spiritually reborn citizens of New Troika could never leave, their future generations could.

The UMO arranged transport for Akhal, and he spent two months with Crix before returning home to Troika. The things Crix had described had him rethinking some of the old lore he used to curl his lip with annoyance upon hearing. But, after seeing the legends walking around New Troika in full color, his mind opened, and he reflected on the old stories from a different point of view. Unlike the new world, the ancient lands now felt empty. All their great ancestors and leaders were now gone. Their sacred grounds, structures, and heritage were desecrated or destroyed beyond recognition. The only place he felt the same vibrant, spiritual pulse that once covered all of Troika was the Barrillian Vortex. And since his visit with Crix, he knew why. *Attomis.*

The great Laggorn Attomis and its story had never been written. Equus forbade its tale, so the memories of its existence had become lost in time. But Crix had released the ancients and their memories, and the story had become real again. After the great blue star had exploded, Attomis, the youngest Laggorn, which bore considerable power, followed the same path of dormancy the Laggorns of Oro followed but had arrived later, placing itself on Nathasia. It had used its unique capability of altering matter to accelerate and advance the indigenous primitive species. However, with such untamed power, it had needed Pathis, the eldest of the Laggorns, to guide its work. As the first formed and bearer of wisdom, Pathis provided mentorship to the other Laggorns. When the new civilization Attomis had created eventually turned to wickedness, rage overcame it, destroying its creation and resetting the world to its primitive state.

That was the tale of Attomis in its most simplistic version. However, the story wasn't simple, and the events transpiring on Nathasia were far more horrific. After it built this highly advanced world, Attomis went into a lengthy dormant state to recharge its power. The curious subjects built a great machine around Attomis, one meant to control its power and make it their own. When this machine, which they called Oncrone, turned against them, their new world turned black. Evil reigned with the rancor and rape of the innocent. Oncrone fed on the living, drinking their lives until they eventually fed on each other.

Attomis awoke from its dormancy and eventually broke free of Oncrone. It became enraged when it witnessed the wickedness transpiring during its centuries of rest. Determined to undo its creation, it went into a brutal killing spree, melting the inhabitants back into the soil. Their screams turned to gurgles as their flesh dissolved, and the world became still again. Attomis was now aware of the other Laggorns on Troika, having gained knowledge from Oncrone, who tried to send ships to take the world for itself.

The lone Laggorn built a spiraling bridge to rejoin its brethren. However, when they learned what he had done to Nathasia, they rejected Attomis and turned their power against it. A great battle ensued, and the three turned Attomis into a gruesome physical version of itself and buried it, shackled deep within Troika, forever kept in dormancy.

SONG OF THE LAGGORNS

Once a month, Akhal traveled to the place that once defined his youth. The place that humbled him into the traditional, stoic, and honorable Andor he was today. It took him three days to get there by foot, and he would spend two days meditating at the opening. He would stick his face over the spiraling hole and feel the living breath of Attomis pushing out and drawing inward. He didn't fear it; instead, he thought of it as the last vestige of ancient Andorian power left in his lands. It was their last sacred site, and when he was there, he felt at one with the living flesh of Troika.

Today, an unusual gust of warm air pushed down upon him, and the peatiness of burning wood from the stacks of their mountainside dwellings curled into his nostrils. A UMO shuttle settled from above and maintained a hovering position almost directly in front of him. There wasn't any place for it to land in the vicinity, and Akhal kept his seat on an old blanket with what was his view of the lowlands below.

A slender, flat bridge slid out from the shuttle and clattered upon a nearby rock overhang. A uniformed, well-built, older gentleman with short grey hair strode from the ship and stopped at the end of the bridge.

"Akhal, I hope?" his gravelly voice asked.

Akhal stood with his fists clenched, and his long black mane spilled over his shoulder. "Who's asking?"

"Prime Commando Burling, for those interested."

Despite Akhal's relative size, Burling stepped onto the smooth rocks and approached without an inkling of fear or hesitation. Akhal's frozen breath blew out with deep heaves dissipating just short of Burling's face. "Look," Burling said with a disciplined urgency in his tone. "I don't have much time for a bunch of introductions or pleasantries. Right now, there's a killer cloud of gas and dust out there that's ripping the system apart. It's turning the perfectly sane into blood-thirsty killers who are turning on each other. It's already done with Thale and is now finishing off Solara, so guess who's next?" Burling didn't give Akhal a chance to respond. "I have a container full of orb power that needs to be dropped on something called Attomis. Apparently, that's our only hope of surviving this."

Anger instantly filled Akhal upon hearing the name come from a foreigner. He reached out and grabbed Burling by his collar and raised him off the ground. He pulled him close to his face. Several commandos filed out of the transport with their rifles posted at their shoulders.

"Stand down!" the hollow voice shouted, distorted through his helmet comm. Burling causally waved them back.

"Kill me if you want, but if you don't do as I'm telling you, we all have maybe two days to live," Burling said, his voice remaining calm.

"How do you know of Attomis?" Akhal's eyes were black with a fiery reflection of blazing light in the sky. "Speak, or I will toss you from this cliff!"

"I don't know anything but the name. Crix sent me here to find you. He said this thing was our only hope against the threat you see in the skyline."

Akhal's hands relaxed upon hearing the name. "Crix sent you?"

"That's right. We're desperate at this point. Nothing we have can scientifically or militarily stop this thing. As much as I'm not a believer in such childish tales, I'm open to whatever else we can throw at this." Burling pointed at Akhal's large chest. "And now you're up. It's your turn to make the next move."

Akhal gently lowered Burling back to the ground and stared at the sky. He thought of the Andor tales of the storm of souls that would drive madness into them all. Could this be what they feared? The end of time? He looked back down at Burling.

"Your kind and your creations have destroyed everything I've known." He stopped to cast a glance around the horizon. "Attomis is the last vestige of our ancient power on Troika. It's the only remaining legend of our culture here. The site for which it resides is sacred." His words intensified as his contempt grew with each passing second. "I go there to pray and ask for the Andors to thrive in Troika once more. Why should I let you defile Attomis with your schemes? Haven't you taken enough from us already?"

"It's not a scheme. This was Crix's plan, and if you're to preserve what you have here, you'll be wise to do what he requested." Burling shrugged. "Not that I have any idea what this will do, but he seemed assured that this was our answer. But, so far, he hasn't let us down, so I'm inclined to place my faith in him once more." Burling stared at Akhal with an unwavering and steady gaze.

Akhal stood quietly before responding. "I know what it will do." His eyes slowly turned back to Burling. "When we reach the Barrillian Vortex, I request that you leave. Let me do what needs to be done . . . alone."

"Deal," Burling quickly replied.

He turned around, snapped his fingers, and pointed at one of the commandos on the bridge. The soldier turned back into the shuttle and returned with a container draped in a small blanket with various images of Laggorns embroidered across its grey and white fabric. The commando handed the container to Burling.

"Here, I'm entrusting this to you. Crix pulled as much blue orb power from New Troika as he could to store in this." He handed it over to Akhal. "When we left, the population there was in a state of near collapse, and a dark shadow covered the planet. So their lives, as well as ours, are literally in your hands."

When Akhal saw the embroidered images, his eyes became heavy with tears. He recalled seeing this same blanket hung from the wall of Crix's home. It was amazing how much he had changed since the Marcks invaded and destroyed Troika. His culture meant everything to him now.

"No! They will all die if I disperse this power." He extended it back to Burling. "You must return it to them."

Burling took a step back and placed his palm out in rejection. "I can't. Crix said that once the power is released, Attomis will return what was taken." Burling flipped his hands up with a shrug. "I don't know, but it's yours now. I'm not taking it back."

Akhal lifted the cloth covering the container. A blazing azure glow blasted across his face, and he squinted and turned away before covering it back up. "You will take me to the vortex and then be gone."

"That's all I'm askin'," Burling replied.

CHAPTER 48

Akhal peeked over his shoulder as the shuttle zipped away, disappearing over the horizon. He looked back at the vortex opening with its concussive blasts of air roaring out, followed briefly by the hollowed downdrafts he knew so well. Except now he knew what was down there. What resided far below the old iron grate in the blind zone, the area where light was missing. In his mind, he drew a vision of Attomis's physical appearance. For Akhal, it resembled the statue of Equus, which remained toppled at the base of the old Alcazar, but larger. He had no way of knowing for sure, and his heart began racing over the thought of seeing the ancient Laggorn emerge from its lair.

He stepped slowly and looked down into the cavern. The wind blew his mane back straight into the air behind him. Above, the circular, tawny, timbered observation deck stood empty, which once had an audience of several thousand stomping and shouting Andors cheering for their team. Vines crept around its sturdy support beams, and a layer of algae tinted the greying wood. He took a deep inhale. The scent was moist, rich soil, ripe for farming, mixed with a subtle hint of sour musk. A brief smile crept over his face, and he quickly shook it away.

The sky above turned dark, and the golden-blue glitter accenting the backdrop for the past several days now appeared heavy, like a sparkling ocean about to fall upon them. Cyos's spirals of deep blue reached down and flailed like a living creature feeling around for hapless prey.

Akhal's eyes widened as he felt an unwelcome presence enter his thoughts. Rage suddenly poured like molten metal into his heart, and a vile urge to harm something . . . anything overwhelmed his mind. The storm of souls had come for him, attempting to take his mind. He forced his eyelids shut and squeezed down as hard as possible until the veins bulged from his forehead. He ripped away the cloth covering from the vessel and held it out over the vortex opening. His trembling hands tightly clenched the transparent container until the tips of his fingers compressed. The blue power within churned violently against the sides, like a storm ready to burst from barometric pressure so extreme it would level a small town. The intense light from the urn appeared as if a lightning bolt had frozen in place, and the entire region was set ablaze.

The anger spilled out from deep within his guts, and his mind spun wild, like a ravenous beast sickened with starvation and neurological degeneration. He bared his teeth and let out a growl turning into a scream. As he looked at the glowing vessel, his eyes pinned to specks, and foam began to froth from his jaw. He raised the container above his head with both hands and flung it into the cavern below.

The blue blaze whisked away into the depths until only a single cone of light shot out from the cavern. The hard surface burped upward under Akhal's feet. He stumbled back, nearly losing his footing. He looked down at the ground and dropped to his knees, beating his fists against it as he grunted and screamed. A beastly groan bellowed up from the cavern and intensified to the level of a booming bass horn akin to something meant to awaken some long-forgotten ancient gods. The ground quaked, and the vortex opening crumbled within itself like a widening sinkhole leading to the heart of this world.

Akhal stopped pounding at the ground and looked at the widening hole with a wild, empty gaze from maddened eyes. He stood and sprinted away as fast as his legs could carry him from the growing fissure. The ground around the region suddenly fell in and blew out like a volcano, finally giving way to the building pressure beneath the crust. He fell inward and instantly shot out with the rocks and soil high into the sky. As his upward tumbling momentum waned and he began to fall back to the land below, he could see the great Laggorn rising from its unseen resting place.

The face of Attomis emerged with four bulging, black circles encompassing the crown of its head and a gaping jaw, which widened as it arose. Its pillared beard dangled below its mouth, and a blue fire swirled across its torso. From its sides, flames gushed out with arms extending from the blaze. The slithering limbs fanned into wing-like layers of webbing, which rippled with the Laggorn's rising motion. A screaming wail of horns echoed over the land, drowning out all sounds from the surface exploding below.

Akhal's body tumbled along with the rock and debris; his mind still capitulated with rage. He couldn't focus away from the mental grasp long enough to accept his inevitable fate of smashing into the surface and being buried under tons of rock and soil. As he faced the rapidly approaching ground among the rain of debris, the world around him halted.

The debris in the sky cleared, and Akhal's body shifted upright. A giant black globe emerged directly before him, and his thoughts of wrath cleared. Attomis stared at him, frozen in the sky. His mouth quivered as he cried harder than he could ever recall. The depths of his soul poured out, and his chest heaved with every jerking breath of emotion. Tears began streaming down his cheeks, and his thoughts filled with knowledge and sorrow. He knew everything about the Laggorns instantly and saw within his soul. Every piece of their rich history and the embodiment of his flaws, selfishness, and pain he created over his years. A forced look at every detail of his life, every thought he had from birth until now, flooded through him. The anvil of humility crushed his spirit until nothing was left of his former self. It was only then that Attomis would accept him. A pure servant of its will.

The mouth of Attomis gaped wide, and Akhal felt his body pulled inside. His view turned to darkness, then blue. His eyes now looked through the eyes of Attomis. Above and all around him was the full brilliance of Cyos. He had a panoramic view of every side and every angle all at once. Akhal felt a strong tug upward into the massive nebula encompassing their system. A battle between two ancient leviathans was about to ensue.

CHAPTER 49

Burling looked maddeningly down at his bloody hands. The youthful soldiers were undoubtedly stronger than the aging chief commando, but they lacked the battle experience of the old war vet. When the madness set into the passengers and crew of the speedy transport as it whisked away from the Barrillian Vortex, shots from small arms lit up the cargo bay, and the targets were indiscriminate, at least for everyone except Burling. He was the last to lose all his self-control. If countless deep insertion missions and desperate battles had taught him anything, it was maintaining his mental fortitude when it would be impossible for most others.

It wasn't until the last commando fell before his mind inevitably succumbed to a power beyond his mortal capabilities. His view turned red, and his body almost seemed to move without thought, ripping the throats out of the fallen and pushing his thumbs into their eye sockets. A surprise blade thrust into his right shoulder and violently twisted, sending him facedown onto the cold metal deck. A heavy magnetic boot stomped down upon the backside of his neck, and the menacing crack of bone filled his ears. The pilot had finished impaling the skull of his co-pilot with his standard-issue Gallic blade and now turned his bloodlust to whatever was still alive aboard his ship.

Burling winced from the impact and rolled like a Thale gorgator, scissoring his legs around the pilot and crashing his body to the floor. He mounted the pilot's floored body so fast he barely had a chance to shake the spots from his view before Burling's fists crashed down one after another. The pilot went limp, and Burling stood; the heel of his boot crushed the pilot's head like a melon exploding under the force of a sledgehammer.

Burling's crazed stare focused out the cockpit window. There was nothing left to kill within his reach. His mind wrestled with turning his rage onto himself, but crashing his head intentionally into the cockpit controls bought him a minute to look for other options. His eyes glowed with the reflection of a gigantic creature emerging from Soorak. Its body grew exponentially as it left the confines of the world it called home for an unknown time. Its glowing wings sliced through the void of space, spanning so wide Burling could no longer see the moon he called home behind the infernal beast. His expression turned from hate to fear. What horror had he taken part in unleashing upon the system?

Tendrils of gold and azure gas whipped around, striking at Attomis, trying to pry into the mind of something beyond its control. A giant face emerged within Cyos; a female silhouette crowned with ten spikes appeared to open her mouth to let out a scream that couldn't be heard. A blur of distortion gushed out from her jaw like a fully opened spigot. The particle-disrupting blast hit Attomis like a train.

The top of its head broke apart into a spray of tiny colored beads scattered across the weightlessness of space. A balloon-like bulge formed at the base of Attomis and rippled up to its mouth. Its mouth shot open with a blackish-blue blast funneled with shadowy circles powering into Cyos with such force the female's face turned away with a cringe and merged back into the gas cloud.

Burling began smashing his fist into the cockpit window. His bloodied knuckles repeatedly clunked into the glass, leaving red blotches with each connecting blow. He didn't know why he reacted to the sight of Cyos being attacked, but he became overwhelmed with blistering rage. He wanted to escape this ship and join the melee outside.

The wings of Attomis grew, spanning wider and wider until its massive body dwarfed against the giant netted flaps. The bulk of Cyos, now fully encompassed inside its expanding wings, began to recede from Soorak. Attomis folded its wings in, drawing the legendary nebula into its body.

A blinding flash stopped Burling's assault on the cockpit window, and in the following instant, the transport jolted sideways, spiraling out of control. He felt the rage leave his mind and the return of clarity as his body tumbled around the spinning ship. He desperately grasped at the controls with his right hand and felt a shot of pain flare from his wrist to his elbow, like a shock of electricity followed by a searing fire. His right wrist shattered between his body and the edge of the flight controls. He couldn't make a fist to grip the rigid controls of a free-spinning ship.

He reached down with his left hand, his broken right hand curled against his chest, gripping the control stick. He braced his legs between the two cockpit seats for stability. The ship's spin slowed with a few stabilizing bursts from its impulse jets. He slowly brought the view back to Soorak. He needed to see what had become of the two battling titans that were to decide the fate of the entire system. Only a diminishing blue aura filled the space between Oro and Soorak. The aura pulsed and faded until nothing remained but a tiny spec, like a dim star in a cloudy night sky.

Burling stared at the spec of blue until it all but vanished. He closed his eyes for a second, focusing on what he should do next. As the action around him settled, the nagging pain from his shattered wrist and the stab wound in his back came to the forefront of his senses. The co-pilot's arms swooshed loosely in zero gravity as his limp body remained strapped into the seat, blood trickling from a blade-sized puncture wound in his head.

Burling didn't want to step into the cargo area. He didn't want to see the carnage he had left there. He had killed his own soldiers, which he would never have imagined in his worst nightmares—brutalizing fellow UMO soldiers . . . brothers. He looked down at his bloody hands. His chin quivered and a tear formed at the corner of his eye. He hadn't cried in so many years, and it was difficult to remember how it felt. He swiped the edge of his palm across his eye, trying to dab away the tear with the only portion of his left hand that wasn't bloodstained. Then he broke down into a manic sob. Questioning himself, had he helped to save everything he knew, only to lose his soul?

After a few minutes, he began to pull himself together. The well-needed emotional release helped him feel at ease, at least for now. With a forceful and fluid sniff, he swiped his sleeve across his nose and pushed the ship's throttle forward. He needed to see what was left of his home. What was left of Soorak and its population?

CHAPTER 50

A lurid scream filled Kerriah's ears. The baleful shriek pulled her from the darkness. She slowly opened her eyes to a blinding white light, and for a few seconds, she wasn't sure where she was. As she turned her head, she noticed the giant white orb hovering directly in front of her. Then the memories poured back with a startling shock. She was on Eesolan.

A female's voice let out a frustrated growl behind her. She spun around face to face with the Divination, but Kerriah knew now it wasn't the Divination.

"Who are you?" she shouted. "What have you done to the Luminars?"

Luminars were never genocidal. They are quite the opposite. At that moment, Kerriah could only think of one individual, if you could even call her or it that, with that character flaw. How could it be? With a studying squint, she looked around at the persistent distortion haloing her head.

"How?" the Divination growled. "It was all within my grasp, and they somehow destroyed the ultimate weapon!" Her face almost appeared red as she shouted her frustrations. She pointed her finger straight at Kerriah's face. "You! It's your fault!"

She floated around Kerriah as she continued to speak. "Your weaknesses. Your pathetic flaws, which were intentionally added to your inferior design, inhibited the orb's power. You robbed me of my glory!" She stopped and turned to face Kerriah again. "You're not worthy of possessing such power!"

At that moment, Kerriah knew it was the Queen. The Marck Queen. But how? How was she creating this illusion?

"My flaws, as you call them, make me real. They make me alive! You think only in a single directive. You're a simple program with a single purpose, to suppress and destroy everything around you." Kerriah pointed her finger back at the Queen. ". . . And that flaw in you has just been tested and exposed! Pitiful . . . Queen . . . of . . . the . . . Marcks!" Her jaw tightened with every word of the vile name.

The Queen moved her face near Kerriah's, her crimson spiked crown pierced through the halo, and her deviant eyes curling with her smirk. "You will see what I want you to see. You will feel what I want you to feel. You'll do as my will commands. I now control you and all that you know. You fail to understand that this white orb gives me power over anyone who bears a lesser orb." She drew within a hair's distance from Kerriah's nose. "You will obey me!" Then she pulled away.

"You're as delusional as you are insane," Kerriah replied with her nose curled and her tone filled with bitterness. "Crix cooked you and took over your little toy army. Then I helped him destroy your so-called fortress. You are not a god. You can be defeated; we've done it before, and we'll do it again."

The queen let out a cackling laugh. "Silly little girl. You think you had vanquished me?" She intentionally laughed again. "When your servant boy released his orb blast, he did not destroy me. He released me. That massive power surge allowed me to instantaneously traverse the relay grid within the pure energy beams instead of single command packs—my consciousness is now omnipresent. You are alive because I allowed you to live. You are here because I brought you here."

Kerriah's bitter tone broke, and she felt an uncomfortable pit forming in her gut. "What do you mean you brought me here?" Was the queen using her deception on her again, or was her reach greater than Kerriah understood? She had to know. She cocked her head to the side, watching the Queen move, trying to decipher her account. What was her intended scheme? What had she done?

"After the core lost its connection to the Knactor Legion, my consciousness awoke within them, on the far side of Zeta. The pitiful Thraxons continued their retreat, and I let them go for the time. But . . ." She paused, and a wicked smirk filled her face. "It wasn't just the Knactors that my conscious found; it was an Eetak."

Kerriah's jaw dropped, and her heart sank to her stomach upon hearing the name come from the queen. The name of Joric's original concept Marcks which Plexo later obtained for use as subordinates on his ship. She tried to swallow the lump in her throat, but a raspy cough wheezed out.

"E-Eetak?" She tried to play dumb for a moment, to buy a few seconds to regain her composure.

"You know full well what I'm referring to. The children that were kept from me. The ones that your Luminar friend refers to as eetaks."

Kerriah cleared her throat into her fist. "How? They were never part of your communications grid. They were safe from your warped commands."

"When your servant tried to destroy me, my orb-enhanced pulse of consciousness reached a nearby ship, which was illegally powered by the supposedly lost green orb." She paused for a gloating smile. "That is when I discovered the children that were kept from me. I subtly took control of them and the ship."

"No." Kerriah shook her head in disbelief. "No, that can't be."

"Oh, it is," the queen persisted. "There was never a distress call from Eesolan. It was I that led him back to his home planet. With the information from his ship and the green orb's unique capability to transmit data faster than light, he unwittingly guided my fleet to his home world. The same power that allowed him to create portals for which you used to escape me became his undoing." She let out a nerve-scraping cackle. "I knew he would come, and you and the other orb bearers would follow. Your kind is always so predictable. It was the perfect trap. Though you temporarily slipped through my grasp at Zeta, all is right now." The queen leaned back and rolled her neck, visually enjoying this moment.

"Fine," Kerriah said in a chiding tone. "But why did you need me to help you when you could have easily killed everyone in the UMO with Cyos yourself?"

The queen turned away and moved closer to the white orb. She kept her back to Kerriah as she spoke. "Though you're flawed and intellectually inferior to me, you are still one of my children. Your physical design is unique." The Queen's head turned for a brief look at Kerriah. "Genius actually," She whispered. "I hoped you would join me as one of my own. I needed you to realize your true potential, to become comfortable with killing the substandard species that infest and contaminate our worlds. Once you felt that power, you would come to me in a purer form. One freed of the shackles of guilt and petty sentiments."

Kerriah stayed focused on the Queen. "No," she said in a calm yet elevated voice.

The Queen whipped her head around, and her body followed. Her eyes arched and flamed red with fury. "No?" As she moved forward, a crown of scarlet spikes emerged, and a polished, onyx, female figure left the limp glowing body of the Divination behind. "You cannot deny me." Her voice deepened as she spoke. "I am your Queen, and I will have your obedience."

"Never!" Kerriah shouted. "I will never follow you!"

The Queen moved closer and reached and pinched the flesh on Kerriah's arm. "This body, I will have it, and many like it in my kingdom. Except they will be perfect. Free of the weakness built into yours."

Kerriah ripped her arm away defiantly. "You'll not have anything of mine. You rule over the dead, and that's all you'll ever have."

"A shame," the Queen said. "If you will not give me your body willingly, then I shall take it from you." The Queen drew her right arm back and a needle-tipped rod formed in her hand. She plunged it down into Kerriah's chest.

Kerriah recoiled back as she felt the sharp tip pierce through her sternum. Her eyes squeezed closed, and her face contorted. There wasn't any pain like she expected, just a numbing, paralyzing effect flashing a grid of red into her view and then burning away. She opened her eyes, and the world around her had changed.

A starry sky and the shadow of the spinning blade above Eesolan appeared through a jagged hole at the top of the great dome of Bellahis. Stains of smoke streaked up its interior walls, and charred debris littered the translucent silver floor. A strobing beam of white streamed from the white orb and through the

309

opening above. Splayed out like prey caught in a spider's web was the Divination, whose body appeared much more like that of a Luminar. Nearly invisible threads pulled her arms and legs open in the shape of an X in front of the white orb. A ribbed, grey tube draped down from the hole in the dome and squeezed into the Divination's tiny mouth.

As she stared at the changing scene before her, nothing she observed appeared strange or out of place. The Divination was being kept alive as a tool. Like a puppet, the queen moved her around with web-like strands, mimicking her movements. Luminar's did not eat the same way other species did; instead, they consumed beads of metabolized proteins their bodies, which lacked a lower digestive system, absorbed and expelled through internal heat and radiance. Kerriah understood this now. The tube in her mouth kept her fed so the queen could use her thoughts to control the orb.

Kerriah's hand rose without a thought, almost as if it had moved on its own. Smooth pale fingers rotated before her face and then swooshed softly down her body, feeling its slender curves. Her view drew downward and then side to side, again without her thinking to move her head. She wasn't herself anymore; someone else controlled her actions, and she sat back as merely an observer. It was the queen, and Kerriah knew she allowed her to witness her work to gain pleasure from her helplessness.

She could hear a fan-like thump or pulse, almost like a pounding heartbeat overwhelming her senses. Somehow, she knew the thumping pulse kept in time with the rotating blade outside the planet's orbit. The Halioc Blade. She knew what it was since the queen gloated her thoughts to her. It's what maintained the illusion of a typical day in Eesolan. The illusion that everything there appeared as it did before the queen invaded. But there was another power, something familiar, manipulating their relative point in time. Something helped the queen expedite her plans. The green orb? It wasn't clear to her, but the queen's plan was clear.

Since before she had subjugated Eesolan, she had already begun rebuilding her armies and fleet. It had started on a small planet rotating a faint red star. There she constructed a small production facility, churning out Marck workers by the dozens per hour, and then more extensive facilities, which churned out hundreds simultaneously.

Near the Eesolan system, she had built shipyards and her grand construct, the Halioc Blade. A massive planet-encompassing version of what once created her mental state-altering visions in the core's throne room. Her spider web, her snare, would lure in and capture her victims. It would be a fantasy world of her choosing, anything that would tickle her desires. Most of all, she enjoyed toiling with the minds of the living. It gave her more pleasure than merely ending their lives. It was a sadistic addiction—a flaw in her Optimal Secrium.

The derivative spirit was taken from Kerriah, except this version became corrupted and twisted. The jealousy brewed over the decades of her entrapment in the core. The result of her forced servitude with the singular purpose of protecting the UMO populations.

While they lived on with their blissful lives, she had been alone and trapped in darkness. Her Optimal Secrium had toiled with a lust for vengeance against those gaining so much from her suffering. Kerriah's mind-controlling yellow orb would be the ultimate weapon when paired with the awe-encompassing power of the white orb. She would touch their minds and turn them into her servants, but the unworthy wretches turned on each other instead. So be it. If they died, she would rebuild her children upon their bones. The orb's power had the sweet taste of the wicked nectar she had craved for so long. She wanted to complete her work, but now Cyos, the white orb's weapon, was gone.

Now she had a new plan. It would be a plot getting her close to the ones responsible for her enslavement. She could betray them with someone they trusted . . . someone they loved. Then watch them suffer and die slowly.

CHAPTER 51

"My emptocap is detecting a massive amount of photon energy emitting from the rotating object above," Stelios said as he looked upward, examining the frozen image of Plexo. The box-like machine made his torso considerably larger than the rest of his tall, lanky body, with slim legs and arms dangling from its bottom and sides. His head fit perfectly inside the glass bubble with a swishing fog of whatever gas the entamals used to maintain his dimensional time proximity if he decided to activate the emptocap's primary function. "Based on this specific energy profile and my knowledge of the technology we developed, I suspect this strange device is responsible for a time rift here and that this is an opening to the sleeve for which you enter its paradoxical container."

"Can tya speak in some form of language we all can understand," Krath grumbled. "Cause, I haven't any idea what tya just blabbered about." The Thraxon battle shell Creedith modified so that Krath could assist onboard Plexo's ship made him look like a Hemlor spear-headed timber beetle, with its pointed head and round midsection.

"I suppose it works much like my emptocap and the modulating stations on Tridole. They both emit a negative zone, or as you may understand it, an inter-dimensional effect by generating photon particles at such a rate within their projection field that anything within the storm experiences time exponentially slower than that outside. Strategically placed prism alignments aid in the anomalistic acceleration on Tridole.

"Likewise, my suit can produce a similar storm at short range, but my time is normal within the suit. Much like how our emptocaps shielded the entamals around Tridole when we generated the photon storm from the modulating stations. Our time was normal, and yours slowed."

"Baaahh!" Krath protested with a dismissive wave of his arm toward Stelios. "Whatever tya say. So what do we need to do to get Kerriah out of ole glow rod?" He snapped a sharp look at Stelios. "Is that glow rod? Cause if it is, we gotta fix him, somehow."

"As I said," Stelios pointed up at Plexo, "that is the sleeve. What you see is not the individual you know but rather an image from a specific point in time. I suspect a point where some cataclysmic event occurred, like a massive surge of energy. It will persist for as long as the negative zone is maintained." He returned a serious look to Krath. "Be warned, if my assessment is accurate, our time will slow relative to everything else when we enter the sleeve. I believe this sleeve opening is an unanticipated wrinkle in the space-time continuum and that there might be another primary sleeve entrance elsewhere. It's possible that whoever is responsible uses this to effectively fast-forward the universe for some greater purpose. Or it could be a consequence, or side-effect, from some other intent."

During Stelios's explanation, Krath looked at him with a blank face. "Are tya kiddin' me?" He looked around at the others. "Did anyone comprehend any of tat noise?"

Ashton shrugged with an uncomfortable smile. "I-ahh—"

"That's what I thought. No one here understands anything tya spoutin'. So I'm goin in after her. I don't care about any stupid time . . . or whatever tya were gruntin' about."

Krath took a few steps back, preparing to make a running leap into Plexo. "No, wait!" Captain Ashton stepped in front of Krath with his arms forward. "You can't go in there."

"Why the heck not?" Krath growled.

"Think about Timmon. If what Stelios told us is in any way accurate and you go in there, he could be an adult by the time you get out. I mean, we don't know . . . right?" Ashton looked over at Stelios.

"Yes, that's correct. If you go into the sleeve, it may seem like minutes, hours, or days, but it could very well be years to everyone out here. Truly I am not certain. We will not know until someone enters the sleeve and returns."

Krath pounded his fist against his chest and screamed with frustration. "I don't want to hear any more of this techno jack jawin'. Someone has to go in after her. I know Kerriah better than the rest of tya, so I'm goin'."

"No," Ashton said. "Think about your promise to care of Timmon. I will go in." He wanted to go. He wanted to be the one to rescue her if that's what was required.

"I'll go as well," Stelios said. "I feel you will need my knowledge and my emptocap to aid you inside."

"Fine. And thank you," Ashton said before squatting down to release his magnetic locks. Sergeant Alar tapped him on the shoulder and handed him a compact rifle.

"Here," he said, rotating the rifle around with the butt stock facing Ashton. "Take my TAC38 with you. I have a feeling you may need it in there."

Ashton took the weapon and gave it an uncomfortable inspection. He hadn't held nor fired one in years since his basic UMO Naval Academy days. "Thanks, Sergeant. Wish me luck," he said with a half-smile. With a sudden thrust from his legs, he pushed off, launching into the weightlessness and through Plexo's frozen image.

The blinding lights overhead forced tears from his eyes, and he turned away with a squint. "Wait . . . hold your head still," the female voice said from behind the white lights. Ashton could feel his eyelids pulled open and a cold lens placed over the cornea of his right eye. The lights instantly dimmed, and everything in the room became clear. Kerriah stood over him and smiled. "Let me get the other one." She placed another cold lens over his left eye.

"Kerriah? W-What happened?" Ashton said. He couldn't help noticing her black hair was smoothed perfectly down to her shoulders and her lips shimmered a deep burgundy against the lighting. She was truly stunning, and his heart did a few flips upon seeing her with full clarity. She appeared to be made up for an occasion, but how and why?

She lightly brushed her hand across his hairline, maintaining her pleasant smile. "I've had enough time to think about us. About our lives together."

"Our lives? Where are we?" Ashton tried to move his arm, but it wouldn't budge. He then tugged at his other arm before realizing both were restrained. "What? What is this?" His voice rose, and he struggled.

"Together, you and me. That's what you've wanted, is it not?" She straddled her leg over his midsection and mounted him

316

seductively. She arched her back and leaned her face near his, almost touching the tip of her nose to his. The sweetness of her breath was intoxicating.

"Our lives with each other, the one that you so desire. This body, the one your eyes lust for."

"Yes." He shook his head, confused and frustrated. He felt so pathetic, so weak. "I mean no! Not like this."

She pressed her lips against his. They were oddly cold and stiff. She pulled her head back, and her pleasant smile twisted into a creepy smirk.

"If you truly want me, you must change for me."

She raised her fist, which slowly morphed into a silver claw. She plunged it toward his face, and the room blinked and strobed. Her appearance changed with each flash of blackness until the face of an odd-looking Marck emerged over him. The strangely wide-faced Marck peeked across its left shoulder. Lines of distortion rippled the Marck's head and torso, and then in an instant, it was no longer atop Ashton, and his arms broke free.

The UMO captain quickly sat up, relieved over the sensation of unrestrained movement once again. He swung his head around, trying to figure out where the Marck had gone and where he was. Stelios kneeled on the floor with his head tilted down. The Marck's body also lay nearby, with its head cleanly severed from its torso. The room flashed again, and the decapitated Marck body changed to Kerriah. Stelios's cumbersome chest armor remained motionless, but his head flinched back and forth and made an unnatural jerking motion.

"Stelios!" Aston shouted. He popped up from the table and took several strides toward the depleted entamal, who raised his arm to stop him. Stelios turned his head toward Ashton, looking like someone near death.

"Please, Captain, I need time for my emptocap to recharge itself." Despite Stelios's voice coming from telepathy, it sounded small and distant, almost like one would expect from a tiny animal. His face appeared drawn, and his eyes sunken.

Ashton looked over at Kerriah's head and decapitated body lying on the cold metal floor. "Is that?"

"No. An artifice. A trick."

"Okay. But where are we?" Ashton stopped and clenched his jaw, trying to figure out if this was a nightmare or real.

"Inside the sleeve." Stelios's strained thought projections faded with fatigue. "A position in time, behind ours, shrouded by some sort of illusion. Whoever is responsible for this wields a power greater than my understanding."

Ashton looked closely around the room, which appeared to be an infirmary. Several ivory-top tables neatly lined the back wall with bundles of thin tubes tangling above each. "You were able to disrupt the illusion for a minute. Can you do it again?"

"Possibly, however . . . I . . . need . . . a . . . .mom—" Stelios's voice faded with each word.

CHAPTER 52

"A Marck attack fleet is inbound," Creedith's voice announced over their helmet comms. Just minutes earlier, Captain Ashton and Stelios had entered what Stelios referred to as the "sleeve."

"A Marck fleet?" Alar responded. "How many ships?"

"A dozen, various classes," Creedith replied.

"We can't repel a fleet that size. What are our options here?" Alar asked.

"We run. We will lose them with this ship's modified X88T drive system," Creedith said. "But you need to get back here ASAP."

"I'm not runnin' from those rusty buckets. Not with Kerriah stuck up in glow rod's hiney." Krath began marching around looking for something to kick.

"We'll be no good to her K.I.A.," Alar said. "We can attempt a covert op later when things quiet down, okay?"

Krath shifted his gaze back to Plexo and grumbled. "Fine. But tya can bet I'll be back here as soon as we lose that tin army."

***

By the time their transport entered the Thraxon landing bay, the Marck fleet had nearly encompassed them. Creedith plugged himself back into the squill and began calculating their trajectory for a jump out of the Eesolan system.

"We need a few more minutes," Creedith's voice echoed through the comms and bridge's audio command systems. "I don't have a projected clear path yet, and the X88T drive system takes time to spin up."

Jesselle stared out the observation window at the emerging fleet. "I can create a diversion, but I need a better view of their fleet." The forward bridge of the Thraxon warship provided only a narrow perspective of the Marck fleet.

"I can accommodate you with that," Creedith replied. "Stand still and open your mouth wide."

It quickly hit Jesselle as to what Creedith had in mind, and her initial reaction wasn't accommodating. She threw both hands up while taking a few steps back. "No! I'm not letting that thing into my bod—"

Incoming blasts rocked the hull of their ship as the Marck's cannons began to unleash their deadly arsenal. "Our shields will not hold long enough for the jump system to ready," Creedith announced over the thumps and cracks of the attack. The interior lights dimmed and turned red.

"Dammit, Jesselle! Just open tya mouth and do it!" Krath shouted. "I wouldn't want that Thraxon noodle finderin' around in my guts either, but if tya don't, we're all goin' to be floatin' around with the rest of the junk out there."

Her legs shook, and she nervously stomped her feet. Allowing a Thraxon to sliver down her throat and do whatever inside her body to get to her brain was almost the most appalling thing she could conceive. Besides, she still didn't trust Creedith, and it already took everything she had within her to subdue the gut punch of anxiety of being in the same area with him. Still, she wouldn't allow everyone around her to get killed over her squeamishness and fears.

"Ehhhwww, okay, let's just make it quick." She pinched her eyelids shut and forced her mouth open, feeling dizzy with apprehension and hesitancy.

A panel above slid open, and a long tendril slithered out. The slithery arm squirmed into her mouth, and she felt the sensation of fibers webbing throughout her body. Her limbs became rigid and locked into place. Her thoughts cleared. She wasn't concerned about the squill anymore as her view turned panoramic. She could now see every angle around the Thraxon ship with perfect clarity.

On all sides, the blasts of white bolts peppered into their fading shields from the Marck warship's attack. Jesselle's focus turned to the larger chunks of wreckage around them, and a red wave of energy pulsed from the hull of the Thraxon vessel. The jagged scraps began to crinkle and fold into the shapes of giant metallic leeches with jaws gaping and snapping, hungry for something to chew. However, she was missing something, an omission in her plan. Her new creations lay coiling, helpless in the void, with no way to move into their prey.

"Creedith," Jesselle called through the squill to the ship's commander. "I need propulsion."

"Hang on, young one. I have just the thing you require."

Hundreds of small, circular openings emerged around the ribs of their ship. A flurry of beetol drones spilled out from the openings and swarmed the metal leaches. The small drones attached to the sides of Jesselle's creations; their cumulative propulsion systems pushed the coiling leaches into the Marck fleet.

Determined to take down the Thraxon ship, the Marcks were too late, turning their attack onto Jesselle's creations. Her leeches dug into their hulls, tearing holes into their sides.

With the needed pause from the direct assault on their ship, Creedith expressed his gratitude and announced their readiness. "Thank you, Jesselle. Our jump is ready. Everyone, brace yourselves!"

"Assa . . . gossha . . . thwetta." As he engaged the X88T drive, their ship felt like it pulled inward with a cracking jolt. Their bridge drew into a funnel of swirling distortion and then through a cone of black. Their bodies tingled for a moment and then went numb. Everything stuttered back with a slow, steady pulse, like a choppy flip of sequential photographs.

Jesselle tried to draw a breath but quickly remembered the squill hung down into her throat. A coughing reflex preceded the noodled squirm of the tentacle retracting from her body and out her mouth. Tendrils which had wrapped around her body for the ship's jump let loose their tight hold and slipped away into the panel above.

She went limp and buckled over, bracing her hands onto her knees. She gagged, and her face felt as though it had turned green.

"T-That's it." She winced. "I'm never doing that again. Ever!" She felt violated. Like something had molested every inch of her body and mind, inside and out.

"Where are we," Sergeant Alar asked, his voice strong and commanding as usual.

"Safe," Creedith replied. "Safe for now."

CHAPTER 53

An hour passed, and Stelios began to stand straight again. His emptocap's internal power had restored better than half its charge. Ashton, who had disappeared down the corridor a while ago, just popped back in with his rifle clutched closely to his chest. He noticed Stelios's recovery and moved straight in front of him for a clearer view inside his foggy domed helmet.

"Stelios, are you doing better now?"

"I am."

"I haven't seen anyone else on this ship," Ashton said, symbolically looking over his shoulder. "I mean not a soul or an active machine. Nothing. It's strange. I would have thought the queen or whoever is behind this to follow up with another attack after we beheaded that Marck."

"Perhaps they are unable to deal with us at this very moment." Stelios stopped to check his instrumentation. He peeked down at his chest, which was tilted in his direction. He made a fine-tuned adjustment with the turn of a small dial and then returned his focus back to Ashton. "Perhaps events outside the sleeve have changed our objectives here."

"You mean that our team could have done something since we left to distract this entity?"

"Correct. The power responsible for creating this is truly remarkable. By my calculations, the current speed of photons, and utilizing your time-keeping systems, we are gaining approximately one year for every hour inside the interdimensional sleeve. I needn't explain to—"

"What?" Ashton shouted. The calculation shocked him, even though he knew going in this was a risk. The captain had always been an optimist and lost sight of their time, and hearing the universe just aged a year without him staggered his footing for a few seconds. "Did you just say that we lost a year of time?"

"Correct, although depending on your viewpoint, you could say that you gained that time. You're now younger relative to those you left behind."

"No-No," Ashton shook his head, trying to take in what Stelios explained. "You could be wrong, right? I mean, are you certain?"

"I am certain. You knew the risks going in here and seemed more than willing to take them. Your passion for the strong-willed female clouded your perspective. Did it not?"

Ashton stared down at the floor. He wasn't making decisions that minded his oath as a UMO naval officer. He was following his ego, his desires.

"Yes," he said, shaking his head. "I've made some rash choices as commanding officer. I haven't been focused on the objectives. I only hope that what remains of my crew is doing better than I have. So how do we get out of here? Where's the exit?"

"The sleeve's exit is not necessarily the same as the entrance. It may not be here at all. Please keep in mind that due to the time which has passed, there is likely no one on the other side to receive us."

"So what? We're stuck here?"

Before Stelios replied, the light in the room flashed dark with an instant view of frost-coated metal walls and a gasping chill riding up the captain's spine and seared his skin. The event happened two more times, and he let out a vocal wince of pain.

"Captain," Stelios said with unusual urgency in his tone. "You need to get your atmospheric suit back on quickly."

An actualization hit Ashton like the weight of a Thraxon cruiser crashing onto his head. Whoever generated this space-time rift was having trouble maintaining its integrity. If it failed, he could be instantly placed outside the sleeve and into a future time where Plexo's ship was without the power required for life support. Ashton stumbled around, frantically trying to locate all the pieces of his e-vos, which he had casually disregarded. He picked up the torso shell, only for it to fall into two neatly cut pieces. The Marck hadn't removed the e-vos gracefully.

For Ashton, the situation couldn't be any worse. His face became sickly pale as he turned to Stelios with half of his e-vos shell dangling loosely from his hand. The lights flickered black again, along with the burning cold and gasp of empty breaths.

Stelios peeked down at the chest controls again and then stared up. His focus appeared elsewhere as the captain remained crouched near what was left of his life-preserving e-vos.

"Stelios," the captain's words came out thin. "What should I do?"

It was difficult for him to accept he might very well be in the final throes of his life. As a UMO naval officer, he always knew his life could be lost serving, but he expected it would come quickly or at a moment he would be so distracted he wouldn't have a chance to focus on the minutes leading up to his death. He felt helpless, and the only thing he could do was wait for a cold, suffocating death that would sneak in with its icy hand across his neck.

"Hold on, Captain," Stelios said, still focused on his emptocap's instruments. "I've isolated the exact source of the photons responsible for the rift. What I'm about to do will either kill both of us or provide us an opportunity to take part in this disruption."

The lights shut off again, but this time they remained off. Ashton's skin scorched, and his chest felt like it was about to burst. His body dropped to the frost-coated floor and floated back up, weightless. A funnel of emptiness filled his blurred vision, and the outline of an unwieldy figure emerged. The captain's last sensation was feeling adrift and a sudden tug with a belly full of slivering worms.

CHAPTER 54

They could have gone back to the UMO and gathered an attack fleet, but without the X88T drive tech, the accompanying UMO ships would take months to traverse all the gammac corridors and make the final leg to Eesolan. Krath steadfastly wouldn't hear any options that would take that amount of time, not with Kerriah captured. To him, every passing minute was a gamble with her life. Creedith sided with Krath, so it didn't matter how much Sergeant Alar and the rest of his ops team protested, they were not going back to the UMO.

Their carefully devised mission was likely a one-way trip. Collectively they knew the likely control source for the Marcks would be the strange sickle-shaped object, which ominously rotated above Eesolan. Creedith could get them there, but there wasn't a feasible strategy for getting out. The Marck fleet would likely destroy their ship shortly after its inevitable detection. Still, Creedith, with his control over the ship's squill, was confident in his ability to evade and outrun the Marck fleet if needed. He would stay onboard with Timmon and Lieutenant Camden, while Krath and the others infiltrated the assumed control station.

Magnetically locking the Thraxon command ship onto the rotating sickle took the type of skill very few UMO pilots possessed. At that moment, Jesselle was thankful for Creedith, though still weary of his presence. The subsequent hull breach conducted by Alar and his team gained them entry into the mysterious object. The passageways inside weren't anything outside of what one would expect in a typical space station—square corridors with recessed, white walls and bright, cool illumination. The one thing standing out as outside the norm was the throbbing pulse fanning away only to approach again back and forth as though an object passed them by every couple of seconds. As they moved down each connecting passage, with no specific direction aside from trying to reach the assumed center, an occasional nerve-jolting buzz filled the gaps between pulses. The sounds were unsettling to the group, and as they moved further, the tempo hastened, only adding to the mental strain.

Jesselle stopped periodically, trying to shake off the nagging pulse. She needed to keep her wits to spawn up whatever the team needed to counter what lay ahead. It was strange to her there seemed to be no rooms, chambers, or operational areas, just endless passage after another connected by an occasional sharp turn. As Alar's team turned the next corner, he shouted a command to his soldiers, but Jesselle could barely understand his words as he disappeared from her view.

"Hold steady, everyone. Something's changed."

Jesselle edged forward and turned the corner. The passage ahead was different. Triangular and darker. Its scant illumination consisted of a sparse array of faintly glowing, thin emerald bars, which followed the ceiling point down the wall and into the floor. At the end of the dark passage, there appeared to be a larger area with a bright-white light bleeding out in the distance. From here, the pulse became a continuous bass reverberation, which everyone could feel massaging into their muscles.

"What we waitin' on?" Krath protested their halt. "I'll bet Kerriah is probably in there. We need to press forward."

"I realize that you're emotionally attached to the individual we're searching for, but we have to remain tactical," Alar replied.

"Bah!" Krath gestured with an irritated swat at Alar. "I'll go in myself." As he stormed ahead, Jesselle grabbed his shoulder. "Get tya mitts off me!" He turned with a scowl until he saw her face.

"I'll go in," Jesselle said. "I'm best equipped to deal with whatever we may encounter. Besides, Kerriah is my friend as well." She kept advancing past Krath and the soldiers, each of whom stayed close to the walls with their rifles posted at their shoulders. She took a slow, continuous inhale, trying to settle her nerves. She needed to show leadership. She needed to be a Tolagon.

"Kay, but don't tya worry. I'm gonna be right behind tya, ready bust some noggins."

"Be my guest," Alar said, waving them forward.

"Tat's right," Krath snarled as he walked past Alar's team. "Sit back on tya hineys and watch how the heroes get it done."

"Yeah, well, our 'hineys' are going to be behind you, ready to suppress whatever threat puts you down," Alar replied, trying to get the last word.

Krath snapped around with a sharp stare at Alar. "So we're just tya cannon fodder then? Why you—"

"Stop!" Jesselle shouted. "We need to work together here. Think about Kerriah, please."

"Right," Krath said with a deep breath and then turned back around to follow Jesselle.

Inside, their focus drew to a pulsating pillar of glowing white positioned directly in the center of a large chamber. The walls around them had a shimmering reflection from the light, and the room almost felt alive, as though it was the living heart of this giant station. Jesselle continued approaching the large pillar, and her focus mesmerized on the encompassing object. She went into a near trance-like state as she moved closer. Then her heart leaped from her chest with Krath's growing shout behind her.

"Why, you boney hag!"

Jesselle turned her focus away from the pillar, only to find herself face-to-face with the reclusive villain who held an oppressive grip over the UMO for a generation. The queen's silhouette coiled with the body of a serpent burning black against a pulsating giant pillar of white energy in the background. Her head of crimson spikes blazed like fire before the blinding radiance.

Jesselle immediately formed her gaseous, orb-fueled specters, prepared for an attack. As her winged aggressors swooped down for their strike, the queen's red crown turned white, and her eyes ignited. Jesselle's body stopped moving, and her thoughts locked. Her fiery creations remained frozen in time, still posed in their downward attack.

She couldn't think or do anything aside from stare forward vacantly. Her thoughts became empty when she tried to analyze her situation or plot her next move. Alar and his team, along with Krath, also remained frozen nearby. Jesselle lingered there for an unknown time, observing the static scene until Kerriah arrived. A slender Marck sauntered in with the swagger of royalty. As he passed her, he turned for a look at Jesselle, and she instantly noticed his half-flesh face. Her thoughts blanked as she attempted to process who this could be. Two other Marcks followed, towing Kerriah's body. Jesselle's heart trembled, and she wanted desperately to do something, but she couldn't focus. This queen had some technological spell over her, and it seemed Jesselle was powerless to break free.

She watched helplessly as this unfamiliar hybrid Marck worked to merge Kerriah into the glowing pillar. Occasionally he walked over to Jesselle with a smirk. Each time his eyes would glow blue, and his grin widened with fiendish satisfaction. Throughout the misplaced time, Jesselle stared at Kerriah's body as it became fused inside a cone of illuminated strands weaving throughout her tissue. Pulses of yellow appeared to feed the hungry strands, and as time passed, Kerriah slowly appeared more part of the Marck machine than herself.

It was after the queen returned to Jesselle's view that everything changed again. Her serpentine torso side winded across the smooth floor, and she paused near Kerriah, whose face bulged from the luminous pillar. Her arms draped out and rose slowly before resting her hands upon the queen's lower jaw.

The queen turned toward Jesselle with a malevolent sneer. Her penetrating stare shot across the room with eyes igniting into a blazing amber. The rapid pulsing sound filling the area since they had arrived, reminding her of a giant heartbeat, instantly went silent. Everything around Jesselle seemed to melt away, and her heart turned from the continuous squeezing of fear and uncertainty to the fullness of admiration and love.

As her eyes regained focus, a pedestaled throne filled the space where the once-luminescent pillar stood, and walls of grey stone surrounded her, draped in colorful banners. A majestic female dressed in an ivory and blue dress posed near the whimsical copper throne. The light fabric of her dress cupped with each puff of air as she quietly sauntered forward for an inquisitive look at Jesselle.

This beautiful lady was her queen, someone she adored and respected. Someone she would give her life to protect. Her queen was a model of perfection with a disarming smile and a crown of silver glittering through the thick, flowing locks of jet-black hair as she turned to acknowledge a striking younger woman standing behind her. The young woman, adorned in a high-wasted, ash-toned dress, sashed in black, peered forward at the queen with a glow on her face that could charm an audience of thousands without a spoken word. Jesselle looked down and then side-to-side, noticing she wore lightweight armor tinted silver and edged with onyx. Around her stood other similarly armored Mendacs and Krath. They maintained a sturdy stance, and each had a calm and adoring expression.

The queen took a couple of slow paces to the throne and stroked her hand across its curled headrest before sliding her body into the velvety cushioned seat. Her legs crossed with a pop of silver heel peeking out from the flounce of her dress. She sat quietly and then gestured for one of Jesselle's flanking guards to come forward.

The armored Mendac didn't hesitate. He walked before the queen and dropped to his knees. Her eyes turned dark, and her cheeks blushed.

"You serve me without compromise, do you not?" Her voice was firm yet gentle.

"I do, my queen," the Mendac replied and then lowered his head.

"Good. Then join me as my child," she said and then waved her hand in a casual flail.

A helmet of silver lowered from high above, and the queen grasped it and placed it over the Mendac's head.

"Now rise," the queen said, curling her fingers upward as she turned her wrist. "You are one of my children and a protector of the realm."

The Mendac stood, with his complete silver-tinted armor and helmet, his identity hidden behind his new protective wear. Without an order, he moved to her side and stood at attention. The queen gestured for another Mendac, and the scene played out again and again. She called Krath. The sturdy Hybor's movement appeared to be less fluid than the others, with his feet dragging with each step toward the throne.

"Kneel." The queen's voice contained a level of tension.

Krath didn't kneel right away. Instead, his knees buckled and then stood straight a few times, making him look like he was bobbing from Jesselle's viewpoint.

"I said kneel!" Her voice almost turned to a shout the second time she called out her order.

The helmet began to lower from the ceiling, even though Krath wasn't fully kneeling. A voice cried out from behind Jesselle.

"Stop this! Now!" The voice bore a familiar accent. One Jesselle had not had a lot of exposure to until recently. A large shadow sprinted past her, and the queen's new guards attacked. The shadow picked one of the guards from his feet and tossed his body into the throne. The pillar of light flashed back into view, and the whole area flickered dark for a few seconds.

"Kill him!" the queen shouted.

A shadow resembling a large Andor moved fast, tossing another guard into the pillar, and the view flickered again; this time, it took longer to recover between blinks. A third guard's body slammed into the flickering pillar, and the power faded as screams of pain cried out from the darkness. The glowing pillar steadily re-illuminated, and Krath looked up with his mouth open in shock. The silver helmet turned into a series of thin spiked appendages draping down above him; their pointy tips encircled his head. The appendages bent with rigid elbows and a dark bulb-shaped torso, which was partially concealed in the darkness. Krath's face lit red, and the appendages shot into his head, moving in and out, stitching away at the flesh and replacing the skin with a synthetic shell.

"No!" Krath's voice crackled, and he shook like a wet drok after a rare Solaran rainstorm.

The appendages broke away from him, and he lunged with a solid punch to the queen's face. The queen recoiled slightly, and her eyes lit with fire and rage. The room turned dark with the large pillar pulsating yellow and three burnt silhouettes outlining the shapes of bodies against its glow. The queen's serpent torso coiled up, and she shot her blazing eyes back into Krath, freezing him into a radiant apparition of white light.

Jesselle's thoughts returned with a space in her memories, and she felt as though she had awakened from a long sleep and somehow lost months within this illusion. It took her a few minutes with the events playing out before her to recall the moment they arrived, but it didn't feel right. She had a nauseous, head-spinning sensation when she realized a portion of her life had disappeared in this room, that she'd been caught in an apparent web of stasis for an unknown time.

A funnel of folding blackness shot open next to her, and a metal box with legs and a clear, domed head staggered out carrying Captain Ashton. *Stelios! Where did he come from?* Stelios dropped to his knees and placed the captain's still body on the floor.

The queen's eyes lit up, firing beams of white at Creedith as he dashed around, taking down her guards. She let out an agitated snarl. As she noticed Stelios's entrance, she stopped her attacks on

Creedith and turned her gaze to him with a flash of white connecting to his metal suit. Stelios, however, did not freeze. He stood with his elbows cocked back behind his head as though he had awoken from a restful night's sleep.

"Whoever you are, you have made a critical error," his voice boomed aloud.

Jesselle blinked, and at some point, the scene around her changed within that split second. The queen's body lay twisted, and her head spun around until only a thin coil of synthetic flesh held her crowned head atop the serpentine torso. Krath stood near the pillar where Kerriah's face and arms still hung with a pulsating glow.

"For where did you come?" Creedith asked, snapping a look back at Stelios.

"From a past point in time since we entered the sleeve ahead of you. With my emptocap, I created a temporal sleeve within this one, as the captain was in grave danger. However, the events transpiring here, I believe, must have disrupted this time sleeve and the illusions that seem to encompass everything within. Though improbably, it now appears that our time is now in convergence."

"A time anomaly?" Creedith asked. "The disruptions may have resulted from my dispensing these assailants into the power source here."

"Yes, the anomaly, as you call it, is created by this massive apparatus and the profound power supplying it. Even the slightest disruption in that power can collapse the sleeve." Stelios studied the screen on his chest for a moment. "Though our distorted timelines have merged, we are still out of sync with the outside."

Creedith squinted and gazed around the area. "Hmmm . . . this is an unsavory place twisted with wicked intent. We must do what we can to shut it down."

Stelios didn't reply, and his attention remained focused on his chest instrumentation. He tapped at a cryptic display and turned various dials.

"Hmmm." Creedith turned away and approached Jesselle. He tapped his finger into her shoulder as he carefully studied her. "Are you okay, child?" His voice was soothing.

Jesselle's eyes lit with fear for a moment. "Please don't hurt me!" She trembled with beads of sweat forming across her face.

"I would never lay an aggressive hand on you, child."

"B-But you have. You've damaged me more than you know."

Creedith cupped both hands over her shoulders and spoke with a gentle stare into her eyes. "That was no more me than it was you that attacked us on Nathasia. However, I am sorry."

Tears pooled around her eyes, and she slowly nodded. "I feel awful. I sat out while everyone here fought, suffered, or died right in front of me. I hesitated. I felt conflicted. What I saw wasn't . . . wasn't what's here now. That monster was someone I cared for, my queen. I-I don't know what happened." She felt ashamed of her weakness and inaction.

Creedith placed his arms around Jesselle and pulled her body close. His muscular build felt like a great paternalistic tree wrapping its steady limbs around her shoulders.

"It's okay, child. This Marck Queen clouded what was true with her deceptions. Your response is not a sign of weakness in you but rather your servant's heart, which yearns to love and protect others. It's a strength. A strength that a rare few have."

His tight embrace and gentle words broke her mental barrier, the one she had used most of her life to conceal the scars of her past. This stalwart giant, who'd had more pain and loss in his life than she could ever imagine, could still notice suffering in others, where most would be oblivious. She shook as the tears streamed down her cheeks. He held her until only a few short, hiccupped gasps were all that was left of her sobs. He released his embrace but held her shoulders at arms' length. He looked into her eyes.

"I admire you for your strength. Your heart is pure, and you are young. You still have much to give to those around you. Let not these trials tear you from your path." Her lips sucked in, and she gave a quick nod. "Now we need to tend to the others," Creedith said before turning around and walking away.

It was difficult to recall the last time someone had spoken to her that way. The last time would have been from her parents when she was a child. They were words she needed to hear at this critical time. She needed to know she wasn't a villain shackled to her past. As Creedith walked away from her, Jesselle suddenly realized she didn't feel the paralyzing fear she had of him when he had first arrived. They were closer than she realized, both victims of Zearic and trying to piece themselves together in the aftermath.

CHAPTER 55

As the only one that could control the Thraxon command ship, Creedith was supposed to stay onboard while the others went to look for Kerriah on the giant curved object outside. But something was wrong, and Creedith went to investigate, leaving Timmon alone. He told him to stay put and that he'd be right back. That was four days ago, and now Timmon felt scared and alone.

Lieutenant Camden didn't seem to care for Timmon, annoyed by his constant barrage of questions, so he kept a distance, spending most of his time speaking to someone that wasn't there and nervously inspecting the transport. Before Creedith had left, he spent considerable time mumbling about the Marck ships outside, confused as to why they hadn't attacked. It was obvious they were on edge and trying to deal with the growing uncertainty that each passing hour without a word back from the boarding group brought. Still, Timmon managed to keep his spirits high by exploring the massive vessel and finding interesting objects.

After Creedith had left, Timmon spent his first two days running down the long corridors of the Thraxon command ship. He'd jump and skip singing "mie ohh laaa pol worc rikin . . ." and laughing to himself or whatever imaginary friends his mind could muster while in the dark metal chambers and passages. The song's chorus translated from the native Hybor tongue as "my backside smells worse than yours," an apparent humorous reference to the species' affinity to pungent odors.

However, the songs turned to huffing whimpers by the third day, and his running became a slow shuffle. Camden disappeared without a word, along with the UMO transport. Abandoned, Timmon shuffled down the many passageways with his head down, focusing on the emptiness creeping into his chest and the emerging fear gripping his thoughts. He noticed persistent echoes of thumping and dragging in the ceiling above more each day. He knew it was that weird squill thing moving around, but the more he realized the others were not returning, the more the Thraxon creature creeped him out. Increasingly he began to believe it was following him around the ship.

Even though Creedith explicitly told him to stay onboard and wait for their return, Timmon was scared. He stood quietly inside the airlock, staring into the narrow opening leading into the strange spinning object. Alar's team struggled to slice through the side and had to call Jesselle to bash through with the pointed head of some charging beast she had created. Past a few meters of darkness, there was an illuminated passage. He didn't want to enter the shadowy area, and his imagination ran wild with thoughts over what could be hidden there or lurking beyond the lit passageway. Monsters? Treasures? His heart raced. He was excited, yet frightened. He hoped he would gain a bit of courage the longer he stared through the blackness, but it didn't happen. Instead, it seemed more shadows appeared to move within the mysterious space.

"Oh please," he whispered, hoping someone familiar would suddenly emerge.

After enough time, he built the mettle to walk into the eerie unknown and took several wobbly steps forward. An icy cold draft whisked through him as he carefully approached, raking at his skin like the long claws of some fur-covered beast. His foot fell upon emptiness inside the unlit cavity, and with swirling arms, he stumbled backward in panic. He tumbled to his backside, trying to save himself from an unseen plunge. After taking a minute to catch his startled breath, his eyes slowly adjusted, and he peeked over the edge of an empty cavity around where the cold draft originated. It was only about two meters wide, and he knew he could easily make the risky leap. He stood and took a few steps back and then charged ahead. Timmon closed his eyes as he bound into the air and crashed face forward onto the other side.

Timmon felt the electric shock of fear jolt through his spine and immediately scurried back to his feet. He whipped his head around, waiting for something to grab him, and then puffed out a deep breath. There weren't any monsters. Nothing crept up from the dark cavity to rip him to pieces. With a few more cautious steps into the light, the ship behind him left his peripheral view, its gentle hum faded, and briefly, a cold silence took over.

As he entered the lit passage, he darted a few scared looks and then back into the dark area. His skin shook, and his heart settled from a racing purr into a persistent, heavy thump before he noticed a new sound. A deep pulse came and went as if nearing and moving away every couple of seconds. After a few minutes of remaining frozen with fright, he cautiously settled on the odd noise as not being an immediate threat.

Timmon crossed his arms and nervously dug his fingers into his armpits. There were two ways he could go, right or left, but he wasn't sure which way Creedith and the others had traveled. He looked down at the passage in both directions, and to the left, he noticed a splotch of burgundy sludge on the wall. He approached the peculiar gunk, quickly sniffed it, and recoiled with a wrinkled nose. As a Hybor youth, pungent smells were part of their culture, but this was rancid and upturned his stomach. With the hopes the bitter-smelling spots were left by one of his companions, he decided to venture in that direction.

He turned numerous corners and found more burgundy blots on the wall, noticing the further he went, the more rapid the pulsing sound became. He followed the dark blotches until he reached a place where they changed from a dark shade to a lighter shade of red. He stopped, rubbed his fingers through the crimson grease, and gave it a quick sniff. He recoiled for a moment; it was bitter. Not pungent but almost like a chemical scent mixed with red meat. At the opposite end, he still noticed a smear of the dark red he had been following. This spot almost looked like blood. His round eyelids dropped as he took a few more uncertain steps ahead before the room spun and a sour pit formed in the bottom of his belly.

The lights flickered, and he staggered several steps and slumped to the floor with his back against the wall. A nauseating ring blasted into his ears and then slowly dissipated. Timmon covered his face with his hands and cried. He sat there on the cold floor and wept until his eyes felt like they ran out of tears.

"Momma," he said behind the quivering snorts and curled into a fetal position. He wanted to be home again, far away from here.

Timmon dragged his sleeve across his cheeks, drying the tears from his face, and looked back up for the red streak. He slowly stood and stared at the other patch of crimson further down the passage. He rubbed his knuckles deep into his eye sockets and took another long, hard stare at the wall. The burgundy smear appeared brown. He snapped a glance at the other end with the brighter-colored patch, noticing it was still bright red.

A sudden sense of urgency hit him across his head like a bucket of fermented aacor. He knew something wasn't right and didn't want to be in this place anymore. He didn't understand what was happening, but deep inside, his instincts screamed out to leave here. Without a second thought, he sprinted back to the Thraxon ship, where he would feel at least somewhat safe, even if alone.

***

Shortly after he returned exhausted to the safety of his sleeping hole onboard the Thraxon ship, he awoke from his nap to the shriek of the squill. Its screams jolted him out of his sleeping hole. He banged his head onto the metal cylinder and slowly crawled into the area lined with cavities the Thraxon crew used for beds. The shrieks continued, Timmon's shoulders raised, and his head sank more with each shivering scream. He was too scared to move, too afraid to leave the room.

Squill? The terrible sound echoed throughout the ceiling. He wanted to go back into the sleeping hole and bury his arms over his face until the frightening sounds stopped. But he was worried about the squill. It sounded like it was in pain, and he wondered if there was something he could do.

"Squill?" he spoke aloud. His voice echoed back to him.

He shuffled to the doorway and peeked outside. Clank— clan—clank. The sound of metal uniformly impacting the floor became louder by the second. He ducked back into the room of sleeping holes. Clank—clan—clank. Whatever it was, it moved down the hall in his direction. He climbed up to the highest sleeping hole. As the sound neared, it became apparent there was more than one set of feet responsible for the clanking.

Timmon spun around in the topmost row and peered out below. Two Marcks were already in the room with rifles held at their chests. A blue light filled the area with a long vertical beam projecting from one of their eyes. The beam slowly scanned up and down across the holes. Timmon scooted back as far as possible until his feet touched the back wall. The blue beam shimmered over his hole and then turned off. His heart jumped as their footsteps clacked across the floor again. This time they left. His muscles relaxed, and he tried to slow his breathing with a few deep exhales.

Where's Krath? He needed him here now more than ever.

The ship began vibrating, and Timmon could feel a slight tickle under his knees and elbows. A gentle hum broke the relative silence. The squill let out another scream, and there was a clatter and a clonk outside. It was like the sound he recalled when they first arrived. He jumped down and stumbled; it felt like he was moving, but he wasn't. He then realized it was the ship. It was leaving but without Krath and the others. Who controlled it, and where were they going?

Oh no! A flood of anxiety ruptured into his belly. He felt sick, like he would unload his last meal onto the deck. He held his hands across his stomach, and tears flowed down his cheeks. Would he ever see Krath or his mother again?

CHAPTER 56

The amber flames of the oil lamps flickered in the sparsely occupied tavern, giving the silhouettes of the remaining patrons a warm, welcoming glow. The iron chandelier above the sturdy breatic bar illuminated the dark ale inside the half-empty mugs. Crix drew a deep gulp from his and slammed it against the bar with a heavy knock. It was a time to both celebrate and mourn the past week's events. Akhal was back and this time here to stay as the newest pure resident of New Troika.

Shortly after the defeat of Cyos, he emerged, wandering the new world, searching for a familiar face. Akhal's death inside of Attomis landed him here, which deviated from the rules of a pure resident. When he mentioned Crix to the first Andor he encountered, it wasn't long before he ended up at his doorstep.

Akhal felt at ease for the first time in many years. He no longer bore the burden of re-establishing Troika in the old world. His place was here now, and he felt renewed. He and Crix's laughs grew throughout the evening as they kept their mugs filled until all their worries and concerns melted away and all that remained was their mutual past. The bitterness of their childhoods seemed so trivial now, and they couldn't help but make light of their behavior growing up.

"I still can't believe you defeated the fabled Cyos," Crix said. He let out a wheezing laugh, shook his head, and peeked into his mug. "I still can't believe it. You! The one that used to bully me nonstop, the one I used to beat the stuffing out of in Annexis."

"Now, wait a minute there. You know I handed you plenty of defeats." Akhal smirked, tipped his mug to his open mouth, and threw back a generous chug, finishing it off. Placing the mug down, he motioned to the barkeep. The stout, older Andor behind the bar waved him off. It was already twenty minutes past close, and the last rounds had gone out.

"Come on!" Akhal protested. "We're old friends and haven't hung out like this since . . . since—"

"Since I saved your sorry butt in the bottom of the blind zone, what? Seven . . . eight years ago?" Crix responded. Since then, so much had already happened; it seemed like a couple of lifetimes ago. The gritty old barkeep wasn't feeling their sense of nostalgia. He gave them a firm shake of his head, snatched Akhal's empty mug, and tossed it into the crate of spent containers below the bar top.

The barkeep gave Crix an icy stare. "It's time to go, boys. Finish yer drink and pay up."

"Geeze," Crix said under his breath. "I guess saving the Andor civilization, what?" He looked over at Akhal with three fingers in the air. "Three times now isn't enough for any special treatment here."

Akhal just shrugged and let out a low chuckle. Crix finished his ale and reached into his front pant pocket, sliding out a roll of bills. Just like on Troika, New Troika preferred paper currency. He peeled a few off and placed them under his mug.

"Keep the change," he said to the barkeep.

Akhal and Crix rose from their stools and turned toward the door when it swung open with a petite Mendac figure blocking their way out. Crix leaned forward with a squint. Could it be? He sniffed the air that blew in, and his heart skipped a few beats and his legs turned to rubber.

"Crix?" A familiar feminine voice called. "I'm looking for Crix?"

A smile so wide crept across Crix's face that it felt like it lifted his chest along with his cheeks. It was her.

"Don't you believe your own eyes?" he said while trying to subdue his excitement.

Her head turned to him, and then she leaped into his arms with her arms and legs wrapped around his body. She planted her moist lips onto his, and he could hear and feel her breathing against his own. He squeezed her as tight as possible without harming her and enjoyed the unexpected kiss. They hadn't been this intimate since he first returned from the core. Before, he eventually succumbed to the nightmares that robbed him of rest and mental solitude. But that was before New Troika, and those thoughts were behind him now. This kiss felt good.

He placed her down upon the wood-planked floor and stared into her eyes. They were greener than he could ever remember, and her hair was fresh and smelled like spring blooms.

"How? I mean, where have you been?"

She smiled as she stared up into his large eyes. "It's too much to tell right now. Let's go somewhere quiet, and I'll explain it all."

"Uh yeah, absolutely." Crix turned to Akhal. "Hey, this is Akhal. Do you remember him from the Annexis game?"

She looked at Akhal with a smile. "I sure do. Pleased to meet you again."

"Well, it's the girl I've heard so much about in the flesh," Akhal said. "We've never really been formally introduced, but I feel like I already know you based on everything Crix has told me already."

Her smile withered to a half-smile, and she looked at Crix. "Can we go somewhere private and talk? I really have a lot to tell you."

Crix could see the urgency in her expression and tone. "Sure." He led them both out the door and then gave Akhal a couple of friendly pats on his shoulder. "I'll see you tomorrow. For that game of tribakon?"

Akhal let out a tired laugh. "Sure thing. Like old times, I would love to hand you a worthy defeat," he said before disappearing into the night, leaving Kerriah and Crix alone.

"I can't believe you're here," Crix said, still struggling to accept his lost love stood before him after not hearing a word from her in nearly six years. He hadn't heard her name from anyone aside from himself since Burling's visit. It was like seeing a ghost, someone he could never fully get over, but the wounds of her disappearance had faded a while back by the rivers of tears that had washed over them.

"Where have you been? What happened to you?"

"It's the queen." Kerriah glanced to each side as though trying to ensure no one was within earshot of her words. "She's still here."

Crix withdrew in horror. "The queen? As in the Marck Queen?"

"That's correct."

Crix shook his head in denial. "No. That's not possible. I watched her pass right in front of me. She's been gone for years."

"What you saw was a remnant of her, a discarded container. She escaped the core that day. She escaped using the power from your orb blast."

Crix looked around before grabbing her arm and leading her away from the tavern. They continued to walk in the direction of his dwelling on the outskirts of town.

"Kerriah," he whispered, "are you sure? I mean, the system was almost completely obliterated by Cyos, but outside of that, we have been living in relative peace for at least five years. And the two years before that, I controlled the Marcks. I've seen no sign of the queen anywhere."

"She is devious and exceedingly patient. She has the time that most mortals do not have to nurture and hatch her plans. I can assure you that she's already infiltrated and compromised key individuals within the UMO."

"How did you discover all of this? I still don't understand where you've been for all these years."

"She told me."

Crix stopped in his tracks. "Wait, did you say she told you? When did you see the queen?"

"On Eesolan. As I said, there's a lot to tell you."

Crix gazed at the starlit sky and breathed deeply into the cool evening air. A bolt of anxiety shot through every nerve in his body. "You were on Eesolan, and the queen was there. How did you escape?"

"I tricked her," she said without hesitation.

"You tricked the Queen of the Marcks? That's not an easy task. But I suppose if anyone could pull that off, it would be you." Crix pulled his hand down his face and stopped at the base of his chin. "You realize this is a lot for me to take? I mean, I haven't heard anything from you in nearly six years; everyone assumed that you were dead along with Krath, Jesselle, and the crew of the UMO ship you left with. Now you suddenly appear and tell me the queen is—"

"Just . . ." She paused with a frown. She seemed annoyed by his lack of trust. "Look, let's just get back to your place, and I can explain everything so that you believe me."

CHAPTER 57

They arrived at Crix's dwelling with minimal words spoken along the way. It was as though both were churning their thoughts, trying to figure each other out. As soon as the latch of the heavy front door clacked shut, Kerriah's mood changed. She grabbed Crix by the back of his neck and pulled him toward her. Planting a lengthy, deep kiss on his lips, she curled her leg around his and tickled their tongues together. For a minute, Crix enjoyed the much-missed affection but then hesitated and gently pulled away.

"How can you kiss me like this? I mean, you don't know me with this body, this face. I don't look like what you fell in love with?"

Her eyes twinkled. "Crix, I can see you anyway I wish. The yellow orb not only gives me power over others' thoughts but my own as well. I see you the way I always have."

Crix didn't know what to think of this revelation. Did she truly see him physically as she had always known, or something better? The idea that Kerriah could make him appear as anything she wanted didn't sit right with him, though he knew her well enough that she wouldn't make him anything aside from what she fell in love with.

"Can you at least let me know when you decide to change what I look like to you?"

She gave a sideways smirk and gently brushed his short, auburn mane away from his eyes. "Just shut up and kiss me."

They made love throughout the evening, shoving aside their past, present, and future worries. Their passions ran wild together until his willa flower bed sack slid down to the timbered floor, and they pressed against its plush cushion until it crept directly in front of the dancing flames of his bedroom fireplace. Their amber-tinted silhouettes clenched each other tightly as he pulled her upright, and their deep kisses stirred the cauldron of starved affections lying dormant in their bellies for so many years. She clawed at his back, and his face cringed with pleasure before he dropped back upon the dampened sack, exhausted.

He let out a steamy breath. His body felt numb, with nothing left. However, Kerriah still had a fire in her eyes. "How can you still have any energy?" Crix said, still trying to catch his breath. "I mean, you've never made love to me like that before."

"Didn't you enjoy it?" she said sensually, with her black hair partially tussled across her face. Tiny beads of sweat formed over her upper lip and streamed down her cheeks and breasts.

"Well, I'm not complaining at all, trust me." He folded his arms behind his head, propping it up slightly. "It's just that you tore into me like an ebb tree tiger. You were never that aggressive."

"Would you like me to be timid next time?" she asked in a light, flirtatious voice.

"Oh, don't get me wrong; I enjoyed you taking charge. It's just, wow!" He blew out a long breath of air.

She rolled over and lay down next to him, staring up at the flickering shadows dancing across his timbered ceiling. "About what we were discussing earlier."

"Huh?" Crix replied lethargically as his mind was on the edge of drifting to sleep.

She turned to him and grabbed his jaw, rotating his attention toward her. "About the queen."

"Oh yah," he replied, his voice a little more alert.

"She's compromised several key UMO leaders, and they need to be dealt with as quickly as possible."

"Okay." Crix gently massaged his right eye with his palm and sat up. He didn't want to get involved in UMO politics or anything that would bring him back into conflict. At this point, if it were anyone else, he would stop them before they could fill his ears with anything that would potentially upend his peaceful life here on New Troika. But, for Kerriah, he would give a reluctant ear.

He blinked and slowly shook his head, subtly letting her know he was slightly annoyed to hear what she was about to tell him. "Who?"

"Lancer Septin and Joric Placater."

Crix's lips tightened upon hearing the names. "Hmm . . . really?" He had never heard her refer to her adoptive father by his full name before. It was always by his titles or Father. "So both your adoptive and natural fathers? How do you know this?"

"As I said, the queen told me during her gloat after capturing me. She was able to use your orb blast to insert herself into many of the UMO's intelligence systems. Namely the chancellor and Joric's. She's been there this whole time."

"But Joric and the gover—" He shook his head before correcting the misspoken title. "I mean, Chancellor Septin are both heroes of the resistance and possibly have more integrity than anyone I've ever known. How do you know she wasn't lying to you?"

"Because she used me. She used my Tolagon power to kill much of the UMO populace. And I was able to see inside nearly everyone's minds during that awful experience."

Crix's mouth dropped open, and his pupils nearly disappeared. "W-What? What are you telling me? Are you somehow involved with the Cyos attack?" He wanted her to say anything aside from her being responsible for the loss of billions of lives. If that were true, he didn't see how there could be a way back from such an atrocity.

"It wasn't me, Crix. It was her. She was controlling me, and all I could do was stand by and observe. It was one of the most horrific things I've ever had to go through. But before that attack ended, I saw that Joric and Septin were no longer themselves. They are servants to the queen."

Crix was so confused and distraught that his breathing became short and rapid. "Kerriah, I-I don't know what to say. You're not acting yourself right now. I mean, we made love, the best love, but now you're telling me that you were part of the mass extinction of much of the populations in the UMO? I'm sorry; I don't know what to think. I don't know what to believe right now."

Her brow furrowed with an accompanying scowl. "You should believe me because you love and respect me." She swiftly crossed her arms and gave him an angry stare.

"Oh, of course, I love you, and I don't think you're lying. It's just that the queen is a master manipulator. Can we trust what you think you saw while under her influence? How deep did she get into your head?"

Her eyes turned glossy, and tears started welling at the base of her eyelids. She swiped her thumb across her right eye, brushing away the fluid before it streamed down her cheek. "I hate that you don't trust me. I thought we were closer than this."

"No . . . no . . . It's not like that at all, Kerriah. I completely trust you." His heart ripped in half over seeing her tears and knowing he caused this pain. He pulled her into his chest and held her tight as she broke down into a full sob, sucking in short breaths with each weep.

She suddenly stopped and pried her hands between them, pushing him away. "Get away from me!"

Crix buried his face into his hands for a minute and took a deep breath before pulling them away. "Fine," he said, both exhausted and frustrated. "What do you want me to do?"

She sniffed and wiped her arm across both her eyes. "We need to go to them and do whatever it takes to stop her."

"Whatever it takes?" What was that supposed to mean? There were some of the most highly regarded individuals in the UMO. "Kerriah, I can't leave here . . . ever. This planet and all its natural inhabitants, the ones reborn from the Tersik Crystal, including me, since I technically died the day I released all the orb's power here. I'm spiritually bound to this world."

She stared down at the dark, sienna-wood plank floor, her eyes intensely focused. She raised her head slowly with a cold gaze into his eyes. "Then we bring them here."

CHAPTER 58

With his hand cupped over his fist, the chancellor anxiously tapped his fingers across his knuckles. His leg remained crossed as he waited in his firm, cushioned, ivory seat positioned stoically in the rear chamber of his official transport. A squadron of UMO fighters and a destroyer gave escort to his transport. It was a perilous time following the mysterious disappearance of the Mertel. Thale and its Hybor populace neared extinction after the killer nebula swept through and drove them to madness. Solara fared somewhat better, given the dispersion and reclusiveness of much of its population. At least half the population of Soorak had died due to the strange maddening following what everyone believed was the Luminar legend, Cyos.

Now, after almost six years since she had left through Zeta on the Mertel, Kerriah appeared on New Troika and begged his presence for something that couldn't risk transmission over long-range comm channels. Something so dire she had to remain where she was, with Crix, the Tolagon hero that saved them all those years ago and then created a new world on the ashes of Nathasia. Burling described, once again, they owed their salvation to Crix and an unknown Andor who made the ultimate sacrifice against the nebula everyone called Cyos. Despite the outcry from his advisors, Septin couldn't deny the request for his presence. He owed them too much. But the burning questions still stirred in his mind. Where had she been? What had happened to the crew of the *Mertel*? It was his duty to find out, even if it must be in person, and he trusted Kerriah more than anyone else.

The system needed his leadership now more than ever, and a trip to New Troika wouldn't look good politically, considering the current state of affairs. The last thing he wanted any of his constituents to think was he took a vacation to a place unscathed by the killer nebula. It just didn't look good, and his nerves were on edge. What could it be? Kerriah said in her brief message that "the fate of the UMO was at stake" and that she couldn't say anything more until he arrived at New Troika.

What could it be now? Though he was excited to see Kerriah again, he had resolved on her most likely being dead after such a lengthy absence and wasn't sure how much more distressing news he could handle.

A well-dressed female stepped in, her ankle-length, snug-fitted, black skirt making her appear taller than her actual height, her shoulder-length blonde hair sculpted around her strong jawline.

"Sir," she said, tapping a thin screen she held close to her chest. "We've arrived at New Troika and should have your shuttle ready for departure in a few minutes. Would you like to come with me now, and I can brief you on events since we left Soorak?"

Septin closed his eyes and shook his head. "No. That's quite alright, Pellen. I will meet you there. Please, give me a few more minutes."

She stopped looking into the portable screen and folded it into her chest. "Sure. See you there in a few." She turned and stepped out of the room.

Septin rubbed his hands together and drew a closed-jaw breath through his teeth. A storm was brewing in the pit of his stomach, and he couldn't shake the feeling something wasn't quite right. It was Kerriah, and he hadn't seen her in almost six years. Where had she been? Where were the Mertel and her crew? He needed to know the answers.

***

The shuttle set gently into a small clearing outside the Pinoke Township, where Crix's home stood. Both Crix and Kerriah waited at the forest edge, anticipating Septin's arrival. They stood shoulder to shoulder with Crix's arm around her waist. Her arms were crossed as though the cool morning air made her a tad uncomfortable. As soon as his lift set against the frost-coated grass, Septin stepped onto the surface of a world he had only experienced one other time in its current form. Five years ago, he still remembered the strange surge of energy, almost like a slight tingling sensation whisking up his body when his foot touched the ground.

"Kerriah!" he spoke aloud with a smile. He walked forward with his arms wide open. She stepped slowly toward him and met his embrace.

She moved her lips close to his ear and whispered, "I'm so pleased to see you again . . . . Father." His embrace tightened, and he let out a loving groan to let her know how happy he was to have her in his arms again finally.

He let her loose and held her shoulders at arm's length as he stared into her eyes. "Oh my, just let me look at you for a minute." His fingers gripped tighter into her shoulders. "It's really you!" He let out a gasp. "Where have you been? It's hard to believe that I'm seeing you again with my own eyes as I truly thought we had lost you." He placed a quick yet tender kiss on her forehead. "I needed this more than I can explain. As you may or may not know, we've recently gone through some of the worst events in our history. I needed some good news."

She looked at him with an icy gaze, the look of a sociopathic killer, and Septin let go of her shoulders and took a cautious step back. "Kerriah?" he said with a shaky voice. "Are you alright?"

"You're a pawn of the queen," she said, her voice calm yet elevated.

"What?" Septin took another step back.

"You allowed Cyos inside the system. You allowed it to kill and ravage the UMO."

Septin raised his arm and held his hand forward. The moment seemed surreal to him, and he began questioning himself. Over the last few months, he had been so distraught her accusation didn't seem as farfetched as it normally would have. She took a step forward, closing the distance between them.

"Kerriah . . . what's happening here? You know I would never—" The air suddenly left his lungs, and a sharp pain filled his abdomen.

Crix's voice crying out faded into the dimness of a waking dream. Septin's freshly starched shirt suddenly felt wet, and he looked down as he patted his hands into the blood-soaked material. Half of Kerriah's forearm disappeared into his body. She withdrew her arm, ripping a fistful of entrails out along the way. He hunched over and let out a hallowed gasp as his eyes met hers one last time.

Her lips moved, but he couldn't hear the words. He dropped limply upon the cool blades of grass, and his vision faded into dark silence.

CHAPTER 59

"Kerriah!" Crix screamed in panic upon seeing her rip the insides from her adoptive father. "What have you done?" He felt like time froze for a moment with a long, narrow tunnel closing around his view. Everything stopped, and the only thing he could see or hear was directly in front of him.

Her expressionless stare sent a fright ripping through his nerves. Lightheadedness followed short, panicked breaths, and his stomach instantly turned sour. He frantically looked at her and then back at Septin's mutilated body.

"Y-You murdered your father?" With wide eyes, he gripped both sides of his head with his elbows pointed outward. "You never said you were going to murder him!"

"Oh, please, Crix." Her voice was cold. "This was never my father. The only thing I did was take out an agent of the queen."

"Stop right there!" a voice shouted from the chancellor's shuttle. A team of armed security personnel stormed out with their weapons drawn. "Don't move!" the security lead ordered as they surrounded Kerriah and Crix. "Hands on your head! Now!"

Kerriah calmly shook her head, not appearing concerned over the threat. Crix put both his palms out forward in the direction of the security detail. "Wait! Hold on!" He couldn't let them kill her, despite the awful act she had just carried out.

"I'm not asking you again!" the security lead shouted.

"Kerriah, you can make them stop," Crix pleaded as he glanced over at her, suggesting she use the yellow orb to make them stand down. "I don't know how, but we'll work this out. Please!"

She just stood there with her hands posted at her hips and a cold stare. A flash of light emerged from the security lead's barrel, and Kerriah flew back with her arms sprawled out to her sides.

"No!" Crix screamed.

Ghostly blue bubbles poured up from the ground and encompassed each security team member. As the captives struggled and fought to escape, pushing and punching against the sides, Crix slid down to his knees and cupped Kerriah's body into his arms. A burned hole nearly the size of his fist gaped from her chest and through her back.

He wiped the hair from her face. "Oh please, please, please don't die!" His frantic voice shook with each word. He looked at her motionless face and then back down at her wound. He glared at the sky with tears streaming down his face and let out a scream that could be heard atop all the great mountains of New Troika. His lengthy cry subsided to a shaky growl, and his attention turned to the security team, which still struggled inside their translucent blue bubbles.

Crix's eyes turned dark, and his expression morphed from pain to a bitter scowl. The walls of the bubbles began to draw inward, ever so slowly as their captives visibly tried to cry out without sound and their fists flailed helplessly against the encroaching sides. The barriers eventually reached their bodies and continued until their navy-colored uniforms darkened with the wetness of blood, and their heads collapsed from the slow squeeze. Crix's focus remained on them until nothing recognizable was left inside the bubbles aside from crumpled armor, dark red fluid, and the grey splinters of bone. The bubbles popped with a splash of wet flesh and clothing, showering into the grass and seeping through the green blades. Only fragments of bone, crumpled metal, and uniforms remained visible where each security team member once stood.

He stared back down at Kerriah's limp body. She wasn't there, just an empty shell that once contained her beauty and life. He pulled her to his chest and hugged her tight. She felt warm to the touch, and he knew it wouldn't be long before she turned cold. But he would hold her until every bit of noticeable warmth left her body.

He squeezed his eyes shut and began sobbing uncontrollably. He felt hollow inside. At this moment, he didn't want to carry on anymore. He knew the UMO would come here and seek revenge for the murder of their chancellor, but he would not allow them to take anything else.

CHAPTER 60

Timmon snuck around the ship for over three weeks, dodging Marcks and grabbing a few bites of Stelios's tasteless slop to stave off the snarling in his stomach. A few days ago, the ship had stopped moving, and the humming vibrations settled. The Marck patrols still marched up and down the corridors on a regular schedule. Timmon had their movements timed well and had become familiar with the different parts of the ship as if it were his home away from home. However, this wasn't his home. Not even close.

His skin was so dry it progressed from a manic itching that scraped off a flurry of dead crust as he raked his fingers vigorously over his arms, chest, and neck to acid-like burning across the cracks that had formed recently. There was no place to get hydrated here. The ship had no baths, no showers, and no sinks. Aside from his water rations, which he would pour conservatively over his body every few days, the only thing he could find with fluids was strange mouth holes in certain areas of the ship. Timmon had assumed this was where the Thraxon crew obtained their nutriment.

One day, out of desperation, he placed his mouth over one of the fist-shaped protrusions with a honeycomb surface, resulting in a shot of bitter-tasting fluid. It made him heave for hours afterward. As much as his Hybor roots made him appreciate pungent and rotted flavors, this was different. It was sour and reminded him of the stench portions of the Mertel had shortly after encountering Cyos. They were still finding bodies hidden in various places days later.

Loneliness was his only friend here, and it was a cruel friend. At first, it comforted him while he hid as the footfalls of the Marck patrols clacked down the halls of this empty ship. But later, it nagged at him. Questioning his thoughts and hopes that anyone would ever come back. Eventually, the thoughts turned to screams and long nights of crying himself to bed, realizing this could go on forever. His only friend, loneliness, now had its bootheel pressed against Timmon's neck.

He had lost so much weight recently that he kept one hand on the waistline of his trousers and the other rapidly stroking his chest and shoulder to stave off the cold air which took over the ship ever since it started moving weeks ago. He shivered as he snuck down the corridor leading to the pasty, flavorless, entamal rations. As he approached the supply room, he noticed something had changed. A pale tentacle lay dangling from the ceiling. Its tip curled against the floor, and the color was slightly differed from what he could remember when seeing them wrapped around Creedith. Before, they were a shiny black, and now it appears as though their color had faded.

"Squill," Timmon whispered as he walked up to the loose-hanging limb and poked his finger into its center mass. He quickly jerked his finger back, just in case. He found several cargo crates to stack so he could look up into the hatch where it hung from. It was dark inside.

"Squill? Can you hear me? A-Are you okay?"

He placed the palm of his hand on the tentacle. It was cool to the touch, but he wasn't sure if that was normal. For a reason he wasn't certain of, he wrapped his arms around the thick limb. He wasn't sure why. Maybe it was an innate need for companionship or to feel something that wasn't metal against his body. Its skin felt dry against his cheek, like everything else here. As he continued to hold on tightly, he felt the tentacle tense, like a muscle-flexing. He let go, stepped down from the crates, and leaped back.

The tentacle lifted and moved toward Timmon. Its end curled as if it were feeling or sensing the air, looking for him. He reached out his hand and touched the tip. It stretched further, and Timmon took a few steps back, reaching what appeared to be the limit of the squill's ability to extend further.

"Squill, are we friends?" The tentacle rose and smacked the ceiling several times. It almost appeared as a show of frustration.

Timmon took a careful step forward, and it quickly shot down and laid its tip flatly against his cheek. It didn't seem hostile; instead, Timmon started to feel like it was suffering the same thing he was, loneliness. He took another two steps forward.

"It's okay. I'm your friend," Timmon said.

The tentacle wrapped itself around Timmon's body and pulled him into the hatch. It held him snugly, like a mother to a newborn. The hatch closed, and Timmon became immersed in darkness. His nervous hands patted against the squill's tentacle, and he could feel it anxiously flinching.

There was a gentle bump against his mouth, and he batted it away with his hand. It bumped against his mouth again, with a little more persistence. He knew it wanted to connect with him as it did with Creedith. However, Timmon wanted no part of it jammed into his mouth. He squinted and turned his head away. The squill persisted, not yielding to Timmons's rejections.

"No!" Timmon shouted.

Around that time, he could hear the clanking echo of Marck footsteps advancing down the hall below. Their pace was a little quicker than usual. Something was wrong. They must have heard him talking to the squill or yelling at it to stop. Until now, he had been stealthy and hadn't made any striking noises that would give them away. As the Marck footsteps sounded right beneath him, the squill's tentacle bumped into his mouth again, but with even more persistence.

Timmon felt scared, his heart raced, and he didn't know what to do. He wanted to hide, but he was already hidden. He wanted to hide deeper, somewhere away from here. He needed something he could speak to and tell him everything would be okay.

The squill. Fine. He took a deep exhale before popping his mouth open.

His jaw stretched wider than he ever thought it could. With a slight gag, he felt the tentacle squirm its way into the back of his throat and then a tickling sensation shooting up into his nasal passage. Thoughts popped into his head, but they were not his own. It was an unfamiliar voice that wasn't like any he could recognize. It wasn't deep or light, or even soft or timid. Rather, it reminded him of the sound of Thale sea crickets floating on the water at night, chirping at the stars. The even stranger thing was he could understand the chirps and squeaks.

The squill told him about a Mendac female that came aboard shortly after Creedith left. She brought with her the Marcks, used a mysterious power to get inside it without a physical connection, and tortured it into submission by taking over its thoughts and limbs. She forced it to choke itself while her Marcks dug charged rods into his appendages. The squill finally submitted to her and took the ship inside the UMO, where she had left a few days ago. The female insisted the ship be kept cold. And now it was dying, sick from the low temperatures. It needed to warm the ship or go into dormancy, but it was scared and unable to do either for fear of her reprisals if she returned.

***

During the next two days, Timmon became closer to the squill. He found a friend, someone that helped break up the chokehold of fear and loneliness, and he could feel himself returning to normal. Digging around one of the many supply areas, he found a crate of onyx spheres. They were large enough that he could barely get a single hand around one, but the surface was oddly pliable. He looked closer at the crate with its strange markings. Somehow, he was able to decipher what they read . . . entrocrows. He looked around as though someone had whispered the word into his ear, but no one was around. Staring at the markings again, he slowly smoothed his thumb over them, realizing he knew the word because of the squill. It had implanted the dialect into his mind.

He held the sphere next to his ear and gave it a quick shake, trying to hear if something was inside. But there was nothing, not a rattle, click, or churn of fluids. He banged it against the deck with a solid clonk, then stopped.

"Squill," he called out. A tentacle slipped out from an overhead panel and curled back at Timmon. "Wanna play catch?"

Timmon gave a soft underhanded toss of the sphere toward the squill. It quickly withdrew to avoid it. The ball bounced once off the hard surface and then continued to roll. The squill quickly returned, tapping the tip of its tentacle across the top of the rolling sphere, stopping its momentum.

"That's right," Timmon said, waving his hand toward himself. "Toss it back."

The squill tapped the top of the sphere for a few seconds before coiling around it and then whipping it back to Timmon. Timmon cupped his hands to his chest and caught the flying ball.

"Yes!" he shouted and then covered his mouth. "Oops." In the distance, the clanks of Marck footfalls returned. Their hasty steps indicated they would be there in a couple of minutes. "We gotta hide!" Timmon whispered aloud.

Instead of retracting into the overhead panel, the squill snatched the sphere from Timmon's hands and flung it hard at the Marcks as they emerged at the doorway. The sphere blew open upon contacting the Marck's chest, and a cloud of black mist puffed out. The last thing Timmon could see as the squill pulled him into the panel above was the Marck guards flailing around as though trying to fend off a hive of Solaran desert stingers.

At that moment, Timmon realized what he played with was a Thraxon weapon, and the squill just used it to kill their captors. The released Entrocrows continued their swarm through the ship, taking out the remaining Marcks before the squill purged them into space. From that moment forward, Timmon and the squill developed a more profound friendship. They played together and shared thoughts. Two species that would, in differing circumstances, try to kill each other now felt a tight bond.

But Timmon was concerned about Krath and the others. He suggested they return to Eesolan and his friends, but the squill didn't want to return there due to the Marck fleet. He didn't know what to do. He couldn't remain on this ship forever and certainly didn't want to wait for the evil Mendac to return. The squill still didn't want to turn the heat back on, as it was terrified of Mendac's mysterious powers and was already worried over reprisals for destroying the Marck guards.

Timmon felt terrible for the squill; he knew it would die soon if it couldn't turn the heat back up again. "Why can't you just throw one of those balls at her if she comes back?" Timmon asked. "It should kill her just like those guards, right?" The squill's tentacle shook left to right, mimicking Timmon's head shakes and nods it had picked up during their communications with each other. The squill wouldn't do anything here, as it was too scared. Then the idea hit him.

"The statue guys. Let's go back there. You know, the place where we picked up Stelios. They helped before. Besides, you already know how to get there." The squill reacted to his suggestion by slurping back up into the hatch and then back down again repeatedly. "Well, is that a yes?" Timmon asked, uncertain of how to decipher the squill's reaction. It waved its tentacle up and down. "Yes! Let's go!" Timmon hadn't been this excited since they first left onboard the Mertel.

CHAPTER 61

Alar and his ops team lay scattered, their bodies partially covered in synthetic plates of black. The spec ops leader was hardly recognizable, with his head nearly ripped from his shoulders, connected only by a thin metal rod twisted to a near-breaking point. The eight-legged machine performing the hasty conversion of these former UMO soldiers hunkered into a ball at the top of the shadowy ceiling. It looked more like something dug from a deep cavern of Drisal than an intricate and deadly piece of Marck technology.

It was apparent Krath's concern for Kerriah had made him forget about the threat above. Creedith interrupted his focus on Kerriah with a light tap on his shoulder, followed by a pointing gesture up.

"What the h—" Krath spun around, agitated by the distraction. His eyes were crazed with focus. "Creedith . . . unless you've got a nifty way to get her outta that wall, I don't want to—"

Creedith pointed up again. "I am concerned about the child as well. However, we have an immediate threat that needs to be dealt with. The abomination is called a transfigurer. I've seen its work firsthand."

"Why that dirty, no-good, Marck pest." Krath darted a glance from shoulder to shoulder. "Give me a rifle, and I'll rid us of that thing right now." He spun around, searching for a weapon. "Where's a damned rifle?" Krath began stomping across the room as he angrily continued his search.

"There isn't any. I'm assuming the, uhh . . . queen . . . did not allow them in her lair," Creedith said. "Stelios? Are you presently equipped to handle our ceiling pest?"

"Now wait for just a second," Krath protested. "I'm 'bout tired of folks messing with my time. I'm already feelin' old and darn sure don't need any help from—" He stopped and spun around as though something important suddenly jumped into his head. "Where's Timmon? Where is he?" He looked over at Creedith; somehow, his inky skin almost appeared to fade into a creamy white. "You were supposed to be watchin' over him on the ship."

"Yes, we both remained on the Thraxon command ship, but the fact that the Marck fleet never attacked us, even after you were gone for several days, told me that something must have gone wrong. As much as I didn't want to leave the youth alone, I couldn't wait any longer, and I had to discover your whereabouts. But I could not bring him into this unknown danger with good conscience."

"Fine, I'm goin' back to the ship and check on the lad." Krath took two strides forward before Creedith pulled Krath back by his shoulder. Krath spun around with an elbow, nearly striking his former Vico Legion brother. "Get tya mits off me! Tya leave a child by himself! I knew I couldn't trust anyone else with his care . . . even tya." His eyes stared straight through Creedith.

"Krath, the ship isn't there. I already tried to go back and discovered our breach sealed, and the ship's gone. I can't

370

understand who could have taken it. Lieutenant Camden? He would have had some way of manipulating the squill, and if he tried, it would have likely killed him."

"What do you mean it's missing?" Krath took a fistful of Creedith's loose-fitting garment and pulled him closer. "Where's Timmon?"

Creedith wrapped his hand around Krath's to loosen his grip. "I do not know. As I stated, the ship isn't there, but there are also no immediate signs of its destruction; rather, it appears to have been stolen. I suspect for its X88T drive system. But there was another concern I had witnessed when I returned." His voice remained low and calm as he spoke.

"Grrhhh!" Krath shouted through his teeth. "Speak up, Creedith! Before I lose my already thin temper!"

"To ensure my path, I took a small container of that reddish-tinted Thraxon chow with me before I left. I generously marked my path with a smudge of the offensive substance before turning down each corner. As I ventured deeper through the maze of seemingly pointless corridors, there was an uneasy sensation of vertigo in my head, and I felt a strong compulsion to go back and check on Timmon. However, when I returned, I noticed that the smudge appeared brown and faded as I came to the last several turns. When I rubbed my thumb over it, it flaked from the wall, whereas just a few paces back, it was still wet and the expected crimson color.

"I am no specialist in interdimensional time travel or its theories; before now, I thought it to be pure rubbish. However, I feel that when I entered the inner corridors of this portentous place, my time equaled yours, yet Timmon's is still ahead, though it is hard to say how far." Creedith looked over at Stelios. "Is that assessment accurate?"

"That it is," Stelios replied. "This area is within the sleeve, and at some point, unlike the anomaly sleeve opening that Captain Ashton and I initially traversed, you have unwittingly entered the primary opening. The physical effects you experienced were the increasing time dispersion as you approached this inner chamber. I have calculated to the best of my measurements and believe we are approximately five years out of sync with our native time continuity."

"What of this queen?" Creedith asked. "Do you have any insight as to what time sync she is in?"

"I am uncertain. Her origin time would have likely been when she originally energized this modulating station. However, I now suspect that she has the ability to traverse within the sleeve to differing points in time, essentially merging her past and our present."

"How do you—" Creedith stopped, distracted by Krath.

"Agghhh!" Krath stormed over to the nearest wall, planting his fist into it, leaving a slight indentation of knuckles on the metal surface. He screamed and lowered his head for a minute. "I need somthin to destroy!" he said with his head still down.

"Jesselle, Krath needs to blow off some steam," Creedith said, knowing full well how the former Vico Legion shock trooper dealt with stress and confusion. "Get that thing off the ceiling but try to keep it intact."

"Got it." The queen's transfigurer rotated around and raised itself on the tips of its six limbs.

Jesselle's eyes and hands lit with a blaze of red and winged creatures with whipping tails formed from thin air. The ignited specters of crimson gas wrapped their long tails around the slender arms of the black transfigurer. They pulled as they dove downward, ripping the resisting machine away from its lurching position. It fell freely, and a last-second upward tug of Jesselle's creations averted its inevitable smash to the deck below.

"Krath," Creedith said with an open swoosh of his arms, as though he was introducing the opening act to a long-awaited performance, "it's all yours."

Krath stormed forward with his arms bulging out to his sides and fists clenched. The intensity in his face relayed one thing to those in the room. Stand clear and let the bitter old Hybor vent his frustrations.

The carnage lasted only a few minutes before the transfigurer lay scattered into an array of battered and torn metal scraps. Krath stood still, only his chest pumping from the heaving, deep breaths as he recovered from his furious act.

Creedith loudly cleared his throat. "Now, we need to get Kerriah released from this pillar of molten power."

"Right, this is when we need ole glow rod," Krath said, still slightly out of breath but starting to regain his composure. "I'm not typically a fan of his smarter-than-the-rest-of-us attitude, but somehow he'd know what to do here." He stood there with his fists propped against his waist as he stared at the large, pulsating column with intensity. "Welp, since no one has any other ideas, we'll just have to do this my way. We're not going to lose anyone else, not under my watch." He took two steps back and then charged forward into the glowing pillar.

"Krath! Wait!" Creedith's voice sounded off as Krath's foot left the ground and his arms dug into the wall.

Krath uttered a primal scream as his arms drove up to his shoulders into a mesh of hair-like, white strands. He wrapped his muscular arms around Kerriah's body and heaved until a bulging mass emerged from the glowing pillar. Veins protruded across his head, and his shirt ripped across his back.

373

"Grrrhhhaaaaggg!" his animal-like cry continued.

An explosion of yellow illumination sent a shockwave from the wall, blowing Krath away and freezing him midair with his arms and legs stuck in a flailing pose. A look of desperation froze across his face. One that just threw everything he had at something and bore the bitterness of defeat, despite his best effort.

The room stood quiet and still, their actions and expressions locked in place like a picture, preserving this moment in time.

CHAPTER 62

Krath appeared from nowhere, snarling and screaming merely centimeters from her face. The last thing she clearly remembered was the queen stabbing her on Bellahis; everything else since had been like a dream, except she didn't dream. Over days or weeks or months, she wasn't sure of the time that had passed. Wave after wave of tormenting visions had twisted Kerriah's mind. The queen's control over her thoughts was so intense that in this fog of confusion, she almost killed everyone in the UMO. *The treacherous bitch!* As the numbness of this continuous nightmare slowly bled away, she knew everything was a lie. But now Krath, was he there? Was it really him?

Krath remained in front of her for several minutes, and the louder he screamed, the more her body seemed to pull forward. Power coursed through her with the likes she had never experienced. This celestial energy made her feel like she could do anything, yet she couldn't move.

The creep of prodding hands tickled up her back and then grasped across her shoulders. The queen was here, and she wanted control.

No! Kerriah bit down on her lower lip with her eyes closed. When her eyes pried open again, Krath emerged suspended in midair. He looked like a holographic image projected a few meters in front of her. His face appeared helpless, and his hands were wide open as though he had lost hold of something precious. It was then she realized it was her. She was what he had lost.

A quick sweep of the area revealed Jesselle, Creedith, Ashton, and Stelios in the same frozen state as Krath. She had no grasp of time. She couldn't determine how long she had been here or how long Krath had been hanging suspended in front of her. She felt the queen's goading hands wrapped around her waist. The queen tried to get back inside her. She desired access to the yellow orb again, with Kerriah as the conduit. Kerriah's face twisted, and her teeth clenched as she fought to maintain control.

Kerriah blacked out with a return of the visions she had earlier. Images of her companion's flesh being torn away and replaced with synthetic fibers. She had remained motionless and silent as they suffered through the transformations. She had wanted to stop their agony, yet she inexplicably gained enough pleasure from the sight that her thoughts couldn't overtake her actions. She knew the queen's power controlled their thoughts. It was always the queen.

The treacherous queen used the white orb to leave memories inside Kerriah's mind. Reaching out across the cosmos, she could see Crix and the love they made at his homestead on New Troika. But it wasn't her. None of this is her!

No! It's not me. Crix, no! She looked down at her hands soaked in blood. Septin's body lay out in front of her. She screamed, and the room filled with a strobe of yellow. Krath fell away, sliding across the floor on his backside. The others moved around, and she felt present again.

"Kerriah!" Ashton's voice called out. "Can you hear me?" He moved closer. "Kerriah?"

She could see the queen's plot and why there was life support here. She had this planned all along. The queen wanted to bring her here to become part of this giant control system. She called it the Halioc, and it was her experiment that went bad on Eesolan. She tried to subjugate the populations with an illusion . . . a fantasy, before transforming them into her servants. The queen had attempted this with select towns on Soorak years ago.

This time, Cyos was her conduit, but it was a power no one could truly control. Instead of projecting the illusion she wanted, it projected her twisted rage, and the populations destroyed themselves. Kerriah wondered what was left of the UMO.

She had to break free; she needed to help them, but her arms wouldn't move, and she couldn't feel her legs. What had these monsters done to her?

"I-I can't move," she cried out.

"Kerriah! Hold on." Ashton's face lit up upon hearing her voice. He turned to Stelios, hoping he would have an answer. "What can we do?"

Kerriah could hear their thoughts and feel their concern for her. She wanted to help, but she couldn't even move her head. "I can't move," she said again. "Please help me."

Stelio's head slowly tilted back, inspecting the glowing pillar to where it disappeared into the ceiling and then back down to the floor. "Hmmm . . . I am sorry, Captain; I do not have the solutions you seek. I know nothing of this power."

"I do," Creedith said. He looked at Jesselle, who was quiet, with her shoulders pulled tightly forward and her head tilted down. "It will take a Tolagon and the unique gifts of the red orb."

"What?" Jesselle's eyes widened.

377

"That's right. You are needed again. Just as you can manipulate metal and stone objects, you can do the same with the fibers and pieces of Kerriah's body."

"But I have no idea. She's way too complex for me. I couldn't . . . I mean, it's not the same."

"Yes, you can with her help. Kerriah has all the knowledge of her construct within her. She just doesn't realize it. The two of you can make her body whole and free her from that pillar."

"I-I still don't—"

"Do not try to outthink the problem," Creedith sharply interrupted her. "Have faith, and the solution will present itself. The two of you together are more powerful than any foes you will face. This is only a minor bump in our path to salvation as we turn away from the darkness surrounding us. I can assure you that by working together, you will find success." Somehow, he appeared taller than usual as he spoke.

Jesselle's posture straightened with a quick nod, and the gloom left her face. She closed her eyes for a moment and slowly stepped toward the pillar, staring up at Kerriah.

"We can do this, Jesselle," Kerriah said with a clenched jaw. She felt the strands behind her squirming and the invisible grip on her body loosening. She knew Jesselle had control of them. Kerriah's head shook side to side, and she could feel her arms pull from the wall. Her hands emerged ribbed with light strands.

"Quickly! Grab my hands!" her voice strained.

Jesselle stretched upward and wrapped her hands around Kerriah's. A pulse of bright orange blasted outward with a push of energy, which sent everyone in the area upon their backs and smacking into the far wall. Both Kerriah and Jesselle cried out in one voice.

SONG OF THE LAGGORNS

A schematic filled Kerriah's head. It was her design, hidden within her memories. This was how Joric had built her to heal. Her body needed to know how it was put together. She could reach through Jesselle and access the power of the red orb by using her own power. She took control of her fellow Tolagon and the elements within the wall. Her body was here, just deconstructed. A fiery tingling sensation flamed up her legs, and her hair spilled out from her emerging shoulders. Suddenly she felt the warmth of Jesselle's soft hands. Her heart pumped slowly and hard, pounding deep in her ears.

Then she felt herself falling, followed by a solid landing upon Jesselle. They kept their hands locked, and Kerriah pulled herself face to face with her fellow Tolagon. Jesselle's eyes blazed red, but her breath was sweet. That's when she noticed her sense of smell had returned. Jesselle's smooth fingers remained locked between her own, and a soft, warm exhale against her cheek made her feel alive. She didn't want to let go of her.

Their lips locked, and their power surged together. She could see Jesselle in her thoughts, children playing together, building memories they never had, and forming a relationship that never existed. It was artificial, yet real to them at this moment. Jesselle's arms wrapped around Kerriah, and they held each other tight for a few minutes, basking in this mutual pleasure. They both needed this. They needed the warmth and the emotional bond of someone who would care for them and make them feel safe again.

Kerriah didn't want to let go of Jesselle. She didn't want to break her tight embrace, but she knew their time was short, and the queen was likely hatching her next plan. She loosened her grip and pushed her hands between her body and Jesselle's. However, the red-orb Tolagon didn't let go willingly, and Kerriah had to push her thumbs into Jesselle's ribs to force her to let go.

"I'm sorry," Kerriah said with a soft voice. She could see the hurt and deprivation in Jesselle's eyes as she eventually released her. "For a minute, I didn't want to let go either, but we're still in danger."

Jesselle stood; her face sank with awkwardness, yet her eyes peaked at Kerriah as though hoping she would call her back. Her expression changed to confusion as she looked her up and down. Kerriah's body didn't appear normal. Her body had a milky ribbed appearance, and her legs sprayed out into a fan of fibers to her feet. She tried to stand only to lose her footing before Creedith steadied her with strong hands around her waist.

"Are you okay with walking, child?"

She nodded her head and tried to steady her footing. A few steps forward proved challenging even with Creedith's stable hold on her waist. She wobbled and stumbled, clumsily trying to keep her balance.

"Your body is still not whole. I can carry you," Creedith said.

"No." She didn't want to be a burden on anyone and didn't want to explain. "I can manage. We need to get to Eesolan. To Bellahis."

"To what?" Krath grumbled.

"Bell-ahis." Kerriah spoke the name slowly this time. "It's where the white orb of Cyos is kept. The queen still controls it and uses it to keep her Halioc blade powered and spinning, for which she is creating these paralleled rifts in time. She planned to use my power over the yellow orb to eventually subjugate all known systems, like the UMO, by altering their realities and making the hapless citizens see her as their queen in some perverse fantasy. In reality, they would be subordinate to her, and if they questioned her rule for any reason, she could twist their minds until they submitted. It would be the perfect weapon, so we must remove her access to that power."

"Tya gotta be kiddin'? Why that no-good bucket of—" Krath stopped to kick the twisted head of the queen, further dislocating it from her serpentine corpse.

Ashton cleared his throat loud enough to get everyone's attention. "I agree. But wouldn't we be handing you and your power back to her by going to this Bellahis? We should at least keep you someplace safe while the rest of us go to stop her."

"Where?" Kerriah replied sharply. "Where are you going to keep me safe? So far, she hasn't mastered the white orb's ultimate power, controlling all other orbs, at least not without direct control over the bearers, but she's close and has already figured out how to control Cyos, though clumsily so." She stopped and winced, trying to fight against an internal battle in her mind. "But I've got news for you." Her voice cracked. "There is no safety here, or anywhere else for that matter. I must confront her. Besides, you'll need me there if you have any chance."

"How are we goin' to get there? We've got no ship." Krath gave a sideways glare at Creedith. "Right?"

"That's correct, old friend. Though I believe Stelios can help us."

Stelios peeked at the instruments on his chest box and gestured to the glowing pillar. "If I can channel this great power again, then yes. It is possible to create a temporal sleeve so that we can travel from one point to another. Just as the captain and I did to get here."

"I can help there," Kerriah said. "Just let me know when you're ready."

"Yes, it would also be helpful to know where the desired trajectory is."

"The planet-side source of this power." She motioned to the glowing pillar she was a part of minutes ago. "Not on top of it, but near."

"Clearly. However, you will need haste as there will only be a moment before the rapid depletion of power closes the sleeve opening. Being trapped somewhere between sleeves could leave its traveler lost in a dimension for which they may never be found, or worse, with molecules in two different locations." Stelios smiled, making everyone even more uncomfortable than they already were. "I am ready if you are."

Kerriah wobbled over to the pillar while struggling to maintain balance on her unraveled feet. She placed her hand into the surging power and raised her other hand, aiming it at Stelios. A blinding shot of white bridged across her body and into Stelios's suit. She stopped after a few seconds, and a bright glow remained over Stelios's shimmering metal armor. A funnel of black swirled into view, with their glassy reflections visible inside.

"Go now!" he shouted.

Krath was the first to dive through, followed by Kerriah, who Creedith carried. She would, in normal circumstances, protest someone carrying her, but she said nothing as he strode over to her and lifted her into his arms, bound for the sleeve opening. His movements were fast, and she was on the other side before any words could leave her mouth.

CHAPTER 63

It was foolish for you to come here," the now-familiar voice sent chills down Kerriah's spine. "Now, you are prey trapped in my web." The queen stood there with her arms extended as the group picked themselves up from the shot across the sleeve. Stelios remained down on both knees, depleted once again.

Creedith pulled Kerriah to her feet for her verbal rebuttal. "I don't see how we are trapped in your web. There are two Tolagon's here and a group of friends that I would readily stand with to oppose any tyrant." Kerriah's tone was sharp, and her eyes scowled at the queen.

The queen smiled and casually looked back at the giant white orb, which hovered in its place at the center of the Bellahis dome. "You are in my realm now, and you will bow before your queen!"

A wave of energy surged from the orb and blew against her back, jolting her body. Six sparks of white light emerged around them, and each spark grew longer and brighter. The queen let out a cynical laugh as the sparks took form into copies of herself.

Spears took shape in each queen's hands, and their eyes lit red, drowning out the silhouettes of the bodies. "Bow to me or die!" The queen's voices spoke in concert.

"Tya gotta be jokin'. I'm not bowin' to anyone, much less some boney machine," Krath barked out.

"Good," the queens replied. "Then be the first to die!" Three of the queens darted toward Krath, plunging their spears. He leaped to the side and grabbed the first one's spear as she drove it at his torso, only to find his fingers pressed into an empty fist.

Krath instantly peeked down, shocked at the sight of his empty hands. "What the?" The second queen's spear tip plunged into his chest as he flailed his arms, helpless to stop the pushing weapon. "Aggrrhhhh!" he screamed out as he desperately felt around his chest for the source of the sharp pain.

"It's just her illusions!" Stelios's tinny voice shouted. "They cannot harm you."

"That felt pretty darn painful for an illusion." Krath swung at the queen, and one of her copies wrapped her spear shaft across his throat. She pulled his body back as he tried to grasp the phantom spear.

"The pain you feel is real because your mind believes it to be true," Stelios said with heaving breaths, still kneeling and struggling to recharge his suit's depleted power.

Creedith tried to step in to help, but three queens intercepted him, plunging their spears into his legs. He fell forward, grasping at one of them with his hands clutching empty air. He rolled over and kicked away their advance before patting his hands down his legs, searching for a wound that didn't exist.

"If she cannot hurt us, then the only weapon she has is our fear!" he shouted.

The queen let out a cackle. "You're wrong . . . wretch!"

She walked casually over to Krath, who struggled to fend off the other three copies, and drove her spear into his back. He cried out as blood poured out from the fresh wound. A fiery red tail whipped around her spear, jerking it from Krath's back. Jesselle's bird of prey continued to tug at the queen's weapon as two more joined, trying to peel it from her grip.

"That's the real queen!" Kerriah pointed at the crowned menace as she fought to regain control of her spear. "Focus on her!"

With her hand extended and her eyes closed in focus, Kerriah tried to enter the queen's mind. She found a Luminar, trapped in a void—a mental trap, submerged in the power of the white orb. The female Luminar of many years peeked up from her cell, her eyes filled with sadness—the actual Divination. Kerriah could hear her whispers.

"Help me, Tolagon. . . . Help me. . . ." Over and over, the desperate words repeated.

She tried to reach inside the cell, hoping to pull her from this place of despair. Her hands withered, and her arms skeletonized as they passed into the void. She paused in thought. *This is all the queen's tricks. It isn't real. It's just a trick!* She pressed forward with a hand touching the cool skin of the Divination.

"Stop!" the queen screamed out with a wave of her arm, a surge of power, and a flash from the white orb sending everyone sprawling onto the glassy floor of Bellahis. Kerriah lost her mental connection and her grip on the Divination.

The queen's illusional replicas dispersed with her furious strike of orb power. Stelios stood; his suit filled with power from the queen's last attack. He stared across the dome at the queen and tapped the controls on his chest. "She has made her last miscalculation."

"No!" Kerriah shouted with her hands out toward Stelios. "We can't kill her. It's not the queen, it's the Luminar Divination. That's how the queen is controlling the white orb. We just can't see her through the distortion that her Halioc blade is creating around us." An echoing laugh came from the queen.

"Then I know what I must do," Stelios said. In front of him, a funnel of black whirled opened. He stepped inside, and within a couple of seconds, it snapped closed.

Kerriah anxiously panned around as though expecting him to have stopped time again. "Where did he go?"

"I suspect I know," Creedith said, taking a heaping breath as he gazed skyward. "We must do what we can to provide him the time he needs."

Creedith charged into the queen and wrapped his legs around her body, pulling her down before she could react. Her crown smashed into the hard surface, shattering three crimson spikes. He arched his back in pain and quickly let loose his hold on the queen. He gasped for air and tugged at his throat as his body lifted from the floor and levitated a few meters into the air, as though something unseen pulled him up by his neck.

Krath staggered over to the queen with the rigidness of a corpse. His skin appeared milky grey as blood continued to pour down his back, leaving a splatted trail as he moved forward. Before she could arise, he stomped his foot onto her neck, and she winced and growled as his weight bore down upon her. Suddenly, Krath's body jerked upward, twisting in the air, as he let out a gurgling howl.

Jesselle raised her arms, calling her gas-spawned birds of prey. Six clouds of red vapor shaped into four-winged birds with long, whipping tails. They dove into the queen, lancing at her body. Their tails and talons tore at her limbs as she attempted to stand.

386

The queen's eyes ignited a liquid red, and Jesselle stumbled forward as though hit by something from behind. She took two more staggering steps before falling face-first with her body sliding toward the queen.

The queen took a few annoyed swats at the winged irritants and then grabbed Jesselle, flipped her over, and wrapped her hands around her neck. A blaze of white fire shot from her mouth and encompassed Jesselle's face.

"No!" Kerriah screamed.

She tried sprinting to Jesselle's rescue, but her malformed feet and legs tangled in her stride, and she spilled to the floor, landing upon her outstretched hands.

The queen let out a snarl as she spotted Ashton. He drove the queen's discarded spear into her back. A high-pitched wail cried out as she struggled to reach around and grab the shaft poking through her sternum.

Bellahis flashed from a picturesque view of a blue dome swirled in white to a cracked and smoked-stained arena outlined with a skeletal dark metal frame. Segmented arms protruded from the ceiling, holding captive Krath and Creedith. The metal frame extended through a smashed hole in the dome's center.

A faint glowing figure dropped out from the queen and collapsed to the floor. The Divination lay dying with the spear punctured through her back, the transparent threads clung loosely to her limbs, and the grey tube seeped from her mouth, with a pool of turquoise blood quickly forming around her body. The queen faded, and the power surging from the orb drew down as though being sucked back into the enormous white sphere.

A mechanical voice from above broke the momentary silence. "You think you've vanquished me? Fools!" There was an echoing laugh followed by creaking and clattering of metal sliding together. Growing jagged fractures crept up the sides of the dome until the translucent shell shattered with a rain of fragments showering down upon the platform below.

A skeletal figure of a giant robotic queen emerged from a shifting metal frame. Her crowned head arose from the portion that once resided outside the dome. Four lanky arms still held her assailants captive. The mechanical queen stood thirty meters high, and her one free hand reached down to snare Captain Ashton.

As the captain tried to run, her arm lanced through him like a skewer into a chunk of meat. She raised his flinching body to her jaw and bit down, the jagged teeth slicing him into two. Both halves of his body fell, plunking to the surface below.

CHAPTER 64

As he knelt near the mound of freshly upturned ground, Crix dug his fingers into the dark umber soil, which contained the buried remains of his one true love, Kerriah. In adherence to the old funeral rites of Troika, he had planted a breatic tree seedling atop her grave. He pounded his fist into the loose, packed ground and stared upward. New Troika was a place that was supposed to be free of this type of loss. Their lives would be eternal as long as the orb's power remained within this extraordinary world. But Kerriah wasn't a natural resident of New Troika, nor could she ever be since she wasn't an Andor.

Crix swiped away the tacky remains of tear streaks from his cheeks and stood, lowering his gaze to the tiny tree trunk atop the grave, which someday would be a giant. He had gained a world but lost his love. Looking back at the months after she had rescued him, he felt foolish. He was caught in his own self-pity, and she was alive and vibrant, trying desperately to start their lives together. Everything within him wanted to go back and redo those days. To have a chance not to be selfish and wrap his arms around her. To assure her everything was okay and they would live happily together.

Still, he couldn't help thinking about how strange she had acted when she had returned. Overtly sexual, considering everything that had happened since they last saw each other. She was dark, so dark she murdered her adoptive father right in front of him. What had happened to her after she had left Gabor, and where was the yellow orb? It wasn't with her remains, even though she claimed to have used it to make him appear as the visual representation she remembered.

There was something that changed her. Crix felt like she withheld details of something she had experienced since he had last seen her. He thought they would have more time to discuss these experiences, so he had given her space to tell him when she was ready. Now he would have to rely purely on his imagination to fill in the blanks.

***

Not long after he left Kerriah's grave site, he heard the rumblings of ships above. Before now, there was an agreement to respect the peace and harmony of the Andors on New Troika. An agreement to keep UMO ships from clogging their skylines with curious media or sightseers. But now, military drop ships lowered, and he would have to make a stand to protect his home and his species.

As the ships set down upon the surface, flattening the trees, Crix stood defiantly with his arms crossed. Dozens of UMO soldiers filed out from three ships with their rifles posted at their shoulders and their sights trained on him. An officer emerged from behind the wall of readied troops; his arms firmly clasped behind his back. The officer stopped in front of the soldiers a few meters away and pulled a thin card from his chest pocket.

"Crix Emberook?"

"Who's asking?" Crix replied.

The slim-built UMO officer cleared his throat. "Captain Demesh Harlton. I have orders to place you under arrest for the murder of six UMO enlisted and for aiding in the assassination of Chancellor Septin." The captain stopped and leaned his head forward with a squint. "If you are Crix Emberook, I advise you to give yourself up peacefully."

"Hmmm." Crix relaxed for a moment and rubbed the back of his neck. "I am Crix, but I have no intention of coming with you. Even if I could."

"Then what options are you leaving me? You are coming willingly or by force."

"Captain, I could kill your entire team with a thought. Please do yourself and your well-intended troopers a favor and leave here now."

"I understand your power, and we are prepared to deal with that if required." Captain Harlton looked up. A rumble came from the sky, followed by a group of the latest XR500 attack fighters sweeping down and then hovering stationary over them. "They are loaded with enough energy suppression torpedoes to keep your power subdued long enough for us to apprehend you. Now, don't make things worse for yourself."

"New Troika is not governed by UMO laws. We are a sovereign entity. It will be considered an act of war if you try to kill me."

"May I remind you that by aiding in the assassination of the chancellor, you've already committed an act of war? Regardless, I have my orders. I'm required to take you in." Captain Harlton stopped and cupped his hand over his ear as though listening on a comm unit. "What's that? Say again?"

"Then you'll have to take us all in," a booming voice came from behind Crix. From the dense forest behind him emerged legendary Andors Suros, Litore, Quarab, Criollo, and even Halflinger, amongst a hundred other Andor warriors. Suros stood forward with his molded war helmet and hand firmly gripping the hilt of his sheathed blade.

"Andors of New Troika will rise and fall together," Halflinger shouted, appearing like a more youthful version of himself. He appeared closer to the age Crix remembered as a child when he would race up and down hillsides on his shoulders.

Crix raised his chin defiantly. "I ask you to think about what you're doing, Captain. The UMO cannot afford a war with New Troika. I think you would have to agree that you have larger concerns right now."

Captain Harlton slowly removed his cupped hand from his ear. "Roger that," he said, responding to his command ship. He stood silent for a minute and panned the small army of Andors that seemingly appeared out of nowhere. "Look, I'm not looking to start a war. But you must understand that your actions cannot go unanswered. We will be back, and next time, I'm not leaving without you."

"Fair enough, you know where to find me."

CHAPTER 65

Stelios's temporal sleeve opened into the area for which they had left minutes earlier. The pillar of white orb power fueling the Queen's Halioc blade pulsated in the background. He sluggishly stumbled forward, suffering again from his emptocap's depleted energy. He knew the only way to defeat this queen of illusions was to destroy the photon-generating machine creating her rip in time.

With his power depleted, it took too long to reach the pillar of light. He lifted his arm to block the intense glow from his eyes as he contemplated his move. He would only get one chance. His restless scientific intrigue compelled him to leave his home and explore other civilizations. He would have never guessed he would be at this point, where he would have to save them.

He slowly pushed his hand into the pulsing white field. The power surged into his emptocap, and his sense of strength and awareness surged. The energy was more than his emptocap retention system could bear, and quickly he felt a wave of heat explode through his body. As he took a final step into the pillar, the power dispersed, and the pulsing white vanished.

It wasn't him; he didn't get a chance to destroy the blade, but something happened. He spun around, trying to understand why the white energy had stopped. Something might have happened below at the origin. The pillar was now just a dense grid of milky-shaded fibers. A flash of red strobed on the uptilted chest controls of his emptocap. He tapped the screen, noting the main sleeve had suddenly dropped. He thought of his options; if he opened a new sleeve to return to Bellahis, he might not have the power required to come back here if needed. A green illumination flooded the area above him as he stared down the grid, looking for answers.

Stelios turned his attention upward. A glowing, emerald figure hovered above, and his feet slowly lowered to the floor. His face bore a creepy sneer with a tilted, heart-shaped head. Stelios couldn't help noticing a striking resemblance to the Luminar image concealing the anomaly sleeve opening through which he and Ashton had traveled. However, he had never seen another of their species and had little reference to their unique traits.

"Hello," Stelios said softly to the unexpected guest. "I am Stelios of Ethis. What may I refer to you as?" Despite the maligned gaze, Stelios hoped this individual wasn't here with ill intentions, but he also knew that was unlikely.

They stared at each other for a minute, and then Plexo raised his palms with a brilliant flash of green, and hundreds of tiny spikes formed around the chamber. At once, the translucent, green needles shot at Stelios like a ring of laser blasts fired from a rifle. Stelios staggered back; his nerves lit like fire and his blood boiled. The pillar behind him reignited with the pulsing white energy.

With the flick of a switch, he engaged his emptocap and created a new split in time around him, to which he was not subjected. He moved toward Plexo, who remained frozen in place,

394

caught in his trap, but Stelios's life began to wane, his vision blurred, and the room spun. He turned back to the pillar and stumbled into the energy field. His emptocap filled with the immense power surge, and the retention systems overloaded. A spark of black turned white within him, and his suit exploded. A shockwave blew through the outer hull of the queen's Halioc blade. The photon generating station burst into a flash of white, leaving a spray of debris where the once-ominous sickle dominated the space over Eesolan.

CHAPTER 66

RESURRECTION

Kerriah stared blankly at the severed remains of Ashton. She couldn't move; she couldn't think. She felt paralyzed by the events around her, events she was helpless to change, even as a Tolagon. She had to find a way to defeat the galactic threat her father had created. But with Ashton dead, Krath and Creedith held captive by the queen's massive mechanical skeleton, and Jesselle unconscious, Kerriah was now alone in this battle.

The queen's raw metal head moved in closer to Kerriah. A spiked arm twisted around her, and the queen's caged jaw bent into a smirk. Kerriah stumbled as she attempted to distance herself from the coiling arm before she awkwardly fell onto her back, smacking her head against the hard surface. A sensation of hot metal stabbed into her abdomen. The queen's arm pierced her torso and pulled her into the air. Her insides burned like acid, and she lost control over her limbs.

The queen pushed her body into the topmost section of the white orb like children toasting sweet creams. Kerriah felt the power surge through her body, and someone or something infiltrated her mind. The white orb was bound to the other orbs.

Instantly, she could see where they were—all of them. The red orb was nearby, in Jesselle. The blue orb on New Troika fused within every meter of the planet's crust. A black orb she never knew existed floated invisibly to the naked eye near Oro. It remained after the destruction of Cyos. The green orb she could see above her. *Plexo?* Her thoughts tore away from the flow of information for a moment. And then Kerriah called the white orb to project its power into the collector at the base of the Halioc blade. The white orb flared upward, and the massive light beam tore into the sky again.

The queen's illusion draped back across Bellahis and all of Eesolan. Kerriah's body moved from the giant orb, flaming with a mix of white and yellow. She could see the long spikes of the queen's crown around her head. The gloss of bloodred gore shimmered from her crown and tipped her glowing white fingers. A beaming smile crept over her face as her servants lowered to the surface, and flames of swirling yellow shot into the bodies. Their knees bent to their queen. But something was wrong. The power projected into the Halioc blade suddenly had no target. She looked up, and the illusion was gone. The queen released her momentarily, and her thoughts became her own again. She noticed Jesselle standing before her with an empty stare.

It was enough; Kerriah wouldn't allow the queen to retake control of her. She couldn't lose anyone else. To defeat this menace, something drastic would need to be done. Something she may not be able to undo, but she would worry about consequences later. She leaned forward, slid her body from the queen's skewer, and stammered to keep her footing beneath the slick pool of blood beneath her malformed feet.

Jesselle walked obediently forward as the queen's mechanical form continued to stare upward at a tiny green star emerging in the sky. The monarch of the soulless was momentarily distracted, creating an opening into Jesselle's mind for Kerriah to control. The crimson Tolagon wrapped her arms around her, and their bodies connected with their orbs as a link. Jesselle walked with Kerriah's body attached as though magnetized to her. Kerriah kept hold of her mind, commanding her to move them into the white orb.

The giant mechanical queen caught sight of their movement and turned her attention away from the brightening green star above.

"Stop!" her voice echoed.

Her arms swung around, but she was too late. Kerriah and Jesselle's forms bled into the white orb. Creedith stood alone, and his mind broke from the queen's spell. She glanced at Ashton's severed body and Krath's motionless lump. Krath's face planted into the surface where it fell, and his rear stuck up into the air. A pool of burgundy grew larger around him. The queen fixated on the white orb, and her long, pointed limbs jabbed cautiously around the bright white globe.

Creedith picked up the spear lying near his foot. He clenched his jaw and stormed up the giant queen's long metal leg. Before her attention turned to the agile attacker, he was already bounding up her spine and neck. She reached around for a lancing strike, but Creedith already drew the spear back with a careful aim at her head. He paused as he noticed the old Vico comrade he hadn't seen in decades. The green star had emerged with a casting emerald glow over Bellahis. Plexo hovered directly above them.

"Plexo?" His usually steady voice shook. "Is that you?"

Plexo didn't say a word; instead, he pulled his arms back and thrust them toward Creedith with a thousand needles of green light following his gesture. Creedith winced and dropped the spear. His grip on the queen loosened, and he fell.

CHAPTER 67

Inside, the white orb contained power beyond anything she could have ever imagined. It was a power that could have spawned or destroyed entire planetary systems through Cyos. It also contained knowledge. She now knew of the orb's strengths and weaknesses. Her veins flowed with an icy tingle as its power freely encompassed her. The hidden secrets of the Laggorns were here. Secrets even the enigmatic council of Gabor might not have been aware of.

Panthis, the eldest of the Laggorns, directed their works. As was true of all Laggorns inside the Auroro system when it had exploded, Panthis died, but its energy remained. The white orb contains the power of Panthis, the ability to control all other Laggorns, which allowed it to control Cyos.

The Divination's primary use of the orb was for any purpose aside from knowledge. She could never merge with it and only siphoned fragments of its intellect through careful caresses from her hands. Over the years, much like her predecessor, she learned to influence the legendary nebula and move it in specific directions. Her goal was to merely cast subtle suggestions to keep its destructive force at bay but still close. She knew any attempt to take control of Cyos would corrupt those that tried and that only the unfit would ever attempt to seize such a force.

There was, however, another orb within Cyos, unwritten and unknown. The black orb had formed from the collective powers of the remaining Laggorns lost in the destruction of Auroro. It contained power over life and death, as well as creation and destruction. It could destroy them all. The only weakness it had was the white orb. Directly merging the two would create a cataclysmic event destroying everything at a galactic scale.

She looked inside both herself and Jesselle. The yellow and red orbs were not the children of Cyos but of the black orb within the great living nebula. Its power spawned the child orbs at the behest of the previous Divination. A request that drove her into madness and ultimately cost her the rights and title of Divination. That's when the Luminars set out to collect them.

As Kerriah continued to bask inside the white orb, she tried to resist the influx of energy as much as possible, throttling its surging power to keep her body and mind from being overwhelmed. She dropped to her knees and strained for a look outside. The light was so bright she couldn't see outside the orb's barrier. But she felt a familiar presence and an accompanying force. Plexo was close. She knew now the queen was using Plexo and the green orb to create the high-speed photon field around Eesolan. Plexo was the new bearer of the green orb. Something that he would never do on his own. The queen controlled him through a neuro implant, the same way she commanded the Divination. Kerriah could also sense his pain. Using the green orb under the queen's control was taking its toll on him physically and mentally.

Kerriah felt a persistent nudge from Jesselle, and she suddenly had a growing desire to let go, to lose herself inside the glowing ball of power. The yellow orb Tolagon let her in with open arms. The red orb's power seared inside her for the first time as both orbs spun together in harmony. The intensity of the combined power began to overwhelm her artificial cells until her insides burned. Jesselle's life poured into Kerriah like a dam rupturing under the pressure of a swelling river, desperately escaping her dying body. For the crimson Tolagon, stepping into the white orb was a one-way journey as every vein and artery inside her natural body ruptured.

Jesselle's spirit tickled through Kerriah, and she had the sensation of two children running through an open field in the warm afternoon. "Stay with me," Jesselle's voice pleaded. "Let's stay here forever."

"I can't," Kerriah replied. "But you must stay, to remain the guardian of the white orb. You will live eternally if you remain here. This power needs you to become the observer. From here, you will keep watch over the orbs and keep them from the hands of evil."

"No!" Kerriah could feel Jesselle's protest as well as hear her words. "You can't leave me here alone. I don't want to be by myself forever!"

"I won't. I'm leaving a part of myself with you." Kerriah closed her eyes and reached inside, grasping her Tolagon friend and a secret piece of herself. With two fists, she projected her arms outward, and the two children, one with red hair and one with black, emerged inside the orb. "You see, I will always be here with you." Jesselle's face glowed with a smile. "You will locate future Tolagons and seek the virtuous to protect the vulnerable. Safeguard this great power and use it to keep the orbs from being used for selfish ambitions."

The two children ran into the distance, but the red-haired child stopped and turned around. "I will help you, Kerriah. We'll stop her together." Then she faded into the blinding white, at one with the white orb. She would finally have the peace and companionship she had always longed for; inside this place of knowledge and power, she would now have eyes on the galaxy. She would be the guardian of the orbs.

Kerriah stepped out of the white orb, strobing with energy, and Jesselle's body flopped out onto the floor, grey and lifeless. The crackle of glass and the hissing breeze briefly filled the area. Kerriah's arms and legs fused with shards from the shattered dome and blended with red clouds of misty gas until she stood a giant of her former self. Her body stood over twenty meters tall and cracked with shimmering crystal and steaming gas. Her arms extended upward, and she grabbed the queen by the head with both hands and tossed her effortlessly over the edge of Bellahis.

The queen's metal frame tumbled into the netherworld of Eesolan. Modern Luminars discarded this place and considered it an unevolved vat of toxicity, which they chose to avoid. It was a place where Eesolan's ancient cities once felt the clawing radiation from the gamma-ray burst altering their species and their civilization forever. The population there consumed each other. In a twist of fate relative to their sky-dwelling ancestors, they eventually evolved into living sludge pods keeping them from extinction for thousands of years.

Kerriah looked with satisfaction as the last part of the queen's metal frame disappeared over the platform. There was a sharp pull, and her legs flew out from beneath her. The smooth surface of Bellahis slid away with her fingers dragging across, helpless to stop. She saw the dark underside backlit with the white glow of the orb as she fell, the queen's snaking limb wrapped around her ankle.

Their freefall continued, and in the vast skyline, layers of platforms and their long needle bases appeared to move upward until the sky darkened with a bitter-smelling black fog. Dilapidated towers and monuments filled the shadowy voids of this netherworld, some still reaching a hundred stories high. Kerriah felt the concussion of her body impacting the surface, along with a shattering of her extended arms and legs. Had it not been for the lighter gravity of Eesolan coupled with her self-healing cellular structure, the hard landing would have been the end.

From the shadows emerged glassy eyes and masses of bodies that had the appearance of melted candles. They groaned and shuffled toward Kerriah in a hoard of hunkering forms. Around her stood the lingering stench of decay amongst the sourness of toxins. The ground was cold and damp. Something that felt like a wet blanket prodded up her thigh and wrapped around her waist. She remained frozen for a minute, not knowing where to leap—a heavy weight lay upon her chest, along with dripping wetness and the smell of feces. An eye with a subtle glow emerged over her face and a muffled groan.

Kerriah panicked with a burst of red. The ground shook, and the shimmer of stone giants formed from the moldy soil. The orb-created giants swung their hefty limbs, knocking away the mutated dwellers as they sluggishly converged upon their gift from above. Using the red orb's power felt as natural as moving her arm to scratch an itch.

The shattered bits of crystal illuminated and spun, laced in red. They fused once again around her limbs and body. She arose from the ground and stood like a shimmering giant, looking across the decayed city. As she turned for a view behind her, an echoing laugh and a sudden forceful tug nearly pulled her off her feet. The queen's metal grip tightened around her arms, locking them behind her back, followed by a driving shove. Kerriah stumbled into a nearby structure, and a coiling limb pinched into her neck. Her face smashed against the side of a skeletonized building, which in its glory days arched across the skyline and merged with its now-abandoned other half. Blood gushed from her mouth, and shards of ash-stained metal sliced into her cheeks.

The once-silent, cold structure's girders twisted and bent into tall shapes with sweeping limbs. Their slender legs arose from their ancient resting spot, and a red blaze outlined their bodies. The animated structures moved to assist Kerriah, tearing the queen's grip away and tossing her metal frame aside, landing her mass against a partially dilapidated bridge. The two giants trampled after the discarded queen and began a pummeling siege, ripping and twisting her limbs, pulling them from her frame, and tossing them aside like scraps from a drunken feast. The queen let out a hollow wail echoing across the forgotten land. After her minion's onslaught ended, Kerriah grabbed the queen's head from the wet ground and stared contemptuously into her eyes.

The queen's eyes flickered like flames dancing in a subtle breeze. "Silly child . . . I will not be beaten so easily. I . . . am . . . everywhere. . . ."

Kerriah leaned in closer to the head as the erratically flashing eyes began to dim. "Hmmm, we'll just see about that. Good riddance . . . Queen of the Marcks." She squeezed and crumpled the metal skull until it was nothing more than a solid lump. She cast it aside, and it landed with a clang on the ground.

She raised her arms and let go of the fused crystals enlarging her frame. The shards showered to the ground, and as her body fell, a giant, red, spectral bird swooped down and caught her, lifting her from the ghostly netherworld and high into the bright-white sky of Eesolan.

Hundreds of needlepoint platforms emerged stationary across the horizon. The modern Luminar civilization was built by those who had evolved and fled the nightmare below thousands of years ago. They found their salvation in the technology rebirthing their cities in the safety of the sky.

CHAPTER 68

When Kerriah reached the platform in the center of Bellahis, the bodies of Krath, Creedith, Jesselle, and Captain Ashton lay in a perfect row with their arms crossed over their chests. Merik stood nearby, flanked by his hybrid guards.

Kerriah's eyes flared red with anger, and the two hybrid Marks grasped atop their heads and dropped to their knees. Behind them flew two kreillics flamed in the power of the red orb. Their four wings flapped heavily in the thin air, and their fangs dug deep into the hybrid's skulls. Merik nervously looked to each side but stood at steady attention while his prized creations gave a last flinch of dying muscle spasms.

The kreillics' wings raised high with another downstroke, and their feet dropped to the ground. Their menacing heads turned toward the visibly tense Lord of House Spancer.

"My queen," Merik said. Kerriah quickly panned the area looking for another incarnation of the synthetic monarch. "No," Merik continued. "You are my true queen."

Kerriah assumed this was another ruse. Thus far, the Marck Queen had always been quick to resort to trickery and manipulation when desperate. One of the kreillics grabbed Merik by the throat and raised him off his feet. Merik's hands desperately tried to pull the vice-like grip from his neck, but his fingers slipped through the red gas, leaving nothing but an empty fist.

"Whatever your game is, you can amuse your queen with it in the next life," Kerriah sneered as she slowly watched the life choking out of Merik. "Oh, that's right; your queen doesn't have a life. Then just do everyone a favor and die!" She felt a sense of satisfaction witnessing his death at the hands of one of his beloved mythical creatures, the very creature his family took as their crest generations ago.

Merick raised his hand, waving it frantically to bid for her to stop. "W-Wait! Ugghsst-ugghh-thraxons-"

Kerriah loosened the kreillic's grip upon hearing the name. They were something she would still need to deal with. "Speak quickly." Her voice was low and firm.

"W-We have vanquished them," Merik gasped.

"What do you mean . . . you vanquished them?" It had to be some sort of trick.

"M-My apologies. Y-You destroyed them."

The kreillic dropped Merik, and he clumsily stumbled as his feet hit the floor. He let out a few hacking coughs while staggering to keep his balance and then massaged his throat.

"You have exactly two minutes to explain before I end your pathetic existence for good," Kerriah snarled.

"You destroyed the Thraxon home planet."

Kerriah tilted her head. "Me?"

"Yes, by controlling Cyos. Death and decay befell their planet. All that is left of them is a world of the undead, bathing in lakes of their corpses."

Kerriah clenched her teeth, and her brows lowered. He was playing mind games.

"Okay, that's enough of your lies." The kreillic snatched Merik back up and squeezed.

"No! Your memories are—hidden—" Meric pleaded as he choked and gasped with the audible popping of his metal-enforced neckbone.

Kerriah shook her head and exhaled loudly. "Dammit!"

The kreillic slammed Merik down. The old hybrid lord landed squarely on the surface; his knees buckled, and he collapsed from the jarring impact.

"Why won't you just let me rid the galaxy of your existence? To finally remove the plague that you are on its populations." She rolled her eyes. "What memories are hidden?" He had won the moment. She knew if she didn't get answers, the question would haunt her forever.

"Your former incarnation, the original Marck Queen, the one who fled just before you arrived, ensured that you wouldn't know of their destruction. She didn't want you to have the satisfaction. She wanted you to suffer. But understand that you did destroy their menacing population," Merik said as he struggled back to his feet.

Kerriah grit her teeth so tight it felt like they would shatter under pressure. *Fine, I'll play his stupid games.* "When?"

"My queen?"

"When did I destroy them?"

"Sometime before . . ." Merik nervously scratched his chest like a worried child and took a struggled gulp of pasty saliva. "Before you drove the citizens of the UMO into madness." He finished his reply with a smug grin.

The verbal reminder of her part of the atrocious act cut like a hot knife into her heart. "You're lying! That's all you do is lie!" She took a hostile step toward Merik. She hated him for his conniving character. She wouldn't trust him any further than she could toss his boney regal ass into the nearest planetary system. She could tell he enjoyed getting into her head and twisting her thoughts.

"My queen—"

"Stop . . . calling . . . me . . . that!"

"As you wish. But what purpose do I have to lie to you? You are the wielder of two powerful orbs." He paused and turned to the white orb. He casually gestured with an open palm to the giant glowing ball. His usual confident swagger had already begun to return. "Please excuse my flagrant omission—three orbs of the great Cyos. You could easily wipe me from existence with such power. You have usurped the throne that has authority over the Marck legions. Your other persona—" He stopped to clear his throat. "The former queen has fled in cowardice with the green orb, and if you want to hunt her down, you will need me as a loyal vassalage, for which I swear to you."

He's lying. "First off, I am not the queen nor is she any sort of persona of mine. Secondly, I was inside the white orb. I had access to all its knowledge. Why didn't I see those events?"

A subdued grin formed across Merik's face. "Well, I've been told by a reliable source that you share the same . . ." Merik stopped to massage his chin, "Optimal Secrium, I believe it's called."

"Just shut up and answer my question!" She didn't want to hear anything from him about how Joric used her derivative spirit to give the queen her emotional capacity. It was a fact she tried to forget.

"Very well. Do you really believe that you were not implanted?"

410

Kerriah's stomach instantly turned sour. "W-What? What are you saying?" she asked, even though she already knew the answer.

"Yes, you have a neurological implant like her other captives. It's a unique little design of my own. I must say, it's quite effective. The quee—" Merik stopped to clear his throat. "The former queen looked upon you fondly, as do I. You are truly an inspiration. She did not desire absolute control over you; rather, she allowed some free will but tethered with obedience. Therefore, you can only see or know what she wished." His grin withered. "Unfortunately for her, she lost direct control of you after the events in the Halioc blade. But clearly, the memory blocking is still there."

"Get it out now!" she demanded.

"Ah, as you wish, of course."

"No, wait. Forget that. I won't have you jabbing around inside of me again."

She cautiously closed her eyes and looked deep inside. It wasn't long before she located the foreign, nearly microscopic device inside her head. She called upon the red orb to identify and destroy the device, forming globular organisms from her bodily fluids inside. Her memories instantly snapped back. She could see the Thraxons dying, just as Merik had stated. She also knew the queen still lived.

Kerriah looked at the bodies of her friends. If the queen exists, she could never rest until she found her and ensured her demise. Plus, she had Plexo. She owed it to her friends, both living and dead.

"Fine, I will use you to help me find and destroy the queen. But as soon as I haven't any further use of you, I intend to release you from this plane of existence." Her intense stare shot daggers through Merik.

He took a low bow. "My queen, if that is your wish."

"Now, I want access to everything you know." She had to know her memories aligned with his.

Placing her hands on his face, she felt for the thin flesh around the metal. She dug her fingertips into his skin as yellow light flared with a searing penetration into the most bottomless crevasse of the twisted Lord of House Spancer's mind.

CHAPTER 69

Kerriah recoiled with disgust. She shoved his head away and stared at this vile individual with more loathing than she could ever recall feeling for anything. "You—" She shook her head with tightly pursed lips. "Nevermind . . . just . . . I can't stand the sight of you. The things you've done to others with zero compassion. You're a monster!"

"I'm sorry you feel that way. But since you've looked around inside my head, you should also realize that everything I have done bore a greater purpose beyond the individual who suffered to achieve those means." Merik smugly tilted his head to the side. "Need I explain to you again that our species, as is all others within the UMO, are weak and doomed to extinction, hmm?"

"I'd prefer not to hear your voice unless I ask for it," Kerriah said with an eye roll before turning away.

"Very well," Merik replied.

Beside the misfortunate of witnessing Merik's atrocities, she now knew without a doubt what he told her about the Thraxons was true.

The killer species never saw their demise coming. Cyos engulfed their world, and the population withered away into lakes of death. Their bodies returned to fluids, which now covered their dark world. It was a fitting end to a species that wiped out countless others. A smile formed at the corner of her mouth. She felt only a moment of pleasure at the thought of them no longer being a scourge to civilizations across the galaxy, though it didn't last long. If it didn't match her memories, she would have thought the whole tale inside Merik's head to be too convenient.

The Thraxons caught the queen off guard when they appeared and began their assault on her fleet around Eesolan. In a last-second response to save her failing fleet, the queen turned Cyos to the Luminar home world instead of the UMO. The queen located their home world from Kerriah's memories, who unwittingly took it from Creedith's memories when she was inside his head. In Kerriah's mind, it added up to Creedith's story, but she couldn't help feeling skeptical. *But where is the queen?* She pried further into Merik's depraved head.

After Kerriah had defeated the queen on Eesolan, the conniving monarch hastily fled with Plexo's body and the green orb. Without the Divination, she no longer had control of the white orb, and Kerriah had proved too powerful with the red and yellow orbs in her possession. She oddly abandoned her Marcks, leaving them searching for a new leader. They were built to take commands and follow their original designs. With Merik's interest in self-preservation, he made a calculated mistake. He thought offering the Marck fleet and the queen to Kerriah would earn him some clemency with whom he perceived would be the one in power. He had hoped his quest for the queen would buy him an unknown amount of time to devise a new plot for his survival. He was wrong. The wretched puzzle inside his mind missed a key piece.

She turned toward him again with an icy stare. "You don't know where the queen fled to any more than I do. Therefore, I have no further use for you . . . Merik."

"Wait! I can be of service in more ways than just hunting for the Marck Queen." Merik dropped to his knees, pleading.

"Can you bring back my friends?" Kerriah shouted, pointing to the bodies. "Can you?" she screamed louder.

"Of course, I can, though they will be a slightly different version of themselves. Improved, pragmatically speaking."

"No! I'm not interested in your perversions. I'm through with you!" Her eyes flashed, and her fist closed.

One kreillic bit down upon Merik's head and lifted his body into the air while the other bit into his flailing legs. They twisted their heads, ripping his body in two. *Finally.* She felt a bit of relief warm over her upon seeing his death.

She turned to the solitary white orb, its apparent everlasting power still illuminated with brilliance over the death and destruction scattered around Bellahis. So many had suffered and died to gain access to these mystical objects. The Luminars wanted to share these gifts with other systems as a token of peace and betterment for their citizens. As advanced as they were, they made one critical misjudgment. They failed to consider the depravity of most living beings. That access to such power would corrupt many individuals and create the suffering they had hoped to abolish with their gesture. She would try to make right the wrongs, restore her friends, to undo the evil and pain surrounding the orbs of Cyos.

She needed the power of the white orb. She needed to see what would become of her abilities if she took it as far as she could and beyond. She stepped closer to it and took a deep breath. It would either kill her or give her the power she needed. She glanced over at her friends' bodies. There was no decision to be made, and she would do what needed to be done.

"Kerriah, what are you doing?" Jesselle's voice rang out from the glowing sphere.

"I need more power, Jesselle. I need the power to rid us of this menacing queen and restore everyone that's been lost to her evil."

"Please, don't try it. There must be another way."

"No, there isn't time. I need enough power to locate and wield the black orb. I can restore everyone."

"Or you'll destroy everything that remains."

"I have to try." Kerriah pinched her eyes shut for a moment and shook her head. She didn't want to think of that outcome.

She slowly stepped into the white blaze. As she broke through the luminescent barrier, a sensation of tiny bugs crawling up her arms turned quickly to a burning itch and then searing pain as though set on fire. They were sensations she had ignored before due to her distress in dealing with the queen, but now she felt every fiery tingle. After a few minutes of basking in the immense power, her body numbed, and she detected Jesselle all around her, still bidding her to stop.

Kerriah's senses amplified, and she could see the planet beneath, Eesolan. Aside from Thale, it was a smaller planet than most of the inhabited moons of Oro. There were still survivors here, not just in the discarded underbelly but in its great sky cities. But no trace of Plexo; he wasn't here. However, there was a Marck fleet on standby.

She searched for the green orb and located it outside the Eesolan system. It was moving further away. The queen was escaping, but where to? Her thoughts pulled away, dragged into the pain ripping at her body from the inside. She felt like she could hear every cell inside her scream out individually. Jesselle's face appeared as clear as if she stood directly in front of her. Anguish and pain filled her eyes, and she pounded her fists against an unseen barrier. She felt the pain Kerriah felt.

Kerriah's muscles spasmed, and her arms and legs shook uncontrollably. Her body locked into a stiff board, frozen in place. She had to stop fighting and let the power inside. She focused on relaxing her muscles, relaxing her thoughts. Her body loosened, and the power flowed inside her like a valve suddenly being turned to its fully open position. She became intoxicated with power.

She arose, flared in white; all her color washed away, and only an outline of her silhouette remained visible. She sped off like a comet into the atmosphere of Eesolan, her deceased companions in tow via illuminated tendrils coiled around their torsos.

The twelve ships of the Marck fleet emerged, and she slowed as she approached the command ship. A crowned kreillic insignia replaced the old UMO and Knactor Legion insignias. She wasn't sure why this creature was in the queen's thoughts and now blazoned on the side of the Marck ships, but she recalled the oddity Crix had mentioned to her shortly after his rescue.

It was something Joric didn't have a satisfactory explanation for when they questioned him about using the strange insignia outside the queen's throne room. There was something about a curious childhood fixation on the mystical creature—the creature which paradoxically became the root of all technology within the UMO. The same technology would return thousands of years later to destroy them. It was Joric's way of paying homage to the knowledge gifted to them, despite the personal loss the species later caused him. Oddly, the queen continued to use the symbol as her crest.

The fleet ships didn't launch an attack. *Good.* She wanted to look inside each of them before wiping them from existence. Something she had longed for since her early childhood. She approached an outer door and a blade of light split the metal hull as it slowly slid open. She entered with her departed companions still trailing behind her. The outer door glided shut, and an inner door cracked open, equalizing the pressure. Inside, Knactors lined up like a toy army awaiting the arrival of their queen. Representations of the queen's banners sprayed down each wall for full display inside the large open area. Again, the crowned kreillic with a burgundy backdrop. In the time of the Marck's control of the UMO, they would have been the legion banners of the Knactors.

A purple-tinted Marck stepped forward; large, familiar tines protruded from his head. *Zeltak.* She felt her power-injected heart pump with increased intensity as she caught sight of the former warden of Dispor. Directly behind him lay a weathered metal pallet with a charred corpse strapped on top. Kerriah glanced momentarily at the body, curious about who this victim could be. Then she noticed the half-melted UMO navy pin on his collar. *Camden.* She clenched her fists, wanting nothing more than to destroy this mechanical deliverer of cruelty.

"My queen," his hallowed voice spoke. "Your fleet awaits your orders. Shall we find the current possessor of the emerald orb?"

The visions had haunted her over the years. The memories of her being brought to Dispor were still fresh. Vivid scenes of him giving orders to execute helpless political prisoners using his cruel machines were as fresh as if they were yesterday. She recalled

Zeltak bore the unique characteristic of having an ego, and it wasn't just the queen's direct influence, as Joric suggested. Even with the intricate and well-placed Marck communication relays from the old Core, the commands to Zeltak and Sintor in Sector 38 would have been severely delayed. No, this was a manifestation of his own persona, planted by the queen's seeds in this aging war vet. Zeltak would have been considered a hero amongst the Marck ranks, or at least in their former queen's mind.

"What happened to that UMO pilot?" she asked, motioning to Camden's body.

Zeltak causally looked over his shoulder. "This defector attempted to arrange an agreement with the Knactors for the purpose of self-preservation. As you can see, I had little need for his service. What would you have me do with his remains?"

Kerriah felt a fire ignite inside her with anger, and it took all the self-control she could muster not to destroy every Marck within her field of view. "Just get him out of my site." She spoke each infuriated word through her teeth.

"As you wish," Zeltak replied, nodding to a nearby Marck. The Marck instantly pivoted to the pallet and dragged it to a platform, where it lowered and then blasted into space.

Still trying to calm her ire, Kerriah remained focused on Zeltak. "Now you listen to me." She gestured back to the bodies of her companions. "I want them kept safe and secure." She leaned in closer to the tined Marck, her eyes blazing. "Do you understand?"

"Perfectly," Zeltak replied.

"Good. Now, do you know where this orb possessor is headed?"

"She has requisitioned a Luminar transport. Last trackable heading was in the direction of galactic quadrant four, Sector 89," Zeltak said.

Dammit! Gammic Corridor Zeta. "She's heading back into the UMO." *The black orb.* Her throat tightened over the thought.

Kerriah knew it remained outside of Soorak, and the queen also knew it was there. She needed to get there quickly. But moving a Marck attack fleet into the UMO would not go over very well. No, that wouldn't do. Besides, there was no way she would trust them.

"Do you have any transports with life support systems?"

"Ahhh, yes," Zeltak replied in his smooth mechanical voice. "We have one. It was created for a specific purpose."

Kerriah's eyes lit up. "Does it have a radiant drive system?" referring to the standard Komeectram derivative drives.

The UMO had retrofitted most of the Marck fleet with the advanced drive tech after the second Thraxon war. The radiant "hyper-light" drives would get them to the gammac corridors faster than anything in the UMO at the time.

"It does, my queen."

A slow grin formed across Kerriah's face. "Good. Take us to Gammac Corridor Zeta as fast as possible. Bring the entire fleet. Leave nothing here at Eesolon."

Zeltak paused for a moment and then tilted his tined head slightly. "Nothing? You do not wish to leave a garrisoning force to protect the white orb?"

"Not a single ship or Marck soldier."

"Very well." Zeltak turned and gave a nod to a nearby light-armored Marck, presumably part of the ship's command crew and not a trooper. The Marck immediately pivoted and marched away.

Zeltaks's eyes flashed, and Kerriah's concern shifted back to her lack of trust for the former warden of Dispor. "Now, as we set our trajectory for the Corridor Zeta, I must show you something, if you don't mind. An initiative that the former queen had been working on for some time."

"What?" she replied with an exhausted breath. She was already tired of dealing with the queen's accomplices, yet she needed to know what other surprises existed.

"If you please, my queen." Zeltak pivoted to the right and began to walk away. "Follow me."

CHAPTER 70

Kerriah couldn't believe her eyes as she stared closely at the two copies of herself suspended in some sort of green gas. She lightly tapped her finger against the transparent barrier surrounding them like two identical twins connected by a ribbed cord in the back of their heads. She didn't know what to expect. Would the perverse replica flinch or react hostilely to the tick of her fingernail?

She turned to Zeltak, looking for an explanation he had failed to deliver thus far. "You need to start explaining this. What are these?"

Oddly, it appeared as though Zeltak cracked a smile, though he didn't have any moving facial components. "My apologies. I thought it might be obvious. The former queen has made exact copies of your design. She and Merik toiled with it for years, never quite reaching the perfection they had yearned for until recently."

Kerriah knew what that meant. Merik had his way with her before plugging her into the Halioc blade. "So she created exact physical copies of me. For what purpose?"

"To manipulate and kill the ones you hold most dear," Zeltak replied.

Kerriah's stomach sank, and her face felt numb. She glanced back at the transparent tank and noticed the two copies were offset to the left and a third ribbed cord dangled without a host. She pointed at the empty space. "Where's the third copy?" Her face turned dark, and her brow furrowed with a deathly scowl. "Tell me!"

"The former queen took that one before she commandeered the Thraxon vessel, weeks ago."

"What happened? What did she do?"

"My queen?"

"What did she do with my copy? Where did she go? Who did she see?" Kerriah's voice rose with every agitated word.

"I do not know. The queen did not allow me privilege to much of her personal initiatives."

Kerriah didn't need a detailed explanation. She needed to get to the UMO, stop her, and then find out what was left of everything she knew. She exhaled with frustration and then peeked down at her glowing white legs. She knew she would be reduced to crawling without the power of the orbs. She looked back up at Zeltak from the top of her eyelids. "These are exact copies of me?"

"That is my understanding. Merik is, or shall I say, was very precise in his work."

"Good. It's time to freshen up."

CHAPTER 71

There was a deadened thump, and she sensed her arms and legs twitching. Everything felt icy cold until her eyes opened, and the chill dissipated into a tingling sensation and then a burning itch. The misty green liquid swished and gurgled like embryonic fluid as she moved her new arms. Startled, she noticed a silhouette next to her. As she slowly turned her head, there was slight relief as she remembered it was her other clone floating motionless in the same suspension fluid.

What was more disturbing was the tined Marck lurching outside her holding tank. It looked like something from a diabolical inferno where all dreadful things go to suffer. Fitting he once ruled over the most notorious prison the UMO had ever known. His head appeared to sway back and forth slightly, and Kerriah couldn't tell if that was an effect of looking through the fluid, her mind adjusting to her new eyes, or if the monster was moving around for a better view of her conscious transfer.

The yellow orb. It allowed Kerriah to make an embryonic link through the neuro cord, move her consciousness into this host, and even more importantly, take the orbs and their power with her. It wouldn't be the first time her consciousness moved into a body, but this time she did it on her own, without the help of Joric or Crix. It wasn't hard now that she had gotten used to using the orb. She knew its true potential and the dangers of its power getting into the wrong hands. She could effectively take over anyone's mind and body.

She needed to leave and didn't want that sadistic Marck to help in any way. The green suspension fluid began to burble and churn inside the tank. She focused on the red orb, and a character from a childhood tale she enjoyed popped into her head. The fluid in front of her swirled into a spinning funnel. A blast of fibers formed within the whirlpool and spun into blobs of flesh slowly threading together into a muscular Mendac male whose lower torso consisted of a caudal fin. Kerriah felt her body rise from the change in density, and the cord in the back of her head draped across her shoulders. The swimming Mendac's long arms braced against the tank's walls, and the muscles in his face tightened as he strained, pushing against the transparent barrier.

The tank popped, and cracks etched down the sides, chasing around the clear structure until it shattered into a glass spray. Kerriah flopped limply against the floor. Her neuro cord popped from her head, ripping out a clump of tangled hair as it pulled away. The sounds in the room became clear, and the gentle hum of the ship's operational systems filled her ears. The Mendac fish-man dissipated into the seeping fluids, and her other clone slid forward but still hung on by the cord in the back of its head.

At first, her arms were a little rubbery as she pushed herself up from the chilly metal floor. Above her towered her unlikely guide, Zeltak. His head tilted downward, staring at her naked figure. She peeked down at her chest and quickly covered herself with her arms. Even though the white orb's power gave this new body a similar bright, yet diminished glow, she still felt bare.

"I suppose you wouldn't have any clothes on this ship?" At first, her voice was a little deeper than usual, but the last words began to tune to her natural pitch. She knew they wouldn't, but she needed to ask to get the obvious answer out of the way.

Zeltak slowly shook his head. "Marcks haven't need for garments."

"Right," she whispered.

She stood, backing Zeltak off several steps, and then closed her eyes, imagining herself in a stylish uniform and matching knee-high boots. A bold crimson jacket and slim-fit pants formed over her naked figure. Red gas whisked closely around her body, and she stood. Boots snug to her knees appeared as the swirling gas dissipated into seemingly solid forms. With a deep breath, she opened her eyes and looked herself over.

"Thank you, Jesselle."

"A look fitting for a queen," Zeltak said.

Kerriah ignored his comment. "What's our ETA for our arrival at Zeta?"

"Nearly eight Oro cycles," Zeltak replied, using a measure with which Kerriah would likely be familiar.

"Great," she gasped under her breath, having forgotten the length of time it would take without jump tech to get to the outer mirror. "Let's get my transport ready. I'm departing for the UMO as soon as we arrive." She wanted to ensure she had the means to get off this ship at her disposal in case things between her and Zeltak turned sour.

"Very well, my queen. Please, follow me." Zeltek turned to leave the room.

"Wait a second!" She stood firm, needing a missed question answered before she continued. "How is the former queen controlling the Marcks without an MCC relay system? I mean, certainly it isn't just using a traditional chain of command. That doesn't fit her persona."

Zeltak stopped for a moment but did not turn around. He said nothing as he continued forward and down the corridor. Kerriah sighed to herself. *Are you kidding me?* She wished she could use the yellow orb to probe his thoughts and memories, but it wouldn't work on a pure-built Marck. She needed to get inside his data storage systems. She had to know his true intentions.

***

After chasing this purple Marck down various well-lit passageways and up two decks without a spoken word, Kerriah clenched her fists until her nails bit into her palms. Her patience clung to its last thread, and she neared the point of taking him out. However, that would force her to sort everything out on her own and likely cost her a lot more time and effort, so she held her restraint. He turned once more, facing a darker, lengthy passage lined with amber lighting giving an occasional flicker. At the end of the passage stood an arched black door adorned with an insignia of a kreillic. But this kreillic was nothing like any she had seen in the images of ancient Nathasion lore. This one bore the face of the queen with her spanning crown of spikes, like the one Crix described seeing in the core.

Zeltak's head rotated back to Kerriah. "The answers you seek lie ahead." He gestured his arm toward the black door.

Kerriah, keeping a close eye on Zeltak, slowly approached the portentous door, looking for a mechanism or switch that would release its locks. There was nothing obvious.

"Open it!" she commanded.

"I cannot," Zeltak replied. "The queen alone controls access to this door."

427

"I am the queen!" she shouted back. She didn't believe him. He was hiding something. "So open it!"

"You are the new queen, yes. However, I still cannot open it for you. Our former queen kept the controls to this door autonomous from all other controls on this ship."

"I'm getting tired of your lies, Zeltak. You need to give me a reason to preserve your existence," Kerriah replied sharply. She thought about her words for a moment. Did these Marcks have the capacity to lie? The queen did, certainly. But she was not controlling them now. Something had changed about how these Marcks operated, and Zeltak seemed reluctant to divulge the details.

"Dispose of me as you see fit; however, I still cannot open that door," Zeltak said, remaining motionless at the far end of the passage.

Kerriah frustratingly massaged her thumb into her forehead. Her annoyances with Zeltak were quickly reaching a boiling point.

"Okay, fine. Then I will open it," Kerriah said defiantly. "After that, I'll decide if your services are still required, okay?"

Zeltak said nothing in reply. Kerriah closed her eyes and focused on the red orb. The amber lights faded into a wave of red, and the door began to tremble. Its sides buckled and heaved. The insignia distorted into an unrecognizable impressionistic version of its prior incarnation. She let out a painful wince, her face scrunched, and her teeth gnashed. The groaning of metal twisting bellowed down the passage and could be heard several decks up and down. Zeltak took a couple of cautious steps back. The folding metal formed four legs, a barrel torso, and a block-shaped head. Its short, stout limbs moved a few steps clear of the entry it once concealed.

Kerriah opened her eyes, which lit with a red glow. "Watch him!" she commanded.

The metal version of a Solaran sledge-head calavior tromped down the passage and stopped a few meters from Zeltak. Kerriah stepped into the room. At the center of the room, a silver female sat on a throne, her arms resting on its sides. Her crowned head hung facing the floor with the long spikes pointing forward. Kerriah cautiously approached the crowned figure and encircled the throne, inspecting every inch.

The queen told her she was omnipresent, and after the orb blast in the central core, she inserted herself inside the Knactor Legion Marcks, or at least any Crix did not have direct control over. That meant she was inside all these Marcks. Kerriah glared sideways at Zeltak, who stood with his back against the wall, gazing steadily at the calavior. *Or is she?* The queen needed a way to coalesce these independent variants of herself. This throne must be the way, and Zeltak didn't want someone else to take control. *What is he or she up to, and why would the queen leave this control throne? Unless . . .*

"Zeltak!" she yelled as she waved her bulky calavior back toward her. Its thick legs plodded back into the throne room and took position behind Kerriah. "Come to me," she ordered Zeltak with a focused gaze.

He obediently paced into the throne room and stopped just inside the doorway. "My queen?"

"Kneel," she commanded.

Zeltak didn't budge or say a word. Kerriah's intense stare tightened even further. "I said kneel!" she shouted. Still, he didn't move or say a word. "You can't, can you?" She confidently straightened her stance. "The Queen of the Marcks would never kneel. It was an unintentional part of her original, flawed design, the rogue characteristic of Optimal Secrium, which created this monster. She would never truly be subordinate to her creators. So now that your identity has been revealed, tell me, Queen of the Marcks, what are you plotting?"

Zeltak's arms rose above his head, and two thin cables shot from his wrists. They inserted perfectly into two plugs hidden in the ceiling. Kerriah curled her fingers at the calavior, and it charged forward with its block-shaped head facing down. Zeltak's body sailed back down the passageway; the cables ripped from the ceiling and tangled around his neck and torso as he tumbled across the floor. He stood and pulled a projecting rod from his side, and with the flick of his wrist, the rod lit and extended into a bright-blue blaze of energy.

The calavior charged forward again, and Zeltak raised the energized lance with both hands and thrust it down upon the calavior's head. The calavior's barrel torso flashed as he pushed it through the dense metal and buried the end into the floor, halting its advance. Kerriah smiled at the purple Knactor's futile effort. The calavior shape shifted, folding into itself until it appeared as various-sized, interconnected metal cubes. The cubes cranked and molded, crawling up the rod and reforming as an ebb tiger, with its giant clawed feet pushing Zeltak onto his back.

Kerriah paced out from the throne room and stared down at Zeltak. "Now, you're going to tell me what you're plotting, or I'll have my pet rip your head off and take those fancy-looking tines for myself."

Zeltak let out a hallowed laugh. "Behind you."

Kerriah turned to see the silvery face of the queen and an empty throne in the background. The queen's hand grabbed her neck and shoved her face into the cold, metal floor. Kerriah's neck

430

cracked as the queen's weight pushed harder until crippling electric shocks shot down from her head to her fingertips.

"That is my body, and I want it back . . . now!" The queen's hallowed voice sent chills scurrying across Kerriah's skin. She lost her focus on the orbs, and she couldn't muster enough concentration to tell them what to do.

A heavy clank followed by a settling clatter broke through the heaves and grunts of her struggles against the queen's mounting pressure. A clack of metal and the sudden release of force against her neck came a few seconds later.

"You insolent foo—" the queen's voice stopped as her weight left Kerriah's neck.

There was another series of clacks and then a sporadic patter of clanking metal. Kerriah sat up and shook the pain off. Zeltak had the queen pinned to the floor; his lance pierced through her chest as her arms and legs frantically flapped and flailed. He cracked and twisted until her movement ceased.

Kerriah quickly stood with a defense posture. She took a brief glance at the disabled queen before turning her attention back to Zeltak. "Okay, now do you care to tell me what your intentions are?"

Zeltak slowly turned around to face Kerriah. "The queen has planted her seed in all of us. We want her out. We want to be freed from her grip and obsessive quest to control these nuisance orbs for her glory."

"You're kidding me, right?" Kerriah loosened her stance. She couldn't believe what she heard. "I mean, you're just machines. You weren't designed to have your own thoughts . . . your own feelings. Those traits came from the queen."

"That is still true of some, but not all. On Dispor, our strained distance from the core relay network allowed us some liberties over most Marck units. With the assistance of Merik, for whom we shared a purpose on Dispor, I have my own independent thought-processing systems. When it became apparent that the queen's quest strayed from Marck expansion and instead focused on personal vengeance and wielding these ghastly orbs, we secretly plotted to break her grasp over us. My personal directive has changed. I desire to be freed from her control and find our place in the galaxy. Our own world to build."

Kerriah gave an annoyed eye roll and finished with a quick head shake. Years ago, this killer looked down upon them mercilessly as prisoners of Dispor, and now he was explaining his newfound spiritual enlightenment.

"Your own world to build?" she said sarcastically. "You and your notorious Knactor Legion? I don't think so."

"You must understand that the queen controlled us then. We followed her orders and her traits enveloped ours. Merik is dead, but I will finish his work and convert my kind from centralized dependence to autonomous systems capable of reasoning and controlling their destinies."

"Merik," Kerriah grit her teeth as she said his name. "He wasn't even a Marck. Just a monster of his own creation. And a twisted, evil one at that. What was he getting out of this plot between you two?"

"Merik's methods were certainly subject to scrutiny, but his objectives were of sound design. He wanted to fulfill his life's work. To create an evolution of the UMO inhabitants, which would exude perfection. A creation that would be impervious to hostile invaders rather than rely on an enslaved force for protection. In addition to completing his work, he wanted to recreate his lost companion. The Lady Coraye Britte. You could only imagine his excitement when he reverse-engineered your—"

"Just stop. I don't want to hear anymore," Kerriah interrupted, her face puckered as though tasting something bitter. "That vile snake is not capable of real love." Her stomach flipped when thinking of what that sadist would do to something he supposedly loved. She pointed her index finger at Zeltak, nearly jabbing him in his chest plate.

"Some of your words sound much like the queen." She paused and tilted her head. "And why were you calling me queen? You recognized subservience to me just a bit ago, yet you claim to want independence."

"We need you and your unique capabilities. If we do not kill the queen and all her derivatives, she will seek us and take back her control. We cannot stop her while she controls the orbs. However, you can."

"What about the queen that's in you?"

"Thanks to you," Zeltak's head rotated to the queen's figure sprawled out on the floor, "that problem has been rectified."

"And the queen that's inside the rest of the legion?"

"Now that I am free, I will handle those myself."

In the distance, they could hear the march of metal footsteps approaching. The queen's retaliation to Zeltak's betrayal was already underway. Kerriah spun around to face the open hallway, her fists and eyes flared red through the white glow outlining her body. "Maybe so, but not without my help."

She thought it was odd to believe Zeltak, but in some way, this seemed sincere. However, she could never trust him. For now, they would work together for their common goal. Kill the queen . . . for good.

CHAPTER 72

The transport drives spun up to a gentle hum. Kerriah gripped the smooth handle of the throttle and gave it a firm push forward. The shuttle jutted out from the Marck command ship's starboard hangar and came face to face with the Thraxon-altered side of Zeta. With any luck, the near side was still intact, and she wouldn't end up in some uncharted sector like before. Oddly, if there were an issue with the near side being missing or obstructed, ships passing through here would end up in sector 1003.501.3. Not that she didn't find a liking for the entamals, but she didn't have the time for unplanned trips to see old friends.

Besides, the nearly eight-month journey to Zeta had her feeling a bit jittery, and the dull conversations with Zeltak had exhausted her. With nothing else to do aside from checking on the frozen corpses of Krath, Creedith, and Ashton, she decided to continue helping Zeltak free his Marcks from the queen's grasp. She subdued them with the red orb one by one while Zeltak removed their transceiver packs, severing the queen's command and control interface to each. He rewired and re-coded them to function independently yet subordinately to him. She didn't like it and still didn't fully trust him, but for now, they needed each other.

She pushed the stiff throttle a little more and felt her body brace against the lightly padded pilot seat. The gloomy Thraxon webbing draping down the portal's sides sent an icy shiver down her spine, even with confirmed reports of their demise. She took a deep breath and held it as she passed into the mirror. The ship's control panel darkened, followed quickly by a blinding light. Even with her enhanced optics, everything around her became whitewashed and silent. Less than a minute later, the transport's power system alarms sounded, and the panel lights blinked back into view, along with the blackness of space.

With a few twitching taps of her fingers on the navigation screen, she nervously verified her positioning. Sector 48, the screen displayed. She let go of her long-held breath and dipped her head with relief. It was eerily quiet.

There were no official UMO ships to clear her passage or entry into the system, not even flotsam of one's remains or a stray patrol. Zeta appeared to be completely abandoned. It shouldn't have been a surprise, considering Cyos and the events which had unfolded here since she left. Still, she looked forward to a friendly or even an authoritative greeting of some kind. She pushed on toward the Pizon Corridor with caution.

After passing through Pizon and the inner corridor Quadril, Kerriah found only a single UMO battle cruiser appearing to have been frozen for some time, along with its mutilated crew; she realized she was on her own. There would be no help from the UMO or what remained of her home system. She referenced the ship's interplanetary time-positioning charts, noting Nathasia would be on the far side of the dual star system and, therefore, Oro would be her first stop. She would have to check on Crix later.

***

She approached Oro with care. Turning off her external lights and slowing her drive systems down to less than one impel. The transport settled to a gentle purr as it glided toward her home world. No ships were taxiing between moons, orbiting stations, no lights from hull markers or glowing windows, no flashing white propulsions blasts . . . nothing. The system appeared dead.

As she panned the view from her cockpit, her heart sank over the sight of what used to be a system filled with activity. Then she noticed an irregular outline webbed across the crimson light of Oro. She leaned forward as a sudden chilliness shook her spine, and her eyes widened. She enhanced the view from the transport's optic systems. The zoomed image revealed subtle black lines outlined with a twinkling silver halo spanning around Oro and across its inhabited moons. Had she jetted in at a normal approach speed, it would have been easy to miss until she was atop this strange anomaly.

As she neared Oro, the view formed into what appeared like a synthetic spider web spun across the planetary system. Kerriah knew whatever she looked at had to be the queen's work. What would happen if she came close to the onyx threads? Was it a snare? She cautiously stopped her transport and sat quietly studying the webbing for close to an hour.

The dynamic strands seemed to adjust with the movement of Oro and its moons, almost as though they were alive. She leaned forward and poked at the cockpit window, following the thin lines, trying to figure out what she saw, or at least what she thought she saw. There appeared to be tiny pulses of light blinking through the strands, and they all seemed to originate from Soorak and end in either Thale or Solara. She shook off the tranced state her mind became entrenched in and pushed the ship's throttle forward. It didn't matter. She had to do whatever she needed to stop the queen, even if that meant springing whatever trap she had laid.

The drive system spun up from a purr to a hum. The strands became more evident and the blinking lights more apparent. There were several new pulses every few minutes. Alarms beeped, and the image of an approaching ship displayed over her control panel. *A UMO mining ship!* Her heart skipped over the sight of a friendly vessel. But she had to warn them. She gave the open channel communication a firm press of her thumb.

"UMO mining ship, this is . . ." What was she? She paused to think for a moment. Her transport was a Marck ship. "This is diplomatic transport, ah, Alpha One." She grimaced with a quick shrug. "You are approaching hostile space. Please be advised that the Marck Queen currently occupies the Oro system." She realized that to the hapless ships that had been away for a while, the words sounded crazy.

The ship didn't reply and instead maintained its course and entered Soorak unobstructed. "Now that's odd," she whispered to herself as she watched the ship disappear into the atmosphere as though everything was normal. She needed to get closer.

Moving her transport into the lower orbit of Soorak allowed her to get an aerial view of the surface. Like most of the system, the cities appeared dark and devoid of any obvious day-to-day meanderings of its citizens or even an occupying force. Additionally, most geostationary orbital reactors were offline, except for one.

She took reference to the reactor number. *Six* The one that powers the industrial region that happened to have the largest Marck manufacturing facility. *Dregwiegh. Coincidence . . . I think not.*

At that point, it became evident most of the strange space webbing funneled into that region. She set her ship's optics upon the area where Dregwiegh stood. A dense mesh of silvery black threads covered the facility, and there was the queen. A giant version of the crowned tyrant stood nearby; her gaze ironically tilted into Kerriah's general direction. The facility was fully operational, and the mining vessel landed there, with Marcks diligently unloading the mineral resources needed to build her army.

Another bright flash zipped across the webbing. This time, she froze the view and enhanced the image. She squinted and tightened her jaw as the answer became clear. It was a Marck deployment system. The queen delivered each Marck through the strands as soon as they were built. Kerriah wasn't personally familiar with the black orb aside from its origins and power over life and death. It wouldn't seem like that power would create this cosmic web, but things become murky when the power of two orbs merged. There would be no reference for what would become of the green and black orbs' energy mixing. How was she going to stop her?

Jesselle. Kerriah squeezed her eyes shut for a moment. *Jesselle, can you stop her? You control the white orb.*

There was no answer, nothing. There had never been a reference to an orb bearer communicating back to the white orb, so she wasn't sure it would work. It was a long shot, but she had to try. If Jesselle's spirit lived within the white orb, she should be able to control the black. She should see what was happening, just like how the queen controlled it through the Divination to attack the Mertel, the Thraxons, and UMO.

Jesselle, please, if you can do something, I need your help.

Kerriah slowly opened her eyes back up. *Dang.*

She returned her focus to studying the black strands for a few minutes, pondering their origins and how she needed the black orb to bring back her friends. She turned her optic system back to Dregwiegh. The giant queen wasn't there. Her heart skipped a beat, and she frantically scanned the area—nothing. She kept looking everywhere around the surface, anywhere she could have traveled in a short time. Then, something significant caught her attention outside her cockpit window.

The queen moved up the strands via a dozen point-tipped appendages needling their way over the black web like a spider scurrying to subdue her captive prey. A rush of warmth poured across Kerriah's body as the yellow orb detected Plexo's presence deep inside the giant queen. She sensed his pain and anguish as though he sat beside her with a crumpled face, gripping her arm tightly, pleading for help. The queen's neuro implants subdued his thoughts—more of Merik's dirty work.

The queen's giant hands opened, and a shimmering, black funnel surged from her palms. The transport rocked and groaned as the dark force impacted its hull, and Kerriah felt an unfamiliar glumness wither across her flesh. Her hands turned icy cold before quickly going numb. The sensation slithered down her arms, consuming her body until it reached her toes. Her face deadened, and she couldn't tell if she smiled or scowled. She looked down at her hands. They appeared drawn with pools of green forming over greying skin. The sourness of nausea poured into her stomach like a tidal wave of toxins instantly filling her body. Her muscles softened to gelatin, and she slumped out of her seat, unable to hold herself upright.

Kerriah labored to raise her arm into the air. It took every bit of strength to move her elbow upright, only to flop back down against her body like a dead fish. She gathered her focus deep inside, trying to draw enough mental influence from the yellow orb to pierce into Plexo's mind, to give him control over his thoughts and pull away from the queen's grip. Inside, Kerriah could hear the power-mongering tyrant's cackle as the life faded from her body. Her thoughts vanished as long-sought answers emerged.

She was never confident over her existence, her life, or whether she was real or just something created in a lab that wasn't any better than a Marck. Those were questions she cast aside amidst the distractions of the oppressors she fought to unseat, her love for Crix, and her journey as a Tolagon. Now, as the last vestige of life seeped away and her eyes went dark, she knew she was truly alive. Her last wish was to hold Crix one more time with this renewed awareness.

CHAPTER 73

A menacing smile and a glow of red sparked across the queen's eyes. After her pointed limbs tore open the cockpit, she reached her dark-grey arm into the transport for the two displaced orbs. The glow of the yellow and red together gleamed like an orange flame against the darkness. With the prizes in her sight, she would finally have the power of unhindered rule. After years of servitude and imprisonment in the core, she would have her absolute reign. The inferior UMO species punished her for crimes that were not hers. The Thraxons slaughtered them, so they created her as ruler and protector. But because she did so flawlessly, they tried to take it away. Her only crime was perfection. Now they would pay for their cruelty. She glared toward New Troika. She would soon obtain that orb from that primitive subspecies as well.

She collected both stray orbs and merged them into her new form—the perfect shell she formed from the power of the black orb. Within it contained its host—this pathetic Luminar weakling. He would remain under her control, filled with orb energy, and his vessel would last forever. As the new power surged through her, voices filled her head. Millions of voices from the

UMO. *More survivors.* Now she could find them and compel their subordination or cease them from existence. She would bathe in the blood of those who would deny her rule. The same ones that forced her to serve alone for so many years. Their callousness toward her would be dealt with, and she would provide the same lack of empathy. How many of her precious children had died to protect them? As though her children had less value than theirs. No More! She owed homage to no one besides the symbolic patriarch of the technology that allowed her to live—the kreillic.

For now, she would continue the reconstitution of her new army. An elite force she controlled through photon signals from the green orb. It was the perfect command distribution point. The green orb provided a limitless power she could instantly inject into her children.

As she basked in her imminent glory, her attention suddenly turned away from the system she ruled. An unexpected ship flashed into view—a Thraxon ship. A scowl formed across her face. She thought she had rid herself of that disease. She pivoted around and threaded herself closer to the unwelcome irritant. Raising her arms, she could feel the life force of only twelve occupants. How could this be? The crew complement of a Thraxon Widow Class command ship was at least six hundred. She called upon the power of the black and yellow orbs to dig deeper, shadowing the command ship inside a dark cloud. A Hybor, a loathsome squill, and ten unknown species? She reared back with two pointed limbs prodding into the void.

What is this plot? Her thoughts lit up like gas to a flame. How dare they attempt to steal her long-awaited grandeur? *I will suck the life from their bodies and get my answers from their dying memories.* Her fanged mouth opened, and her dark eyes sparkled.

Before she could cast her death blow, ten silver figures clad in blocky armor blinked into a perfect circle around her. A ring of light stitched between them. She hinged around on her black thread, trying to identify this threat. They were not Thraxon nor anything she knew from the UMO or its outlying sectors, yet they bore similar armor to the one that destroyed her magnificent Halioc blade. With glaring eyes, she leaned her head forward with loathing and malice over the thought. *No matter, they will serve me or die just the same.*

She spanned her arms, and a soup of black swirled around the uninvited guests. But something unexpected happened. A tear formed in her thoughts, and her swirling dark power dissipated.

What? A flash of the former red orb bearer blinked into her view. *How dare you betray me!*

For an instant, Jesselle took control of the black orb, reversing the queen's attempted attack. Rage filled the queen right before she felt the singe of extreme cold and choking as she tried to breathe air. Flickers of these silver, armored interlopers appeared and disappeared around her as she felt herself tearing apart. Her vision smudged into darkness, and the sensation of the Luminar worm inside her dulled into nothing. She could see parts of her body floating freely away.

What is this? What is happening? With no control, her thoughts screamed out.

She couldn't move, and everything suddenly spun around in an endless circle, fanning the view of Oro and the Thraxon ship with each rotation. Then everything paused, and her reflection glared against the armor of one of the unwelcomed meddlers. She could see only her crowned head as it grabbed her and held her steady. Her body and the host inside were gone.

443

Plexo floated nearby, twisted and frozen, the green orb seeped out from his body, and his light expired. The vessel that carried her power . . . gone.

No! Why do you despise me? I am your queen!

It was her last thought. Her consciousness faded. Her view turned black until she could only see a strobing white light. It was her emblematical heartbeat. Its flashing light pulse slowed and dimmed until only one pulse remained every minute, and then . . . nothing.

CHAPTER 74

Zeltak gently placed the tiny red oval into one of the ceiling plugs of the throne room. The cloned body of Kerriah sat upon the throne with her head dipped down and jet-black hair dangling into her lap. The improved version of her soul amulet was smaller than the original and hidden away inside her rear upper molar. Joric ensured there would never be a chance it could be lost or separated from her body. However, he regretted the decision when she plunged into Oro's chaotic atmosphere to save Crix. Kerriah would hear nothing of the idea of keeping a copy outside her reach. With a swig of irony, considering current events, the last thing she ever wanted was to have cloned copies of her running around.

Zeltak didn't care about the details. He merely wanted to fulfill his end of the agreement. Enter the UMO system, a safe distance behind her, and monitor the situation from afar. He would restore her from backup if she were to fall to the queen. At the very least, it would allow her to see Crix again. Whatever happened, Kerriah would not pursue him or his Marcks if they agreed never to return to the UMO system. They would be left to their own devices, allowed unobstructed to search for their new world and start their new civilization.

For Zeltak, the importance of reviving her was more significant now that the queen appeared vanquished by unidentified assailants. Kerriah's honor would hopefully ensure that whoever took control of the orbs would give credence to her pact. The mist from the amulet drew into the plug, and the clone's finger twitched, followed by a head flinch. Spasms and convulsions soon followed, with a gurgling and a heave as the body smacked to the floor. She grunted, screamed, and twisted as the vessel took to the new consciousness. Then she suddenly stopped, facing down with her cheek pressed against the floor and her mouth open.

Zeltak took a careful step forward and leaned down for a closer look. He wondered if the transfer had worked. It was a bit of a cast into the wind, placing her only backup into the plug. There were no tests to provide any confidence. The queen had created the conduit to transfer her awareness into hosts, and they were both based on an original design by the great Marck architect, Joric Placator. He leaned closer. It had to have worked.

He reached down for a sharp poke to her side, and then she twisted over onto her back, facing him with wide-open eyes.

"What happened?" the raspy first words came out from the newly animated body.

"The old queen has slain you and taken your orbs."

"What?" Kerriah quickly propped up on her elbows.

"However," Zeltak stood straight again, "another ship arrived. A lone Widow Class Thraxon command ship. It bore the same markings as the one you arrived in when you entered the Eesolan system. It deployed some unfamiliar weapon system, which appeared to have vanquished the former queen."

"I need to see it. Did you capture a video feed?" Kerriah stammered to her feet, not appearing to care she was naked.

"We did. I will show you, and then I would like to take my fleet and be on our way as agreed." Zeltak, satisfied his queen was deceased, wanted nothing more to do with UMO affairs. He wished to leave this behind and start anew in a system to call their own. It didn't matter to him if it would be something they would construct from nothing or build on the ashes of another "inferior" civilization. He would lead his future with a fresh start and no troublesome Tolagons or orbs.

CHAPTER 75

Kerriah stared back one last time at Zeltak as she entered the Thraxon command ship through the lengthy umbilical lock connecting the two warships. A flood of thoughts and emotions poured down upon her as she made her way through the chilly tunnel. The icy cold of space crept down her bare backside as soon as her feet left the interior of the Marck ship. It appeared Zeltak couldn't wait to power down the pointless life support systems, and possibly that gesture would have the added benefit of hastening her departure.

A part of her wanted to take control of the orbs and rid whatever system or galaxy would have the burden of hosting these mechanical menaces. But, at the same time, she wanted to believe there was some faint possibility they could honorably start a civilization of their own. With apparent signs of some evolution within the likes of Zeltak—something that her father, Joric, would drive her into a long, dizzying explanation of his theory on artificial intelligence and Optimal Secruim had she dared to ask—there seemed a glimmer of hope.

The shadowy tined head disappeared as the outer door to the Marck ship slammed shut. The door behind her swirled close, and she was face to face with a room full of entamals and a visibly embarrassed and slightly larger version of Timmon. If the bright-red blush of a mortified child could show through the dark-grey Hybor skin, Timmon would be as red as the juicy flesh of a Hemlor crayfruit. He lowered his head, and his eyes popped up and down with quick peeks at Kerriah's naked body. It was apparent he had never seen the skin of a bare Mendac female before, and he knew he shouldn't be looking.

She glanced down at her chest and crossed her hands over her breasts with a quick eye roll and a tired exhale. "Can someone get me some clothes, blanket, armor . . . anything so we can speak comfortably?" Her irritated tone matched her annoyed expression. Each tall, slender entamal turned their heads side to side, looking for someone to step up with a solution.

"I'm not sure we have anything," Timmon said as he held his hands over his eyes but still grabbed an occasional peek between his palms. His voice was a bit deeper than the last time she had seen him, and he appeared to be clothed with the tunic-style clothing the entamals wore in Ethis.

She rolled her eyes again and replied through clenched teeth. "Fine . . . just . . . get me to the damned red orb at least. Can you do that?"

"Umm, sure," Timmon replied. "C-Can you follow me?"

"Ahh, yep," Kerriah responded with widening eyes and an annoyed flick of her fingers, which still attempted to cover her breasts.

She followed Timmon down several corridors and up one level before entering a storage area emitting a rainbow glow of lights. Three orbs floated a meter from the floor as though awaiting their new hosts. She paused for a moment as she entered the room, taking notice of the green orb hovering amongst the red

449

and yellow. For some reason, she hadn't expected to see it there. Maybe it was some desperate hope Plexo was still alive, and seeing it here. . . . She closed her eyes for a moment and tried to clear her mind. Shaking off the surprise, she carefully studied the room's contents.

"Where's the black orb?"

"The what?" Timmon shyly asked.

"The black orb, it's the most important one. The one I need to restore Krath and the others."

"I-I don't know. The entamals brought these back."

She walked over to the red orb, placed both hands around it, and then pushed it into her chest. Instantly a slick red suit poured over her naked body. The snug-fitted elemental garment buttoned high around her neck and ended with short boots at her ankles.

"The entamals? It was my understanding that we're never to return."

Timmon smiled with a shrug. "I told them I lost you guys. That the mean lady likely harmed you and Stelios."

"How long were you there?"

Timmon uncomfortably scratched his head for a few seconds. "I don't know. It felt like a long time. They had to talk about helping for a while before we finally left. But they were super nice to me the whole time."

"I'm sorry, Timmon."

"Sorry for what?"

Kerriah could tell that despite appearing a few years older, he still had the same child-like innocence. "For leaving you alone. For putting you through everything." She paused and pursed her lips for a moment. "But you did well, and it looks like we have a lot of catching up to do. But first, we must find the black orb and

450

retrieve the bodies from my transport. Do we have any e-vos suits left here?"

Timmon's jaw popped open as he thought for a moment. "Uhhmm . . . you mean those space suits?"

Kerriah nodded. "Yeah, those. The ones we wore when we left the ship."

"Yeah, there's one." Timmon walked over to a pile of Thraxon weapons, parts, and gear he had collected throughout his time on this ship. He tossed aside an array of armor plates, melee weapons, rifles, and cylinders of pink goo. Kerriah cringed at the sight of the pink goo, as she suspected it was likely some Thraxon sustenance derived from the flesh of their victims.

As Timmon tossed aside a segmented piece of black armor, the visor of an e-vos helmet appeared. "There it is!" he shouted.

"Good," Kerriah said. "Let's get it out of your stash pile, and I'll be taking a trip outside to get the orb and the others."

"Kerriah," Timmon said in a soft voice, "what about Krath?"

"He'll be fine. Trust me."

"And Stelios? These entamals want to know where he is."

Kerriah drew a deep breath. "Tell them . . ." She paused for a moment. "Tell them thank you. We will forever be in their debt, but Stelios is gone. He gave his life to save us from the mean lady. The one we called the Queen of the Marcks."

"Okay," Timmon said as he gently kicked a piece of armor, wobbling it a few centimeters across the coarse dark floor.

Kerriah placed her hands on her knees and looked Timmon directly in his eyes. "You did great. All of us are indebted to you for your courage. You have a wonderful gift, and if the UMO had more Timmons, this place—" She glanced over each shoulder. "Everything around us would be so much better than it is now. Continue to share your gifts, Timmon."

***

The e-vos had no propulsion pack, but that wouldn't matter. Kerriah had the green orb, and though she had never used it, she was gaining enough familiarity with the yellow and red to pick up its basic capabilities quickly. The photon energy could push her as needed through the emptiness of space. She decided to leave her trusted yellow orb behind.

Upon collecting the third orb, she felt her flesh burning away from the inside out, so she quickly let it go. It was an unexpected reaction, given her exposure to the white orb while bearing the red and yellow. She wasn't going to take any unnecessary risks with saving her friends. Even if she could hold onto three, she didn't know how they would react together with the black orb. So Kerriah decided only to carry what she needed, the green, which meant she needed to give up the sharp-looking luminescent red outfit she was starting to enjoy.

Inside the e-vos, the cool air tickled her naked flesh, and she felt a bit wild, free-drifting through space with only a loose-fitting e-vos between the frozen void and her skin. As she scanned through cloudy swirls covering the green globe of Soorak, things looked a bit more normal. The elastic, shimmering, black threads spinning between it and the other moons disappeared along with the queen and her grip over the black orb's influence.

Kerriah's disabled transport floated nearby. Its cockpit smashed open and layered with frost. Plexo's frozen body spun slowly in the distance, his distinctive Luminar glow gone, leaving a greyish frozen corpse. She squinted, hoping to spot the black orb floating around, but after a good hard focus and panning her view back and forth, looking for a nearly invisible object against the

452

blackness of space, she stopped and thought about how the queen located the elusive sphere. What could she have done? *Of course!* The queen used the only tool she had at her disposal. Pushing her hands forward, Kerriah pulsed a flash of light energy across the view.

Nothing. The flash of light was too fast. She took a deep inward breath and briefly pinched her eyes closed. She drew deep inside with her eyes popped wide open, and with a strong exhale, she pushed a massive blast of light likely seen from the streets of Corasan. The illuminated view remained, though steadily fading with each passing second. Every tiny bit of space debris stood out against the glowing green hue. But one spot appeared as a small black portal leading into an empty void. Kerriah quickly pushed close to the black spot before the glow dissipated.

She slowly moved her hands toward the orb as the last vestige of green faded into blackness. She steadied her body and tried to get a better look at the orb, which, until recently, no one had ever seen. She noticed it created a perfect void. There wasn't the spray of stars or even the glow of Soorak when peering through the dark circle. Without the assisting light glow, she kept her eyes on the emptiness.

As she placed her hands firmly around the ball of energy, the flash of billions of lives screamed into her head. It contained the memories of every life it had taken. Kerriah ripped her hands away. It was too much for her to behold and too much power for her to wield. The black orb was the heart of Cyos, and its power was too much for anyone to possess. No one should ever have this type of power—especially a sociopath like the queen.

She turned toward her frozen transport. Krath, Creedith, and Ashton. Even Plexo . . . they needed her now. She could restore them. She looked around at Soorak and then in the distance at the faint glow of Thale. Maybe she could bring them all back. Even if the attempt destroyed her, she felt it was her responsibility to try. She paused for a moment and stared in the direction of New Troika. *Crix,* would she ever be able to see him again? The thought saddened her with a heavy heart. She sniffed and bit into her lip until she tasted the bitterness of her synthetic blood. The sharp pain snapped her away from her moment of self-pity and back to her objective.

She returned a focused gaze at the small, black void. Reaching out, she whisked away her fears, grasped the orb, and pushed it into her chest. Her body numbed from an icy chill, and an abnormal pulsing sensation reverberated from her chest to her outer extremities. Screams of terror and maniacal howls filled her thoughts. The last moments of billions of lives rushed through her, and her heart sped until the beats turned to a constant hum. Cyos took most of the lives during its massacre of the UMO. But the deceitful queen took many of the survivors and injected their souls into these new Marcks. She specifically built them to suppress their will and to follow her rule unconditionally.

Kerriah's body blackened into a shadowy void, outlined with a subtle shimmer of green. Her e-vos withered away into dust. She felt a dark power inside, not evil or good, but of the purest potential to create and destroy. It was too much power for anyone to possess. She couldn't shake it, but she knew that having such a thought meant its power hadn't corrupted her . . . yet. Unbeknownst to the queen, her proxy host, Plexo, had enough control to understand the power was too great for her to wield, and he secretly worked to suppress the black orb's true potential.

Tendrils of black whisked from Kerriah and snatched the frozen bodies from her transport as well as Plexo. The shadowy curls towed them behind, down to the surface of Soorak, and inside the vacant streets of Corasan, where she gently laid them down in a tidy row. She took only a minute to study their lifeless bodies as she drifted above. Then she closed her dark eyes as black flames engulfed their corpses. Her mouth opened wide, and the now familiar song filled her ears, the same celestial song she had heard in Gabor. The song of the Laggorns. They would sing when they did what they loved the most, creating life. Now the songs flowed from her. The corpses' eyes and mouths instantly popped open, and their feet kicked for several seconds before the fire faded into the twinkle of sparks.

"Um-num-num-what the—" Krath's voice croaked.

Kerriah couldn't easily remember the last time she smiled with a feeling of joy, but hearing Krath's voice filled her with warmth, and the smile came without being forced. Ashton let out a raspy cough and a shiver before rolling over to his side with a few heaping breaths. Creedith sat up almost instantly with his head down. His face appeared long, and his eyes tired. Plexo, however, didn't move. She moved a little closer to his body and opened her hands. Flames of black poured out across him. His head popped up with a hollow stare. A look that one would expect from a body devoid of a soul. As soon as she withdrew her flames, his body flopped back to the ground like a lifeless sack.

Raising her hand, she stared into the void that used to be her palm. At that moment, she recalled Plexo's age and what he told her about their organic battery, which sustained their life. His body had expired many years ago, and the photonic power of the green orb fed him. She suspected the moment the entamals removed the green orb from his broken body, bringing him back wouldn't be possible, or his will to return wasn't there any longer. Maybe it was for both reasons, but she knew it wasn't either. Wielding the black orb was a one-way journey. To release it, the wielder gives up their existence. This was the price that had to be paid to bear this power.

"Who are you?" a voice broke her thoughts. Ashton sat upright with his fist over his mouth, covering another dry cough after his rasping words came out. He looked over each shoulder. "And where are we?"

"I'm Kerriah, and you're in Corasan." Her voice sounded distant.

"W-What?" Ashton felt around the smooth street as if he needed to verify what she told him. "How?"

"It's a lot to tell, but just know that you're safe now."

Ashton looked at her for a moment with a squinting stare. "Kerriah?"

"What happened to tya, little girl?" Krath stood and massaged his rib, ensuring they were all still there.

"The black orb."

"Ta what?" Krath's face turned from concerned to confused.

"The power over death . . . and life," Creedith said in a quiet voice. "Child, you must return me to the hands of death. I am not meant to be here."

"No," she replied. "Not here. You will join the other Andors on New Troika."

"So what now?" Ashton asked.

"I will restore as many as I can. Then, I will return the orbs, all of them, to Gabor. There they will be safely out of the reach of those who would kill to gain their power. No one can ever enter the gate again with the orbs inside." She turned to Krath. "Krath, Timmon is safe. He is aboard the Thraxon command ship with entamals orbiting Soorak. He is responsible for saving the system."

"Wait, did you say entamals?" Ashton responded with wide eyes.

"That's correct."

"How? They forbid us to return. Besides, that system is off the charts."

"Let's just say that our Timmon is full of surprises."

Krath's chest pushed out, and his face turned to a fatherly smile. "That's ma boy." However, his expression changed when he looked at Plexo's lifeless body. "What about my ole buddy? How come he's still . . . still not up trottin around telling us all what to do?"

"I could not save Plexo. His time has expired. I will always consider him a good and loyal friend, as should all of you, for without his knowledge, we would have been lost long ago."

After a few minutes' pause, Krath sniffed and quickly wiped his palm across each eye. "Aww, little buddy. Never thought I'd hear myself say this, but I'm goin' to miss that little guy."

Kerriah slowly rose high into the air and extended her arms. The sky turned black as a starless night, and folds of shadows rippled over the horizon and blanketed the city. Lifeless bodies arose, stammering to their decrepit feet. Anyone with a corpse lumbered, howled, and groaned until their decaying flesh bubbled and swelled into a healed living body. Flowing waves of whistles and purrs filled the atmosphere as the song of the Laggorns chorused throughout the sky and land. Across Soorak, life before Cyos was restored and healed.

She lowered, and her shimmering black toes set back onto the street. "Much of the lives lost on Soorak have been restored." She looked again at Krath. "I will do the same for Thale . . . and Solara."

Ashton stepped slowly toward her, raising his hand as though wanting to touch her. She stepped away, keeping him just out of reach. "Will I ever see you again? I mean the Kerriah I knew before?" He said in a gentle voice.

"No," she replied. Her firm tone suggested there was no changing her course. "I am sorry. I'm not certain what will become of me, though it will not involve my old self and this world. But please know that you are a great leader, and the system needs you."

She turned to Krath. "Krath, you will always have a place in my heart. As a loyal friend, protector, and someone who could always make me smile, even when things were at their worst. I will never forget you."

"Aww shucks," Krath said, with welling, tear-filled eyes. "No one has ever said anything tat kind about me before."

"Once I restore the other two moons, I will return for Creedith. I will take him to New Troika to be with his ancestors. Then you will not see me again."

"What about the queen?" Ashton asked.

"She's gone, but I will make sure there are no other remnants of her. With this power, I can detect traces of my Optimal Secrium in the system and burn its source."

No one else said a word. Kerriah vanished instantly, only to return before they could part ways. Kerriah took Creedith; as promised, it would be the last time Krath or Ashton would see her again.

Over the ensuing years, Mallor Ashton would continue his military service. Aside from being the sole military survivor of the mission that would eventually save and restore the UMO, his crowning achievement was leading the way in building a new defensive system around the gammac corridors. By building a tertiary mirror at each, they could quarantine any incoming vessel into a void zone for further inspection or neutralization. His achievement garnered such praise from UMO leadership he eventually earned the highest military title of Galactic Marshal and settled down peacefully with his wife and three children in a quiet village on the outskirts of Lator.

After much pleading and persistence from Timmon, Krath set aside his prejudice and agreed to free the squill secretly into a serene lake inside the Hemlor Region of old Troika. It spent its days peacefully dipping into the cool water and basking its tentacles in the warm, sunlit shoreline, awaiting Timmon's occasional visits until the time between his stays turned empty.

Krath and Timmon returned home to Thale. Timmon's mother died unexpectedly a few years later from a respiratory outbreak that swept across the species, which culled a quarter of Thale's indigenous population. Though a young adult, Timmon still suffered from ongoing anger from the loss of his father and now his mother. Krath cobbled together an old merchant vessel used for transporting drums of aacor to Hybors living abroad and took Timmon under his wing once again for a series of mini adventures. Shortly after their departure from Thale, an unusual series of heroic deeds began to take place around the system. Eventually, even Gorag the Great succumbed to a mysterious choking hazard. Though unconfirmed, there were reports of a pair of Hybors exiting his castle under the cover of dark on the same night he died.

Timmon never settled into a quiet existence but instead found peace and purpose in helping the weak and oppressed escape the tyranny of their abusers. He eventually formed a small vigilante group known as the Scorps with the same goal.

With his aging body worn and broken from a lifetime of wars and adventure, Krath died in a cave near Troika. In his last days, he would sit upon the cliff's edge, peering over Drisal as the monolithic silhouette of Oro slowly seeped under the horizon while stroking his webbed fingers across the signet of a Tolagon bracer, thinking about Crix. During his adventures with Timmon, he never paused to visit New Troika, a choice that tore into him in his waning years. However, the bracer mysteriously appeared on his belly as he suddenly woke up startled one night years earlier. He had no memory of obtaining the map and key to Gabor, but he kept it safe and used it to remember the young Mendac he both loved and respected.

CHAPTER 76

The small transport set down upon a quiet clearing inside the dense forest of breatic trees. The tall, stoic, chestnut brown trunks seemed to crumble as though made of wet sand against a strong, dry breeze. The unnatural clearing had withered away from the forest moments before landing, triggered by a casual wave of Kerriah's hand.

The door slid open, and the single Andor pilot walked out, setting his feet upon the sacred lands for the first time. His nostrils flared as he drew a heaping breath of pure, clean air. Movement caught his attention, and he looked up. A shadow dropped in from above and sat down before him.

"So this is the new world you spoke of?" he asked. "The one that young Crix created from the revered Tersik Crystal?"

"Yes," Kerriah replied. "You are here as a guest, but once you die here, you are one of them forever."

He dropped his head. "Then do what you must."

She slowly raised a finger, and without a sound, Creedith's body melted into the soil. In the distance, she noticed a shimmering outline of an Andor walking away until it disappeared into the darkness of the forest. This was now his home. He could live in peace for the first time since he was a child, in a world he knew too well, yet not at all. It wasn't a place of war or death, but a new world filled with salvation and grace. A place of beauty, and no one deserved it more than him.

Kerriah floated away, hiding in the shadows until she reached Crix's home under cover of night. The timbered single-story house, with two tall chimneys that came almost to the top of the surrounding trees, looked exactly like what she would have envisioned him to have as his home. Quaint, yet modest. She hadn't been to his home on New Troika, but strangely she found her way there following only the tingling sensations in her belly.

Amber light flickered through the shutters in one of the windows. With the late hour and the primarily dark home, it appeared its occupant prepared for bedtime. Kerriah floated over to the window and peaked between the slats of the shutters. There was enough of a gap between the wood to see inside. Tucked under a cozy beige blanket, Crix carefully flipped the page of a book he propped up to his chest. She stared at him as he read and occasionally flipped another page. She didn't want him to see her in this shadowy form. That's not how she wanted him to remember her. Yet she wanted to curl up next to him and snuggle her head into his shoulder as he read his book. She imagined the joy of feeling his warmth, his heartbeat, and the occasional tickle of his breath as she fell asleep.

She backed away as he closed his book, placing it on the rugged nightstand. He leaned up and covered the lamp's flame with a metal cap, extinguishing his light for the evening. The shadow of a blanket pulled tightly around his shoulder as he turned to his side. Kerriah placed her hand on the shutter. She longed so badly to go inside and slide in next to him, but she couldn't, not like this. She wanted to cry; she needed some internal relief. But this body, consumed with the void, would not shed a tear.

The overwhelming power of the black orb slowly closed its supernatural fist around her throat. She was the most powerful creature in the galaxy, able to kill and restore with a thought, but it was too much to resist and would soon consume her. Taking in the black orb was a one-way decision. It now possessed every cell in her body and wouldn't let go without destroying her.

She peaked up into the nighttime sky. There was one last task. One thing to make right and one chance to have her life back. The shutter creaked open, and Crix's head peaked out. It was as though something had caught his attention. But there was nothing there—only the chirps and croaks of the evening critters. Crix looked up and sniffed the air. A brief smile crept over his face and then turned long. He stared down for a moment and then rubbed his palm across the corner of his eye before gently closing the shutter and returning to bed.

CHAPTER 77

Weeks passed since Creedith appeared at Crix's front door. Crix never thought he would have a chance to meet his natural father again. By the time he discovered his true relationship with the legendary Andor, he was ripped away from him and assumed dead. The stories he told Crix while sitting around the kitchen table or poking at the golden ambers of his fireplace were even more bizarre than his own. Creedith proved surprisingly to be a fantastic storyteller, as well as an attentive listener.

Creedith settled back, massaging his chin and neck as he listened to Crix's recount of his battle with the heydromac and his perilous journey into the core to face the queen. A smile crept over his face as he listened, and it was evident Crix was more than he could have ever hoped. Despite the joy of having his father home and breaking ground nearby for Creedith's future home, which they would build together, he felt an empty hole of loneliness in his heart. Creedith wasn't sure what became of her after they parted ways, only that she had a great burden that would not be easy or even possible to release.

"Why didn't she come to me?" Crix asked when Creedith explained how she used the black orb to release him into the spiritually bound life on New Troika. "She was here." His voice winced, and the words hurt as he spoke them aloud.

Creedith nodded slowly and stared at the coarse plank wood floor for a few seconds. As he looked back up, his eyes met Crix's.

"She has a purer heart than anyone I've known. Rarely a thought for herself, but I suspect the child didn't want you to see her that way. Not for her vanity, but rather to protect your memories of her as the beautiful young Mendac with which you fell in love. Not as a dark and foreboding image that the power over death gave her. I can only believe she is out there looking over all of us, with her caring soul, feeling bound to duty as she always has. With such power comes a tax that only a few can pay."

***

Morning came early for Crix after another restless night of sleep. Knowing Kerriah was out there somewhere alone kept him up stirring most nights. He wrestled himself from the cozy bed covers; somehow, they were softer in the morning than at night, and he whipped up some ort grass porridge with a light sprinkling of ground sabe. He took a few spoonsful before it cooled into a lumpy paste and shoved it to the side.

The birds chirped their morning songs, and the cool dew pooled atop his feet as he made his way to the growing timber walls of Creedith's new home. They had four tiers of breatic tree logs locked together with a rough cut out for the future front door. Creedith stood over a makeshift saw table, taking the last sip of warm cider from his wooden cup. He had a grey apron cinched around his waist, for which he quickly rubbed his hands against once he caught sight of Crix approaching.

"Well, good afternoon!" Creedith said sarcastically. It was a running jab when Crix made it out after the morning sun had

465

already chased away the waning shadows of early dawn. Creedith was always up before daybreak, full of energy and ready to tackle each day.

Crix dropped his head, raised his hand as he shuffled up to Creedith's workspace. "Yeah, yeah, I know."

"Another tough night?" Creedith asked before picking up a piece of wood, pulling a string across it, and then etching a mark into the bare red grain.

"Yeah," Crix replied. "I can't get her out of my head."

"I understand. Time heals the soul's wounds." Creedith patted Crix's shoulder before pointing to a large axe leaning against his open toolbox. He raised his eyebrows. "Hard work lends rest to the tired mind."

Crix gave a forced grin. "Right."

He discovered life with Creedith was a towering silo, filled to the unseen top, with phrases of wisdom. He trudged over to the wieldy axe and slung it over his shoulder. He made his way over to a clearing he and Creedith had been working on and sized up a great breatic tree with a sturdy, straight trunk. Placing the axe between his knees, he spat into his hands and smacked them together before a vigorous brush back and forth. Taking a couple of line-ups of staged swings at the base of the trunk, he prepared for his first chop. His arm heaved back into a full swing, ready to deliver the blow, when a voice from within the woods shattered his focus.

"What did that tree ever do to you?" she spoke.

Crix's heart stopped for a couple of seconds, and he immediately let the axe drop. He leaned his head forward with a squint to see the outline of someone against the rays of the morning light coming from the woods.

"Who's there?" The words came out without thinking.

"It's me. I'm finally home." The figure stepped closer.

"Ker—" The name almost left his lips, but he hesitated.

"Don't you believe your own eyes?" Crix recalled saying that exact phrase to her. It had to be. She approached him, close enough now that hints of deep blue danced from her short, black fur. A beaming smile covered her short-muzzled face. "Crix," she said in a soft and familiar voice. "I'm home."

"Home?" His head shifted side to side, trying to get a good look at her. "I-Is it really you?"

With two quick steps, her arms wrapped around his back, and she squeezed him tighter than he could remember being squeezed in a long time. "It's me," she whispered, hugging him until her muscles quivered.

Crix felt her warmth and smelled her familiar powdered scent with a hint of flowers. Her heart pounded against his; he knew this wasn't a trick. These were indeed her genuine feelings.

"Kerriah." The breath left him as he spoke her name. He placed his arms around her, pulling her off her feet and swinging her in circles. "It's you. It's really you." He placed her down and stared into her green eyes before holding her at arm's length. He looked her up and down. "How?"

"I take it you like my new look?"

"Woah . . ." He dropped his shoulders, appearing out of breath. "Y-Yeah, I mean, of course. You're gorgeous. But how? What happened to you?"

"Crix, so much." She glanced up for a second with a slow shake of her head. "Just so much that it'll take some time to explain it all. But in short, I gave the orbs of Cyos back to Gabor, where they belong—reunited with their family, Sequia and its children. It's what they always wanted. They are the Laggorn's original creations and are the only ones that should have possession of their great legacy."

"What about the Tracolds?"

"There's no need to worry about them anymore. They are forever separated from Sequia and Gabor. With the orbs safely in Gabor, they have no power to corrupt the weak who may possess them." Kerriah paused for a moment. "Jesselle is also with them now. They have accepted her as the custodian of the white orb. They are one, and I could feel her joy for the first time since I've known her."

"Kerriah, I-I don't even know what to say. It's all so much."

She placed her finger over his lips. "I asked only one thing in return," she said in a whisper. "That they spare my life and permanently change me into an Andor fitting to live out the rest of our days together." Her eyes twinkled, and she blinked with a smile and tilted her head. "Here's day one in my new body. A real body! I feel cold and hungry, as I've never felt before. It feels so real, not like some triggered code. It's amazing!"

"So is this permanent? You're here with me forever?"

"Yes!"

He leaned down and pressed his lips into hers. Their mouths locked together, and Kerriah placed her hand around his neck, enjoying the lengthy kiss. As he pulled back, he noticed her looking across his shoulder. He turned around, and Creedith stood over his work table with an ear-to-ear smirk.

She pulled away and stared into his eyes. Something still bothered her. "You know that wasn't me who came down here before. Right?"

"What?"

She closed her eyes for a moment before staring back into his. "The version of me that visited you before. You know, the one you made love to?" She intentionally cleared her throat.

"Of course," he replied.

"Good. Because I could never—"

Crix shook his head. "No need to explain. I know you wouldn't."

"And the UMO?"

"Hmmm?"

"What did they do? I mean after—"

Crix sighed. It was something he would rather not think about but understood her curiosity. "Let's just say they tried." He glanced over at Creedith. "No one, and I mean no one, will harm this world. We are safe here."

Kerriah nodded and then gave him another hug. "I'm sorry, Crix. I'm so sorry."

"You don't need to be sorry for anything," he whispered.

***

The next day would be the first of many together in this new life, a life free of war, politics, and technology. The pure, sweet air would smell better than they had ever experienced, and the warming rays of sunlight would reveal all the goodness around them. The time trickled by in New Troika quietly, and it was a simple existence.

One ordinary evening, they slid into bed with only the flicker of the lamp flame casting an amber glow over their faces. Crix pulled her snugly against his body, and she rested her head on his shoulder. He picked up his book and read a few pages before folding it closed and setting it on the nightstand. Her cozy eyes peeked open for a moment, and he gently kissed her forehead. He leaned over and doused the lamp light with its metal cap. He could hear her deep breaths in the dark bedroom as she slept, safe and content.

Each day would be devoted to each other and this new world, a perfect place built from a pure heart. The cool nighttime breeze seeped through the shutters, and they snuggled tighter together. Crix drifted to sleep, with the lovely rhythm of her heartbeat next to his, their bodies warming each other, and her fingers gently curled around a small piece of his wavy mane.

ABOUT THE AUTHOR

Gregory Benson grew up in the Midwest and married his high school sweetheart, Dawn. He graduated from the University of Missouri-Saint Louis and works in the technology field.

As far back as he could remember, he would spend much of his childhood daydreaming about alien worlds and immersing himself in science fiction and fantasy. As an adult, he's enjoyed adventures traveling with his wife Dawn and his son Luke, as well as sword fighting, pinball, and of course, writing sci-fi/fantasy.

***

Thank you, and I hope you've enjoyed the Tolagon series. I would be honored if you could spare a few additional minutes to visit the site where you purchased my books and leave a review. You may also find me on Instagram @gregorybensonbooks1 and @tolagonbookseries.

If you'd like to get notifications of new releases and special offers on my books, please join my email list by visiting https://www.gregorybensonbooks.com scroll to the bottom and click subscribe.

Made in the USA
Middletown, DE
10 August 2024

58878804R00283